The Meaning of Gay

The Meaning of Gay

Interaction, Publicity, and Community among Homosexual Men in 1960s San Francisco

J. Todd Ormsbee

LEXINGTON BOOKS
A division of
ROWMAN & LITTLEFIELD PUBLISHERS, INC.
Lanham • Boulder • New York • Toronto • Plymouth, UK

Published by Lexington Books
A division of Rowman & Littlefield Publishers, Inc.
A wholly owned subsidiary of The Rowman & Littlefield Publishing Group, Inc.
4501 Forbes Boulevard, Suite 200, Lanham, Maryland 20706
http://www.lexingtonbooks.com

Estover Road, Plymouth PL6 7PY, United Kingdom

British Library Cataloguing in Publication Information Available

Library of Congress Cataloging-in-Publication Data

Ormsbee, J. Todd, 1970–
  The meaning of gay : interaction, publicity, and community among homosexual men in
1960s San Francisco / J. Todd Ormsbee.
    p. cm.
  Includes bibliographical references and index.
  ISBN 978-0-7391-1597-8 (cloth : alk. paper)
  ISBN 978-0-7391-1598-5 (pbk. : alk. paper)
  ISBN 978-0-7391-4471-8 (electronic)
  1. Gay men—California—San Francisco—Social conditions—20th century. 2. Gay
men—California—San Francisco—Social life and customs—20th century. 3. Gay
community—California—San Francisco—History—20th century. 4. Gay culture—
California—San Francisco—History—20th century. 5. San Francisco (Calif.)—Social
life and customs—20th century. I. Title.
  HQ76.2.U52S356 2010
  306.76'62097946109046—dc22   2009043597

⊖™ The paper used in this publication meets the minimum requirements of American
National Standard for Information Sciences—Permanence of Paper for Printed Library
Materials, ANSI/NISO Z39.48-1992.

Printed in the United States of America

For Ken

Contents

San Francisco Gay Organizations, 1961–1972

Organization	Abbr.
Bay Area Gay Activists Alliance (1971)[1]	BayGay
Committee for Homosexual Freedom (1969)	CHF
Council on Religion and the Homosexual (1963)	CRH
Daughters of Bilitis (1955)	DOB
Gay Liberation Front (1969)	GLF
Gay Sunshine Collective (1970)	*none*
League of Civil Education (1961)	LCE
Mattachine Society (1949?)[2]	*none*
National Council of Homophile Organizations (1965)	NACHO
Society for Individual Rights (1964)	SIR
Tavern Guild (1961)	TG
Vanguard (1966)	*none*

1. Years provided are starting dates; many of these organizations waxed and waned through the period.
2. The Mattachine Society began in Los Angeles in approximately 1949, but it is unclear when a San Francisco group first organized. Leadership moved to San Francisco after the 1953 ouster of the organization's founders at the national meeting.

San Francisco Gay Publications, 1961–1972

Publication	Abbr.[1]	Dates Consulted & Cited
LCE News	*LN*	Oct. 13, 1962 to April 29, 1963
The News	*TN*	May 13, 1963 to Dec. 23, 1963
Citizens News	*CN*	Jan. 13, 1964 to Vol. 4 No. 8 (Jan. 1965)[2]
Town Talk	*TT*	July 1965 to Jan.–Feb. 1966[3]
Vector	*VR*	Dec. 1964 to June 1972[4]
Vanguard	*VG*	Sept. 1966 to Vol. 2.2 (Fall 1967?) & Spring 1969[5]
CHF Newsletter	CHFN	April 22, 1969 to Oct. 16, 1969
San Francisco Free Press	*SFFP*	Oct. 1, 1969 to Vol. 1.1 (Spring 1970?)
San Francisco Gay Free Press	*SFGFP*	Nov. 1970 to Dec. 1970
Agape and Action	*AA*	June 23, 1970 to Feb. 1971
Gay Sunshine	*GS*	Aug.–Sept. 1970 to July–Aug. 1972
The Effeminist	*TE*	May 1971 to Vol. 1.1 (June 1971?)
Adz Gayzette	*AG*	Oct. 9, 1970 to June 28, 1971
I Am: Oracle of Gay Emmaus	*IA*	Feb. 1971 to Vol. 1.3 (Summer 1971?)
Bay Area Reporter	*BAR*	April 1, 1971 to June 23, 1972[6]

1. All citations in this book use these abbreviations; page numbers are given where known; formatting, grammar, and spelling is retained from the original.
2. *LN*, *TN*, and *CN* were begun as the publication of the League of Civil Education and produced by Guy Strait. Strait continued publishing *CN* as a bar rag after the dissolution of the LCE through mid-1966.
3. Bill Beardemphl published *TT* independently; not paginated after the first issue.
4. *VR* continued publication until 1975.
5. As a cottage newsletter run by a youth organization at Glide Memorial Church, *VG*'s run was erratic; issues often weren't dated and rarely paginated.
6. *BAR* continues into the present, having gone through several iterations; it was published bi-monthly during this period and was not paginated until 1972.

Preface

The fact that homosexuals are marching in the streets in large numbers, unafraid and unashamed, forces heterosexuals to re-evaluate their attitudes; it puts an end to the stereotype of the homosexual as a timid, fearful, guilt ridden, effete faggot who can be shoved around and walked over. It tells the world, homosexuals are dissatisfied with their status and are demanding social justice and the full equality they deserve as human beings. But most of all, the parade is for the closet queens ... [and] a large element of teenage Gays who don't have access to other media.

—Rev. Robert Humphries.
Bay Area Reporter, March 1, 1972

San Francisco's first Gay Pride celebration provoked anger, frustration, and conflict among the city's competing gay organizations. Some felt that such an event would merely reinforce stereotypes; others worried that it would flatten the differences among gay men and women; still others contended that such a parade threatened the lives of gay men and women who were working to integrate into society; and many argued that the event would be racist and sexist, so they could not in good conscience participate. Interestingly, nearly all activists, regardless of their political programs, urged their memberships not to participate. But the Bay Area's gay men and lesbians did finally gather on June 25, 1972, three years after the Stonewall riots they commemorated and a year after the city's first Stonewall memorial demonstration. Planning for the event had begun only three months earlier, when Rev. Robert Humphries, who had organized the Christopher Street West parade in Los Angeles in 1971, convened an "open committee" to plan a similar event in San Francisco, his new home. *The Bay Area Reporter* announced the event, starting a non-stop rhetorical and ideological battle in the pages of the city's gay publications. Such disagreement was a hallmark of San Francisco's gay life, as the gay men and women of the city continually locked horns over what it should mean to be gay.

xiii

Humphries hoped the event would offer "something for everyone—bar owners, lesbians, bike riders, drags, militants, conservatives, street queens, freaks, and every other segment of the Gay Community" (*BAR* March 1, 1972). Organizers of the event hoped the parade would show the gay movement's strength and would raise the consciousness of gay men and lesbians. A month later, the open committee announced that the parade would be inclusive and non-judgmental, allowing anyone to participate who wanted to. For them, New York City's Stonewall uprising against the police and the mafia-owned bars had "marked the beginning of a tremendous surge in Gay Pride all over America" (*BAR* Apr. 1, 1972). San Francisco's new celebration event would include a town hall meeting on the history of gay liberation, a "gay rap" session, a plenary on the meaning of gay liberation, several dances, a bingo game, a bar night, and ultimately, the parade (see June 14, 1972). Organizers gushed that the parade would instill "gay pride" in the city's homosexuals, and indeed in the homosexuals of the entire nation (see Apr. 1, 1972).

In the pages of *Vector*, the Society for Individual Rights complained that the ad hoc committee had acted on its own, and they were convinced that the parade would fail (*VR* June 1972, 4). SIR doubted that such an event was even necessary in San Francisco, where gay men and women had been fighting for their rights for years before Stonewall had even occurred on the other side of the continent. Indeed, the main problem they saw in the city was arrests for public sex, which they felt were not really opposed by most gay men and women. Many SIR members also objected to Ray Broshear's participation in the parade. As head of BayGay, the local version of the Gay Activists Alliance, Broshear was an outspoken critic of other gay organizations and activism in the city. GayBay had circulated a "zap" flier against the gay organizations and businesses that didn't want to participate in the gay pride celebration. Humphries and Troy Perry responded to the flier in the *BAR*, arguing that BayGay sought to repress gay men and women from the inside, trying to coerce participation; they also argued that Broshears had not approved the flier with BayGay's steering committee (*BAR* May 15, 1972). In *Vector*, Clark Fulmer boosted the parade and insisted that it was to promote homosexual unity (41); and SIR did eventually encourage its members to participate.

Gay Sunshine Collective, the Bay Area's homegrown gay liberation group, likewise rejected the idea of the parade outright, calling it a rip-off of the "real" Christopher Street. Winston Leyland argued that although such a parade had the potential to raise consciousness, the San Francisco parade had been co-opted by the "commercial capitalist gay interests" (*GS* May 1972, 2). For Leyland, the parade committee was overrun with "the capitalist bar/bath syndrome which so exploits gay people." In *Gay Sunshine*, Don Kilhefner of the Los Angeles Community Center underscored the cultural tension within the gay community when he accused the San Francisco organizers of being "gay pigs" who had co-opted the culture of gay liberation for their own ends. Leyland told "true" gay libbers to avoid the parade, first because it included an "Imperial Ball," a drag competition that would "reinforce [straight people's] stereotyped thinking about homosexuals"; and second, because lesbians were not included in the planning, so the "Parade is basically a male chauvinist trip." For Leyland, gay men with no real interest in gay liberation were organizing the event, so the event would actually suppress gay consciousness instead of raising it. The Collective urged its members not to participate in the pride event.

The controversy kept boiling for months after the event, as the gay publications offered conflicting evaluations and interpretations. Gay liberationists could only see a failed, oppressive event. Skip Reed wrote that the parade, for all the consciousness raising it may have done, had raised the wrong consciousness.

> Gay Parade puts me down. It tells me that I must be stereotypically gay. It tells me that gays are sex-objects worthy of straight society's ridicule. It tell me that the social life of gays is cruising, drag, and the bar scene. Those are sexist lies. Smash them, brothers! ... In choosing to live in a gay society represented in Gay Parade, brother, you are choosing self-destruction. *GS* July–Aug. 1972, 14.

And John Williams echoed the complaint, declaring that the parade made clowns out of gay people. "If straights need to see a circus let them contact Barnum and Bailey. After four thousand years of oppression isn't it time to get off the stage and onto the battlefield? Give us justice not a parade." Conversely, the *BAR* saw the parade and events as gay ecumenicalism at its best, presenting a united front to the straight world and offering a larger community experience for gay men and women. Weeks before the parade, Donald McLean had argued that the parade was a chance for "peaceful solidarity," where no matter what "scene" a gay man or woman was in, they could come and express themselves. "Let the Silent Majority be someone else," McLean had argued. "Why not be part of the Working Minority?!" (*BAR* June 14, 1972). So not surprisingly, the *BAR* gave the parade positive reviews, dismissing a few scuffles during the events as the sour grapes of "lady libbers" and "spaced-out, head [hippie] homosexuals." *BAR* felt the parade was a success because it had been extensively covered by local media and had brought together gays and lesbians across the political spectrum for the event. Writers noted that the vast majority of the attendees were celebrating and happy, and that any controversy occurred among organizers and activists, revealing what may have been a wide gap between the gay-on-the-street and the activists of the period (see *BAR* June 28, 1972).

Looking at the contentious interactions surrounding the city's first Gay Pride event, it becomes clear that there never was a settled, stable gay community, no golden age of harmony among gay men and women. When I began poring through San Francisco's gay publications from the 1960s, I had expected to find a political roadmap for gay activism. Looking to the origin of late-twentieth-century gay activism, I had hoped to find a clear framework for how gay men and women should organize their lives, politics, and community. What I found instead were actual people, real human beings simply struggling to make sense of their experiences and to create social connections, groups, organizations, and political ideologies that would fulfill their needs and desires and allow them to live as they wanted. Whereas I began by asking what queer political strategies were worthwhile and effective, I ended by seeing human beings creating meaningful lives. It also became clear early in the process that although gay men and lesbians were acting together in their organizations, their different experiences of gender identity, expression, and sexism led to different experiences of homosexuality and a different set of meanings for the increasingly common framework of *being gay*. Ultimately I decided to focus on gay men's experiences, but could not do so without also talking about lesbians, with whom gay men continually interacted and upon whom gay men depended for much of their movement's success. The events of June 1972 help us not to understand which point of view was *right*, but rather help us to understand the competing values and contradictory experiences of gay men and women that led to such vehement fissures among the gay people of San Francisco; and they open a window into the reasons why individuals and groups interpret their sexual experiences in the ways that they do.

Along this personal and intellectual journey many champions, advocates, and friends have offered emotional, intellectual, and financial help, without which this project would not have been possible. Robert Antonio still shows a constant and unfailing faith in my intellect, inspires me to be both rigorous in my analysis and compassionate of my subjects, and offers the best advice both personal and professional. Several mentors had particularly strong impacts on my intellectual development, evident in the pages of this book. Angel Kwolek-Folland, Joane Nagel, and Norm Yetman shared their knowledge and insight, showed unbelievable patience, and introduced me to the pleasure of academic work and friendships; Jim Woelfel revealed to me the interconnection of careful critical thought with leading an ethical life worth living; and Barry Shank taught me passion, enthusiasm, care for detail, and kindness in the life of the mind. My parents', brother's, and baby sister's contributions are invisible in the text, but evident in the man that I am. George Leylegian's stunning generosity literally made this book possible in its early years, supporting me financially as I completed a year of research. Many men and women have collected these materials and preserved them for future generations; they made this research possible in their archives at the GLBT Historical Society in San Francisco and the San Francisco Public Library. Numerous colleagues and friends offered invaluable feedback in the preparation of the manuscript, to them I am indebted. And finally Kenneth Baker, I could never have done this without you and your undying friendship, loyalty, and love.

Introduction

Homosexuality and Meaning

We are blind and unimagined. We are only just beginning to create a culture and an identity. . . . No one man can create a subculture by himself, and by the time homosexuals find one another, the unsympathetic society has so much distorted their views of themselves that the culture they have created in the past has been shaky, campy, without real depth.

—from *Agape in Action*, July 20, 1970.

Communication is consummatory as well as instrumental. It is a means of establishing cooperation, domination, order. Shared experience is the greatest of human goods.

—John Dewey, *Experience and Nature*, 1925

Something dramatic happened in the lives of San Francisco's gay men during the 1960s. Homosexuals had started the decade interacting mostly in private, informal groups, meeting in bars and house parties, and a few of them in a small, behind-the-scenes movement. For the most part, they had let bar owners fight their legal battles for them and focused their attention on hiding personal lives from family, employers, and the law. But by 1972, San Francisco had a "gay community" and "gay pride," declared publicly in a parade. Gay organizations, both political and social, were numerous and diverse. Gay male life had become a public cacophony of competing ideas and practices. Gay men had widened their interactions with each other and with lesbians into political, social, and religious organizations, and they had expanded the city's gay publications into a homegrown, tumultuous, competing set of periodicals.

Since the 1960s, gay men have been through much, from the sublime to the horrific: the bathhouse and disco years of the 1970s; AIDS and a renewed asso-

1

ciation of gay men with disease in the public consciousness; ACT UP and Queer Nation; ballot initiatives and "anti-special-rights" campaigns; *Lawrence v. Texas*; and most recently, legally recognized gay marriage. The experience of being gay in the twenty-first century is surely different from what it was during the 1960s, as gay men and women are now simultaneously integrated and excluded in American society in an odd kind of social tug-of-war. But the dramatic explosion of possibilities for gayness that emerged during the 1960s may serve as a touchstone for those concerned with the problems of gay male life in the twenty-first century. In 1960s San Francisco, gay men created increasingly diverse kinds of social interaction, which in turn enabled the creation of wide range of meanings for gay-maleness. This social fact from the past points up the centrality of maintaining the social and communicative spaces for gay folks to interact with each other, so that they can keep the power to make their own *meaning* of being homosexual. In the 1960s, the many conflicting ideas about what it meant to be a gay man grew out of the ground of diverse contexts for social interaction among the city's homosexuals and with the dominant society. Indeed, these contexts for communication and interaction provided them with the ability to create meaningful lives for themselves.

Many gay bars, a couple of gay activist organizations, and a handful of national publications already had served gay men in the previous decade, so clearly the transformation of the 1960s was one of scale and scope, not necessarily of kind. When I looked closely at gay men's lives in the 1960s, what I found was a significant shift in the way gay men (and lesbians) interacted with each other and with the dominant society, and a resultant burgeoning of *meaning production*, which in turn created the experience of increasing freedom among San Francisco's gay men and women. Although the idea of "gayness" had significance prior to the 1960s, two specific shifts in the way gay men interacted with each other, with lesbians, and with society at large changed the context within which gay men could understand themselves and create meaningful lives: first, they moved their efforts into the public sphere, and second, they self-consciously tried to create a "gay community." These two changes opened up the social space necessary for gay men to give new meaning to their experiences as homosexual and to their desires for freedom, relationship, and sex.

Moving their debates and struggles into the public sphere, activists in the early 1960s expanded a strategy begun by the Mattachine Society and the Daughters of Bilitis during the 1950s. Whereas the 1950s groups had tried reconciliation with American society and sought legitimacy by calling on experts to represent them in public, these new activists demanded they be heard on their own terms. They wanted to participate as full citizens in the democracy of San Francisco. By the end of the decade, younger gay men and women adopted the language and tactics of the anti-war movement[1] and argued that as gay people in public, they could show America how to liberate itself from worn-out sexual rules. This shift in the way gay men and women engaged the public sphere opened new fronts in the struggle of gay men to define gayness itself. Most scholarship about this period characterizes these movements in a kind of binary, with the "homophile," liberal, or assimilationist politics on one side, and the radical, revolutionary, or gay liberationist movement on the other side. However, by focusing on the micro-social level of individual experiences and feelings, I found instead a great deal of overlap and interplay among the city's activists, where gay men were arguing with each other, moving from group to group (or refusing to join any group), and constantly adapting and changing their views to match new experiences and ideas. More importantly, as activists worked to establish an effective social movement, they unintentionally created a communication community wherein even gay men who weren't activists could participate in important arguments over meaning. The struggles over political ends and means had the fruitful side effect of providing a platform from which gay men could work out the meaning of being a homosexual man.

The second shift in interaction ran parallel to the new gay publicity, as gay men increasingly expressed the desire to establish and participate in a "gay community." They wanted interaction with men who were "like them"; and they wanted interactions beyond bars and fleeting sexual encounters. In practice, they discovered that gay men were diverse, not only by race, class, and gender expression, but also in the ways they wanted to *be* gay and express their gayness. Because lesbians participated in and spearheaded much of the activism and they insisted on having a place in the community, gay men had to confront their sexism and the meaning of their gender identities. As a result, they argued continually over whether or not such a gay community could even exist. Nevertheless, they desired a community, even as they foundered on what exactly such a community should be. They worked hard, often in competing and contradictory ways, to establish institutions, organizations, physical spaces, and weekly meetings that would provide such a communal experience. It is difficult to say whether or not they ever succeeded, because as much as they desired the community of acceptance, they also felt sharply its shortcomings and failures. Regardless, their community-building efforts provided a context for gay men to consummate certain desires, both sexual and social; and it provided the second context for new kinds of interaction, out of which grew a variety of functioning gay male communities tied together through affective bonds. Gay men were able to figure out what gayness would mean precisely because they were trying to form a community, even though that community arguably never materialized.

This book isn't a history in the conventional sense. Although it treats a time period in the past, it is not a narrative of past events or of the actions of particular groups or individuals. To understand the interactions that occurred during a period of time and gave rise to meanings of gay-maleness that continue to be salient nearly fifty years later required a thoroughly interdisciplinary approach, both in research and analysis. And so I have borrowed from traditional historical method, employed a hermeneutical analysis inflected by mid-century symbolic interaction, and engaged in several of the key questions of John Dewey's pragmatism, namely, how is knowledge produced in the process of problem solving in a social environment, how do publics arise and to what effect, and what are the implications of both of these for democratic citizenship. This book, examines the kinds of social interactions gay men established and engaged in during this period, and to ask how that set of interactions produced those meanings for gay-maleness.

In order to drill down to the relationship between individual experience and meaning production, I have chosen to focus on a single location, the San Francisco Bay Area, in order to be as specific as possible about the environment and context of their experiences. In the American imagination, the city of San Francisco had become a homosexual Mecca by the early 1960s. By limiting this study to a particular location, it is easier to focus on the day-to-day conversations and struggles gay men were having with each other. San Francisco was a relatively open city sexually speaking well before the 1960s; and in California, a series of court cases had begun both opening up gay men's public lives and bringing gay men into the general public's awareness by the late 1950s. To frame the period in time, I chose two years that saw significant changes in gay men's interactions with each other and with society at large. In 1961, a popular drag entertainer, José Sarria, ran for the Board of Supervisors; also that year, the largest vice raid in the city's history arrested over eighty people at the Tay-Bush Inn, and the infamous Gayola extortion trials took place. On the other end of the decade, activists organized the city's first Gay Pride event in 1972, marking the beginning of a somewhat more centralized cultural practice that spanned across gay men's and lesbians' various communities.[2]

The surprisingly large and diverse body of gay publications from San Francisco during this period[3] contains a trove of experiences and feelings that gay men left in their own words, as articles, letters to the editor, editorials, photographs and illustrations, and design choices. Unconventionally, I elected to read the entire set of publications that began after 1960, rather than to sample. In a humanistic reading mode, I sought to tease out the connections between experience and meaning formation. Although these periodicals' distribution in bars and newsstands around the city and the array of views expressed in them do not give us any idea of the proportion of gay men who felt any given way, they can illustrate the range of ways that gay men experienced their gayness during the decade. From these data, it appears that individuals and groups moved through meanings contextually, changing as often as their experience required or allowed. My purpose here is to underscore this *accumulating* and *conditional* property of meanings, which are in effect the sum of the experience that preceded them, and the contingent nature of meaning formation, which occurs in particular contexts by embodied individual "experiencers."

Such archival primary source material has the limitation of possibly silencing groups of gay men who did not have access to these publications or to other means of leaving a trace of their experience and asserting a place in the gay public, including perhaps poor and working class men, and some men of color. The experiences of gay black, Latino, and Asian-American men are present in my data, but are difficult to mine, often only identifiable in the ethnicity of a last name or in the occasional self-identification of a writer. Despite this difficulty, race and ethnicity and class were key aspects of the arguments gay men were having with each other about what it meant to be gay in America; and I strive here to set the stage for what happens in the 1970s, as gay men of color began forming groups and movements of their own. Similarly, lesbians are present in the book but not the focus of this study. The gender differences between gay men and women during an era of intense sexism means that gay men and women had vastly different experiences of working out the meaning of their sexuality; by the end of the 1960s, lesbians were focusing most of their attention on sexism itself, which they experienced as the primary source of their oppression. Nonetheless, gay men and lesbians participated together in the formation of their publicity and their community, and gay men's efforts to understand gay-maleness cannot be separated from their interactions with lesbians. So throughout this book, I explicitly keep lesbians present to highlight the presence of gay women in gay men's lives and the centrality of gay women's efforts in gay men's ability to create a meaningful gay-maleness for themselves.

The increase in the scope and kind of interactions of publicity and community building bore diverse and contradictory ideas about what it meant to be a "gay man." As gay men and women interacted in new ways, gay men claimed power to define and control the meaning of their sexual desires, relationships, and communities. They confronted the meaning of "homosexual" as given them by the law, by the church and synagogue, and by medicine. And they fought to replace these outsider meanings with meanings of their own. For gay men, these battles linked up with struggles over the meaning of gay masculinity, male-male relationships, and homosexual sex. So a set of practices, institutions, objects, representations, and ideas about gay male life grew and evolved during this period, forming what I am calling here the *meaning of gay-maleness*. Some practices, like drag performances, originated in earlier gay male cultures and accrued new meanings and significance during the decade; other practices, such as the Community Center opened in 1966, were new experiments in what it might mean to be gay. But all of these practices, discourses, and experiences accrued and transformed the meaning of being a gay man. More important than their political activism or their new social movement, the meanings of gay-maleness that emerged during this period, with all their contradictions and paradoxes, proved to be the ground from which the long-lasting, widening, dynamic, and, most important, unsettled arguments about what it means to be a gay man have continued to grow. Even as they fought, argued, and zapped each other over meanings they didn't like, San Francisco's gay men worked throughout the period to create and sustain the social interactions necessary for them to workout the meanings of gay-maleness that answered their needs and supported the lives they wanted to lead.

The Nature of Meaning:
Experience, Environment, and Desire

To understand how and why gay men created the *meanings* of gay-maleness they did during this period and in this city, I begin with some important assumptions about the nature and origin of human interaction and of meaning itself. The way I describe the tangled systems of meanings gay men created follows closely what Clifford Geertz called "thick description," that is, a description not only of gay men's beliefs, practices, objects, responses, and feelings but also of their relationship to their social and cultural context and in their interaction with each other. Geertz posited "that man [sic] is an animal suspended in webs of significance he himself has spun." I argue with Geertz that "those webs, and the analysis of it to be therefore not an experimental science in search of law, but an interpretive one in search of meaning."[4] To this end, I strive to pay close attention to the actual process of meaning production, that is, how gay men attached significance to their experiences. The immediate difficulty of seeking to describe the "webs of significance" is that they were infinitely complex, with every practice, idea, word, or symbol carrying with them and number of possible meanings relative to the social contexts individual gay men were participating in. More difficult yet, any symbol, word, object, or act could have multiple simultaneous meanings for any number of gay men. The process of "thick description," then, is an analysis that seeks to sort out the relationships among the possible meanings, the social context of meaning-production, and the import or power of the meanings once they are formed.[5] I hope to expose gay men's distinctiveness, but also their "normalness" or banality as human beings, doing what humans do: making their lives meaningful. I make 1960s gay men understandable to us today, with all of our new and changed ideas about gay-maleness, by seeing them in their contexts. To this end, I lay aside as much as possible the notion of "gay male culture" as a category of analysis in favor of seeing *meaning* as the fundamental category of analysis, the particular and specific meanings that gay men were using and creating in the 1960s to make sense of their experiences as homosexuals in San Francisco.

The intellectual framework I employ is an empirical application of John Dewey's theory of mind and experience, which forms the underlying assumptions of my analysis. In that spirit, I have strived to treat gay men as individuals and groups who intelligently sought to create new meanings, as their circumstances allowed or required. More important, I have worked to consider these meanings in relation to the social and historical world they inhabited. This world was an infinitely complex social, cultural, physical *environment*, consisting not only of objects and not only of social relationships but also of all of the meanings ascribed to objects, individuals, practices, and signs within the environment and through its history. Through interaction with their complex environment, gay men's knowledge and their goals were linked together; and they garnered meaning from practice, action, and embodied experience, not from a priori truths. The relationship between the individual gay man and his complex environment was mutually transforming: as the environment shifted and changed through the 1960s, so did gay men's response to it; likewise, individuals and groups effected substantial changes in their environment by becoming conscious of it and choosing to shape it to meet their ends.[6] (In a broad sense, change happens over time precisely through this inextricable relationship between the individual and its environment.) The environment in which gay men lived—the national, religious, state and local cultures, their physical bodies, desires, and sex acts, their social interactions, language and discourses, and all the circulating meanings and signs extant in their cultural milieu—shaped them by provoking responses. Conversely, simultaneously, and necessarily, gay men sought to understand and change their environment to meet their needs and desires.

Consciousness of their needs and desires came from the constant problems gay men encountered, as their environment thwarted their efforts to fulfill their sexual, social, political, and relational desires, indeed, as the environment sought to arrest, harass, prosecute, excommunicate, and reject them. In daily living, when individuals' behaviors are supported and sustained by their environment, they act from what Dewey called "habit," which is to say, non-consciously or without thinking. For Dewey, it is when we encounter a problem, when we cannot for whatever reason consummate a desire, that we become aware of our environment and seek to adjust it or ourselves or both so that our desires can be met. The environment of 1960s San Francisco consisted of an ascribed perversion, illness, and criminality to same-sex desire, and social institutions sought, through direct and violent means, to prevent gay men and women from consummating their social and sexual desires. These were the "problems" that brought gay men to seek new ways of interacting with each other and with their environment (i.e., with the rest of society) in the 1960s.

Here I adapt George Herbert Mead's social-behaviorist definition of meaning to the task of interpreting 1960s gay publications. To wit, meaning arises in a three-phase process, as humans interact with each other and their environment and as they use language and communication and shared experience to figure out ways to make sense of their experiences. First, meaning must not be reduced to its linguistic component, but must always be conceived of as having the phase of the physical, embodied interaction with the environment and with other people; second, meaning has a phase of thinking, ruminating, examining, and communicating about experience; and in the third phase of meaning-making, new thinking and communication is used to transform the environment or the individual's perception of the environment in order to change future experience. From that three-phase, never-ending cycle emerges meaning. Said another way, meaning can only be described and understood operationally, that is, how it actually works in the world.[7] To be clear, then: I am employing a social-behavioristic view of meaning, where meaning is larger and more inclusive than rhetorical, semantic, or discursive understandings. Gay men of 1960s San Francisco, like all humans, were knowing and feeling individuals who experienced their world, their environment, and reacted consciously to reshape it and themselves to resolve the problems they experienced as men with same-sex desire. In *The Meaning of Gay*, I work to discern what the experience of those gay men might have been. The meanings they lent to their experiences to gayness itself were no mere rhetorical turns, nor were they simply political strategies of an "identity politic," nor were they broadly "discursive" or "linguistic." Rather, they emerged in thought and deed in the constant give and take between the their experience and their meaning-making.

So far I have used the term "experience" as if it were a self-evident concept, but I want to use the idea of experience in a specific way to describe the process whereby an individual interacts with its environment to produce culture. The concept of "experience" has been much criticized as an attempt to lend authenticity and authority to the individual, thereby making subjectivity into something it cannot be.[8] But for my purposes in this book, I want to think of experience as a *process*. In this sense, experience is neither observation, nor is it knowing, although knowledge arises from experience; rather it is *undergoing*, "a process of standing something; of suffering and passion, of affection, in the literal sense of these words. The organism has to endure, to undergo, the consequences of its own actions. Experience is no slipping along in a path fixed by inner consciousness."[9] For Dewey, experience is both an *activity*, something we do and have agency over, and an *undergoing*, something that happens to us over which we have no control. As an activity-undergoing, experience can be neither dualistic, with a mind existing apart from the environment, nor subjective, with experience being knowable only to the experiencer. To remain analytically useful, experience must be held as distinct from the thoughts experience produces, that is to say from the evaluation and appraisal of experience, which are the cognitive effect of experience.[10] But it is likewise an analytical error to separate the experience from that which is experienced; experience must not be reduced to the process of experiencing as if it were complete in itself. That is to say, gay men *actively-underwent* their environment, making meanings inextricably linked to the environment that produced them.[11]

Finally, my move away from culture to meaning, and from meaning to experience, leads to the centrality of *desire*. Perhaps in queer studies more than any other, desire already plays a huge role, precisely because the object of desire is at the center of queers' difference and hence their social position. But in thinking about experience and meaning, the notion of desire must be expanded. As gay men experienced their environment, what desires did they feel? What desires were suppressed or encouraged? What desires were easily, habitually consummated and how? What desires were not easily consumable and therefore created problems for gay men, requiring conscious efforts to adjust themselves and their environment in order to consummate them? Why were some desires difficult to consummate while others could be consummated habitually? Desire must be reconceived in much larger terms to understand why and how this homosexuality, a particular set of meanings for gay-maleness came to be between

1961 and 1972. A narrow, erotic, or Freudian understanding of desire could never explain the struggles for meaning or for community, nor could it explain why and how gay men fought for recognition in the public sphere. To answer that problem, we must greatly expand our understanding of desire and both its individual and social functions.

Desires begin with what Dewey called "impulses," which are sort of amorphous biological functions: you have a crick in your back, a hunger pang, a sexual desire, a yawn. The problem with such impulses lies in their unintelligibility—to know these impulses as desires is already to have interpreted them. All we have to evaluate such "impulses" is either their material effect (i.e., the individual's behavior) or the meaning we ascribe to them or their concomitant behavior. "In short, the meaning of native activities [impulses and their behaviors] is not native; it is acquired."[12] Inasmuch as gay men were, by definition, social organisms, their impulses were from the beginning experienced in a social context which lent to them significance. In the best of cases, impulses meld nicely into the environment and their significance takes on the form of habitual action, where their expression and regular consummation are supported by the environment. Many impulses are dealt with habitually, in predispositions to act in certain ways under certain circumstances. For example, the majority of people's sexual impulses are successfully guided and tracked into habitual forms that are intelligible to and morally resonant with others in their environment. But for gay men, their desires were neither guided into habitual forms of expression, nor were they intelligible to or morally resonant with the majority of society in the 1960s. Thus, gay men continually "tripped" over their sexual desires, bringing them out of habitual consummation and demanding that they be fulfilled. In short, gay men's desires were problems that could not be ignored.

In the end, what came of my immersion in their periodicals and in these men's lives was a view into the complexity of how their interactions and experiences created meanings to solve the problems presented by the social setting they lived in. Gay men's desires arose precisely because their environment thwarted the habitual consummation of their various sexual, social, political, relational impulses. That is, something was wrong or lacking in their environment, so their impulses rose to consciousness as desires and problems that must be addressed, demanding interpretation and adjustment.[13] I seek here to lay bare gay men's desires as they were connected to their environment, in order to understand and thickly describe the interaction, experience, and especially the *meanings* that emerged among gay men in this particular time and place. In each of the following chapters, I sift through the multiple aspects of gay male life, paying particular attention to the affective quality of their experience and the discursive contents of their arguments, as well as to their conflicts and points of rupture. I also focus on their strategies or proposed strategies to try to discern what their desires were by looking at their hoped-for ends. And finally, I strive to reveal where gay men's lives intersected with the dominant culture and the effect that such interaction had. The end result is a map of the field of possible desires, strategies, and behaviors, the very *meaning of gay* is it came to be for homosexual men by 1972 in San Francisco.

Notes

1. See Justin David Suran, "Coming Out against the War: Antimilitarism and the Politicization of Homosexuality in the Era of Vietnam" in *American Quarterly* 53, no. 2 (Sept. 2001): 452–488.

2. There had been at least one Christopher Street Memorial march before 1972. For a detailed description of San Francisco's gay history and for the general historical context of the 1960s, see the Appendix.

3. I have excluded from my body of evidence two publications from the period, *The Mattachine Review* and *The Ladder*. I did, however, skim through them as a point of reference and to answer questions I had as I was researching. The former was a publication anchored in the older forms of gay activism from the 1950s. Although I don't reference the publication specifically, I do give voice to the political stances of that style of gayness inasmuch as those men were also participating in the publication of the newer periodicals. *The Ladder* was a lesbian publication of the Daughters of Bilitis; it did contain a number of articles by, for, and about gay men (see Chapter 6). I chose to focus on the publications of organizations that were seeking new and more expansive methods of dealing with their experience of gayness, so I didn't treat directly the publications that preceded the period.

4. Clifford Geertz, *The Interpretation of Cultures* [1973] (Basic Books: New York, 2000): 5.

5. See Geertz, 9.

6. See John Dewey, *Individualism Old and New* [1930], in *John Dewey: The Later Works, 1925–1953*, Vol. 5, ed. Jo Ann Boydston (Carbondale: Southern Illinois UP, 1988, 112.

7. This is a modified and, for my purposes, simplified rendering of George Herbert Mead's definition of meaning from *Mind Self and Society: From the Standpoint of a Social Behaviorist* [1934], ed. by Charles W. Morris (University of Chicago Press: Chicago, 1962), 75–80.

8. See Joan W. Scott, "The Evidence of Experience," in *The Lesbian and Gay Studies Reader*, eds., Henry Abelove, Michele Aina Barale, and David M. Halperin (New York: Routledge, 1993): 397–415.

9. From "The Need for a Recovery of Philosophy," quoted in Robert. B. Westbrook, *John Dewey and American Democracy* (Ithaca: Cornell UP, 1993): 127.

10. See Westbrook, 323.

11. See Westbrook, 345.

12. John Dewey, *Human Nature and Conduct* [1922] (Dover Books: Toronto, 2002): 90.

13. John Dewey, *Theory of Valuation* [1939] in *The Later Works: Vol. 13* ed. by Jo Ann Boydston (Southern Illinois UP: Carbondale, 1991): 220.

1

The Origins and Values of
a Gay Male Public

Never fear, we shall win—for the fight for personal freedom is a growing thing
and VICTORY IS IN THE WIND.
                                                    —from *The News*, Aug. 5, 1963

It is even more important to realize that the conditions out of which the efforts
at remedy [of shared, public problems] grew, and made it possible for them to
succeed, were primarily non-political in nature. For the evils were of long
standing, and any account of the movement must raise two questions: Why
were efforts at improvement not made earlier, and, when they were made, why
did they take just the form they did take?
                              —John Dewey, *The Public and Its Problems*, 1927

In 1964, Washington D.C. police arrested Walter W. Jenkins, a member of
President Johnson's administration, for soliciting a lewd act in the YMCA men's
restroom. On the other side of the country in San Francisco, *Citizen's News*
commented on the "Jenkins Affair" with a blasé tone about the bugaboo of public sex.[1] Guy Strait, *Citizen's News* publisher, was more interested in how much
of a non-issue Jenkins' arrest seemed to be. Strait used the dalliance in a public
toilet stall to argue that Jenkins, who had served with Johnson for years, proved
once and for all that homosexuals were trustworthy and stalwart citizens who
should be given security clearances and equal access to public service jobs. For
Strait, the only thing Jenkins was guilty of was being "one of the majority of
American males who have in their adult life sought out the sexual companionship of the same sex" (*CN*, 4.1, 5–6).[2] But after the D.C. YMCA had closed the

bathroom where Jenkins had been arrested, Strait bitterly noticed that when a public official had sex in public, it was attributed to "'overwork' and 'intoxication,'" rather than to immorality of a homosexual (*CN* Nov. 1964, 2). For its part, *Citizen's News* continued to print warnings about sting operations by the San Francisco Police Department[3] and even maps of local public restrooms where officials were spying on patrons and entrapping gay men.[4]

Men have used so-called public spaces to have sex with each other in many different times and places.[5] In the twentieth century, certain parks, YMCAs, men's boarding houses, wharves, and restrooms often gained reputations, for those "in the life," as areas where sex could be had with other men. By 1961, these meeting spots in San Francisco and the cruising habits of homosexual men were used in the official public sphere as proof-positive of the moral degeneracy of gay men, where "the mere presence of deviates is enough to scare many people" (*CN* Feb. 24, 1964, 1–2). In 1970, one man who claimed to have overcome his homosexuality through psychotherapy summed up the fears about gay men's public acts. "I could really have more compassion for your [gay] cause . . . if it weren't for the roving eyes and hands, the succulent voice, the nudging and nestling up to perfect strangers that so many gays do . . . and on and on. And always in public" (*VR* July 1970, 18–19, 41). Comments such as these show the general association of homosexuality with public sex. In San Francisco, an all-out war raged against gay public sex throughout the 1960s, with the SFPD training young police recruits in "homosexual styles" to solicit sex from men in public places.[6] Local police even raided private parties.[7] San Francisco Parks and Recreation department even went so far as to cut down the bushes and shrubs in Buena Vista Park, a popular cruising area for gay men, hoping to discourage sex in the underbrush.[8] In California's penal code, solicitation of someone of the same sex was a lewd act that carried severe penalties.[9] Even when the charges didn't stick, the arrestees' names were regularly printed in local newspapers such that they were exposed to friends, family, and employers, who more often than not would fire the sex offender employees.[10] The city's police continued this practice even after a 1971 Mayor's committee endorsed gay rights and recommended stepping back from spending so many resources on "victimless crimes" of public sex.[11] Indeed, between 1961 and 1972, gay male public sex arose again and again as the primary point of conflict in the relationship between gay men and the official public sphere in San Francisco.

The issue of "public sex" points to a particular way that gay men encountered publicity in the post-war years, and also points out the particularly vexed notions of the public itself. Inasmuch as the United States is a pluralistic, democratic society, in many ways, something that seems so obvious as a "public sphere" often defies definition. The idea of a public remains useful, nonetheless, and indeed paramount to understanding what happened to gay men during the 1960s. John Dewey's notion of fluid, overlapping publics offers a useful hermeneutic for understanding the complex ways that gay men adjusted and recreated their publicity and how their collective move toward the public sphere served as a foundational cite of social interaction where gay men made sense of their lives during the 1960s. For my purposes, I will be employing Dewey's definition of a *public* as a social effect, not necessarily a physical space or institution, emerging out of specific circumstances and experiences and interactions of specific people. Individual gay men's experiences in aggregate led various groups of gay men to discover that they had shared problems or interests (social, economic, emotional, sexual, etc.) and pushed them together to solve those problems or meet their collective needs. A gay public arose out of that interaction.[12] *Publicity* as I will be using the term is the state of taking part in an existing public or in the formation of a new one. Gay male publicity arose through, among other things, the ongoing controversies surrounding public sex in 1960s San Francisco, which pushed them to engage with each other and with the official public sphere in new ways.

The idea of an *official public* bears some explanation. In coming together to talk about the ramifications of public sex, gay men encountered and modified existing publics even as they formed new ones. And clearly, some publics have more power than others to control and shape the environment and to enforce their values on those living under their influence. In gay men's experience in the 1960s, the public sphere of the American liberal democratic system, as it was practiced in San Francisco, exerted control over their lives through its legal, medical, and police institutions. I will be using the phrase *official public* to indicate this dominant social space and the institutions and agents that had the power to enforce its norms on gay men, especially through the law, police, court system, government regulation, governmental agencies, and policies. Nancy Fraser has argued that the official public sphere by definition excludes those who do not meet certain minimum requirements for participation; that is to say, it excludes those who violate the norms of the society that produces the particular public in question. The official public sphere, then, is the "institutional vehicle" of social control based "primarily on consent supplemented with some measure of repression."[13]

In an official public sphere that rendered their sexuality illegitimate and that devoted much time and money to suppressing their sexuality, the list of the ways gay men were excluded from participating in "normal" society grew long. In addition to the city persecuting gay men for the crime of public sex, insurance companies denied coverage for "moral reasons"[14]; Ronald Reagan's tax reforms doubled taxes on single men[15] and rewarded married couples (de facto heterosexual) with decreased taxes; the Supreme Court ruled that the Immigration and Naturalization Service could exclude homosexuals from entry because they were psychopathic by definition[16]; the *San Francisco Chronicle* refused to print SIR's advertisements[17]; the media regularly censored materials containing homosexual content[18]; and the California Public Utilities Commission ruled that the phone book did not have to carry listings for gay organizations.[19] Gay men were seen as unstable employees, prone to alcoholism and blackmail, and thus security risks.[20] It wasn't until the end of the 1960s that Assemblyman Willie Brown and Supervisor Diane Feinstein in San Francisco politics courted the gay vote; Brown actually fought for years in the California Assembly to decriminalize homosexual sex between consenting adults. It wasn't until the McGovern campaign in 1972 that a national public figure in a major political party argued for the first time that sexuality should have no bearing in employment.[21]

Thus, this official public sphere unavoidably formed gay men's experience, their activity-undergoing, during this period, as the institutions and agents of the official public constantly intervened and thwarted their efforts to consummate their sexual desires, to form lasting relationships and communities, and to create meaningful lives. Combined with the immediate danger of police harassment in their day-to-day lives, these other forms of institutional discrimination created an environment in which *gay man* would become increasingly salient as a category of exclusion vis-à-vis the official public sphere starting in the 1950s and coming to a head in the 1960s. These kinds of public, material repressions were embedded in the institutional structure of the public sphere, and as time wore on, would form the ways individual men constructed the meaning of their gayness, or in other words, the ways they were able to understand their sexuality.

The repression of the public sphere motivated gay men's production of particular meanings, symbols, and practices in response to and in transaction with it. As gay men became aware that they were no longer satisfied with their status in the official public, that the official public was indeed a "problem" in and of itself, they had to come up with means of dealing with and transforming it. But experiences of institutional repressions were not equally distributed among gay men. Races, ethnicities, classes, occupations, religions, and gender expressions all created vastly differentiated relationships to the same official public among gay men. This varied experience of public oppression gave rise in part to the greatly differentiated (if often overlapping) modes of gay male expression. That is to say, a more effeminate gay man experienced public repression differently than a more masculine gay man; a Mexican-American gay man experienced public repression differently than an Asian-American gay man; a working class gay man experienced public repression differently from a professional gay man. Despite these differences, gay men had discovered in the 1950s that if they presented themselves as "normal" or if they hid their sexuality, they could often participate in the official public sphere unmolested. However, the scope and scale of institutional discrimination led many, but not all, gay men to conclude that such "respectability"—that is, entering the official public sphere on its own terms—came at too high a price. It required the individual to hide or manage parts of himself as a precondition of participation in the official public; it required gay men to *pass* as heterosexual. This would form the backbone of many disagreements among gay men throughout the 1960s.

Gay Sex and the Experience of Gay Publicity

As I have already strongly suggested, the issue of public sex itself formed the center of gay men's debates with each other (not to mention with lesbians) about

what a gay publicity would or should look like, revealing the tensions and contradictions gay men experienced as they tried to participate in the official public
between 1961 and 1972, in various ways, *as gay men*. During this period, some
gay men in San Francisco began to shift their political engagement with the official public by refusing to conform to heterosexual society's mores, and insisting
on a fundamental transformation of the official public sphere to accommodate
their sexual and gender differences. The controversy surrounding gay male public sexuality reveals the basic tensions and contradictions that gay men encountered as they attempted to access the public sphere. Gay men encountered an
official public that constantly challenged and foreclosed their personal integration as gay men by reducing them to a small set of sex acts (performed in public
spaces and presenting a "danger" to society) and by tightly corralling their sexual activities through the intervention of the official public's agents (regardless
of where the acts actually took place). In other words, interaction with the official public vis-à-vis public sex produced an *experience* of publicity that demanded that gay men take steps either to confront the power of the official public, to claim a place in that public to transform it, or to form a counter-public. To
experience publicity, then, in the Deweyan sense, meant an active-undergoing of
the interactive processes among individuals and with social institutions and
symbol systems, out of which emerged a gay male publicity, identifiable in its
effects among gay men and in its interactions with the official public.[22]

To understand these dynamics, I turn to a close examination of the arguments gay men had with each other about public sex and the connections those
arguments had with their experience of repression. In 1967, SFPD Officer Elliot
Blackstone, of the community relations unit, told members of the Society for
Individual Rights[23] that "more bad things happen to the homophile than to the
'straight' guy because of the homophile's indiscretion. Self-policing was urged"
(*VR* March 1967, 5). This officer's view—that gays were to blame for their harassment and that the only way they could stop harassment was to police each
other's behavior—is indicative of the overall relationship that gay men had to
the institutions of the official public during the 1960s. Agents of the official
public (in this case, a police officer) felt repressive actions against gay men were
justified and that only by changing their own behavior would gay men be freed
from harassment in the public sphere.[24] A couple months after Officer Blackstone's speech, *Vector* ran an Open Forum, "Sex In Public Places," which aired
the feelings within the San Francisco gay male community about public sex.
Gay men offered conflicting responses, revealing internalized conflict as they
struggled with their abjection vis-à-vis the domination of the official public and
their efforts to "self-police." The forum also laid bare key areas of social conflict
among gay men who effectively "self-policed" their behavior to fit the expectations of the official public sphere and those who resisted the notion that they
were responsible for their own persecution. By 1972, not much had changed in
terms of gay male sexual practices in public and police efforts to control them.
"The police, alarmed by the falling arrest rate, sent in a large number of hand-

some vice officers in skin tight clothing to make entrapment arrests" into Land's End, a beach park in the northwest corner of the city (*BAR*, May 31, 1972).[25]

From the official public's repressive actions came the knowledge that simply talking to a man you didn't know while out in public could land you before a judge. Gay men had to make personal, day-to-day decisions accounting for the possible public consequences of their private sex lives. *LCE News* began to report on specific judges and their excessive penalties for these victimless sex crimes in 1962.[26] If a man was ever actually caught having sex with another man, the maximum penalty could have been life in prison.[27] It continued to amaze gay men that such overblown means were used to control their sexual behavior. When security officers began to arrest gay men in the Union Square Macy's bathroom with some regularity, a *Vector* report took a stand, questioning the zealousness of the District Attorney's office in prosecuting these cases as felonies (*VR* Aug. 1970, 50). More important, these kinds of experiences with police sweeps and public punishment taught gay men that to enter the public sphere *as gay men* was to put themselves in danger. Wrote one man, "Am I the only one who is outraged that just to be a homosexual in public is to be subjected to beatings and possibly murder for not reason other than you ARE a homosexual?" (*VR* June 1967, 17). And so in transaction with their environment, with the official public, gay men shaped their views of themselves and their sexual desires and practices and reacted by modifying their behavior accordingly.

This was no easy process, as gay men's experiences arose within an official public that granted and withheld privileges and powers; so gay men were torn between their desires to fulfill their sexual needs and desires and their desires to be recognized within the official public. In the early 1960s, Guy Strait embodied this ambivalence many gay men felt about so-called public sex. On one hand, Strait championed a conservative citizenship, where allegiance was owed to the state and rights were a privilege. Strait argued that "calling the police is fully justified" in cases of public sex, and that "public sexual display is not and never will be tolerated in this country" (*TN* Sept. 16, 1963, 1–2). Strait blamed men who have sex in parks for delaying the day when "consenting adults may enjoy sex acts in private" (*CN* Feb. 24, 1964, 1–2). At the same time, he also acknowledged that "most people, at one time or the other, have committed lewd acts of one kind or another in public" and defended peoples' rights to use public places without danger of unconstitutional spying[28] or entrapment by undercover police (*CN* Jan. 27, 1964, 1, 5). In fact, in the same stories where Strait condemned public sex, he often also clearly stated where such sex was to be had and how to avoid arrest, as if with a sly wink. This ambivalence about public sex—between acknowledging that real people are sexual everywhere, including in public spaces, and the desire to conform to dominant mores—is the hallmark of a bifurcated perception that gay men developed of the official public sphere.

On one hand, gay men attempted to explain and understand why some among them sought sex in public places.[29] One letter writer asked, "Why in heaven's name did they go out there [to Land's End] in the first place? . . . Do your thing, but do it at home and not in public places" (*BAR* July 15, 1971).

Charles Davis actually offered a classification of the kinds of men who sought sex in public places: "masochists" or those who seek the thrill; those who don't know there are communities and organizations; those "who find it almost impossible to make out [successfully find a sex partner] in the other places"[30]; and "the closet queen who doesn't want to associate with her sex partners" (see *VR* May 1967, 14). Some men argued for public sex on practical erotic grounds: quite simply, it was where sex was available.[31] Spaces where gay men sought each other for sex offered "ready availability to contacts for quick sex acts" (*VR* May 1967, 14).[32] Perhaps the most candid explanation of all came from someone calling himself An Old Bush Queen. "No homosexual in his right mind should condone sex in public places, but let's face it: It's fun!" (*VR* May 1967, 14).[33] E. Barlow wrote, "As a person near 40 years of age, I have enjoyed sex in public places for most of my life. . . . Although I practice sex in public, I try to do so in secluded spots where no one but those involved will be exposed to what I am doing." [34] For many men, the meaning of public sex was quite simply as a physical release, in many cases, the only available means to consummate their sexual desires.

On the other hand, some gay men argued against public sex and for the arrest of gay men who engaged in it. They did so from several standpoints. One was simply that the general population (the majority of whom participate in the official public) would be offended by public displays of sexuality.

> We cannot condone the set of participating in open and public display of sex appetites. . . . Buena Vista Park [is] amply stocked with the Nature Boys who dart hither and thither with a lean and hungry look for something. . . . [An offended park patron] only knows that these people make the parks unpleasant and therefore should be controlled. *TN* Sept. 1963, 1–2

Aceydecy, a letter writer from New York, argued that public sex was even more offensive than effeminacy.[35] Another blasting critique came from Fred, an exgay man: "Those gays so hot for cum down their throat they commit sexual intercourse (anal or 69s) right on the floors of the public toilets. . . . I never have known a law-abiding gay to get arrested" (*VR* July 1970, 18–19, 41). This image of the sex-crazed gay men who couldn't control himself circulated regularly among gay men themselves, and often with condemnation for bringing shame to the gay community.[36] Thus, in many ways gay men reproduced the attitudes and values of the dominant culture, agreeing with the judgments made of them by individuals such as Officer Blackstone. Guy Christien wrote, "I don't think any group, including us, has the right to thrust our pleasure or sexual activities down anyone's throat (you'll pardon that)" (*VR* March 1970, 32). Thus, many gay men ended up accepting the inherent lewdness of public gay sexuality, even as they regularly availed themselves of sex in public places.[37]

At the same time, this ambivalence did not prevent gay men from making direct critiques of the official public's regulation of their sexuality. Inasmuch as the public had been structured to render gay sexuality illicit per se, the "implica-

tion that we had better operate within the law has no merit for us [gay men]—
any of us. For our very sexual orientation leads to an illegal activity in the consummation of our natural sexual desire" (*BAR* March 1, 1972). Gay men also
began speaking out about the hypocrisy of the double standard that allowed
straight public sex to go not only unpunished,[38] but often completely unnoticed.
Strait had pointed out a *San Francisco Examiner* article on public sex that completely ignored the places that are "filled with men and women necking" (*CN*
Feb. 24, 1964, 1–2). And one letter writer wrote, "To say such conduct [flirting
in bars] is obscene is absurd, unless the courts were to hold that a man telling a
woman in a heterosexual bar that 'You're a cute little doll' is equally obscene"
(*VR* Jan. 1966, 3).[39] This disconnect between the way heterosexual public sex
was treated and the way homosexual public sex was treated stood as a stark reminder of their abject position in the official public.

A further contradiction became clear to gay men later in the 1960s, that they
were being arrested merely for associating with each other as openly gay men.
Gay Sunshine ran numerous editorials excoriating the double standard, and criticizing gay men for going "out of their way to avoid offending heterosexual sensibilities" by associating openly with each other in public (*GS* Oct.–Nov. 1971,
6). What gay men came to realize was that they weren't being arrested for having sex in public, but merely for flirting or cruising or most egregiously, just for
congregating together. By 1972, the anger had grown at the way the official
public sought to control their sexuality. "And in fact, 'public sex' . . . is not an
issue here. What is at issue is the abuse of police power and the right of gay
people to ask other gay people to ball [fuck]. 'Public sex' has nothing to do with
it. People are not being busted for balling in public." This ultimately boiled
down to the rights of gay people to use public spaces to meet each other and
even have sex with each other, just as heterosexuals did.[40] How could it be
against the law just to ask someone to have sex with you? Gay backlash against
this repression raged more pointed in the early 1970s when gay men began to
see how the laws against public sexuality played to the economic and political
benefit of straight institutions. When the YMCA refused to hire gay employees
but continued to charge higher rates for single men, critics began to argue that
the Y was exploiting gay men for the money, because they knew they provided
one of the few spaces for gay men to meet.[41] Gay men also noticed the political
advantage of maintaining the strict control of their sexuality in public. Quoting
an editorial from the *Chronicle*, "'Many of our law enforcement people . . .
would rather that certain crimes especially those of a sexual nature, continue to
exist. The elimination of these crimes would deprive certain politicians of votes,
and certain cops of a reason for being,'" (*VR* Oct. 1970, 10). To get around this
differential treatment, gay men had established separate and clandestine institutions and small associations (such as bars) years earlier, in order to meet each
other and have sex; but for many gay men at the end of the 1960s, gay bars and
private clubs were no longer a good enough response to the repression.

As gay men grew in their political power toward the end of the 1960s and
support was growing to overturn California's sodomy statute, state officials

drew a connection between legalizing private consensual behavior and the "menace" of public sex. Beginning in the late 1960s, the official public exercised its dominance as it fought against these efforts. A state lobbyist, Carl Anderson argued in favor of the continued legal proscription of homosexuality, insisting that they "'do not practice in private, but rather in the men's rooms, bus stations, and bowling alleys,'" thereby causing public danger (quoted in *VR* June 1972, 23). Even as San Francisco's Assemblyman Willie Brown led the fight to repeal the sodomy statute, the city's gay men were subjected to the argument that if gay sex were decriminalized, the police would be unable to enforce public lewdness laws and ultimately would lose the ability to prevent child molestation.[42] The institutions of the official public again and again exerted a tight control of gay sex. What gay men had to confront, subconsciously or consciously in their day-to-day lives, was that their sex would never be private; it was, by definition a minority sexuality and therefore a public and criminal sexuality.[43]

Given the structure of social relations in the official public as it emerged in the battles over public sex, many gay men saw their fastest way out of hot water was to position gay sex firmly in the realm of the private sphere.[44] Strait argued that gay men should "learn to live [their] private lives privately" (*TN* Aug. 18, 1963, 3–4), and a young man recently kicked out of the Navy declared, "I say that what a man does in private is his own business" (*CN* June 22, 1964, 6). It was hoped that by making a claim to privacy, they would be treated like heterosexuals (assuming, of course, that heterosexuals likewise bracketed their sexuality when in public).[45] By the mid-1960s, privacy had emerged as the foremost right that many gay men desired in a list of other rights[46]; they saw privacy as the means to attain "sexual freedom in private" (*TT* Feb.–March 1965).[47] They hoped that by removing gay sex to the protection of the private sphere, it would somehow lift the stigma upon homosexuality in the dominant culture.[48] This, they hoped, would be attained as privacy created an imaginary wall that would keep the government from interfering with gay men's lives.[49] By the late 1960s, arguments for privacy morphed into arguments for equal protection, where "sexual practices between consenting adults are not a proper subject for state regulation" (*VR* June 1969, 5).[50] At the same time, for many others, privacy was not merely the politically expedient strategy, but it was the *morally correct* thing to do. Indeed, for them, sex really did belong in the private sphere.[51]

Placing gay sex in the private sphere in this way required on one hand that the dominant culture recognize gay sex as a legitimate sexuality and on the other hand that gay men agree to completely bracket their sexuality in public. So even as gay men hoped that privacy would lead to their ultimate sexual freedom, their experiences in public provoked pointed doubts. "We have been brainwashed by the 'right to privacy' into believing that liberty means . . . get in your little cubicle baby, lock your door behind you, and stay there and ONLY there have you the right to be a human being" (*VR* June 1967, 17). Whereas some gay men saw privacy as their only way into the heretofore closed public sphere, others felt that privacy only offered partial personhood. Gary Alinder highlighted this with his description of a run-in with a lawyer in Los Angeles who defended gay men in court. "'What I do in bed is nobody's business' [said the lawyer]. I wanted to scream, 'Honey, I don't care what you do in bed. I just asked if you are Gay,'" (*GS* Aug.–Sept. 1970, 12). Fundamentally, for most gay men writing in the gay publications of the period, the unequal control of same-sex acts trumped the argument for privacy: "Nor does the public demand protection from the sexual solicitation of heterosexuals" (*GS* Oct.–Nov. 1971, 6). The relationship between "being gay" and "fucking in private" was made explicit in their argument for privacy, as admission into the official public required hiding one's sexual difference.

These ongoing arguments that gay men had with each other about public sex reveal a four-point relationship to public sexuality in particular, and ultimately, to publicity writ large. First, if there weren't always immediate institutional consequences to their sexuality, there was always the threat (of repression, arrest, imprisonment, loss of employment, etc.). Thus, sexuality expressed in any public, open way—from solicitation to effeminate behavior—carried with it real consequences that threatened these men's lives. Second, there was not only a negative valence attached to same-sexuality, but there was attached to it the insistence by the dominant culture that gay male sex was *always* public by definition; thus, there was in practice no space where their sexuality could possibly be completely private and unregulated. Third, there was great confusion over the notions of lewdness and public decency. Since gay sex was by definition lewd, normal sexual activities—from flirting to seeking sexual contact to expressing a gender that challenges social norms—were denied gay men, creating a double standard.[52] And fourth, this double standard allowed straights to express their sexual-ness in the public sphere unthinkingly—or *habitually*, in the Deweyan sense—thereby foreclosing a full publicity to gay men who must always bracket their sexual-ness when in public. The official public, then, seems to have defined "public sex" not as an actual place (e.g., a park) or a particular interaction (e.g., cruising), but as the possibility of witnessing a gay act by individuals who did not wish to see or acknowledge the existence or possibility of gayness at all.

Gay men experienced publicity in tandem with their sex lives, in opposition to police intervention in their sex lives and in the context of 1960s America. They reacted in varied ways to the repression of their sexuality and they contested each others' experiences, arguing over what it meant to be gay within that environment and with that particular official public. Ultimately, these experiences could only be interpreted within gay men's communities and associations, which in turn pushed them to rethink their fundamental values as they interacted with each other and with lesbians. The values that gay men produced out of their experience in the official public sphere were the first steps toward producing a new publicity, a gay male publicity (overlapping with a larger gay and lesbian publicity). Fraser calls such a publicity a "counter-public," one of multiple competing publics in any given society. Whereas official publics have institutional power to enforce its cultural norms, counter-publics form "where subordinated social groups invent and circulate counter-discourses to formulate oppositional interpretation of their identities, interests, and needs."[53] This proved to be the impetus necessary to produce a gay male public with a dominant culture all its own, albeit a hotly contested and unstable one. Indeed, in many ways, these active-undergoings of publicity produced gay men themselves in the self-conscious, public formation we have come to expect in democratic societies. This nascent counter-public grew in response and transaction with other, more broad forms of repression.

Oppression as Thwarted Individuation

The public sex controversy was only one aspect of the official public's repression of gay men. They also had to withstand the constant intrusion of the police, the courts, the church, and medical professionals into their lives. Through these incursions, the official public constantly interfered in gay men's association with each other and with the other publics within which they interacted. This disrupted association was the locus of gay men's experience of what they called alternately oppression, discrimination, repression, domination, inequality, slavery, abuse, and violence, among other things. Without the ability to freely interact and associate with each other without interference, to form relationships, and create meaningful lives, they did not, and I argue indeed could not, feel free. John Dewey argued that associations provide individuality through interaction in a counter-intuitive way, where "individuality demands association to develop and sustain it and association requires arrangement and coordination of its elements, or organization—otherwise it is formless and devoid of power."[54] The consequence of official interference, then, was that it forestalled the development of an affective association wherein gay men could individuate. Rather than a mere attack on rights or an abstract kind of freedom (which was how gay men framed their experience in the pages of their publications), these intrusions from the official public actually repressed their ability to individuate, in a Deweyan instrumental sense. Such repression took the form of legal maneuvering and enforcement, violence against gay men, institutionalization, incarceration, and the continual threat of all of the above. What I will loosely call *oppression*, then, originated in the interference of the official public in their emerging gay publics and works by disrupting their ability to interact with each other in productive ways for their personal individuation.

In an article that appeared in *The Nation* in December 1965 and reprinted in *Town Talk*, the editors argued that "instead of protecting citizens from criminals, a substantial part of the police department devotes itself to harassing and persecuting homosexuals, who almost always are harmless" (*TT* Dec. 1965, 11). Through their relationship with the police department, gay men most acutely felt the oppression of their sexuality by the official public, thereby rendering their oppression intelligible and material, that is, as a problem to be worked out. "Our reward [for seeking publicity] . . . is ostracism and jail, blackmail and entrapment, the back alley and the drag ball" (*VR* Jan 1965, 5). In its inaugural issue,

Gay Sunshine ran a consciousness-raising, graphic-laden list of gay men who had been beaten, harassed, and killed by the police (see *GS* Aug.–Sept. 1970, 7). The need to directly engage with the police had begun before 1961 and continued through the period and beyond. In the early 1970s, the newer gay organizations saw themselves as being those who would finally change that relationship, often ignoring the work of their activist forebears. "Every day gay people are unjustly arrested for lewd conduct, prostitution, loitering, etc. . . . With the advent of the gay liberation movement, things are beginning to change" (*GS* Oct.–Nov. 1971, 2). And so, among all the sources of oppression, many gay men saw the government as its primary source.[55]

Nonetheless, the forms this oppression took were varied. Legal hurdles were erected to prevent gay men's sociality. The SFPD and the Alcoholic Beverages Commission enforced a series of laws meant to discourage the incursion of homosexuals into the city. Loitering laws were modified making it illegal for a single man to walk alone or to linger in the street without a purpose, and police were given the authority to stop anyone and ask for that purpose. It was against the law to dress in the opposite gender's clothing with the "intent to deceive." Through a series of lawsuits, bar owners had secured the rights of gay men and women to assemble and consume alcohol in California by the early 1960s.[56] But this fight continued, as a legal loophole allowed the continued closing of gay and lesbian bars.[57] The California Supreme Court had ruled that to be a homosexual and serve alcohol to a homosexual could not be constitutionally forbidden; but their ruling had left also said the state could regulate lewd behavior, which by legal definition, all homosexual behavior was. So rather than loosening the associative possibilities of gay male life, the California Supreme Court decision tightened anti-homosexual legal precedent, such that any homosexual act—including flirting, talking about sex with someone of the same sex, dancing, kissing, and holding hands—was grounds for arrest of the individual and closure of the establishment where it occured.[58] For example, the ABC announced that the alcohol license of the Black Cat at midnight on October 31, 1963, because of lewd behavior on the premises. Guy Strait covered both the events of that last Halloween and the subsequent legal battles.[59] It was common knowledge among gay men that agents of the state made false arrests[60] and lied on the stand[61]—guilt or innocence played little role in the execution of the law.

The SFPD's primary tool of enforcement, as mentioned earlier, was entrapment.[62] Plain-clothed, young police officers were routinely sent into bars, bath houses, parks, streets, anywhere where gay men congregated; they would make a pass at a man they suspected was gay; if the man accepted, he was arrested. Violence often followed arrest, as in the case of Roberto Bacigalupi, a gay man arrested and brutally beaten after he was handcuffed in Dolores Park in 1971.[63] According to one police officer, the SFPD trained its officers to "'look and act like a social variant.' There was no formal school, but there were lectures with slides and the idiom was given to us" (letter from Confused, *TN* June 24, 1963).[64] This method of police control, which showed young officers "horror movies of the most bizarre 'homosexual murders'" ignored the experience of gay men that "it is the homosexual who falls *victim* to the cruel and inhuman action of the cop" (*VR* Sept. 1970, 13). Gay publications singled out notorious officers for their continual entrapment of gay men, including one Officer Bigarani, whose patrols meant that "shit house and bush queens should not get a false sense of security" (*BAR* Oct. 15, 1971). Interestingly, such facts of life were often met with humor. "Gays on seeing the photo [of Bigarani] say 'I'd never be entrapped by that mess.'"

Gay men tended to reject the SFPD's and the ABC's legal arguments as mere crutches justifying unconstitutional actions and a complete misapprehension of the concepts of *victim* and *perpetrator*.[65] When the police added to their tactics in 1966, asking the board of supervisors for the power to issue and revoke licenses for bathhouses and dances in the city, gay men scoffed at their legal reasoning.[66] After a SIR meeting where a police officer had argued that the police had to control the crime within the gay community, a letter to *Vector* responded, "What officer Nieto failed to mention was the fact that the homosexuals involved were victims, not perpetrators, of the crimes . . . without mention of robbery, beating, mugging, theft, attempt at blackmail or even murder" (Sept. 1967, 17). Gay men felt the local police and the state were moving to regulate morality and to deepen their control of the private lives of gay men.[67] Police action was experienced as "more and more legislation to give Big Brother Blue more and more power to regulate our lives and our minds" (*VR* Sept. 1970, 13).[68] In regulating moral behavior in this way, the police in fact exerted control over gay men's lives, enforcing social norms, rather than tracking down criminals.[69] Although gay men criticized the legal system for prosecuting "victimless crimes" rather than real criminal behavior, in practice, they had little recourse in an official public that used its institutions to expand and perpetuate their oppression.[70] It is important to note that, in distinction to what seems to have been a general consensus, some gay men thought the legal actions were justified and that gay men brought it on themselves. This kind of sentiment was not uncommon: "Have you ever wondered . . . what provocation earlier caused the *necessity* of the raid?" (*VR* July 1970, 18–19, 41). Often, gay publications even lurched into a sycophantic editorials, in what seems in retrospect to have been an effort to gain the favor of the police and legal system.[71]

The very real oppression by the official public, however, was often punctuated with bloody violence perpetrated against gay men in the Bay Area and around the country. Both actual violence and the constant threat of violence weighed heavily on the minds of men writing in the gay periodicals and in the minds of the men I spoke with. The cover of the February–March 1968 issue of *Vector* depicted a shirtless young man lying dead on the floor, a bloody pillow nearby with the caption "homosexual homicide." The 1968 "homosexual homicide" issue of *Vector* published the first debate about violence against gay men in the San Francisco gay press and included statements from the police department.[72] In that and later publications, gay men angrily discussed police reactions to violence against gay men and, worse, violence perpetrated by the police themselves. Several instances came to be emblematic in discussions of violence and gay men's responses to violence in the official public. In 1967, a member of SIR was beaten and killed at Land's End.[73] In 1969, a gay man, Frank V. Bartley, was shot in the back of the head by Officer Kline of the Berkeley Police Department, who had been posing as a homosexual to entrap men in a Berkeley park. These officers were never brought to trial on any charges; Officer Kline claimed Bartley resisted arrest. And in December 1969, the police shot a young San Francisco State University student in the back as he fled from a police raid at the Stud, a bar south of Market.[74] One supposedly straight letter writer, calling himself Ex-Navy, exemplified what gay men faced: "Maybe if all you cock-suckers would leave us normal guys alone, you wouldn't get killed" (*VR* Feb.– March 1968, 16–18). Gay men feared from their past experiences that the police were not there to protect gay men from violence, but to antagonize them. One man using the name Old Timer wrote of his firsthand knowledge of the police refusing to investigate murders when they knew the victim was homosexual.[75] "Is it any wonder," he wrote, "that those who may have information. . .stay clear of the police department, which in fact couldn't care less if the killer of a homo-sexual is caught or not?" For this reason, some argued that gay men did bear some responsibility, because they let their fear keep them from reporting crimes and testifying in court against perpetrators.[76]

And so gay men were left with trying to figure out how to think about the fact that the official public actually perpetrated and allowed violence against them, and to reconcile that with what they felt it meant to be a citizen in a de-mocracy. In a more general sense, gay men had to grapple with why they were targets for violence. From the earliest publications, gay men connected the treatment they received at the hands of the police to larger social attitudes. Old Timer, quoted earlier, believed that gay men would have to accept murder and violence as part of gay life "until the police departments of the country begin to recognize that homosexuals are also people who contribute their share." For the gay men living through the 1960s, many of whom had also experienced the 1950s and 40s, it was obvious that the official public's treatment of gay men undergird the more general tendency of violence against gay men. Of the brutal murder at Land's End, Beardemphl reported that the gang who killed Soltz be-lieved their actions were sanctioned by the police. "Those criminals that beat and murder gay persons are an ever-present outgrowth of society's sanctions against homosexuality in general" (*VR* June 1967, 17).[77] Interestingly, I did not find in their published writings the idea of police sadism, nor of the psychologi-cal connection between the power of the police and their violence against gay men in the city, as many later critics would do in the 1970s. Whatever the source of police antagonism, gay men experienced it as being persecuted by those who should be protecting them. Although the vast majority of gay men weren't vic-tims of violence, the threat of violence—the knowledge that the agents of the official public were at best indifferent violence against gay men, the knowledge that they could be a victim—acted to control gay men's day-to-day lives and forestalled their associations, thereby truncating their individuation.

Gay men who were institutionalized, either in prisons or mental institutions, bore the brunt of the public sphere's controlling power and they stood for gay men as the possible outcome of living life as a gay man in America. One man, Frank, had been sentenced to a state prison when he was in high school because he was caught having sex with a schoolmate. Lucky for him, his parents had connections in the government and were able to get him out after just over a year.[78] In the mid-1960s, activists became increasingly aware of the plight of gay men in prison—men who had usually been arrested for loitering, lewdness, etc.—now living in maximum security penitentiaries. By the late 1960s, these issues came to the fore as evidence of the brutality of the "Establishment" against gay men. One prisoner, named Joel, wrote an article for *Vector* in 1969, where he told of being denied parole over and over again, "the reason used is the man is a suspected or known homosexual" (*VR* Dec. 1969, 19). He goes on to say that prisoners caught having sex with each other can expect twenty-nine days of solitary confinement. Lawrence A. Bennett, Ph.D., worked for the department of corrections in the late 1960s and early 1970s. He justified the treatment of homosexual prisoners who "flaunt their homosexual orientation," because they cause "disruption to the interpersonal relationships among prison society" (*VR* June 1972, 9). *Gay Sunshine* lamented the "thousands of our brothers incarcerated in prisons, jails, and mental institutions" (*GS* Jan. 1972, 4) and reminded its readers that gay sex was punishable by life in prison.[79] When one gay man, Westley Ashmore, committed suicide at Vacaville State Prison, his death became an emblem of brutality: "His suicide was the result of cruel treatment by the staff, general neglect during his incarceration, and specific medical neglect at the time of his attempted self-hanging" (*GS* April 1972, 1).

Throughout the country, various kinds of medical treatments were under consideration, ranging from institutionalization and therapy, to brain surgery, to castration.[80] In 1970, California amended its sexual criminal law with the Mentally Disordered Sex Offender Act, which allowed a judge presented with evidence of mental disorder to order mental treatment instead of prison. If ever that person were found to be mentally competent, he or she could then be sent back to the courts for sentencing to prison. Further, anyone so committed to a mental institution could be held indefinitely by the state.[81] In 1969, gay activists learned that men accused of homosexual crimes were being sentenced to mental hospitals and state prisons for the insane. By 1972, this had exploded into a full-scale scandal within the gay community, as information about Atascadero State Mental Hospital, which some referred to as the "Buchenwald of the Reagan Regime,"[82] became more widely available. It was rumored that patients at Atascadero were routinely subject to medical experimentation, torture, pain-causing drugs, and electroshock therapy; these experiments were ostensibly aimed at discovering a cure for homosexuality. *Gay Sunshine* reported that Dr. Martin J. Reimringer, was using a drug called succinylcholine, which induced near-death, as a means of behavioral modification.[83] Patients were tricked or forced into giving consent, despite the fact that both state law and the AMA's ethics board prohibited such human experimentation. Because the state criminalized gay sex, these brutal punishments came to be seen as the foreclosure by the state of gay love and of human interaction writ large. This was experienced as the ultimate in state brutality. "To my Gay sisters and brothers, I say Reagan's paradise is re-staging Dachau here," wrote Don Jackson (*GS* Nov. 1970, back cover).

Taken together, the law, violence, and institutionalization created a general atmosphere of fear among gay men. Although during this period they spoke openly and began to push back, the experience of this repression had direct con-sequences on gay men's ability to produce meaningful interpersonal associations beyond the reach of such repressive action. Not dissimilar to lynching in the African American community, it was the constant threat of legal police action, violence, and institutionalization that served to direct and shape the feelings, practices, and associations of gay men. The associations formed by gay men during this period and the meanings those associations produced as gay men interacted with each other emerged in and from this repressive environment.

The Gay Male Reformulation of Liberal Democratic Values

Not surprisingly, as gay men experienced their sexuality in conjunction with the repression of the official public, they most often framed their experience and evaluated it in terms of the value-terms of liberal democracy: rights, freedom, equality, and justice. These value-terms, anchored in the American version of democracy as it was constituted in the early 1960s, served San Francisco's gay men as a sort of clay from which they molded particular understandings of de-mocracy; that is, they actively rethought and restructured the meaning of these value-terms themselves through their experience of repression at the hands of the official democratic public. These revaluations provided moral standards for evaluation of their experiences as sexually different individuals, members of a "minority" group, and subjects of official reppression at the Federal, state and city levels. They made their experience of the hidden stigma[84] of intelligible through the cultural structures they already possessed, most prominently, through liberal democratic values. This process of engaging known values with experience had a two-fold effect. First, in concert with gay women, gay men necessarily reformed and reshaped these values to better meet their needs as a group within a democracy that failed to recognize them. Second, again alongside gay women, they used those values as a guide for intelligent action in the world, aimed at reshaping their environment—ranging from the official public sphere to their bedrooms, bars and politics, personal relationships and families, thoughts and feelings—to meet their needs as gay men, to create a kind of de-mocracy that would account for them and recognize them as full citizens. The kinds of meanings that gay men had developed on the ground by the time of San Francisco's first Gay Pride Parade in 1972 could not have existed without American democratic values as they were commonly constituted in 1961 and what gay men and women made those values in the intervening eleven years.[85]

Many historical and social factors played directly into the emergence of the conflicted meanings of gay. The two arguments circulating most frequently among historians are on one hand the materialist argument, that the cultures of capitalism created an environment that allowed individuals to separate from familial responsibilities and seek other forms of sexual bonding[86]; and on the other hand that the discourses of the dominant culture in the form of sexology and psychoanalysis produced the knowledge necessary to create a new kind of person.[87] And more commonly in sociological discussions about the 1960s, scholars point to the social movements of the time as the source of a gay identity, that social movements moved toward identity movements.[88] It is historically evident that other identities based on same-sex desire have existed in various social and economic conditions throughout the history of the United States.[89] But in the case of 1960s San Francisco, neither the economic conditions, nor the social movements, nor the discursive construction of gay identity can adequately describe the complex interactions among gay men and their transactions with the dominant culture. The form of gay identity that emerged in the 1960s, the one with ongoing salience in late twentieth and early twenty-first century America, emerged specifically out of the conditions of the 1960s when gay men and women engaged in a reformation of liberal democratic ideas in order to lay claim to a place in the public sphere. The meaning of gay as it came to be by 1972, with its emphasis on individual freedom and its supreme value of self-expression and self-fulfillment, could not have existed without the foundational values of the culture of American democracy. That is not to say that democracy or American institutions produced or determined the meaning of gay; rather, it is to argue that the values of American democracy functioned as ends-as-means among gay men, and impelled them toward a particular iteration of their self-conception, their role in society, and their cultural expressions. As they "tripped" on their repression, they both reformed their conceptions of basic democratic values—freedom, rights, equality, justice—and sought to reshape their environment (i.e., the official public) to meet their needs as gay men and women, to create a kind of democracy that would account for them and recognize them as full citizens. The kind meanings that gay men developed on the ground at the time of San Francisco's first Gay Pride Parade could not have existed without American democratic values and gay men's revisions of those values.[90]

Despite a forty-year history of gay men and women struggling against the dominant culture of the official public, the particular experience gay men had in American culture of the 1960s meant that they had a conflicted relationship to democratic values, which as often as not seemed to them to be void of content. This led to a particular rupture in the gay male consciousness, analogous but not identical to W.E.B. du Bois's "double consciousness" of African Americans[91]: Gay men's faith in democracy's ability to secure their rights pulled against their lived experiences of democracy as a corrupt system that actively sought to repress their lives and expressions and associations. Both their faith in liberal democratic values and their disillusionment with American democracy accreted within their individual experience, so that when they came together to talk about democracy with each other and with the larger public, they seemed to speak out of both sides of their mouths.

Democracy during this period was marked in gay men's consciousness as a failed experiment, or at least an institution which had failed them. During the 1960s, World War II remained strong in the collective memory as a time when American democracy stood for "the individual over an oppressive state"; but for gay men like Robert Cole, in 1960s America, "justice is now tempered with injustice, freedom is a thing which we graciously give to people in South Vietnam, equality is equated with 'black power' and the right of the individual is a mocking bird hill" (*VR* Oct. 1967, 23). By the mid 1960s, gay men's suspicions of democracy had grown. When the Society for Individual Rights was founded in the spring of 1965, it actually defended its appeal to democratic values, unintentionally revealing the feelings of its membership: "We also are aware of the many pitfalls of democracy. . . . Indecisive and cumbersome and slow moving and intellectually banal and shallow in concept, and blah and more blah" (*VR* Jan., 1965, 2). A couple years later in an even more frank tone, *Vanguard* editors realized the inherent difficulties of democracy. "Democracy's a word. In action, what comes out is equality and justice for all. To work it, everyone's got to try in sincere humility. You must shit on your pride" (*VG* 1.6). Even as it was critiqued in the gay press, democracy's value-terms—rights, freedom, equality, and justice—continued to circulate both as ideals to strive for and as standards of evaluation, as gay men appraised their relationship to the public sphere and struggled to formulate strategies to change it.

Beginning with their earliest attempts to form a gay male publicity in 1961, there was the faith in democratic principles married to the suspicion that democratic values were defunct and could never lead to a true freedom for gay men and women. Showing his faith, Guy Strait wrote early in 1963, "Never fear, we shall win—for the fight for personal freedom is a growing thing and VICTORY IS IN THE WIND" (*TN* Aug. 5, 1963, 4). Interestingly, Strait and other contributing writers also deployed discourses of freedom, justice, and the American Way *against* their common Cold War usage. In a story about five presumably gay men arrested at a Halloween party, the editors called for the judges to rule "in the American Way, based on law, not the little minds of people who have their own prejudices" (*LCEN* Nov. 13, 1961). Editors, especially Guy Strait, made constant appeals to this "American Way" and looked to the law, specifically the Constitution, as the final say in what constituted freedom. One such example, a front page story in 1963 discussed the implications for gay people of a recent Supreme Court decision that made it more difficult for police to arrest individuals for drunkenness, removing such actions from municipal jurisdiction (*TN* June 10, 1963, 1). Between 1961 and 1972, the faith that the U.S. Constitution could answer gay men's problems[92] eroded first into a belief that they would have to struggle for it[93] and finally into a total disillusionment of the power of the Constitution to do anything for gay people at all. "Among these groups there stands one group who have been persecuted as long as we have had the Constitution. This very Constitution that said that ALL men are free. Of course, the group I am referring to is the Homosexual" (*VR* July 1969, cover).

Guy Strait's newspapers and, later, *Vector* made repeated use of a particular kind of Americanism in their repetition of familiar patriotic tropes. In 1962, *The League of Civil Education News* reproduced "The American's Creed" written by William Page in 1913, and adopted by the House of Representatives in 1918, which read in part, "I therefore believe it is my duty to my country to love it" (*LCEN* March 4, 1962). In the first issue of the *LCE News*, the Declaration of Independence was cited three separate times as the foundation upon which "social deviants [homosexuals]" of San Francisco should fight police harassment and brutality (Oct. 13, 1961). By the second issue, the masthead bore the phrase, "We hold these truths to be self-evident," taken from the Declaration. Following issues would refer often to the mythologized figures of George Washington, Thomas Jefferson, Benjamin Franklin, and Thomas Payne as they constructed the LCE newspaper's raisons-d'être. But Strait's papers also published materials that simultaneously turned Americanism on its head, pointing out its inconsistencies and using patriotic rhetoric against gay folk's oppressors. In 1964, D.L. of New York wrote an open letter to Mayor Shelley reprinted by Strait. "Justice requires us to remember, when any citizen denies his fellow saying, 'His color is not mine' or 'His beliefs are strange and different,' in that moment he betrays America, though his forbears created this nation" (*CN* vol. 4.8, 5). And Strait himself wrote, "Of course, on the other hand, if a person has the right to wear whatever he sees fit without regard to what our Big Brother in the National Capitol, State Capitol, and in city hall might think, then we shall again be happy to say that this is indeed the land of the free and the home of the brave. But then even we are sometimes taken" (*CN* Aug. 17, 1964, 7). In sum, these men in the early 1960s argued that if we are free to do as we desire when it harms no one else, this is America; if not, we know we've been duped, or at least denied our Americanness.

As gay men continued to see their experience as a particularly American experience, their disillusionment about American institutions grew stronger and stronger through the 1960s, both as they experienced the social upheavals of the 1960s and as they experienced their own repression in San Francisco. Strait had mocked President Kennedy (and by extension Cicero), by declaring, "ASK NOT WHAT YOUR COUNTRY CAN DO FOR YOU, RATHER ASK WHAT YOU CAN DO FOR YOUR COUNRY—unless you are a homosexual" (*TN* Dec. 6, 1963, 2, emphasis in original). Such wry wit gave way to open skepticism by 1965, as gay men integrated their experience into their evaluation of America. "[T]he American perspective has become unrealistic, hypocritical and filled with conflict" (*VR* June 1965, 6). Gay men had became aware that dominant cultural beliefs functioned in the public sphere to trump America and democracy, for, to the American public, "all Negroes are dirty and lazy, all homosexuals are effeminate and unmanly, all Christians are saved." And eventually, the prominence of the idea that American democracy could be the locus of possible freedom for gays dropped from the gay publications just as the counter-culture came

into full swing. "Let us always remember that we are human beings and homosexuals before we are Americans or political partisans," wrote Jim Gradford,
who had been president of Mattachine Midwest in the mid-1960s (*VR* Nov.
1967, 15).

By the late 1960s, disillusionment led to outright cynicism. "The inalienable
rights of 'life, liberty and the pursuit of happiness'—consistently abridged by
the federal government—have now become empty rhetoric for these millions of
America's 'Invisible Minority'" (*VR* Aug. 1968, 7). Indeed, by 1969 all of San
Francisco's gay publications had begun to refer to the United States as
"Amerika," either consistently or from time to time for rhetorical effect, using
the common idiom of the anti-war movement. "Amerika" underscored the incommensurability of the active-undergoing of being gay with the accepted values of American democracy. Thus, among the city's gay men, Americanness
moved from being prized—that is from being a value in itself—to being the subject of scorn and critique. When Carl Whitman wrote his now famous "Refugees
from Amerika: A Gay Manifesto" in 1969, he was essentially penning a statement of the otherness of gays in American democracy. He described eloquently
the experience of that otherness, where Amerika was an empty promise to anyone who was different.[94]

As these contradictory feelings toward America accrued in individuals to
varying degrees and at different times through the period, the already problematic notion of the "democratic citizen" became almost schizoid for gay men. Full
citizenship was an oft-stated goal of the pre-gay lib publications.[95] In the early
and mid-1960s, *citizenship* commonly denoted the responsibilities of voting,
paying taxes, and obeying the law, responsibilities that should guarantee in return a fair amount of freedom. *Town Talk* actually argued that citizenship for
gays would mean conforming to the expectation of the public sphere that citizens exhibit decorous behavior (first issue, 4). But soon others made demands in
exchange for citizenship. Vector demanded federal employment, security clearances, the end to military discrimination, and an end to legal enforcement of sex
laws.[96] But the promises of American citizenship were also experienced as a
fraud by many gay men who refused to accept the ethic of conformity that
seemed to be required for full citizenship during the 1960s. The realities of their
experience were simply too starkly contrasted against the ideals of democratic
values, which they often did not even see as democratic. "There are those who
say the song ["My Country 'Tis of Thee"] is a lie, and for good reason. These
people have felt the denial of liberty, the inequity of justice, the sting of bigoted
inequality. Black, brown, yellow, red, and yes even many white people have felt
the sting of the power structure. . . . Liberty? Justice? Equality? For a queer?"
(*CHFN* May 20, 1969). Ultimately, gay men's relationship to justice and equality flipped to a negative, statements of what these values were not. "[B]ring
these injustices out into the open so that the 'straight' community can see them
for the damnable things they are," declared the July 1969 cover of *Vector*. And
because the experiences of oppression were varied from homosexual to homosexual, *Gay Sunshine* would simply conclude that homosexuality could not be a

political category at all for thinking about equality and justice (*GS* Aug.–Sept. 1970, 2).

This debate over citizenship served as one of the primary community boundaries gay men drew among themselves. This was a division of gay male community based on a relationship to American society, perceived or real, imputed by gay men onto other gay men. Among the many in/out boundaries gay men struggled to establish during the period, these political boundaries which arose in the late 1960s were among the more powerful and still constitute serious community divides among gay men to this day. They divided each other into the "truly" oppressed and the "middle-class Bourgeois" gays who were, ostensibly, not oppressed; or they divided themselves into the "duped" who still believed in America and the "aware" who saw the lies and understood true liberation; or they drew the line between those who saw the possibilities of democracy and those who had withdrawn. Interestingly, even as some gay men rejected the idea of an American citizenship, at least in its 1960s Cold War form, they practiced a different kind of citizenship: the citizenship of the outsider, the abject. As abject citizens, they argued from their passion and experience, but continued to be inspired by democratic values they held, even when they went unspoken. Indeed, they often did not see a connection between their value critiques and American democracy itself. In sum, this abject citizenship criticized the shortcomings of the society that purported to protect them, but in effect denied them freedom, equality, and justice.

The clash between the democratic values gay men held dear (even if unconsciously) and gay men's experience of oppression in the official public sphere led to a significant rethinking of what "freedom" and "rights" should mean, not only to gay men but to Americans at large. Although they continued to demand freedom and rights in traditional meanings,[97] gay men also knew from experience that rights, supposedly universal, were selectively granted. Throughout the period, they nonetheless continued to speak of rights in universal terms, arguing for example, "We must not forget that there are certain rights connected with being a man which are, despite peculiarities of color, of creed or of sexual orientation, guaranteed to all men" (*VR* July 1968, 16–17). Further, they continued to invoke the classic harm principle of democratic theory,[98] repeating often the argument that "'Liberty consists in being able to do all that which does not harm someone else.' . . . Therefore, homosexual acts between consenting adults, whether some regard them as sinful, immoral, or diseased, are within the constitutional rights of all" (*VG* Feb. 1967).[99]

By 1972, gay men had been fighting harassment and violence for years and had come to realize that intimidation as they experienced it—causing another human being to fear—was the primary means whereby their freedom had been and continued to be denied at the deepest and most personal level. Intimidation hit "at the core of a person's being. It robs him of his freedom; the state of feeling free. Intimidation is rooted in fear and executed in emasculation. Freedom takes a little guts" (*VR* Feb. 1970, 24). They also saw that this intimidation and its resultant fear was deeply ingrained in American society, going far beyond mere harassment of the police. "Homosexuals are in an especially vulnerable position, having been taught from childhood that they are without rights" (*VR* Feb. 1970, 24). So they came to believe that they had to actively assert that they had any rights to begin with. "[H]omosexuality does not bear a direct relationship to an individual's human worth nor logically disqualify him from human rights" (*VG* Feb. 1967). For a gay man in 1967, an assertion of rights began as a claim to his own humanity.

So "freedom" for a gay man came to mean significantly more than freedom of the press or freedom of speech as enumerated in the Bill of Rights; indeed, during the socialist revivals of the 1960s, some gay men also expressed how this kind of freedom was equally thwarted in socialist, and supposedly more free, countries as well (Tom Hillan, *VR* Feb. 1972, 7). As with many oppressed groups, freedom became for gay men and women to mean something more personal, cultural, and social. Through their experiences, gay men learned that freedom meant at its base every day things, like "jobs, homes, friends, social lives, safety, and security. Here is our challenge to San Francisco: Face reality—Face homosexuality" (*VR* Sept. 1966, 2). These statements of personal freedom grow stronger and stronger through the period; and by the early 1970s, meaning-statements about "freedom" delved even deeper into the psychological well-being of gays. "We [homosexuals] all want to be truly free, . . . free from our own guilt and fears . . . free to live as we will, and yet be able to live peacefully with those around us" (*VR* Aug. 1970, 27). And by the time of the first Gay Pride celebration in San Francisco in 1972, and parallel to the conclusions drawn in the counter-culture, freedom and rights had been inextricably linked to *the right to be*, per se: "[T]he homosexual has a moral right to be a homosexual and being a homosexual has a moral right not only to live his or her homosexuality fully, freely, openly, and with pride, but also has a right to do so free of arrogant and insolent pressures to convert to the prevailing heterosexuality" (*VR* June 1972). The activity-undergoing of *mis-recognition* by the American democratic official public sphere caused gay men to rework the very notion of freedom itself: to be recognized by the official public was to live free of fear, guilt and intimidation; to have access to the most basic necessities for a free life, both material and spiritual; and to be who one was without intervention or threat of intervention. This rethinking of freedom, the most central of American democratic values, in the context of gay male repression forced "gayness"—gay men's self-consciousness as gay men—to the center of the formation of the meaning of gay. Simply put, personal freedom made the idea of gayness, or gay identity, salient to gay men themselves, even among those gay men who denied the salience of gayness to begin with, where the freedom to be gay, whatever that may mean in actual behavior, became a value proposition in itself.

If from their experience of being gay in America, San Francisco's gay men were considering the notion that their homosexuality could not, indeed must not, be separated from their humanity and, concomitantly, from their rights; and if they also knew that the culture of the official public sphere denied them basic humanity and rights; then freedom and rights came to be seen as things that must be achieved, fought for, or taken. Freedom and rights had ceased to be, for gay men, conditions granted by their democratic society. "Freedom must also be won, for ourselves, not granted by politicians" (*GS* may 1972, 7). And so among the gay men who participated in the gay public in opposition to the official public, the argument evolved into the claim that the individual and group had to claim freedom in the face of intimidation by the dominant culture. "Only we can change society. . . . Demand and Get equal rights with heterosexuals" (*VR* June 1967, 17). There began to be frequent insistence that gay men claim their freedom, regardless of the law and government. "And in spite of all the fences and all the difficulties we will continue to love, to make love, to need whomever and whatever we must" (*VG* Feb. 1967). Rather than hoping to transform the public sphere, many gay men began to think that claiming their rights meant acting as if they already had those rights, and doing so loudly and publicly. "Our approach to social action shall be to act out our rights as legally as possible and letting society adjust to us" (*VR* Sept. 1966, 2). The experience of being a gay man and a citizen in the United States belied the American construction of citizenship. The gay experience of citizenship in America gave rise to a homosexual demand for a new kind of citizenship, particular to their needs and lives, with rights connected to personal expression and fulfillment, what I will refer to hereafter as *freedom of personhood.*

Out of gay men's counter-publicity—that ever-widening, ever-changing social space where gay men struggled against the repression of the official public, and where they insisted on their humanity and therefore their freedom to be—sprang the debates and discussions about the meaning of gay. The work to create a gay publicity had begun much earlier, as homosexual activists between the world wars and in the first fifteen years of the Cold War had laid the ground work for gay men to conceptualize themselves not only as a different kind of a person, not only as a group bonded together in their oppression, not just as a sexual desire apart from the norm, but as a potential public. Many factors accreted from the complex environment within which gay men lived, to shape their experiences of themselves and of their world. With the increasing social conflict of the 1960s as backdrop, gay men came to understand themselves in their abject position to the public sphere and ramped up their struggle for inclusion as they felt their oppression and framed it in increasingly intolerable terms. The inspiration they drew from the Civil Rights movement and the radical social and cultural movements of the 1960s provoked debates about gay men's role in the public sphere and pushed them toward thinking of themselves in terms of a group that could act accordingly in the public sphere. And the hippie movement provided a freedom of thought that allowed many to shake off their enculturated notions of what their sexual desires might mean.

In confronting the life-and-death problems of arrest, harassment, entrapment, job loss, getting beaten up and even murdered, gay men had to conceive of possible means to alleviate their oppression and to create a social environment that would enable their pursuit of the consummation of their sexual and relational desires without the intervention of public institutions. To maintain status within the public sphere, gay men had to adopt strategies of splitting— where their public self was dramatically and necessarily different from their private self—that created a necessarily fragmented personhood; the only other choice was direct state intervention to prevent them from expressing their sexuality freely. The public sphere treated gay men as a group, a coherent thing that could be dealt with en masse; so they were arrested in groups; hung out in groups at bars, clubs, parties, and bath houses. But gay men also dealt with individual agents of the public sphere—police officers, politicians, clergymen or doctors. And these agents also acted in conceptually coherent groups, the police department, the court system, the Board of Supervisors, etc. Gay men's consciousness of themselves in their difference as it emerged in their experience in the public sphere produced in them a contradictory yet powerful understanding of the official public's meaning. By virtue of the structure of the American public, gay men by definition had a different experience of the public sphere from other Americans, even from other oppressed groups, one that by definition was oppressive to gay men who had to suppress their sexuality to safely participate in the official public. But the public sphere paradoxically required gay men on one hand to lay aside their differences in public, but simultaneously actively sought to eradicate their difference and specificity by insisting on the intelligibility and illegitimacy of homosexuality.[100] The lie of the social formation of the official public sphere is that because it is inextricably linked to cultural norms, only some of its members may retain truly private lives that are protected by interventions in the public sphere.

Most important, however, it was the direct and constant intervention of the state through the ABC and the SFPD that served as a continual reminder to gay men of their abject status and the illegitimacy of their sexuality, which they experienced as inseparably connected to their personhood. The particular combination of all of these aspects in this particular time and place provided the cultural and social tools gay men needed to assert a new kind of publicity, a gay publicity, a counter-public set explicitly to fight for recognition in the official public sphere, armed with new understandings of the base value-terms of American democracy. But such a gay counter-public could never have emerged without the values gay men engaged from the democratic culture of America. The dialectic between their lived experiences and the values the dominant culture purported to hold dear created in gay men a heightened understanding of the foundations of democratic culture. Surely, "personal freedom" was a contested idea among gay men; but the nature of their debate and the modes of the discourses constructing ideas of freedom and rights took on a particular valence for homosexual men who had experienced the necessary splitting of their selves in the public sphere and the constant threat of retribution against them if they failed to enact the split. Two related problems emerged for the fledgling gay male public: first, if their experiences were real and reliable, then what should the goal be of their new counter-public; and second, how should they combine their diverse and contradictory experiences of abjection into a coherent, meaningful, and effective political strategy?

Notes

1. For more information and a critical analysis of historical importance of the Jenkins Affair, see Lee Edelman, "Tearooms and Sympathy, or the Epistemology of the Water Closet" in Henry Abelove, Michele Aina Barale, and David M. Halperin, eds., *The Lesbian and Gay Studies Reader* (Routledge: New York, 1993), 553–574.

2. Interestingly, for Strait, the only known case of homosexual blackmail was one of two Republican senators blackmailing a democratic senator from Wyoming when his son was arrested for public sex in a D.C. restroom. "Please note that the blackmail was perpetrated by two Republicans then in Congress and not by Communist agents attempting to subvert an honest America. We must note that this blackmail was performed by two highly moral men, 'protecting America.'" Strait goes on to relate the story of how Styles Bridges (R-NH) and Herman Welker (R-ID) blackmailed Lester Hung (D-WY) when his son was arrested by D.C. vice squad on homosexual charges; they threatened to reveal the scandal to the press unless he agreed not to seek reelection. Hung killed himself a few weeks later, according to a report by Drew Pearson in the *Washington Post*. See *CN*, Oct. 1964, 5–6; and *CN* Nov. 1964, 1–2.

3. See for example, *CN* Feb. 24, 1964, 1–2.

4. See for example, *CN* Jan. 27, 1964, 4.

5. See George Chauncey, *Gay New York: Gender, Urban Culture, and the Making of a Gay World, 1890–1940* (Basic Books: New York, 1995).

6. See *VR* Aug. 1970, 50. One of the primary civil rights arguments gay men made by the early 1970s was that police should patrol 'problem areas' in uniform, not in disguise. See *VR* Sept. 1970, 12.

7. In September 1964, for example, County Sheriffs raided a Coit Club party at a private Russian River resort. See *CN* 4.1, 1, 4 and *TT* Oct. 1964 for reports on the raid and subsequent arrests.

8. See *CN* Feb. 24, 1964, 1–2.

9. An undercover policeman solicited sex with a gay rights activist in a Los Angeles Park in late 1971. See *GS* Oct.–Nov. 1971, 2. When he was finally sentenced in April of 1971, Richard Nash was given penalties that far exceeded normal punishment. He was forbidden from *associating* with "known homosexuals" or coming within so many yards of a homosexual establishment or of participating in any way in the gay movement. The judge effectively cut him off from his social world. See *GS* April 1972, 5.

10. In an informal survey of its readers conducted by *Citizens News*, 15 of 101 respondents said they had lost their jobs because an employer found out they were homosexual. See *CN* May 25, 1964.

11. See *VR* July 1971, 10; Sept. 1971, 37.

12. See John Dewey, *The Public and Its Problems*, in *John Dewey: The Later Works, 1925–1953*, Vol. 2, ed. Jo Ann Boydston (Southern Illinois UP: Carbondale, 1988), 243.

13. Nancy Fraser, "Rethinking the Public Sphere: A Contribution to the Critique of the Actually Existing Democracy" in *Habermas and the Public Sphere*, ed. by Craig

Calhoun (MIT Press; Cambridge, Massachusetts, 1992), 117.

    14. See *VR* Jan. 1966, 1.

    15. See *VR* July 1967, 26.

    16. See *VR* July 1967, 10; and Sept. 1969, 17.

    17. See *VR* Dec. 1967, 6.

    18. The arguments about censorship raged during the 1960s, both within and without the gay male community. See for example *TN* May 27, 1962 1; June 10, 1962; *VR* Dec. 1966, 2; Sept. 1967 8; and Feb.–March 16–18.

    19. See for example *VR* July 1969, 13; Oct. 1970; and April 1971, 4.

    20. Emerging especially from the Cold War and McCarthy era witch hunts, the notion that homosexuals were security risks was long in the dying. For gay male critiques of this argument, see *TN* Dec. 1963, 2; *CN* July 1964; and *CN* 4.4 (Nov. 1964), 7. See also David K. Johnson, *The Lavender Scare: The Cold War Persecution of Gays and Lesbians in the Federal Government* (Chicago: University of Chicago Press, 2004).

    21. See *VR* Jan. 1972, 15.

    22. This approach to experience turns out to be somewhat intuitive to members of oppressed populations, as they seek to understand the environment producing their experience. "[T]he homosexual needs to understand that the difficulties faced by the [gay] community grow from a basic sickness in a society which must be transformed, in radical ways, before any minority including the homosexual one, will be allowed to live as tit wants, developing its own culture" *VR* Oct. 1968, 20–23.

    23. Hereafter referred to as SIR, this was a gay rights and social organization that began meeting in the spring of 1964 after the dissolution of the League of Civil Education.

    24. For a detailed discussion of the multiplicity of publics and their interrelationship, see Dewey, *The Public and Its Problems* [1927], 235–372.

    25. Gay publications frequently published warning of increasing police presence or arrests in given areas or at certain times. In 1970, there was a concerted effort on the part of SFPD to step up arrests of gay men for "lewd acts" in public, and undercover agents were sent in droves to Land's End, Golden Gate Park, Buena Vista Park, and Macy's Department Store. See *VR* Aug. 1970, 50.

    26. See *TN* May 27, 1962, 1.

    27. See *CN* Feb. 24, 1964, 1–2.

    28. See *CN* Feb. 24, 1964, 1–2.

    29. *Vector* published a review in September 1970 of sociologist Laud Humphreys' *Tearoom Trade* which has since come under fire for what has been seen as unethical research techniques. For the original text, critical responses to his research, and defense of the importance of his research, see the 1975 revised edition. Laud Humphreys, *Tearoom Trade: Impersonal Sex in Public Places* (Aldine de Gruyter: New York, 1975). And for more detailed recent work on public gay sex, see William Leap, ed., *Public Sex/Gay Spaces* (Columbia UP: New York, 1999). For my purposes here, what is of most interest was the response *Vector* writers had to Humphrey's findings. The following details were what *Vector* pulled out of the study: Studying the T-Room habits of men in Chicago, Humphreys sought to understand "covert homosexual behavior." In conducting his study, he posed as a gay voyeur and asked men about their backgrounds. To the extent that his data was reliable, the findings were significant. More than 50 percent of the men were married and about 10 percent were servicemen. He broke the men down into types. 38 percent were "trade" (men who did not in any way identify as homosexual, but who regu-

larly used T-rooms); 28 percent were closeted and generally hostile to gay society; 24 percent claimed bisexual identities; 14 percent claimed gay identities. He also found that these men were often blackmailed by the local police who extorted money from them in exchange for not arresting them. Most interestingly, he reported, "[T-rooms are] easily accessible, 'private,' (they do not identify people the way entering a bar or bath would), and because they provide what many males appreciate—sexual variety." *VR* Sept. 1970, 14–15.

30. See also letter from Acedecy and Strait's response, *TN* Oct. 14, 1963. Strait argued that "It is true that a great many people have problems of social contact (on both sides of the street) but you would agree with me that if it was open and notorious conduct in public that it would offend you."

31. In *CN* Jan. 27, 1962, 1, 5, Strait goes so far as to list the public restrooms in the city where gay men can find sex.

32. According to Humphreys, one informant claimed, "'I'm here for the sex—not friendship,'" quoted in *VR* Sept. 1970, 14–15.

33. From Guy Christien, "I think the articles in *Vector* concerning T-room arrests are a bunch of bullshit! . . . The real issue concerns the fact that a lot of faggots dig sex in public places!" *VR* March 1971, 32.

34. Throughout the 1960s, the burden for giving gay men the bad reputation of public sex was placed on the backs of "secretive" (i.e., closeted) men. According to the gay papers, those engaged in public sex were those who were fearful, worried about appearing masculine, married, suburban, those who refused to identify with other "social variants," and those who were simply ignorant that there was an (underground) community. See *CN* Jan. 27, 1964, 1, 5. This was, of course, disingenuous, as gay men of all ilks sought sex in the means available to them, which included, of course, public cruising. This tension between the closeted and the out homosexual functioned as a primary boundary marker for the gay community throughout this period. I will return to this rift between the "closeted" and the "blatant" or "out" homosexual in subsequent chapters.

35. See *TN* Oct. 14, 1963.

36. *VR* May 1967, 14 "Responsible action by responsible people" was one of SIR's mottos.

37. See also Tom Harrison, *BAR* June 14, 1972, "Don't you agree those of the homophile community who engage in 'public' sex are expressing a type of self-destructive behavior?"

38. "However acceptable ordinary petting may be to the American Public, no homosexual petting has aver been allowed in public. . . ." *CN* Feb. 24, 1964, 1–2.

39. "Straight people have it much better. They take it for granted that they may cruise and solicit wherever they choose. They do so on public beaches, in their bars, in shopping centers, movie theaters, at the library, and at high schools, colleges, and universities. Even right out on Market St. in broad daylight," *GS* Oct.–Nov. 1971, 6.

40. See also *BAR* March 1, 1972. Fred, the ex-gay cited earlier, denies that straights use the public sphere for sexual purposes. "It's funny, but you never see this with the heterosexual in public. He makes his advances (and conquests) in private, contrary to the public gay" *VR* July 1970, 18–19, 41.

41. See *BAR*, May 1, 1972, 1.

42. See *VR* June 1972, 23.

43. *VR* June 1967, 17

44. The private sphere had historically been viewed as that which is outside the pur-

view of the government, the home and family life; so in this context, gay men were seeking to remove their sexuality from the enforcing institutions of the public sphere.

45. See *TT* Jan 1965, 1–2, 4.

46. See for example *VR* April 1967, 9.

47. For more information about privacy arguments, see *VR* Aug. 1971, 50: "It is our opinion, however, that laws which make a felony of homosexual acts privately committed by consenting adults are morally unsupportable, contribute nothing to the public welfare, and inhibit rather than permit changes in behavior by homosexual persons."

48. See *VR* Nov. 1971, 10.

49. See for example, *VR* Nov. 1967, 7.

50. See also *VR* Sept. 1970, 36–37.

51. See for example letter from E.L.K, *VR* May 1967, 14; and *VR* Aug. 1971, 50.

52. "What makes an act lewd in public and not in private? What makes an act lewd when performed between two in most places yet not lewd when done before thousands [speaking of athletes hitting each other on the ass]?" *CN* April 6, 1964.

53. Fraser, "Rethinking," 137.

54. John Dewey, *Freedom and Culture* [1938] (Amherst: Prometheus Books, 1989), 127.

55. See "Government Is the Primary Oppressor" *VR* May 1972, 41. Others argued that the oppression came from the unevenness of the laws and their various instantiations around the country. See *VR* June 1972, 34–35.

56. See Nan Alamillo Boyd, *Wide Open Town: A History of Queer San Francisco to 1965* (Berkeley: University of California Press, 2004).

57. See for example coverage of the closing of the Jumping Frog, *TN* Sept. 2, 1963, 4.

58. See *CN* March 23, 1964, 1.

59. "[Witches' Christmas] had been marred by the announcement from the Department of ABC of the State of California that the license of the Black Cat, traditional Halloween gathering spot, would be revoked at Midnight on the 31st. . . . There had been talk of violence against the agents of the ABC, but this did not develop since the license was lifted at 2:10 AM on the morning of the 31st. . . . However, as the large crowd congregated they all went to the center of the street that had been blocked off by the San Francisco Police Department and only those persons in costume were allowed to enter the area in vehicles," *TN* Nov. 11, 1963, 1–2. Strait reproduced the *San Francisco Chronicle*'s article about the Black Cat's closing; charges declared that "lewd and indecent acts took place there" and that Sol Stoumen, owner, was trying to fight the charges. "'Sure,' Stoumen conceded, 'alleged homosexuals—we have quite a few, but I don't know if they're really homosexuals, and it's none of my business as long as they behave.' 'It's a witch hunt,' he said," quoted in *TN* Nov. 25, 1963.

60. See for example *CN* April 6, 1964, 6.

61. See letter from Confused, *TN* June 24, 1963; and Dec. 23, 1963, 1.

62. Guy Strait actually reported that there was a Grand Jury report in San Francisco instructing the police to "'harass habitual criminals and violators of vice—presumably prostitutes and homosexuals—to keep them from being lulled into a sense of well being in San Francisco." See *CN* 4.7 (Jan. 1965), 4.

63. See *VR* Oct. 1971, 11.

64. Gay publications often made campy jokes of police training. One cartoon showed a well-appointed man walking a poodle, with a couple of whispering behind him.

"Too bad—occupational hazard. I hear that he collects disability, too. He used to be an ABC agent" *CN* Feb. 1964, 12.

65 See for example *TT* Jan. 1965, 1, 3, 5.

66. See *VR* April 1966, 3–4; Sept. 1967, 16–17. Earlier, police had used their control of pinball machines to justify raids on gay establishments. See *TN* Dec. 1963, 1–2. And later, police tried again for licensing control of dances and movie theaters. See *VR* Sept. 1970, 13.

67. In Los Angeles, these dynamics were magnified by a much more conservative history and bitter relations between the police and the gay community. See *VR* Oct. 1967, 5. Gay men felt that the police were enforcing a specific moral code. This critique of the police's enthusiasm often lapsed into a crude anti-Catholicism. See for example, *CN* 4.8, 5.

68. Guy Strait had the most detailed and vociferous critiques of the moralizing aspect of American law. "The object of the various assorted busy-bodies appears to be 'vice,' particularly when engaged in by 'undesirables.' Vice should be defined as anything that does not fit into the picture of those that are too old to engage in such things' or activities that see to be too much fun for those who engage in them; or anything that does not add to the economic wealth of the 'civic minded citizens.'" *CN*, Feb. 1964, 1–2. And "In the United States, the various states have set themselves up as arbiters of what is morally right and sinful and have enacted statues against sinful practices, but these laws have no connection with offenses against life, liberty, or property. Instead these laws mitigate against life and liberty. . . . Most sex laws have been found unconstitutional in some lower court or another but since that rule is binding only in that court it has no effect on other cases in equal or other lower courts. . . . It is not an American principle to force the belief of anyone onto anyone else, therefore the theoretical Christian belief of sexual abstinence, copulation for procreation only or any other practice belongs to that faith and that faith only and has no place in the American law." *CN*, 3.23, 5–7.

69. See *VR* July 1971, 10.

70. *Vector* illustrated the concept of victimless crime with marijuana use: "Getting drunk, smoking marijuana, gambling and copulating with someone of your own sex are relatively harmless acts that rarely infringe on the rights of others. . . . The police and the church work hand-in-hand to see that people who have sex out of marriage, gamble, use drugs or get drunk are punished for their 'sins.' . . . Recently, SIR's membership voted twice to endorse the legalization of marijuana. . . . [T]he right of a citizen to do so if he pleases without police harassment should be no more questioned than the right of a citizen to copulate with someone of his own sex in private. . . . Possibly, by assisting in the formation of a coalition to fight all the victimless crimes, we can more effectively eliminate injustice for others and for ourselves." *VR* May 1972, 4.

71. See for example *VR* Feb.–March 1968, 16–18; *VR* May 1970, 6. Sometimes they even made excuses for the police, that it was because their training was lacking. See *VR* April–May 1968, 29. And the arguments continued on all sides. One letter writer excoriated Strait for his praise of the SFPD: "I resent your wishy-washy attitude regarding the police department of San Francisco. . . . Call the bastards what they are," *CN* 4.8, 5.

72. See *VR* Feb.–March 1968, 16–18, where Capt. Martin Lee, SFPD, argued that most violence against gays was homosexual upon homosexual. In 1970, the police issued a description of the 'composite murder' to aid its officers, "22 years old, Negro, single, unemployed, having a moderate police record, and 'usually a homosexual,'" *VR* Jan. 1970, 7.

73. See also *VR* June 1967, 17; Feb.–March 1968, 16–18.

74. For coverage of the shooting and subsequent trial, see *VR* Jan. 1971, 18–19 and *SFGFP* Dec. 1970.

75. Old Timer describes one murder where the police dropped a case when they found gay pornography in the victim's apartment; and another when the victim was found choked with a chain, which they said was a gay S/M murder.

76. See *VR* Sept. 1967, 14. See letter from Nauseous, *VR* Feb.–March 1968, 16–18.

77. This link between police attitudes and sanctioned violence against gay men was underscored when J. Edgar Hoover died in 1972. Gay men in San Francisco rejoiced, hoping that his demise, at long last, had "cleared the way for a fresh opportunity for change in 1972" William Lockhart, *VR* June 1972, 9. They would be sorely disappointed.

78. Letter dated July 12, 2002.

79. Although this may have been technically possible, given the severe sentences for sex crimes, I couldn't find any cases of a man being jailed for life because of gay sex.

80. See *VR* Aug. 1970, 13; Jan. 1971, 30–31. In California, some judges gave men the choice of castration or life in prison. See *GS* Nov. 1970, back cover.

81. See *VR* Jan. 1970, 21.

82. See *GS* Feb–March 1972, 10.

83. See *GS* Nov. 1970, back cover.

84. See Erving Goffman, *Stigma: Notes on the Management of Spoiled Identity* [1963] (New York: Touchstone, 1986).

85. See Morris B. Kaplan, *Sexual Justice: Democratic Citizenship and the Politics of Desire* (New York: Routledge, 1997).

86. See John D'Emilio, "Capitalism and Gay Identity" [1980] in *Making Trouble: Essays on Gay History, Politics, and the University*, ed. by John D'Emilio (New York: Routledge, 1992). In this highly influential essay, D'Emilio argues that gay identity in America did not exist until capitalism had developed sufficiently to support such an identity. John D'Emilio argues that capitalism privatized the nuclear family and elevated it to an almost sacred level within society, that capitalism separated sexuality from procreation, and finally that capitalism ultimately undermines the family it extols by destabilizing the material conditions of its existence. Surely, the move to a more atomized and competitive labor market contributed to the social conditions necessary to foster gay identities, but D'Emilio overstates his case on many counts (to say nothing of his claim that contemporary gay and lesbian movements are "changing consciousness" which create "ideological conditions" that will allow more and more people to "choose homosexuality").

87. Following from the highly influential work of Michèle Foucault, *The History of Sexuality; An Introduction Vol. 1* [1978], trans. Robert Hurley (Vintage Books: New York, 1990).

88. See for example Barry D. Adam, *The Rise of a Gay and Lesbian Movement* (Boston: Twayne, 1987); Elizabeth A. Armstrong, *Forging Gay Identities: Organizing Sexuality in San Francisco, 1950–1994* (Chicago: University of Chicago Press, 2002); Margaret Cruikshank, *The Gay and Lesbian Liberation Movement* (New York: Routledge, 1992); Craig A. Rimmerman, *From Identity to Politics: The Lesbian and Gay Movements in the United States* (Philadelphia : Temple UP, 2002).

89. David Halperin offers a valuable historical corrective to the overly simple contention that sexual identities did not precede the sexology movement. See "Forgetting

Foucault" in *How to do the History of Homosexuality* (Chicago UP: Chicago, 2002), 24–47.

90. See Kaplan, *Sexual Justice*. Kaplan argues the place of gays and lesbians in democratic public spheres has an underlying assumption of the role democratic values made in the production of gay and lesbian cultures in the 1960s.

91. See W.E.B. Du Bois, *The Souls of Black Folk* [1903] (New York: Dover, 1994).

92. See *TN* Dec. 6, 1963, 1–2

93. See *TT* Jan. 1965, 1–2, 5

94. See *SFFP* Dec. 22–Jan. 7, 1970, 3–5

95. See for example, *TT* Jan. 1965, 1–2, 5

96. See *VR* Aug. 1968, 5

97. See for example *VR* Jan. 1965, 6; July 1970, 36

98. See John Stuart Mill, *On Liberty* [1859] (New York: Penguin, 1974).

99. See also Dec. 1966, 2; July 1968, 16–17; and *BAR* Nov. 1, 1971.

100. See Michael Warner, "The Mass Public and the Mass Subject" in *Habermas and the Public Sphere*, ed. Craig Calhoun (Boston: Massachusetts Institute of Technology Press, 1992), 377–401.

2

Sickness and Sin:
Gay Men Confront Symbolic Domination

In our society, the simple fact that I love other men means (for the most part) that I must swish, that I must slur my words, that I must be an alcoholic, that I must be a "mamma's boy," that I must be subservient (a waiter, artist, or busboy), that I must hate women, and that I must sexually desire anything with a cock!

—from *I Am* 1.2 (1971)

To speak of domination or symbolic violence is to say that, except in the case of a subversive revolt leading to inversion of the categories of perception and appreciation, the dominated tend to adopt the dominant point of view on themselves.

—Pierre Bourdieu, *Masculine Domination*, 2001 (1998)

By 1961, an entire system of knowledge had been generated in the U.S. culture regarding the meaning and role of homosexuality, including the overlapping fields of medicine, the law[1], and religion. Prior to World War II, the official medical, scientific, political, religious, and legal discourses concerning sexual behaviors and desires had worked to make homosexuality intelligible to a heterosexual society and to thereby render it containable and non-threatening to the heterosexual order. The production of this kind of knowledge about sexuality continued after World War II, growing more intense as the culture of the United States tightened and grew more restrictive at the onset of the Cold War.[2] With few exceptions, this flow of information about homosexuality served to produce dominant *meanings* ascribed to homosexuality, meanings produced from the

43

outside by non-homosexuals with particular ends, namely the containment of a "social disease." Starting in the late 1940s, some gay men had begun to reconsider their sexual experiences and desires and, more important, to struggle against these dominating official discourses. This continual stream of information, quasi-facts, and normative judgments about homosexuality circulating at the time provoked in gay men a particular experience of domination and a concomitant response that built upon activism in the 1950s, but which also sought to redress and counter these dominating meanings of homosexuality and replace them with what I am calling here "gayness."

During the 1960s, the medical discourses, which had established the pathology of homosexuality well before 1961, combined with the religious discourses, which had long affirmed the immorality of homosexuality, to justify and enable the coercive state and interpersonal interventions into gay men's lives. The direct violence of both official and unofficial agents of the public sphere added a physical dimension to the domination of the heterosexual order and effected its internalization within gay men, who self-surveilled in order to avoid the consequences of their sexual difference. Thus, gay men experienced the dominant meanings of homosexuality in their bodies, rendering the experience personal, internal, emotional, and cognitive. They felt their domination as a series of outside forces continually battling in their psyches and on their bodies for control of their lives.[3] The dominant meanings of homosexuality had the power to discipline not only gay men's behaviors but also their feelings and self-perceptions. This kind of oppression was more personal, more inward, and in some ways more profound than the oppression of state and legal institutions. A version of Pierre Bourdieu's concept of *symbolic domination* seems to be the best approach to understanding how this worked.[4] This was mastery or control, that is, domination exerted through symbolic means (language, ideas, images, representations). This was a kind of domination[5] that evoked in individuals feelings about the self, particular self-perceptions, an affective orientation toward the self that had potentially dire consequences for the life of the individual. Given that these symbols were internalized by gay men to their detriment, I will also use the phrase of *symbolic violence* to denote the deleterious effects of what appeared to be neutral, scientific, just, legal, and moral ideas.

But their lived experiences ultimately gave them the will and power to resist and refuse symbolic violence and to create something else. Gay men had noticed far before 1961 a fundamental disconnect between the dominant symbolic order's intended effect and their actual experience of sexual desire and social life. What we see in the 1960s is an escalation of gay men's and gay women's willingness to use that contradiction to counteract the effects of symbolic domination. Indeed, gay men's increasing frustration arose out of this disjuncture between what authorities argued should be homosexual experience and what they *actually* experienced. They did not feel sick, lonely, incapable of love, attracted to children, immature, underdeveloped, or woman-hating. Rather, they found that in their gay communities they thrived, and that their same-sexuality was as integral to their well-being as any form of sexual desire and relationships.

Gay men and women, then, were fighting for the power to create their own meanings for their own sexuality as they experienced it. In earlier periods of American history, most folks with same-sex desires had to either succumb to the pressures of the dominant symbolic order and live their lives in the ways dictated to them, or they had to create alternative meanings on their own in private and out of reach of the symbolic order. Sometimes these men were lucky enough to find one of the various urban homosexual communities that gave a sub-cultural and communal context to their alternative meanings. What was different in the 1960s was the scope of those sub-cultural contexts, which were then being redefined as a public in itself, and which actively and publicly engaged and fought against symbolic domination, most famously by extolling the virtues of "gay pride."[6] San Francisco's gay publications record how gay men experienced symbolic domination and how they fought against it. They preserve for us the traces of the specific ways that gay men worked to reshape the dominant symbolic order into a gayness that made sense to them and which would enable them to live out their lives in a way of their choosing. They were continuing the battle over symbols started in the previous decade by the Mattachine Society and the Daughters of Bilitis. San Francisco's gay men were seeking self-consciously to understand their sexual desires and behaviors, generating new knowledge about their gayness for themselves, making it intelligible to a gay audience in ways commensurate with *their own experience* of their desires and behaviors. This new knowledge ran counter to the official discourses of the heterosexual order, so gay men had to work hard to create a cognitive space, a framework of meaning that would nurture their own meanings of homosexuality and that would support their emerging gay communities. The struggle to replace these oppressive self-perceptions with positive ones they created for themselves sets the larger symbolic ground out of which gay men would create their multiple and conflicting meanings of "gay." [7]

Homosexuality as Mental Illness

The most common and pervasive meaning of homosexuality arose out of the nineteenth century sexology movement and twentieth century psychiatry. The medical discourses equated, quite simply, homosexuality with disease. At best, the homosexual male was a mistake of nature who would lead a troubled life; at worst he was mentally ill and a danger to society that must be institutionalized, castrated, or worse.[8] Gay men dealt with all sorts of mental defects attributed to homosexuality: alcoholism,[9] the inability to love or to maintain intimate relationships,[10] gender identity confusion, hatred of women,[11] depression, suicidality, antisocial behavior, criminality, perversion,[12] and in the Cold War, vulnerability to blackmail and treason. Experts even blamed the spread of disease on homosexuals.[13] Among gay men's archenemies was one Dr. Socarides, who argued through books, on the radio, and on television that gay men were profoundly ill individuals in desperate need of medical help, could never achieve real happiness, and were incapable of love.[14] Another expert laughingly dismissed the gay movement, arguing that homosexuality produces such profound guilt that they would never coalesce into an effective social movement.[15] In a kinder vein, some psychiatrists argued that since homosexuality was an illness, society should have pity upon them. This view often argued that homosexual acts should be decriminalized, but from a condescending and paternal position of power.[16] Unfortunately, this was always coupled with a description of the illness. One psychiatrist argued that gay men so desired to be masculine that they would experience extreme duress if denied access to sex with other men, regardless of which position they took in anal intercourse. Therefore, these "sick" people should be allowed to practice their sexualities without government interference. For gay men, the problem with these psychiatric explanations was two-fold: one, they inevitably classified gay men as mentally ill, because sex with another man could only be psychologically unhealthful, "a denigrating experience" (VR Aug. 1971, 12–13); and two, the description of illness didn't seem to match their lived experience of homosexuality.

Because homosexuality was a mental illness, mental health and medical professionals believed that gay men could be cured of their homosexuality, and they publicly advocated various treatments. They argued that gay organizations "'perform a disservice when they insist that homosexuals cannot change,'" (VR April 1967, 10). A "good, respectable" homosexual, then, would seek out help and participate actively in his cure.[17] On a couple of occasions, Vector printed articles and letters from men who had been cured of their homosexuality. These men, whom today we would call "ex-gay," echoed the psychiatric diagnoses that brought them to therapy and cure. This handful of men told of their deep unhappiness in homosexuality and repeated many of the tropes of the medical discourses regarding homosexuality, including the lack of love and the obsession with sex.[18] Interestingly, all three ex-gay men published in Vector placed the onus of change on gay men. They argued that it took discipline and that you had to want to change.[19] Echoing the psychiatric discourses of the period, this idea that you have to "want to change" demonstrates how the symbol system dominated, by building blame and guilt into the mental frame through which gay men could understand themselves.

Gay men worked to counter the equation of homosexuality with mental illness and the push for a "cure" in many ways. They responded with anger at the cures, which ranged from brain surgery,[20] to castration,[21] to aversion therapy,[22] and to hormone therapy.[23] The promise of a cure was seen as a new way that gay men would be oppressed, and even came to see "curing" as a kind of genocide.[24] That gay men saw psychiatry as engaged in an effort to eradicate them may have been hyperbolic, but it seems that their feeling of the threat was very real, and this feeling of threat of annihilation fed their growing resistance to the medical establishment's views of homosexuality. In a nutshell, gay men came to simply refuse the diagnosis: Homosexuality was not a disease.[25] "Homosexuality can no more be 'cured' than color-blindness. . . . Although a left-handed person may learn to write with his right hand, he really feels it more natural to use his left hand" (*VR* March–April 1968, 20–21). Another way to counter the dominating effect of psychiatry was by making fun of it.[26] One letter writer joked that only doctors who were hard up for money would try to convince the public that homosexuals could be cured.[27] Responses often took on a vengeful or bitter tone, as with one man who joked, "Show the psychiatrist a picture of Sigmund Freud and feed him a powerful laxative. After enough of this shock treatment he may leave us alone or assist in helping others to adjust to their life style" (*VR* Jan. 1971, 14–15).[28] After $2000 worth of therapy, one patient complained, "Came to find out my therapist was just as gay as I was" (*VR* Aug. 1971, 36–37). Others claimed that those who are "cured" are simply men who weren't really gay in the first place.[29] Importantly, gay men argued that to stop having sex with other men was not to be cured of homosexuality.[30] Often, the counterarguments were quite sophisticated. When castration was proposed in California as a punishment for homosexual sex offenders, *Vector* argued that it was the most direct way that the majority could alleviate its fears of gay men. "The use of castration in most instances is viewed psychologically as a counter-phobic procedure projected upon others. . . . He attempts to overcome his fear (phobia) by castrating others. . . . If another person, group, can be made more acceptable through castration then one can accept it more easily for oneself" (*VR* May 1972, 17).

Gay men weren't naïve, however, and readily admitted that many among them experienced mild to severe emotional problems because of their homosexuality.[31] They argued, however, that it was the experience of oppression, *not* homosexuality, that caused their mental health problems; and that sadness, depression, and loneliness were normal consequences of the kinds of oppression they experienced because of their sexuality. Because they are forced to lead a double life and take on the dominating meanings of homosexuality from their cultural milieu, gay men suffered emotional and mental breakdowns.[32] This often led to a rupture among gay men, especially late in the period, where those who kept their homosexuality a secret were seen as bringing upon themselves their own problems by refusing to accept who they were.[33] Because they saw their mental health problems as coming from the domination they experienced socially, some gay men blamed psychiatrists for perpetrating and perpetuating mental harm on gay men.[34]

By the early 1970s, gay men increasingly argued that they were curing themselves and simply didn't need they help of medical professionals anymore.[35] "Something is on the rise, however. That is the ability of the homosexual to accept himself. Isn't that the real purpose of psychiatry?" (*VR* Jan. 1971, 14–15). And so they simply rejected the legitimacy of the psychiatric profession and medical health professionals, engaging in direct attacks on the psychiatric establishment. "It is time that homosexuals rejected a philosophy that considers them 'sick' by definition" (*VR* June 1967, 23).[36] Both their experiences as gay men and their experiences with psychiatrists and psychiatric discourse led many to conclude that psychiatry had been completely discredited *because the psychopathology of homosexuality made no sense in their experience.*[37] Psychiatrists were dismissed as uninformed, biased, bigoted, driven by their identities as experts, dangerous, and even criminal.[38] In response to this threat, gay men and women across the nation began a tradition of zapping American Psychiatric Association meetings, including the 1970 meeting in San Francisco.[39] During the early 1970s, the publications claimed repeatedly that psychiatry's purpose was simply to reproduce society's bigotry rather than to seek the truth. By 1972, I could find no defense of psychiatry in San Francico's gay publication.[40] By refusing the legitimacy of the psychiatric profession and the power of the diagnosis, gay men created a symbolic space to rethink and re-define gayness. By reacting against and interacting with psychiatry's symbolic domination, gayness came to take on the meaning of happiness, emotional adjustment, and normality. By refusing mental illness, gay men created a way for themselves to see gayness as healthful. In this symbolic space, many saw an ever-more important role for gay *pride*, one that led to self-acceptance, which enabled gay men to overcome the effects of being told they were ill, and which would build a positive, affirming way of being gay.[41]

Jesus Was a Homosexual:
Gay Men Stand Up to Religion

While there clearly were gay men of non-Western backgrounds living in San Francisco during the 1960s, it was Christianity and, to a lesser extent, Judaism that dominated gay men's discussions of religiosity and homosexuality. In religious terms, the world is divided into the sacred and profane, with human beings' strong disgust reflex often tied to religiously constructed categories of profane or unclean. In general terms, as reflected throughout this period in gay men's writings, Christianity and Judaism saw homosexuality as *sin* and therefore *unclean.* It carried with it a heavy presumption of disgust and revulsion, accompanying the social consequences of expulsion and shunning. Religious definitions of homosexuality haunted many gay men their whole lives as they tried to leave behind the cultures of their youths. One man wrote that having been raised Southern Baptist, "as I hit adolescence, I had strong doubts about the worth of my intellect, my physical appearance and strength, my sexual desires, my ability to relate to people—in short, about myself" (*GS* Aug.–Sept. 1970, 14). For many men, separating from their religious upbringing was a painful and life-shaping experience.[42] In San Francisco, the church sought actively to intervene in the public sphere to control the sex lives of citizens,[43] as the archdiocese had a disproportionate impact on the running of the police department,[44] or at least what gay men felt as the inappropriate power of the church in the government of the city as it directly affected them.[45] But here I want to examine how gay men engaged the idea that they were *sinful*, and how they dealt with the social ostracism and the emotional burden sinfulness could carry with it—in short, the symbolic domination created by religious views of sexuality. As reflected in their publications, gay men were well aware of a wide array of religious views regarding their lives and sexuality, ranging across the spectrum of Christianity and Judaism,[46] and including a range of stances from the supportive to the adversarial. Gay men's lived experience of religion included both the power of religion to help and free them, as an activist institution and as a moral authority[47]; and the power of religion to dominate them and thwart their efforts to create a meaningful gay life. Dealing with religion was significantly different from dealing with psychiatry, because individual gay men differed in their religious beliefs, religiosity, and upbringings.

Some gay men sincerely and deeply believed; others were culturally religious; others were secular or atheist. Yet they all shared the experience of religious ideas of homosexuality permeating the culture and the effect that these ideas had on them. Sometimes, the effect of religion was individual and personal, where a gay man was raised a certain way with a set of beliefs that shaped his self-perception; other times it was very public, when the church or synagogue intruded into the public sphere to assert its moral authority on law enforcement and politics. So gay men at once experienced a specific, personal aspect of religion connected to their own histories and beliefs; and a generalized social aspect of religion that was not dependent on their beliefs or history. The reality was that many gay men were gay and religious at the same time, which caused division among gay men as they engaged religious symbolic domination. For example, Bois Burk, an elderly man who considered himself a gay libber, argued that religion only seemed to be a problem for people who are recently out or who still believe their religion's teachings about salvation. Burke argued that for those gay men, if religion is so important, they have to accept the double life of being gay and being part of an organization that hated them.[48] In an informal survey, *Vector* readers responded overwhelmingly that gay men could be homosexual *and* Christian and that the ethical stances of Christianity did not conflict with homosexuality.[49] But again this was complicated as some believing gay men chastised others for being atheistic or non-religious.[50]

For those who saw religion as a possible source of empowerment, they sought to reinterpret traditional religious beliefs and practices to accommodate homosexuality. For them, religion could offer a comfort and moral legitimation to gay men who sought reassurance about the fundamental goodness of being gay. Many churches and synagogues offered their support, including most famously Glide Memorial Church and Rev. Cecil Williams. One reverend told *Vanguard* that "contrary to common belief, the homosexual act in itself is not necessarily a sin" (*VG* 1.7, 29). But the Unitarians rejection of homosexuality as a disease in 1970, and the United Church of Christ's ordination of gay ministry in 1972 also stand out in gay men's thinking about the intersection of religion and sexuality.[51] A handful of gay men and women in Berkeley took Christian theology into their own hands to remake it for gay people. The radical gay Christian publication *Agape in Action* argued that "the locus of sin with respect to the homosexual is in the imposition of the concept homosexuality, and not in the self-identity or expression of homosexual" (*AA* Aug. 25, 1970, 1). They argued that justice for homosexuals was an obligation of Jewish and Christian ethics. The Church's "silence will not do. Unspoken concern will not do. Rap sessions and lectures alone will not do. Justice is being demanded, and to render justice, for Christians and Jews , is not less than a requirement of our faith. One cannot choose not to render justice or to break the yoke of oppression. One must" (*AA* June 23, 1970). So by seeing homosexuality as one possibility for human sexuality and rethinking homosexuality as an issue of justice and ethical obligation, religion became a tool for seeing homosexuality as a moral Good.

At various times, writers attempted to engage and challenge directly religious symbolic domination by recasting traditional Christian views and reinterpreting scripture. One piece in *Vector* imagined Jesus as a human being with sex drives and included images of male nudes. The article gave scriptural evidence that perhaps Jesus was himself homosexual.[52] Laud Humphreys, a sociologist and a minister,[53] wrote a similar essay in 1970, arguing that Jesus as a human had to be sexual.[54] And Dr. Paul Roberts argued that Paul was probably gay and gives a radical rereading of Romans 1, wherein he says that Paul only condemns "unnatural" same-sex sex; so if it is natural to you, it cannot be a sin (see *VR* May 1971, 24). So for Dr. Roberts, trying to change one's natural homosexuality to heterosexuality was the real sin. Throughout the latter part of the period, numerous articles appeared engaging in theological debates concerning the morality and spirituality of homosexuality, often with humor.[55] Paul Bernadino, writing in *Gay Sunshine*, theorized that traditional Christianity was a "Phallic Christ Imperialism. . . . It is repressed humanism and sexuality and the Christian desire for sublimated phallic-sexual union with the worshipped phallic god 'Jesus Christ,'" (*GS* Aug.–Sept. 1971, 11). In this line of thinking, religions are seen barriers to community and humanity.[56] These examples demonstrate how gay men, believing or not, took and transformed religious thought for their own ends, and created out of them a view of homosexuality commensurate with an emerging gay-friendly Christianity.[57]

Because of the history of intense persecution and the equating of homosexuality with sin that arose from religion, many gay men insisted that to be truly liberated, one must leave the churches and synagogues behind. Anger and frustration at religion's power to define the morality of sexuality and to influence the state permeates the entire period; gay men saw religious condemnation of homosexuality as hypocritical.[58] Robert Koch illustrates the anger that was often aimed at religion: "[It] is the most retardant, destructive, regressive power in our culture. . . .The most abominable edicts . . . are the sexual ones delineating who with and how to have sex, and even so far as why to have sex. . . . I think this [religion] is the sickest thing in our society. Who's worried about drag?" (*VR* June 1967, 18). Gay men saw that sex negativity in general came from Christianity and that "homoerotophobia" (later shortened to "homophobia") was born of Christian parentage.[59] For these men, it was at best problematic and at worst self-hating for gay men to be religious.[60] Gay religion was seen as taking gay men away from what really mattered: fighting oppression and gaining liberation. For those critical of gay religiosity, religiosity could only be a sycophantic pandering to the heterosexual culture. But those who considered themselves religious were numerous, and they were equally loud in demanding their rights to create religious identities compatible with their homosexual identities.[61] When seen from our position in the twenty-first century, it becomes clear that regardless of their individual positions on religion, it served for many as a starting point for thinking about the social ethics of homosexuality and for the formation of new kinds of gay communities.

Gays in the Media: The Mass Production of Symbolic Domination

A man writing for *Vector* in 1970 argued that gay men had to begin using the tools of the mass media to overcome the negative images and assumptions of the dominant culture.[62] Mass media through the 1960s and early 1970s did more than reinforce negative images of homosexuals—it was the primary means of the reproduction of they symbolic domination. The local newspapers, both the *Chronicle* and the *Examiner*, frequently commented on the "homosexual problem" in the city[63]; but no less important was the coverage of the national media, radio,[64] television,[65] film, and books. Gay men had an uneasy relationship to these representations. On the one hand, they were at least *some* kind of representation.[66] On the other hand, such representations were overwhelmingly inaccurate and sensationalized, reflecting the predominant views of the psychiatry and medicine. Especially problematic, media tended to be completely uncritical about *why* gay men may have lived or behaved they way the did. By mid-1967, gay men were beginning to feel overwhelmed by the coverage given homosexuality in the popular media.[67] Gay men in San Francisco had little means to engage mass media directly, so they used the tools available to them to respond to the representations of homosexuality they saw in national magazines, television, film, books,[68] and at least one treatment of advertising.[69] In these responses, we find another field in which, by engaging and challenging symbolic domination, gay men were able to make meaning of their homosexuality through their interaction with each other.[70]

Notoriously sensationalistic, magazines in the 1950s had painted homosexuality as the perversion that threatened society, most commonly linking it with pedophilia. National coverage shifted slightly in the 1960s, however, to treat the emerging public face of gay life and the little-by-little more open lives of gay men and women. San Francisco's gay publications took numerous tacks against magazine representations, but the foundation of their resistance was that it was inaccurate and unfair. *LIFE Magazine*'s now infamous 1964 cover story

"Homosexuality in America" is emblematic of how gay men re-framed the media coverage among themselves. They saw *LIFE*'s story as a money-making
scheme and as a blatant effort to support the legal oppression of gay men.[71] But
their rebuttals grew more sophisticated as the decade wore on. When *Time* ran a
similar piece in its January 22, 1966, issue called "The Homosexual in America," Frank J. Howell used *Time*'s portrayal as an opportunity to rethink how
representation functioned and what gay men should do about it. He argued that
gay organizations focused solely on civil rights and not on the day-to-day lives
of gay men, thereby allowing the mass media to portray them as isolated and
lonely, without peer or friend, because such an image was never countered.[72] He
wrote, "The time has probably come for the bewildered homosexual to arise
from the church altar or the analyst's couch and shape the environment and his
destiny by his own will and actions."[73] Most reviewers, however, focused on the
barrage of negative images about gay men they saw in the media. They found
that *Look*'s coverage in a story called "The Sad 'Gay' Life" failed to acknowledge the humanity of homosexuals, that gay men and women were actually people with complex lives.[74] They accused *Look* of condescension and ignorance.
When *Ramparts* magazine claimed that a homosexual syndicate ran the creative
industries, gay men turned the accusation on itself, arguing that to the extent that
gay men have influence in creative fields, it was because they were shunned in
other fields.[75] Rather, it was because society shunted, they argued, homosexuals
into "acceptable" fields.[76] When the Nixon's U.S. Attorney Foran railed against
the "freaking faggot revolution" going on in San Francisco, *Vector* blamed his
reaction on the representations "available on homosexuality from the popular
straight press and magazines [that] would tend to support Mr. Foran's deepest
fears" (*VR* April 1970, 11). Given *Time*'s December 31, 1969, *Esquire*'s November 1968, and *Holiday*'s March 1970 issues, *Vector* claimed it was no wonder Foran thought gay men were sick, silly, drug-crazed, and hippie-radicals.
Although there was no focused or cohesive response, we find that gay men attacked media on a piece-by-piece basis that showed a growing confidence in
rejecting dominating images of homosexuality.

Gay men also engaged in debates about the nature and effect of fictional
representations of gay men in cinema. Several films, now famous for their early
portrayals of gay men, appeared during this period, ranging from a Jean Genet
film[77] to mainstream Hollywood fare. As one might expect, the conflict seemed
to center around gay characters that were possible in real life, but not necessarily
representative, or perhaps that don't represent the gay life of the viewer.[78] This
is the classic dilemma of minority representations, when the representations may
represent some aspect of truth and yet they still feel oppressive in their effect. Of
Staircase, the *Vector* reviewer complained that "The gay characterizations are
the projected stereotypes of the straight community" (*VR* Oct. 1969, 17). No
movie with gay themes or characters received more attention than *The Boys in
the Band*, which was actually based on a play written by a gay man. John
Ferguson, a reviewer, complained that the characters were simply neurotics who
were incapable of enjoying their lives, nothing more than maladjusted homo-

sexuals who were incapable of happiness.[79] In a review of *Geese*, a stage play, the writer reveals the core of gay men's feelings about their representations in the mass media, that gay characters are there to die for the plot in "murder, madness, suicide or VD" (*VR* Feb. 1970, 25). One reviewer lamented that if a movie depicted actual gay life, it wouldn't sell tickets because gay life is actually too much like straight life.[80] And that's really where most engagement with these representations ended up: Gay men rejected them because they were incomplete or outright false, and failed to actually represent a gayness that they could identify with and relate to.

One form of knowledge production, however, sought to counter the unthinking images circulating in the public sphere. Several important academic studies began appearing at the end of the period, many of them conducted by gay men themselves, that began a shift away from homophobia in the academy, which became the prototypes of gay and lesbian studies and of queer theory. Tom Mauer came to San Francisco to head up a research project for the Kinsey Institute in 1970, looking into the actual sexual habits of gay men, comparing over sixty different categories of race, ethnicity, gender expression, outness, and age.[81] Martin S. Weinberg of Indiana University published a study of older gay men in 1971 that sought to measure the social adjustment and attitudes of older gay men in comparison to younger gay men.[82] And Dr. John Gigl published the results of his readership survey of *Vector*, which he used in his doctoral dissertation aiming to describe the life styles of "overt" gay men. He concluded that "no striking characteristics of the sample that would make them obviously identifiable from other male members of society."[83]

Even these more positive approaches to representation met resistance, however. The *San Francisco Free Press* objected to the academic study of gay men, particularly what they considered the prurient Kinsey study. "The only valid study of homosexuality is the one which operates on the political level to ascertain the causes of our oppression and quickly gets down to the real business of deciding what the hell we're going to do about it" (SFFP Jan. 1970, 12). They feared that such studies gave credibility to "the liberal shtick of understanding but condescending interest, 'Some of my best friends are queers.'" Academic study, they felt, were straight Ph.D. carpetbaggers to the community, another form of exploitation; ultimately, they felt the academic study, no matter how positive, did nothing to address the actual source of oppression.

Experiencing Symbolic Domination

The combination of psychiatry and religion with mass media representations created an environment in which powerful negative images of the homosexual male circulated. This cluster of images served to justify, in the minds of the American public, the suppression of gay men and gay groups and the repression of their behaviors and desires. As many have noted, these images served to reinforce heterosexuality in the negative.[84] To the heterosexual culture, gay men were effeminate,[85] irresponsible and free,[86] sex-crazed,[87] alcoholics,[88] members of a nationwide crime syndicate or secret society with plans to subvert America,[89] the cause of the decline of Western Civilization,[90] dangerously spreading throughout the country,[91] and the "Typhoid Mary" of America.[92] A story in *I Am* addressed the effect these images of gayness had on gay men, revealing the depth of the psychological and emotional impact of this kind of symbolic violence and pointing us to the primary strategy gay men employed in combating it. These were *meanings* of homosexuality assigned from the outside by non-homosexuals that gave substance to homosexuality vis-à-vis the dominant culture. From the beginning of the period in 1961, many of San Francisco's gay men rejected those images and tried to replace them with images of gayness of their own making, and with some kind of meaning that would sustain a healthful and happy life.

It was really at the end of this period that gay men began seriously confronting the psychological effects of symbolic domination.[93] As a passing comment, one writer for the *San Francisco Free Press* revealed the fundamental wound: "[S]ubjected to a barrage of straight propaganda . . . we grew up thinking that we're all alone and different and perverted. . . . The television, billboards and magazines pour forth an unreal idealization of male/female relationships, and make us wish we were different, we were 'in,'" (Dec. 22–Jan. 7, 1970, 3–5). It's the feeling or sense that one does not belong, that one is outside, different, or bad that cut so deep throughout a gay man's life. One strategy to deal with difference was to embrace it and minimize its significance.[94] But for others, ignoring the very real differences was to impose a silence, or an imposed conformity; it was like ignoring the person.[95] The idea that gay men needed to ignore the dominating symbol system, that it is wrong, is so often repeated that one must conclude that there is something to understand from the repetition. The effort to counter a symbolic domination is ongoing and requires constant attention and work, symbolic work. But this is no mere rhetorical exercise. Gay men were actively in the pages of these publications generating new symbol systems through which they could see themselves and which, they hoped, held the potential to change the way they experienced life. They were fighting against "powerlessness, incapacity, [a feeling of] smallness" (*TE* 1.2, 5–6) a tyranny of their very consciousness (*GS* Aug.–Sept. 1970, 14).

One particular understanding of the experience of domination surfaced several times in the early 1970s, that of sickness. We saw earlier that gay men often argued that their mental health issues were the result of their oppression as a way to counter the domination of psychiatry; but there were also discussions of sickness disconnected from psychiatry, where gay men framed their experience of life as one of sickness. One writer, Ralph Schaffer, coined the term "oppression sickness" to describe the feelings of guilt, shame, fear, and inadequacy that plagued gay men's lives.[96] For Schaffer, one of the primary effects of symbolic domination was to cause gay men to value heterosexuality, which he connected to the value of "respectability" espoused by many gay men. For better or worse,

Schaffer uses his analysis to draw distinctions among gay men and to condemn those who are "sick" with oppression, seeing them not only as self-hating but as a wounded homosexual who hurts others like him. The next issue of *Gay Sunshine* carried several critical responses to Schaffer. One response argued that Schaffer conflated social liberation with psychological liberation, and that the two weren't necessarily the same thing. For this man, to blame a gay man for being sick from oppression was to remove him from the social context of his oppression. Becoming psychologically free does not guarantee your social freedom; nor does social freedom necessarily provide the means to overcome the effects of psychological oppression.[97] What seems clear is that symbolic domination produced a fundamentally negative affect in the gay male psyche and that gay man were trying non-stop to counter that negative affect. Their efforts to replace the negative images from religion, psychiatry, and the mass media were heroic; but there seems to be franticness about their efforts, as the domination they were confronting is so much bigger than they were.

So part of the process of addressing the experience of domination was to try to understand its source. Although there were clear institutional sources (the church, the medical establishment, the law), gay men's thinking started looking deeper in the early 1970s. Berkeley's *Gay Sunshine* contained numerous articles trying to analyze how exactly gay men internalized the meanings given them by the dominant symbolic order, really to understand the source of their domination. One idea that appeared in 1970 was that gay men had, consciously or not, accepted the idea that heterosexuality is superior and "good," and therefore lived their lives as "heteroseuxalized homosexuals," that is, homosexual men with heterosexual values.[98] Heterosexual culture produced in gay men expectations, desires, and social statuses that were at odds with their experiences of themselves and their lives and their sexual desires, leaving them with the feeling of incompleteness or inadequacy.[99] One gay man wrote of looking at pictures of women with his father, even while he was thinking of boys from gym class[100]; he concluded that this was the result of living in a society that would not accept his love of men and required the love of women. Others located the source of their domination in the homo/hetero or a male/female binary, where being forced to choose one or the other is the cause of the negative affect. For these gay men, they binary caused gay men to question their masculinity.[101] When there are only two choices, and when heterosexuality is dominant, homosexuality becomes nothing more than a degenerate or degraded form of the true or correct form of sexuality.[102] In this conception, the domination arises because homosexuality becomes not just a degeneracy, but *the* degeneracy, the sign of all that could go wrong with one's sexuality and gender.

So symbolic domination was not merely the circulation of oppressive images or ideas about homosexuality, but the requirement put upon gay men to live according to heterosexual practices and standards. The symbolic order tells you that you're wrong, and then socially, you are forced to live differently than you otherwise would. Heterosexuals were directly blamed for creating the world that

perpetrates violence against gay men.[103] One man wrote of going home for the
holidays without his partner, because the expectations were that he bring a
woman home. A small heterosexual practice had the consequence of "once again
disavowing the validity of gay life and helped to further, permanently establish
our lives a second-best, transient, lightly, unimportant" (GS Jan. 1972, 11).[104]

Previously I noted that the fundamental quality of the negative affect created by symbolic domination was loneliness or unbelonging (to coin a word).
And so more than any discussion of heterosexual dominance, "alienation" appeared more and more often as a descriptor for the experience of being homosexual in America as the 1960s came to a close. As young college students and
graduate students moved into leadership roles in the emerging gay liberation
movements and as the overlap of revolutionary ideologies from various movements and the counter-culture progressed, certain aspects of a sometimes quasi-
Marxist and sometimes explicitly Marxist critique took prominence in the gay
men's discussion of their domination. Robert Cole wrote, "A homosexual, no
matter how integrated into the heterosexual society, is alienated from that society by virtue of the fact" (VR Aug. 1967, 14–15). Alienation meant a hyper-
awareness of one's socially unacceptable differences, of ones "faults" (VR Dec.
1967, 18). Some gay men began to rethink their behaviors in terms of alienation,
such as when one writer linked cruising to protection against the "fear of abandonment and the need to be dependent on others" (VR June 1968, 12). Another
man wrote of how the social conceptions of homosexuality put him in the mental state where he thought the only way to be accepted or to find peace was as a
second-rate man, a sorry substitute for a woman.[105]

To the extent the homosexuals suffered from extremely low self-esteem or
unbearable feelings of guilt, the cause was not a natural defect in the homosexual, but a flaw in society—alienation resulting from domination—that constantly
fed him "an unpleasant image of himself from the behavior of others towards
him" (VR March 1969, 16–17).[106] Oppression emerged out of the unfortunate
meeting of "his own sexual predestination and society's outdated moral standards" (VR April 1969, 13–14, 25).[107] Some gay men began to look with compassion upon each other, understanding the link between their suffering and the
environment they lived in.[108] Of course, the most devastating effect of domination was an inner pain so intense it led to utter hopelessness and suicide. Rev.
Ray Broshears exclaimed, "Due to the oppression by the heterosexual society,
most gay people are forced to take their own lives in great numbers each year"
(GS Feb.–March 1972, 10). In this view, alienation came to be seen as the primary barrier to self-acceptance. Alienation, unbelonging, "crippled the human
potential" of gay people[109] and made self-acceptance into a hard-fought battle.[110]
Some gay men optimistically believed that by removing the social stigma, they
could remove the experience of alienation and thereby remove the obstacles to
gay men's self-acceptance.[111] For many gay men, in the context of symbolic
domination, there was no other possible outcome than alienation from the self:
to be self-hating. "I felt I was queer, that I'd always be a queer, that every-

thing—when I got to the bottom of things—was hopeless" (*GS* Aug.–Sept. 1970, 14).[112]

Some gay men experienced another form of alienation, in that they were alienated from their own bodies. *The Effeminist* ran a series of articles in 1971 explaining how an anti-homosexual culture cuts gay men off from their bodies. First, *The Effeminist* made a feminist- and anti-war-inspired argument about the control of men's bodies in general, seeing unmarried or young men were simply fodder for the heterosexual order's violent needs, seeing the gay male body as "already a conquered territory" (*TE* 1.2, 5–6). But more to the point, another writer argued that heterosexual culture "mystifies" the gay body, keeping the gay man powerless, frozen, and small by keeping him from feeling and understanding his own body. "It is important you see that we be taught not to listen to our bodies, not to listen when our bodies know better than we do . . . when we are being raped and fucked over" (*TE* 1.2, 5, 12). They advised gay men to "pay attention to your body," and that you would know what was best for you and your life and could wade through the false consciousness of heterosexism. Only by paying attention to your own body intently, they argued, could a gay man overcome the pressure of the dominating heterosexual order to ignore the gay male body. "The system exploits the individual's intense longing for a bodily sensation of transcending the experience of alienation by promoting institutions which reinforce the tendency of alienated persons to misread body messages in their searches after pleasure. . . . It goes for sex, too—that is the alienated contact that passes for sex in the so-called homosexual world."[113]

The 1970s gay libbers had returned to discussions that began in the early 1960s about the meaning of gay sex and the possibility (or impossibility) for gay men to make true intimate connections with one another. Gay men, they argued, lived out their alienation through anonymous sex that perpetuated their alienation rather than alleviating it. Some writers blamed gay men for their own relegation to backroom and public restroom sex and one-night stands; others recognized the social structures that forced this kind of sexual practice on gay men by enforcing heterosexuality in the public sphere. "First they made it dangerous for us to be open about sex in our regular relationships. Then they provided meeting places, which, because we were so easily exposed, were also dangerous. Anonymity became necessary for survival. . . . Impersonal sex became an imposed way of life. . . . Our oppression reached into our bedrooms" (*GS* April 1972, 10). So anonymous gay sex could be both the cause and the effect of a hollow alienation, deepening the alienation of gay men from their bodies and of reproducing the "stereotypes," the very vehicle of symbolic domination.[114]

Fighting Back: Refusing Domination and Its Effects

As we have already seen, the primary means gay men employed to fight against symbolic domination was to refuse it, that is, to deny, counter, reject, and resist the meanings of homosexuality in their dominant forms. In so doing, gay men (perhaps unknowingly) were simultaneously creating new and different *meanings* of gay, in the sense that George Herbert Mead described.[115] Here we have seen gay men interacting with each other through and around the very broad, national (and even international) meanings of gay, that is, the symbol systems they received from their social context and which they worked to shape into something more resonant with their experience of gayness and with their desires for a different kind of social position in the United States and the City of San Francisco. Because the actual sources of this symbolic domination were distant and anonymous, most of this work happened among and between gay men and women themselves and most of it was at the level of symbols, of reforming and replacing the symbolic structures that gave meaning and salience to homosexuality, but hopefully on their own terms.

By the early 1970s, many activists had grown impatient and angry; they had come to see oppression as a direct result of gay men's refusal to fight for their own lives.[116] The volume of these symbolic refusals had gradually mounted over the decade, but make no mistake about it that the refusals had started early. From the beginning of this period, gay men felt they had to shatter stereotypes, to throw off the oppressive definitions imposed from the outside. But the 1970s gay libbers did change the direction of the debate somewhat, producing what we might call a "gay self." This was not just a resistance to the a transformation of the meaning of gayness that had roots decades before in the activism of Harry Hay, but which came to fruition during this period. Gayness came to be seen as a form of self-expression,[117] where language and the power to control the language about the gay self became increasingly important, as the right to define the self was a constitutive feature of the gay self.[118] So gay-maleness was conceived of as a kind of person with the agency and the ability to choose his own way of being and who could express himself as gay, where gay was a constitutive part of his being. This is a particular kind of self, a gay self, that arose in specific response to and interaction with the kinds of symbolic domination that gay men were undergoing and building on notions of self-hood already present in American culture at the time.

In a larger sense, this gay self was conceived of as capable of rejecting the social acceptance of the dominant heterosexual order altogether. For some gay men in the early 1970s, doing so was actually an imperative.[119] One of the most enduring ways that gay men refused the heterosexual culture in their publications was to produce campy spoofs of heterosexual fears of gay men.[120] Indeed, why ask for acceptance when you have your own culture? "We also find that even though this society has tried to crush our ideas of culture and society they have survived and now are surging toward a greater uniqueness and awareness" (*GS* Nov. 1970, 8–9). The rejection of straight society sometimes found expression in symbolic violence of a different kind, as in Charles Thorp's poem about raping a straight man[121] or Keith St. Clare's poem about the violent side of gay male sex.[122] Especially the tone of *San Francisco Gay Free Press* and *The Effeminist* grew more and more confrontational and threatening.[123] This often involved a repudiation of straight-male privilege and the forms of masculinity that bestowed said privilege and the sexual violence that was their prerogative.[124] "I'm rising up gay to smash your cock-power, understand?" (*SFGFP* Dec. 1970, 5). *Agape in Action* took a similar tack in the rejection of straight-male privilege, seeing straight-maleness as the source of domination.

> It's hard to hold onto what you [straight males] do to us [gay males]. I've even got a cock, too, just like you. Just so, I'm still just the hole in your head. I don't exist except in your head, you, the all-absorbing cosmic one. I'm just a queer. I'm just like a woman. . . . You stick all sorts of instruments up me, thermometers, fingers, fingers with rubber protective coverings, sterilized metal probes, some with lights to see the cavities, the ruptures. You poke and cram. You shoot, you kill. And still you can't find me. You've got radar, you've got lasers, in hopes I'm nowhere. I'm just the hole in your head. I'm the other, the other person you're not, the outside world. You call me woman. You call me queer. You call me slave. You're too busy to know me. You define me. You steal my life to fill the hole in your head. You tell me who I am. You never let me be. Poke, push, and scram. Student, workers, woman, queer. *AA* Feb. 1971.[125]

So gay men took up the task of the continual assertion of the self along with their refusal of the straight norm. Although it had started in the early 1960s, it really came to bear fruit in the early 1970s. Notice in the following quotes the insistence on self-hood and personal identity. "'We must give up the "Amos and Andy" syndrome,' SIR President Tom Maurer, told this crowd. 'Let us stop playing society's game. Begin to say, "*I'm me*—and if you don't like it that's YOUR problem,"'" (*VR* Oct. 1970, 13, emphasis added). *Gay Sunshine* echoed Maurer's sentiment. "Straights have ruled us too long. It's time to be *YOURSELF*! Don't blend in with Straight people—oppressing yourself. *BLATANT IS BEAUTIFUL!*" (*GS* Oct. 1970, 9, emphasis added). The feeling had become, by the 1970s, that gay men should no longer have to adjust to society, but that they were fine as they were. "The societal norm must adjust to us, must adjust to the fact that we exist, that we emerged out of and were conditioned by a straight/queer society, and that we have as rightful a place in society as the next person" (*GS* Oct.–Nov. 1971, 7).[126] For many gay men, these intense feelings of anger, frustration, and violence underlay their continual (re)assertion of the gay self, an ongoing project of claiming their "gay self," insisting on their existence as gay individuals, whole human beings. In the oppressive cultural environment of 1960s America, gay men had had to continually remind themselves that they were even human.[127] What so frustrated gay men was that it seemed with each step toward building a life for themselves, the dominant culture responded with renewed efforts to oppress.[128] As gay men were fighting these symbolic battles, they were also confronting the very real, embodied power of the state as they confronted legal institutions and agencies of the official public, their struggle for the meaning of gay took on a political and activist tone. Indeed, the struggle against symbolic domination cannot be fully understood outside of the context of gay men and women's emerging formation of a gay counter-public.

Notes

1. I will be leaving aside an in-depth analysis of the law for Chapters 3 and 4.

2. See for example Robert J. Corber, *Homosexuality in Cold War America: Resistance and the Crisis of Masculinity* (Durham: Duke University Press, 1997); John D'Emilio, *Sexual Politics, Sexual Communities: The Making of a Homosexual Minority in the United States, 1940–1970* (Chicago: Chicago University Press, 1983); and David K. Johnson, *The Lavender Scare: The Cold War Persecution of Gays and Lesbians in the Federal Government* (Chicago: Chicago University Press, 2004).

3. Here, I am adapting concepts gleaned from Foucault's analysis of the nineteenth century prison. See Michèl Foucault, *Discipline and Punish: The Birth of the Prison* [1975], trans. Alan Sheridan [1977] (New York: Vintage Books, 1995).

4. I am adapting this concept from Pierre Bourdieu's *Masculine Domination* [1998] (Palo Alto: Stanford University Press, 2001). See especially pp. 9–23 and 34–38. I find the term "symbolic domination" prefereable to "discourse" and "oppression," both of which seem to have lost their analytical specificity in their common usage in the social and cultural sciences. I will use "symbolic domination" and "symbolic violence" to refer to the domination produced by systems of symbols which are in turn enacted and internalized by individuals who incorporate them into their perceptions, their attitudes, their dispositions, and their practices (or as Bourdieu would say, in their habitus). Herein I will refer specifically to the "heterosexual order" as the dominating symbolic system that legitimates the practices of a kind of heterosexuality and instills in individuals the values of that order to the effect of structuring the culture and social relations of those who live under its regime.

5. Sometimes symbolic domination came from enforced silence, which served to keep gay men separate from each other; at other times, it took the form of the general disapproval of the majority of Americans. Most often, domination came from the "experts" who expounded to the public the "truth" about homosexuality. See for example *VR* Dec. 1969, 10: "The status of the homosexual in our society today is extremely low. In a recent Harris Opinion Survey 63% of a cross section of the American population thought that homosexuals were 'harmful to American life.'" And also, "The established institutions perpetrate the silence about love between men in order to keep the homosexual isolated from his sexual peers," wrote one gay man. *VR* March 1966, 11.

6. "One is willing to excuse stupidity and fear in the uneducated, but the tolerance level is suppressed rapidly when the person spreading bilge is a 'learned' one" (*VR* Aug. 1968, 7). Joe Amahein of Milwaukee wrote that "Oppression flows from social attitudes and not a legal system. . . . What I am saying is that the attitude of a president toward gays is much more important than legal reforms that he may endorse" *VR* May 1972, 16).

7. A 1972 *Vector* article made a parallel between scientific explanations of homosexuality and the old scientific explanations of racism and anti-Semitism. The author argued that science allowed the majority to feel comfortable in their prejudice. See *VR* Feb. 1972, 35.

8. See *VR* Aug. 1971, 12–13.

9. See *VR* Dec. 1967, 26–27.

10. See for example *VR* April 1967, 20–21, 29; Dec. 1967, 18; March–April 1968, 16–18; Aug. 1971, 12–13.

11. See VR Aug. 1971, 12–13.

12. These were "The old standard belief that many homosexuals are perverts and dangerous." *VR* April 1967, 10).

13. See *VR* April 1967, 10.

14. "'The fact that somebody is homosexual, a true, obligatory homosexual, automatically rules out the possibility that he will remain happy for long.'" *VR* April 1967, 20–21, 29. On another occasion, Dr. Socarides appeared on New York television where he was publicly humiliated by a local representative from Mattachine New York. See *VR* March 1969, 7. "'I asked if the "treatment" would be free, [at Socarides treatment center for homosexual men]' Leitsch writes. 'Socarides said he hoped the government would subsidize it. I asked where the centers would be located. He hadn't given it any thought. I suggested that he make them in Puerto Rico, Hawaii, and other vacation areas, and told him I thought sending all homosexuals to one place like that was the best idea since Fire Island, only better, because we'd be subsidized." See also *VR* Oct. 1970, 48.

15. See *VR* Feb.–March 1968, 11.

16. One psychiatrist argued, "It is neither inborn nor instinctive but is a 'learned' style of behavior. The sexual drive however, *is imprinted*, (instinctive) in all people. Its object is *reversed* in the homosexual." *VR* Sept. 1970, 26.

17. At the American Medical Association meeting in San Francisco in 1968, Socarides lobbied for funds to create a treatment center for gay men who desired cure. He expressed shock and dismay "that homosexuals 'do not cry out and demand medical attention.'" *VR* July 1968, 5. From earlier work, such as Edmund Bergler's, doctors in the 1960s argued that gay men had to *want* to change, or cure would be ineffective. See letter from T.P., *VR* Jan. 1969, 16–17, in which he reviews the literature on the cure for homosexuality.

18. Letter writer Fred wrote, "And when it gets right down to it, Frank, I don't think that you are happy [as a gay man]." *VR* July 1970, 18–19, 41. Fred went on to argue that homosexuals could never be happy, by definition. They can "never be satisfied," because they engage in a "constant search for the prefect cock."

19. Another ex-gay man, calling himself Marcus Veritas, wrote, "I am saying I left homosexual life where I thought I was happy for a real life where I KNOW I am happy. In short, yes, there is away out. You must want out, but this can only come when you can take no more." Another ex-gay man reported that to cure himself of homosexuality, he went for two years without sex. See *VR* April 1967, 20–21.

20. See *VR* June 1972, 6–8.

21. See *VR* May 1972, 17.

22. "So science in all its Mesozoic Miracle Work invents electric shock therapy, [and] castration to cure its patients, whose sickness is love and life with the same sex." *SFGFP* Nov. 1970, 4–5, 12. This article pointed out that the North Koreans used aversion therapy on prisoners of war. "Vomit away your perversions! Patients (yea, victims) are shown pictures of men and then administered apomorphone to make them vomit." *VR* Jan. 1971, 14–15.

23. *VR* Feb. 1972, 45.

24. "The most tragic aspect of this outright lie is the many latent homosexuals who will continue to live with their suppressed pain and the terrible blow this strikes against all of our efforts to enlighten an already prejudiced public." *VR* Aug. 1970, 9. For discussions of "gay genocide" see *VR* June 1972. Responding to a National Institute of Mental Health report in 1970, *Agape in Action*, a radical gay Christian publication, argued that

mental health experts refuse to speak of heterosexuals in the same terms that they use for homosexuals, assuming that heterosexuals are uniformly well-adjusted. "The real meaning of this report is very simple: the government and the professions are engaged in a deliberate program of genocide—the destruction of a people." *AA* Oct. 28, 1970, 7–8. This was not an extreme or isolated view. *Gay Sunshine* reported that efforts to "cure" homosexuals amounted to nothing less than the mass murder of gay people as a people. As the public debates about homosexuality increased in the early 1970s, so did the proponents of cure. "Gay Liberationists take all this as evidence of a monstrous conspiracy for the genocide of homosexuals." *GS* June–July 1971, 11–12. *Gay Sunshine* called this trend a neo-Eugenics movement.

25. See *CN* June 22, 1964, 6; *GS* Jan. 1972, 5.

26. In response, *Vector* printed a campy review of a book by an ex-gay calling himself William Aaron in 1972. "Aaron falls in love with a lively Christian group and finally makes it in the sack with a real live woman. Conversion gradually takes place. To this we can hardly object." *VR* June 1972, 18. In his book, Aaron "pities anyone who is gay and believes old-fashioned morality offers the one rewarding answer." Bob Reader of San Rafael riffed on an extended joke that eating turnips would cure homosexuality, and asked how, if that were true, the turnips remained unbought at the grocer. "I guess we can conclude that if homosexuality is a 'sickness' and curable, there are some 90,000 of us in the Bay Area who are not interested in a cure." *VR* Jan. 1969, 16–17. When Primal Scream creator Arthor Janov claimed that he could cure homosexuality, *Vector* panned him. See *VR* July 1971, 45.

27. See letter from U.R. Long, M.D., *VR* Jan. 1969, 16–17. And Helen Warren of Chicago wrote, "I guess if I was making $40 an hour 'curing' homosexuals, I would also try to convince the world that homosexuals are sick." *VR* Oct. 1970, 48. See also *VR* Feb. 1972, 35.

28. In a similar vein, another joked that "I am certain electric shock treatments will recondition the religious among us to a more mature conceptualization of God." *VR* July 1967, 13.

29. See for example *VR* Jan. 1971, 14–15; 30–31.

30. "The person who has been 'cured' of homosexuality has often only modified his genital relationships." *VR* Aug. 1970, 6.

31. See for example *VR* March 1967, 17, 23; Jan. 1969, 7, 22

32. Oppression could even produce a "crippled person." *VR* March 1967, 20. D.F. Hering described social attitudes as "crippling blows" for the homosexual. "It takes a most unusual person who can be a homosexual in our society and not have emotional and mental health problems. The guilt of being what others about you consider loathsome, the strain of leading a 'double life,' the trauma of exposure, etc., all have their impact on the personality of the homosexual." *VR* Dec. 1967, 26–27.

33. *VR* Jan. 1969, 16–17.

34. "[P]ersistent efforts by psychiatrists to convert homosexuals to heterosexuality instead of inculcating them with pride in their homosexuality. . . . When society generally, and psychiatry particularly, have 'brainwashed' homosexuals into a belief in the inferiority of their homosexuality, the homosexual who asks to be changed is merely the creation of a self-fulfilling process." *VR* June 1972.

35. "We don't even need you [psychiatrists] any more. We'll define ourselves, thank you. And we won't do it just in terms of sexuality, either. We are not homosexual, we are gay. No, I mean Gay. And it isn't homosexuality that we're talking about, it's gayness.

Transvestite, transsexual, homosexual, bisexual, maybe even straight . . . we are Gay. And we say to you. . . . We know who you are now, and we won't trust you or submit to your subtleties again." *AA* Oct. 28, 1970, 7–8.

36. See also *CN* May 25, 1964, 8–9. The easiest critique was that doctors' "studies" used psychiatric hospital patients as their samples. See *VR* Nov. 1970, 14–15; Feb. 1972, 35.

37. From time to time, the gay press published positive notes from psychiatrists who had similar findings to Evelyn Hooker's in the late 1950s. William Walker, M.D., Oakland, wrote, "I have discovered that the great majority of homosexuals are remarkably well-adjusted individuals. . . . Careful analysis has revealed an emotional equilibrium that I wish my other patients could attain." *VR* Oct. 1970, 48. *Gay Sunshine* published the theories of a gay-positive therapist in Jan. 1971, 5: "Freedman holds that the etiology (causes) of homosexuality is relatively unimportant; what matters is the operational behavior of the individual and his self-concept in relation to his life-situation. . . . First, there is the stereotyped 'homosexual' who willingly subordinates his own uniqueness to the role of 'fag' that society lays out for him, resulting in a wasteful self-contempt. Secondly, there is the 'pragmatist' who disguises his sexual identity in society, learns to function effectively. . . . More rare is 'creative oppositionalism,' in which the creative direction of an individual is determined by social pressures exerted against the minority group to which he belongs."

38. "Homosexuals are sick—sick of hearing uninformed, self-appointed authorities airing their personal prejudices and distortions as facts." *VR* March 1967, 8. Frank Kameny of D.C. wrote, "It is psychiatry and psychoanalysts which are sick and psychiatrists and psychoanalysis who are suffering from a faulty scientific identity and so are pathological." *VR* Nov. 1970, 14–15. Don Jackson advised one young man *not* to see a psychiatrist because "psychiatrists are moralists and are unable to give good advice to homosexuals." *VR* April 1971, 20–21.

39. In 1971, gay men and women zapped the Washington, D.C., APA and were able to get on the program and addressed directly their medical oppressors. That year, the APA voted to reclassify homosexuality as a "sexual perversion." They disrupted a panel discussion on aversion therapy, participated in a panel with Dr. Bieber, an anti-gay hawker of gay cures, and held an independent panel on the last day they titled, "Life Styles of Non-patient Homosexuals." See *VR* July 1971, 34–35 and *GS* June–July 1971, 11–12. Frank Kameny read a statement at the panel, wherein he asserted "that we consider them THE enemy incarnate; that we feel that they have been waging a relentless war of extermination against us. . . . I pointed out to the psychiatrists that if psychiatry were to attend to its proper responsibilities, to help dispel prejudice and bigotry, fear and misinformation, people would cease to be afraid of homosexuality, in themselves and in others, and pseudo homosexual (and homosexual) panic was cease to occur." See *VR* Aug. 1971, 36–37. In 1972, another group zapped the APA in Dallas. In Dallas, *Vector* reported, "Dr. Robert Seindenberg [a panelist] . . . was saddened now to find the gay psychiatrist seated on the panel wearing a mask (a hideous thing completely covering his face). . . . [Judd Manor, professor of psychology at UCLA said,] 'I submit that the entire judgment that homosexuality is an illness has no basis in fact. Just as women were supposed to hate being women, there is a prejudice in psychotherapy which reflects the dominant ideas of our times. . . . No heterosexual is really mature unless he has resolved his own prejudices toward homosexuality.'" See *VR* June 1972, 38. For these gay men, psychiatry is based on "a misinterpretation of cultural artifacts of the particularly dis-

torted, warped, perverted sexual attitudes of the Victorian era in which Freud grew up." *VR* June 1972. "That a noted psychiatrist should refer to two people of the same sex who enjoy each other as 'an affliction' illustrated his unscientific and moralistic judgment." *VR* March 1971, 38–39.

40. Some gay men concluded that the very purpose of psychiatry was "To support and buttress the prejudices of society and to assist the bigots in the perpetration and perpetuation of their bigotry; and at least equally important (2) To destroy the homosexual's self-confidence and self-esteem, impair his or her self-image, degrade his or her basic human dignity." *VR* June 1972. Thinking historically, one earlier *Vector* article foreshadowed Foucault as it traced the cultural history of the transition from controlling sex through "sin" to controlling sex through "sickness." "So a new vision of hell was created: That of Freud." *VR* Jan. 1969, 16–17. Another expert, Edmund Bergler, and his book, *One Thousand Homosexuals*, resurfaced during the 1960s and was duly excoriated in *Vector* as so much Freudian mumbo-jumbo based on a non-scientific sample of mentally ill men who happened to be homosexual. See *VR* Jan. 1969, 16–17.

41. "To give them pride is even more devastating" to the status quo. *GS* Nov. 1970, 7. For *Gay Sunshine*, power came when an "oppressed people get pride about themselves as meaningful individuals." See also *GS* June–July 1971, 11–12. Don Jackson wrote that "Gay Is Superior" in 1971. Using somewhat dubious scientific evidence, Jackson sets out to demonstrate that gay men are smarter, live longer, and are more masculine than heterosexual men. Regardless of the scientific basis for such claims, what stands out is Jackson's insistence on the *goodness* of being gay. "Ever since Plato observed that most of his brilliant students were Gay, underground Gay supremacists have lurked in the lurch. . . . Ever since then, many Gay intellectuals have been obsessed with the notion that Gay is better, but few have the courage to openly admit their closet beliefs." *BAR* Oct. 1, 1971.

42. "My homosexuality is what separated me from religion," wrote one man. *VR* Nov. 1970, 39, 43–44.

43. See for example *VR* Nov. 1968, 5.

44. See Chapter 1.

45. See *CN* 4.8, 5; *VR* June 1971, 34–35.

46. "Clerics pitied the homosexual whose 'unnatural' behavior condemned him to one of the Dante fiery tortures." *VR* Jan. 1969, 16–17. And Rabbi Schoel Myers, with extensive quoting from both the Torah and the Talmud, explained in no uncertain terms that "The attitude of the Jewish religion is, then, clear and unambiguous: homosexual relations are sinful." *VR* May 1971, 24. In a backhanded effort to be charitable, the American Presbyterian general assembly in 1971 both affirmed that homosexuality is a sin, but urged the government to legalize it because making it illegal simply persecuted the sick and afflicted. For a full reprint of the statement, which was not officially accepted by the General Assembly, see *VR* Aug. 1971, 50.

47. See for example Glide Memorial Church, *CN* 4.5, 1. Even a Catholic priest wrote to *Vector* encouraging gay Catholics to remember the love they felt in communion with the church. See *VR* July 1969, 17. And a gay Catholic group met with the Diocese in 1971. See "Gay Catholics: A First Step," *AG* April 22, 1971, 1.

48. See *VR* June 1967, 18. Burke also wrote a series of newsletters that he sent to friends, expounding his experiences as a gay man in San Francisco. A few of these survive and are held in the GLBT Historical Society's archives in San Francisco.

49. See *VR* June 1967, 18: "(6) do you believe a homosexual can maintain a 'religious ethic' outside of an organized church? yes 38, no 2; (7) Have the ethical values of

Christianity made your adjustment of being accepted as a homosexual more difficult? yes 26, no 14; (8) Does religion create a moral conflict for the homosexual? yes 36, no 4. ...." In a later survey, readers refused to disclose their religious affiliation. See *VR* April 1971, 5.

50. See letter from anonymous writer, *VR* Sept. 1967, 16–17.

51. In 1970, the General Assembly of the Unitarian Universalist Association declared that "homosexuality as an inevitable sociological phenomenon and not as a mental illness." *VR* Sept. 1970, 22–23. Ironically, in 1970, the UU would reject a gay candidate for ordination to the priesthood because he was openly gay. Gay men and women of the Bay Area ended up zapping a UU General Assembly meeting. See *VR* Nov. 1970, 22–23: "[UU]that the denomination would prefer if I sought other employment. . . . About 300 'freaks' showed up at the Unitarian General Assembly in Seattle and involved themselves in dialogue with the 1200 delegates . . . . most of our group were under 23 years of age, but there were maybe 50 of us older freaks working with the young people. . . . [In a speech Stoll said] I wish to identify myself with the many, many people who are not only disenfranchised in this society, but in our churches [UU] as well." The United Churches of Christ did eventually ordain a gay minister in 1972; *Vector* reported it was the first of its kind in the nation. See *VR* June 1972, 9.

52. See *VR* Dec. 1969, 20–21. See also a similar argument in *GS* Aug.–Sept. 1971, 11.

53. See Chapter 1, footnote 29.

54. "Had I proceeded with the logical extension of this central, Christian doctrine to proclaim that Jesus 'jacked off' as a teenager, my active ministry would never have lasted ten years." *VR* Dec. 1970, 13–14, 38. He went on to claim that St. Paul was a closeted queen and that although the Bible doesn't say that Jesus had orgasms with the Apostles whom he loved, it does demonstrate special attention for his favorites, and notes that this was after all the Hellenistic world where teachers would have been expected to have sex with their students. This essay was also illustrated: a photo of naked young guy, smooth, water in the background, arms outstretched in a crucifix.

55. See Dr. Fredrick C. Wood, Jr., "Sex within the Created Order," *VG* 1.8 (June 1967?), 5–6; Rev. Michael Itkin, "Christ and the Homosexual," *SFFP* Jan. 1970; Paul Bernadino, "A Gay Theology," *GS* Aug.–Sept. 1971, 11; Dr. Paul Roberts, "Gomorrah," *VR* Jan. 1972. For example, "If the raping of males in Sodom condemns all homosexual acts, then certainly the raping of females in Gomorrah would condemn all heterosexual acts." *VR* Jan. 1972, 33.

56. In line with gay liberation's authenticity values, Bernadino asserted, "The Brave New World is our world; where with love, there is neither Christian nor Jew, neither Greek nor Roman; neither male nor female; neither 'homosexual' nor 'heterosexual,' and neither slave nor master. But all are as one in the human family. Let us exchange the terminal City of God for the Secular City of Gay humanism."

57. During this period, there is precious little else but Christianity in these gay publications, with the exception of the occasional reference to Judaism and the appearance of one anti-gay Rabbi. Other religions are talked about as interesting, but outside of the gay experience.

58. See "To make a spectacle of the variant to the exclusion of other forms of sexual expression is hardly becoming to those professing their beliefs." *TN* Aug. 19, 1963, 3–4. Or "The church has been responsible for and has aggravated more wars and hatreds among men than any other source." *VR* June 1967, 5.

59. See *VR* Feb.–March 1968, 11.

60. "In America today, the gay churches stand spiritually vacated. Homosexuals are on their knees—a frightened and infernally dull lot—instead of on their feet. . . . We don't want what heterosexuals have; heterosexuals should not want what we have." *VR* Oct. 1971, 35.

61. "What right has one gay brother or sister to tell another to get out of their churches, to give up their religious beliefs; attacking them in a most hateful and destructive way? There is something very wrong in all this. If some gays feel that their religious practices, faith and fellowship, bring more meaning into their lives, so be it. With all this talk by gays about 'liberation,' 'dignity' and 'the right to live as we desire,' perhaps all of us should rethink what these words mean when dealing with our gay brothers' or sisters' religious convictions and activities." *VR* May 1972, 41.

62. "[T]he mass media could break down the stereotyped images, whereas now they only reinforce these images." *VR* Nov. 1970, 39, 43–44.

63. See for example: Kenneth Rexroth, "About the Homosexual," reprinted from *The San Francisco Examiner* 14 June, 1964, *CN* 22 June, 1964, 8. "American society is coming to accept homosexuality between consenting adults, not as an unfortunate but tolerable affliction, like epilepsy, but as a condition like albinism or color blindness which should not enter into the judgment of most of our relations with our fellow humans. . . . It is true that most of the sickness connected with homosexuality is due to the lack of virtues in this context—to conflict, ostracism, neurotic compulsive drives, guilt, emotional instability, and not least, the resulting difficulty in forming enduring love relationships. Many wise men who have come through the fire of these struggles have matured to be of vast help to others—the 'normal' people."

Guy Wright, "You Fellahs Should Be Discreet," reprinted from the *San Francisco Call-Bulletin*, *CN* 4.4 (Nov. 1964), 5. "'Please, gentlemen, try to be a bit more discreet. . . . This unfortunate [a guy with pink hair and makeup and tight pants] was taking a delicious pleasure in the distaste which he caused among the other customers. . . . It has become almost commonplace to see young men holding hands as they stroll down the street. . . . But we don't dare use it ['gay'] anymore because it has been sullied by overtones of perversions. Queer, fruit, swish, drag—these and other perfectly good coins of the king's English now draw a smirk. . . . So for your own sake, gentlemen, please respect the sensibilities of the rest of us. In your case all the world doesn't love a lover. Be a bit more discreet.'"

64. One young gay man was interviewed on the radio, and experienced the way the media controls information. Guy Strait was critical of the man's behavior on the air: "The brash young men who did not understand the difference between publicity and notoriety arranged for radio time on KMPX-FM. The first program was cut off the air when the word 'gay' was mentioned." *CN* 3.22, 7.

65. Televised coverage of homosexuality was new during the 1960s, but only in news formats and exposés. Because there were no fictional gay characters to speak of (at least not open ones), gay men tended to counter television coverage as they did magazines. *Vector* titled a review of Mike Wallace's 1967 "Homosexuality," "CBS remains Perplexed. . .So Does Its Audience" and called it an abdication of journalistic responsibility. *VR* April 1967, 20–21, 29. This was the documentary that made Dr. Socarides famous and served to launch his career as a reparative therapist for gay men. *Vector* felt that the overall effect of the broadcast was to convince America that homosexuals were nothing more than "wounded animals at best, or dangerous psychotics at worst." *Vanguard* also

responded to the CBS program, noting "Mr. and Mrs. America were reminded again and again that we are one of the most despised minorities." *VG* March 1967.

66. This is a similar dynamic to the way black folks in America used to consume *Amos and Andy*, despite their profoundly racist representations.

67. "In the past few years we have been subjected to a barrage of information on homosexuality from the press, television, radio and the national magazines." *VR* May 1967, 10.

68. Reviews of mass circulation books, fiction and non-fiction alike, also served as a platform to address gay representation. When a popular novelist, Merle Miller, came out in 1971, *Vector* complained it was too little too late. But they ate up his firsthand account of being gay in America, focusing especially on his experience of difference. "'As a child I wanted to be the girl my mother wanted—or else the all-American boy that everybody so admired.' Here we see the apple pie American conflict. The battle between compelling inner desire and the need to be just like everybody else was never stilled." *VR* March 1971, 45. The reviewer doubted that Miller could ever step completely out of the closet, but delighted in the cultural effects of a well-known author coming out. "Who will be next to yank down the lavender curtain and cause the establishment to eat crow?" The gay press of San Francisco continually reviewed non-fiction books treating homosexuality. In a couple of reviews, we discover what gay men were looking for in reading non-fiction literature. In *Town Talk*'s review of *In Defense of Homosexuality*, the reviewer appreciated the frank and rational tone discussing sexual matters, which he considered to be adult and mature. The book supported the notion that homosexuality was a choice by arguing that it was one of many valid sexual expressions open to human beings. "For the homosexual, this book will serve as a first step toward his unashamed self-recognition and to his emergence as a whole person." *TT* Sept. 1965, 1, 4. Another review that same year of *Attitudes To(Ward) Homosexuality* confronted another common image of the homosexual: "Envy of the so-called homosexual freedom, to be promiscuous, to have no lasting ties or emotional bonds." *VR* June 1965, 9. *Vector* attributed this distortion to heterosexuals' own emotional weakness and inability to adapt to the lifestyles they chose.

69. Some gay men began to pay attention to the effects of advertising on the gay community as well. In "Selling the Groovy Guy," Craig Hanson argued that advertising perpetuated images of the perfect male body which can only produce inferiority complexes and feelings of worthlessness." *GS* May 1972, 3. Because gay men liked to wear "modish clothes," they were regularly exploited by the fashion industry, which used gay men's youth-consciousness to ensnare would-be buyers. This, Hanson argued, came from the pornography industry, which exploited young men and sold to gay men "the groovy ideal." Ultimately, this lead to "Much of the gay world consists[ing]of selling the body as a commodity and offering the promise of youth and beauty to men who can neither become younger nor more 'beautiful.'" Hanson argued that three kinds of commercial exploiters used gay men's insecure body awareness for profit: "1) those who mold the body and face to ever-changing standards of male beauty; 2) merchants who emulsify the flesh with cosmetics and dress it in the latest fashion; 3) commercial interests who profit from the use of fashionably clothed or nude groovy guys by displaying them in various ways."

Another format, a lost art of the 1960s, was the production of informational, spoken word LPs. One such LP appeared in 1967 called "Homosexuality in the American Male," complete with interviews from the usual experts, including Dr. Socarides. *Vector* critiqued the LP for using experts who do little more than offer personal opinion, serving to lend credibility to the false representations of gay men, giving a "rationalization for every repressive moral and legal indictment of the homosexual." *VR* June 1967, 23. Importantly, the critic complained that the LP left out completely the political and social efforts of the "homophile organizations, which are becoming increasingly important in the lives of many of us."

70. Many more examples of gay press reactions survive the era, especially relationships with local radio; what follows is a selection of the most significant media events in terms of how gay men reacted to them.

71. Harry d'Turk wrote, "When a publication begins to have circulation problems, they only have to print an article on homosexuality." *CN* 4.6 (Dec. 1964), 7. Both *Citizens News* and *Town Talk* blasted *LIFE*'s dramatized and baleful depiction of gay life. *CN* did so mainly through camp. In a mockery of the "facts" presented by life, and an assessment of the effect of the piece. "WHAT WAS ACCOMPLISHED: It would appear that with the play-up of the extremes of homosexuality, *Life* would like to see the status quo maintained. No good reason was put forth to change any existing injustice. In fact, every reason was depicted to maintain the laws exactly as they are." *CN* July 20, 1964, 1–2. *CN* also included a mock spread titled "Heterosexuality in America," campily dismissing and rejecting the power of *LIFE* to depict their lives.

Paul Welsh responded for *Town Talk*. "And with such information, with its negative as well as its positive aspects of homosexual behavior, proof is ample that this age-old and pervasive human condition fails to pose threat which uninformed alarmists claims it does." *TT* July 1964, 1. And later that year, they reconsidered the effect of the media coverage. "[A] greater demand for recognition of the right for individuals to be different and accepted as such is being voiced over the U.S. and Canada today. . . . 1. LIFE Magazine's discussion June 26 of homosexuality . . . 2. University of California Medical Center . . . [announced] that the phenomenon of 'cross-gender identification' . . . and transsexualism . . . is now receiving serious study by its medical and psychiatric authorities . . . 3. New organizations and publications." *TT* Oct. 1964.

72. *VR* March 1966, 11.

73. Only one pro-gay article appeared in the mass press, albeit in the alternative left magazine, *The Nation*, which ran its argument in favor of gay rights in its November 8, 1965 issue, reprinted in *TT* Dec. 1965, 11.

74. Reviewing the January 10, 1967 issue in *VR* Feb. 1967, 1.

75. *VR* March 1967, 17, 23.

76. In addition, a couple of dramatic television shows caught the eye of the gay press. The debut episode of a half-hour drama called *NYPD* ran on ABC in the fall of 1967, called "Homosexual Extortion." It depicted a homosexual man blackmailed by hustlers in which the gay character died. See review, *VR* Oct. 1967, 7. And when Marcus Welby found a sidekick in 1972, John Bennett campily reread the drama as a gay love story. "Neither Welby nor Kiley has any regular female companionship. . . . Meanwhile, we can enjoy the very warm relationship between these two virile men who live together—without women—as a TV testimony that this is not only a healthy but a most natural relationship." *VR* Feb. 1972, 54.

77. When a gay-positive Jean Genet film came to Berkeley in 1964, Guy Strait complained that "The film was so full of symbolism that it was almost beyond comprehension," which was too bad because "the story of sex in prison is one that sorely needs to be told." *CN* 4.1, 2. Later, another art film, Fellini's *Satyricon*, brought down the wrath of *The Effeminist. The Effeminist* excoriated the film for making hatred of homosexuals easy in its portrayal of degeneracy and with little hope of anything else. "Fellini, after all, is an

old queer who could not help finally ripping off all of us by positing a future based on the inter-relation of two or more pretty young men," *TE* May 1971, 1.

78. Revealing the complex reception of mass representations, Magdalena Monte-zuma, a campy movie reviewer, thought that although *The Gay Deceivers* was a bad film, its representations weren't all that bad because she knew gay men who were like the ones in the film. *VR* Aug. 1969, 14.

79. *VR* Oct. 1969, 22. The film and stage versions were reviewed twice more. See *VR* Nov. 1969, 30–31; Jan. 1970, 18

80. See *VR* Aug. 1971, 36–37. Several other films of note received reviews. *The Story of Christine Jorgensen* received positive notes for telling the transsexual's story from the transsexual's point of view. See *VR* July 1970, 30. *Zachariah* attracted attention mainly because of its young star, Don Johnson. Magdalena also read it as a gay story and actually interviewed Johnson. "Homosexuality plays an underlying theme in *Zachariah* as the two lead males obviously groove on each other more than they do on Belle Star. . . . [Don Johnson] said, 'You don't have to fuck to show homosexual love.'" *VR* March 1971, 20–21. A few films received positive reactions, including *Bloody Sunday*, which was seen as an accurate and important film by *Gay Sunshine* Jan. 1972, 5. *Bay Area Reporter*'s review of *Lawrence of Arabia* was equally glowing. Terry Smith, the reviewer, saw the film as a lesson in what being closeted can do to a man. "Lawrence's masochism is the key and he is called upon to use it to the greatest degree in his quest for recognition. . . . And since he suppressed his homosexuality, he wouldn't be detected, would he? . . . Lawrence's flaw was not his latent homosexuality, but his overt megalomania . . . the [Turkish] General simply had him anally raped and thrown out into the street—secure in the knowledge that this one, initial act of homosexuality would crumble the foundation," *BAR* Apr. 15, 1971.

81. See *VR* Jan. 1970, 16–17.

82. See *VR* March 1971, 16–17.

83. See *VR* April 1971, 12–13, 36: 3/5 came from intact families, 68.09 percent fa-vored their mothers over fathers; "In this study, 276 or 31.12 percent of the respondents claimed that their homosexuality never made them feel guilty"; "(48.24 percent) of the respondents indicated 'no response' regarding their own religious affiliation"; "the educa-tional achievement (of the respondents) was considerably higher than the males of the general population"; "the man age of first homosexual contact was 13.35"; "Only 7.98 percent of all responses indicated genetic etiology"; 81.9 percent of respondents covered upper half of Special Hollingshead Occupational Scale; 62.01 percent only children or firstborn; "The mean sexual contact with the same person, in any given month, is 8.21 versus a mean contact with strangers of 6.99. It is concluded that the male homosexual is promiscuous, but not as highly indiscriminant as is generally speculated."

84. Much work has been done expounding the meanings of homophobic images and their effects, both intended and accidental. My purpose here is to talk about gay men's strategies for dealing with these images and their responses to them, not the meaning of such images for heterosexuals.

85. See *TN* Sept. 16, 1963, 1–2; *CN* May 25, 1964, 8–9; June 22, 1964, 6; Aug. 3, 1964, 6–8; 4.5, 1, 2; *TT* Oct.–Nov. 1965, 8; *VR* May 1967, 13;

86. See *VR* June 1965, 9.

87. See letters from J.F.K. and from R.L.J., *VR* Dec. 1968, 16–18.

88. See *CN* 3.22.

89. See *CN* Feb. 1964, 1; May 25, 1964, 8–9; April 1967, 20–21, 29; letter from R.P., *VR* June 1967, 33;

90. See letter from Hans Shultz, *VR* Sept. 1971, 36.

91. See *CN* May 25, 1964, 8–9.

92. See *TN* Dec. 23, 1963, 1; *CN* May 4, 1964, 10;

93. To be fair, these kinds of analyses had appeared before the 1970s. Some gay men had started to think critically about the personal effect of socially constituted regulations of their sexuality. "Like most of them, [the homosexual] is brainwashed into following rules which are privately flouted by almost every [heterosexual] citizen every day. . . . Empty, frustrated and lonely heterosexuals are forced to compare themselves with what seems to be defiance of law and freedom incarnate: the gay boy—ever promiscuous, ever laughing, ever drinking, and whoring the night away." *VR* Jan. 1965, 5. But what the straight coveter missed was the oppression perpetrated by the very rules the homosexual seems to flaunt. "The only difference is that when he [the homosexual] faces up to his moral convictions and acts on them, he invites police harassment and often jail. The homosexual is required to be homosexual in a hypocritically heterosexual culture." So gay men felt their oppression not as simply the experience of being harassed by the police, but more the experience of knowing that the simplest form of self-expression was forbidden, strictly patrolled and brutally punished—expressing oneself became the source of danger. The daily task of the homosexual was "to grapple with the alienation the individual homosexual experiences between himself and his fellow man." *VR* Aug. 1967, 14–15.

94. "He is different. That's all that is wrong. He is the solitary white crow in the flock and all other crows peck him to death because he is not like them." *SFFP* Oct. 1, 1969, 12.

95. "'I was Homosexual and you oppressed me in silence.' Silence surrounds us like an unfriendly night, it stands before us like a wall one can see and touch, but it is never really something you can come to grips with. . . . We are what the heterosexual wants to be blind to." *AA* July 20, 1970.

96. *GS* April 1972, 15. As was typical, Schaffer then turned his critique of the dominant culture into a moralizing critique of his fellow gay men. He categorized types of men suffering from oppression sickness: the Princess (older, effeminate gay men: chronic liar, the hustler syndrome, intensely selfish, incommunicado and closeted); the homosexualized heterosexual; and the heterosexualized gay. He then designed a questionnaire in the style of tabloid magazine's sex quizzes, for gay men to evaluate their level of oppression sickness by taking stock of their sexual habits.

"Sexuality Test for Gay Males:

1. Are most of your sex partners within five years of your own age?

2. Do you kiss your lover's mouth before, during, or after intercourse?

3. Do you enjoy all possible sex acts?

4. Do you usually perform a sex act which results in your partner's orgasm?

5. Do you often have sex with close friends?

6. If a friend of yours were very horny and had no means of finding a sex partner at the time, would you attempt to gratify him sexually in some way?

7. After having good sex with a stranger, do you attempt to contact him later for further sexual enjoyment?

8. When entertaining either a friend of lover, do you shut off the television?

9. Do you often find yourself unable to find a sex partner when you feel the need for sex?

10. Do you feel flattered if friends or acquaintances embrace or kiss you?

11. Do you sometimes have warm feelings for female acquaintances?

12. Do you usually get along with lesbians?

Scoring: The more 'yes's' the better.

1 to 4. Your sexual expression is limited and you probably are not very good in bed in the opinion of most.

5 to 8. You are an average gay guy.

9 to 12 You give a comparatively full range to your expression of gayness; you are probably great in bed." *GS* April 1972, 15.

Analysis of responses were as follows:

"I dare say not one gay man has escaped oppression sickness." *GS*, April 1972, 15.

97. *GS* May 1972, 7. Ned Tuck, Michael Cox, and Ralph Hill all weighed in to counter Schaffer's theory of oppression sickness. See *GS* May 1972, 14. Cox inveighed against Schaffer's mistake in only seeing the sickness without accounting for the "social pressures that provoke their responses." For Cox, this pointed to the necessity of the Gay Community to produce its own politics and values, "a world-view which does not see men and women as passive, vicious stereotypes, and which does not assess people in terms of their sexual performance." This was the only way to stop reproducing the vicious lies of the dominant culture.

98. This reads as a proto-version of Michael Warner's notion of heteronormativity. See *Fear of a Queer Planet* (Minnesota UP: 1993).

99. "Some of my expectations are thinking I should be heterosexual, thinking I should fall romantically in love with someone and that any relationship short of this isn't worth my time that I should achieve success, that I should be productive." *GS* Aug.–Sept. 1970, 14.

100. *GS* Oct. 1970, 10.

101. *GS* Oct–Nov. 1971, 7.

102. *TE* May 1971, 1.

103. See for example *GS* Jan. 1972, 3.

104. Pinney hoped that a real gay community that believed that "Gay is Good" would alleviate this kind of domination in the future. "At every possible point, we must make those moves which re-affirm our homosexual relationships—and we must do so in the face of innumerable aspects of our culture which tell us differently. Only we can liberate ourselves. One suggestion? Let's make certain that we spend Christmas with our gay families."

105. "The homosexual life was a desperate mirage and the most I could expect to find in the way of a personal growth or expansion was to be accepted in more oppressed parts of society as a poor man's 'woman.'" *GS* Aug.–Sept. 1971, 11.

106. See also *VR* Sept. 1969, 20–21, 30; *SFGFP* Nov. 1970, 4–5, 12;

107. See also *VR* Nov. 1970, 14–15; Jan. 1971, 14–15; and letter from Bob Hart, April 1971, 20–21.

108. One reviewer of *Boys in the Band* argued that what made the performance he saw so powerful was that one of the actors "allowed his audience to see that beneath the 'screaming fag' lurks a sensitive and deeply hurt human being." *VR* Jan. 1970, 18. Fred, the ex-gay, argued that his behaviors were "used by me in an attempt to cover up my corrupt crumbling life by wildly attacking society and everyone in it." *VR* July 1970, 18–19, 41.

109. *GS* Jann. 1972, 5.

110. "And the degree of misery or happiness in their lives depends on their level of consciousness. Self-acceptance in a hostile society is not easily won." *VR* July 1970, 12.

111. "[T]he homosexual. . .usually goes through years of conflict in our society. Why not remove the conflict by removing the social stigmata associated with homosexuality?" *VR* Jan. 1971, 14–15. James L. Stoll wrote hopefully, "So our work is paying off! Future generations should be free to enjoy sharing love with any person. Repressive prejudice robs people of their self worth and, by establishing that some people are better than others, gives 'the betters' power over others." *VR* Oct. 1971, 9.

112. While this experience was surely real, it also became another point of moralizing, where gay libbers distinguished themselves from older gay men and from older cultural forms of gayness. If you were self-hating, it became a sign that you weren't strong enough or out enough or moral enough to shake off the effects of domination. Only a self-hating gay man would go to bars; only a self-hating gay man has multiple partners; only a self-hating gay man enjoys drag. Old-school "fairies" had, for some gay libbers, internalized the heterosexual's hatred of homosexuals. See *GS* Jan. 1972, 3. "They [older gay men] are unable to imagine that gay is good. . . . Gay traditionalists are drawn towards astrology, the occult, and superstitious ideas of every sort. They desperately want to be heterosexual, but they believe the hand of cruel fate is set against them."

113. In some ways, this reads as a recapitulation of discussions of disillusionment with gay life from earlier in the period. As early as 1963, in a piece about James Baldwin, *The News* pondered how gay men's relationship to their own bodies foreclosed the possibility of real, connected relationships. This was a disillusionment with the "gay underworld." Baldwin had been highly critical of gay men's lifestyles in the early 1960s and Guy Strait zeroed in on this particular aspect of Baldwin's critique. In the gay underworld, "'it is impossible to have either a lover or a friend, where the possibility of genuine human involvement has altogether ceased.' I would recommend the rest of the quotation as good advice." *TN* Oct. 28, 1963. This feeling that real human relationships were impossible for gay men continued through the period, but the critique shifted focus with the gay libbers.

114. See *IA* 1.2, 3.

115. See Introduction.

116. "In our society, nobody cares what happens to a fag. We believe the homosexual is also to blame for the depressing life he often leads. He has allowed it to happen. He has allowed society to force him into a subordinate position. He has not fought back. Many homosexuals have depended on and supported a society which rejects them. Too often the homosexual has played the role." *IA* 1.3.

117. For example, "The best news is that many young people are coming out vocally as homosexuals and expressing themselves. There is a great deal of 'Well, fuck you, if you don't accept me." *VR* March. 1972, 4.

118. For example, "The term 'fag' when used by a heterosexual (or even a homosexual for that matter) is not innocent, no matter how offhanded it seems; it reflects the same old condescending attitude, the same disgusting overtones of 'queer' and 'pervert' and degenerate' by which 'right thinking' heterosexual attempt to maintain their supposed superiority to homosexuals." *VR* July 1970, 10–11.

119. See *GS* Oct.–Nov. 1971, 7.

120. "The straight people of San Francisco are hurriedly looking for a community in which they can live and form some identity. . . . The President caused an uproar in the nation today by lifting the ban on heterosexuality." *AG* April 15, 1971, 1. Guy Strait had

started this practice early on in his publication of a satire of *LIFE Magazine*'s issue about homosexuality. *Citizens News* spoofed *LIFE*'s photos and captions, July 20, 1964: Under a photo of four Ku Klux Klan members ran the caption, "The group to the right is a posed picture of active, practicing heterosexuals who wear white robes and make a show of masculinity and scorn effeminate members of their world"; and under a photo of Elizabeth Taylor, the caption read, "Flagrant heterosexuals such as Elizabeth Taylor ignore the stares of other people. Such people are unabashed by reactions of shock, perplexity and disgust." Strait attacked heterosexual fear of the "spread" of homosexuality. "But today especially in big cities, heterosexuals are discarding their furtive ways and are openly admitting, even flaunting their challenge to sexual conventions. Heterosexuals have their own bars, their special assignation streets, even their own organizations." And *LIFE*'s prurient interest in hustlers. "And midtown off Broadway, their more professional counterparts, dressed in sexy dresses and continental suits, loiter everywhere. Few of the passers-by recognize them as hustlers. In Chicago, the near north portion of Michigan Boulevard is a swarm with heterosexuals looking for a bed-partner for the night." He even spoofed heterosexual efforts to understand the homosexual. "They [heterosexuals] have good jobs and families; they go to church. . . . The only difference between them and the conformists world is the fear of exposure and their troubled conscience. Then there are also the 'respectable' heterosexuals who pair off and establish a 'marriage,' often transitory but sometimes lasting for years."

In the early 1970s, *Vector* ran several such spoofs. The first was a two-issue "exclusive," "I Am Straight: The Heart Rending Story of One Man's Failure as a Homosexual," in which they panned the coming-out process. See *VR* July 1970, 27. In May 1971, the second one was entitled "Heterosexuality Exposed! The Private and Public Life of the Straight Ones." This exposé ran with photos to illustrate the life of a straight man. One was a photo of a woman with large breasts on all fours, under which the caption read, "Mammary glands drive some men wild. Tavern owners make fortunes by having women bounce their nude mammaries for hetero male voyeurs"; another photo of two men in the military carried the caption, "The Army keeps putting up photos of Ann Margaret to remind the men that they are straight"; and another of a wedding, "The church encourages male-female relationships." See *VR* May 1971, 10–11. The article evaluates straightness harshly: "The story of heterosexuality has been one of wars, conquests, enslavements, exploitations and every form of oppression. Those practicing these unnatural sex acts have gone on to loot, burn, and butcher." Taking a crack at the image of San Francisco as a gay haven, the writer contends, "San Francisco is reported to be the 'straight' capital of the world. Here, heteros have their own hard-core porno movie houses, sex massage parlors, and pick-up bars. In their own entertainment section called 'North Beach' you can observe men and women in the nude together on stage and 'topless and bottomless' dancers." And he spoofed other straight stereotypes. "Some heteros also walk funny. They have firm (not limp) wrists. . . . [They like] particularly telling tales of when they were in the service. Killing animal and fish is very 'masculine.'" And finally, he jabbed at the prominence of heterosexuality in American public life. "Heterosexuals are very religious and very American. . . . Just being a heterosexual is a great burden to carry and it requires a great deal of time in itself. Psychiatrists and psychologists have many theories about what causes heterosexuality. Some claim it is an imbalance of hormones while others say it is an over-dominant father." See *VR* May 1971, 10–11.

In February 1972, the *Bay Area Reporter* began a series by Don Jackson titled "Everything You've Always Wanted to Know about Heterosexuality but Were Afraid to

Ask." Jackson's primary target was the psycho-babble that sought to "explain" and "cure" homosexuality. This series would become hotly controversial in the *BAR* as some men objected to what they saw as Jackson's alienating rhetoric—many of the readers of the *BAR* it appears continued to hope for straight allies and acceptance. From Jon Lastala, "The 'Hetero' series and his recent article 'Gay Is Superior' cannot ultimately help the homosexuals' craving for equality, or help the broader Gay Liberation Movement." *BAR* April 15, 1972.

121. See *SFFGP* Nov. 1970, 11.

122. See *VG* March 1967.

123. "I want to tell you that I'm proud of me, what I am, my culture, my openness, my gayness and what I do, feel and say, so damn it, leave me alone, stop interfering or else." *SFGFP* Dec. 1970, 5.

124. "And what does sisterhood actually mean to you? You don't even know because you've never experienced brotherhood. You still want to exploit and use women as sexual objects for your pleasures and bondage just to keep on provin' you're a masculinity, to cover over your errors and frailties. . . . I can tell you right now, straight man, I'm not going to feed your feeble-minded ego any longer and neither will my sisters." *SFGFP* Dec. 1970, 5.

125. Similar views of straight men were published in *The Effeminist*. "And Elijah, writing for *The Effeminist*, took it to violence. "My brother says I am a pig—a straight man—because I wanted a gun to kill straights last week. . . . No brother, they do have power. I am unable to fight them one body alone without help (none of you faggots are showing solidarity, that's for sure). I demand to be free of their daily assault on my body, my mind, on my soul. They will back off or die. . . . But the demand is met at once by force. . . . You who sit and do not help when I am under attack—what do you know of queerness? . . . Did you ever feel the assault of gestures, his loud voice, his eyes with their gestures of dominance, his controlling handshakes, his assumption of his right to fully occupy any assumption of his right to rule, to be heard, to be desired, to have all he wants and to destroy all else? . . . You [my gay brother] dare to say I am straight when I defend my life? You pig." *TE* 1.2, 6.

126. And at its core, this most often amounted to insisting, over and over again, on their basic humanity. "The next time someone tells a 'queer' joke, don't laugh, look at him and say, 'I'm gay.' . . . We are humans, not something to be laughed at." *IA* 1.2, 3.

127. "The Navy says I am undesirable. The sexologists say I'm sick. The government says I'm a poor security risk. The law says I'm a criminal. The Church says I'm a sinner. The man in the street thinks I'm queer." *CN* June 22, 1964, 6.

128. "We Gay males discover our histories, our lives. The Man suppressed our existence and isolated us from one another. We discovered we were human and they called it homosexuality. We discovered what it means to be a man in America and they called it self-hate. We discovered ourselves, and they said we were afraid of women. We discovered their secret, their empty and vicious lives, and they called us outlaws." *TE* 1.2, 11.

3

Conflict over the Ends and Means of Gay Counter-Publicity

Timid leaders with enormous ego-trips, middle class bigotry and racism, and too many middle-aged, up-tight conservatives are hurting almost every homosexual organization on the West Coast and probably throughout the nation.

—from *Vector*, April 1969

. . .[The] uninhibited militancy of today is obviously generating antagonism in the heterosexual society, the society that we must live in. . . . Continued progress will be made only when the heterosexual community is convinced that we are not a threat. . . .

—from *Vector*, Nov. 1970

A large part of forming a new gay publicity, or counter-public, as I have called it, was the effort to create a coherent strategy for a gay movement, and to devise tactics that would get gay men and women the kind of outcome they desired. Not surprisingly, gay men and women differed not only on strategies and tactics, but on the desired outcomes as well. Because my goal here isn't to conduct a political analysis of the various ways that gay folks tried to engage the official public, but rather to understand how these debates produced a meaningful gayness, I will be using the more basic Deweyan terms of *ends* (the goals or desired outcomes) and *means* (strategies, tactics, and forms of activism) to frame this discussion. By seeing this hotly contested, central argument among gay people during the 1960s in terms of ends and means, I hope to both minimize the tendency to judge and evaluate their politics in favor of focusing on the kinds of meanings that these debates enabled.

Building on the efforts of the 1950s homophile organizations, San Francisco's gay men and women had begun more adamantly to refuse the meanings of homosexuality assigned by psychiatry, religion, and the law, which were spread by the mass media, in their efforts to overthrow the symbolic domination of homosexuality. These parallel struggles necessitated that gay men and women strategize their engagement with the official public, including how and when to interact, how and when to fight back, how and when to withdraw, how and when to use official means (such as the courts), and how and when to resort to civil disobedience.[1] To repeat, I argue that when taken in the context of the push to create a gay publicity and the fight against symbolic domination, the conflict among gay men and women over their *ends* and *means* of engagement created an ever-widening, ever-changing pattern of social interaction that provided gay men the context to try to create a meaningful gay-maleness, a way of being a gay man that would answer their needs in the complex environment of 1960s San Francisco.

In forming its ends and means, the emerging gay counter-public drew inspiration from the Civil Rights movement, the Free Speech movement, the counterculture movements, and the Anti-War movement. But it also provoked debates about whether or not their needs as "sexually different" individuals could be met with the strategies and tactics of other movements; these arguments led them toward increasingly daring and confrontational tactics as the decade wore on. Further, as early as 1966 the hippie and free love movements in San Francisco had already inspired a framework for a kind of freedom of thought and action and an openness of gay practices that had before been secretive or closeted. As we have already seen, the official public as it was then constituted required gay men to adopt strategies of psychological and behavioral division that created a necessarily fragmented personhood, where whole pieces of their personality must be set aside and actively suppressed in order to participate in the official public. The only other option was to suffer direct intervention into their lives aimed at preventing them from expressing and experiencing their sexuality freely. Gay men appear to have wanted to change their environment such that they could pursue the consummation of their sexual and relational desires without the intervention of official public institutions or the unofficial regulation of their lives, such as anti-gay vigilantism, or the symbolic domination of mainstream culture.

The official public sought to suppress homosexuality by treating homosexuals as a totality, as a group; but gay men and women were individually the objects of that suppression and experienced it on an often very personal level. This complicated their efforts to come up with coherent ends and means of engagement.[2] In addition, the sense that there was a broader kind of freedom that gay people needed, a *freedom of personhood*, clashed with the older, dominant definition of *freedom as rights*, a classical "freedom from" model of liberty. And so the uncertainty about what exactly freedom should mean for gay folks led to additional conflicts over the means—the strategies and tactics—of fighting for liberation. These battles over political means and ends are the most common object of scholarly study about gay culture during the 1960s. Because gay folks' emerging conception of the *freedom of personhood* remained poorly articulated through the period (indeed, the phrase is my own effort to give a name that will capture the essence of the direction of their arguments, which actually remained relatively inchoate throughout the 1960s), the ends and means they proposed for public action were highly variable and contradictory.

By reading gay men's proposed ends and means for public action as expressions of values, we gain a crucial insight into how these arguments served as the foundation for arguments about gay-maleness. John Dewey linked the process of *valuation* to the notion of a public, by connecting the *prizing* (valuing) of an object to the social action required to achieve it. In Dewey's terms, gay men's experience of their environment, their interaction with the dominating official public, produced in them a need or lack that required directed thinking to fulfill. The arguments and conflicts gay men were having over the meaning of their repression and domination were the literal process of gay men working out new possibilities for the meaning of freedom, foreseeing the possible consequences of a new and different kind of freedom that would resolve their discomfort in American (and San Franciscan) society[3]—in Dewey's terms, ends-as-means of public action for the procurement and retention of freedom of personhood. In Dewey's theory of values, this is the very process of *valuation*, where freedom of personhood was proposed as a possible *end*, where desires coalesce into a proposition of what *should* be, knowledge gained from their activity-undergoing.[4] What remained for the gay men of the 1960s was *appraisal of means*,[5] whereby they could separate meaningful and effective means from those that did not work. The problem for the nascent counter-public was that neither the full meaning of freedom of personhood as an end, nor the means to achieve it, could be settled upon, as in practice, different gay men literally needed different kinds of freedom, from their experience, and as in practice, different means produced multiple and contradictory consequences, which turned out extremely difficult to evaluation. For Dewey, humans "struggle for things they prize, spending time and energy in their behalf: doing so indeed to such an extent that the best measure we have of what is valued is the effort spent in its behalf."[6] For better or worse, much of their own efforts to understand the value battle among gay men and women revolved around how radical their various ends and means were or should have been, a battle which continues along much the same lines into the twenty-first century.

This battle revolved around a kind of ideological divide: on one side is the assimilationist program, also called conservative, and sometimes liberal, as in, wanting to be a part of liberal democratic culture as it was constituted; on the other side was the liberationist or radical camp. Indeed, much of the research about this period relies heavily upon this particular political binary (which is common to many political analyses of the period) to effect its critiques.[7] This political binary framework functions as a *normative value position* that can be applied uncritically to evaluate the cultural actions of gay and lesbian movements to this day. In this radical-vs.-assimilationist binary, cultural, social, and political means are evaluated based on their relationship to the values of "radical" politics as they emerged during the 1960s. However, a detailed mapping of the struggle gay men and women were actually having over the political meanings of their practices, feelings, and cultures hobbles the utility of such a binary to help us understand the culture as it emerged. Indeed, this binary was inherited directly from the political conflicts among the gay men of the period, as they became the first generation of gay historians and social scientists. Continued reliance on such a binary framework, one that emerged during the period in question, produces three problems: first, it occludes the real and contextually radical political and social practices of earlier gay men and women; second, it renders invisible the complexity and overlapping nature of the cultural struggles gay men and women were engaged in at the time as they moved between and among possible ends and means; and finally, it hides their effects of this struggle on the development of the homosexual activism prior to Stonewall Inn riots in June 1969.[8] In sum, this political binary enables a potentially facile and inaccurate evaluation of the complicated reasons why gay men ascribed certain meanings to certain practices and desires in different times and places by applying a normative evaluative standard; it renders unintelligible the range of actions that individuals and groups engaged in different settings and contexts.[9]

A careful, empirical examination of the debates gay men and women were having over means and ends reveals two specific complexities that must be held in mind. First, which social problems gay men targeted for solution varied within the same period and among groups and individuals. The application of their revised democratic values produced a range of possible ends and means, which defies an either/or binary categorization; further, individuals and groups held a complex of values that spanned the range between conservative and radical, and which were often contradictory. For example, so-called "conservative" groups like SIR had many radical qualities, such as a commitment to being open to all queers, including bisexuals, married men, and men with handicaps; simultaneously and contradictorily, gay liberation groups such as the Gay Sunshine Collective often displayed an almost reactionary cultural politic, which drew sharp boundaries between good gays and bad gays based on their gender expression, in much the same way their hippie forebears had done. A second complexity lies in gay men's experiences with their environment, which gave rise to a complex and divided consciousness to explain and deal with their environment and to reshape it to meet their needs.

So it is more accurate and more historically and sociologically useful to think of gay men's conflicting ends and means not as a binary struggle, but as the organic begetting of knowledge from experience, from activity-undergoing, through which gay men made their environment intelligible and therefore moldable to their needs and desires. And so the values, the ends-as-means, of gay men in the past—including those that conflict with our own, present values— become intelligible for what they actually were, for the meanings they generated and supported in their contexts. The various ends and means created in 1960s San Francisco were specific strategies to solve specific problems in specific times by specific individuals and groups. But this can be difficult to tease out, because they were modifying the language of classical democratic theory, which they had inherited from their environment, such that gay men of the period often saw each other split into binary camps in a way that occluded the complexity of their multiple positions and strategies. But the effort to undermine the assimilationist/radical binary proves invaluable in that it enables an appreciation for the diversity of gay men's approaches to dealing with their oppression. It also foregrounds the fact that whatever the proposed ends happened to be, they were necessarily overlapping, contradictory, complementary, and accrued with past, contemporary, and later proposed ends, and eventually to the analysis of the strategies they proposed and employed to achieve their ends.

Recognition and a Fundamental Contradiction in the Meaning of Gay

Gay men's differing experiences of repression produced a wide range of desires that were translated into differing valuations and meanings of freedom from domination. As gay men experienced domination and began to engage publicly to alleviate it, they necessarily had to decide what life should look like, absent the repression they had experienced. These normative discussions about freedom evolved into more and more detailed and specific propositions for possible ends for a gay counter-public. Over the years of this study, gay men thought of and tried out numerous and often contradictory possible ends for their publicity in a kind of ad hoc experimentation, both conceptual and in the real world, seeking the magic formula for a public action that would lead to the end of their subordinate status and to their symbolic domination. Among these was the desire to be recognized in the official public sphere as full and equal citizens; indeed, one of the major shifts between 1950s gay activists and their 1960s counterparts was their desire to participate in the official public sphere and be recognized as gay men, that the public sphere should no longer require the bracketing of their personhood for full participation and citizenship. Another conflict emerged between the desire to be recognized as individuals and the desire to be recognized as a group; this debate focused on whether or how gay men and women might constitute a minority, and if so, how to maintain their cohesion as a group so to effectively demand recognition. From here, the arguments narrowed down to specific goals within democracy, ranging from changing the law to allow homosexuality, to rewriting sexual mores more generally to include a positive role for same-sex love; from democratic tolerance to full-blown social acceptance and approval; and from the general stance for a liberal freedom of personhood to a wholesale overturning of society.

The struggle for recognition—social, political, cultural, etc.—has been the central political problem of minorities and outsider groups in the United States for centuries. Much of the historical work and the sociology of social movements focuses on these efforts and evaluates the goals, strategies, and tactics of these movements in terms of their ability to achieve recognition. My goal here, however, is somewhat askew of that earlier work; I want to know what kind of *gayness* is created from the conflicts that gay men (and women) had over ends and means, and what kinds of *meanings* are created both in the process of struggling to articulate various ends and means and in adopting those ends in means as values and practices. As noted earlier, the primary conflict among San Francisco's gay men over recognition during this period was whether it should be individual-based or group-based (i.e., minority-based). By examining closely their arguments, we can see that behind the arguments over means and ends, gay men were arguing about different ways of being gay or different possible meanings of gayness.

As we have already seen, the need for recognition, either group or individual, arose so often in gay men's published discussions precisely because their day-to-day life was one of *mis*recognition, that is, a misfiring of the democratic process that worked not to free them but to enthrall their feelings and behaviors to the will of the dominating official public. In fact, the dominant culture, the culture of the official public, already did recognize homosexuals as a group. I would argue that the public's misrecognition of homosexuals as a kind of person that must be contained actually provided the conditions under which the groupness of a homosexual minority could (had to?) form in the first place.[10] The official public, through the law and through its officials, excluded and denied rights and participation to gay men and women. At least a decade before 1961, some gay men had come to see themselves as having a common oppression that united them in some way, so much so that by the early 1960s, they often compared themselves to African Americans and even referred to their status as one of "niggerhood." And this abject status ascribed by the official public and by the dominant culture it supported created a social experience from which homosexuals had to fight as a group. This emerging group consciousness emerged out of a common experience of domination and led to a demand for a true and full recognition that would enable the freedom of personhood gay men came to value during this period.[11]

The goal of individual recognition crops up more in the early part of the decade, but is common across the period and throughout the various publications, regardless of their politics. As a strategy, many gay men believed that seeing themselves as individuals making individual choices would be most successful in overcoming the discriminatory repression of the official public. Here, they connected a conception of individual rights to what I have called *freedom of personhood*, as the "right to care and feel in one's own individual way" (see *VR* Sept. 1970, 22–23). Often, writers made clear connections between the 1960s social movements as a movement for the individual. Later in the decade, when it became clear that the Civil Rights movement had seemed to fail to secure substantive freedom for African Americans, the individual lost some of its appeal as a category for activism. Yet in the publications, many continued to defend the individual as the best way to conceive of a gay rights movement, and categorization as a minority group was distrusted as a sure means to the erosion of individuality and difference (see for example *VR* Aug. 1971, 4). For these men, gayness boiled down to a set of personal choices over which they believed the government (and by extension, society at large) should have no direct control over. For them, to be gay was to be an individual free to make one's own sexual and relational choices.

The arguments for recognition as a group, a minority, had begun just as early, back in the 1950s. The Mattachine Society's founders had argued that homosexuals were a specific and, importantly, *different* kind of person who were therefore a group that functioned as a minority.[12] Nan Boyd has argued that the legal battles fought by gay bars in the 1950s were primarily about minority or group recognition, in that they centered on the right to assemble. However, minority rights as articulated by gay men in the 1960s went further than a mere legal tactic, inasmuch as they were articulating their desire for minority (group) recognition. This seems to have arisen out of a sense or feeling that, as a group, they shared a common experience of oppression. Guy Strait referred to the "variant community" as a minority for the first time in the very first issue of *The LCE News* (May 27, 1963), and reference to the community of gay men and women as a minority was commonplace within the first two years of a small, but active gay counter-publicity.[13] Whereas the early Mattachine Society saw themselves as a minority based on a shared difference, in early 1960s San Francisco, the more common conception of minority was as a potential political bloc; but this particular interpretation of the gay minority (clearly growing out of the conservative turn the Mattachine Society took in the early 1950s) was only one of many. As gay men interacted with the official public as openly gay men, their experiences of their *minority-ness*—that is, their shared, undergone abjection—refined and reshaped their conception of minority (and ultimately of community, which will be addressed in later chapters).

For these men, it had become obvious that gay men and women did constitute a minority of some kind. Their emphasis on the gay minority indicates that they saw gayness as a shared state of being, a shared social position, and a shared experience. But they also recognized that a gay minority was significantly different from other minorities vis-à-vis the official public: unlike other minorities, a homosexual minority had to be consciously built and nurtured; it didn't just arise spontaneously nor was it inherited from a family. Nonetheless, the fact that they had to work to maintain their group-ness, their cohesiveness as a minority, never seems to have completely undermined their feeling of minority-ness. So gay group-ness, the uneasy identification with other gay men and women as some sort of social reality, had to be worked for, itself an end to achieve, and end deeply connected to its relationship with the official public. The future of gay community, as it came to be called by the mid-1960s, and of freedom of personhood rested in gay men's efforts to establish and maintain that relationship to the official public. From the perspective of those advocating group or minority recognition, the dangers were seen to come from the insistence on individuality, which felt like a danger or threat to group-ness. Where

the meaning of gay was connected to the idea of the shared experience, the minority-ness of gay men, it was also explicitly connected to the social reality that
gay men came from all different possible backgrounds and so maintaining the
group in practice required a lot of work.

Ultimately, out of the interaction of these two conflicting ends—recognition
of individuals vs. recognition of a minority—arose what I will call an *ethic of
difference* that could exceed the boundaries of a gay community and be applied
to the broader public. This ethic was often expressed as an appeal to gay men to
love each other despite their differences, or even to value those differences. But
the fact that many gay men of the decade refused a group identification also
constantly undermined any such appeal to an ethic of difference, as they insisted
on a gayness that was above all an individual choice. When examining how gay
men argued about this problem, I found two divergent and contradictory strands
of experiences expressed over and over again. On one hand, gay men's differences and their desire to be viewed as an individual created a sense of revulsion
or suffocation in regards to a "gay minority"; on the other hand, their similar life
experiences and shared social status as outcasts led them to see each other as
members of a group and to desire association with each other, often being expressed as a vital need. Although the evidence for such a conclusion is sparse, it
does seem safe to speculate that any given individual gay man could have both
of these feelings to a greater or lesser degree at various times and maybe even
simultaneously. They dealt with this contradiction in a variety of ways ranging
from rejecting any group identification at all, to a wholesale effort to build a
complete Gay Culture with a history and social institutions and cultural signs
and meanings. This contradiction seems to span the entire political spectrum,
popping up in the politics of a "radical" group like the Gay Sunshine Collective
as well as in a "liberal" group like SIR. It would seem, then, that this tension
between individual difference and group-ness in the public sphere had become
constitutive of gay publicity, and more to the point, constitutive of gayness itself. The argument over how gay men ought to be recognized reveals to us a
fundamental problem at the heart of the meaning of gay: Is it an individual experience or a group identity?

This contradiction in the meaning of gayness was even reflected in the most
simple of all proposed ends was a straightforward *legal reform*, which required
gay men to grapple with the meaning and structure of the law itself. Reform
proposals ranged from a simple liberalization process, an opening up of the law
to include gay lives, to overturning and transforming social-sexual mores altogether. Proposals to liberalize the law, it was hoped, would change the structure
of the institutions of the public sphere. Very early, however, gay men realized
that there was a possible problem: would changing the law be sufficient to effect
a freedom of personhood? Despite this nagging question, various forms of liberalization were fought for as ends throughout the decade, most notably, the freedom of assembly[14] and the liberalization of sexual laws to allow gay male sex
and prostitution.[15] But the contradiction between freedom as *rights* (i.e., legal
reform) and freedom of personhood would haunt gay politics in San Francisco

through the period and caused no insignificant angst among many gay men.[16] In evaluating the liberalization of the law, many gay men moved to the obvious, if onerous, logical next end: They would have to change the very culture they lived in, and freedom of personhood for gay men would never be possible until such a fundamental cultural change had occurred.[17] Liberalization of the law seemed empty of redemptive promise.

Another possible goal was the *integration* of gay men into society, a restructuring of day-to-day interactions with non-gays that would eliminate the problems gay men experienced in their social interactions and remove the barriers to the consummation of their sexual and social desires. Always underlying many gay men's understanding of their experience of exclusion was the desire to be accepted, not merely to be citizens but to be supported and esteemed in their difference. The desire to be accepted permeates the arguments about appropriate ends for a gay movement, simultaneously bolstering and undermining various efforts to crack open the official public. And surprisingly, various forms of integration appear across the political spectrum as a possible end for gay politics. But integration and acceptance were hotly contested goals, and they reveal not just the political differences among gay men but how they imbued their own gayness with meaning vis-à-vis their relationship to the dominant culture.

Men who preferred integration feared that the growing group identity of homosexuals would lead to a permanent foreclosure of social acceptance by preventing "heterosexuals from knowing homosexuals as persons" (*VR* Aug. 1966, 2). Indeed, one of the original stated purposes of SIR was to overcome the "ingroupness" that was felt to separate gay men and women from society writ large[18]; throughout the period many gay men felt that separation from the rest of society was a mistake.[19] Some gay men noted that the African American experience pointed up the weakness and perhaps futility of acceptance and integration as an end for their movement.[20] For still other gay men, unless society changed, integration inevitably would mean the oppressed group "must face adaptation to the present society" and would therefore lose control over the meaning of gay, and that they would be required to shed their gayness, the very thing they were seeking freedom to express (*VR* April 1967, 14–15).[21] In other words, many gay men were "not willing to surrender [their] central identities in order to achieve integration" (*VR* Aug. 1967, 14–15). So when gay was experienced as a central facet of one's personhood, integration and acceptance were possible threats to personhood. The arguments over the idea of integration indicate a tension over the relative salience of gayness to the rest of one's personhood. For those seeking integration, their proposals would reduce the salience of gayness vis-à-vis the rest of society and therefore vis-à-vis the individual.

Many gay men seemed to struggle with this contradiction: If gayness becomes less socially salient as a *kind* of person, then does gayness disappear? What happens to gay men who are different or who want to be different? Would integration into the society benefit them at all or would it be another kind of oppression? One writer argued that the only acceptance that wouldn't be damaging to gays and lesbians would be to "demand that we are accepted as such and not let it ride along with our friends and families for the sake of peace" (*SFGFP* Nov. 1970, 4–5, 12). But others felt that "gays are accepted for themselves only when they cater and serve the general public as busboys, hairdressers, and decorators. Gays are the subservient slaves of modern society. They are dupes and scapegoats" (*IA* 1.3). The overwhelming feeling among these gay men was one of fear of being forced to be something they were not, of having their freedom of personhood further abridged through an imposed necessity to conform in order to integrate. *Gay Sunshine* often argued that a cultural transformation that removed the stigma of gayness would allow integration without conformity.[22] By the 1970s, many found integration to be a retrogressive goal that would ultimately be counterproductive[23] and insulting. "Who is the [straight man] with his perverted asexual notions and behavioral patterns to accept us?" (*GS* Oct.–Nov. 1971, 7). For these men, the cost of integration, the loss of saliency, was a loss of personhood and anti-individuality.[24]

Yet another goal or possible end for the movement, *tolerance* arose in the publications often from the very beginning to the end of the period in question. Sometimes it was that a bare classical tolerance was all that could possibly achieved in the society as it was then constituted.[25] Among the earliest articulated movement ends,[26] tolerance seemed to open the possibility of having a socially sanctioned basic humanity, such as was hopefully articulated after the second CRH Mardi Gras Ball went off without police interference in 1966.[27] This kind of liberal tolerance—where gay men's difference were allowed to exist without either sanction or censure—was framed in terms of a bare minimum, overcoming the prejudice and eliminating state oppression, so that gay men would have access to the official public sphere,[28] while allowing them to explore their lives as gay men. This position harkened back to more traditional democratic constructions of the public, seeing gay men as citizens.[29] From within the gay community itself, however, tolerance came to signify a fundamental hypocrisy, because either gay men were themselves intolerant of each other[30] or because it was gay men's own fault that the public was intolerant of them, that they brought oppression upon themselves.[31] Tolerance, too, was fraught with contradictions as an end for gay men's publicity, similar to those of social acceptance. The Man, said one writer to *Gay Sunshine*, "tolerated us as long as we stayed in our place and shut up (just as women and blacks did)" (Oct.–Nov. 1971, 7).[32]

With the inadequacy of liberalization, the improbability of overturning sexual mores, and with the unlikelihood of achieving integration or tolerance without also losing what was meaningful and distinctive about gay male lives, gay men's discussions inevitably returned to their foundational value of freedom of personhood. Moving with the politics of the times, many gay men across the various organizations began to question whether or not a liberal democratic political movement could succeed in "true liberation." And so emerged the common 1960s conundrum: Freedom within a liberal-democratic framework[33] or freedom through revolution? But as we saw in gay men's conception of publicity, for freedom of personhood to have meaning as an end, freedom would have to expand into the realm of personal fulfillment. So many had begun to imagine social-sexual revolution, one freed from the legitimizing institutions of the public sphere that foreclosed their desires, relationships, and communities, their very personhood, very early in San Francisco. In a 1965 *Town Talk*, one man wrote that "sexual pleasure . . . should be determined by the person or persons concerned and not limited in legitimization by a group or structure" (1, 4).[34]

Inasmuch as none of the traditional democratic ends-as-means (i.e., legal reform and tolerance) seemed likely to bring about freedom, gay men began speaking of simply laying claim to it, as if they already had it. This marked a subtle but key transformation in the meaning of gay, as it inflected upon gayness an existential valence. That is, in the move to more radical rhetoric in the late 1960s, gayness became intrinsic to the individual and constitutive of the individual's very being. Whereas early conceptions were about the freedom to *choose*, the language became one of the freedom to *be*. Although this is related to Foucault's thesis about the development of sexology, I see here something far more important: The transformation of how gay men and women saw themselves as emergent in a particular effort to gain publicity without intervention by the state, religious, and medico-psychiatric apparatuses. One *Vector* writer argued that "the homosexual has a *moral right to be a homosexual* and *being a homosexual* has a moral right not only to live his or her homosexuality fully, freely, openly, and with pride, but also has a right to do so free of arrogant and insolent pressures to convert to the prevailing heterosexuality" (July 1970, 39, emphasis added). Such a *moral right to be* would mean, they hoped, the end of the duality gay men experienced in the public sphere.

Hence the introduction of revolutionary rhetoric to the conversation. "Revolutionary consciousness does not suffice anymore. Revolutionary action is inevitable and necessary. Gay is beautiful" (*SFFP* Oct. 1969, 8). Many gay men came to believe that *the moral right to be* could only be brought about through revolution. Seeing heterosexuals as the natural subjects of the liberal society, *San Francisco Free Press* frequently contained the notion that homosexuality was inconsistent with and detrimental to the liberal democratic order. "Society's ethics are always enslavement; the homosexuals are every liberation. . . . Every homosexual is potentially a revolutionary" (Nov. 1, 1969, 7). The men and women whom historians and activists would eventually call "gay libbers" made explicit connections between a sexual revolution and the social revolution they believed was going down around them.[35] Indeed, for one *Vector* writer, seeking a Sexual Revolution was part and parcel to the Social Revolution.[36] Gay men and women of color were rarely heard from (at least explicitly and identifiably as such), but in this late era, the meaning of race turned from an example of another oppressed group to some beginning critiques of the race privilege of the white men who were leading the movement.[37]

The salience of gayness arose again as gay men began to align themselves for or against the revolutionary perception of the problem of gayness. Many readers wrote in to *Vector* to protest the magazine giving coverage to the revolutionaries, and argued that such coverage equated the homosexual movement with socialist movements that they knew were just as oppressive to homosexuals as capitalist ones.[38] SIR's membership was by and large older and it responded with fear to the rhetoric of revolution; their fear centered on being further alienated from the society by revolutionaries' public, angry critique of the dominant society.[39] The battle between SIR and the gay libbers grew fierce as the 1970s dawned. The gay libbers saw themselves not only as revolutionaries against the dominant society, but as liberating themselves from the "Gay Establishment" which they saw as middle-class, white, bourgeois, and liberal. Libbers defined themselves as fighting to establish not a mere freedom, but a new way of life.[40]

These were ultimately normative arguments over what the ends of the movement should be, and as such, they were also subtly normative arguments about the meaning of gayness. I found five general categories where gay men placed their values-as-ends: social recognition, liberalization of the legal structures, integration, tolerance, and revolution. What was fascinating to me was that almost without exception I found examples of all positions in all the gay organizations of the period, demonstrating a high degree of overlap and cross-conversation, and suggesting a degree of uncertainty and porousness to their positions. While these contradictions can be easily seen socially, I have also speculated that individual gay men may have also moved in, around, and between positions as they worked out the meaning of their gayness. These struggles over possible ends do not reveal to us any clear winner in the struggles, as all of the possibilities not only survived in print, but were enacted in their political activism and day-to-day lives. As the arguments over ends proceeded through the decade, they revealed more fundamental contradictions in the meanings of gayness from which gay men as a group were working. Gayness could lie along a spectrum between an individual characteristic, implying individual choice and rights, and a group, shared experience, implying minority-ness or group-ness. Gayness could hold a minimum salience socially, being reduced to a mere quirk or superficial difference of no meaning in the public sphere; or it could be a fundamental difference that stood in stark contrast to the majority; or it could fall anywhere in between. Gayness could be a matter of action and choice; or it could be a matter of an existential right to be. My purpose here is not to choose which end these gay men should have chosen. Rather, my hope is that by seeing how the context of American culture in 1960s and especially the culture of San Francisco combined with the experience of being sexual different, created a historical moment in which the argument over ends was actually in fact an argument over the meaning of gay.

Means to Ends and Gayness

The multiple ends and the battles over them had become, by the early 1970s, constitutive of gay publicity itself, such that the actual public *deeds* of gay men in the public sphere often took on a divided quality, where gay men and women ended up fighting each other as much as the "Establishment." The social battles among gay men were fought primarily over the power to conceive of and enact the *means*, that is, the actions to be taken as a counter-public directly in the official public. The means actually proposed and employed in San Francisco between 1961 and 1972 ranged from the homophile strategy of using heterosexual experts to advocate for the cause, all the way to a sort of militant, counterculture style of direct confrontation. The means debate ultimately served to shape the gay male publicity of the period, thereby reflecting more intensely the meanings of gayness that we saw in the symbolic battle over ends. By the end of the decade, it seemed that gay men were struggling to find some new way to get what they wanted, seeing the movement as stalled and even as failed; but they couldn't find the necessary effective means to do so.[41] But gay men had always disagreed on the efficacy of the means they had used and new means they were creating to achieve their intended ends. And because all gay men, regardless of politics, tended to point toward *freedom* as some form of self-fulfillment, and because they disagreed intensely on what that fulfillment would look like, they of course could not easily resolve their conflicts over means to achieve that freedom. As the 1960s passed, various strategies were considered and reconsidered, recycled in new ways, with new hopes for their possibilities.

As I noted earlier, the scholarly work on gays and lesbians of this period often relies on the categories that originated from the period, namely the assimilationist (or liberal) vs. radical (or revolutionary) split, an empirical description of these arguments over means can get bogged down in trying to make them fit into this binary category scheme or in inadvertently assigning a label to a particular means. To further complicate matters, various groups and individuals of the period critiqued each other using those very binary categories, treating the radical vs. assimilationist divide as a given.[42] Given the history of American culture during the 1960s (and especially the history of the Bay Area), this comes as no surprise. This binary view of politics reflected the deep philosophical and experiential divisions within the left and socially progressive communities of the period. But having been steeped in the writings from gay men of the period, I would argue that for this current project in symbolic interaction, in my attempt to understand how gay men created meaningfulness, it is more fruitful to see gay men and women as interacting with each other across political and ideological boundaries during this period and how their conversations were fraught with contradictions, overlaps, and accretions. The social change during the 1960s was extensive and rapid, such that the context of the struggle over means and the meaning and consequences of proposed means and by extension of gayness itself greatly changed over a relatively few short years. Nevertheless, the changes were not so vast that there were wholesale changes in the complex social environment; rather, the environment by the early 1970s had expanded slightly the possible iterations of a public gayness, which allowed for further expansion of what could be imagined as possible ends and means by the gay men struggling for freedom of personhood. A careful scrutiny of the means considered and employed by gay men during the period illustrates the complexity of the connections between these means and the ends discussed above, gay male interaction, and the meanings of gayness produced during this period. Indeed, there emerges a continuity among the various ideas of means (and gayness) rather than a rigid political binary. The standard distinction between the "homophile" movement (seen as assimilationist) and the radical or "gay liberation" movement crumbles when examined at this micro level.

To be sure, the role of gay organizations (regardless of their politics) increased in scope and power throughout the 1960s.[43] The San Francisco organizations served gay men by directly engaging the public with protests, legal action and court cases, public interviews and speakers bureaus; they also spent a good deal of their energy in community building[44] through social activities and direct cultural production, such as through their publications. Being pulled between engaging the public and creating a social space for gay men created both common and creative means for fighting the repression and domination of the official public. The relationship of proposed ends to the actual gay organizations has always been an uneasy one, as evidenced by San Francisco men complaining about the constant "bitch fights" that dominated meetings. But these meetings within gay organizations were the social space wherein the conflicts I've been discussing were actually fought out, in the real interaction of gay men and women.[45] The local organizations that grew up between 1961 and 1972 in San Francisco Bay Area were not isolated, but also participated with national gay organizations, carrying national problems and achievements to the consciousness of their local constituents. But San Francisco's participants often came away from these national conferences frustrated. San Francisco organizations had achieved a level of publicity within the city and state by 1965 that would not be achieved elsewhere until after Stonewall.[46] So they often didn't understand the particular brand of militancy of Mattachine D.C. or the complacency of Mattachine New York. Still, the movements were nationally connected during the 1960s through organization such as the North American Council of Homophile Organizations, and although the gay male experience in San Francisco was constantly localized by their interactions with the police and other public institutions, they had a consciousness of being connected to a national movement.[47] Indeed, the disjuncture between local and national organizations often undergirded conflict over means, where SIR hosted a radical, national gay liberation conference in August 1970; and a few months later, gay libbers and feminists "zapped" the SIR-hosted NACHO conference.[48] This invasion of NACHO by gay radicals typified the conflicts among gay men and women over the production of a gay publicity and the meaning of "gay." The proliferation of gay organizations in the early 1970s reflected the depth of the disagreement over ends and means.

Although it is important to give voice to the feelings and experiences of the men at the time—they did indeed feel that the "homophiles" were dramatically different from the "radicals"—it is equally important to take a critical stance in comparing the actual values (in the form of their proposed ends) and actions (means) among the various groups. Of course, the various groups did not want exactly the same thing, and espoused differing ends; but speaking movement-wide in the San Francisco Bay Area, there was a great deal of overlap and accretion among the groups, which in practice moved around and between various political positions. Individuals also carried on value debates, which were refracted across the organizational boundaries rather than distinguishing among them. The means that arose most often in these struggles were modification of personal behavior (respectability), political action to change the law, participation in electoral politics, and coalition building across groups. John Dewey argued that *meaning* at its most basic form is an awareness of the possible consequences of an idea (object of thought) when put into action—in this case, the possible consequences of potential actions to be taken in the public sphere. Dewey further suggests that among the methods available for a imbuing a particular public action with meaning in the abstract is to consider it in relationship to already-existing meanings.[49] Gay men indeed conducted mental experiments with their proposed means in order to work out what their effect might be; and they made sense of these means and their possible consequences in terms of what they already knew, from their past experiences and the experiences of other groups. In the end, the combination of arguing about means and then actually trying them out and arguing about the actual consequences provided yet another context within which what gay men were actually doing was working out the meaning of gayness. To say that differently, by working out means, gay men were coming to understand how homosexual desire and sex fit into their experience of American society in the context of San Francisco.

Persistence of 1950s Means: Respectability

Drawing from the experience of the 1950s Mattachine Society and Daughters of Bilitis, gay men and women in the 1960s continued their efforts to appear "respectable" to the American public as a direct means to their social integration and the liberalization of the law. Nineteen-fifties-style *respectability* served as the jumping off point for the new LCE and SIR, but rethinking it to match their new goals and the changed context of the 1960s. In the 1950s, gay organizations in San Francisco had tried to build respectability by presenting heterosexual advocates from psychiatry, church, and the law to the public, to imbue homosexuals vicariously with public respectability.[50] In significant ways, this tactic carried through the 1960s and formed the center of debates about possible means.[51]

Although many of the specific tactics of old-style homophiles quickly died away in the surge for counter-publicity of the 1960s, the central value held by the homophile movement stuck.[52] "Respectability" as a value grew out of gay men's experience of repression by the public sphere. Gay men often felt that the reason the official public came down on them was because they did not conform to social expectations. Thus, the most persistent strategic means espoused during the 1960s (and arguably to this day) was for gay men to tightly monitor and control personal behavior, to internalize fully the values and strictures of the dominant culture, and to live accordingly—that is, to be respectable. So respectability as a means was transformed into something that individual gay men were responsible for in their own behavior. But with the formation of the LCE in 1961, what exactly constituted "respectability" was up for debate. For some, respectability came from demonstrating true citizenship; for example, many writers criticized gay men's lack of political participation as evidence of their lack of respectability.[53] For others, it was demonstrating behavior that was in "good taste" according to dominant standards.[54] In the late 1960s, respectability came to mean staying clear of radical social movements, such as the Black Panthers.[55] Others simply feared that non-conformist behavior, i.e., any behavior readily identified as "gay," would render it impossible for freedom to be achieved.[56]

Importantly, the evolving 1960s-style respectability differed significantly from of earlier 1950s homophiles in its adoption of the idea of "openness" (and later "outness") to respectable behavior. To wit, the 1960s version of respectability was responsible public action as an openly gay man. Building on what they saw as the ambivalence of the 1950s call for respectability,[57] "[We] are steadfast in our attempt to change society by *openly joining in activities as homosexuals*, working within established structures to qualify all injustices in a responsible manner" (*VR* Aug. 1966, 2, emphasis added). But as gay men began to insist on openness, they also began to think critically about respectability and its relationship to the dominating symbolic order. They came to see the dominating symbolic order as producing their behavior and practices, that is, that the repression itself causes the "unrespectable" behavior.[58] This desire for openness not only redefined respectability, but ultimately it seemed to undermine the possibility of "responsible action" ever working effectively to free gay men; for, as we saw in Chapter 2, responsibility was and is always defined by the official public, and gay men's formulations of responsibility were, even in their goal of placating the dominating order, by definition counter to the dominant order's definition of gayness, which had already established the abjection of same-sex desire and behavior. Importantly here is the effective equivalence of openness to gayness, or at least openness to a *good* gayness.

Given the multiple and various experiences of gay men in relationship to the official public and dominating symbolic order, "openness" necessarily took on various forms. For those gay men who leaned toward integration as an end, openness became an assertion of "quiet dignity and self-respect," in other words, of respectable gayness (see *VR* July 1966, 4).[59] This connection of openness to responsibility brought with it new tensions. Just what should a gay man be open about in the public sphere? Many aspects of gay life remained hidden.[60] Some men frustrated with a lack of progress toward the alleviation of repression argued that it was the fault of the "unrespectable" among them. They feared that irresponsible gay men supplied "ammunition to guns that have too long held us down" (*TT* Aug. 1965, 11). But this argument was problematic for many, because it meant, yet again, that they had to conform, that they couldn't be gay as they chose to be gay.[61] As conformity became more and more unacceptable to many gay men, respectability as an effective strategy came to be seen as a myth.[62] Employing respectability as a means meant necessarily leading a double life, where the values of the dominant culture regulated and contained gay male behavior in the official public sphere,[63] thereby foreclosing the creative possibilities of self-determination and fulfillment, which were for many the desired ends of the movement. Notice again the tension between the relative salience of gayness to personhood and how that plays out here: If gayness bears a great deal of weight for the personhood of an individual, the prospect of conformity looms large and oppressive. Rejection of respectability as a means was often anchored in the refusal of social integration as a desirable end in the first place.

By 1970, "social responsibility" as espoused by SIR came under particularly vehement attack from those who saw respectability as a kind of *false consciousness* they called "establishment thinking." "[W]e find 'good queers' eating up the crap that straights drop on us and then thanking master for token-life. . . . The straight establishment has taken any notion of identity from us by trick-or-treating us into believing that we are a sexual entity, therefore, we'll suck cock and be quiet (it's hard to speak with a cock in the mouth)" (*GS* Nov. 1970, 8–9). Respectability, it was feared, led to gay men condoning the oppressive actions of the state.[64] So many gay men's rejection of respectability as a means was concomitant with their refusal of America as a possible arbiter of freedom and meaning for gay male life at all; this disagreement about the meaning of America and, therefore, of freedom led to confrontational modes of protest that deeply frightened the advocates of respectability.[65]

The Law as Means

Beginning with the LCE in 1961[66] and emerging out of the earlier court battles that San Francisco bar owners had fought for homosexuals' freedom of assembly in California,[67] the most straightforward and expected tactic of gay organizations was to engage the law, the very institutional structure they saw as the source of so much of their oppression. Even those later gay-lib organizations that rejected this "liberal" approach continued a tradition of critique of the legal institutions' treatment of gay men and lesbians. All groups through the 1960s recognized their reliance on the courts to overturn unfair and discriminatory laws.[68] What emerged out of their engagement with the law was a three-pronged approach: educate individuals about the law so they could protect themselves, use the courts as a means to effect structural change, and take direct political action to reform the law.

The effort to inform gay men and women about their legal standing was a carry-over from the 1950s and was a tack taken by all the organizations in the San Francisco Bay Area between 1961–1972, although later organizations took a more defiant stance to the law than did LCE. Information included ways to get around laws that forbade cross-dressing,[69] monitoring pertinent court cases,[70] publishing lists of penalties for sex crimes,[71] SIR's 1965 "Pocket Lawyer" for bar-goers in 1965, monitoring Sacramento for changes to state law,[72] legal advice for military personnel to be able to fight discharge,[73] and U.S. Supreme Court information and news.[74] Age of consent laws were especially important during this period for a couple reasons. First was that the age of majority through the period was twenty-one, which meant that many of the gay youth were excluded from the movement to liberalize sex laws no matter what; and second, because it was felt by many that homosexual teenagers (particularly university students) could often make choices for themselves and should be counted as capable of giving sexual consent.[75] Gay publications served the default role of keeping gay men and women abreast of legal developments not only in the city, but around the country, that affected gays and lesbians directly.[76] Writers would then use court decisions as rationales in their arguments for civil rights.[77] These included discussions of cases involving bathroom solicitation,[78] obscenity laws and court cases,[79] free speech laws and issues,[80] freedom of assembly,[81] and the right to work.[82] Within the complex environment of the official public, as gay men and women underwent the effects of the legal institutions in their lives, they worked through the 1960s to keep each other informed through organizations and especially through their publications.

But staying informed wasn't sufficient, and some advocated using the courts as a direct means to effect homosexual freedom. Californians in San Francisco and in Los Angeles had begun using the court system to establish their rights in the 1950s. The efforts to challenge the laws had begun to spread and through the national networks, gay men in San Francisco watched court challenges at home and across the nation. When Frank Kameny led court battles in Washington, D.C., to reinstate three federal employees fired for homosexuality, his tactics were described in depth in *Vector* as gay men in San Francisco were working out how to use the law to their advantage in similar court battles.[83] In San Francisco, these kinds of court cases had become less common after the bar cases of the 1950s and early 1960s were decided. One significant battle was SIR suing the local Bell telephone company for refusing to print contact information in the yellow pages for SIR and other gay organizations.[84] Police entrapment cases, however, remained common throughout the period and by the late 1960s, SIR had begun to press against the use of decoys by police departments throughout the Bay Area. On June 25, 1969, SIR filed a suit requesting an injunction against such entrapment tactics.[85] In another case, a gay man successfully argued that an undercover officer posing as a gay man had violated his right to privacy by entering his home under false pretenses; the municipal court judge agreed.[86] Although unsuccessful through much of the decade, entrapment cases began to succeed late in the period, and entrapment came to be used as a defense in public cruising trials.[87]

Unfortunately, using the courts to redress grievances was as often as not unreliable as a means to achieving gay men's freedom; one case in particular highlighted the difficulty of relying on the courts for justice. In December 1969,

SFPD surrounded the Stud, a gay bar in SOMA, at closing time. One young man, Charles Christman, panicked and ran from the police to his car, trying to escape arrest. Police shot into the car, hitting Christman, who then tried to get out of the car and run away; he was shot in the back by police officers who, witnesses reported, were shouting, "I killed the fucking faggot." With permanent disabling injuries, Christman was then brought to trial for resisting arrest and attempted murder of a police officer with his car. SIR established a legal defense fund for the twenty-sex-year-old man, but his trial demonstrated the flaws in the criminal justice system as it became clear that the courts functioned according to peoples' cultural predispositions, not according to the legal standards (see *VR* April 1971, 4; 30–31). The first trial ended in a hung jury only because two young women refused to convict; when the new trial was rescheduled for the spring, the district attorney pled him out to three misdemeanors (see *VR* June 1971, 28).

If the courts couldn't solve their problems, many gay activists hoped that changing the law would. That the law had been an instrument to contain homosexuality through intimidation should, by now, be evident. Prominent among these efforts, the Committee for Homosexual Freedom supported an initiative among the Board of Supervisors to add homosexuality to the city's nondiscrimination clause. Although both these reform efforts were direct means to alleviating gay men's repression by the official public, both efforts in the real world brought to the surface the ambivalence and fear gay men felt about their relationship to the official public, as they fought each other over these potential means and sabotaged each others' efforts. The CHF began pushing to get the San Francisco Board of Supervisors to add homosexuality to its employment nondiscrimination statutes in late 1969, working to put it on the June 1970 city ballot with a coalition of other gay groups in the Bay Area. But they were rebuffed in their efforts. SIR's Vice President Perry A. George did not want his organization involved and began a campaign to withdraw SIR's endorsement of the ballot initiative. CHF decided to take the action alone, refusing to be limited by what they considered the shortsightedness of "gay shopkeepers."[88] This conflict between SIR and the CHF eventually developed into what the *San Francisco Free Press* would dub "The Homosexual Civil War." In what seems an eerily familiar debate in the early twenty-first century, SIR president Larry Littlejohn argued that it wasn't the time to push the issue of non-discrimination. He feared a loss and a backlash.[89] *SFFP*'s staff felt his arguments were insufficient.

> Still unanswered is the apparent anomaly of a homosexual organization refusing to back a petition calling for non-discrimination against homosexuals. . ..
> Mistaking the tolerance of the police and city officials for acceptance, and an organization unwilling to see that the reason the establishment is leaving the homosexuals alone is because it has its hands full with the blacks and the hippies.

Notwithstanding the arguments, SIR did not budge from its position as a group (although apparent from some letters to the editor in *Vector*, many SIR members disagreed with the group's leadership). Although the CHF's 1970 campaign was unsuccessful, the Board of Supervisors eventually did pass such a code in 1972, City Ordinance 96–72, making San Francisco the first municipality in the nation, according to *Vector*, to protect employment rights of homosexuals working for contractors or sub-contractors of the city.[90]

But it was SIR's support of a Willie Brown's State Assembly bill to change California's consensual sex laws—starting in 1969 just before the CHF initiative—that captured the attention of the official public and mainstream press. The elimination or reform of the state's sodomy statute, it was hoped, would bring with it the kind of freedoms gay men and women needed. Brown brought the bill before the California Assembly yearly starting in 1969. Conservative legislators threw procedural blocks up against it, preventing it from coming to vote, and then when it did come to a vote, they used fear to garner the votes they needed to defeat the bill every year until May 12, 1975, when it finally passed (although only after the Lieutenant Governor broke a tie in the Senate). When the bill failed for the third time in 1971, *Vector* reported, "The religious fundamentalists who hold Assembly seats had a field day with the bill." Assemblyman E. Richard Barnes spearheaded the campaign against consensual sex bills through the period. *Vector*'s editor published a redux of Barnes' arguments so that readers could understand the aggressive opposition they were experiencing, a rehashing of the argument that homosexuality is pedophilia and the moral decline of society.[91] Gay activists hoped that changing the sodomy laws of the state would open the way for a full citizenship and gay publicity.

But many gay men opposed these efforts as a mere "reformist" strategy. Many articles even referred to this as an "'Uncle Tom' bill," because it bowed to the requirements of the system and sought legitimation through the established order.[92] Some saw the effort to overturn sodomy laws as an extension of the move to become "respectable."[93] Those who saw themselves as "revolutionary" argued that working for a "liberal" bill would only aid "liberal politicians and a few middle class homophiles who sill desperately crave the acceptance of some tired old men in Sacramento. Is there really any choice [between revolution and liberalism]?" (*GS* Feb.–March 1972, 2, 7). Some younger gay men found the primary weakness of the proposed law was that it discriminated by age, only protecting legal adults, which left out not only a significant number of youth, but a huge proportion of gay activists themselves.[94] Clearly, the experiences of gay men of different ages often played a significant part in the particular ends and means they espoused, although there relative ages are often difficult to discern in the texts they left us.

The primary argument against legalization of sex between consenting adults as a means was the fear that it would ultimately be ineffectual in achieving the desired ends. "Bills very similar to Brown have passed in states like Illinois without noticeably diminishing police harassment of gays." (*GS*, Oct.–Nov. 1971, 6). In responding to a report about a police raid on a model agency (i.e., an escort service), letter writer Darryl Hall pointed up the grave weaknesses in the Brown bill, which would have left in place laws that make it illegal for homosexuals to talk about sex with each other and to propose sex to a potential partner. Under the existing laws, solicitation—not sodomy—was what gay men were arrested and prosecuted for.[95] When gay proponents of Brown's bill met at the SIR Community House in 1972, a coalition of the groups in the city decided to "zap" the meeting, printing up a pamphlet to distribute as they protested, explaining their actions and asking others to withhold support from Brown's consensual sex bill.[96]

Their action underscores the intense emotional attachment that gay men had to their respective values; the pressures of dealing with oppression divided gay men and had deleterious effects on the fledgling gay community. The conflicts that gay men had with each other about their proposed means had spilled out onto the streets and taken shape in public conflicts between their organizations. Although arguably these conflicts over reform weakened gay men and women's power to provoke change in the official public, they did serve as a crucible for refining the meaning of being a gay man itself, as gay men interacted with each other interacting with the law-making bodies of the city and state, they inevitably produced meanings of gay-maleness that revolved around public power, or the ability and necessity of direct engagement with the institutions of the official public. Regardless of where gay men seemed to have fallen on an assimilationist vs. radical continuum, these battles over means were an extension of the battles over ends, with related outcomes: gayness could be open, salient, and existential; or it could be private, minimized, and behavioral; or it could be anywhere in between and in any combination. When examining gay men's arguments over these legal tactics, it becomes clear that the legal structure of San Francisco, California, and the United States constrained and shaped the possibilities available to gay men as possible meanings for gayness.

Electoral Politics

Historically, gay men and women's effort to enter the electoral arena began in 1961, when José Sarria, the Nightingale of Montgomery Street,[97] entered the Supervisorial race as the first openly gay candidate for office—a drag queen, no less—in U.S. history. Sarria's campaign followed the founding of the League of Civil Education and marked the beginning of a more concerted effort on the part of gays and lesbians in San Francisco to directly affect electoral politics. Beginning with elections that fall, gay organizations in San Francisco ran voter registration drives, endorsed candidates, and courted politicians they thought would be sympathetic to their goals in the public sphere. This would dramatically reshape the relationship of gay men and women to the electoral politics of the city: in 1959, homosexuality had been used to slander a mayoral candidate, but by 1968 Diane Feinstein actively sought the gay vote to put her on the Board of

Supervisors. As a possible means to achieve their ends, gay activists hoped that by publicly and openly supporting candidates and forming electoral blocks they would have direct power in the official public. Gay men who valued traditional citizenship and saw liberalization and integration as the best ends seem to have been the most likely to support electoral politics as a means.[98] Between 1961 and 1972, the power to vote, presidential elections, and Diane Feinstein's campaign reveal what gay men expected to get out of electoral participation.

Not surprisingly, Guy Strait's publications focused on the power of the vote[99] and urged the "variants" of the city to vote in a political block to demonstrate their potential power. Early in the decade, the LCE publications urged gay men to cross racial and class lines to vote as a block in their interests, thereby hopefully eliminating the motivation for elected officials to prosecute homosexuals.[100] SIR continued the LCE's strategies, urging its members to register and vote.[101] The CRH and the Tavern Guild began holding candidates nights in the mid-1960s, asking candidates to take public stands on the issues that concerned the homophile community the most.[102] And SIR began taking credit for affecting election outcomes.[103] By 1969, *Newsweek* was reporting that San Francisco indeed had a powerful gay voting bloc, and the *San Francisco Chronicle* echoed that opinion in 1971.[104] But some gay men complained that voting didn't help homosexuals run for office; and others argued that while it was important to vote, it was inappropriate for SIR to ask gay men to vote as a bloc.[105] In urging their constituents to vote, gay publications ran commentary about candidates and ballot measures that focused on their stands on issues affecting the gay community.[106] All gay organizations and their publications commented on electoral issues and candidates and advocated voting for candidates who would further the gay cause.[107] Publications across the board also opened their pages to alternative parties such as the Socialist Workers Party[108] and the Peace and Freedom Party.[109]

The Presidential elections of 1964, 1968, and 1972 were carefully watched by the gay publications.[110] In 1964, Strait even went so far as to speak admirably about the Goldwater campaign; but he would eventually endorse Johnson "against his better judgment" because he would be better for "social variants."[111] One letter writer argued that Nixon-Agnew's "law and order" policies would end up being anti-homosexual.[112] In 1972, most gay people involved in the political discussion agreed that McGovern was the best hope for gay rights, and the only candidate to promise to end discrimination in hiring and firing of homosexuals in civil service.[113] But there was opposition among gays to McGovern in the Bay Area. Among these, some supported Shirley Chisolm, a female Democrat whom they felt would have been the better candidate for the Democratic Party to represent more fully gay male and lesbian issues.[114] In all three elections, the federal executive was seen to be of vital importance to gays and lesbians.[115] One more *BAR* writer hoped that gay issues could have a significant impact on the 1972 convention in Miami, the first presidential election after Stonewall.[116] But other gays pooh-poohed the idea that you could end oppression by electing a pro-gay president. "It is not within the power of the president to end gay oppression," wrote one writer (*GS* July–Aug. 1972, 2).

By the 1970s, many gay men in San Francisco had grown cynical of electoral politics as an effective means, having seen that voting alone did very little to advance their cause or get them any closer to a freedom of personhood. Diane Feinstein was a primary cause of this disillusionment among Bay Area gays and lesbians, who had supported her run for the Board of Supervisors.[117] After her election in 1968, Feinstein began publicly reversing her positions on issues important especially to gay men (a reversal that would prove devastating to the gay community when she was mayor during the early days of the AIDS epidemic).[118] She became an outspoken advocate for keeping homosexuality out of public view and protecting children from homosexual influences, favoring a rigorous censorship of all materials dealing with sexuality of any kind.[119] Feinstein made one alienating blunder after another when speaking at gay groups.[120] Feinstein foreshadowed her 1980s politics when she defended her reversal on gay rights by making an assimilationist argument, that gay men should become "mainstream" to be accepted (see *VR* June 1971, 13). The problem, however, was that as gay men caught on to her politics, they withdrew their support of Feinstein's bid for Mayor in 1972, and the homophobic incumbent, Joseph Alioto, mastermind of the 1960s anti-public-sex campaigns in the city, was reelected.[121] And so some gay men began advocating a withdrawal from electoral politics.[122] They criticized all politics as usual and accused the liberal groups of being Uncle Toms (or Auntie Toms, as they often put it) for participating in electoral politics. They continued to argue instead that "it is pointless to undertake such political activity until the oppressed segments of society are organized enough to make their own campaigns and present their own program" (*GS* July–Aug. 1972, 2). By 1971, even *Vector* was musing, "Perhaps we need a gay candidate for the San Francisco Board of Supervisors" (April 1971, 4).[123] In the end, gay men's engagement in electoral politics did not bring the hoped-for results before 1972, although their support of Brown for State Assembly would ultimately lead to the change in the consensual sex laws of the state in 1975.

Coalition with Other Abject Groups and Social Movements

For men who believed in social-sexual revolution as the best among possible ends, coalition building with other oppressed groups rose to the top of their list of necessary means. Not surprisingly, coalition building brought to the fore many problems and tensions among gay men. But the notion that there were other causes with which gay men should be allied could be seen as early as 1965, when a lesbian SIR member, Nancy May, accused SIR membership of being too narrowly focused, pointing to racial inequality and pollution as possible issues gay men and women should be engaged in.[124] This was a different kind of gayness, one which was not merely open and public, but one which was expansive and extended beyond the individual rights of a liberal democratic citizen. This is a gayness that sees itself as connected to other injustices and social problems.[125] Those men identifying as gay revolutionaries argued that gay men could only be free by supporting the freedom of all oppressed peoples, that modes of oppression were interlinked.[126] And in his "Gay Manifesto," Carl Whitman pointed out that many gay men have multiple identities, and therefore, multiple political needs beyond their oppression as gay men.[127] The movements considered as possible allies ranged from the anti-war movement, to Women's Liberation, to the Black Panthers, to the growing environmental movement, and the newly emerging Third World movement. Whether or not a gay man saw his gayness in the expansive mode or in the narrowly focused mode could determine his status in a particular circle of gay men.[128] Like most issues, these arguments erected boundaries drawn on moral grounds as gay men belittled and mocked each other's values and lifestyles as means of building moral hierarchies between their groups.

Some gay men feared that building coalitions would weaken the fight for gay rights; or when seen in terms of the meaning of gay, they feared that an expansion of gayness would dilute its power. They often used their organizations and publications to ponder the connections between the gay movement and others of the period.[129] Other gay men were more forceful in their argument that gay men should be fighting for gay rights alone. The *Bay Area Reporter* argued that the homosexual movement should work for homosexuals and homosexuals alone; it even went so far as to argue that Women's Liberation was actually destroying the homosexual movement by putting "lesbians back into a thumb sucking fetal position, and [has] effectively taken lesbians out of the homosexual movement" (*BAR* Jan. 1, 1972). Even activists sympathetic with the idea of coalition building recognized the problems in gay men's involvement in other movements, especially the interrelationship between gay liberation and women's liberation.[130] More importantly, *Gay Sunshine* argued that the American left and the feminist movement were themselves being exclusive and unwelcoming of help from gays and lesbians.[131]

But homophobia stood as the highest hurdle to gay men's coalition with other movements. Sometimes this homophobia merely took the form of denying the role of homosexuals within movements, such as within socialist parties.[132] In other cases, this homophobia progressed to outright oppression and provoked a new level of outrage in gay men who had tried to participate in other movements. The *San Francisco Gay Free Press* published a furious rebuke of straight male activists' treatment of gay activists, rejecting their sympathy as condescending and blasting them for their sexual exploitation of women.[133] But the most scathing of all critiques, from *The Effeminist*, argued that straight male activists were actually sexually exploiting gay men.

> They kept trying to tell me it was a sexual freedom thing—people are basically "bi" and should have the freedom to do what they pleased sexually. But gay men's oppression is not necessarily a matter of sex, and what they meant was

that they wanted to be free to indulge their occasional "homosexual" urges while I remained categorized and apart. They would stick their oppressive cocks up my ass now and then and allow me to suck them off, but the constructs "homosexual" and "homosexuality" would remain for me and my brothers, and our oppression as a people would not change. *TE* May 1971, 1, 4.

The Effeminist argued that no movement run on the assumptions of straight men, the "genitally-oriented dominant class," could ever lead to liberation for gay men. And so the urge to identify with other oppressed peoples conflicted with the urge to effect the freedom of gay men themselves; and problems within other liberation movements often prevented participation of out and activist gays within them, as gay men and women encountered homophobia and sexual harassment. As far as the begetting of a gay male culture, the key to understanding the conflicts over respectability, legal reform, electoral politics, and coalition building is that they were constitutive of the meanings gay men formed of themselves and their experiences in the 1960s.

Militancy and Direct Confrontation

Nearly all gay men active in the San Francisco gay public favored direct forms of activism, but they disagreed, often vehemently, on the form direct action should take. What developed, then, was a debate about what would actually constitute a direct activism, specifically in comparison to the developing value of militancy. While gay men of all political stripes threw around the idea of "militancy," it actually seems hard to define and seems to be time- and context-dependent. The debate revolved around three central questions: what would a militant gay strategy mean, when would it be appropriate, which actions would actually be militant, and what militancy could and could not accomplish? Given that gay men tended to agree about taking public action, starting with the LCE in 1961, it is again important not to too easily see militancy in terms of the radical-vs.-assmilationist binary discussed previously. Militancy for gay men in San Francisco was a way of talking about the potential danger and social power of a particular means and of an individual. It could be either a badge of honor or an albatross, depending on the social context and how the gay men you were with constructed militancy. Ultimately, the argument over means and militancy reveals gay men's relationship to the dominant culture and the official public, and combined with what I've discussed above regarding respectability, the law, electoral politics, and coalition building, the way gay men used the idea of militancy reveals to us in the strongest of terms how the environment within which gay men lived produced their response to it and the kinds of meanings of gayness available to them.

Clearly, the social environment of San Francisco frightened many gay men, who foresaw retaliation and increased repression as a result of public action. These were often men who had managed to organize their lives in such a way that they could consummate their same-sex social and sexual desires with a minimum of interference.[134] These men resisted efforts to become more public and especially reacted against actions that they feared would disrupt the lives they had made for themselves.[135] In 1971, an informal (i.e., non-scientific) survey of *Ads Gayzette* revealed that gay male readers were nearly evenly split on the question of using militant, direct action as a means, with those opposing increasing militancy in the majority.[136] Militancy for these men was seen as self-defense[137]; but civil disobedience shouldn't be part of it[138]; and direct action would be okay, but only "within the system" (Two Peaceful Lovers, *AG* Dec. 17, 1970). Even among those who felt that more militant action was the only way to get results, they feared the violence it might provoke.[139] In 1969, the CHF had instructed its members "to be a militant group, a revolutionary group" (*CHFN* Aug. 13, 1969), and by the early 1970s, militancy became associated with the gay liberation movement and the idea of militancy was closely tied to the assimilationist-radical binary discussed earlier.[140] But merely to react to issues and doing so "in unison" became highly problematic[141] inasmuch as direct action actually brought as little social change as other strategies did.

Such conflicts over militant strategies had their roots in the Mattachine Society's efforts to control its membership during the late 1950s, and grew in pitch and furor between 1961 and 1972. From the beginning, the LCE's methods of what was, in its time and context, direct militant action, caused dissension in the San Francisco gay community. Guy Strait worked tirelessly to motivate his readers to action, sometimes any kind of action; and often defended his own public actions in the pages of his publications. Others criticized the League from the other side, saying that it "does nothing but talk, talk, talk."[142] SIR began thinking seriously about direct action from its inception, but its members argued among each other over what would be appropriate action.[143] SIR's membership expressed openly their frustration with a lack of progress and argued for direct actions; it was clear historically that militant, direct action had been the only effective means for securing the most basic of rights.[144] But many were unhappy about SIR's increasingly militancy, and in November of 1967, SIR President Dorr Jones stepped down in protest of SIR's increasingly direct confrontational methods; the new president pledged to increase militancy within the organization. Still others were calling for other forms of action, such as gathering financial strength to gain power, because pickets were getting them nowhere.[145] And other SIR members were mortified by the actions of revolutionary activists who advocated social revolution.[146]

A handful of groups sprung up in 1969 and early 1970 with the hopes of bringing about an even more militant action than SIR had been able to muster; these groups were a sort of middle-ground between SIR and the groups that arose after 1969. Of these intermediate groups, the Sexual Freedom League sought to bring about the sexual liberation not just of gays and lesbians, but of all Americans.[147] Another example, Continuum, was a student group formed on San Francisco State University's campus, in mid-1970, to compete with the Gay Liberation Front on campus. Continuum saw itself as a group that would radically transform society by bringing gay and straight people together in action.[148] The most militant of these middling groups, the Committee for Homosexual Freedom, sprang up to protest the firing of Gayle Whittington from State Steamship Company in April 1969.

Emerging from these "middle" groups were the gay men who saw themselves as the most militant, a loosely allied bunch of organizations that called themselves collectively "Gay Liberation"—specifically, Gay Sunshine Collective in Berkeley and the Gay Liberation Front,[149] which had chapters around the Bay Area. These activists complained that the other groups weren't militant enough (or at all) and were therefore "Timid leaders with enormous ego-trips, middle class bigotry and racism, and too many middle-aged, up-tight conservatives are hurting almost every major homosexual organization on the West Coast and probably throughout the nation" (*VR* April 1969, 11, 25). As evidenced here, these gay militants saw themselves in generational terms; those who disagreed with them were old and "out of touch." So militancy came to be seen as a conflict of generations (not unlike other radical movements of the late 1960s), where "the old-timers are scared that these kids will come in and really create a gay revolution." For the most part, Bay Area organizations forged their own way. And interestingly, many SIR members also considered themselves Gay Libbers, and crossed those boundaries frequently. Gay Liberation, San Francisco style, saw itself as "a new style for the movement, a style that sharply sets apart Gay Lib from the older and more staid progenitors" (*VR* Oct. 1970, 38). Some SIR members criticized the liberation movement for its incoherence and lack of leadership and of a unified plan of action.[150] And SIR resented how self-described gay libbers viewed themselves as being the source of a social movement and progress, a view which ignored preceding activists' actions and accomplishments, as evidenced in a disappointed 1971 review of Donn Teal's *The Gay Militants*.[151]

Despite these internal struggles over the meaning of militancy and who would take credit for advancing social change, gay men and women did actually engage in direct actions against the dominating official public, and not just against each other. And all of the Bay Areas groups were involved to some degree in the protest movement of the early 1970s. The most common direct action taken, as might be obvious, were protests and demonstrations.[152] The protests movement in San Francisco actually began in 1966, following coverage of the protests of the Washington, D.C., Mattachine Society in front of the White House.[153] SIR's May 1966 demonstration in front of the federal building protested draft policies[154]; a second protest followed on July 3, 1968.[155] It was a poor turnout, with press outnumbering protestors, but it set the precedent for what would become regular actions in the city.[156] In California, self-styled militants hoped that direct action would change the minds of the general public.[157] Nineteen-sixty-nine was a year of protests in San Francisco, beginning with CHF's protest of State Steamship Company that April (see *CHFN* Apr. 28, 1969). This protest energized those in the gay community who craved more confrontational action, and they protested the State Steamship offices every lunch hour for weeks. In May, another action began as CHF protested Tower Records for the firing of Frank Denaro for "acting gay" on the job.[158] The Tower Record protest was used as a way to differentiate between the "truly militant" and the "pseudo-hip, anti-gay, and super uptight gay people [who] crossed the picket line" (*VR* July 1969, 8). The Tower Records protest was the first recorded incidence of San Franciscans shouting the now famous slogan, "Out of your closets; into your streets." One writer saw protesting as a way to distance homosexuals from the effeminate stereotypes of the weak, cowering homosexual and associated militant direct action with masculinity.[159] In these two CHF-organized protests, gay men had moved to define gayness by masculinizing it and by insisting on openness.

Still more protests were organized. In November 1969, the *San Francisco Examiner* published a blatantly homophobic article, to which The *San Francisco Free Press* responded with a spoof.[160] In response, the CHF organized a protest of the *Examiner* building south of Market, which activists from many different organizations attended, circulating in front of the building shouting "We're gay and we're proud" (see *VR* Dec. 1966, 9). Workers in the building threw ink at the protesters, who in turn used the ink puddles to make handprints on the building, making the purple hand a short-lived sign of protest among San Francisco gay activists. "Laughing and running, the beautiful people tracked through the ink and decided to make pretty purple hand prints on the face of the fortress" (*SFFP* Nov. 15, 1969, 2). Police beat up and arrested several protesters.[161] Another wave of protests came in the fall of 1970. Mayor Alioto and the SFPD had engaged in a large-scale crack down on gay men and so-called public sex. A coalition of gay groups banned together to protest in front of Macy's department store on Union Square, where the bulk of arrests were taking place. Gay men organized to warn men to stay away from public restrooms in Macy's and leafleted in front of the store.[162] And Union Square became the site of another demonstration on June 19, 1971, when another coalition of gay rights organizations planned a protest event to commemorate Christopher Street (i.e., the Stonewall riots in New York) in the Bay Area by staging a march to Sacramento in support of Willie Brown's consensual sex bill, discussed earlier.[163] The march to Sacramento had a galvanizing effect on many gay men and Douglas L. Brown's account reflects the more expansive gayness described earlier.[164] Some militants rejected the march on Sacramento, criticizing both its intentions and its possible effects. *The Effeminist* felt that the march played into heterosexual men's dominance by accepting their terms to describe and experience sexuality.[165] Two other major demonstrations took place toward the end of this period, a third protest at the Federal building and a protest of the YMCA.[166]

During this period of intensifying protest, gay men in San Francisco began to insist not just on entering the public sphere as gay men, but to be openly, blatantly gay, to take their distinctiveness into public with them and insist on their right to do so. This was the now well-known "come out of the closet" cultural moment. The problem was whether or not coming out itself was militant, or rather, militant enough. To be clear, in the early 1960s, Guy Strait had talked about being open in public, especially being honest in court; and we have already seen that part of the development of values as gay men interacted with the official public was to develop an open homosexuality as part of their gay publicity. But in the early 1970s, the argument became an imperative to effect social change, a means in itself, and with a new militancy that would have baffled Strait in the early 1960s. Many gay men across the spectrum believed that "coming out" would somehow force the hand of the dominating official public by forcing it to face the realities of gay men's and women's lives.[167] For gay libbers, coming out meant a rejection of passing and of respectability, which were "old-style homosexual" attributes. They replaced it with, "I'M GAY AND I'M PROUD—OUT OF THE CLOSETS AND INTO THE STERETS," (*VR* Oct. 1970, 38).[168] But suspicion also grew about the effectiveness of coming out as a strategy; it was feared that it would become the excuse for inactivity and passivity, that coming out alone would be seen as gay men as all they had to do.[169]

Although social-sexual revolution was a prized end for many gay men, the revolutionaries never really created means beyond the protest. In many ways, revolutionary gay men seem in retrospect to have been more about a particular type of gay man rather than about the particular means they employed. Although the frequency of protest definitely picked up after 1969, there doesn't seem to be much different about the protests themselves. What was different was the kind of gayness they saw themselves creating. We have already seen that the revolutionaries associated themselves with a more expansive and porous kind of gayness. But it was also an identification with the time and with peers, a cultural moment that sought to hook gayness and gay men and women to the liberation movements of the era. Militancy came to serve as a constant backdrop to discussions about whether a particular means was in fact revolutionary.[170] Throughout the first three years of the 1970s, there played out an endless back and forth: Does liberation require militant action, and is the only real militant action a revolution, and if so, what would that revolution look like?[171] By 1972, revolution had not materialized beyond the strategic means already known within the American context. The meaning of militancy and revolution remained an open question.

Gay folk's struggle to formulate and enact effective means to engage with the official public and bring about their freedom of personhood reveals that the means themselves seem to have been shaped by the context gay men were living in. The personal modes of social control (the internalization of external standards of respectability), the structure of the law and the courts, coalition building across social groups and problems, and the mode of "militant" democratic protest so much a part of American history were all reformulations of the cultural tools available to gay men to meet their specific needs at the time. These specific means, the experience of putting them into action, and gay men's responses to them repeat and perhaps amplify the meanings of gayness that we saw evident in their argument over ends and values, namely that gayness in the context of

1960s San Francisco had to be defined along several continua of openness, ex-pansiveness, individual or group identification, choice or state of being. These were not accidental formulations of gayness, but the necessary range of possi-bilities enabled by the complex environment in which gay men interacted.

Gay men's individual experiences of repression were articulated through the structures and relationships of groups of gay individuals; where gay men en-gaged in direct struggle with the official public, this interaction took place pri-marily in gay rights organizations. The establishment of gay organizations pro-duced a social interaction where ends and means were hotly contested and in which gay men allied themselves to particular groups, events, strategies, and values based on their own activity-undergoing within the official public and in their personal lives. These organizations in turn fought to achieve dominance among gay men by convincing them that their means and ends were the right ones. Even as they worked to fight the dominating official public, gay organiza-tions worked to control the gay movement as a whole, to assume a role of lead-ership for the entire gay community.

In their arguments over what ends were worth fighting for and which means to employ to achieve those ends, there emerged a kind of gayness, a particular meaning of gay that we can formulate as a gayness in relationship to a liberal-democratic public sphere. Indeed, the contradictions in the meaning of gay that I have enumerated here are all about the relationship of the individual to the state and the kind of "self" that might be produced within that structure. For all their talk of revolution, the later gay men were as engaged in conceptions of freedom and individuality as the earlier ones. Here among San Francisco's gay men, the possible gayness that emerged was one that could be laid out as the tension be-tween the freedom to be and the freedom to choose, and the relationship of the individual to the society. Whether it was the desire of professional white gay men to enter the public sphere as it was constituted as full citizens or the desire of gay youth in the 1970s to effect a complete sexual-social revolution, the end always seemed to be one of integration into society in one form or another: inte-gration into the legal system or the labor market; integration into church; inte-gration into revolutionary movements; integration into a new society they would create together; or even just integration into the society of gay men. What comes out of the period is an underlying feeling that permeates the gay publications by the 1970s that merely to enter the official public sphere and gain a place therein could never bring about the kind of self-fulfillment gay men lacked. So many gay men sought a gayness that exceeded the boundaries of a classical liberal-democratic public sphere, one where there were not satisfied merely to be a citi-zen, but also demanded the right to be difference. At a social level, the points to a particular tension within democratic societies generally speaking: That they are *societies*, that is, groups of people with shared values (at some level), that cohere around those values. Gay men were bumping up against those shared values of the dominating society and insisting on their expansion to include gay-ness. Regardless of the outcome, they formulated a gayness that could include a kind of person that was outside the dominant version of liberal democratic citizen, even as they fought to be just that.

Here in their actual practices in engaging the public sphere directly, gay men continued the experiential process of meaning making. Through their efforts to enact a respectable public homosexuality (or not), to take on and reform the legal establishment (or not), participate in electoral politics (or not), and build bridges with other oppressed groups and social movements (or not), gay men came to understand gay-maleness as *engaged*. While political scientists may argue about the relative success or failure of particular strategic means, my point here is a larger one: through the layers of interaction with each other in their conflicts over means, gay men created the meaning of gayness itself and set the terms of gayness, many of which persist into the twenty-first century. Having seen how gay men resisted symbolic interaction, how and why they joined with gay women in creating a gay publicity, and the variety of ends and means they desired for a "gay movement", there remains one final piece of the puzzle: the gay community itself.

Notes

1. Although gay men and lesbians worked together in strategizing (indeed, lesbians were front and center in these efforts), the debates over strategy reveal the first clues that gay men and lesbians might have differing needs and desires.

2. The official public simultaneously required gay men and women to lay aside their differences in public, while it called their sexual differences out through public suppression, which, it was hoped, would eradicate sexual difference and specificity by insisting on the intelligibility, singularity, and most importantly the illegitimacy of homosexuality. See Michael Warner, "The Mass Public and the Mass Subject" in *Habermas and the Public Sphere*, ed. Craig Calhoun (Boston: Massachusetts Institute of Technology Press, 1992), 377–401.

3. See John Dewey, *The Quest for Certainty* [1929] in *The Later Works, 1925–1953: Volume 4: 1929*, ed. Jo Ann Boydston (Carbondale: Southern Illinois University Press, 1984), 239.

4. See John Dewey, *Theory of Valuation [1939]*. In *The Later Works, 1925–1953: Volume 13: 1938–1939*, edited by Jo Ann Boydston (Carbondale: Southern Illinois University Press, 1988), 219.

5. See Dewey, *Valuation*, 212.

6. Dewey, *Valuation*, 71.

7. For examples of this political binary as applied specifically to San Francisco's gay movement, see Elizabeth A. Armstrong, *Forging Gay Identities: Organizing Sexuality in San Francisco, 1950–1994* (Chicago: University of Chicago Press, 2002); Nan Alamillo Boyd, *Wide Open Town: A History of Queer San Francisco to 1965* (Berkeley: University of California Press, 2004); and John D'Emilio, *Sexual Politics, Sexual Communities* (Chicago: Chicago University Press, 1983).

8. See for example the problematic, Stonewall-centered narrative in Roger Streitmatter, *Unspeakable: The Rise of the Gay and Lesbian Press in America* (New York: Faber

& Faber, 1993).

9. For a superior discussion of this problematic, see Martin Meeker, "Behind the Mask of Respectability: Reconsidering the Mattachine Society and Male Homophile Practice, 1950s and 1960s" in *The Journal of the History of Sexuality* 10, No. 1 (2001): 78–116.

10. For a recent, thorough discussion of this dynamic, see Margot Canaday, *The Straight State: Sexuality and Citizenship in Twentieth-Century America* (Princeton: Princeton University Press, 2009).

11. See Paul Jacobs, *VR* Oct. 1968, 20–23; the complexities of their identification with African Americans will be discussed later. For more on their feelings of misrecognition, see also *VR* June 1969, 6; July 1969, 13; June 1972; and *VG* 1.10.

12. See D'Emilio, *Sexual Politics*, Chapter 4: "Radical Beginnings of the Mattachine Society."

13. See *TN* Oct. 14, 1963, 7

14. See for example, *CN* March 23, 1964, 1.

15. See for example *CN* Jan. 27, 1964, 1.

16. See for example GS Oct.–Nov. 1971, 7.

17. See *VG* Feb. 1967; VR Dec. 1966, 2; *TN* Aug. 19, 1963, 3–4; *VR* Oct. 1968, 20–23; and *VR* Dec. 1967, 10. Also, a student group was formed at SFSU called Continuum with the express purpose of breaking down sexual barriers between homosexual and heterosexual groups by changing the value systems that defined them. See *VR* June 1970, 35.

18. See *VR* July 1965, 2.

19. In explaining why "integration" was one of SIR's goals, *Vector* editors explained, "There is no answer in pulling apart into separate or segregated institutions. . . . We should not want to separate ourselves in our living areas or our social activities or our church participation, etc." *VR* July 1970, 39.

20. See also *VR* April 1967 and 16–17; and *VR* Feb.–March 1968, 16–18.

21. Some men argued that normalizing homosexuality would simply turn it into another kind of relation governed by strict rules and obligations. For others, this wasn't necessarily a bad thing, because it would separate homosexuality from those who choose it merely as a social escape from obligation. See *VR* March 1969, 16–17. Other gay men argued that they had a moral obligation to heterosexuals to "understand them," or else they could never expect heterosexuals to accept them. See *VR* April 1969, 13–14, 25.

22. See for example Oct.–Nov. 1971, 7.

23. See *VR* Jan. 1972, 13.

24. See for example, *VR* Sept. 1970, 9.

25. See *VR* April 1972, 13; and *CHFN* Aug. 13, 1969.

26. See *TN* Sept. 2, 1963, 1–2.

27. See *TT* Jan.–Feb. 1966, 1.

28. See *VG* 1.7, 2 & 5.

29. See *VR* March 1969, 16.

30. See for example, *VR* Apr. 1967, 16–17.

31. See for example, *TN* Dec. 23, 1963, 1. This particular dynamic will be discussed in depth in Chapters 4 and 5.

32. See also *IA* 1.1, 2.

33. For example, making a classic liberal argument to the newly formed SIR, Beardemphl argued that "society must support action that accords with human nature and

guarantees the right of man to pursue the fulfillment of his nature." *VR* March 1965, 4. He went on to define the social contract as one that nurtures an environment where individuals can not only seek their individual fulfillment, but where they can form groups wherein individuals may fulfill their nature.

34. See also *CN* May 25, 1964, 8–9 and *VR* July 1969, 14.

35. See also *SFFP* 1.9, 12; *SFGFP* Nov. 1970, 4–5, 12; *VR* April 1969, 13–14, 25; and *GS* Jan. 1972, 2.

36. *VR* April 1969, 13–14, 25. There was a decidedly Marxist bent to some of the revolutionary rhetoric, which played into Cold War anti-communist culture. *Gay Sunshine* referred to "straight capitalist chicken shit" and the *Committee for Homosexual Freedom Newsletter* printed extended arguments employing Marxist critique to explain the oppression of homosexuals. See *CHFN* Aug. 25, 1969; Sept. 8, 1969; *SFFP* 1.9, 12; *GS* Aug.–Sept. 1970, 2; and *BAR* Jan. 1, 1972, where gay libbers are referred to as "little Trotskyites."

37. See *VR* April 1972, 13.

38. See for example, *VR* Jan. 1970, 11; 28; and 36.

39. See for example *VR* July 1970, 36; and Oct. 1971, 7.

40. See *AA* July 20, 1970, 1; and *GS* May 1972, 7.

41. Tom Mauer, SIR President, argued for "NEW WAYS OF EFFECTING SOCIAL CHANGE: [. . .] I doubt the claim that homosexuals are more creative than heterosexuals, but we surely ought to be as creative and therefore ought to be able to create our own methods for changing society." *VR* July 1970, 39.

42. Gay men themselves originated this distinction, so it is no wonder that the scholarly literature has reproduced it. First, LCE and then SIR tried to distinguish themselves from the old Mattachine Society, which they saw as a kind of Uncle Tomism. They saw themselves as militant in approach and strategy, and contextually, indeed they were. The later gay liberation movements and organizations used the same distinctive language to separate themselves from SIR (LCE had long since dissolved) and the Tavern Guild. Because both SIR and Tavern Guild members continued to use the term "homophile" the distinction between radical and homophile stuck. But the gay libbers added the critique, common of the cultural movements of the period, that SIR was merely a "liberal" organization, pandering to the values of the white, middle-class, and sexist values of the "establishment."

43. For a historical sketch of the birth of the major organizations in San Francisco, see Boyd, *Wide Open Town*, Chapter 5.

44. See for example *VR* Aug. 1967, 14–15. And see Chapter 4 for an extended discussion of this aspect of organization building in detail.

45. See for example *VR* Aug. 1967, 14–15.

46. See Boyd, *Wide Open Town*, for a clearer understanding of why Stonewall played such a small role in San Francisco's activist consciousness.

47. See *CN* 4.1 (Oct. 1964), 1; and *VR* March 1966, 1. The disconnect between San Francisco's gay men and women and national gay organizations came to the fore in 1968, at the NACHO conference in Chicago. At those meetings, the national body remade itself into an oversight organization with powers to dictate policy for local organizations; this Chicago body passed motions to exclude both the Daughters of Bilitis and SIR in order to get rid of what they called the "west coast liberals." According to San Francisco coverage of the events, parliamentary procedures weren't followed and delegates from the west (particularly the women) were ignored and publicly ridiculed. See *VR* Sept. 1968, 5. The

San Francisco delegates felt that the responsibility of their organizations was first and foremost to the gay men and women of San Francisco. "The purpose of SIR is to respond to the needs of homosexual individuals in San Francisco. Our concept of the planning conference was to respond to the needs of the indigenous organizations across the country and strengthen us all by mutual cooperation and communication. The highly structured NACHO supersedes, engulfs, destroys these very simple needs." *VR* Sept. 1968, 5. These tensions between San Francisco's activists and activists from across the country were typical of the period.

48. See *VR* Aug. 1970; and Oct. 1970, 14–15.

49. See John Dewey, *Experience and Nature* [1929 (1925)] in *The Later Works, 1925–1953: Volume 1: 1925*, ed. Jo Ann Boydston (Carbondale: Southern Illinois University Press, 1988), 156–57.

50. As an example of how this strategy continued through the 1960s, see *VR* Sept. 1969, 20. It is important to include a few important caveats here. First, the homophile movement itself was not a unitary thing, and was torn by conflicts about how to proceed, from the early 1950s on. Although the assimilationist stance had dominance prior to 1961, it was far from uncontested. For example, *ONE, Inc.* in Los Angeles continued to insist on the fundamental difference of homosexuals. In the early 1960s, the Daughters of Bilitis slowly but surely became more and more activist and directly feminist in its orientation; and the Mattachine Society chapters in New York City and in Washington, D.C., moved significantly away from the San Francisco Mattachine after the organization was decentralised. Martin Meeker has amply demonstrated the complexity of community actions of the Mattachine Society in San Francisco, showing that despite their public face of respectability, the society worked among gay men in ways that, although not explicitly intended to do so, laid important groundwork for the communities that would spring up in the 1960s. See Martin Meeker, "Come Out West: Communication and the Gay and Lesbian Migration to San Francisco, 1940s–1960s" (Ph.D. Diss., University of Southern California, 2000).

51. In 1964, *Town Talk* reported that "numerous professional persons and public and private agencies benefit from the helpful liaisons contracted with the Mattachine Society, and in turn these benefits are passed on to the public in the form of enlightened social action" (Dec. 1964, 6).

A related and long-lasting tactic, groups also worked with a police liaison officer to address the problems of police harassment, unlawful arrest, entrapment, and general curtailment of gay men's rights to self-expression in public. Blackstone spoke frequently to SIR throughout the 1960s, always with the same arguments. He argued at a SIR meeting "that only responsible communication will dispel the commonly held stereotypes of the homosexual (as an empty effeminate or as a sexual psychopath lurking in parks and restrooms) and eventually lead to the repeal of repressive laws." *VR* July 1966, 1. Working through Blackstone created a bind for gay men wherein they were responsible for their own harassment and only a certain respectable image of gay-maleness would dispel the oppression they experienced. See also *VR* March 1967, 5. One letter from an ostensible police officer argued that "you [homosexuals] are a long way from achieving what you seek, if it can ever be achieved. In this I speak of 'creating a sense of social responsibility.' How can you expect to do this when among your ranks are welcomed the bad with the same open arms as the good?" *TN* July 22, 1963, 4.

52. See for example *VR* Sept. 1965, 2 and *GS* Feb.–March 1972, 2, 7.

53. See for example *TN* Oct. 14, 1963; Thomas M. Edwards, *VR* Oct. 1967, 18–19.

E.L.K. wrote, "There are many of us, probably a greater majority, who desire to live our lives as respectable citizens making useful contributions to society and maintaining a conduct which is expect of all adults." *VR* May 1967, 14.

54. When the Beaux Arts Ball was discussed in *Town Talk*, the editors encouraged partygoers to behave. "At all times, play it cool, don't parade on the street, and don't push your luck. Authorities are not so hostile to the person having fun within the bounds of good taste as they are toward the individual who wants to stretch the season into an unlimited license for wearing drag anywhere he chooses. Regardless of what we think our rights should be, such conduct is not yet permitted." Oct.–Nov. 1965, 8.

55. See for example Dan, *VR* Oct. 1967, 18–19; *VR* March 1972, 16.

56. In objecting to drag as a cultural form, Jim Ramp wrote to *Vector*, "[It is] of no use to say we have rights. Morally we do; but the law says no. . . . Therefore, our public behavior is of supreme importance. To ignore public criticism, vicious as it may seem, is to delay our final recognition by society." *VR* April 1967, 16–17. See also *VR* March 1972, 16.

57. One letter writer described the older 1950s movement that "sought desperately to prove that they really belonged in [Eisenhower's America] . . . for [these] homosexuals [in the 1950s] themselves did not really believe they were the same as Middle America. . . . One senses a tension between the desire to conform and a strong camp, 'Boys-in-the-Band' mannerism that is beneath those protestations of respectability." *VR* Oct. 1970, 38.

58. For example, "[H]omosexuals often behave as irresponsibly as they have been branded by society and by themselves. . . . It is probably true that had we, upon coming out, learned that 'gay people always help one another and never lie to each other,' we would have adopted a different pattern in our gay dealings." *VR* Jan. 1966, 8.

59. Yet others continued to deny the salience of homosexuality in the public sphere at all. One letter writer, Thomas M. Edwards, echoed a perennial argument in gay politics: "If a homosexual runs for office, it should be on the bases of his political conviction—not his sexual choice. . . . The homosexual in the political arena is no different than the heterosexual, the bisexual, or the asexual. . . . The ever-present issue is one of conservative, responsible citizenship prescinding [sic] from sexual persuasion." *VR* Oct. 1967, 18–19.

60. In a meeting of homophile organizations in Washington, D.C., in 1967, for example, the official press was not contacted for fear that the debate and conflict within the movement would be aired to the general public. One columnist was irritated at the secrecy and argued, "[H]omosexuals must leave off spinning myths about our unblemished virtue. . . . [We] are duty bound to present our opinion and observations as to its goodness and badness. . . . Let us assume command of the dialogue (as the Negro is doing for himself today), for it is our dignity, our lives, our future at stake here." *VR* March–April 1968, 15.

61. As early as 1963, Guy Strait was defending his decision to publish pictures of men in drag from the Halloween street party. He responded that "Public Image" should not be affected by modes of dress. See *TN* Dec. 23, 1963, 1.

"The first hang-up that revealed itself in these letters [to the editor] was our group's acceptance of the concept of 'social acceptability.' It goes something like this: 'WE MUST CONFORM! We are no different than heterosexuals except in sexual preference. We will gain social acceptance ONLY when we conform to conventional dress and societal standards'" *VR* May 1967, 13.

62. In a speech to SIR, Willie Brown said that "homosexuals might pay heed to this

analogy [with race], for they too cannot be 'safe' from the reality of prejudice. 'If you believe that being presentable and getting a good education will give you full respectability you aura living a myth,' Brown stressed." *VR* Oct. 1970, 13.

63. See for example , *CHFN* May 13, 1969.

64. From Darryl Hall, in response to a February 15th report of police raids of "model" agencies, "It is people of your ilk and attitude that help keep minority groups in the minority. For so long as you accept and condone discriminatory use of discriminating laws, you are setting precedent for the discriminatory use of other discriminating laws." *BAR*, March 1, 1972.

65. But by the end of the decade, even some *Vector* writers had grown weary of the call for respectability. "Society's concept of respectability is a sham . . . Anyone ashamed of effeminate men, masculine women, long hair, public use of words depicting reality (such as 'suck cock,' [or] 'beat the draft!') or the nude body has been duped by a hypocritical society, which is frightened by harmless deviations. . . . To all those homosexuals who want to 'be just like them' and who will continue to do 'what they are told' by a Government which hates them, I say your lives are in vain." *VR* April 1970, 26. As Jim Castleberry wrote, "I may not be the sign-carrying picket type, but I'm glad that someone is."

66. For example, the LCE wanted the elimination of sex laws between consenting adults, and looked to the example of the state of Illinois, the first to overturn its sodomy statute in 1961. See also *TN* Aug. 19, 1963, 3–4.

67. See Boyd, *Wide Open Town*, Chapters 2 and 3.

68. See *VR* Sept. 1965, 1.

69. For example, *The News* suggested that drag queens and butch lesbians wear signs that read "I'm a boy" or "I'm a girl" to take advantage of the "intent to deceive" loophole left in the cross-dressing law. See for example *TN* Oct. 14, 1963, 8.

70. See *TN* Oct. 14, 1963, 8.

71. See *CN* 4.5, 11. Perhaps more important, the LCE educated its readers about ABC tactics for entrapment. Strait informed readers that the police used drugs as an excuse to raid gay bars. See *TN* July 22, 1963, 4. Later, Strait wrote, "All the charges that are leveled against a bar owner for any type of conversation that a customer carries on with another customer is nothing more or less than an attempt to close him. Neither Malcom Harris (Chief of the ABC) Pat Brown [governor of California], or for that matter anyone in the world can regulate this conversation. Stalin, Hitler and company have been only partially successful" *TN* Sept. 2, 1963, 1. Strait also spoke at length about proper comportment when out in the bars to avoid harassment of the ABC. "Let us talk about tight fitting pants—and those numerous fine, and not so fine, manufacturers who will, be surprised to learn that they might contribute to the moral degeneration of the country. . . . If the ABC really is interested in what is worn in bars in our state, may we suggest that they publish an 'Approved Wear' list; and we think that the general public would tell them to go to hell, in no uncertain terms. . . . The ABC has built its entire case on the fact that this bar is allegedly a place where social variants can come to drink. The case is built on the basis that they sent social variants . . . into this establishment to provoke a variant into making an overt act. This act might not have been made had it not been for the gentle coaxing the eager skillfully drawn out invitation and enticement" *TN* Sept. 16, 1963, 1–2.

72. See *VR* March 1967, 9, 13 for coverage of Gov. Ronald Reagan's effort to put vice enforcement back into local law enforcement's hands. For coverage of the original *Lane v. Los Angeles County* case, see *CN* March 23, 1964, 1.

73. See *VR* March 1969, 8.

74. One of the most interesting stories treated Warren Burger's appointment to the Supreme Court, wherein *Vector* warned readers of a coming calamity for the homophile movement. "[Burger believes that] the Government may properly discriminate against homosexuals, and rejects the concept that homosexuals as a class come within the Equal Protection Clause of the Constitution." *VR* July 1969, 12.

75. See for example *TN* Aug. 19, 1963, 3–4.

76. See for example, *Robinson v. California*, which ruled that homosexuality alone could not be used as a category for discrimination, only homosexual behavior could be regulated; covered in *VR* April 1967, 9. And *Scott v. Macy*, covered in *VR* Oct. 1968, 8–9, disallowed the federal government from using homosexuality per se in refusing or terminating employment.

77. For example, two commonly referenced cases were *Vallerga v. Department of ABC* which held that homosexuals could not be held to a higher standard than heterosexuals and *Guarro v. U.S. Government* which held that if flirtation is encouraged or if it leads to intimacy that is not repelled, such action cannot be criminally classified as assault. See *VR* Dec. 1965, 5.

78. For example, Strait covered the court decision that ruled that spying in bathrooms violated the expectation to privacy and the efforts around the Bay Area to subvert the decision in schools and public restrooms, reminding his readers that "the California Supreme Court has held that any use of mirrors or spy pipes in public places is unconstitutional." *TN* Dec. 6, 1963, 2. See *TN* Sept. 16, 1963, 1–2. For story about high school's using two-way mirrors, see *TN* Dec. 6, 1963, 2.

79. Obscenity laws were covered most thoroughly in the early period when censoring public actions against gay publications, movies with gay content, and books were more common. "We Would Like to Know: What Is 'Smut?'" asked the *Citizens News* 4.4 (Nov. 1964), 8–9. Obscenity charges related to homosexual content continued through the period, despite the 1958 U.S. Supreme Court's overturning the Postmaster of Los Angeles County's confiscation of *ONE Magazine* (made without written decision). For in depth discussions of this issue, see See Streitmatter *Unspeakable* and D'Emilio *Sexual Politics.*

80. In the late 1970s, freedom of speech became an issue as gay and lesbian protestors would be arrested for using obscene language, when straight protestors were left alone. See letter from Don Jackson about *People v. Mathews and Brown* who were convicted by a straight jury for vulgar and profane language at a protest. "[T]he statutory differences between the legal status of homosexuals and heterosexuals in America is greater than the differences between commoners and peers in England. . . . [They were] prosecuted only because they are admitted homosexuals. Heterosexuals frequently say fuck, cocksuckers, etc., in presence of policemen. They are never arrested. Indeed, policemen frequently use such words themselves. . . . David Hilliard and other Black leaders say 'motherfucker' and 'punk cocksucker' over public address systems [and aren't arrested]. . . . It is disgusting that the law sets up homosexuals as a type of third class citizen." *VR* June 1970, 37.

81. See for example Boyd's description of the events surrounding the 1964 Mardi Gras Ball, and the relevant court cases in *Wide Open Town*. For contemporary coverage, see *CN* 4.4 (Nov. 1964), 1; 4.7 (Jan. 1965), 1–2; *TT* Dec. 1964, 3–4; and Jan. 1965, 1.

82. One key case, in 1970, the California Supreme Court ruled that a homosexual act did not constitute "immoral conduct" *per se*, and so did not necessarily render an individ-

ual unfit to teach in public schools. But their decision left open the possibility that "ongoing homosexual acts" might constitute immoral conduct. See *VR* Jan. 1970, 25, 28.

83. Primary among Kameny's tactics as descried in *Vector* was to come out, admit to being homosexual, and then to argue that you could not be subject to blackmail if everyone knew already you were homosexual. Kameny wrote, "We have tried to use these cases as a device for teaching the Pentagon something about the real world around them, and the real facts of the real of life homosexuals around them." *VR* Sept. 1970, 10–11. Kameny had three legal arguments: first, homosexuals cannot be asked to live up to higher restrictive standards than heterosexuals; second, homosexuals cannot be required to divulge more than heterosexuals for civil service; and third, the conduct of homosexuals cannot be subject to harsher judgment than heterosexuals. When probing, detailed questions were posed of the defendants, "We objected to the questions on grounds . . . of irrelevancy, of unequal administration of regulations (heterosexuals are not asked about their acts of 'sexual perversion' of 'criminality' (sodomy, fornication) despite the wide prevalence of these 'perversions' and 'crimes' among heterosexuals). Predictably our objections were overruled." A year later, the *Bay Area Reporter* reported that "U.S. District Judge John H. Pratt ruled that government security evaluators cannot subject homosexuals to 'probing personal questions' about their sex lives or withhold security clearances for refusal to answer such questions." *BAR* Oct. 1, 1971.

84. "A representative of the telephone company testified that the advertisement would be offensive to most users, and that many would not allow the directory into their homes." *VR* June 1969, 6. But SIR argued that "neither the state nor its protected monopolies can censor political or social views on the ground that the public is not ready for them." The battle finally went before the California Supreme Court in 1971, and SIR hoped that "a favorable decision for SIR . . . could also be an influence on minds of the general public that the homosexual is not a 'criminal' or 'sick' . . . ." *VR* July 1971, 21.

85. "SIR takes the realistic view that even homosexuals have the right and necessity to use public restroom facilities and that those homosexuals who would not otherwise be involved should not be exposed to the enticing blandishments of plainclothes police officers any more than heterosexuals should be exposed to the antics of these officers." *VR* Aug. 1969, 9.

86. see *VR* Sept. 1969, 23–24.

87. For example, in *People v. Lawrence More,* a black man arrested for cruising in Dolores Park was acquitted due to police entrapment. *VR* Jan. 1972, 17.

88. "While recognizing the contributions SIR has made toward organizing the gay community, we have no intention of allowing ourselves to be limited by the shortsightedness of gay shopkeepers and ghetto empresses aspirant. Such people simply have not recognized the depth or meaning of the social changes that are occurring in this country and the world." *CHFN* Oct. 16, 1969.

89. In an interview with the *SFFP*, SIR President Larry Littlejohn explained that the major issue was "whether the petitions are a worthwhile political move at this time. . . . when the gay community had the resources to make it successful would be the appropriate time." *SFFP* Oct. 16, 1969, 1, 5. Littlejohn said the use of the word "homosexual" in the petition draft and CHF's involvement with draft resisters would be too damaging to the homosexual's image in the city. Littlejohn did eventually endorse the initiative at a SIR board meeting, despite the board's rescinding of its original endorsement. See *VR* April 1970, 6 and 36. "On behalf of SIR, Larry Littlejohn, SIR Board Member, initiated the proceedings. . . . He asked the committee to support a resolution that would recom-

mend to the Board of Supervisors that the city Non-Discrimination in Employment Ordinance be broadened to include prohibition of discrimination on grounds of sex or sexual orientation. . . . A stand on the issue of equal employment rights for homosexuals and other sexual minority groups by recommending to the SF board of Supervisors that the City non-discrimination in employment ordinance be broadened. . . . Almost all homosexuals (even here in liberal San Francisco) live in a constant fear that their private sexual being will become known to their employer. . . . Most homosexuals are extremely careful to hide their homosexuality."

90. "[T]he city of San Francisco shall not discriminate against present employees or applicants for employment because of their sexual orientation. It further requires equal treatment of employees regardless of their sexual orientation, in regard to training, apprenticeship, layoff or termination, rates of pay or other compensation, demotion or transfer and recruitment." *VR* May 1972, 17. The National Organization of Women had also participated in the negotiations for the ordinance which in the end included "sex" in its list of protected categories.

91. Barnes resorted to the by now old argument that gay men were pedophiles who prayed on children: "What is destructive of society is that when one of these older men, who have learned to do this sexual perversion, entices some young boys." *VR* March 1972. Police and District Attorneys also opposed the bill and testified at hearings against the bill in 1972, arguing that it legalized public sex and child molestation. "Charles R. Gross, for the D.A.-Police associations, claimed that 'the homosexual is discontent, aggressive, and attempts to convert others to his ways.'" *VR* June 1972, 23. Gay men encountered opposition in the City as well. San Francisco Board of Supervisors voted down a resolution to support AB-743. See *VR* June 1969, 8. And when they passed a resolution to endorse 1971's iteration, Mayor Alioto vetoed it, saying it would protect "sex in bushes and in Macy's restrooms." *VR* Sept. 1971). Gay folks' legal argument for the bill was simple. George Mendenhall argued that AB-701 (1970's iteration of the bill) would reduce blackmail and release police officers to fight real crime. See *VR* May 1970, 6. AB-701 redefined "deviate intercourse," limiting criminality to non-consent and underage. See *VR* Sept. 1970, 36–37. Consensual sex laws would make "it legal to practice oral and anal copulation in private . . . would particularly open up new employment opportunities for homosexuals, restrict the police in their spying into bedrooms and eliminate the stigma which says that some sex acts are 'unnatural.'" *VR* Nov. 1971, 10.

92. See for example *VR* Oct. 1970, 13.

93. *Gay Sunshine* was profoundly skeptical of Brown's involvement, suspecting that it was a political ploy. "[Both attitudes make people] willing to spend a great deal of time and energy into a project which will benefit almost nobody—with the possible exception of Willie Brown who would no doubt get credit for 'saving the faggots'. . . . [Brown said his bill was] analogous to anti-lynching bills in the south. Then he went on to suggest that homosexuals waste their time and money trying to get local referendums on the bill." *GS* Feb.–March 1972, 2, 7. And Aubrey Bailey wrote, "I was ashamed of the homosexual community for having to depend on leadership from a member [Assemblyman Willie Brown] of a minority more oppressed than we are in demanding our rights." *CHFN* May 6, 1969.

94. "Laws legalizing private sex acts between 'consenting adults'—the key word is *adults* defined as 21 or over. . . . I want laws that don't just *hint* that my love is all right, but directly *state* it. . . . I can't vote or make love. What is the homosexual community doing for me?" *VR* Nov. 1970, 39, 43–44. Before Willie Brown's campaign, SIR's legal

committee was contemplating a change to the consensual sex laws. In 1968, Charles Thorp, a young SFSU student and activist, argued that "the law changes that organizations like SIR are supporting are also not going to help the teenage homosexual—for instance, the law legalizing private sex acts between 'consenting adults'—defined as 21 and over. Where does this leave me if I'm 20 or 18 or 16?'" *VR* Dec. 1968, 34–35.

Thinking about sexual freedom, some gay men even went so far as to contemplate what freedom would look like for people of all ages. In *Vanguard*, Keith St. Clare wrote, "Not only 'minors,' but also children should be allowed to engage in sex play. It's healthy. Group: Little girls and boys who are repressed and given guilt complexes about their penis or vagina are often poorly adjusted for the major part of their life." *VG* 1.7, 30.

95. *BAR* March 1, 1972.

96. For a full description of Gay Sunshine Collective's objections to Brown's consensual sex bill, see "Zap," the pamphlet reprinted in full in *GS* Feb. –March 1972, 2.

97. For more about Sarria from contemporary news coverage, see *TN* Dec. 23, 1963. Also, Boyd, *Wide Open Town*, treats Jose Sarria's career at length.

98. Assemblyman Willie Brown told gay men that they *had* to vote or risked admitting that democracy was a failure. See *VR* Oct. 1968, 20–23.

99. See for example *TN* Oct. 14, 1963, 1–2.

100. See *TN* Aug. 19, 1963, 1.

101. See *VR* Sept. 1967, 36.

102. See for example *TT* Oct.–Nov. 1965, 7; *VR* Sept. 1965; Dec. 1969, 7; Oct. 1971, 24–25.

103. See *VR* Sept. 1967, 36.

104. See *VR* Dec. 1969, 7; and *VR* Nov. 1971, 41.

105. See letter from Dan, *VR* Oct. 1967, 18–19. The debate about whether gay men should vote for conservative candidates, even if their conscience so dictated, became a sharp issue in the 1970s, a tension that resonates today in arguments about the Log Cabin Republicans. "Only the sickest masochist could vote for any of these queer haters. Many 'Gay conservatives' are politically innocent. . . . The authoritarian rightists, who are in control of the nation now, hate liberty. . . . They are attempting to suppress freedom of the press, and to destroy the Bill of Rights. . . . This is not conservatism. It is fascism," *BAR*, Nov. 1, 1971.

106. For SIR, a gay electoral strategy would consist of "1, the election of a Supervisor to the Presidency of the Board who is the most friendly and supportive to the gay community, and 2, the defeat of the Supervisor who is most likely to be antagonistic to the gay community." *VR* Oct. 1971, 24–25.

107. See for example *TN* May 13, 1963, 1; Aug. 19, 1963, 1; *VR* Oct. 1967, 7; Oct. 1967, 14; Nov. 1967, 5; Oct. 1969, 12; Nov. 1969, 16; *BAR*, May 31, 1972; and June 14, 1972. Concerning Ronald Reagan's gubernatorial campaign, *Vector* published a scathing article about Ronald Reagan's platform, which included "the elimination of 'beatniks, communists, and homosexuals' from the Berkeley campus; 'work on programs to control our soaring crime rate'; ways to 'beef up local autonomy to regulate such things as topless waitresses'; and his first statement after being elected was . . . to 'get a law to control pornography so that we can protect our children.'" *VR* Dec. 1966, 2.

108. See for example *VR* Sept. 1971, 9. There was also an article by the Socialist Workers Party presidential candidate, Linda Jenness, explaining the cross-over between gay rights and socialist ideologies. See *VR* May 1972, 15.

109. *VR* Oct. 1968, 20–23; *GS*, Oct. 1970, 5

110. *Vector*'s 1968 rundown of presidential candidates reveals the growing ambivalence in the American electorate as it was experienced by gay men in San Francisco. See *VR* Oct. 1968, 20–23.

111. See "Political Opinions," *CN* 4.1 (Oct. 1964), 6.

112. See letter from M.R.P., *VR* Oct. 1968, 20–23.

113. See *VR* Jan. 1972, 15. A paid political ad ran for McGovern in *BAR* May 15, 1972, advocating many of the primary issues of concern to gay men: "Has Anybody Spoken Up for You Lately" included his stance on homosexual issues. Don Jackson conducted a survey of Laurel Heights and found that "the tally shows McGovern leading Humphrey by a 3 to 1 margin [in the Castro]" *BAR* June 14, 1972.

114. See from Gary Miller, *BAR* June 23, 1972: "I've learned that politics is a white man's game." And for a feminist critique of why gay men didn't vote for Shirley Chisholm, *BAR* June 28, 1972.

115. "The only real hope for freedom in the foreseeable future lies in electing a Gay rights advocate to the presidency. Much of the oppression of homosexuals results from executive orders and policies made by the President. . . . Employment discrimination, immigration discrimination, and the criminal and civil sanctions against homosexuals by the Federal Government and armed forces were created by an executive order written by Richard Nixon and signed by President Eisenhower during Nixon's term as vice-president." *BAR*, June 14, 1972. From Joe Amahein, Milwaukee, "Oppression flows from social attitudes and not a legal system. . . . What I am saying is that the attitude of a president toward gays is much more important than legal reforms that he may endorse." *VR* May 1972, 16.

116. "When Gays, during and before the McCarthy-Nixon witch hunts of 1950, were so immersed in fear, so intimidated by psychoanalytic dogma, so surrounded by ignorance of their own character. . . June 28, 1969, was our 'Battle of Bunker Hill' . . . mobilizing tens of thousands of 'new Gays' who had no intention of waiting 40 more years for stingy gains. . . . Gays have contributed much to the American heritage. Both Europeans who came to these shores and the native Americans [native born, not Indians] they inundated included Gays. Some of the proudest names in American history, both poets, and Presidents, were secretly, OUR names. WE SHALL BE HEARD: Some Gays, enraged by unending injustice, have given up faith in America, and have indeed joined that 'freaking fag revolution' set off by our party's 1968 disaster in Chicago. We understand their anger—even if we are not yet ready to give up on 'the System.' . . . We sincerely hope that the aspirations and needs of Gays will be heard, in this Summer of '72, INSIDE the Democratic Notational Convention in Miami." *BAR* April 15, 1972.

117. See *VR* Sept. 1969, 8; and June 1971, 13.

118. After her election, gay men felt that "[Feinstein] wanted their [homosexuals'] votes and the enthusiastic volunteer support they offered, but she did not want that support publicized." *VR* Feb. 1972, 11.

119. In an interview with *Vector*, Feinstein clarified some of her positions. "*Vector*'s concern was not with her personal reaction to such films but her comments about them, that indicate an underlying rejection of homosexuality. . . . She did not approve of gays renting public building for gay dances, but now she states she was in error. . . . She has recently made statements to the effect the heterosexual activity is permissible on the movie screen but that 'other activity' is 'sick.' . . . On another occasion she said the 'homosexual cruising' resulted from seeing homosexual movies. . . . She stresses that she has a teen-age daughter that she wants to protect. . . . We are concerned when any public

official believes that laws should be based on moral judgments and not on facts that are readily available." See *VR* March 1971.

120. "[Feinstein] strongly denounced: 1. cruising; 2. gay marriage (this was a maybe. She wanted to mull over it); 3. and pornographic pictures of 12-year-old boys." *GS* Oct.–Nov. 1971, 6. "When questioned on homosexual marriages, Mrs. Feinstein stumbled over admitted 'bias' when she said marriage means different things to different people." *BAR* June 1, 1971.

121. See letter from Jon Kroll, *BAR* Nov. 1, 1971.

122. By the 1970s, *Gay Sunshine* was urging "gay people [to] save their enthusiasm for political activity until such time as there are political forces seriously at work to achieve economic, social and sexual democracy for all oppressed people." *GS* April 1972, 3.

123. The only other openly gay candidate for a public office between 1961 and 1972 was Rick Stokes, who ran for Community College Board in 1972. See *BAR* June 14, 1972.

124. *VR* June 1965, 9.

125. "We who presume to love and who demand understanding open minds, deserve the latter only if we ourselves are willing to concern ourselves with the world's problems [poverty, racism, and the war in Vietnam]." *VR* May 1970, 12–13. See also *VR* Jan. 1970, 10: "This position holds that homosexuals as homosexuals and homosexual organizations as representatives of the homosexual community should take stands on issues such as abortion capital punishment, draft resistance, Vietnam, the Grape Boycott, student strikes, and so called 'militant' political activity."

126. See for example *VR* Jan. 1970, 11; Apr. 1972, 13; and "Refugees from Amerika" in *SFFP* Dec. 22–Jan. 7, 1970.

127. See *SFFP* Dec. 22–Jan. 7, 1970, 3–5.

128. "Homosexuals are involved in activities other than homosexuality. The Queen who is only interested in size, the Drag who cannot leave her sewing machine, or the Stud who exhibits only his leather are pitiful period pieces and inadequate caricatures of to-day's homosexual." *VR* June 1971, 34–35. Some gay men saw coalition building as a means to the future end of full integration with society. See letter from Tip Hillman, *VR* Sept. 1971, 9.

129. "There are times when I as a militant homosexual feel that some gay militants are in danger of dissipating their strength by taking up other causes when, after all, the number one battle is homosexual civil rights. However, we cannot lose sight of the fact that homosexuals civil rights is wrapped up in the struggle for the rights of everyone." *VR* Dec. 1971, 5. Even Carl Whitman had earlier worried that if gay organizations took stands on other issues it would weaken the cohesion of gay groups. "We should be held together by one thing only: That we as homosexuals have the right to be full human be-ings." *CHFN* Apr. 22, 1969. SIR's official position was that as an organization, it would only advocate for homosexual issues; but that SIR members should freely participate in other activist groups important to them. See *VR* Jan. 1970, 10.

130. *GS* June–July 1971, 2, 5.

131. This writer also condemned gay men for being judgmental of straight men: "I cannot accept the way that gay liberation people totally deny the humanity of straight men. . . . Of course, straight men wield power and have privileges. But it is absurd for us to label as a 'pig' or the enemy every male who fails to establish a gay identity. . . . Is it not possible that a straight man may be unable to express himself homosexually? For this,

is he to be condemned as a person? I cannot find the emotional basis to cut myself off from straight men who, over the years, have been my friends. . . ." *GS* June–July 1971, 2, 5. A writer from *The Effeminist* offered a different take on this topic: ". . . any discussion of sexuality where straight males are involved must be taken with a grain of salt, and even regarded with great suspicion. Especially when the discussion centers around other sexualities than their own" *TE* May 1971, 1, 4.

132. See *GS* Dec. 1971–Jan. 1972, 1, 13. "[W]ithin the Straight establishment, within the revolution itself, and even within the Gay world, I see people who are skeptical of the validity of the Homosexual Liberation Movement," wrote one man. *SFFP* Oct. 16, 1969, 11.

133. See *SFGFP* Dec. 1970, 5: "How manly, how brotherly, how vanguard, how strong your [straight activist's] up-front rhetoric was and we [gay activists] weakened you by challenge rather than by competition and you were offended and backed away from us, and more often than not you kicked us in the balls and laughed (oink!) like the pigs you supposedly hate and disassociate from being. . . . Prove yourself worthy of my brotherhood. I'm sick of the abuse and the ways you closet me and my sisters and brothers. . . . I don't need your straight ideals and political philosophies to guide me or support me. . . . My liberation will be accomplished my way on my terms, liken to that which my brothers and sister agree will best free us, totally and complete. . . . You don't like gay men and women around your women because we treat them as women, as equals, as sisters, as humans. You stigmatize us as all being feminine and nelly and detest our cultural camp. You fear you might like homosexuals and going gay. You fear us because you feel all we want is to get at your 'meat' and that we'll stop at nothing, even rape. . . . Men (hah!) Men who cannot love themselves or members of the same sex are also incapable of loving women. . . . Radical gay men, white and third world, have learned a lot about sexism and racism from our sisters and brothers and you can bet your life you're not going through with this revolution without us. . . . You don't have to be homosexual to love another man. . . . It's an expression of brotherly love, not necessarily sexual, unless and although it can be that too, depending on how you express your love or come across. Why do you associate sex especially gay sex, with aggression and fear? Hmmmm."

134. An anonymous reader wrote to Vector that the "uninhibited militancy of today is obviously generating antagonism in the heterosexual society, the society that we must live in. . . . Continued progress will be made only when the heterosexual community is convinced that we are not a threat . . . not when it learns that we are a threat. . . . It seems that they [gay militants] are working out their aggressions by attempting to shove gay ideology down heterosexual throats." *VR* Nov. 1970.

135. Other men were simply products of the Cold War culture and feared that militant action would lead to the United States losing the Cold War. See for example *CN* March 23, 1964, 4. See also *AG* Dec. 17, 1970: "The people who think we should prance down the streets proclaiming against all the fascists pigs, establishment, etc., etc. They had better go to Eastern Europe first and count themselves lucky; they wouldn't be tolerated for one second over there."

136. See question #22, "Should gays be more militant to achieve goals: no 55%, yes 45%." *AG* Jan. 7, 1971.

137. *VR* Sept. 1965, 2.

138. See *VR* Aug. 1965, 8.

139. "In social rights movements, is violence, such as recently erupted in Los Ange-

les [Watts], inevitable? . . . [Violence] is the failure of the 'establishment' more than a failure within the movements' leadership, but both are at fault." *VR* Sept. 1965, 2. Such men hoped that the "homophile revolution" would be a "bloodless revolution."

140. See *VR* march 1971, 32; and June 1971, 4.

141. For example, following an action in 1969, a SIR participant wrote that CHF protesters should dress conservatively. A CHF protestor replied, "'You get us the men in suits to picket and we'll gladly welcome them.'" *VR* Sept. 1969, 20–21, 30.

142. For example, *TN* Sept. 16, 1963, 1–2: "How long are you going to let your Governor go unaware of what his men are doing? It is just this simple. We are paying taxes to provide funds to have men go into bars and proposition others to commit lewd acts so that if they accept they will be arrested. If you object to spending money for this then write to Pat Brown, governor of California, Sacramento, today. Ask him to remove Malcom Harris [chief of ABC]—NOW."

143. This was in an article about Saul Alinsky's visit to Benjamin Franklin High School on Sept 10, 1965. "'It is a fight,' [Alinsky] said, 'and being decent just isn't effective.' . . . [Alinsky's method involves] any program confronting the establishment with the reality that formerly subservient and disunited groups are now working together and are determined that 'change will come.'" *VR* Nov. 1965, 4.

144. "[H]omosexuals as a minority have been waiting for breaks one hell of a long time and rarely if ever see them extended gratis. What homosexuals have attained . . . they have attained by themselves and by insisting on their right to do so." *VR* March 1967, 17, 23. From the editor, "Only with the advent, in the last four years, of a new kind of societal involvement of homosexuals . . . have social conditions begun to be changed in SF. In most other parts of the country the conditions are abominable. . . . I could not agree more that we need to be united and effective but we also must allow for open honest disagreement on ideologies and then find the best possible compromise solution." *VR* Oct. 1967, 32–33.

145. See letter from John Callahan, *VR* March 1970, 12–13.

146. Roy Ledbetter wrote, "When the GLF recently picketed KGO-TV, they conducted themselves in a most disgraceful manner. Yelling 'we suck cock' and similar obscenities at the top of their voices." *VR* March 1970, 26. To such complaints, the editor concurred that public militancy put "too much emphasis on the surface 'war' than on the tedious work in the courts and in professional publications like *Vector* that are not as glamorous but are most vital." *VR* Oct. 1970, 9. As SIR entered into deep conflict with CHF and then with the Gay Sunshine Collective, SIR leaders claimed that SIR "is more than inside the gay liberation movement. . . . We are leaders in that movement." *VR* Nov. 1971, 4.

147. See Thomas W. Palmer, "Sexual Freedom League: A Gay Invasion," *VR* April 1969, 5: "The primary purpose of the SFL when it was founded was to further acceptance and tolerance of any sexual activity, and to work toward altering, or doing away with, any laws restricting private, adult, sexual activity. . . . We get to the public in speaking engagements. . . . As a group advocating acceptance of any sexual persuasion we appear rather heterosexual. . . . These reasons for homosexual non-interest in the SFL are fairly understandable to me. . . . I believe that although SIR, CRH, etc., pushes 'Gay is Good' the biggest part of the gay world is isolationalistic [sic]. . . . But any group (gay or not) that is trying to find an acceptable place in the great American Sunshine should reach for any possible forms of communication."

148. See "S.F. State Group Gets Official Approval" *VR* June 1970, 35: "Aim of the

group is to 'bring together people of all sexual persuasions and stimulate critical analysis of existing sexual mores and public laws relating to sexual behavior. . . . [The] group hopes to break down barriers between people of different sexual orientations and bring new respect and understanding between gays, bi's, and straights. . . . They hope to free the climate of public attitude towards sexual minorities, break down the myths and prejudices and replace the puritanical mores that govern our society with a more just code." Charles P. Thorp, a Bay Area activist and leader of the San Francisco State's GLF, complained, "*Vector* has chosen to give space about *Continuum* at SF State without any space to GLF which will make the bigger mark for gay people at State than *Continuum*." To which the editor replied, "We will be glad to give you space when you send us something besides *Examiner* clippings." See *VR* Aug. 1970, 9.

149. Interestingly, it was in San José that the New York–inspired Gay Liberation Front took hold, and not in San Francisco or Berkeley. San Francisco's and Berkeley's GLFs were short lived and other liberation organizations took their place, but remained connected to the New York GLF and other New York and Los Angeles militant organizations.

150. See for example, *VR* June 1971, 4.

151. See *VR* July 1971, 4: "By what [*The Gay Militants*] leaves out it misinforms. Significant achievements in the area of homosexual rights are passed by for the sensational. . . . Many will question that the homosexual was in hiding until Stonewall (1969) where Teal said 'gay liberation' began. . . . Someone like Don Jackson, a gay 'underground' writer gets significant space but many significant and dedicated fighters for homosexual freedom are missed completely or only mentioned in passing. . . . He does not, however, make it clear that this movement [GLF] is generally disorganized due to lack of mature leadership and its confused involvement in non-homosexual causes. . . . Hundreds, sometimes thousands, of young homosexuals were marching together—demanding their rights. This was a useful and significant historical development. Two factors weakened much of this original movement, however. One was that it was watered down when many of these new groups became involved in endless non-homosexual causes and the other was the belief that the LACK of organization was an attribute. . . . They were able to draw together large numbers of homosexuals for a specific cause and garner good media publicity for that cause."

152. The gay liberation groups also took action against other gay groups, which they called "zapping." The idea of "zapping" was adapted from the New York Gay Activists Alliance, although the GAA didn't originally use the idea against other gay groups. See *VR* June 1971, 4: "The formula of GAA is simple and effective: A tight active membership and a large non-member following. . . . 'Zapping' is a GAA word that has proven to be most effective: GAA moves before legislatures, boards, commissions, psychiatrists, etc., with various plans and actions fro homosexual freedom. If no one will hear them or they are not getting results they 'zap,' meaning that they disrupt the person or meeting until they are heard."

153. See *VR* Dec. 1965, 1.

154. See letter from Jack Parrish, *VR* July 1966, 5. Also in 1966, a Sacramento gay rights organization, the ARC, tried to get a booth at the California State Fair; officials said it was too controversial, but allowed planned parenthood and the anti-war movement to have booths.

155. 1968 to "remind Americans that homosexuals do not have the rights granted to all other citizens of this country." *VR* Aug. 1968, 5.

156. Interestingly, as the San Francisco protest movement got underway, the gay press in San Francisco virtually ignored the Stonewall riots in New York City in June 1969, most likely because the basic kinds of issues New Yorkers were fighting for (i.e., freedom to assemble) had been won much earlier in California. Even gay liberation publications (*GS, IA, CHFN, TE, SFFP,* and *SFGFP*) only mentioned Stonewall much after the fact; but when they did, they tended to see it as the beginning of gay rebellion, ignoring the work that had been done before gay liberation hit the scene. See for example Charles P. Thorp, "June 29, 1970 Christopher Street First Anniversary," *GS* Aug.–Sept. 1970, 17.

157. Leo Laurence wrote, "Our picket line is beginning to show the public the beauty in homosexuality as they see our marchers singing freedom songs, laughing, holding hands, and even kissing in public." *CHFN* Apr. 29, 1969.

158. Although the group was unsuccessful against State Steamship, Tower Records capitulated and reinstated Denaro. See *VR* July 1969, 8.

159. "The confrontation must be nonviolent, but must show the public that we are committed to winning our freedom. We must prove that all homosexuals are not the scared, limp-wristed types typical of the stereotyped homosexuals." *CHFN* May 6, 1969.

160. "Once upon a time, in Amerika, there existed a kingdom known as San Francisco. . . . [The evil reporter] called them [homosexuals] such unbecoming names as 'semi-males,' 'drag darlings,' and 'women who aren't exactly women.'" *SFFP* Nov. 15, 1969, 2.

161. See *SFFP* Nov. 15, 1969, 2: "The people screamed and ran; the Pigs clubbed and maced. The people gathered at another point to count their lost brothers. . . . Now 15 people face jail sentences for daring to admit that they love their fellow man. Is there no justice for the just? Power to the People!" See also the firsthand accounts of the arrestees in "24 Hours: From Bust to Bail," *SFFP* Nov. 15, 1969. The CHF representatives organized the remaining protestors into a march on Mayor Alioto's office to protest the police brutality. See *VR* Dec. 1969, 9. When CHF criticized SIR for being part of the establishment, SIR was quick to point out that Al Alvarez, a SIR protester at the *Examiner*, was the only arrestee to fight the charges. "[Alvarez] refused to cop out [like CHF arrestees]. Instead he chose to defend his constitutional rights openly as a homosexual." *VR* Jan. 1970, 7.

162. The men who had been arrested were being brought up on felony charges, which carried a possible life sentence. A representative from Macy's told a *Vector* reporter "that there would be no reduction [in charge] and the 'perverts can go on picketing for as long as they wish.'" *VR* Sept. 1970, 32–33. SIR members organized a boycott of Macy's and argued that it had been effective in getting the store to call off its crack down, and SIR President Tom Maurer resigned because he objected to the boycott of Macy's. When Macy's refused to ask the District Attorney's office to reduce the felony charges to misdemeanors, SIR continued the boycott.

163. Demonstrators at the rally carried provocative signs, one reading "I am going to commit a felony tonight!" See photo, *VR* July 1971, 33. Some activists hoped that the march to Sacramento would inspire the reticent, non-militant homosexuals of the city to action and to convince straight revolutionaries that homosexual rights was a legitimate cause. See *CHFN* Oct. 16, 1969.

164. "We're Gay, good, proud and angry. We are angry because we are discriminated against, in the laws, in the churches, in the feelings of other human beings, who don't share our sexual preference. . . . We marched for love, for dignity, understanding,

humanity, our rights, and your rights. We ask you—Gay, Het, religious, agnostic, Black, Brown, Yellow or White—we ask you to consider, to think, to ponder human dignity. Think about man's natural or, if you will, 'god-given rights,' ponder your role in the struggle not just for Gay Liberation, but in the never ending every growing expanding, overpowering struggle for Total Human Liberation. Where are you?" *GS* June–July 1971, 5.

165. See *TE* 1.2, 11: "We refuse to march [to Sacramento] under false leadership that would dupe and confuse Gay people that our lives will somehow be better if certain powerful straight men permit us certain 'deviate' behavior. White homophile leadership is using a Third World male, Willie Brown, to sell us, the Gay people, out and bring us under the regulation and control of a powerful state apparatus. . . . Perry and Night [gay religious leaders] would allow straight men to define our lives. Powerful straight men dichotomize heterosexuality and homosexuality. . . . You're playing the straight man's game. And we ain't marching anymore."

166. See *BAR* June 15, 1971. The federal building protest appeared on the evening news nationwide. Walter Cronkite covered the federal building protest on the *CBS Evening News*, commenting, "'I don't know anything about the organization, but it certainly has guts.'" *VR* July 1971, 12–13. NBC had broadest coverage of events, enumerating the actions of the movement in the Bay Area. This protest went a little differently, as demonstrators pinned placards to themselves that read, "I am a homosexual working for the federal government," and then entered the building to circulate among federal employees. They handed out leaflets explaining that hundreds of federal employees were gay and discriminated against. Both Larry Littlejohn and Leo Laurence were arrested for their actions in the building.

The protest was only days after Mayor Alioto had said he favored consensual sex legislation and the San Francisco Mental Health Association had announced that it would no longer consider homosexuality a mental illness. "All of this was not by accident. Careful contacts and the long range educating of public officials is not bringing the homosexuals in San Francisco closer to first-class citizenship. It is still true. . . . United We Stand, divided they will pick us off one by one." *BAR* June 15, 1971. The second major protest of the early 1970s, gay men protested the YMCA's hypocrisy of basically running a "male brothel" while condemning homosexuality. Rev. Robert Humphries organized the YMCA protests, arguing that the Y's double standard perpetuated the myths of the gay sexual predator and profited from the oppression of gay men by providing a place they could meet when no other places were available. See *BAR* May 1, 1972, 1: ". . . hypocrisy of the Y in making money from a male brothel while condemning homosexuality. . . . [from Rev. Humphries' letter:] 'Since your Embarcadero facility is one of the oldest, most famous Gay houses of assignation in the world, it is important that you relate to the Gay Community.' . . . When the Y did not answer after three weeks, Humphries called for picketing to expose the closet queenery of Y officials. . . . The Y knows that homosexuality is not permitted elsewhere, so it steps in to provide a meeting place—for a high price; it exploits the sexual needs of homosexuals for financial gain. Humphries says that this position is a form of closet queenery which should be exposed. . . . 'The YMCA is a Gay Community institution,' Humphries said. 'They don't call it the French Embassy for nothing. . . .' 'Gay doesn't mean just sex,' he continued. 'Gays are whole persons who have needs other than sexual—needs for social activities, educational activities, physical activities and the like. If the Y is to profit by exploiting the sexuality of the homosexual, it should also provide for his other needs as a whole person.'"

167. See *VR* Oct. 1970, 38. "There is a risk involved [in demonstrating] and not everyone needs to fly a banner for the cause. . . . However, I also know many 'closet types' who are suffering because they never took a stand on anything. I dare say that many of them are known to their families, friends, and business associates. A little honesty about their own self-acceptance might work wonders." *VR* Sept. 1969, 20–21, 30.

168. "Homosexuals who beat the giant drum so that the world will know that they are demanding freedom do a service for the others who are less demonstrative because they make the public aware, aware that the homosexual exists. . . . The counter-reaction has also been a polarization but wasn't that polarization there anyway?" *VR* Dec. 1970, 6.

169. But it is also true that we must live the things we say and not just mouth revolutionary clichés. Anyone who shouts 'out of your closets' had damn well better be speaking from a 'decloseted' position. . . . CLOSETRY. It seems especially unfortunate that 'out of our closets' may have become just another cliché mouthed by closeted homosexuals, for there is nothing more basic to anyone's liberation. GS Oct. 1970, 13.

170. For example, after hearing a speech by Tim O'Leary in Golden Gate Park, a Gay Sunshine writer mused, "Marching in circles in front of the White Horse bar won't close the bar. Marching round and round at Macy's won't save our brothers. Marching against ABC Radio-TV wont' stop their lies. . . . I feel it is necessary now that the Gay Liberation Front issue a warning to the world: 'We should be considered dangerous to anyone who threatens our life or our freedom.'" *GS*, Oct. 1970, 7.

171. If so, wrote one man, "Then [he], as a revolutionary, would see the importance of destroying SIR and completely closing off any avenue of possible success in dealing with the establishment." *VR* Jan. 1970, 11, 28. Others argued that it was Uncle Tom's methods that brought freedom to blacks, and so would it be for gay men. See *VR* Oct. 1971, 7. Others feared anarchy from the ever-more confrontational methods being employed by gay lib activists.

4

The Struggle for a Gay Community

It was felt that a "better social fabric" was needed for the ordinary homosexual, for at that time, there really was no Gay Community per se. At the present time, it appears that that fabric has been attacked by many moths and presently seems to look more like last year's Cockettes costumes.

—from *Bay Area Reporter* June 14, 1972

[T]he way the term [community] is widely used implies two necessary attributes: first, a web of *affect-laden relationships* among a group of individuals, relationships that often crisscross and reinforce one another, and second, a measure of commitment to a set of *shared values*, norms, and meanings.

—Amitai Etzioni, "Is Bowling Together Sociologically Lite?" May 2001

In San Francisco before 1961, gay men's social interaction had largely focused on informal associations and relationships formed at bars or cabarets, meeting in bathhouses, through networks of friends and private parties, and chance public encounters. The new kinds of publicity-seeking organizations that began to emerge in 1961 brought about new kinds of social imperatives in addition to their political goals.[1] In other words, efforts to establish an effective counter-public made it necessary for gay men to associate with each other in ways they weren't used to; at the same time, gay men increasingly wanted to associate with other gay men and establish social institutions and groups that would meet more of their social and cultural needs than earlier forms of gay community in San Francisco had been able to provide. Even gay men who eschewed gay political organizations encountered a new and evolving community of gay men and women that both flowed out of and reinforced the growing counter-publicity;

this evolving gay community in turn served as the locus of a growing and rap-idly evolving meaning of gayness and all the interconnections between cogni-tion, psychology, language, symbols, social interaction, and symbolic domina-tion that entailed. As a consequence of the growing public community, gay men in San Francisco were forced to expand their self- and social conceptions to in-clude individuals who fell outside their immediate circles of friends, to see strangers as *like-others*. So gay men's desires for more and deeper associations were folded into their political goals in such a way that they must begin to ask what a gay community would mean and to widen the commonalities they felt with other gay men.

In the publications of the period, gay men left evidence of a broad undercur-rent of desire, a yearning for meaningful social interaction, for social support, and for recognition by other gay men—like-others who understood not only their abjection, but also the joys and pains of their loves and relationships; cul-tural tastes and burgeoning cultural production; experiences as gay men in other social settings such as family, work, and religion; and of course their sexual re-lationships. The struggles over ends and means for their counter-publics inevita-bly led to trying to define what exactly a gay community could and should be and what an individual gay man's relationship to it could or should be. The de-bates about community formation engrossed, divided, confounded, nurtured, tortured, supported, welcomed, and rejected the gay men of San Francisco throughout the 1960s. Gay men's abjection, their symbolic domination, with their diversity complicated their efforts to understand and direct their own com-munity. But the need for new kinds of social interaction and their desire to asso-ciate with each other in meaningful ways pushed them to forge ahead in their community-building efforts, even when many doubted that a gay community could exist at all. What they ended up with was an astoundingly porous, highly textured community with intricate tiers and layers, some of which reached back into the nineteenth century and others of which were newly formed in the 1960s.

Under the best of circumstances, the term *community* can confuse important issues. The word is commonly used to connote everything from a close-knit, small group of like individuals to a broadly defined, shapeless group of loosely allied individuals lumped together for semantic ease. In the case of San Fran-cisco's gay male community, it was empirically comprised of men who came with allegiances and bonds to other communal value systems (e.g., religious communities or ethnic communities) but who at the same time wanted a gay male community but didn't agree on what that meant. To fully understand these complex dynamics and contradictions among 1960s gay men in the Bay Area, I will be using a four-part definition of community for the rest of this book. These four aspects of community are sometimes conflicting and rarely clear-cut, as the men on the ground pushed and pulled with each other to enact their varied ideals of community; but these contradictions and conflicts must be held in solution with the practices and meanings gay men produced on the ground, with the ac-tual community they created, and with their notions of the ideal community they desired.

A theorist of communitarianism, Amitai Etzioni offers the first two aspects of community that I will be using here, namely, that communities are characterized by *affect-laden* interaction and a set of *shared values*.[2] For my purposes here, at the heart of gay male community, the affect-laden bonds were extremely tenuous. Some bonds carried over from previous communities, others were newly forming through efforts to identify with other gay men, and still others were only imagined or hoped for. But the existence of the *activity-undergoing* of such bonds cannot be denied from the evidence they left. Gay men either experienced themselves as members of a community, or they at least felt the presence or absence of a community of some sort that they longed for. For some, the feeling of membership was a consummatory experience, an end in itself. John Dewey described the experience of these affect-bonds and experience: "Whenever there is a conjoint activity whose consequences are appreciated as good by all singular persons who take part in it, and where the realization of the good is such as to effect an energetic desire and effort to sustain it in being just because it is a good shared by all, there is in so far a community."[3] The second aspect, shared values, is really at the core of gay male community development in this period. Gay men were fighting to understand what it would mean to be gay openly, in public, with full freedom or personhood, and in community with one another. The establishment of some form of interpersonal connections was a necessary step in providing the social context wherein those conversations could take place; and as those conversations progressed, they served to reinforce, expand, and ultimately establish a kind of community. Gay men have never, as a group, settled on a clear set of shared-values or meanings of gay-maleness, but they have continued the dialogue for going on fifty years now. As we will see in the later chapters, it is this ongoing dialogue about values and meanings that keeps the gay male community together, inasmuch as that community is necessary for the conversation to continue.

A third aspect of community is its *multiplicity*. Like Dewey's conception of public discussed in earlier chapters, community must be conceived as having layers and tiers, and individuals must be seen as having allegiances to multiple communities at once. Within any given community are smaller communities of individuals uniting and interacting for different reasons. And individual members of a community may also have simultaneous allegiances and bonds with other communities that are completely unrelated or unconnected from the community in question. Although for my discussion here, I will be referring to "gay community" and in San Francisco, I will insist that it always be seen as a field of social interaction comprised of a loose conglomeration of smaller communities and whose members are multiply allied to various other non-gay, and often oppositional, communities. For example, gay men had small interpersonal communities of friends and acquaintances, such as the informal networks of house parties; groups of men who frequented specific bars and neighborhoods also formed communal relationships and values; and communities formed from subcultures such as leather, S/M, and drag shared affect-bonds and values.[4] These informal associations persisted through the 1960s in a kind of cultural accrual and continuity—indeed, these older informal associations undergirded the community building of the 1960s. They did, however, change in character, composition, and meaning during the decade as they were exposed to the publicizing efforts of activists who questioned the validity of older lifestyles and sexualities. Although they retained their sub-cultural and resistant character, many of these smaller communities evolved from underground, secret social structures into open and often counter-public structures during the 1960s.

Fourth and finally, again from Dewey, community is a particular kind of social space that facilitates *meaningful communication*. As such, community is vital to the realization of both collective and individual ends. "To learn to be human is to develop through the give and take of communication an effective sense of being an individually distinctive member of a community; one who understands and appreciates its beliefs, desires, and methods, and who contributes to a further conversion of organic powers into human resources and values."[5] For Dewey, the primary social function of a community is to provide the context wherein communicative interaction can occur to lend meaning to experience and where individuals and groups can work to create a social context for the consummation of their desires. Seeing community as a context for communicative interaction for the consummation of desires gives a groundwork from which we can evaluate the successes and failures of gay community formation in this period. We have already seen in Chapter 2 that this kind of communicative interaction allowed gay men to combat the symbolic domination of the psychiatric, legal, and religious institutions of the time. But more than a mere reaction to the dominant culture, gay men successfully created a community where they could struggle and work out the meanings of their lives and experiences and where they could establish new social spaces for the consummation of their various desires. Gay community emerged as, among other things, the social space where important arguments could be had, allowing gay men to talk and argue about their experience of same-sex desire, of sex and relationships, of gender, their experience of oppression, and their reactions to various anti-gay discourses. In Deweyan terms, *meaning* itself arose among gay men directly out of this kind of communal interaction; indeed, it could not exist without it. The meaning of gay desires and practices accrued over time as gay men debated the potential conflicts and consequences of their desires and practices. This association of particular practices and meanings with particular social outcomes and effects is the very core of meaning formation. Having sex with another man, dressing in drag, going to a gay bar, or participating in a "zap" action were all necessarily marked by the meaning they acquired in gay men's communicative interaction.

Gay men who would establish a community functioned under the assumption that gay men could indeed form meaningful communal bonds and that community formation was worthwhile for both personal and political reasons. The actual community they ended up with, which I will be describing in detail over the next few chapters, emerged out of a complex interaction between individual gay men, their desires for community, the meanings they imputed on their communal interactions, and the conflicts they had over values and normatives and boundaries. As the community emerged, it automatically increased the number and scope of gay men's social interactions; it reflexively reshaped and formed gay men themselves as they adopted the meanings they were begetting in their communal interaction. With the individual and the community shaping and being shaped by each other, the community became more, rather than less, rife with meaningful conflict.

Gay Organizations and Community before 1969

While the various gay organizations formed between constituted the social space necessary for the formation of gay publicity, they were also the social spaces necessary for the creation of new kinds of gay communities, in whatever form they may have taken. Of particular importance in the first two-thirds of the decade, the League of Civil Education and the Society for Individual Rights left a detailed account of the relationship between political organization and community building, as they served as major points of face-to-face and symbolic contact among gay men and women. Vanguard also was founded during the middle part of the decade and, serving those who were excluded from SIR, brought more nuanced and critical views of community to the table. Building community upon the foundations set by pre-existing sub-cultural communities (e.g., bar communities) from previous decades and the work started by the 1950s organizations, these groups had the new task of incorporating their emerging publicity into notions of community. Leaders touted the possibility of "gay community"[6] (or "deviate" or "homophile" community), and their members endeavored to understand, express, and consummate their desires for community belonging. Whereas the LCE wondered if such a disparate group of individuals could form a community at all, SIR came to see gay men's social lives as integral to their political cause; for its part, Vanguard saw itself as a foil to SIR, highlighting the weakness of SIR's community. All three groups, however, included men with competing desires: they didn't agree on whether or not a community was necessary or desirable; those gay men who desired community with other gay men disagreed on what constituted a community and how to organize it; and the organizations had political goals that sometimes conflicted with community building.[7] By trying to define gay community out of gay politics, these men were simultaneously giving a social depth to their understandings of the meaning of "gay" as such.[8]

During the early 1960s, the League of Civil Education was focused primarily on securing individual rights (at least that's how it presented itself in Guy Strait's publications). This focus on individual rights coupled with a view that gay men were a shockingly diverse bunch led Strait to the conclusion that gay community may not be possible or even desirable. And so in articles and letters to the editor, gay men expressed an interesting tension: the doubt that a community could exist, but the hope that it would. Early on, Guy Strait argued that the LCE[9] should be single-issue driven, that "social deviants" have nothing in common but their deviance.[10] So the LCE espoused a community that was limited to a constituency of political and legal *like-others*; but the kinds of intimacies and social bonds found in the bedrock sub-cultures and informal associations of the pre-existing homophile culture (e.g., bar communities, circles of friends, house parties) frequently erupted into discussion about community, as LCE members, readers, and observers wanted more than a mere political organization. But Strait rejected the personal role a community could play and argued in 1963, "We use the word 'Community' in the sense that we have, in our ranks every facet of life necessary to qualify as a true community. . . . We do not think of a 'community' as a place where one person looks after the other" (*TN* Dec. 23, 1963, 1–2).[11] This ambivalence about what a community should mean grew out of Strait's insistence that the community was merely a collection of "deviants" who formed a political minority. Interestingly, for Strait, this was a minority that had to be formed through "constant vigilance and comment" (*TN* July 22, 1963, 1).[12] Reflected in Strait's arguments with himself, there emerged a context-specific mode of thinking about sexual community that would be powerful but short-lived. Interestingly, this concept and its concomitant experiences rejected a homosexual identity as an adequate basis upon which to build a meaningful gay community. Instead it relied upon the democratic interests of "individual dignity and protection of civil rights" as the basis of the community the LCE sought (*TN* Oct. 14, 1963).[13]

But others argued against Strait and observed that the LCE was serving to foster more broadly defined interpersonal relationships. From the first year of the LCE's existence, gay men had argued that the community must be something more than just a collection of individuals with similar political interests. For example, a guest columnist suggested that more national and international news should be included in *The News* to be interpreted from the "variant viewpoint"; he obviously believed there was a more salient commonality, a perspective that went beyond political interest. He also suggested a "Sound Off" column about local theater and arts that would cover events beyond the sub-cultural coverage (e.g., drag shows), which were already included in *The News*. This guest columnist also suggested changes for LCE itself, that it should have a legal advisory committee and have direct fund raising campaigns. "I have more ideas," he concluded, "but I am sure that every member of the Community has something constructive to offer" (*TN* Oct. 14, 1963, 7–8). So at least by late 1963, some gay men in San Francisco were seeking a more expansive and encompassing kind of community than the one they saw reflected in Strait's small publication, distributed in bars.

In 1964, when a group of dissatisfied LCE board members walked out of a board meeting to form a new group,[14] another way of conceiving of gay community manifested itself in the Society for Individual Rights. Despite its name, SIR greatly expanded the role organizations could play in providing a community. Namely, it saw itself as a source of security, a refuge from social alienation, where gay men and women could interact, form bonds, share views, and help each other. In this view, organizations served as a kind of community of refugees, of people who needed escape from a dominating society. They connected this kind of community with their political, liberal democratic core values, namely the need for individual rights and for political recognition.[15] But in its conception of gay community, SIR took several steps beyond where the LCE had stopped, by seeing one of their primary tasks as providing a "social fabric" wherein gay people could come to understand and feel their own dignity and worth.[16] Seeing themselves as beleaguered by the dominant society,[17] SIR anchored its conceptions of community in the lived experiences of gay men. SIR's Statement of Policies argued that among the primary needs of members of the gay community was "the need to provide our people with an honorable *social fabric*. . . . In particular to provide an attractive, meaningful and healthy social fabric for the well-being of our Members" (*VR* Dec. 1964, 1, emphasis added).[18] This addition of "social fabric" to the understanding of community was a dramatic departure from Strait's and the LCE's insistence that community should be limited to the political needs of a deviant minority. This change in focus would set the stage for the development of a new kind of gayness.

The hints and traces of the experience of belonging and the desire to belong that poked through in LCE's publications became explicit in SIR's. Within the first year of its publication, *Vector*'s pages began to speak of "a feeling of community" and a "community spirit"[19] evident among gay men. This raised conflicts with older homophile organizations, which argued that SIR was merely doubling the efforts they had already done.[20] But SIR leadership forged ahead, starting all sorts of new activities, committees, and projects to form a new kind of community that included group affiliations and interpersonal associations under the aegis of the counter-public organization: through its existence, such groups included the SIRporium, a thrift store to fund SIR; the SIRcapades, a yearly variety show; a support group for deaf gay men; art classes; health and fitness classes; and political discussion groups. Even as they set up a membership organization, they envisioned SIR's importance as universal among homosexuals. "We are meant to include all expressions of the homosexual community. Each member fits into those aspects he wishes, but no member has a right to exclude anyone but himself" (*VR* Dec. 1965, 2).[21] This fed into an idea that the "feeling of community" would create a unification of homosexuals and become a "gay movement."[22] SIR tried to present itself as open to all and used the prospect of community to recruit[23]; and many wrote *Vector* talking about how SIR met their needs and desires for community.[24] SIR was obviously filling some deep need for many of its membership. In the end, at the level of gay men's communal experience, SIR's efforts to create a social fabric and foster a communal feeling had as great an impact as their efforts to form a counter-public; both served to meet the needs of men who experienced abjection in the public sphere.

But not everyone's needs were met by this community. Because of California laws, young homosexuals were excluded from joining SIR until they were twenty-one. The young, often poor youth of color, along with other outcasts from SIR's social fabric, such as the transgendered and hustlers, found a different kind of organization in Vanguard. Sponsored by Glide Memorial Church. Like SIR had done before it, Vanguard saw its mission as primarily to protect against the negative effects of what I have called symbolic violence.[25] Calling themselves the "idealists of the slums," Vanguard moved beyond political activism, but in a way that no other group of the period would do: they spoke explicitly of the difference poverty and racism make on homosexuals' experiences of oppression and domination, and they specifically geared themselves to serving youth up to the age of twenty-one, whom SIR explicitly excluded. In many ways Vanguard advocated the values of social revolution a few years before Stonewall and connected to the imagery and ideas of the counter-culture, which was then flourishing in San Francisco, seeking to "promote an environment of love and understanding between all the peoples of the earth" (*VG* Feb. 1967); but they also sought the basics of recognition, appreciation, and dignity.

Among the first publications to speak explicitly of a "sexual identity," *Vanguard* writers spoke often of a "search for identity" that would be fostered in the kind of more encompassing and wide-reaching gay community Vanguard sought to create. Much of this arose from the values and experiences Rev. Williams brought to Glide from the Civil Rights movement, combined with the brutal poverty and violence of the Tenderloin neighborhood, and the awareness that comes from being gay in the dominant culture. Vanguard's social actions ranged from encounter nights at Glide Memorial church to the publication of the organization's newsletter, all with the highest of hopes and ideals driving their push toward community. Vanguard's community, then, was a community built in a deeper, more complicated abjection, one fraught with other social divisions of age, race, poverty, and gender identity. This was, in many ways, a gayness outside of gayness.

These early years saw gay men coming to terms with several hard realities about their community and about the meaning of gay. Gay men were so diverse, that at any given moment they could meet another gay men with whom they had nothing in common except their "sexual proclivity." And so gayness seems to be a very narrow, individual affair. Yet they experienced a shared domination, and they came from already-established sub-cultures that allowed some kind of cohesion to form, as evidenced by the existence and persistence of gay organizations in the Bay Area. And so gayness seemed to be amenable to a communal definition, that is, that when interests and experiences and desires coincided, gayness could be conceived of communally, as something enacted with other gay men. Around the fringes in these early years was the idea that gay community should be conceived of as a collection of disparate homosexuals who, together, could be empowered to *be* gay. Harry Hay, for example, argued in several different publications and articles that building a community comprised of a coalition of kinds of gay men would actually enable the social and political needs of gay men to be met. Where men continued throughout the period to insist that gay community wasn't desireable or necessary, others continued to insist that gay community was the source of empowerment.[26] As we will see, despite all their efforts, there were many gay men who remained dissatisfied gay community as it had been constituted organizationally in San Francisco.[27]

Gay Religious Movements as Community

As we saw in Chapter 1, many gay men were religious or had attachments to their cultural identities as being religious, and many gay men found meaning and power in religion. Not surprisingly then, one of the ways that gay men worked to form community was to form religious groups. These gay religious movements and gay religious sensibilities led to slightly different conceptions of gay community. As some gay men sought to transform their religious lives into something that made sense of their experiences of homosexuality, they created communities of religious gay men who engaged each other on different terms than those of the political organizations. Here, gay men's community were defined in terms of the sacred and the moral Good. Nelson Chuang, for example, thought a religious gay community would bring a "more *wholesome social recreation* as well as promote *deeper and more meaningful social understanding*" (*VR* July 1968, 16–17, emphasis mine). Chuang's argument reflects both the overall desire for "deeper" social interaction and also the belief that religion could be one possible source for such interaction that drove much of the gay religious community building efforts. As William James described the religious experience as something *MORE*[28]—a higher or transcendent experience of the self, the loss of the self's boundaries, the expansion of the self—so did gayness take on this desire for something *more* in these religious contexts.

In the early part of the decade, churches formed service and outreach groups for homosexuals, bridging the gap between homosexuality and religiosity in interesting ways, given the times. The Council on Religion and the Homosexual, founded in 1964,[29] saw as one of its primary purposes to bring about full acceptance of homosexuals in mainstream churches. The CRH explained itself in *Vector* as "an attempt to realize the identity of the homophile in today's society and to provide an ecumenical and inter-sexual ministry to people who are deviant from generally accepted norms" (*VR* March 1967, 20).[30] Because its goal was integration into existing churches, CRH's members often shied away from gay community building as such.[31] But the CRH set the groundwork for other gay men and women to consider their communities in religious terms. Between the founding of CRH and the first Pride Parade in 1972, ads for gay church services had become common in San Francisco's gay publications, including not only new gay denominations and congregations, but gay versions of established churches, even including for example Monday afternoon services for gay Mormons.[32]

Glide Memorial Methodist Church in the Tenderloin and Cecil Williams' ministry to gay men and lesbians in the mid-1960s were key factors in the development of gay community, as Williams explicitly encouraged community building among gay men and women. Glide worked culturally to shift the meanings of homosexuality both in Sunday sermons and in holding conferences about homosexuality. In October 1968, at a conference on "The Lifestyle of the Homosexual," Williams gave a pro-gay speech in which he argued that the role of the church was to "'create a new concept (other than pervert) for homosexuals, a concept that will allow gay people to become fully human individuals free of fear and guilt about their homosexuality,'" (*VR* Nov. 1968, 5). A later "Gay Symposium" at Glide in 1969 sought to bring together mental health workers and ministers from around the Bay Area to educate them on gay issues. But for community building, it was the Glide chapel itself that played the most significant role. Glide provided the space for SIR's early meetings and community events before they built their Community House. And when it formed Vanguard, Glide proved a diverse and welcoming space for the most tread-upon homosexual. A young man described a Vanguard meeting in the basement of the Glide chapel in 1967: "Then the drags were there. Food for anyone in the basement. I saw pornographic movies in a room while a political discussion was in progress. We moved to Indian Chanting in the Sanctuary. . . . The church is a live building. Look around" (*VG* March 1967). The Reverend in charge of Vanguard insisted that the combination of religion and gay liberation could produce a powerful resistance to injustice in American society and could create a more fulfilling community for gays (see *VG* 1.7, 29).[33]

Outside of the mainstream church, gay folks began forming their own separate, explicitly gay religions and religious organizations. Most famously, Rev. Troy Perry started a gay denomination in Los Angeles in 1969 called the Metropolitan Community Church. Perry came to speak to SIR in August 1969 and spoke of a gay Christianity that both reached beyond the boundaries of gay community by engaging in charitable service, but also would insist on its gayness (his congregants handed out cards that read, "You've just been helped by a member of the homophile community).[34] The combination of religious values with gay culture often led to tensions in the community, where religious gay men often moralized against gay male cultural practices, such as bar-going and casual sex. A *Vector* writer responded to one such incident by arguing that there was an inherent disconnect between Christianity and homosexuality that brings judgment, division, and self-righteousness into the community.[35] In the Bay Area, a combination of gay liberation and radical Christians formed a group called Agape in Action, which saw the MCC as just a gay version of what was wrong with Bible Belt fundamentalism.[36] Agape hoped, nonetheless, that a gay religious movement would necessary challenge the assumptions of traditional Christianity and bring about the possibility of a gay Christian theology. Other gay religious groups formed as service organizations, such as The Community of St. John the Beloved, which provided housing, food, employment counseling, draft counseling, clothing, and legal and medical referrals.[37]

These religious organizations didn't so much redefine gay community as transform ideals of Christian community for gay adherents. They overlapped gay organizations in their activism and provided contexts for the affect-laden bonds necessary for community formation, adding the powerful bond of religious identification and experience to that of sexual difference. Although these groups represent a range of possibilities for gay Christianity, they all imbue gayness with a transformative possibility. Building on themes common in Christian mythos, they saw gayness as a reminder for heterosexuals about their ethical and moral responsibilities to the downtrodden and as a possible conduit to restore a more authentic, more deeply ethical kind of Christianity.[38]

But as much as some gay men found community and meaning in their religious endeavors, other saw religion as hindrance to community and as detrimental to gayness. These gay men and women attempted to take part in alternatives to religious organizations, rejecting the religious for the secular, yet often seeking something more than the organizations could offer. Among those secular movements that appealed to some gay men by 1972 was American Humanism. The Humanist Movement grew out of a 1933 effort by John Dewey and other American intellectuals to create "non-theistic alternative to the Judeo-Christian religions" (*VR* Feb. 1972, 11).[39] Gay Sunshine rejected the religiosity of gay people, but adapted religious rhetoric both to reject religion and to effect its revolution. They often used the rhetoric of religion to make revolutionary value statements, and in this case, used it to reject religion itself.[40] Still others actively fought against gay religiosity, seeing religion as an unnecessary drag on the homosexual movement that, in their view, held no positive reward for gay men.[41] As should be expected, the primary argument against the involvement of religion in the gay movement was the history of oppression, especially spiritual oppression based on faulty morality, perpetrated by the Christian Church in particular. Religious rules proved to be, for these critics, anti-human and by nature, anti-gay. The *BAR* argued that gay churches were destructive to homosexuals because they "narcotized so many homosexuals [and] are nothing but a drugging drag. Spiritually starved queens should get themselves to a nunnery" (*BAR* Jan. 1, 1972). Another critic, Steve Ginsburg, couldn't understand why gay folks even cared that churches rejected them. "Who cares except them and what for? Most gays don't give a shit about the church; and then there are others who don't belong to any of the Christian faiths" (*GS* April–May 1971, 16). *Gay Sunshine* ran an anti-religious political cartoon in 1971 that depicted a bunch of animals in ecclesiastical garb approaching a gay rights rally. The caption read, "Let us prey" (*GS* Oct.–Nov. 1971, cover).

It is clear that many overlapping desires were converging in these religious efforts at gay community formation. These men carried with them their religious values from childhood or perhaps discovered religion anew as they came out; regardless, there was a desire among many to continue their religious lives and religious affiliations. The affective aspects of religious experience leant themselves to the formation of gay communities centered around religious practice and served for a reformulation of the meaning of gay in particularly Christian

terms. Whether it was the early advocacy of pastors from the protestant communities, the use of the physical space at Glide Memorial, or the efforts of gay men
and women themselves to form gay religions, the role of religion in San Francisco's community formation must not be pushed aside. Clearly, just as religion
imputed abject meanings, symbolic domination, upon homosexuality forcing
gay men and women to shirk religious oppression, so did religion provide contexts, spaces and meanings useful to gay men in building their communities and
creating a meaningful gayness.

Gay Liberation as Community:
Authenticity as a Value

Members and leaders of the gay liberation organizations in the Bay Area infused
their notions of community (and consequently, their notions of gayness) with
some of the language and values of the counter-culture movement and other
political movements of the time.[42] Gay men across the political spectrum and
from various organizations had begun to argue for the *specificity* of gayness, that
is, the *difference* of gay men and women; and they believed that a "true" gay
community was needed to nurture this uniqueness within gay individuals.[43] As
with the battles over political values discussed in Chapters 1 and 3, the battles
over what a gay community should look like often boiled down to arguments
over *authenticity*, what it should mean to be authentically gay. These arguments
about authenticity anchored gay community well below mere sexual desire, to
the presentation of and the deepest personal feelings about the self; this view of
community focused on the psychology of the individual and had personal *identity* at its core. This notion of authenticity had deep ties to the values of the hippie movement's communal lifestyle of the mid-1960s (before its popularization),
and it insisted on the fundamental difference between gays and straights and
sought to produce a social environment that would nurture self-fulfillment for
gay individuals through personal expression that could be classified as authentic
to the individual but simultaneously gay, which was conceived as a shared characteristic of the authentic individual.

But the liberationist community was fraught with deep contradictions. Following the convention of the times, gay libbers called each other "brother," in-
voking the language of fraternity and acceptance even as they condemned and
rejected the communities and cultures of the older forms of gay communal life,
such as bar communities and the leather and drag communities.[44] In their writings and actions, they assumed the possibility of establishing a coherent homosexual community, even as they idealized an essential (Freudian) bisexuality and
argued that humans ideally should be open to all sexual relationships without
sexual orientations impeding the way.[45] These kinds of inherent contradictions
drive San Francisco gay liberation's antipathy toward older gay men and older
gay organizations[46] as they struggle to create a new kind of gay community.

In the most general of terms, gay liberation took the notion of pride (which actually first appeared in Guy Strait's papers in 1961) and elevated it to a normative that would serve as the foundation for a generally more thoroughgoing (albeit sexually diverse) community. Whereas earlier organizations had spoken of pride, they had done so in terms of the individual's psychological well-being. For gay liberation, pride grew out of interaction with like-others and out of a purposeful effort to create a new kind of community and a movement. Pride was the rallying call both for political activism and for rejection of other forms of gayness.[47] These calls for Gay Pride gradually produced a kind of gay authenticity that consisted of the personal liberation centered around coming out, political activism, and association in the activist community; it wanted to "turn other gay people on," to raise consciousness and build a community of love and acceptance; it sought not only to free homosexuals, but to "free the homosexual in everyone" (see *SFFP* Dec. 7, 1969, 6).

The Gay Sunshine Collective, formed in Berkeley in the early 1970s, produced some of the most complex arguments on the meaning of gay community and authenticity to come out of the period. At the end of 1971,[48] when a handful of Gay Sunshine founders met to discuss the practice of "Gay Rap"—gay consciousness raising groups being held in the Bay Area—they ended up instead trying to figure out what a gay community should be. They saw both false and true communities; and they confronted the tension between the individual and the community head on. Winston Leyland argued that the individual could not actually be liberated (have his consciousness raised) in isolation, that it required a community.[49] Whereas a false community was an unrealizable "feel-good" community, a true community provided the context necessary for liberation, and they feared that gay liberation was failing to establish a true gay community. This was partially the fault of older gay men, according to this group, who weren't part of the movement and refused to change.[50] Here as in other areas, gay liberation experienced a "historical forgetfulness" about the gay organizing and community activism that had preceded them. They saw themselves as the first to get people to think positively about being gay. They thought they were the first to tackle unemployment and poverty among gays and lesbians, as well as the first to tackle the psychological problems of being gay.[51] So authenticity emerges here as the boundary dividing true gay community from false.

The Emmaus House, a short-lived gay commune on Polk Street, had a notion of community and authenticity more closely allied with the counter-culture. Here it was an authenticity of being true to oneself in a communal setting.[52] The project was to bring people together by turning them inward to their authentic selves; if this could not be achieved, there would never be freedom from oppression. Like Gay Sunshine, Emmaus House sought to differentiate itself from the existing older-form communities; but rather than do so from a moralizing stance, Emmaus thought to include all kinds of gayness in a kind of psychic wholeness of the individual.[53] This was the most open form of authenticity I discerned among the gay liberation groups, where what was sought was a space for gay people to be gay, where gayness could emerge from a safe social environment;

Emmaus saw authenticity as something that emerged and could be nurtured, not something that was already known that could be defined and defended. *I Am* articles consistently referred to the authentic gay community as a kind of gay, chosen family that would, through its love and communion, free the individuals who chose to be there.[54] Emmaus's gay community was something created, chosen, and nurtured, which would change to meet the needs of those in the community. In its second year, Emmaus House added the idea of social revolution to its understanding of community. The gayness produced in Emmaus House was, then, familial, flexible, deeply in touch with true core self, and in so doing, was enacting revolution. This kind of gayness was deeply individualistic, but in a more existential way. Whereas the LCE had seen individuality as both the political basis of its actions and the impediment to community, Emmaus House sees the individual as an end in itself and gay community as the context for the discovery and expression of that almost sacred self.[55]

These gay men believed that only gay liberation could provide authentic gay life and community. Even in the pages of *Vector*, they argued that a true community, a gay liberation community, should offer a "way of accepting himself that semi-private and adult-oriented liberal groups cannot" (Oct. 1970, 38). Older communities were not only inferior, but false. Authenticity, true gayness and true community, would be the natural consequences of the "new way of life" gay liberation worked for.[56] Often, this authenticity was conceived as a community of "soul" or of affect, in a kind of qualification of the affect-laden bonds necessary for community formation. Turning to Tina Turner and Janis Joplin for support, Charles Thorp conceived of a true community thusly: "'Workin' together we can make a change. Workin' together we can have better things,' Tina sings. It's really the only moral to this tragic story. We got to do, as Janis screams, 'try just a little bit harder—so I can give, give, give every bit of my soul.' And with the giving of our soul will come the strength and answers" (*SFGFP* Dec. 1970). Importantly, the gay libbers saw community as something to be actively sought out and created, not something that appeared of its own accord.[57] But such a community had to be a *gay* community, with "its own politics, and also its own values . . . but we must start with radical new ideas and not repeat those old lies under which we have lived for so long" (*GS* May 1972, 7).

Whereas for LCE, the problem with gay community had been about the heterogeneity of homosexuals and the resulting difficulties for political unity, let alone community formation[58]; but for gay liberation, the problem lay in the contradiction between the exclusivity of their ideals of "authenticity" and their professed values of inclusiveness and acceptance. Although in the drawing of their in/out boundaries, the gay liberation groups were often blind to this contradiction, some were keen to it and criticized Gay Sunshine and gay liberation in general for its exclusivity, seeing gay liberation as a movement of "negation." Allen Young argued that gay liberation's community used revolutionary language and cultures of personal presentation in dress and gender expression as tools of exclusion. "But I was not prepared to take—and I now more than ever firmly reject—total negation of myself as a person and as a brother because I would not embrace the pierced-ears, semi-drag appearance which some gay men enjoy and insist is the proper revolutionary behavior" (*GS* June–July 1971, 2, 5).[59] Other gay men experienced gay liberation as an elitist group. Dick Jones observed, "One reason I left gay lib was the development of gay elitism, an 'I'm more liberated than you are' competition, and hostilities based on political ideologies—and a tremendous tendency for many people to label and classify others." (*GS* June–July 1971, 14). Jones elaborated the hierarchies of liberation, which excluded "closet queens," those who didn't engage in gender fuck, and those who didn't present with the correct politics. Jones concluded by saying that the social pressure of a meat market gay bar was no worse than the political pressure of a typical gay liberation meeting. "As for me, let me laugh at my oppressors—at all these political, metaphysical, pseudo-ethical ideologies—at all their blindness and stupidity—even if I die laughing."

The problems of exclusion were common across all the organizational communities that formed during the 1960s, but they often arose from different sources. Even as gay organizations struggled with the notion and formation of gay community, they also inevitably left many gay men out (and some gay men chose to remain outside). Gay liberation's focus on authenticity created a community that sought a kind of political or cultural purity, even as it often claimed to provide the only space for true individuality. This reveals a conflict in the meaning of gay as it was being produced among gay liberation. On one hand, gayness was an intensely individual aspect of the self that could only arise in true community, but there was also clearly a right and a wrong way to be gay. Gayness, then, was the gayness that conformed to the libbers particular brand of politics and cultural presentation. By 1972, some gay men outside of the gay lib movement felt that liberation had actually weakened (or maybe even destroyed) the community that had developed through the 1960s.[60] when many gay men felt more and more alienated from gay liberation, they argued that it was actually leading to the dissolution of the community that had already been on the scene when gay liberation arrived in 1969. Much of the time frame of this disillusionment with gay liberation coincides historically with the demise of the hippie movement and of the New Left in general. Activists were exhausted from such hard work with no discernable results; the hippie ideals had given way to a burned out war zone in the Haight-Ashbury district; Reagan had won his war against the radicals at Berkeley. For gay men disillusioned by the community that gay libbers advocated, the contradictions, the impossible moralizing, and the lack of tangible progress had exhausted them.

Strategies of Community Building

It was one thing to talk about community and ponder its meaning and extol its virtues and decry its vices, but actually creating community and maintaining it required constant work and attention. Indeed, the discussions I have outlined above are part of the work: By engaging in the discussion about what community is, gay men were in effect producing community. From the outset, the LCE hosted an intense, ongoing dialogue about how to create a more satisfying community that would fulfill the social needs of the "variant community." This dialogue persisted through the decade, and I would argue continues into the twenty-first century. Because of the persistent tension among gay men's different kinds of communal desires, values, politics, and gay practices that constantly threatened the dissolution of the community, activists found that once the base of a community had been formed, it required unending vigilance to ensure sufficient affective bonds and shared values just to hold the community together.

Discursively, gay publications throughout the period, regardless of their respective visions of community or politics, all insisted on a kind of *mutual recognition* among gay men to form *group identifications*. We have already seen how the tension between the individual and the group complicated their efforts to formulate effective ends for their counter-public; I found this area of debate to be yet another in which the relationship between the individual and the group formed the boundaries for discussions about the meaning of gay. From the archival record, it appears that this strategy arose organically out of the experiences of entering the public sphere, which required a degree of group cohesion absent in the earlier forms of cultural and citizen community of the 1950s. The idea of recognition provoked intense cultural conflicts as gay men tried to articulate what exactly they recognized in each other and why. The various answers they came up with moved through the period and accrued to form the constitutive dialectics of gay male community: not just whether or not to be part of a gay community, but when to belong, when to withdraw, why, with whom, to what ends, where, and how.

In the early 1960s, recognition meant a simple shared oppression and therefore of a shared interest in reforming the official public sphere to accommodate sexual difference. This notion of recognition of oppression lasted through the period and across community formations, and indeed continues to this day. Even *Gay Sunshine* wanted to be a newspaper for "those who understand themselves as oppressed" (*GS* Aug.–Sept. 1970, 2). Later, recognition became a moral imperative not just to recognize the common oppression, but to consider the good of the group.[61] As the Committee for Homosexual Freedom began its short life, its leaders argued that commitment to the cause came from a knowledge that activism without group identification was a form of death.[62] Gay liberation believed that their movement would generate a group identification requisite for community formation, and perhaps even so powerful that it might provoke violent backlash.[63] Here again, the relative salience of gayness comes into play. Is it merely your choice of sex partners, or is it your entire being? One gay libber argued, "I am not Gay because of where I put my cock or whom I sleep with. I am Gay because everything about me is Gay, because I am part of a Gay community. I was Gay long before I admitted my homosexuality to myself, long before I ever had sex, long before I knew what sex was" (*GS* Aug.–Sept. 1970, 12). In this mode, recognition requires a very wide view indeed, where whole people are "gay." Here, gayness exists prior to community, before self-awareness even, creating a mutually constitutive relationship between sexual desire and identity.

A second means of community building, service and social activities, could serve as the impetus for collective action and the founding of the affective bonds of community. *Citizens News* publicized a community service called Coffee Break in 1964, hoping that it would serve to "broaden the friendships" and "the base of social life of the Community" (*CN* 3.24, 11), as a sort of clearinghouse for community services ranging from bail bondsmen to employment counseling.[64] Gay organizations constantly produced social events ranging from picnics to drag balls, often as fundraisers, but apparently always well attended.[65] Pictures from *Vector* in February 1972 show such diverse goings-on as a karate class, a dance, a New Year's party, and an art class.[66] On at least two occasions in the early 1960s, funerals were organized either for gay men and women without family or for gay individuals' family members.[67] Both the LCE and SIR sponsored health initiatives such as blood drives[68] and VD clinics.[69] In the early 1970s, SIR envisioned a retirement home for aging gays and lesbians (a still unrealized dream in San Francisco).[70] Numerous educational forums, such as SIR's "Friday Series," came and went during the period.[71] SIR even started a support group for married men, those who "discover their sexual preferences too late" (*VR* March 1972, 16).[72] Gay activists organized numerous phone banks and hotlines, to report police harassment or to provide an understanding person to talk to.[73] Many groups also provided counseling services for their members.[74] And even more common were counseling and legal services for military servicemen kicked out of the military for homosexuality.[75] SIR would even eventually start a group for deaf gay men and women, called The Silent Society.[76] Such activities served to strengthen the notion of a gay community that transcended the boundaries of the various organizations and often of other kinds of identities as well. This is the most basic of social-psychological observations: interaction produces social bonds.

In the early 1970s, echoing the cultural efforts in other movements of the period, the gay libbers adopted consciousness raising groups such as "Gay Rap"[77] as a means to foster community. Believing that community (and gayness itself) required the right attitude,[78] they called together groups of men to "encounter" each other in honest dialogue and deep sharing. The belief was that such activities would make gay men aware of their oppression and their shared experiences with other gay men, and ultimately would create the consciousness necessary for the gay liberation community to cohere.[79] Lee Atwell wrote, "Maybe it [gay rap] didn't produce that [a sense of community] for you, but it has for a lot of other people. A lot of people have been coming regularly week after week and it's a really important part of their lives" (*GS* Dec. 1971–Jan. 1972, 1, 13). The social activities and consciousness raising groups, according to the accounts left by men from the period, were perhaps the most salient loci of the *activity-undergoing* of being gay in 1960s San Francisco Bay Area. They provided the social spaces necessary for actual face-to-face interaction with other gay men, and through their interaction, gay men did as a group cohere into loosely organized communities.

Finally, gay organizations came to understand from the beginning that community required not just social interaction, but the physical space for that interaction to occur. In the early part of the decade, gay men and women mostly congregated in bars or at people's homes, so there was already a shared knowledge of the importance of shared physical space. By the mid-1960s, this came to be seen as inadequate if a real community was to be formed. Soon after the demise of the LCE, members of SIR and CRH proposed the idea of a "half-way house" that would serve the homosexual man who was "jobless, broke, emotionally sick, on dope or drink"; this house would not only be a place where bodily needs could be met, but where a homosexual "can feel the warmth of people caring about him just because he is a man" (*CN* 4.5 (Dec. 1964), 2). And so the first gay space emerging from the newly forming gay publicity was conceived for the San Francisco Bay Area. This first iteration of a community space was positioned specifically to meet the problems gay men faced in a society that oppressed them and would serve the personal needs of individual gay men, to provide psychic safety and to provide a sense of belonging.

Although this halfway house was never built, SIR took up the idea and transformed it into the SIR Community House, with much broader social and cultural goals. SIR leadership felt like alienation from society created a situation that foreclosed the possibility of meaningful relationships with other homosexuals, so the Community House was to provide the actual space necessary for those relationship to form. The discussions about the space need to be taken together with the understanding of the breadth of activities that would eventually be hosted there, listed above. SIR hoped the space would encourage individuals to bond together and help each other, evoke a sense of compassion, and help "the individual homosexual in finding his own place in the larger human community" by providing "an accepting, loving environment" (*VR* May 1965, 1). The Community House opened on April 17, 1966, and quickly became one of the key cultural and social centers of the gay movement in the city, outside of the bars. The significance of this community space for those with access to it cannot be underestimated: it served as meeting space for numerous groups affiliated with SIR, it was a locus for the public side of drag culture through campy reviews and theater productions, community service projects such as employment boards, and even for a center of militant activism in the early 1970s.[80]

Other groups tried to establish physical spaces for social interaction as well, including Gay Sunshine and the MCC. Gay Sunshine tried to create an informal coffee house, called $5^2 \ 4^2$ that was held once per week in someone's house.[81] They wanted to offer alternatives to what they saw as the regressive spaces of gay bars and bathhouses.[82] Gay Sunshine looked to the community center in Los Angeles as the model they wanted to follow to provide services to the gay community, but outside the "radical ghetto."[83] In fact, by early 1972, they had begun to reformulate their notion of radicalism to be one that would work out of Community Service Centers like those in LA and Seattle.[84] Again, the libbers ignored or rejected the existence of existing community centers, such as SIR's Community House. Despite their dreams of a community house for gay liberation, Gay Sunshine's plans never gelled during this period. The MCC House was established to help homeless gay people in the city, aimed to relieve their oppression and meeting the physical and emotional needs of individual gay men and women.[85] Doug Brown hoped that MCC house would alleviate some of the effects of what I have called symbolic domination and begin to create a better life for the members of the community by getting gays involved in serving and helping other gays.

Finally, the Emmaus House, discussed earlier, differed from other organizations' spaces in that its main purpose was to provide a communal social space, in the mode of counter-cultural communes. As we have seen, the ends of Emmaus were internally focused, about consciousness raising creating an authentic gay community made up of authentic gay individuals. This space was conceived of as a place apart, a different social world from that of the domiant social order of modern "Amerika".[86] The founders of the house believed that the worst part of gay oppression was that society worked to keep gay people from each other, keep them separated; their response was to form a quasi-separatist space for gay people to be together. But the Emmaus House also believed in education and invited non-members to workshops and consciousness raising activities as well.[87] Whereas the other community spaces were conceived as the location of community forming activities, the Emmaus House's commune saw the physical space as constitutive of the community itself. Without the House as context for chosen families and day-to-day engagement, the true authentic community could not form. Based on the New York Emmaus House, the founder of San Francisco's all-gay iteration argued that no liberation could take place unless homosexuals themselves came together to form such a meaningful and supportive community (see *IA* 1.2).

Political Barriers to Community Building

Many sources of dissension—ranging from simple personality differences to significant differences in values—continually threatened to undermine gay community building, not to mention the counter-public or the political actions of various organizations. Individual gay men came to gay community with vastly different values, needs, and desires, which in turn created diverse and contradictory relationships to their like-others. For many, their experience made them fear that a gay community would be counter-productive, that it would incite repression by the official public (e.g., the police entrapment or loss of employment). Others rejected the idea of gay community altogether as a strategy to position themselves in the official public sphere and in their other community affiliations, such as with their family and friends. But during the 1960s and early

1970s, as San Francisco's gay men sought interactions beyond those offered by the older-style bars and sub-cultures, and as they came to desire their *freedom of personhood*, the meaning of gay community shifted and along with it, the meaning of gayness itself.[88]

At the micro-political level, throughout the decade many gay men resisted both counter-publicity and community-building efforts. Such men's voices were powerful enough that activists often addressed their critiques and concerns both in meetings and in publications. And for their part, these resisters attended meetings and wrote for the various publications to express their dissatisfaction, fear, and anger. Activists and organizers saw the range of men who withdrew or resisted their efforts as barriers to progress and as complicit in gay folk's domination in the public sphere. From Guy Strait to the San Francisco GLF, organizers blamed continued oppression on the apathy of such resisters.[89] For organizers, resistance to the publicity and community they were building was seen as acquiescence or capitulation.[90] For many, a refusal to participate was a form of selfishness.[91] Others attributed the movement's failure to complacency, that many gay men had made worlds for themselves and were relatively safe, and so they did not feel the need to make it better for others.[92] And still others blamed it on fear.[93] Whatever the source of the refusal, it caused great frustration among the community activists. "In the face of tremendous discrimination, abuse, and persecution what does the homosexual citizen do? He does nothing! . . . It is fair to say that the homosexual is scarcely doing anything to help himself" (*VR* Dec. 1969, 10).[94] The men who distanced themselves from community formation responded to such accusations with equal emotion, sometimes expressing outright shame at gay organizations.[95] But many gay men were simply happy with the small, informal communities they had enjoyed for years. "We enjoy very much going to brunch with friends, a drink or two, then leave; because there are so many wonderful things to do and see [in San Francisco]" (from "Two Peaceful Lovers," *AG* Dec. 17, 1970).

It is difficult from the traces left in these publications to see specifically why individuals would specifically resist the emerging community and publicity, but a one major complaint ran through the decade: the gay organizations and communal spaces only represented the interests and needs of some gay men, but not theirs. Indeed, many gay men wrote of their doubt that any gay organization or community could meet any *individual* gay man's needs at all, although they wish there were such a gay space. When one reader complained that Strait was covering drag events in *The News,* he revealed something deeper when he asked, "What about people like me?" (*TN* July 22, 1963, 3). [96] This seems to have been a relatively common response to the forming organizations, community, and publicity, that they didn't belong in the gay community as it was then forming. The gay liberation movement had their share of these complaints as well. "Why is Berkeley Gay Lib like a shitty joint?" asked one reader. "With a shitty joint, you smoke and smoke and smoke but never get stoned; with Berkeley gay lib they rap and rap and rap but nothing ever happens or gets accomplished for all" (*GS* April-May 1971, 16). The sentiment among many gay men that they really didn't belong in the community seemed to persist well into the end of the period.[97]

At the larger, more traditionally political level, as we have seen, gay men disagreed intensely about the ends and means of a gay movement, and these disagreements served as background for competing meanings of gayness. While the organizations provided the context for communicative interaction to lay down communal values, they also provoked oppositional interaction that threatened the dissolution of community. These divisions, discussed in earlier chapters, worked to counteract efforts to produce the affective bonds necessary for community and especially thwarted efforts to agree on values around which to organize a community. For many, these disagreements felt like evidence that gay men could not form a community, that they did not, indeed, have anything in common upon which to build. Although early in the decade there was hope that divergent organizations could work together,[98] rivalry among bar owners and conflicts among activists made this impossible, and competition and conflict became the hallmark of the interaction of gay organizations.[99] Nonetheless, few activists felt that "controversy" was a positive aspect of the movement. Frequent accusation of "ego-trips," racism, middle-class bigotry, and sexism were hurled back and forth among various organizations, especially at SIR meetings and in the pages of *Vector*.[100] The activists who saw themselves as revolutionary accused the less militant of being afraid and hypocritical; and those from more staid organizations who held to more reformist means saw the revolutionaries as counter-productive, dreamers, and ne'er-do-wells. Despite their overlapping goals and crossing of organizational boundaries, this struggle between the gay libbers and the existing organizations came to be seen in binary terms, which I have simplified as the "radicals" vs. the "assimilationists."[101] In terms of community building, as we have seen, many of the "assimilationist" actions were quite progressive, and many of the radical gay liberation actions were regressive.

Although this binary was contested both in argument and in practice, it would eventually anchor itself in the consciousness of the San Francisco gay community. During the period, a few saw through this easy bifurcation. "[W]e feared the mindless labels like 'homophile' and 'radical' that such a confrontation would be sure to foster. We believed that the gay movement should avoid dividing up into arbitrary little sects like a bunch of Marxists" (*GS* Feb.–March 1972, 2, 7). And in the 1970s, some voices raised in agreement with Rev. Williams, that diversity of thought and strategy was healthy for the movement.[102] But those who eschewed rigid distinctions between radical and assimilationist, were overwhelmed by the realities of political activism in the late 1960s and early 1970s, which tended to see all liberation politics in binary terms. Much stronger and louder voices and action in the gay counter-public and in the official public ensured that the binary would stick and survive as a constitutive feature of gay community. By the 1970s, the primary conflict lay between the perceived divide between liberal reformers (what the gay libbers called the "Gay Establishment" or assimilationists[103]) and the radicals (or the "radical element" or "militants"[104] as SIR members called them). Assignment to one or the other category seems to have depended largely on who was doing the evaluating and their social position, rather than on an objective evaluation of means and ends, which, on the ground, tended to span across political categories and were agnostic about effectiveness.[105] In fact, from the publications of the period, it seems that many men circulated among various groups, so that on the ground, individuals participated in communities across the political spectrum. For community builders, this political conflict, framed as it was in terms of a stark binary, plagued their efforts from beginning to end.

The key here, though, is that in the minds of the gay men of the time, the perceived divide was huge, perhaps even insurmountable, making political enemies of other gay men. Men of both "sides" located their gay identities in the side where their political sympathies lay. The two sides maintained a dialectical relationship, as they forged their communities oppositionally and confrontationally. Hopefully it is obvious by now that this symbolic binary, whether real or perceived, framed and constrained the meanings that gayness could accrue during the period, creating very real social boundaries against which individual men had to align themselves. In making this alignment, they were in fact imbuing gayness with a particular meaning, through their interactions and the social structures in which they enacted it.[106] In the end, this conceptual divide was so powerfully anchored in gay communal consciousness, that it remains to this day a constitutive feature of gay community and culture. In many ways, the distinction between radical and assimilationist/liberal was deleterious to the community, as it threw up real barriers to communication across organizations and the kinds of social interaction that may have produced a different kind of coalitional public. At the same time, those divisions, especially as Bailey described them, arose not just out of men's political values, but out of their experiences in the official public, interacting with contemporary political movements, fearing arrest and harassment, and longing for more meaningful social interaction. In other words, in Deweyan terms, gay men *underwent* this bifurcation, they felt it deeply, and it became constitutive of their consciousnesses as gay men.

For the so-called assimilationists, that is to say, the liberal reformers, the revolutionaries were lazy freeloaders, ungrateful, unwilling to work, and lived off the dole.[107] To the liberals, the "revs" were brash, rude, and loud—and ultimately unproductive.[108] They saw themselves as being open to diverse opinions and different kinds of gay people. SIR members and gay men who aligned with them saw their form of activism as promoting stability and long-term results.[109] Most biting, however, was their critique of the so-called radicals' lack of organization, arguing that it lacked any sense of coherence or unified action, and predicting its quick demise. Yet many "assimilationists" also admired the demonstrations organized by the libbers and felt they would be effective where liberal methods had not been.[110] Others argued for accommodation to gay liberation and agreed with some of its critiques, for example of SIR's refusal to allow men under twenty-one to join.[111] But many others merely saw a hodge-podge of infighting and confusion among the gay liberation groups.[112] SIR members countered critiques with the argument that the gay libbers were being divisive and counter-productive.[113] SIR's efforts to answer the gay libbers' critique reflected their frustration. In answer to the charge that liberals were "Uncle Toms," one writer noted, bemused, that the accusation implied that "there are those of us who choose to remain loyal to a social system that causes us anguish and humiliation" (*VR* Oct. 1971, 7). And when an anti-SIR cartoon appeared in *Gay Sunshine* depicting SIR as the Mad Hatter, the editor devoted the masthead spread to a response. He noted that, while some of *Gay Sunshine*'s critiques were warranted, that they had nothing to offer but the label *radical* with no clear strategy or plans for the actual liberation of gay men and women.[114]

Individuals in and out of SIR levelled intense critiques at its membership and liberal strategies.[115] A central critique of SIR's strategy was that it was sycophantic (i.e., assimilationist).[116] Gay libbers resented and bucked against the fear and reticence of both SIR members and non-activist gay men. Charles Thorp expressed this well: "This has seared the Don't-Rock-The-Boat older gays. . . . So the gay Estab-in-the-back-lishment will try to prevent us from doing our freedom in the ass, but we can't stop, it feels too good" (*SFGFP* Nov. 1970, 4–5, 12).[117] Libbers also called "assimilationist" gay men of being racist in their political assumptions.[118] From burning their SIR membership cards[119] to zapping meetings, the "radicals" expressed a deep distrust and disdain for the older organizations.[120] Photographs of protestors handing out leaflets[121] at the 1972 SIR zapping showed gay men with signs that read, "SIR does not speak for all gays" and with "Gay Love" painted on their foreheads (see *GS* Feb.–March 1972, 2, 7).[122] *Gay Sunshine*'s relentless criticism of SIR emerged during tense times when the police were launching a new entrapment campaign.[123] They excoriated what they felt was SIR's sycophantic response to police harassment, when SIR argued simply and publicly that entrapment of gay men for public sex was inefficient use of police resources.[124] They criticized SIR for supporting the older sub-cultures (especially drag and camp), or rather, for working to maintain their integrity through legal action.[125]

Gay Sunshine Collective members felt that *Vector* ignored their efforts and demonstrations, and took credit for actions that weren't theirs. The libbers took credit for the social change they perceived around them, with a sort of wilful ignorance to the previous decades: "It has been the appearance of the spirit of gay militancy which has radically altered both the self-concept and the public image of gay people. Our lives are enormously healthier and better-balanced because of gay liberation movement—and no one doubts this but the SIR-domites and their cronies" (*GS* Jan. 1972, 2).[126] Perhaps the most pointed and trenchant of the critiques, however, was that SIR and gay men who ascribed to its ends and means were trying to "pass" as straight.[127] Foremost among these was an early article in *The Effeminist*,[128] where they accused organizations both in San Francisco and Los Angeles of conciliating and participating in the oppressive power structure of American society, which keeps gay men from understanding who they *really* are, by maintaining false consciousness.[129] To be fair, there was also a good deal of self-critique among gay libbers, including the same problems pointed out by SIR and even the possibility that gay lib was out of touch with average, day-to-day gay men.[130]

This binary view of gay politics and its concomitant competing meanings of gay emerged out of the experiences of the gay men at the time, given the number and diversity of their organizations and the depth of their disagreement about values, ends, and means. When young gay men joined gay liberation organizations, they did so partly because it was the "thing to do" among their cohort, but also because many young men were constantly frustrated by the oppression they felt on a daily basis and their desires weren't fulfilled either by the existing gay organizations or by the bar, drag, and leather sub-cultures. At the same time, older gay men (including men in their 50s and 60s) joined gay liberation organizations because they had been working long in strategies that didn't seem to be working, and the hoped that gay lib would offer something new and finally push them over the edge into equality and/or freedom in America. Likewise, many younger men did find their way into the bar sub-cultures and into organizations such as SIR, because they also experienced social needs and the need to express themselves in those ways. In the end, this binary view of gay male politics combined with community building efforts to produce a social context within which gay men produced, through their social alignments and interactions, different styles or gayness, or in Deweyan terms, different *meanings* of gay. One writer of the period actually noticed this phenomenon as it was happening. "But in [San Francisco] we are beginning to engage in dialogue over the kind of community life we wish to encourage. Only in San Francisco, of all American cities, does the gay community enjoy the kid of relative safety from harassment that such a struggle can be joined" (*GS* Feb.–March 1972, 2, 7).

A Community of Difference

The most pervasive problem gay men encountered in trying to build a gay community was the inherent diversity of gay men themselves. From the beginning of the LCE,[131] to the first Gay Pride Parade in the city, gay men struggled with how to account for the vast differences among them and to form a coherent social movement and a community from that group of constitutively difference men. Interestingly, from the outset, they acknowledged the inherent heterogeneity of gay men and framed the question not of how to make everyone the same, but as how to account for the differences.[132] This insistence on the multiplicity of political[133] and cultural standpoints within the gay community would be reiterated time and again during the period, as different kinds of diversity were also recognized and added. Community builders acknowledged differences in the ways men expressed their genders, their professional lives and careers,[134] their cultural community identifications,[135] class status and ethnic group,[136] education,[137] and region of origin.[138] Yet Guy Strait's description of the community's diversity reveals the structural problems of diversity: even as he insisted on the possibilities of group cohesion *with* diversity,[139] he also privileged one kind of gay man in his vision of what that community would look like, the so-called "socially responsible." In other words, with a group of people as diverse as gay men are, it seems perhaps inevitable that some kinds of gayness will be privileged and recognized about other kinds, that various possible meanings of gay will be necessarily hierarchalized and that power within the community will be distributed unevenly among the different kinds of gay that arise.

In their actual face-to-face encounters with each other, in their interactions in bars and organizations, drag balls and cruising for sex, gay men already knew from the outset that they were not in fact all the same. The knowledge of their own diversity, however, would not prevent them from transposing many of the dominant forms of American social hierarchies and stratifications onto their budding gay community. In other words, American society at large divided its people by race, ethnicity, class and gender expression; and so gay men brought those stratifications with them into the gay community. Gay men were also different from each other in terms of cultural values and practices. Many men, already in an abject position vis-à-vis American society, vied with each other for dominance within the community based on these social distinctions. These power struggles served to demarcate complex and overlapping in-groups and out-groups, and gay men used them against each other in the struggle to represent and create a moral rightness within the gay male community and for individual expressions of gayness. A fundamental problem of community building—to what degree and in what ways must we be the *same* in order to share values and affect-laden bonds—became the primary symbolic apparatus within gay community for policing and enforcing privileged kinds of gayness. Among the salient differences, class often determined how an individual could participate in the community; racial and ethnic differences often went unspoken, but constantly exerted pressures on the ways the gay community was forming; and age differences served as a sign of "liberation" or "internalized hatred," a constant division within the community.[140] Diversity notwithstanding, the urgent feeling that formation of a cohesive gay community alone could potentially lead to liberation undergirded all community building efforts.[141] Despite this optimistic and perhaps naïve belief in the power of community building to effect the liberation of gay men and women, the many ways that gay men differed from each other was always apparent and had a direct impact on their ability to maintain community ties.

Rarely discussed outright, class differences were always present and deeply problematic. Gay libbers was actively critical of what they saw as "middle-class values" among older gay men. Otherwise, I had to search for clues of class positions among gay men.[142] As early as 1964, The *Citizens News* noted the difference in jobs of its readership.[143] And Strait wrote a story about the economic power of the gay community in September 1964, oddly prefiguring the arguments about disposable income and consumerism made by marketing firms in the late 1980s.[144] Strait saw a primarily middle-class constituency of gay men and women with great spending power, especially in the areas of recreation and entertainment, thereby ignoring the poor and working class who made up much of the community he purported to represent.[145] *Ads gayzette* reported its readers' yearly income in a survey: "5K 28%, 5–10K 41%, 10–15K 19%, 15K–UP 12%" (*AG* Jan. 7, 1971). Yet at least a few gay men throughout the period sought to poke holes in the facile middle-class assumptions. Robert Cole spoke of growing up in the depression and the experience of being poor.[146] In the 1970s, many gay men began agitating for organizational communities to pay closer attention to economic disparity among gay men.[147] The *BAR* reported that changes in Reagan's economic policies made it impossible for gay men to receive public relief from poverty and unemployment; the article further noted that community houses and social services run by gay organizations were deluged with homeless and poor gay folks. By the early 1970s, many turned these economic critiques on gay businesses, which, it was felt, took advantage of a rapt market for their own profit, without consideration for their effect on the community.[148] These class tensions are subtle and often hidden (as they often are in American culture at large), but emerge throughout the period when middle-class sensibilities are violated or when gay lib economic values were at stake.

In addition to class divisions, race and ethnicity posed the most troublesome problems for gay community building. Despite their constant identification with blackness and the black civil rights movement and later with the Black Panthers, gay men throughout the period, even gay libbers, produced a discourse of community in their publications that belied an assumed *whiteness* of their community. This presumed whiteness would become entrenched in the dominant forms of gay male community as its primary racial articulation. It must be noted that San Francisco by the mid-1960s had a dramatically diverse population consisting of, in addition to people of European descent, Japanese, Cantonese, Mexican, and African American; and smaller populations of Filipino and Korean immigrants. Following the lifting of immigration restrictions during the Johnson administration, this racial and ethnic diversity would only increase among gay men. Using the gay publications of the period, I have found only faint traces of the lives of gay and lesbian people of color during this period, either men whose last names make it probable that they were men of color or, on the rare occasion when they designate their race or ethnicity.

This is not to say they did not exist or weren't active in the gay movement; rather it is to point out the particular formulation of race and ethnicity in the production of gay-maleness during this period. The public voices of gays and lesbians of color would cry out with force during the 1970s, after the gay Pride parade of 1972,[149] when the gayness had already been thoroughly inscribed as white. Thus, race is most often revealed as an *absence* in the discourses that survived among gay men during this period; it was simply rarely (if at all) talked about, as if the race of gay men of color didn't matter. Racial politics made this an exceptionally complicated matter for men of all politics and races. If gay men of color were participating in SIR organizations and events, and if the men there considered themselves "integrated," what was happening with race in that setting? Or if Gay Sunshine espoused an anti-racist, pro-Third World politic,[150] but has little participation of actual gay men of color, what is happening with race there? In other words, on both sides of the political-social divide, the erasure or absence of explicit racial difference often happened in combination with an anti-racist politic. This is difficult to see in many ways, and can only be demonstrated archivally through the traces left in the historical record.[151] It is exceptionally difficult to quantify, but a casual perusal of some key facts points up the difficulties race and ethnicity posed for a community that prided itself on being open to all diversity.

The primary clue to the dominant construction of *gay* as *white* lies in the dearth of representations of men of color in any of the publications. Of those that could be visually racialized, most were representations in the form advertisements,[152] reviews of popular cultural productions, such as a *Boys in the Band* review in 1970,[153] or in pornography.[154] And a fashion spread for The Raza Power Company appeared in 1970 that included a presumably Latino model.[155] Other brief mentions of racial difference included Guy Strait's note of the presence of the "Oriental and Polynesian community"[156] among the Halloween revelers in 1963, the year the Black Cat was closed by the ABC.[157] And from time to time, publications would run pictures from social events, and by the late 1960s, these nearly always contained images of men of color.[158] The gay lib publications had an equally small number of representations of men of color in their pages, including one story about the Third World gay Revolution, a reprint from *Gay Flames*, a New York gay publication.[159] There were also a series of articles both in *Vector* and in *Gay Sunshine* about gay life in Cuba.[160] Other key clues remain of the lives of gay men of color. In a report about the oppression of gays in the Bay Area during 1969 and 1970, *Gay Sunshine* broke down their violence and suicide statistics by race,[161] and noted that "The high rate of suicide among Black gays is alarming" (*GS* Feb.–March 1972, 10).

Those scant clues notwithstanding, for all intents and purposes, the different life experiences and social positions of gay men of color were virtually invisible and unspoken within the gay public during this period of gay community building, despite the community's hyper-awareness of the black civil rights movement. Sometimes people of color were simply ignored or subsumed in the exotic cultural practices common to the 1960s, such as when SIR held a "Hawaiian Night" in 1965 and ran pictures of white men dressed in grass skirts (see photos, *VR* Oct. 1965). In a rare instance of someone self-identifying as a man of color, Gene Gonzales, of Honolulu, wrote that he wanted to be pictured in *Vector*.[162] *Gay Sunshine* ran a long article by a gay black man in Chicago, Ron Vernon, about his experiences being black and gay,[163] but nothing comparable by gay men of color in the Bay Area was published during this period.[164] Thus, the gay community that was being created was paradoxically aware of race and silent about it; gay men of color were put in an awkward position of having to shed their race or ethnicity in the gay counter public in a way that either cut out their different life experiences and ignored the ways their race and ethnicity were used to give them a lower position within the gay community; or they were exoticized into a special kind of sexual object.

Discussed far more often than race, the perceived generational differences between "old" and "young" gay men came up with increasing frequency; this was a generation gap that was greatly heightened by the counter-culture and the radical politics of the decade, as gay men young and old aligned themselves according to the social movements of the day, many of which were centered in the Bay Area. Complicating the generational gap, gay men's sexual desire often crossed age boundaries.[165] Thus, although the animosity often arose out of the political differences, it also came from the push and pull of sexual attraction and repulsion. Some saw youth as a desirable attribute that should be cultivated and welcomed in the growing gay community to keep it vital and forward-thinking[166]; whereas others saw age as having more wisdom and experience.[167] Some saw youth as dangerous, selfish, and disinterested in real work for the movement.[168] Beyond these perceptions, however, there were practical reasons for gay organizations to be wary of youth. The sexual age of consent laws were twenty-one, the drinking age was twenty-one, and the stereotype of the child-molesting homosexual was rampant in California culture, so SIR expressly forbade younger men from joining.[169]

This provoked a great deal of resentment among younger gays, especially students, who were excluded from one of the central and most powerful gay organizations in San Francisco. These young gay men often resented or feared the sexual advances of older gay men, and they thought of them as being lonely, old, and closeted,[170] a view that *Vector* attempted to counter on numerous occasions.[171] The gay libbers were relentless in their equation of SIR and its "conservative" politics with being "old." Younger gay men perceived themselves as being open-minded, free from social definitions of sexuality, and happy in their homosexuality; whereas they perceived elder gays as having internalized oppression, closed to new ideas, and miserable in their homosexuality.[172] Some voices called for generational reconciliation. Dan Allen concluded, "All [age] groups of gays have been mother-fucked and father-failed. . . . Peace within the homosexual family is a desirable aim. . . . The enemy is not within; he's barely out yonder, right outside the wall, so all gays must stay together, away from the wall" (*SFFP* Dec. 22-Jan. 7, 1970, 10).[173] Others admired older gay men, but lamented that they weren't available as role models.[174]

Divided as they were by class, race, and age (not to mention their gay sub-cultures and politics), the gay community seemed doomed to dissolution. But as mentioned previously, a handful of thoughtful men hoped that the inherent diversity of the gay community would lead to a community ethic of acceptance of difference, even for an ethic of compassion, mutual respect, and affection.[175] Harry Hay, ever the spiritual guide, laid out a series of ethical guidelines for the community that he hoped would guide the community toward cohesion and strength. He suggested "respect [for] the integrity and the underlying purpose and aims of all the others, withholding neither constructive criticism nor well-earned praise for the acts of others"; he argued that members of the community should refrain from personal attacks against those with whom we disagree; and to renounce ego in dealing with the community (see *VR* May 1967, 21, 25). For gay men who valued the diversity of the community, they did see it as a strength; yet that value was always undercut by the fear that heterogeneity would preclude community building and, ultimately, gay liberation itself.

The acknowledged and obvious diversity of gay men evoked fear and provoked in many men a yearning for unity. The necessity of being unified enough to form a political bloc was already apparent, but the added dimension of community building greatly complicated the *meaning* of the community's diversity. We have already seen numerous times that gay men feared that only their sexual desire unified them as either a counter-public or as a community, or more precisely, their shared domination stemming from their sexual desires.[176] Ultimately, a central question that gay men began to ask themselves was what exactly constituted a first-person plural identification with gay community: was there a "we" among gay men and could there ever be one? For some, there emerged out of this conundrum the minimalist *gay* that we saw above, one that was more or less like straight people except for this small difference in sexual behavior.[177] Community advocates had to constantly argue that their only commonality, or "sexual proclivity," was strong enough to form a community (see *TT* Sept. 1965, 5). Later, some men with liberation values denied that homosexuality should even be an enduring category of human social relationships at all, and even suggested that by trying to "be gay," gay men were playing the role that had been given them by the dominant culture.[178] But as we've seen, others argued that not all homosexuals were equally oppressed, thus oppression was not adequate for community formation either.

And so out of this confusion arose a peculiar dialectic, a constant struggle between the desire for unity and belonging, and the reality of and desire to maintain diversity[179]; the ideal of a unified group of *all* homosexuals was constantly undercut by the heterogeneity of homosexuals. For some, the answer was to leave open the definition of gay community, to maintain a sort of fluidity of boundaries.[180] Two drag queens suggested on two occasions how the fight for unity would ultimately lead to both empowerment and the retention of individual differences.[181] Unity as a value never died during the period, and some even claimed that it was the diversity that leant strength to the unity.[182] But this particular kind of diversity of opinion, a classic democratic problem, had very real difficulties in practice, because the diversity was more than just a difference in values, means, or ends. The life experiences of gay men from different American strata converging in San Francisco were so different that they often spoke past each other through their different needs and desires for the community.[183] And the naysayers and critics were equally vocal and dubious of the prospect of gay unity. Ultimately, gay men simply forged ahead, working for community and unity even as they experienced and articulated their differences and heterogeneity. It remains an open and vexing problem in gay community formation to this day, and constitutive of the meaning of any individual man's gayness.

As we have seen, these were uneasy formulations of gay community. Early on, many gay men had distrusted what they called the "ingroupness" of community building altogether. The danger of community building, for some, meant cutting oneself off from the citizenship of the public sphere[184] and the possible loss of individuality. By the 1970s, these fears had largely abated, simply because by then a gay community, however conflicted and tumultuous, undeniably existed. Gay community had entered public consciousness of U.S. culture at large and had come to be seen as a political and cultural force; and San Francisco's gay community had become more and more interconnected to a national gay community that transcended geography to connect gay men together across the continent.[185] In 1971, *Vector* claimed that the homosexual was the most average person in the city, because the heterosexuals had fled to the suburbs (*VR* June 1971, 34–35). And just a year latter, the magazine observed the bustling community with pride. "Amidst this the youthful gays are uniting in situations that best meet their needs; gay liberation communes and gay newspapers abound. Amidst this a gay church has emerged, maybe shaking up some people . . . but, nevertheless, meeting the needs of many homosexuals" (*VR* March. 1972, 4). Amid all the conflict, there was one constant strand as gay men described their experiences of community: they felt relief from the pressure they felt from the dominant culture when they were "in" the community. This seemed to hold true whether they were describing informal associations of friends, cultural sub-communities, organizations, or just "gay community" writ large. So perhaps more than the influence of the counter-cultural emphasis on authenticity, it was the experience of symbolic domination and public oppression—the double-life of passing, the pressure to conform to avoid negative and sometimes violent consequences—that produced in gay men the very real sense that they needed a space to be their true selves and that they needed a social identification with like others.[186] Community provided a space to have the conversations, both internal and social, necessary to make sense of one's homosexuality.[187]

Gay organizations and the social spaces they created provided safety, shelters from the external tirade of harassing representations of homosexuality[188] and from the intervention of the official public into gay men's freedom of personhood, and even from physical violence.[189] This shelter allowed gay men to come to terms with who they were and to live accordingly.[190] In their conversation about the meaning of gay liberation, the Gay Sunshine Collective expressed similar sentiments.[191] The kinds of safety organizations provided were numerous. Community, then was an effect, the result not only of the discursive work of the publications, but of the social interactions organizations and informal associations and sub-communities engendered. It was further the effect of the push for publicity and recognition, where the process of becoming open and the public battles gay men fought (and continue to fight) with each other about the appropriateness of their individual gaynesses produced a context wherein, if they chose to embrace it in some way, many men thrived. If community is an effect, then it is also an *affect*, a feeling that gay men have about each other, about gay men they see but don't personally know. But it is also a particular relationship to an argument. As gay men fought over boundaries, all kinds of men participated in the struggle. Thus, community as affect is also a feeling that you have a stake in the struggle and have the power to speak up and be heard. I do not mean to dismiss the centrality or importance or power of the divisions and conflicts within the gay community as it emerged, nor to ignore the fierce battles they had with each other over the meaning of community and over means and ends in the public. I wish instead to argue that those conflicts are in and of themselves constitutive of gay community; and that in the fighting of those battles with each other, gay men shaped their communities and associations. Indeed, the feeling of belonging and meaning—solidarity—itself arose out of engaging in these battles over meaning, organization, ends, and boundaries.

With mutual recognition and group identification as the conceptual backdrop, and with an ever increasing array of social and service activities for gay men and women, and with the establishment of physical spaces that guaranteed the possibility of real interaction, the gay community seems to have been well established by 1972. The reality is far more complicated, as gay men were divided by generation, politics, ends and means, and even the meaning of gay itself. So the communities they formed were always in flux, and many gay men experienced them as ephemeral or temporary, unreliable or fickle. Gay men never agreed whether or not there should be a community or what that community would look like if it should exist. To be clear, these kinds of spaces and interactions had begun before 1961 in the bar sub-cultures and, in San Francisco, in the gender tourism of the drag performers in North Beach. But the publicity-seeking organizations expanded the possibility of gay spaces beyond meetings for sex and out into an open, integrated part of gay life, rather than the clandestine sub-cultural spaces of the 1950s. From SIR to Emmaus House, the experience of domination, that is, the consequences of being a homosexual in this society, motivated the creation of gay community. So many men felt (and perhaps even proved?) that the effects of oppression were most directly and immediately remediated through community interaction in safe gay spaces.

The gay communities that came to exist arose out of a complex relationship between the emerging counter-public organizations and the gay male sub-cultures already in place by 1961, especially the drag and bar cultures, which they brought with them into the newly forming communities, as we shall see in later chapters. Gay men's multiple gay affiliations often served different purposes—going to a bathhouse and going to a SIR meeting were not the same kind of interaction, but they were also not completely different, and both seemed to have served a role in the on-going meaning-making which is the subject of this study. Importantly, each group affiliation, each association, each organization and sub-culture to which a gay man belonged served as one among many social nexuses that gay men had to navigate as they made sense of their experiences as gay men and sought to consummate their various desires and solve problems within that environment. As they discussed and debated the merits of each of these organizations and their particular communities I discussed earlier, the older practices were always visible and present in their evaluations.

Ultimately, there was no resolution among the primary competing visions of gay community in the city, as gay men today still variously see their community as one of political organizing, one of social connection, identity formation, or of the locus of their authentic selves. What is clear is that the means gay men used to build their community—from pushing for mutual recognition, to sponsoring service and social activities, to the establishment of physical spaces for face-to-face interaction—provided the critical foundations upon which a gay community could be built. Although the community has been torn down, rebuilt, wings added and demolished, and regularly remodeled over the years, those patterns of interaction—in bars, clubs, bathhouses, community centers, and political organizations—remain foundational and still serve to produce, in their effect, gay male community, as fractured and unkempt as it may be. No single cohesive community emerged, with affect-bonds and shared values. Rather, they remained a point of as gay men stretched to see themselves in each other despite massive differences, as they worked to conceive and establish a community that would meet their conflicting needs and desires. And so in the end, the salient aspect of gay community is that it was a space for communicative interaction where those struggles over meaning could take place. Community building fostered and nurtured the contested view of gayness as communal. This in turn created the paradoxical outcome where a communal gayness fostered the interactions that allowed the liberal-democratic, individualistic gayness to flourish. Gay men speaking and writing of their experiences during this period most often formulated meanings for their experiences and found fulfillment, however fleeting, in their interaction with other gay men in gay spaces.

The social work necessary to create the affect-laden bonds and the shared values that would nurture a gay community and the cultural work needed to imbue that community work with *meaning* stumbled along despite the many roadblocks. Judging from the reactions of men at the time, community building was a messy and confrontational process; even the most ardent proponents of community seemed taken aback by the extent of the dissention among gay men in their community building efforts. Indeed, the paradigmatic "bitch fight" was bitched about throughout the period and across the political spectrum.[192] In the early 1970s, when community for many was *the* answer—providing safe social spaces, acceptance, belonging, and even spiritual fulfilment—men at the center of the community-building effort felt that gay community might not be possible.[193] Two primary ruptures of imagination bedeviled gay community formation between 1961 and 1972: the search for enough commonality to form a community in the first place and the underlying fear that any gay community would be fake, unreal, or otherwise false.

But in its effect, this new kind of community, gay and public, would transform the very *meanings of gay-maleness* by transforming the social interaction gay men had with each other: the meanings of going to a bar, of doing drag, of being in a musical review, of cruising for sex, of having a boyfriend, of *being* a homosexual man. In their efforts to produce a community, to bond together emotionally and through shared values, gay men ended up creating the Deweyan communicative space they needed to rethink, revamp, and recreate gay-maleness. Given that these community building efforts were fraught with struggles over power within the counter-public and community, many individuals and groups protected their ways of life from the encroachment of the new community; that is, they resisted the new gay community and pushed back with their already-held meanings of gay-maleness. As the process progressed, the men (and women) who actively sought to form a counter-public were also those who ended up with the power to shape and represent the emerging community through their activism and their publications. Community activists struggled with each other over the community they were building, and they struggled with and against the gay laity whose needs they claimed to represent. This emergent and conflicted gay community, comprised of multiple organizations, sub-cultures, and informal associations, traversed and nurtured all kinds of communal experiences and interactions, and meanings, reflexively transforming them all.

Notes

1. This is not to argue that the men of the 1950s did not have arguments about publicity or that they did not have organizational associations; rather it is to say that the scale of those interactions greatly shifted in San Francisco in 1961 and that the LCE began a trend that would transform whatever idea gay men had of their associations such that by 1972 there existed something they called a "gay community."

2. Amitai Etzioni, "Is Bowling Together Sociologically Lite?" in *Contemporary Sociology* 30:3 (May 2001), 223–224, emphasis mine.

3. John Dewey, from *The Public and Its Problems*, quoted in Robert B. Westbrook, *John Dewey and American Democracy* (Ithaca: Cornell University Press, 1991), 365. Important here, Etzioni argues that community formation is fraught with problems, especially for the democratically minded, because by definition, community formation entails the drawing of social in-and-out boundaries. Such boundaries might contradict liberal democratic assumptions about freedom and equality as espoused by the gay organizations of the period. Uncritical advocates of community often see the affective bonds of community as ends in themselves and don't honestly consider the potential pitfalls of community formation. Another problem, for Etzioni, emerges as a community seeks to "bridge" with other communities. Such bridges may lead to a loss of control over the values and normatives of the community.

4. For a detailed history of the development of the earlier community formations of gender performance, see Boyd, *Wide Open Town*; for a good introduction to history of these leather and S/M communities, see Rubin, "The Miracle Mile."

5. Dewey, quoted in Westbrook, 365–66.

6. For example, in 1967, SIR's newly elected president, Dorr Jones, argued that the goals of SIR should combine community building with activism, that the two were connected. See *VR* March 1967, 10.

7. To illustrate this point, after the suicide of a young gay man, R.D.H. wrote to *Vector*, "I will again ask myself whether or not SIR should be an activist organization or just a social club? Have fun! While others die?" *VR* Oct. 1967, 32–33.

8. In addition to the explicitly activist groups discussed here, the San Francisco Tavern Guild had served San Francisco since its humble beginnings at the Suzie Q on Polk St. in 1963. See Stryker and Buskirk, *Gay by the Bay*. The social activities sponsored by the Tavern Guild will come up throughout the dissertation, in conjunction with the activities of other groups and in terms of their effect in community building efforts (e.g., monthly meetings, picnics, newsletter, Beaux Arts Ball, and Auction Series). For a good brief history of the Tavern Guild's actions through the 1960s, see Bob Peck, "San Francisco Has America's Most Successful Tavern Guild," *VR* Feb. 1971. Peck argues, "T.G. history has been, largely, a chronicling of some people in our community who cared. They all helped the entire gay scene, each in his (or her) own unique way."

9. See Boyd, *Wide Open Town*, for historical details.

10. In a particularly revealing article, Strait encouraged disagreement and criticism from *The News* readers, saying that he hoped that the LCE could act on behalf of the common interests of deviants. Strait's "community" was a conflicted one; he believed that its members had nothing in common, but, at the same time, that they shared something salient that allowed them to form a community. "But even if we disagreed in many ways, so long as the eventual and primary goals are the same, we feel a kinship." *TN* Aug. 5, 1963, 3. See also *TN* Sept. 16, 1963, 1–2.

11. But Strait was conflicted, and also considered individual needs important and argued that social action had to be careful of individual's privacy and be for the good both of individuals and the community as a whole. See *TN* Oct. 28, 1963.

12. Strait saw the efforts of the LCE as the glue which held the fledgling Community together, and published laudatory letters often. See for example *TN* Oct. 14, 1963; and Aug. 5, 1963, 2: "We of the social variant community owe you a huge debt of gratitude. It is difficult to believe that there are people in this Community that criticize you for your activities on the behalf of their rights and freedoms."

13. W.E.B. of San Francisco wrote *The News* to say that he would join the LCE if it truly were just an organization advocating such "non-partisan" values and social action limited to "promot[ing] our ideals, ideas, and civil rights"; but that he wouldn't join because what he found instead was the LCE was in fact trying to be more than that, a community of homosexuals. See *TN* Oct. 14, 1963, 7. There is good evidence to support the belief that WEB was William Beardemphl, the founder of the Society for Individual rights in 1964 and activist columnist for both *Vector* and *BAR*.

14. See *CN* June 8, 1964. Strait pledged in this issue of *Citizens News* to be a non-partisan forum where all gay organizations in San Francisco would have access to publication of their ideas and efforts, following the dissolution of LCE.

15. Like all these organizations in the 1960s and early 1970s, there is a historical forgetfulness, where as identities are formed against existing and older organizations, the work of those organizations is elided from history. One member wrote just three years later, "SIR was the forerunner in getting homosexuals into organized action that causes constructive changes and in bringing dignity to members." *VR* Jan. 1967, 2. In 1967, Robert Cole, SIR President, wrote "A homosexual, no matter how integrated into the heterosexual society, is alienated from that society by virtue of the fact. . . . He nonetheless must feel a sense of security that [a gay organization] does exist. . . . Such an organization is constructive to the individual homosexual. . . . It is the direction of the particular homophile organization that will determine its accomplishments, constructive or destruc-

tive. . . . It is a part of society, a part that recognizes that society and demands recognition." *VR* Aug. 1967, 14–15.

16. In the first issue of *Vector* (originally published by SIR as its official newsletter), the new board laid out its policies and goals, which on the surface focused on the same democratic values of the dignity and rights of the individual. See also *VR* Dec. 1964, 1. SIR's Statement of Policy reflects the classical democratic values with their focus on the individual, on rights, and on freedom, as laid out in the previous chapter. But notice also their groping to redefine freedom into something more than the classical definition allowed. "By trying to give the individual a sense of dignity before himself and within his Society, [SIR] answers the question of how we can maintain our self-respect. SIR is dedicated to [a] belief in the worth of the homosexual and adheres to the principle that the individual has the right to his own sexual orientation so long as the practice of the belief does not interfere with the rights of others. . . . [Rights inhere] despite peculiarities of color, of creed, or of sexual orientation, guaranteed to all men. . . . These inalienable rights must be constantly defended against the erosion of public power and ruin by personal apathy. . . . We believe in the necessity of a political mantle guaranteeing to the homosexual the rights so easily granted to others." This also reflected SIR's commitment to democratic organization, a commitment that would later open them up to harsh criticism from more revolutionary activists. See also *VR* Jan. 1965, 2; June 1969, 14. They hoped that this emphasis on individual expression would eventually lead to a change in social status, creating a more friendly society where homosexuals could live freely. "We are a societal gadfly that shall change social status in all these areas though a personal expression of the individual which evaluates self and his relation to his environment." *VR* Dec. 1965, 2. See also *VR* Feb. 1970, 9, 19.

17. "We find ourselves scorned by the very society which may in fact be largely responsible for our creation, our rights as persons and citizens before the law imperiled, our individuality suppressed by a hostile social order and our spirit forced to accept a guilt unwarranted by the circumstances of our existence." *VR* Dec. 1964, 1.

18. A few months later, *Vector* was claiming that they had indeed done just that. See *VR* June 1965, 9.

19. See for example, *VR* Jan. 1967, 2.

20. See *VR* Jan. 1965, 2. In some ways, they were right; but in SIR's publicity, its reach was far greater and potentially far more effective as a community builder than the Mattachine Society could ever have been.

21. See also *VR* June 1969, 6.

22. See *VR* Aug. 1966, 2: "Our work is to create a Community feeling that will bring a 'homophile movement' into being. Every homosexual must commit himself to the overriding necessity that we all be united. When this feeling comes into being within the 'gay world,' then we will see the implementation of programs that will provide the way for substantial sexual maturing of our country."

23. Robert Cole wrote, "I urge every man or woman who is by nature a homosexual to join SIR. . . . If you find your nature to be homosexual, then stand not alone." *VR* Aug. 1967, 14–15.

24. See letter from George Mendenhall, *VR* July 1968, 16–17: "The effect of SIR is constantly being felt. Our extensive flood of mail, phone calls, and personal visits to the Center indicate increased interest. . . . So let's not sit back and by cynical." Another man, F. Lehman, focused on the interpersonal associations he found at SIR events. "It is then that I have to say a polite 'thank you' to SIR, because it was through SIR that I was able to develop such friendship." *VR* July 1968, 16–17. Nelson S. Chuang wrote, "SIR has

given me an unmistakable, an undeniable sense of direction—like a beacon light to a floundering sailor at sea, or like a welcome oasis to a wayward wandering in a desert." And J.B. praised SIR for providing a social context that was broader than the sexual environments he found elsewhere. "SIR has given me a place to go and become acquainted with people without them thinking I am only interested in having sex or without being looked upon as a sex object. . . . I wish more people would become involved in the works of SIR so that they can also have that wonderful feeling of accomplishment."

25. "VANGUARD is an organization for the youth in the Tenderloin attempting to get for its citizens a sense of dignity and responsibility too long denied. We of VANGUARD find civil liberties imperiled by a hostile social order in which all difference from the usual in behavior is attacked. . . . We are forced to accept an unwarranted guilt which is more the product of society's hypocrisy than scientific fact." *VG* Sept. 1966.

26. See *VR* Feb.–March 1968, 15, 28.

27. See for example *Ads Gayzette*'s reader survey, *AG* Jan. 7, 1971. See especially question 23, wherein 88 percent of readers responded that the gay community was disorganized and unsatisfactory.

28. I'm adapting this conception of the qualia of MORE in religious experience from William James, *The Varieties of Religious Experience: A Study in Human Nature* [1902] (Mineola: Dover Publications, 2002).

29. See Boyd, *Wide Open Town*, and D'Emilio, *Sexual Politics*, for historical details.

30. The police commonly used the existence of the CRH as a twisted way to justify their actions. In 1968, Police Chief Thomas Cahill told a meeting of CRH ministers, "If you (the churches) won't keep the moral laws, then the police will." *VR* Nov. 1968, 5.

31. See *BAR* May 15, 1971.

32. See for example *AG* Feb. 25, 1971, 7, where an ad for three church services appeared: Metropolitan Community Church; The Community of Love of Christ, Oratory of St. Francis; and on Monday afternoons, a gay Mormon church service.

33. Late in the period, Rev. Mikhail Itkin of the Evangelical Catholic Communion, an Eastern Orthodox denomination, began officiating the Divine Liturgy for Homosexual Liberation and Peace, the rite of St. Serapion. Itkin argued that "a complete sacramental and mystical communion [for gay men and women] is a historical part of the Orthodox Church. . . . [It] offers to the Gay a valid and legitimate sacramental marriage without considerations of gender-identity." *GS* Nov. 1970, 7. See also *GS* Aug.–Sept. 1970, 17.

34. See *VR* Aug. 1969, 10. Perry had also begun conducting same-sex marriages. He had strict rules for this, insisting that gay male couples be together at least six months prior to marriage and that they have counseling with him.

35. In San Francisco, Howard Welles, MCCSF pastor, had criticized a Tavern Guild event, calling the participants "sexually promiscuous and drunken." For his part, however, Perry continued to be a activist in Los Angeles and met with stiff opposition not just from the L.A. Police, but from his own congregants, who discussed dismissing him. See *VR* Dec. 1971, 18–19.

36. See *AA* Aug. 25, 1970, 5

37. See *AG* June 10, 1971.

38. Other religions would follow afterward. Perry told his Jewish congregants sometime in the first two years of MCC that it was their responsibility to create a gay Jewish synagogue. Other gay religious movements sprung up after this period, including the efforts of gay men and women to create a place for themselves in the now infamous San Francisco Zen Center.

Many other gay Christian groups and churches formed during this period, ranging from changing existing churches from within to formation of new religious traditions. The church served as a temporary community when Frank Bartley was murdered by the Berkeley police. The Catholic priests in charge of Bartley's funeral lamented the fact that traditional funeral masses only offered a "Save him from hell" theme. See *VR* July 1969, cover. They tried to create a service "to be of joy that he is with his Maker." In the November 1969 *Vector*, there appeared an ad for a new church, with a drawing of a naked man, praying with genitals exposed. The ad copy worked to establish a kind of Christian community that refused traditional moral boundaries and focused on acceptance and ministry to the outcast.

See also See *VR* Nov. 1969, 14: "Community of Jesus our Brother: A house of prayer for all people. The Good News, the Gospel of Jesus our Brother and liberator, calls us to those of His brothers and sisters that have been written off by the establishment, those He called 'even the least of these my brethren' (Matthew 25). The Community of Jesus Our Brother is a non-denominational community of the concerned, ministering to the needs of their brethren even as they themselves are ministered to, and also a community of dialogue, worship, prayer and above all of the celebration of life in loving encounter."

39. The Humanist Movement of the Bay Area accepted gay membership early on, and argued for the belief that "humanity is a part of nature and that we emerged as the result of a continuing evolutionary process. . . . Genuine religion, we believe, consists of those actions, purposes and experiences which are humanly significant. Nothing human is alien to the truly religious." Following the basic tenants of Dewey's pragmatic philosophy, humanists maintained that morality arose out of human experience and could not be derived from ancient texts.

40. "We as an assertive gay revolutionary force are an eschatological community and a prophetic witness in the world. . . . The Brave New World is our world; where with love, there is neither Christian nor Jew, neither Greek nor Roman; neither male nor female; neither 'homosexual' nor 'heterosexual,' and neither slave nor master. But all are as one in the human family. Let us exchange the terminal City of God for the Secular City of Gay humanism." *GS* Aug.–Sept. 1971, 11.

41. Don Slater, a Los Angeles activist, argued in *Vector* that religious activism within the gay movement was detrimental to the cause. "The homosexual movement in America has sunk to new depths as 'homosexual churches' continue to appear. . . . But they are not necessary nor essential to the welfare of homosexuals. . . . The religious proposition that God's laws guide the affairs of men with an unseen hand has taken the positive action out of the movement." *VR* Oct. 1971, 35.

42. Another short-lived organization, formed primarily to protest discrimination, the Committee for Homosexual Freedom, discussed in Chapter 3, had a self-conception that bridged the interpersonal and citizenship values of SIR and LCE with the authenticity values envisioned by revolutionary activists. Like SIR, they advocated the need for the homosexual community to be united in its public action. See *CHFN* Aug. 13, 1969. And like the LCE they saw themselves as heterogeneous and un-unitable. See *SFFP* Nov. 1, 1969, 15. But they took their cues from the other radical movements of the 1960s, taking direct action in the public sphere and insisting on their gayness in their actions, thereby extending a kind of militancy into the possible meaning of Gay Community.

43. In many ways, this hearkened back to the ideas of Harry Hay in the late 1940s, when he had first argued that homosexuals were a different kind of person, in need of their own communal spaces and cultural life.

44. See Chapter 5.

45. See *VR* Apr. 1972, 13.

46. Again we find a historical "willful obliviousness," to use Benedict Anderson's phrase, where the work of preceding organizations is ignored and where the value of other community formations is rejected out of hand. At least one gay libber argued against this forgetfulness in 1969, but his voice was only a single voice among many opposing voices: "The first ancestor of gay liberation was the old homophile movement. . . . Without the pioneering efforts of such organizations much of the homosexual ideas and literature which provided the philosophical roots [of gay lib] would scarcely have existed. The second leg of the foundation was the Black civil rights movement and the white radical movement catalyzed by it." *SFFP* 1.9, 12.

47. For example, an advertisement in the *San Francisco Free Press*, with a back shot of a naked young man, asked readers, "Gay? Bi? Tired of Hiding? JOIN GAY LIB-ERATION—A group dedicated to ending all erotic oppression through education and action projects. BE GAY AND PROUD OF IT! Help us free ourselves and our brothers and sisters from oppressive straight society and from the plastic world of the gay ghetto bars." *SFFP* Dec. 7, 1969, 16.

48. Winston Leyland argued that only Gay Activists Alliance was left in New York and two strong GLFs, one at Cornell and the other at University of Kansas. See *GS* Dec. 1971–Jan. 1972, 1, 13. They discussed why GLF had collapsed, and Morgan Pinney asked, if individuals were the most important, "Why do we need organization? Aren't you on an old-fashioned establishment trip to relate to organizations?" To which Leyland replied, "It's not a complete anarchistic thing. There has to be some form of basic structure. . . . GLF was unstructured to the point where a few people could come in, take it over, and destroy it."

49. *GS* Dec. 1971–Jan. 1972, 1, 13.

50. For Lee Atwell, the antagonism older gay people had toward liberation undercut gay liberation's efforts. He lamented, "In the Bay Area I don't see any evidence that gay liberation has made much of an impact in peoples' lives." What little success gay liberation had had they attributed to other social movements, especially black and women's movements. See *GS* Jan. 1972, 2.

51. Around the same time, the Bay Area Gay Activists Alliance was established in San Francisco, or BayGay, as it was known. In an interview in *Gay Sunshine*, two founding members described what GayBay would be about: "True to the traditional San Francisco style, some of the earlier gatherings were marked by stormy exchanges and political intransigency; but gradually, as the established stars of the movement walked out on each other, one by one, over doctrinal disputes, a group emerged with a definite perspective for a new organization. . . . Our first priority was to avoid the mistakes and narrowness of both [old homophile and GLF] tendencies. . . . Our criticism of the homophile movement was of course that it is imbecile to limit one's struggle to appeals to society's institutions for 'emancipation' through liberal social reform. . . . The Gay Lib movement on the other hand allowed itself to be taken over successively by one or another more or less arcane political tendency. . . . It made in other words, no effort to be a 'front' in any true sense. [The four goals of GayBay are:] 1. There must be a modicum of organizational structure. Gay lib was terribly undemocratic in that it could be taken over by any faction which could muster four or five loud voiced stalwarts to a meeting. 2. We decided to stress activity. . . .the value of activity in attracting new people into an organization and keeping up he morale of older members. 3. We decided that BayGay must relate to the community. . . .their failure to relate to anything like a significant part of the gay community . . .

SIR to the middle age and respectable; GLF to the hip-young-movement type." *GS*, June–July 1971, 12.

52. In the House's newsletter, *I Am*, the House's founder wondered, "How can I with these people, with this person—bring out who they are and who I am. . . ?" *IA* 1.1, 2.

53. "Why not a Gay Way: A fulfilling, 'whole' life for homosexuals. . . . I speak about Gay Self-Determination: Coming out of the closet, not just physically (or sexually); but physically, psychologically, and emotionally: Coming all the way out of the closet." *IA* 1.1, 4–5.

54. "We can be Human with one another. We can be a family. I am referring to a chosen family of gay individuals. . . . A family coming together to 'free' the individuals involved: To free them from the anomie of modern life. . . . The family structure must be informal and changeable. . . . The gay family will exist when each individual member knows himself." *IA* 1.1, 1.

55. For example, "The See-er foresees a liberation-community where roles and stereotypes are meaningless and where individual uniqueness is cherished." *IA* 1.2, 2.

56. See *AA* July 20, 1970.

57. In their call for writers to submit to *Gay Sunshine*, the editors declared: "Keep us [Gay Sunshine] pure. Rise up and demand that you be heard! If you are Gay, you have something heavy and beautiful to say. . . . Add your energy to the community by letting the community in on your creativity. If you believe in Gay community, make it real." *GS* Nov. 1970, 2.

58. BayGay had pulled away from authenticity as a communal value and had made appeal to the older liberal democratic values and the value of interpersonal association as it tried to rectify the problems caused by Gay Liberation Front's undemocratic structure. "BayGay hopes that militants from many different life styles, ages, sexes, sexual orientations, etc., will come together to fight the common interest against all forms of gay oppression—and not just that narrow range that encompasses one's friends. . . . However, we feel that our major problem at this point must be to build a strong viable gay movement around those issues that affect us directly." *GS* June–July 1971, 12.

59. Young's passage in full: "I am fed up with the way that gay liberation shifted from essentially a movement of affirmation to a movement of negation. We started out committed to expressing love and solidarity for each other and we ended up bad-mouthing, complaining, hating, even being physically violent with each other. . . . My own experience shows how affirmation was overwhelmed by negation. . . . [J]ust as I was beginning to enjoy the sunlight of being out of the closet, I felt a very strong rejection from many of my gay brothers and sisters. . . . It was suggested not that I use these [journalistic] skills and contacts to help the gay movement (which seemed logical enough to me and still does) but abandon them as products of my 'male privilege.' The heaviest pressures came from brothers who attacked my 'butch image.' It is true that for years I put considerable effort into passing for straight (isn't that what most gay men do?), but this was not the cultivated masculine image one would associate with John Wayne or a football hero. . . . It is also true that I had many negative attitudes toward 'effeminate' men. . . ." *GS* June–July 1971, 2, 5.

60. For example, "It was felt that 'a better social fabric' was needed for the ordinary homosexual, for at that time, there really was no Gay Community per se. At the present time, it appears that that fabric has been attacked by many moths and presently seems to look more like last year's Cockette's costumes." *BAR* June 14, 1972.

61. "The individual dedication to oneself must grow into a dedication to our groups; our group dedication to all homosexuals plight; our dedication to the homophile move-

ment must grow into a dedication to humanity. Still we must not lose sight of being true to ourselves or our groups." *VR* July 1965, 2.

62. *CHFN* May 13, 1969.

63. *SFFP* Nov. 1, 1969, 10.

64. See for example *TN* Aug. 19, 1963, 1.

65. For example: a TG picnic on Angel Island, April 25, 1965; a SIR campout at Big Sur, April 30, 1965; hiking on Mount Tamalpais, May and June 1965; the COITS Western Jamboree March 5, 1966; Gay Sunshine's campout at Yokut Campground in Kearn county, fall 1970; etc. See also *TN* May 17, 1963, 1; July 22, 1963, 1; Aug. 19, 1963, 1; *TN* Oct. 14, 1963, 7; *CN* April 6, 1964, 6; *VR* Oct. 1967, 5; *VR* Dec. 1967, 22–23; *VR* Jan. 1971, 35.

66. See *VR* Feb. 1972, 10–11.

67. For example see TN Dec. 6, 1963, 1–2 (a benefit held for the late mother of pianist Sidney Blackman (known among the "cocktail set")); and *CN* June 22, 1964, 1 (a memorial benefit for Carol Berg, a lesbian activist killed in a motorcycle accident).

68. See for example *VR* June 1965, 2.

69. See for example *TN* June 10, 1963, 1; and *VR* July 1967, 17.

70. See *VR* April 1971, 4.

71. See for example *VR* Aug. 1969, 9.

72. From Editor, *VR* March 1972, 16: "We are asking married men who also have homosexual inclinations and who desire to rap with other married men to write to The Married Men's Group [address] We assure all responding that names will be kept confidential and that there is no implied sexual intent in this announcement." See also *VR* June 1972, 41. "Married Men is a new San Francisco group organized by SIR. It has been meeting recently for dinner parties and informal discussions that are of mutual benefit. . . . Only married, bisexual men may join."

73. See for example talks for Citizens Alert, *VR* Sept. 1965; and discussions of the Berkeley Gay Switchboard, *GS* Aug.–Sept. 1970; and Emmaus House Switchboard, *BAR* Dec. 1, 1971.

74. See for example *VR* Oct. 1967, 32–33; *VR* July 1970, 39;

75. See for example *VR* Oct. 1967, 11.

76. See *VR* March 1972, 31.

77. See for example *GS* Dec. 1971–Jan. 1972, 1, 13.

78. See Mark Ryan, *GS* Dec. 1971–Jan. 1972, 1, 13.

79. "'Gut-level encountering between eight males . . . to get individuals to openly and honestly feel their emotions and to assist others in the same process. It is an attempt to overcome the superficiality that is normally common in day-to-day contact." *VR* Feb. 1970, 15.

80. "We have made significant progress in changing our social setting from the city streets and 'tea rooms' to be a responsible environment. . . . Can you imagine how radically it would affect our social lives if there were no Community Center now?" *VR* Jan. 1967, 2.

81. "A fulltime coffeehouse and community center is one of Gay Liberation's goals," *GS* Aug.–Sept. 1970, 8.

82. See *GS* April–May 1971, 16.

83. Winston Leyland said, "The gay community center [in L.A.] provides services for gay community. . . . They are not staying in a radical ghetto. They still have a radical perspective on things but are trying to get rid of the radical rhetoric." *GS*, Dec. 1971–Jan. 1972, 1, 13.

84. See *GS* April 1972, 3.

85. Doug Brown, "Every day, when people walk in the door seeking food, housing, jobs, or counseling or maybe just rapping with someone else like them to help them deal with their gay identity, we come face to face with oppression. The master of the 'meat rack' is oppressed and exploited but so is the employed closet queen who hides for fear every time the word 'gay' is used. These are real, everyday problems which are fucking over the lives of real, everyday human beings, causing them to turn to us for something. . . . The theme of the entire project is 'gays helping gays' as opposed to using establishment or straight resources. . . . This is not the glamorous part of the revolution, the spectacular headline stuff Gay Lib was based on. This is the gut level, meet the basic needs of survival, function that was so often neglected in the past." *GS* Aug.–Sept. 1971, 11.

86. "We must get inside one another (physically, mentally, and spiritually) in order to free each other. Once we are free we can build a world within a world, a society within a society. . . . WE will be able to take the accumulating waste of modern Amerika and build a 'nation-within.'" *IA* 1.1, 1.

87. See *IA* 1.1, 8.

88. See Chapter 5.

89. *TN* Sept. 16, 1963, 1–2; see *GS* Nov. 1970, 16.

90. *VR* Sept. 1967, 15. One letter writer suggested that raising SIR's membership dues would winnow out the freeloaders. See from H.C., *VR* July 1969, 16–17.

91. *VR* April 1969, 11, 25.

92. See *VR* July 1969, 14; March 1970, 12–13.

93. See *VR* Sept. 1969, 20–21, 30.

94. Emmaus House demanded, "WE MUST COME AND WE MUST DEMAND THAT OTHERS COME, NOT MERELY WITH COCK AND CUNT, BUT FROM MIND AND HEART, COME TOWARD THE WHOLE PERSON FROM THE WHOLE PERSON." *IA* 1.1, 2, emphasis in original.

95. *VR* Aug. 1971, 9.

96. For example, one reader believed that a good gay organization should meet the needs of all its members. See *BAR* July 15, 1971. W.E.B. had complained much earlier that LCE could never build an effective community because it didn't appeal to all gay men. "And believe me, I would never be caught dead at one of your 'Smash Picnics.' Who needs to play baseball (ugh) in high heels (sick not sic) and drink beer until they fall on their face." *TN* Oct. 14, 1963, 7.

97. Nonetheless, by 1971 *Ads Gayzette* was reporting that over two thirds of its readers felt they were part of the gay community—bearing in mind that this statistic came from readers of a publication whose purpose was to advertise sex.

98. See *TN* Dec. 6, 1963, 1–2.

99. Some saw conflict as natural to a social movement. See from "reader," *BAR* July 15, 1971. When SIR broke off from LCE, Rev. Williams advised them to "not be afraid of controversy or tension. We in the civil rights movement have learned how to rock the boat, how to disturb complacent middle class people, how to root out complacency. . . . controversy is the need; it stimulates communication and the exchange of ideas." *VR* Jan. 1965, 10.

100. See *VR* April 1969, 11, 25.

101. See for example *VR* Aug. 1970, 27.

102. From Bob Russel, Sacramento, "[T]here would seem to be no reason why there should not be a 100% dialogue with the gay Lib." *VR* Jan. 1971, 30–31. A BAR reader argued that the community could encompass multiple means and ends (notice that he

speaks of the community as a fait accompli). For this reader, the community benefited from the diversity of organizations. "The community is united with its many organizations, for within each organization the membership has found an activity they believe in and can advance." *BAR*, July 15, 1971.

103. See for example *SFFP* Nov. 1, 1969, 7; and *GS* Jan. 1972, 2.

104. At least one older radical had a different idea. From Don Jackson, "Your equation of radicals with socialists shows how little you know of the radical movement. Most radicals are libertarians." *VR* March 1972, 7.

105. One writer complained that the entire homosexual movement was schizophrenic because the various organizations "put down one organization or the other—hoping that their 'demands' won't be met and end the attention-getting thunderbolts." *VR* Feb. 1970, 12–13. The binary organizing in gay community formation frustrated Aubrey Bailey, a SIR volunteer. "SIR is called 'too radical' by those who won't participate because it is so up front by those who fear losing their jobs or are just plain scared. SIR is condemned as 'too conservative' by self-proclaimed radicals who are so hostile that they sometimes verbally spit in my face when I approach them about really helping their own people." *VR* March 1972, 7.

106. "The central conflict was on how to deal with reality. . . . It was that there was a deep division as to what the goals ought to be. . . . The older group felt it had to justify itself to the world, become part of it, let straights into leadership roles, keep the movement a 'one-issue' trip. Be wary of dealing with youth, and in general conform to the reality the heterosexual oppressor imposed. The others replied that the whole thing must be turned upside down for the values had been inverted: 'Don't adjust your mind: reality has a flaw in it.' Right on!" *GS* Oct. 1970, 4.

107. See for example, *VR* Jan. 1970, 11, 28.

108. See *VR* March 1970, 26.

109. See *VR* Feb. 1970, 9, 19. One *Vector* reader argued that gay liberation were homosexuals "who themselves hold a low opinion of homosexuality," because they were so vocally critical of most of the sub-cultures to which gay men belonged. "Some of us see this as the problem underlying gay militancy: if you can't love yourself then you'll get everyone else to dislike you through hostile behavior," he continued. *VR* Jan. 1971, 4.

110. See for example *VR* Nov. 1971, 4; from Michael Cooke, Jan. 1972, 7.

111. "[O]ur organization [SIR] has not attracted the mature young person. . . . We must now open the doors to the young; reorganize our large, awkward Board; find funds for at least one additional paid staff member, and most important—begin to plan and discuss homosexual liberation as much as we do mall activities, dances, and stages shows." *VR* June 1971, 4. Another reader, Bob Russel, Sacramento, commented that "[I] sometimes think that American homosexuals who condemn these young people have never been in love or are so old they've forgotten." *VR* Jan. 1971, 30–31.

112. "Since 'gay liberation' is the exclusive property of some gay lib groups who attack SIR continually for its politics, just what are the specific politics of such groups? Being 'radical' and 'revolutionary' and 'libertarian' is not enough for us." *VR* March 1972, 7. And the *BAR* called gay liberation "nebulous" and complained that the gay liberation movement was completely out of touch with the gay community, arguing that the "1970s homosexual movement has NO connection with the homosexual community." *BAR* Jan. 1, 1972.

113. "If some poor neglected soul wants to burn a SIR card or scream 'Dirty Gay Revs,' that's their trip, let them go on it, but don't furnish the gas—your attention." *VR* Feb. 1970, 12–13.

114. "The implication is either that SIR should be offering free food to the gay community or that it is insensitive to the needs of that community. . . . This simplistic solution [proposed by gay lib] to the world's ills does not necessitate much action—to do anything other than criticize and damn others would evidently be participating in the system." *VR* Feb. 1972, 8. The editor continued, "Aspects of the *gay Sunshine* attack are justified, but we ask, 'So what?' . . . The effort to resolve problems at SIR is an exhaustive task to which many are now dedicated. . . . *Gay Sunshine* offers criticism, not a helping hand." Exasperated, he continued, "[M]aybe a 'clear program' would be to claim that we are 'radical'—which seems very vague to us. Maybe calling for the 'revolution' would be a 'clear program.'" These kinds of sarcastic defences were common in the last three years of the period.

115. One critique of SIR argued that its activism "substitutes frenzied activity for a clear political program and self-righteousness for any real understanding of the revolutionary impact of the gay movement. . . . [It will] convert the gay community into a special interest group to be bartered to the liberals. . . . Unable to perceive the relationship between the sexual oppression of gays and the oppression of other minorities. . . ., [liberals] do nothing to promote viable alternatives to the bar-bath-modeling-agency syndrome." *GS* Jan. 1972, 2.

116. "SIR gets so involved competing with CHR that it too often withholds its support from CHF," wrote Don Collins. *VR* Feb. 1970, 12–13. As we already saw, when CHF tried to get an anti-discrimination clause put on the ballot, SIR opposed it. See *CHFN* Oct. 16, 1969.

117. *Gay Sunshine* complained that "Liberal reformers meet problems on an issue-by-issue basis. They are too lazy to try to discover the interrelationships of evils like imperialism, oppressive economic institutions, and negative social attitude towards sexuality." *GS* April 1972, 3. Responding to an editorial in *Vector* that argued that televisions and new houses proved that poverty was not a problem, readers responded that SIR was a dupe of capitalism, choosing suburbia over justice. See letters from Jay Wallach, *VR* Feb. 1970, 12–13; and from Andrew Betancourt, *VR* Feb. 1970, 19.

118. "They chastise radicals for our 'confused' participation in 'other people's movement,' as though gay people had no stake in ending the war, eliminating capitalism and poverty, or ending racism. SIR clearly assumes that gay people are all white, rich, and somehow unaffected by American foreign policy. They declare that we have been disorganized." *GS* Jan. 1972, 2.

119. See photo *SFFP* Nov. 1, 1969, 7.

120. For example, Gay Liberation Theatre's disruption of a SIR meeting in October 1969, *SFFP* Nov. 1, 1969, 7; zapping 1970 NACHO conference, see Chapter 3 and *GS* Oct. 1970, 4, "The radical-conservative conflict became bitter indeed," noted Jim Rankin of the zapping of the NACHO conference; zapping SIR's 1971 fundraising dinner ["The gay People's Action Committee . . . demonstrated against a fund-raising dinner sponsored by the Society for Individual Rights, a large conservative gay organization . . . to protest what militants called a waste of the energies of the community on the Brown consensual adult sexual freedom bill. . . . Another purpose was to protest the exclusion of many gay organizations from the sex law reform conference being held over the January 15 weekend." *BAR* Feb. 1, 1972, 1]; and the meeting protesting Assemblyman Brown's consensual sex bill [See *GS* Feb.–March 1972, 2, 7: ". . . giving the SIRdomites an educational experience in the power of direct-action politics. A meeting devoted to proper lobbying techniques and how to appeal politely to the liberal middle class would earn firsthand the power of a spirited picket line. . . . We forced the homophiles to consider a whole raft of

issues they had never confronted before . . . the very basis of gay Liberation movement. . . . This piece of proposed legislation has seldom been discussed rationally in gay circles. . . . Emotional attachment to legal reform as the 'respectable' route to wider acceptance."]

121. The protest leaflet was reprinted in full in *Gay Sunshine* Feb.–March 1970, 2: "This meeting [with Brown] is being held to plan activity to speed the passage of Willie Brown's consensual sex bill. We oppose both Assemblyman Brown's bill and SIR's convention. . . . We deny the state's right to regulate anyone's sex life. The only acceptable sex law is no sex law at all. While the Brown Bill permits most sex acts between 'consenting adults,' it increases penalties for sex acts with (and in some cases between) minors. We hold that an active sex life is both necessary for physical and mental health and an inalienable right of all people, regardless of sex, age, or sexual orientation. . . . The bill will not reduce the present persecution of gays. . . . The police bust gays under a variety of vague and contradictory local statutes against such 'crimes' as loitering, prostitution, lewd conduct, or soliciting. It will not affect the common police tactic of entrapment. . . . We feel it shows a lack of judgment on the part of the SIR leadership to attempt to direct the energies of our community into such useless activities . . . energy in developing community services for gays, including alternatives to the exploitative bar and bath scene, services for teenage gays in juvenile homes and mental institutions, and for our gay sisters and brother in the prisons of this state. We must not allow the pursuit of 'respectability' to blind us to the plight of gay sisters and brothers more oppressed than ourselves. SIR is clearly concerned only with rich and middle class gays who can be satisfied with a hollow symbolic victory. . . . SIR has included only token representation from the gay Liberation community at its meeting. . . . [SIR kowtows to businesses] which reap huge profits out of the ghettoized condition of gay people. It is time SIR began to relate a little less to its friends in the police department and a little more to its gay brothers and sisters."

122. The cultural tensions strained to breaking at the 1972 zap. "This sort of thing is alien to the spirit of the Gay Liberation movement, and it clearly gives the lie to *Vector*'s recent claims that SIR is a Gay Liberation group," wrote Zack Mansfield. *GS* Feb.–March 1972, 2, 7.

123. "Who can we turn to? Why not to the Society of Individual Rights? . . . What vigorous & RESPONSIBLE steps are the SIRdomites taking to meet the rising tide of police harassment?" one writer asked. *GS* Oct.–Nov. 1971, 6.

124. See *GS* Oct.–Nov. 1971, 6.

125. "Right on! Gay power to the SIRdomites is keeping the bars full! 'Gay power,' quoth *Vector*'s editor, 'is here and it comes from self-respect.'" *GS* Oct.–Nov. 1971, 6.

126. The *BAR*, in its turn, countered that gay liberation would not have even existed without "many years of hard work on the part of numerous devoted members of our community working independently in politics, and collectively through such organizations as the Tavern Guild, SIR, CRH, and DOB." *BAR*, June 1, 1971. But the liberal editors and writers of *BAR* also had sharp words about SIR: "It now seems that the organization [SIR] has back-slid into a rather non-volunteer, 'professional homosexual' slump. It reminds me of the very thing we were trying to fight, in the old 'Mattachine days' with our star 'professional homosexual' Harold Call. . . . [SIR] is too general and alienates many members. . . . For those that are interested in working with homosexual improvements, SIR's present attitude is self-defeating." *BAR* June 14, 1972. Chuck Thayer argued in his column that because of SIR's reticence, *Vector* failed to reach its potential as a national magazine and the SIR community center was a "waterfront dump."

127. "The Society for Individual Rights, also known as the Society for Idle Rap, is a good grey organization dedicated to total integration within the establishment and to the proposition that, with a little help from a haircut and a suit, and tie, all men can look equal. Passing for straight is SIR's ideal, and 'Really? You don't look it' the highest compliment it can receive. . . . Its members see homosexual freedom as conformity to the universal dissatisfaction and as safety within the shelter of anonymity and oblivion. . . . NO VIETNAMESE EVER CALLED ME A QUEER." *SFFP* Nov. 1, 1969, 7.

128. An especially bitter cultural critique of the pre-1969 organizations and older bar sub-cultures came from the men of *The Effeminist*. They argued that *Vector* and the Los Angeles publication *The Advocate* were in substance straight magazines that pass as gay. They saw S&M and leather as a form of "straight sexuality" based on power. They accused *Vector* and *The Advocate* of being part of the "power structure" that oppresses gay men by keeping them from seeing who they *really* are (i.e., their authentic selves), perpetuating a false consciousness. "They, like every pseudo-groovy old queer ripping off the Avenue, are predators (straight men) and have no place yet within revolutionary process except to make us fight that of them in each of us. They cannot tell us who we are." *TE* 1.2, 5–6. Their response, like Emmaus House's, was for gay men to turn inward: "[P]ay attention to yourself, pay attention to your body. You will probably begin to notice that they are either really straight men on power trips or just gay men freaking out loudly while you freak out quietly in your chair."

129. Not all gay libbers were so harsh. Carl Whitman's "Gay Manifesto" had a more restrained and appreciative view of what he called "homophile" movements. He advocated that the ethics of gay liberation be extended to more "conservative" brethren. "[R]eformists, as pokey as they might sometimes be, they are our brothers. They will grow just as we have grown and will grow. Don't attack them, particularly in a straight or mixed company. 2) Ignore their attacks on us. 3) Cooperate where cooperation is possible without essential compromise of our identity." *SFFP* Dec. 22–Jan. 7, 1970, 3–5. But even here, clearly Whitman sees a meaningful difference between him and his "pokey brethren," and although he doesn't want to air dirty laundry in public in front of the straight people, he nonetheless feels the superiority of his own view. Later that year, *Gay Sunshine* claimed that zapping the NACHO conference at SIR had destroyed the homophile movement.

In a sort of premature eulogy, an *Agape in Action* writer reflected, "[The homophile movement and SIR] produced men and women of great stature, it had its martyrs, it made possible to a large degree everything that a new movement is going to do. It was a noble thing. We respect it. We love those who were a part of it. They were brave and strong when it was difficult. We fear having to match their stature." *AA* Aug. 25, 1970, 3. See also *GS* Oct. 1970, 4.

130. "[We radicals have an] equally irrationally fixated on the necessity of 'getting things done' . . . a failure to come to grips with the intellectual problems of definition, strategy, the over-all view—faults which we hold in common with the rest of the left." *GS* Feb.–March 1972, 2, 7. And others agreed with the assessment that gay liberation was out of touch with real, everyday gay men. "I want to be part of a movement that will not alienate the average gay person," wrote one gay rev. "One gay brother who has had passing contact with gay liberation said to me recently, 'They want to take away everything we have, but they offer nothing in return.'" *GS* June–July 1971, 2, 5.

131. In December 1961, Strait had already begun to explicitly address the various opinions of the community of social deviants in relationship to their own liberation. Seeing "divergent factions" among gays, Strait hoped to bring them together. "We shall plug

away at those who could scoff at our feeble attempts to get the 'community' to stick together." *LCEN* Dec. 25, 1961.

132. Mid-decade, a *Vector* writer explicitly rejected the necessity of sameness for social cohesion in the gay community. "The assumption of homogeneity of man's nature has created the assumption of the need for a homogeneous social contract." *VR* March 1965, 5. He argued instead that a group of divergent points of view allowed for individuals to be fulfilled through interaction with difference. Another *Vector* writer later proclaimed, it should always be remembered that homosexuals have many differences. Among these differences are varying life styles (from drag to leather, from complete openness to the closet queen, from persons who have long-term relationships to those who prefer one night stands); different backgrounds (from the white, middle-class, middle aged to the young black); different political beliefs (from McCarthy Democrats to Goldwater Republicans); in short all those differences which we find among the whole of the American people. IT IS IMPORTANT TO EMPHASIZE THAT S.I.R. HAS CHOSEN TO ORGANIZE AROUND THOSE COMMON INTERESTS THAT UNITE US ALL." *VR* June 1969, 6.

133. See for example *TN* Sept. 2, 1963, 1–2; *VR* Sept. 1969, 20–21, 30; *VR* July 1970, 9; *VR* Nov. 1971, 41: "gay leaders themselves emphasize that it would be a mistake to assume the homosexual population has a common and predictable political leaning. 'We have arch-conservatives, extreme liberal Democrats and everything in between. We run the full spectrum in politics, thought and religions,' said [James] Foster [chair of SIR]"; and *AG* Jan. 28, 1971, 1.

Only one significant article appeared during this period about gay Republicans (although Strait was a self-proclaimed Republican). It should be remembered that the Republican party of the 1960s was significantly different from that of today. See *BAR* June 14, 1972: "A second problem is the gay Republicans. There are no recognized gay Republicans and there won't be. The Republican Party wouldn't permit the formation of a gay Republican organization. . . . Gays who vote for these bigots are equitable with the masochistic Jews who voted for Hitler as an act of self-destruction. . . . The phenomenon of gay Republicans may be due to the 'princess syndrome.' Many gays . . . fantasize that they are members of the Establishment. In their delusions of grandeur, they identify with people in the million dollar per year bracket, and so vote Republican as a status symbol. Some 2800 homosexuals get arrested for sex acts in San Francisco every year. More often than not they lose their jobs, their mortgaged homes or flats get foreclosed, their business licenses get revoked and they go to the welfare line. . . . The princess must be educated to the fact that he will never be secure in his job or possessions until the anti-homosexual criminal laws and employment discrimination are abolished. And that's not going to happen while Nixon, Reagan and their cohorts are in power."

134. See for example *VR* Aug. 1968, 7.

135. See for example *VR* Sept. 1969, 20–21, 30.

136. See for example *SFFP* Oct. 1, 1969, 12.

137. See for example, *CN* May 25, 1964: "[Of 110 readers of *CN*] PhD 2; Masters 20; Bachelor's 30; some college, 33; completed high school 24; two years of high school 1"; 3.22: "READING AND EDUCATION: . . .1) the cosmopolitan atmosphere of the homosexual community is such that a greater variety of knowledge is required for intelligent conversation, 2) since there are no children to detract, it is possible for a man to appreciate some of the better literature on the modern market, 3) interest in clothes, styling, and photography makes the reading of magazines devoted to these fields a necessity"; *VR* April 1971, 5: "The educational achievement (of the respondents) was consid-

erably higher than the males of the general population"; and *AG* Jan. 7, 1971: of readers, "education grade 3%, HS 34%, college 60%, trade 3%."

138. See *TN* August 1963, where it was reported in the results of a survey that of sixty-five respondents, it found eleven raised in the south, twelve in the east, twenty-five in the Midwest, and twenty in the west. Forty-one resided currently in the west, none in the east.

139. Strait recognized cultural differences and insisted they were irrelevant to community building. "We [social variants] differ in the type of dress; we differ in the way that we want to have our hair cut; we differ in our mannerisms; we differ in our tastes in food, clothing, as sexual practices. AND NONE OF US IS ABSOLUTELY RIGHT." *TN* Dec. 23, 1963, 1.

140. These points of difference in turn produced problems and tensions as the attempt to meet the needs of such a profoundly heterogeneous group stretched resources, challenged assumptions and values, and required constant vigilance against community dissolution. Some feared that diversity would always undermine community. "Heterogeneity among homosexuals is in constant evidence. . . . Co-genitality has never been a cohesive force in the community because sex has a different meaning to every individual." *VR* Aug. 1971, 4. The *BAR* reported these tensions in interpersonal terms and reported their incommensurability with community formation. "It does not take a gigantic intellect to realize that the leather set won't associate with the teen set; that drags won't be caught dead with a head; that gay women cannot care less about the super-masculine body freak; and that the homosexual intelligentsia can't abide any other homosexual. The divisions within our community are real." *BAR* July 15, 1971. Others saw gay folks' diversity as evidence of their normality. "We represent a cross-section of modern society: wealthy, middle class, poor; educated, experienced, illiterate; well-mannered, careless, rude; well-groomed, careless, dirty; religious, uncommitted, atheistic; adjusted, uncertain, lost. These conditions are found to the same degree in the heterosexual, the normal segment of civilization. Therefore, we are as normal as they." *VR* Jan. 1965, 3. SIR continued this theme of diversity throughout *Vector*'s run. See for example *VR* July 1969, 14: "Most of our members live in the Bay Area but there are members throughout the U.S. and even in foreign countries. Members are male and female, young and old, gay and straight, rich and poor, religious, and agnostic, Ph.D.s, and high school dropouts, New Left radicals and Goldwater conservatives, and all shades of color"; and June 1970, 12: "The homosexuality community, however, speaks in many tongues, which gives *Vector* many voices to serve."

141. "We cannot exclude any homosexual. We all must have loyalty to homophile considerations if we are to have real worth to society and to ourselves. We must never accept, and we must actively oppose, social-political oppression. We must continue to develop knowledge of ourselves so that we do not pervert ourselves." *VR* Dec. 1966, 2.

142. For example, "Two Peaceful Lovers" eschewed gay community, but then noted that they were in the process of buying recreational land, revealing their own class position as well above the majority of gay men. See *AG* Dec. 17, 1970.

143. See *CN* May 1964,

144. See for example M.V. Lee Badgett, "Thinking Homo/Economically" in *A Queer World: The Center for Lesbian and Gay Studies Reader*, ed. by Martin Duberman (New York: New York University Press, 1997), 467–76.

145. See *CN* 3.22.

146. See *VR* Oct. 1967, 23. Another writer noted that "Homosexuals are represented on all levels of our society, running the gambit from the degrees of social acceptance

(based on wealth education, etc., at the top of the scale) to those numbered among the disadvantaged." *VR* Sept. 1969, 20–21, 30. See also *VR* April 1970, 36.

147. For example, Don Jackson complained, "Instead of having a Christmas party with food and gifts for the street gays of the Tenderloin and Skid Row, S.I.R. had its 'Members Only' party." *VR* Jan. 1971, 30–31.

148. "The gay community has been indifferent and ignorant about the gay poverty problem. Greed-obsessed gay businessmen are concerned only with profits. The bike clubs are more concerned with their image as bike riders and as pseudo-heterosexuals. Too many gay leaders are overly concerned with their ego trips and ripping off publicity for themselves. Individual gays are more concerned with getting another trick." *BAR* Dec. 1, 1971.

149. During the summer of 1972, the Community of Oriental Gays (COGS) was formed in San Francisco. "Its main purposes are to bridge the cultural gap between Oriental and non-Oriental gays; and to increase a sense of gay pride among its members and make this group more active in the gay community." *GS* July–Aug. 1972, 1.

150. Among the other rare voices of men of color during the period, Michael Robinson, a spokesman for the Third World Gay People of Berkeley, connected racial invisibility to class issues when he wrote, "The main reason I feel that most homosexuals don't care is that they are mainly upper-class." *GS* March 1971, 17. Perhaps his impression of gay men's class status came from the fact that he was dealing with UC Berkeley students, a relatively privileged group.

151. Other scholars have worked in this period through interviews of people of color, in an effort to draw out how their experiences may have differed or developed during the same time. See especially the work of Horacio N. Roque Ramírez and Nan Boyd, for examples (although Boyd's work is mostly before the period covered here).

152. See for example ads for the Hula Shack which often depicted line drawings of young Polynesian men in lavalavas and laes, throughout the run of Guy Strait's papers.

153. See *VR* Jan. 1970, 18.

154. See for example ads for *Blackmale*, *VR* July 1970, 37.

155. See *VR* 1970, 22–23.

156. From what I can tell, Filipinos of this period referred to themselves or were referred to as Polynesian.

157. See *TN* Nov. 11, 1963, 1–2: "Next in front of the Cat came 'A night in Shangri La.' This was a procession staged by the Oriental and Polynesian community. . . . Following the musicians was a sedan chair made in the Philippines. It was pagoda shaped, red with black panels. . . . The chair was especially made for this event. It was a creation of the relatives of the participants. It was carried by 8 boys from the outside. The Queen of Thailand Sirikit was riding in the chair as depicted by Haku. Following him was the depiction of Miss Korea, Mel; and Miss China, Ricardo. Preceding the whole entourage was red smoke carried by a man playing the gong."

158. See *VR* Dec. 1968, pictures from the SIRcapades included usual costumes and drag queens, but also an African American couple with a caption reading "What would Stokley say?" and an Asian couple, one in drag, with the caption reading "Mme Butterfly and her escort." An advertisement for SIR's *Revolution* show depicted an African American performer in a turban and a long-haired, bespeckled Asian man alongside white performers. See photos, *VR* Oct. 1970.

159. See *SFGFP* Dec. 1970, 14.

160. See especially Gina Larouch, "Gay in Cuba" *VR* May 1971, 61: "My first sexual encounter happened when two other neighborhood boys called me over to the apart-

ment next door. for the first time I was kissed and fondled and from that time on, sex became a very important part of my life. . . . But as Castro and his forces moved across the country, I didn't really care about it. I was entering my first romance with a married man and I was only fifteen. . . . Many of my friends were associated with Bautista and at one time I was the lover of an official in his ministry of Labor. . . . My biggest job was to plant a bomb in a police station, which I did but the damn thing never went off. . . . Castro unleashed a savage hunt on the gay community. Many homosexuals were sent to concentration camps and Havana was no longer gay in all ways. . . . It is good to live again in a country where people sing and dance, where there is a new life for me, where a homosexual can live without much trouble"; and June 1971, 29: "Mating and courtship do differ between Cuba and here but, let's fact it, the goal is the same—get the trick to bed. . . . The effeminate 'queen' gets more tricks but his lovemaking is limited to the 'bottoms up' type of sex. The 'butch' homosexual has more sexual choice. . . . Wealthy homosexuals were openly accepted and even sometimes preferred as friends but the poor ones didn't have such good luck."

161. See *GS* Feb.–March 1972, 10: "Of the sixty-eight gay suicides in 1969, twelve had lost recent employment due to the discovery by their straight bosses that they were gay. . . . Eighteen of the sixty-eight were Black, and four were Chicano. Forty-three of the sixty-eight died due to an overdose of barbiturates. . . . Of the forty-seven known gays who took their lives in 1970, six were Black, two Oriental, and seven Chicano. . . . Of the twenty-nine suicides in 1971 that have been determined to be gay, nine were Black, four Chicano, and one Oriental. . . .This most certainly does prove that being a 'closet-queen' can kill you in the ultimate way."

162. "I am a Polynesian [probably Filipino] and I would like to be 'Man of the Month' in Vector. . . . I thought it would be far-out to represent the gay society in Hawaii in your magazine." *VR* March 1971, 31.

163. See Ron Vernon, "Growing Up in Chicago: Black and Gay," *GS* March 1971, 14–17: "I acted in sort of a way of always being with girls . . . being fem, and eventually the word 'sissy' arose and I was classified. And that's when I really became aware that something was different about me"; [author recounts horrible experiences in prison, juvenile hall, and school or discrimination based on his sexuality and race]; "[When I used to turn tricks] I was the homosexual and he was a straight man, you know, and I related to him that way. My consciousness is entirely different now. I think that having to play those roles was extremely oppressive for many of us. . . . I'm really struggling right now with developing my own gay consciousness. . . . I think the people I still have the most difficulty understanding are white people . . . because of their racism. . . . White straight people bring about this whole shit. . . . I'm able to see better is the white gay person's point of view, and I'm able to identify—have something to identify with in a white gay person . . . and I'm sort of able to understand white straight women because they're sort of able to understand black gay men. . . . Women's liberation has an awful lot of racism to deal with before they can really understand the whole point of view [of blacks]. And I think that black gay men and white gay men have an awful lot of consciousness raising before they can understand women's oppression. . . . Black people are consistently raising their own consciousness about their Blackness, and so that's how I relate to it. . . . Like I've experienced oppression from white gay men. . . . My roles were reinforced by white men at that time. . . . In fact they were white gay men that I was having sex with [as a hustler]. Most of them married, suburbia with two children. . . . Because they lied about themselves, they had to deal with me, and that really turned me off."

164. Vernon spoke of the exploitation he experienced as a hustler and as a prison inmate; and then after he came out, Vernon spoke of being frequently exploited by white gay men who saw him only as an object of their sexual fantasies. A picture of Vernon and his Asian boyfriend ran in *GS* March 1971, 16.

165. Indeed, *Vector* reported that the average age of its readers' first gay sexual experience was 13.5 years. See *VR* April 1971, 5. In 1970, *Vector* reported a phenomenon of the "auntie," or older gay man who takes care of younger gay men in lieu of a sexual relationship. See *VR* Oct. 1970, 4, 12.

166. See *VR* Jan. 1971, 30–31; letter from Del Martin, Nov. 1968, 16–18; April 1969, 11, 25. Harry Hay, already in his fifties, argued, "We elders have not yet perceived that we must release ourselves from servile adulation of the now shoddy and worn self-images on which we have lavished our energies over the years. . . . We elders . . . are but wickedly wise . . . merely once vital, are now grown monstrous, blind and destructive. . . . [T]he young of today are not as we were—they are far closer to one another; much more ready to extend the hand of fellowship. The middle groups meanwhile suffer in silence the anguish of our obscene struggles with one another. . . . [I]n utmost humility we [the elders] must make prodigious amends." See *VR* May 1967, 21, 25.

167. See *VR* June 1969, 24.

168. See *VR* Dec. 1967, 31.

169. See letter from Wayne Whitecotton, *VR* Nov. 1968, 16–18; Charles Thorp Dec. 1968, 34–35; April 1970, 26; letter from K.W. Loring, May 1970, 12–13; Nov. 1970, 39, 43–44.

170. See letter from B.A., *VR* Jan. 1969, 27.

171. In one review of a study of older gay men by Martin S. Weinberg of University of Indiana, *Vector* argued that images of the lonely sad old queen just didn't bear out in fact. "With regard to loneliness, Weinberg found no differences between younger and older gays. . . . Older homosexuals were the best adjusted on these same [psychological] dimensions . . . younger homosexual was more apt to desire psychiatric treatment." *VR* March 1971, 16–17.

172. See *GS* Oct.–Nov. 1971, 7; *BAR* July 15, 1971 and Dec. 1, 1971. Interestingly, readership of the explicit publication *Ads Gayzette* skewed to the under-forty age group. See *AG* Jan. 7, 1971: "age 21–30 46%, 31–40 37%, 41–50 13%, 51–60 3%."

When the Young Homosexual Committee met in Los Angeles, a San Francisco gay youth, Keith St. Clare, told the attendees, "I'm the youngest person attending this conference. It is my opinion that the kids feel you don't know a fucking thing about reality, real value things [sic]." *VG* 1.7 (May 1967), 30. The article titled "Young Fruit" continues: "The Young Homosexual Committee [at the LA Homophile Conference] met three times one day to quibble over problems pertinent to the chicken queen, the chicken, and the organizations that involve them both. . . . There is a basic problem finding out [about homosexuality for young gays]. Then there are the difficulties of self-acceptance which many seem to have. . . . They [homophile groups] should try despite the legal problems to counsel, serve and represent the interests of minors. . . . Dorr Jones, SIR: . . .We are afraid the center will fold if we deal with [minors]. . . . Keith [St. Clare]: . . . Not only 'minors,' but also children should be allowed to engage in sex play. It's healthy. Group: Little girls and boys who are repressed and given guilt complexes about their penis or vagina are often poorly adjusted for the major part of their life. . . . Rev. Mamiya: There is a lot of freedom and experimentation [among hippies]. They are largely bisexual. Part of the long hair thing is to change male and female concepts."

173. He wrote a thought piece for the *San Francisco Free Press* in 1970 in which he laid out the five generations of gay men. "Nearly all members of the youngest generation consider those in the two oldest groups to be babushka-head Auntie Toms," he wrote. The two oldest groups he called the "Oldies," born before World War II, and the "Middle-Agies," born between WWII and the end of the Truman administration. He argued that the Oldies were "sweet below that rhinoceros epidermis" but that the Middle-Agies were holier-than-thou. To be fair, Allen was also critical of the younger men, calling them "Darlings of America's press" and "sanctimonious Red Queens."

174. "They [men old enough to be our father] were all the kind of men that my generation could have honored and much respected, had they been visible to us. That they were not was—and is—their tragedy and ours. Watching them during the [church] service, I felt like crying for them and for myself, wondering where they had been when I (and many others like myself) had needed their wisdom, their courage, and encouragement, their guidance." *AA* Aug. 25, 1970, 5.

175. A letter from Mitch made the oft-repeated argument, "[I]f we can honestly expect the straight community to tolerate us, we must learn to tolerate the least lovely of our own community." *VR* Oct. 1967, 32–33. These men argued that the ethics of openness and acceptance would overcome the divisions and separateness that diversity engenders. "The most important strategy for homophile organizations lies in treating all men and women, especially their own members, with respect . . . with affection. Respect and affection strengthen people and make them very hard to subjugate." *VR* April 1967, 3.

176. The idea that homosexual commonality came not from same-sex desire but from a shared oppression had roughly equal coverage by the latter part of the decade. "Our homosexuality is a crucial part of our identity, not because of anything intrinsic, but because social oppression has made it so." *VR* Jan. 1972, 32. Or as *The Emmaus* put it, "Our commonality is not homosexuality. Our only unity is the common, but deeply personal experience of resisting, usually in isolation and terror, the pressures to become a 'man' from the ongoing society." *TE* 1.2, 11. See also *VR* May 1970, 12–13; Aug. 1970, 27.

177. "There is absolutely nothing that can be said that will apply to all homosexuals except that they either have, will, or want to engage in homoerotic practices." *CN* 3.22. See also *CN* May 25, 1964, 8–9.

178. "[B]iologically speaking, people are not compartmentalized into homosexual, heterosexual, or bisexual. Homosexuality is not a condition—it is a sex act like any other socially non-conforming sex act. . .; homosexual persons are not a class; their minority status stems solely form society's label, and the willingness of homosexual lifestyle cultists to continue to act the part." *VR* April 1972, 6. When the Gay Sunshine Collective considered the issue, they wondered if homosexuality were enough to even justify a newspaper, let alone a community. See *GS* Aug.–Sept. 1970, 2. And *BAR* reminded its readers, "And remember, there is only one issue that binds all homosexuals together and that is homosexuality." *BAR* July 15, 1971.

179. Guy Strait called it the "disturbing problem of political unity." *TN* Oct. 28, 1963.

180. "Since the homosexual community is composed of all types of persons, we feel that the movement ought not be constricted by any limiting concept of public image. The homosexual has no reputation to protect. . . . But we should support the right of individuals to do what they want and should educate the homosexual to accept himself as a homosexual and to accept all other persons . . . to help individuals achieve full personhood. . . .

As human beings and as homosexuals, we have a special interest in understanding all sexuality." *VR* May 1967, 3.

181. Roxanne (stage name of Jeff Hrock) argued that oneness came from coming out and being yourself, whatever that might mean. See *BAR* July 1, 1971. Ginger Snapp argued quite simply, "If we stay together, help each other, we can do it, or is it back in the closet queer?! Whatever our sex desires are has no bearing on why we can't unite. . . . Fight if we must to keep together and once we're together, the fight is over." *BAR* Oct. 1, 1971.

182. "We need the power and strength that comes from a large and diversified membership." *VR* Dec. 1969, 10. A self-identified conservative letter writer, E. Thompson, argued that "only thru expressions of diversity of opinion do we really go forwards. It is in UNITY as adverse to conformity that we really accomplish something worthwhile. And by spreading out all the ideas in a public forum sort of we can truly work for a democratic society." *VR* June 1972, 9.

183. Dan Allen observed, "My observations had been that Young gays and Old gays were out to drive each other up against the wall. More than that, there were stirrings of other confrontations: Gay Brother vs. Gay Sister, Black vs. White gay, Poor vs. Rich, Revolutionary vs. Passive, Obvious vs. Closet, splintering, splintering." *SFFP* Jan. 1970, 2. *Gay Sunshine* bemoaned the audience-driven content of gay publications, suggesting that this was what kept gay men divided from each other by always exaggerating their differences. "Existing gay publications—such as the *San Francisco Free Press* on one end and SIR's *Vector* on the other—almost deliberately appeal to only one sector of the total gay community in the area. That's the way the powers that be want it. They want to keep the city's 90,000 homosexuals divided among themselves." GS, Aug.–Sept. 1970, 2.

184. See for example *VR* July 1965, 2.

185. See Meeker, "Come Out West."

186. "Many homosexuals feel that they must impress the world that they are really more than meets the eye. . . . Is there a place in town where he could just be himself?" *VR* Jan. 1966, 3. To repeat a man cited above, when gay men were with each other, they experienced "the opportunity to take off one's mask to be oneself, for however short a time. For many homosexuals, it is unquestionably the only reason they seek the company of fellow homosexuals; not for the promise of sexual conquest, but simply for the exquisite release from the tension of playing a role they play every moment they move in a heterosexual circle." *VR* April 1967, 20–21, 29. More personally, Jay confessed that SIR's organization was "of great help in realizing the fact that one is not alone in a world of straight people. I find it a great help in times of stress to be able to hold my head up and say, 'I am not alone.'" *VR* July 1968, 16–17.

187. "How one 'comes out' is the basis for a very necessary conversation [with] our world. It teaches us what to expect in others. Without our gay friends, who confide their secrets and experiences, we would be lost. Our directions must be plotted in a hostile world, a world that we must take laughable when seen from the gay way, for sanity's sake." *VR* Nov. 1968, 16–18.

188. *Vector*'s editor claimed that SIR activities provided the context for self-acceptance and personal relationships. "We can only open doors; we cannot force persons to enter." *VR* Oct. 1967, 32–33.

189. Another man who had been beaten by a trick insisted on the importance of the safety offered by a true, open community such as that provided by SIR. See from "Left for Dead," *VR* Feb.–March 1968, 16–18.

190. "For the first time in my life, I have absolutely no recriminations about being a homosexual. I credit SIR, and other organizations like it, for seeing that one can live reasonably free of harassment." *VR* Nov. 1968, 16–18.

191. To repeat Winston Leyland's words, "I do feel for myself that my involvement in Gay Sunshine is where I belong—in this kind of creative activity." *GS* Dec. 1971–Jan. 1972, 1, 13. And Mark Ryan agreed, "I find a kind of a community, at least friends in the gay rap group, something I never felt before. Of course, I had to move to this city [San Francisco]."

192. See for example *VR* March 1972, 31: "After weaving in and out of homophile organizations for the past eight years and witnessing endless 'bitch fights' I question that love and unity is that evident [as Fisher argues]."

193. Zack Mansfield argued, "People really don't have common interests, they don't really belong together. But they're getting together and saying, 'Tonight, let's pretend that we're really a big happy family.'" *GS* Dec. 1971–Jan. 1972, 1, 13. To which Morgan Pinney responded, "I almost think, Zack, that any time you get together any community, it's a pretend job."

5

The Meaning of Gay Sex: Intimacy, Love, and Friendship

I get off the Polk Street bus several blocks before my stop. To cruise. That's what it is—cruising. But in my mind, I just want to walk home slowly. In my mind, I picture meeting some nice young man standing alongside a building and we'll chat very harmoniously and we'll walk on to my place and, and etc. And someday far in the future, when he and I are still lovers, I'll be saying to someone, "Oh, I met him one evening walking."

—from *Gay Sunshine*, Jan. 1972

As with other aspects of human behavior, the concrete institutional forms of sexuality at any given time and place are products of human action. They are imbued with conflicts of interest and political maneuvering, both deliberate and incidental. In that sense, sex is always political. . . . It is difficult to develop a pluralistic sexual ethics without a concept of benign sexual variation. . . . One of the most tenacious ideas about sex is that there is one best way to do it, and that everyone should do it that way.

—Gayle Rubin, "Thinking Sex" 1993 [1984]

San Francisco's gay men occupied a layered social world in the 1960s, one characterized by a dominated position vis-à-vis the symbolic order, oppressed by the official-public and its agents; yet their efforts to establish a gay publicity and act as a gay counter-public, and their desires for and work to build a gay community constituted other layers of their world. In this context, gay men were having a depth of conversation about the meaning of *gay* that hadn't occurred ever before. Surely, this was a new and different social context, one in which gay men could produce a meaningful gayness built upon but starkly unlike those that had preceded it. Marked by the political struggles within the community and the perceived assimilationist-radical binary, gay men had an extended (and ongoing) conversation about the most personal and individual aspects of their lives, including sex and intimacy, gender and masculinity, and identity and authenticity. In the following three chapters, I will examine in detail the range of meanings gay men were able to ascribe to these aspects of their gayness, beginning here with sex and intimacy.

Throughout the 1960s and peppered throughout their publications and in many different contexts, gay men's conversations always seemed to return to the meaning of their sexual desires and sex acts, and to a basic desire for relationship, for interactions with other gay men that would satisfy what many experienced as the need for emotional, social, and sexual intimacy. In many ways, this desire for connection with other gay men, sexually and emotionally, underlay many other conversations. From the LCE to gay liberation, gay men worried that the bonds they were able to form with other gay men should be meaningful and "real" and substantive in ways that could actually fulfill their needs. As I explained in the introduction, John Dewey wrote extensively about the "drives" that underlie human action and interaction in the 1910s and 1920s, as he worked out the dynamics of social interaction. For Dewey, drives such as hunger and sex were unknowable in themselves because they are always interpreted through our interactivity within social systems. Nonetheless, these drives are at the base of many of our social actions, but already refracted as "desires," that is, as an undergone *affect*, knowable and intelligible through the meanings emergent in interaction. Indeed, much of our life is aimed at satisfying these drives, however we may interpret or make sense of them. The pervasiveness of gay men's desires for relationships and intimacy, to say nothing of sex, speaks to something fundamental about these men's experience of their gay-maleness at the time. What remains for us here, in Dewey's estimation, is to understand the desire, that is, the set of meanings these gay men set up as paramount in their experiences as gay men, how they made sense of the desire for social, emotional, and sexual contact, the meanings they ascribed to relationship and interaction at the base, personal level of intimate bonds.

Clearly, for many if not most gay men at the time, it was not enough merely to be recognized in the official public, merely to be free of dominating meanings of homosexuality. Intimate friendships and relationships, sexual or otherwise, had to be formed and meaningful intimate bonds established. We have already seen the traces of these desires in gay men's intense and ongoing criticism of the failure of the political organizations and the community writ large to be an inclusive and meaningful social interaction. We have also seen that gay men were savvy to the ways in which their abject position in American society and in San Francisco specifically thwarted their efforts to form such intimate bonds. Yet beyond what can be deduced from these other cultural struggles, in the publications of the time, there are only the barest clues about gay men's significant friendships and relationships, which one current sociological study has demonstrated to be central to gay men's lives.[1] Other than the occasional picture of friends at SIR activities or a drag ball or at a Tavern Guild picnic, the men of the time didn't discuss their friendships or relationships very often in the gay publications.

I do not wish to romanticize gay male relationships, but I also don't want to underestimate their centrality in the experiences of gay men of the period. Both the meaning of sexual encounters and the formation of intimate bonds, both friendships and pair bonds, seem to have been the unspoken (and perhaps unintended) end of most of the counter-public and community building efforts, the struggle to create overarching social spaces within which these kinds of intimate relationships could be founded and flourish, in the way that they ebb and flow for most individuals in American society. Although the publications contain only the sparsest of references to specific experiences of these kinds of intimate relationships, writers did pay a constant attention to them, albeit abstractly or indirectly. Gay men across the political spectrum and in all the various subcultures and in the fractured community at large seemed to worry constantly about their inability to establish meaningful, intimate relationships with other gay men. And so the quest for liberation, for integration, for community, for normality, in short, nearly all their efforts during the period seem to have fallen back onto a quest for gay intimacy.[2]

Gayness and Sex

Within this context of an emergent counter-publicity and community building, and in their response to symbolic domination, gay men necessarily confronted the meaning of the sex act itself. As with most aspects of gayness, same-sex sexual acts could be imbued with an all-encompassing power to define the individual or they could be reduced to have barely any salience at all, or anywhere in between. But at a fundamental level, the question became, is same-sex sex alone *enough* to demand a more robust meaning, indeed, a *gayness* at all? This unspoken problem surfaced over and over again in gay men's ongoing arguments over what the male-male sex act itself should or could mean. This often resulted in gay men comparing their experience of sex with the dominant views of sex and sexuality at the time, and also of framing homosexual sex as being opposite heterosexual sex. Gay men worked between several tensions in lending meaning to male-male sex, between heightened meaning and meaninglessness, between sexual recreation and sexual objectification, between mimicry of straight sex and the democratic possibilities of male-male sex. The meaning of gay sex emerged in relationship to a dominant heteronormativity, as well as the experience of gay sex itself and the desire for gay sex.

Early in the period, Guy Strait's papers took a surprisingly positive tack in dealing with sex, although often indirectly. There were occasional discussions of sex, as when one letter writer, John Smith, wrote that when "social variants" finally accepted the truth about themselves, they often found that they were cut off from all social contact and that they had no rules guiding their sexual conduct anymore.[3] This lack of "rules" would be a recurring theme throughout the period, as gay men realized that they were refusing the dominant culture's rules and definitions of sexuality writ large. For Smith, sex *had* to be something more than *just sex*.[4] This was a lamentation heard from 1961 to 1972: gay sex had to be more than just cruising and anonymous sexual encounters, didn't it? This became one of the hinge points of the arguments about the meaning of gay sex, where men who wanted "more" argued against those who said "more" was an imposition from outside of gay life, and that gay male sex was good as it was. But the question remained open: if *more*, then *what*?

By mid-decade, other ideas began circulating more and more frequently. At first, following the San Francisco zeitgeist, gay men made oblique references to sex-positive attitudes had just become common in the city.[5] Soon they began more directly engaging the meanings of sex that had been imposed on them. Having been called sinners, gay men actively sought to dissociate sex from morality and associations of sexual rules with religion.[6] Indeed, as gay men responded to religious notions of sex, many flipped the moral question on its head. "'Homosexuals should not feel guilt or shame about their sexuality,' the SIR official concluded. 'Sex is God-created. We should learn to be proficient in it, using it to make our lives more beautiful'" (*VR* July 1970, 31).[7] Some simply took a matter-of-fact attitude about sex,[8] while others questioned the centrality of sex at all for a gayness.[9] Yet many insisted that yes, sex really was important. In 1971, a Sex and Drug Forum with gay men and women on the panel concluded that all people simply needed to be appropriately educated about sex so that they would enjoy it.[10] The Forum argued that sex was central to any human's life, and that all had a right to access to information and stimulation.

And so it was really in the early 1970s that the gay publications began directly tackling the problem of the meaning of gay sex itself, and often concluded that gay sex was purely recreational, about fun and celebration. In a review of a novel about a gay man trying to find his way, *Vector* began exploring what the meaning of gay sex might be, looking at the volatile issue of anonymous sexual encounters, implying that one possible meaning of gay sex was recreation, fun, sex as pleasure.[11] Part of this shift was to see homosexual sex as superior to straight sex. "The homosexual tends to bring more variety and fewer inhibitions to the bedroom," argued one writer (*VR* March 1972, 31). At the same time, the 1970s brought a heightened awareness of sex as itself oppressive, and many were wary, that sex-for-fun would lead to sexual objectification, which they saw as oppressive.[12] One gay libber was worried that he was messed up sexually, because "I want sex in such huge never satisfying quantities and because I want to commit every nice-looking man to my bed" (*GS* Jan. 1972, 11). So the meaning of gayness contained this tension between a celebratory or fun sex and the experience of objectification, and the meaninglessness of sex versus the possibility for gay sex to mean more.

As gay men worked out the meaning of gay sex, they also confronted the thorny problem of what makes a particular sex act *gay* in the first place. The obvious answer was that gay sex was between two people of the same sex and oriented toward "sameness."[13] But saying gay sex is *only* sex with someone of the same sex was too simplistic and was the starting point for detailed and extended discussions, especially among libbers, about the meaning of having sex with a man. Carl Whitman's definition of sex, for example, went further to include objectification as a positive aspect of sexuality, when it is mutual. But he also undercut the idea that homo-sex is different simply because it is *homo* sex, suggesting an inherent possibility of bisexuality.[14] At the same time, Whitman criticized gays for basing their sex on a "mimicry of straights." For him, gay sex "must transcend these roles—we strive for democratic, mutual, reciprocal sex . . . but that we break away from roles which enslave us" (*SFFP* Dec. 22–Jan. 7, 1970, 3–5). And so gay sex could be more than merely two men "balling," and it definitely shouldn't be like straight sex; but it could (even should) also hold the possibility of an egalitarian and more ethical sexuality.

For its part, *Gay Sunshine* addressed the meaning of gay sex often. Many of *GS*'s writers tried to be sex-positive, but were also highly critical of gay sexual practices and concerned about the personal effects that such practices had on individuals and on the community, which is to say, on the meaning of gayness. Like Carl Whitman, *Gay Sunshine* writers also criticized the dominant meanings of sex and connected them to other forms of oppression, from patriarchy and sexism to imperialism and nationalism.[15] Near the end of the period, one *Gay Sunshine* writer made an expansive argument for gay sex and its multiple meanings. He drew a sharp distinction between gay sex and straight sex—namely that procreation plays no role—and argued that out of that distinction arose the fundamental difference of gay sex. For him, gay sex was about communication and a heightened intimacy with all people.[16] Gay sex as a "means of relating" became an ideal for some gay men during this period and is a mode of gay life that endures to this day for many gay men. This same writer argued that for gay men, sexual pleasure can be in or out of a relationship, and that it's a personal preference; for some, emotional attachment enhances sex, but not necessarily so. Whereas some gay libbers were bitterly critical of cruising and anonymous sex, this writer argued that sex had many forms and meanings and shouldn't be limited, in order to facilitate a greater human connection.[17] For him, then, gay sex could sometimes rise almost to the level of something spiritual. "A hard dick is something very beautiful. . . . Then to come and give your lover the product of your body's love, or to receive the love juice from your partner, is a sweetness to be savored as you collapse and perhaps go to sleep in each other's arms" (*GS* April 1972, 10).

Men who saw homosexuality as something greater than its bald sex act fought to expand the meaning of gayness through the meanings they attached to the gay sex act. For men who saw homosexuality as merely a difference in their "proclivities," their effort was to strip sex (and gayness) of as much meaning as possible. And as these arguments played out in the pages of their publications, most men actually fell somewhere along the spectrum between these two possibilities. Importantly, the minimalist stance could actually be as sex-positive as the stance for a more meaningful sex, but the two poles often saw each other as sex negative. That is, men who argued that gay sex was meaningless were often quite sex positive, but because they refused gay publicity and community, they were seen as sex negative by activists of all political stripes. Conversely, those who argued that gay male sex be imbued with meaning and connected to gay identity could often be sex positive, but were seen by minimalists as sex negative because they were simply creating new rules for gay male sex. That said, it seems clear that for many, maybe even most, gay men, the notion that a same-sex sex act was the bare-bones meaning of *gay* made no sense to them in their experience. In all the publications, and across the political spectrum, gay men argued that homosexuality simply could not be reduced to its sexual function.[18] To illustrate, in their engagement with ex-gay men, gay men simply refused to believe that just because you stopped having sex with men you were no longer gay, insisting that to do so was merely to give up the act, not the gayness. "Were every anal canal equipped with a bear trap and every penis coated with strychnine, we might see a decline in the incidence of sodomy and fellatio, but not in homosexuality. The bars and baths would be as busy as ever, because homosexuality is something much more than homogenitality [having sex]" (*VR* Aug. 1970, 6). For this *Vector* author, a homosexual who rejected same-sex sex was therefore rejecting something deeper and more important than a sex act.

By 1970, it was most common to read ethical critiques of reducing gayness to the sex act. *The Effeminist* argued that when gay was nothing more than fucking, it could be nothing but exploitive, empty, and alienating—"the alienated contact that passes for sex in the so-called homosexual world" (*TE* 1.2, 5, 12). And indeed, the point was that gay sex was more than what one did with one's cock and ass.[19] Many gay men began to feel that the argument that being gay was just having gay sex was an oppressive and homophobic argument that served to keep gay men in their place. "Well I am tired to the bone of being told what I am. I am Gay. Yes, yes, my cock, my mouth, and my asshole is Gay. So is my fingernail, my big toe, my nose and my brain. I am not Gay because of where I put my cock or who I sleep with" (*GS* Aug.–Sept. 1970, 12). The difference, the *more*, was often located in the shared experience of symbolic domination and oppression.[20] Going even further, *Gay Sunshine* argued that the "establishment" had tricked gay men into thinking that their only difference was what they did sexually, so that "we'll suck cock and be quiet (it's hard to speak with a cock in the mouth)" (*GS* Nov. 1970, 8–9). For this writer, the internalization of the notion that gayness was nothing more than sex was why so many gay men refused gay male community, why they refused the idea of a gay brotherhood, why so many gay men got married to women. But, he declared, gay men were something much more that their sexual practices. "We are Homosexual-Sapiens (how's that for a scientific bag!) not just physical entities."

Some kinds of sex were derided as regressive, self-hating, or simply dangerous. Most gay men of the time, for example, distanced themselves from the practices of hustling and public sex. The hustler and his john represented a way to refuse publicity, to secretly (and illegally) engage in gay sex without suffering the consequences of being gay.[21] Gay organizations feared the hustlers for the violence they often perpetrated against their more vulnerable johns. Even in 1963, Guy Strait saw this as a form of self-hatred, where the hustler was praying on his own kind. And hustlers became one of the points of conflict over gender, as many men through the period observed that those who went out of their way to appear masculine were often hustlers.[22] In 1968, intrepid *Vector* readers mused together over why someone would want to be a hustler, with several "experts" weighing in. Most commonly, they concluded it was either the result of oppression from society or the "deprived background" where young men desperately needed love and acceptance and sought it in their older johns.[23] One man noted that hustlers were often violent against those johns with whom they might have an emotional attachment.[24] Perhaps such conclusions were drawn from experience, as surely many gay men used hustler's services, during a time when it was more difficult to find sex or companionship. But one man with whom I corresponded stumbled into hustling accidentally. Having only recently had his first sexual experience with another man, this man had come to San Francisco on leave from the Navy and quickly found that he could make a lot of money hustling. "I looked forward to seeing the Golden Gate Bridge and getting back to San Francisco where all the action was, and there was plenty of it for a young sailor in uniform and I soon learned that a hard cock brought in big bucks."[25] This man's experience as an openly gay man who enjoyed sex and the money he made from selling his services undermines the moralizing stances of the critiques of hustlers, but leaves open the critique of their johns. This contradictory evidence seems to point to the contradiction between the meaning of hustling and the actual experience of hustling.

As we saw in Chapter 1, public sex, whatever that might mean at any given moment, was often legal excuse for the persecution of gay men. As men in the counter-public argued about the meaning of public sex, they often associated a man's relative "outness" with his participation in public sex; that is, they saw public sex as evidence of a man who wasn't out or who hadn't fully accepted his gayness. This became a moral position, across the political spectrum, where a man caught having public sex could be seen as bearing individual responsibility in bringing about the oppression of the entire community.[26] The counter-public also saw such men as those most likely to appear threatening to straight people.[27] But there were also those who challenged these assumptions, as when Strait noticed the hypocrisy of those who shunned "swishes" but themselves got arrested for public sex.[28] For Strait, in the dominant culture, there was only one kind of homosexual, the one who gets arrested for public sex. But Strait still saw them as closeted and self-hating.[29]

And so the argument turned increasingly normative as the 1970s got underway, trying to figure out the appropriate relationship between sex and gayness, and returning often to the questions of multiple partners, cruising, and anonymous sex. Indeed, for many, meaning they hoped to create for gayness depended upon disarticulating gayness from sex, or more accurately, to make it about much more than sex, indeed, gayness for these men had to be political and communal, as much as it was sexual.[30] Others were already on to imagining the possibilities. One young man argued that gay men had the potential to create for themselves a new and vibrant "creative life style." Indeed, for him, it was an imperative to work toward this life style, and sex should be at the center of its creation. A truly good gay life style "means that sex becomes not an end but a means to embellishing and enhancing life" (*VR* July 1970, 39). And as we saw in Whitman's "Gay Manifesto," gay sex came to be seen as the possibility for intimate egalitarianism, often a morally and spiritually superior form of sex, "higher reaches of personal and intimate interrelationships . . . those of sexual and psychic love between equals on a subject-to-subject basis" (*VG* 2.1). These expanding meanings of gay sex were nearly always framed as fundamentally different from heterosexual sex, which was seen as constrained, hierarchal, and oppressive.[31] As usual, *Gay Sunshine*'s discussions were the most frank and idealized.

> What equality means in the sexual relationship is the question central to all sexual liberation movements. For gays, I think, its essence is that what I can do my partner can also do, how I feel he can also feel. In this sense we are biological and psychological equals. I can love being sucked and I can love sucking. I can love being fucked and I can love fucking. I am not limited to one or the other experience or feeling. . . . It is not one of us who is the giver and the other who is the receiver. Each of us is both. . . . In fact, we tend to embrace more of the polarities within us and relate to more of the polarities in our partner, rather than to suppress half our polarities in an effort to accentuate the polarities between the sexes. *GS* April 1972, 10.

In the end, then, the meaning of gay sex spanned every possibility between no meaning at all, to pure pleasure and fun, to deeply intimate human connection; and the range of those possibilities lent to the idea of gayness a breadth and significance. "Homosexuality is the great capacity to love a member of the same sex. It is a beautiful and varied aspect of human sexuality" (*IA* 1.3).

The Meaning of Pornography

In the first years of the LCE publications, there appeared a handful of line drawings of nearly nude men in advertisements, most notably the bare back of a cowboy in an ad for a bar in Phoenix in 1962 (only six months after the paper's first issue), a nearly naked Hawaiian youth in an ad for the Hula Shack, and drawings of Egyptian warriors, and the nearly naked body of a minotaur.[32] In the gay magazines of the period, following the advertising practices of the dominant culture, eroticized images of men's bodies were included for everything from clothing, exercise machines, pet stores, and of course bath houses, film houses,[33] gyms, "model agencies,"[34] and adult magazine stores.[35] By 1968, the images still either blocked out the genitals or discreetly hid them; but in 1969, more explicit images began to appear, especially in ads for pornography vendors. By 1971, the owner of Le Salon, an adult newsstand, worried that the proliferation of pornographic images in gay publications would be bad for his business.[36] I am using the idea of "erotic" and "pornographic" interchangeably here to reflect the slippery way that gay men of the period understood the phenomenon.

Erotic or explicitly sexual photographic images of men had begun to circulate among gay men in San Francisco before World War II. Men would exchange photographs with each other, and some had photo labs where copies could be made without notice by the authorities. The archives at the Gay Lesbian Bisexual Transgender Historical Society of Northern California contain several personal porn collections from men from the period.[37] What emerged between 1961 and 1972 was a battle between and among gay men about the meaning of such erotic imagery, its value for the community, and what the consumption and production of pornography would ultimately mean for gay men.[38] Besides its obvious sexual use,[39] gay men saw pornography and its consumption as being used in their oppression, their respectability or lack thereof, their liberation, and even in their aesthetics and ethics. Many believed, early in the 1960s, that pornography (at his time, this meant primarily physique magazines) was consumed almost exclusively "by latent or repressed homosexuals and if anything are used as outlets for emotions that may not be expressed in any other fashion" (*CN* 3.22).[40] This was a powerful idea that survived through the period.[41]

Whether or not these men were right about the closetedness of porn consumers, the observation that it served as an outlet for the consummation of desires that couldn't otherwise be met is significant. Beyond the usual playout of fantasy life often associated with pornography, the images of naked men, either by themselves or engaged in sexual acts, gave to gay men a connection to something they may have had no other connection to, to the positive images of men as sexual objects of desire and as sexually appropriate for each other. The emotional importance of these images for gay men must not be underestimated. Access to such materials was obviously important to Strait as he frequently discussed issues of censorship and informed on more than one occasion as to the laws referring to obscenity.[42] Some gay men seemed to have grasped that erotic images were fulfilling needs in the community.[43] Importantly, for a group of men whose sexuality was so tightly controlled and monitored by the dominant culture, seeing erotic images of men could play important roles beyond the merely prurient by providing psychological reinforcement to the moral goodness of their desires.

Whereas before 1968, pornography was mostly treated obliquely, as an a legal issue of censorship, after 1969, when nude and sexual imagery began appearing in gay organizations' publications, the arguments over the meaning and role of pornography in the community escalated into a heated battle. Gay men who had come from a culture where pornography was a primary sexual outlet in an oppressive society clashed with younger or more recently "out" gay men who wanted to rethink pornography's role. Many feared that pornography distracted from what the homosexual movement was really all about.[44] One oft-repeated claim (although sometimes with an implied wink) held that the majority of gay men did not consume pornography, thus, pornography should not be associated with gay men per se. Frank J. Howell argued that pornography in the gay world is simply part of the male psychology; this connection of pornography to masculinity was another oft-repeated trope.[45] Pornography then could be seen as a nuisance and distraction, an outlet for an oppressed people, or the expression of normal male sexuality.

In January 1968, *Vector* published its first full-frontal nude as part of its Forum on pornography.[46] The resulting controversy revealed much about the ways that gay men positioned themselves in relationship to the consumption of pornography, ranging from "pornography is degrading" to "pornography is alright by me." The following month, the controversy began. Ron K. Clark argued that any association of pornography with the movement was offensive to the entire community.[47] Men who criticized the nude cover attempted to de-sexualize homosexuality, not because they wanted a larger definition of "gay," but because they saw respectability as a political means of the movement; this is evident in how their arguments center around keeping the erotic part of homosexuality "private," or hidden from the larger public. Others used the occasion to argue for a different view of pornography altogether, using the occasion to add pornography to the list of sexual practices that should be morally rehabilitated, that is, seen in a sex-positive light.[48] Still others congratulated the magazine on its bravery.[49] An anonymous writer turned the objections around on the objectors, arguing that they reveal a hyprocrisy.[50] This first round discussion set the stage for much of what followed in the early 1970s.

In 1970, the editor of *Vector* started printing full-frontal nudes on the cover of the magazine. The first such issue had a naked young man standing outside on a dirt road in a natural setting (*VR* April 1970, cover). The community reacted strongly. The Ramrod, a leather bar, refused to sell *Vector* with a nude on the cover.[51] One of the editors reported a conversation he had with the bartender of the Ramrod, which had murals of male nudes on its walls. The bartender "carefully pointed out that they were nude, but all without a single penis. It was my opinion that paintings of eunuchs or castrated males were more obscene than a photograph of a man with one" (*VR* May 1970, 21). The editors argued that erotic representations of naked men that failed to show their genitals were in fact far more offensive than a penis, and urged its readers to compare them. Reader responses to the controversial cover ranged from embarrassment[52] to satisfaction. As with the 1968 controversy, the primary complaint was about the public image of the community. But some readers saw the covers as positive step toward refusing the rules of straight society imposed on gay male sexuality.[53] One reader, G.V. Lonsdale, added that it is simply the wrong choice to fight for acceptance by self-censorship. And at least one man found the controversy to be nothing more than another way for gay men to judge each other.[54]

At the same time, gay men also engaged the moral issues surrounding pornography in ways that echoed discussions then occurring in American society at large during the 1960s, attempting to make the difficult distinction between pornography and erotica. Frank J. Howell argued that something truly pornographic (i.e., immoral) would be a depiction of violence, not sex.[55] He argued that no evidence linked depictions of sex to any sort of mental harm and questioned why its consumption was then associated with mental illness. Others simply argued that it was a matter of personal morality.[56] And others pointed to the arbitrary definitions of pornography.[57] Such arguments centered on sex-positive messages, refusing not only the negative worth of homosexuality but of sex in general. Martin Stowe argued that those who were anti-pornography are simply anti-sex and sexually repressed.[58] For Stowe, pornography's true harm lay in how it might lead to a decline in real, human-to-human sexual contact; not that it was sexual per se. Indeed, many felt that pornography was simply irrelevant.[59]

Gay men understood from their experience that American culture was firmly anti-sexual, or sex-negative. That was why the gay press seemed to threaten "the very foundation of what we stand for, legal and social acceptance" (*TT* Aug. 1965, 11). For the publishers of *Town Talk* that meant that pornographic images were negative ammunition for the dominant culture. But even they felt that only "irrational thinkers" disapproved of sex between consenting adults.[60] What ultimately emerged out of their understanding of American anti-sexuality was an understanding of its hypocrisy, that pornography was simply a reflection of the natural interest in sex.[61] Indeed, this writer felt that Americans' crusade against pornography revealed not their desire to be rid of pornography, but their desire to enjoy it without having to possess it freely. For him, espousing anti-pornographic values was a way to have access to pornography.[62] And here we find another oft-repeated refrain, that pornography is merely the depiction of the beauty of the human form and of human sexuality, and that finding it offensive or disgusting amounted to a stunted view of aesthetics and morals. Yet others argued that real bodies, not pictorial bodies, were where true beauty lay.[63] Still, the majority of writers seemed to take the sex-positive tack, arguing for the aesthetics of the male body.[64]

By the 1970s, the arguments were getting more complicated as gay men had begun to address the objectification that feminism had begun to criticize in pornography. Interestingly, the critique often went side-by-side with a defense of pornography.[65] In contrast, Leo Laurence wrote a scathing critique of *Vector* in the *Berkeley Barb* arguing that it had become a porno magazine that served the needs of pornographers and gay bar owners.[66] Also paralleling the emerging feminist critique of pornography, in 1970 gay men began to critique the production of pornography rather than its consumption. George R. Coffman wrote that the nude images in *Vector* were obscene not because they were nude, but because they were hawking the wares of pornographers, who exploited young and poor men.[67] *Gay Sunshine* made the criticism explicit: the models were being exploited where they are required to sell their bodies for someone else's profit.[68] The paper accused *Vector* of contributing directly to the exploitation and humiliation of their gay brothers by using nudes in its pages.[69] *Gay Sunshine* insisted that the production of pornography was only a sanitized kind of prostitution, and even more horrifying, it was gay men exploiting other gay men to make a buck.[70] This was at the heart of what many gay libbers found bankrupt about the gay culture they inherited. "Much of the gay world consists of selling the body as a commodity and offering the promise of youth and beauty to men who can neither become younger nor more 'beautiful.'" (GS, May 1972, 3).

For some, the purpose of gay liberation was to create a culture where the sexual fix of pornography was no longer necessary, where "gay brothers and sisters are able to communicate with one another verbally and sexually without being unduly constricted by considerations of age, beauty, and other limitations which are now so emphasized in the gay subculture" (GS Jan. 1972, 11). Thus, a gay pulp novel shouldn't be judged on its pornographic content, but on whether or not it idealized "gay institutions such as bars and baths out of recognition and stereotype gay roles do the characters use one another impersonally?" For Rink, the impersonality of pornography made it automatically "offensive to anyone who connects sex with love, affection, tenderness and meaningful relationships between people as a rip-off" (GS Feb.–March 1972, 3).[71] But the arguments spanned the political spectrum and confounded the publications and individual gay men alike. Was pornography merely a celebration of the beauty of the male body? Was it a normal expression of male sexuality? Or was it immoral to consume as objectification of the oppressed? Did consuming pornography implicate the consumer in the exploitive means of producing the image? Or was the consumption of pornography a useful and normal outlet for a homosexual man's desire? Obviously, these are questions that remained unanswered but which continued to vex men throughout the period and perhaps into the present.

Evolving Gay Male Sexual-Social Spaces

Not surprisingly, the cultural practices that enabled same-sex-attracted men to find each other and to have sex with each other and, sometimes, to form longer-lasting relationships with each other—indeed the practices of gayness itself, as it was defined by these men—received unending scrutiny. The practices of going to bars and to bathhouses to "cruise" for sex—not to mention the practice of seeking sex in public parks and restrooms—and all the particular modes of dress, speech, and behavior that accompanied seeking sexual partners preoccupied many gay men, activists, and community-builders during the 1960s. Guy Strait's papers covered gay bar culture with several regular columns,[72] and the LCE News ran ads for gay bars and eateries, a practice that would be carried on in Vector, Adz Gayzette, and the Bay Area Reporter.[73] In the pages of Strait's publications, a rich culture, with its own codes and practices was recorded, where bars, after-hours hangouts, and bathhouses not only provided gay men with places to hook up for sex, but to form relationships and communities, to watch movies, organize picnics and outings, softball games, and even to establish lifelong family-like relationships. The social spaces that were primarily designed to facilitate sexual contact in fact served much larger roles, so that sex comes to overlap with other social activities and functions, expanding the meaning of gay male sex beyond the sex act to a social and communal activity. Although this is sociologically true, it must always be held in contrast with the experiences of many gay men who found such sexual-social spaces unwelcoming and even oppressive. So they did serve much expanded social roles, thereby expanding the understanding of sexual spaces; but they also were hot points for debate, exclusion, and contested meanings of gay sexual-social spaces.

The meaning and value of bar-going and the role of bars in the gay male community was hotly contested. Before the Black Cat was closed, Strait reported that the popular tourist gay bars actually mainly catered to straight people. For Strait, there were three kinds of bars: the "gay yet straight" bar like the Black Cat, where it was gay for show, but primarily a heterosexual patronage; the "homosexual but not gay" bar, where closeted men could hook up for sex[74]; and the authentic "gay" bar, where men who knew who they were and desired more than quick sex could hang out with each other and without being overrun by straight people. Strait, like the gay libbers after him, saw many gay bars as exploitive and detrimental to gay men's efforts for justice and to have a healthy self-acceptance. On the other hand, and in contrast to many later gay libbers, Strait also lauded the role of the "honest gay bar," where there was more than mere gay sex, but also a brief experience of the freedom of personhood gay men sought.[75] Bars that served more narrow cultural needs, such as leather, biker, S&M, and cowboy bars, also were often seen as safe spaces where patrons could be themselves while consummating their particular desires for sex and gender expression.[76] This idea that gay bars were larger sexual-social spaces persists through the decade, but is especially prominent outside of gay liberation.[77]

Yet for many gay men, the bars tended to be exclusive social spaces. This is most easily seen in the more specialized bars, such as leather bars, which met the needs of a narrower cross-section of gay men and actively excluded the men who didn't conform to their sub-cultural norms. In addition to a generalized gender anxiety,[78] these conflicts between the sub-cultural bars and the larger community were located in very specific sexual desires, that is, desires for particular kinds of sexual experiences and expressions, with particular kinds of men. So particular bars became social spaces to enact and consummate particular sexual desires. One *Vector* editor explained that leather bars don't seem like homosexual hangouts, which is part of their draw. Rather, it is a place where an emphasis on "masculine identification" is achieved through dress and self-conscious behavior.[79] But that notion of "masculine drag" held some power in and out of the leather community, as leather bars insisted on their gendered identity for sexual purposes, and created highly specialized cultural spaces that were quite accepting, but only to those who matched the cultural expectations of leather-gender. So leather bars became spaces for a particular expression of gay maleness and gay sex. This inevitably excluded as many as it included, as described by Richard M. Morton of Petaluma.

> I [no longer] go cruising on Folsom St. [an area with a high concentration of leather bars] because of the wretched state of mind I had to get into in order to 'fit-in' or 'make-out' [find a sex partner]. True it was that I milked the 'motorcycle-image' for what it was (not) worth; in a desperate attempt to compensate for the masculinity I thought I didn't have. *GS* Oct.–Nov. 1971, 13.

So leather bars could either be safe havens for men whose particular sexual desires for that kind of masculinity resonated with the cultures in the bars; but could also be highly judgmental and exclusive spaces that discriminated and created a kind of society apart.

But some gay men experienced exclusivity in all gay bars. These men argued, against my claim earlier, that gay bars oppressed the very men they purported to serve, because they failed to provide the social spaces where gay men could form meaningful relationships with other gay men. One letter writer went so far as to say that public, anonymous sex was actually created by the exclusivity of gay bars.[80] Gay liberation publications joined this critique, adding that such exclusive spaces were an inauthentic form of gayness.[81] So gay men from across the political spectrum often felt that gay bars failed them.[82] Like other gay male practices, bar-going could only do so much to meet gay men's needs. For others, gay bars in general came to be seen as oppressive in and of themselves, as evidence of the exclusion of homosexuals from society at large.[83] During the early 1970s, gay libbers extended their critique of bar culture to see bars as evidence of self-hatred, inauthentic gayness, and internalized oppression. An ad to join gay liberation in the *San Francisco Free Press* asked readers to "Help us free ourselves and our brothers and sisters from oppressive straight society and from the *plastic world of the gay ghetto bars*" (Dec. 7, 1969, 17, emphasis mine). For men who valued the counterculture, gay bars were "plastic" and fake. Bars, they argued, catered to gay men who were "so integrated (closeted) into straight society that they are all but impossible to reach"—they are "too far gone" (6). For this, only gay "heads"[84] outside of the bar culture could understand the arguments of gay liberation; gay bars produced a "sickness" and "polluted" gay men, and only those free from this sickness, uncorrupted by gay bars, were welcome in gay liberation.[85] These two arguments—that gay bars produced inauthentic gay culture and that they were run by capitalists to exploit gay men—became the core of the libbers' critique of gay bars and bathhouses.[86] So in the gaze of gay liberation, participation in these bar or bathhouse practices was to oppress oneself, to be inauthentic, and to further the exploitation of all gay men.[87]

Beyond the social, economic and cultural problems of the gay bars, the personal, relational effects on gay men were deeply felt. Morgan Pinney, for example, argued that gay bars perpetuated the culture of one-night stands and ghettoization.[88] For Pinney, liberation meant freedom *from* bar culture and the kinds of sexual practices it, in his experience, fostered. "[T]he point is that you can't expect to be liberated in a non-liberated territory which gay bars are." Thus, some men experienced the bars as harmful to the personhood of the gay man, against the very liberation they were working toward. Richard M. Morton wrote, "Many a night I would leave bars in tears—tears of rejection and regret, and tears of hot rage" (*GS* Oct.–Nov. 1971, 13).[89]

Critiques of bar culture after 1970s held that older forms of gay social life in bars had centered around getting a quick fuck and going back to a closeted life as soon as you'd had an orgasm.[90] Some men hoped for a way to "make yourself known, to make it known that you are seeking a meaningful relationship with someone" (*GS* Jan. 1972, 2). For many men, gay life in the bars ended up being nothing more than sex.[91] They hoped for a broadening of gay community that could foster what would be to him, deeper, more meaningful relationships. For many gay men, bar and bath culture hampered their ability to foster more substantive, emotional intimacy. For one Emmaus House writer, having sex at a bath was following a forewritten script rather than thinking and acting for himself.[92] Douglas Brown wrote that gay bars in San Francisco, with loud music that allowed no conversation, were only for cruising. For Brown, bars were alienating, where the possibility of a real, authentic sexual connection was foreclosed.[93] Gay bars, for many men, offered only a venue for a quick pick up, "sex, but love, never." And moreover, it was exploitive as gay bars took gay men's money, charging more than straight bars, and alienated gay men from each other. But away from the bar, "In bed at night, our hands clasped, legs entwined, we know we love each other and we love honesty and always will, wherever we are" (*IA* 1.1, 2).

Interestingly, gay publications across the political spectrum simultaneously voiced these concerns about gay bars and bathhouses, and continued to report and revel in the goings-on at these establishments. They widely noted that gay bars served some purpose in gay men's lives, even if incompletely or problematically, and that the critiques seemed to miss for the most part. And so the negative experiences of gay bars were always contradicted by others' positive experiences. The meaning of the gay bar, then, was continually negotiated and fought over; gay men experienced the gay bar as not just a site of exclusion, disappointment and oppression, but simultaneously as a valuable social space where they met not only for sex, but to make friends and form significant and lasting relationships and for political organizing and activism.

Wanting Something "More"

Two contextual issues pushed many gay men to demand more from their gay relationships. On one hand, among the many dominating ideas about homosexual men that circulated in American culture at the time was the idea that two men could never honestly love each other at all. To put it more bluntly, many believed that deep, abiding love between two men was simply impossible. Many gay men, working from their own experiences, held this idea; but many others resisted it and took it as a challenge to prove that gay men could have successful relationships. Many gay men seemed to have struggled against these dominating notions that foreclosed the very possibility of intimacy and that argued that homosexual love could never be as meaningful as heterosexual love.[94] On the other hand, as the 1960s moved forward and as gay men gained more sexual freedom and more visibility, some gay men began arguing that merely to have sex with another man was not sufficient to meet their needs, indeed, to reexamine what they really desired in the first place. And many concluded that they wanted something more. This again was an expansion of the meaning of gay beyond the mere sex act, pushing into the realm of intimacy and relationship and pair-bonding.

One man interviewed in a 1967 CBS documentary, reviewed in San Francisco's gay press, felt that the notion of a lasting gay male relationship was simply "gay folklore."[95] In answer to such fears, Don Burton, a gay folksinger, sang to his gay audience that it didn't matter whom they loved, because "love is always real" (SFFP Oct. 16, 1969, 11). In their struggle to move into the public sphere, gay men realized that they could have other kinds of relationships that, in their estimation, had been all too rare, in their estimation, in previous generations. "I need to be together with other Gay men," wrote one man. "We have not been together—we've not had enough self-respect for that. Isolated sex and then look for another partner. Enough of that, that's where we've been. Let's go somewhere else. Let's go somewhere where we value each other as more than just a hunk of meat" (GS Aug.–Sept. 1970, 12). So while many gay men were fighting to remove the stigma from gay sex in particular and sexuality in general, many were also feeling that sex alone was not enough for a meaningful gay life.

The search for some kind of intimacy, sexual or emotional, seems to have driven many gay men in their activism and their frustration with gay male culture. Morgan Pinney described a gay dance at San Francisco State University, where they perceived the desperation of alienated people.[96] Lee Atwell added that in his experience all gay people "are very lonely and very frustrated by their inability to cope with loneliness."[97] The frustration led many gay men to try all sorts of things to fill the void of intimacy in their lives, including trying to go back to loving girls or even trying to have relationships with straight men.[98] The men of Gay Sunshine Collective concluded that perhaps there is no solution for gay loneliness.[99] It is hard to tell where the symbolic domination ends and real gay male experience begins, or rather, what is the effect of the social environment gay men lived in and what was being produced by gay men themselves. Regardless, it is common throughout the period to read of gay men describing their lives as lonely and disconnected.

The desire for intimacy ranged from wanting long-term, committed relationships to simply wanting real friends, whatever that may have meant to the individual. Many men felt that gay culture actually prevented true friendships from forming. When Vector published an article in 1971 by a therapist who treated homosexuals, whom Vector was trying to discredit, he revealed something that resonated with many of the magazine's readers. He wrote, "The homosexuals I have seen [for therapy] were in the main disgusted with the brevity of their relationships, disgusted by how they squandered their time, interfered with their work, dispensed with their integrity, and sacrificed hopes of an enduring relationship and family life by their driven pursuit of homosexual sex partners" (*VR* Aug. 1971, 12–13). It is this brevity or the ephemeral nature of gay male connections that seemed to be at issue. Another author, arguing against public cruising and the YMCA, wished that gay men would understand that their basic humanity demanded more intimate bonds than the fleeting sexual encounter could provide. For him, it was about seeing each other not as sexual objects, but as human beings.[100] This longing for something more, a deeper sense of connection with other gay men, pushed many men into involvement in the community and in public activism.

But if some gay men wanted something more, they had to grapple with what that "more" would be. Even as they strove to form intimate bonds, they had to define what intimacy should actually mean, what kinds of practices that would actually provide the kinds of relationships and bonds they desired. Following from that need, the role of sex in gay men's relationships was under constant scrutiny. Many observed that after "coming out," many gay men engaged in lots of anonymous sex and ended up feeling as empty and lonely and they had when they were closeted. Tricking and cruising came to represent for some gay men evidence of an individual's oppressed state of being, one which rendered gay men incapable of meaningful relationship. Sometimes they blamed this inability to form intimate bonds on oppression.[101] Another writer argued that cruising was a way to cover up the fear of abandonment.[102] And in his article "Liberation Beats Masturbation," Douglas L. Brown said that anyone who gives in to the kind of guilt that prevents real intimacy has built their own prison. For many, the fight for intimacy "is our fight for Life and the right to live it. It is up to us to be involved with the entire gay community, not just the next trick!" (*IA* 1.2, 3). What is missing here is any concrete suggestions for what would constitute "intimacy" at all, other than that it was *more* than sex.

For many, living in a culture that dominated them sabotaged gay men's relationships before they began. To have a relationship under such circumstances required an amazing amount of psychological work. Libbers hoped that forming the new counterculture would create a new social context wherein gay men could have real, intimate bonds[103]; they looked to the future, when a different kind of society would enable more "authentic" relationships. Gay men's perceived inability or unwillingness to form meaningful relationships arose, from many men's experiences, from their place in society. For libbers, gay men's obsession with sex and their inability (or lack of desire) to establish long-term relationship reflected that oppression, not something intrinsic to masculinity or to gay-maleness.[104] The stereotype that gay men are incapable of relationship "is straight society's cop-out criticism of the gay world. . . . They are symptoms of a pattern of behavior forced on us by the extreme social, psychological, and legal repression the straight society has brought down on gays" (*GS* Nov. 1970, 17). So gay libbers thought that gay liberation and self-acceptance were the only way for gay men to throw off the straight lie about gay men, reject the "meat-market" atmosphere of the bars, and produce a new and more supportive gay culture.[105] Still, others argued that the nature of gayness meant that their relationships would be different and that straight values could not be applied to gay relationships. "Dr. Hatterer, as well as many homosexuals, apply heterosexual criteria for successful relationships to homosexuality, principally the criteria of longevity, sexuality and fidelity. . . . What takes over [in a gay relationship] is more important than the homogenitality and cannot be denied. To continue to harp on the sex of the object is futile to understanding this more significant relationship" (*VR* Sept. 1971, 30–31). And so the search for something more often returned to the question of whether gay love was fundamentally different from straight love and, if so, what should it look like?

Sex, Love, and Relationships

Starting in 1968, San Francisco's gay publications began to more and more often run photographs and line drawings of gay couples, rather than individual men. This is both a stage in the ongoing process of claiming a gay publicity, and a significant shift in gay men's self-representation. Some of these images depicted men engaged in sex acts, but more often, they were just male-male couples. It was a subtle change, but a significant one. This shift in the visual representations of gay men from individual shots and sexually explicit images to couples embracing, holding hands, or kissing (as opposed to simply fucking) signaled a shift in gay male culture of the city vis-à-vis their relationships with each other and how they saw those relationships.[106] But the change in imagery did not mean that gay men had figured out what their relationships would mean or what a relationship between two men even was in practice. Introducing its "Lover's Column," *Gay Sunshine* marked the shift between casual sex and meaningful relationship.[107] This sharp distinction between the "meaningless" sexual relationships and the "meaningful, authentic" relationship proved a slippery distinction to maintain, primarily because as the decade wore on, gay men didn't switch from one to another form of relating to each other, but instead worked to achieve intimacy and friendships in addition to their already established sexual practices and cultures.

As a group, gay men incorporated many different relational practices and their meanings into gay male cultural life, which included the anonymous sex of cruising and ranged all the way to gay marriage. In other words, the sexual practices of cruising and tricking did not decline during the period, from the anecdotal evidence available; but other forms of gay male relationships arose, or at least gained notice and recognition within the counter-public, and discussions about what kinds of sexual and non-sexual long-term relationships gay men could form occurred with increasing frequency, as least at a public level. I do not mean to imply that there weren't gay male couples prior to the 1960s.

Rather, I mean to argue that during the 1960s, the possibility of living openly with a lover and of being recognized as a couple, combined with a more open sexual culture in general among gay men produced a cultural imperative to define and understand gay male intimacy beyond fucking. Despite many men's insistence on the "closeted" nature of such practices, different kinds of gay relationships coexisted in the gay community of San Francisco. All of these kinds of relationships had to be given meaning in relationship to each other and from the context of the struggles produced by gay men who now felt that the possibility of establishing long-term, recognized, intimate relationships was available to them.

Among the most common meanings ascribed to gay male relationships was the insistence that gay male coupling demonstrated a real love between men, in defiance of the dominant culture's view of homosexuality. For example, *Citizens News* ran a series written by a man who was in a long-term relationship called "The Homosexual Ethic" (see CN 3.25 (1963), 2, 10, 12), in which he discussed the challenges of establishing long-term loving relationships with another man. In contrast to the men we've seen who felt that gay men's oppression foreclosed the possibility of real relationship, this author argued that young men coming to San Francisco for the first time could actually find true friendships that would allow a kind of physical intimacy that went beyond a quick fuck, which they wouldn't otherwise find possible. He also argued, however, that intimacy could be short lived in a place like San Francisco where so many gay men were all seeking the same thing. So "most young men end up with only acquaintances who often fail to provide the minimum comfort." The author argued that gay men needed to overcome infatuation, which is only fleeting sexual fulfillment, and extended the idea of gay relationship to *love*, which he defined as working together toward common goals. The argument of "The Homosexual Ethic" borrowed amply from the dominant notions of love and relationship as it defined bonding as respect, sharing, and mutual building-up. For this man, gay men simply don't want to take the time to actually build such a relationship; the writer argued that it takes a willingness to open oneself to another person and honestly listen to their desires and then to work for it.

Given the symbolic domination that insisted gay men were incapable of love, it is no surprise that throughout this period, gay men constantly insisted on the reality of gay love and attached gay love to gay relationship. However, such insistence was nearly always qualified.[108] Two men, Gorgeous and Mike Smith, declared that gay love is real and powerful in their lives; but another writer felt that too often gay men relied on sex as their proof of personhood, when in fact, love was that proof. [109] But if the meaning of gay relationships was to be anchored in gay love, then gay love itself had to be defined. Some libbers worried that seeking after "gay love" was "just trying to play bourgeois heterosexuals," to be play-acting.[110] But others unashamedly pulled upon traditional notions of familial, friendly, and wedded love.[111] Ultimately, many gay men concluded that what they wanted was intimacy, closeness with another man, rather than just sex with one.[112] And so they were left with a more specific question: what is love between to men? Commonly, gay men saw sex and love as being separate things and sometimes even mutually exclusive.[113] Often, they felt that if consummating a sexual desire were the purpose of an encounter, sex would foreclose the possibility of love.[114]

The confusion over the connection between love and sex produced interesting ideas, ranging from the more traditional ideas of sex dominant in Cold War America to the free love ethics of the late 1960s. These ranged from one man arguing in 1963 for a gay "law of chastity" that demanded a certain degree of restraint.[115] Surprisingly, this love/sex split reappeared through the period; even the gay libbers had their own version of it.[116] When sex and love were seen as being so disjointed, it tended to divorce sex from any sort of intimacy or meaning when it did not occur "as part of a total intimate relationship."

What gay men ended with was a vast array of ways to organize their relationships, ways to structure their intimacy with and without sex. Thus, the meanings of those relationships were equally diverse and wide ranging. To be clear, at least by 1972 it was by no means settled that individual taste and preference would be the rule of thumb for gay men's relationships. The emphasis on "love" and "authentic" relationship inherited from the counterculture seems to have claimed the dominant role in gay male culture at that time, at least in the publications; yet the actual relational practices of gay men were far more diverse than the prevailing ideas of the publications. Just as gay men understood their own diversity on many levels—without stating it that they were different from each other—they also seem to have acknowledged each other's different kinds of relationships even as they moralized about them.[117]

At its most traditional, the emerging desire for new forms of gay male relationship was the desire for fully legal and publicly recognized gay marriage. In February 1970, *Vector* ran a short man-on-the-street piece in which people were asked if two people of the same sex should be allowed to marry. It is plain to see that this particular rift in gay culture and politics had its birth more than thirty years ago. On the culturally conservative side, Paul Miller responded yes because he hoped it would reduce tricking.[118] On the "revolutionary" side, Peter Abinanati argued no, saying that relationships are about respect and consent, not about socially sanctioned institutions. And Don Young said yes, but that group marriage should also be legal. On the traditionally liberal side, Ben Olson argued that the legal benefits were the only reason for gay people to marry. And on the side of doubt, Gene Olson argued that homosexuals aren't ready for marriage because they "have to accept one another first." Interestingly, in the same issue, *Vector* explained to gay couples how to protect themselves legally (14–15).

Marriage was a polarizing issue in the early 1970s, not because it was a politically possibility as it is in the twenty-first century, but because of what it meant for gayness. In September 1971, *Vector* ran a feature about two men, Bob and Rick, who worked together at the American Conservatory Theatre in the city and decided to follow as closely as possible their Christian upbringing in setting up their marriage. For Bob and Rick, their marriage was a public statement of their devotion and to show younger homosexuals that happiness is possible (*VR* Sept. 1971, 40–41). In that image of gay marriage, the institution was cast in very conservative and, objectively speaking, assimilationist terms. An example from the opposing side, Whitman's "Gay Manifesto," argued that marriage was an inherently oppressive institution, and that gay people who wanted marriage were trapped by the desire to imitate straight life.[119] Rev. Perry of the MCC started marrying gay couples in 1970, "but only after they have been together for six months and have made a firm commitment to one another" (*VR* Aug. 1969, 10).[120] While not necessarily an important ends for gay publicity, the notion of gay marriage was already powerful by 1972 and reflected the deeper conflicts among gay men of the period.

Despite marriage's appearance on the scene, more common was the argument that a good gay relationship was a long-term affair based in mutual respect and commitment.[121] In part 2 of "The Homosexual Ethic," the author argued simply that honesty is the basis for any long-lasting gay relationship.[122] As gay men discussed their relationships they tended to be realistic about the difficulties. Part three of "The Homosexual Ethic" explained the difficulties of the gay relationship, especially of jealousy.[123] Real Married wrote that he'd left his partner three separate times, but that the relationship ultimately made him happier than anything else he'd experienced. In an early iteration of "open relationships," he described their commitment as one in which they allowed each other the space to experience life beyond their companionship.[124] Toward the end of the period, gay men began discussing more openly the multiple ways that they organized their sex lives within relationships, both undercutting the normative ideals of "authentic love" and demonstrating a substrate of different relationship of sex to love in their intimate relationships. In *Vector*'s Forum on gay marriage, there emerged a rare glimpse (for the period) into the actual practices of gay men in their relationships. One letter writer referred to "modern marriages" where "occasional outings" were allowed and mutually consensual. In an interesting twist, open relationships reproduce the disjunction between sex and love.[125] Another writer told of how his partner could not live with him having sex with other men outside the relationship, and eventually left him. And yet another, calling himself P.K., argued that it was unfair for gay couples to expect sexual fidelity from each other; he argued that the love and commitment were the actual substance of a gay relationship.

Another pattern that peeks through the record is men who have series of relationships, rather than one long-term relationship. Again in *Vector*'s Forum on marriage, Smith took a tolerant and open stance to other gay men's relational decisions, implying a communal ethic where gay men decide for themselves as individuals and as couples the kind of relationship they want. Beginning with Carl Whitman, many men argued that it was necessary simply that gay relationships discard a set of destructive expectations from the straight world. First, an attitude that we own our partners and they are exclusive to us; second, that we promise the future when we have no control over it; and third, that we establish inflexible roles based on social expectations.[126]

Other gay men, however, took a more expansive view of sex in gay relationships. Here, these gay men wrote of the intimacy and connection they found
in all kinds of sexual encounters. Tony Rossi wrote, "Is there 'love' in such sud-
den sex experiences? I believe there is to some extent . . . there is something of
each partner that transfers psychologically as well as physically" (*VR* March–
April 1968, 16–18).[127] Rossi resisted the argument that sex is superior in a relationship, arguing that there are kinds of intimacy to be found in all sex. And to
be clear, many men simply preferred casual, anonymous encounters over emotional connections; they wanted the sex for the pleasure of sex.[128] *Gay Sunshine*
also often wrote articles arguing that there is a place for casual sex in gay men's
lives.[129] For them, the problem with casual sex is that it often becomes a goal
that we have to achieve to see ourselves as successes. So the relationship between sex and love vexed gay men's search for intimacy throughout the period
and is never resolved. But for the meaning of gay, clearly for many gay men, it
had to be more than sex; they added *gay love* and *gay relationship* to the understanding of gayness.

Meaning and Gay Interaction

As gay men worked to build a community and a counter-public, the ways they
related to each other increased and broadened in scope, forming a constitutive
part of gay men's experience living in San Francisco. Not only were gay men
struggling with the repression of the public sphere, but they were struggling with
each other to create a social context that would give meaning to their experiences of same-sex desire and which could sustain both their cultural practices
and the relationships they forged in the context of an emergent gay community.
Here were the actual processes, discursive and performative, of establishing
meaningful social bonds that could support a social movement, a gay community. An equally important part of their environment, the most intimate social
bonds, friendships, sexual liaisons, and pair-boding relationships drill the gay
male experience down to the most personal level, the meaning of intimacy for a
gay man. In terms of these interactions, gay men wanted their community to
mean something to them, to fulfill a need, to satisfy a desire, often only barely
known to them. Mark Forrester of Vanguard argued that the very raison d'être of
organizations was to meet the *personal* needs of its members, and that political
benefits were secondary.[130] Such a community—a social environment of belonging where personal needs can be met—must be chosen: it does not exist of itself.
For these gay men on the frontlines of gay counter-publicity, the experiential
meanings of community emerged out of a *process* of achieving an end-in-
view,[131] subject to constant evaluation in terms of its effectiveness in creating
senses of belonging and meeting personal needs. And these evaluations seemed
to have focused on the interaction of gay men with each other in community.

Most prominent among the feelings gay men recorded was their need to feel a part of something, a yearning for a social reality that would support them in their difference.[132] As early as 1963, one guest writer for *The News* suggested that the community of social variants had to establish three modes of *belonging* within the community—Political, Intellectual, and Social—which included an understanding of homosexual history to help them feel more connected to each other.[133] One gay libber echoed this emphasis on belonging nearly a decade later when he described his feelings about belonging to the Gay Sunshine Collective.[134] Expressed in many different ways, gay men longed for the feeling of being in a place where an individual was accepted as he was. Some held out the desire that that acceptance would ultimately extend to the larger American public,[135] but most hoped simply for acceptance from other gay men.[136] The gay hippies used the ideals of the hippie movement to formulate their notion of what acceptance would feel like, a counterculture of young people creating a new society.[137] And by the early 1970s, the notion of *brotherhood* merged with acceptance. "I have heard many of our people say that it is foolish to claim a brotherhood, yet may I say that we are our own and only self defense" (*GS* Nov. 1970, 8–9). This sense of belonging, however it was conceived, from "homophile" to "revolutionary," stood at the core of what community meant to gay men, and brought to the surface the primary lack they felt in their oppressed existence and also their profound disappointment when the community failed to live up to its promise to deliver the sense of belonging they so desired.

Others found a kind of "spiritual," almost quasi-religious fulfillment that went beyond communal bonding or social belonging. This idea emerged late in the period and was associated with men who wanted saw their gayness as a uniqueness, and who valued creating social spaces that would preserve and nurture that uniqueness. The Emmaus House borrowed religious metaphors in its self-understanding; they saw their goal as to find the divine within gayness.[138] Emmaus, housed in a church on Polk Street, didn't see itself as Christian but sought rather to expand religious notions to constitute a spiritual community. Harry Hay, a granddaddy of the post-war gay movement, argued that the dominant culture had perpetrated spiritual violence, suppressing "ways of the spirit that should never have had to be stated, being as they are in the inmost guides of men and women of true maturity and integrity, in whom they lie too deep for words" (*VR* May 1967, 21, 25).[139] For men such as these, the spiritual significance of relationship with other gay men was that it opened up the inner truth of gay men's souls by putting them in communion with each other.

Many men believed that it was only through building relationships with other gay men that it would be possible to replace the symbolically dominating values with values that gay men themselves produced. Only then could gay men emerge "proud" of who they were, supported by others like themselves.[140] Thus, according to Hay, through interaction with other homosexuals, gay men could create and realize the full potential of a homosexual life. For the Gay Sunshine collective, a sense of pride among gay men would "liberate our minds and help bring about Identity-Community. We must develop our Art and Energy in order to assault the system with an alternative and with a show of the total beauty of our life-style" (*GS* Nov. 1970, 8–9). Others were aware of the diversity of homosexuals, but thought "pride" might give a way to gay unity despite diversity.[141] But such was only possible if a community helped "the individual gain a better understanding of himself and also other homosexuals" (*VR* Aug. 1967, 14–15). This would provide not only group acceptance, but self-acceptance.[142]

For some gay libbers and other men in the last few years of the period, gay male interaction was the most direct route to social transformation, to the creation of something new, a place for liberated individuals and free expression. Charles Thorp's poem, "June 29, 1970: Christopher Street First Anniversary" (*GS* Aug.–Sept. 1970, 17), directly connects community formation to revolutionary action. In another poem dedicated to two victims of violence (*GS* March 1971, 7), Thorp continues this theme, but adds to it that it's a community of lovers. He calls on the members of the community to come to each other's defenses like an army of lovers. The poem ends in bright optimism that the gay community will be victorious. Here, Thorp integrates the notion of a community of acceptance and love with the militant stand against oppression. The power of togetherness was the power to throw off oppressive forces and free the community of lovers. Ultimately, gay men turned to their hopes for what association with other gay men could provide them. The desire for interaction with gay men and the formation of bonds that were more than sex and that were more diverse than pair-bonding resulted in heightened expectations for what such relationships could provide.

For gay men who imbued interaction with other gay men with more broad and far-reaching emotional import, community was more than the communicative interaction I have been describing so far. For them, gay community was the very possibility of intimate relationships with other gay men, emotional, social, and sexual.[143] The sex act between two (or more) men held a range of possible meanings, depending on the experiences, expectations, and social positions of the individual gay men. It could be as narrow or as expansive as the situation called for, and it could be as connected or as separated from relationship and intimacy as desired. Despite gay men's arguments, the evidence seems to indicate that no matter how narrow some men desired their sex acts to be construed, they held a huge significance socially, as they took place within a dominating symbolic order that imbued their sex acts with consequences that far outstripped what they would hope. Indeed, I would argue that the minimalist meaning of gay sex was contrary to their lived experience, or perhaps hopeful. They seemed to misapprehend their private, secret, anonymous sex as "free" as meaningless; the very fact that it was constrained as it was demonstrates that gay sex acts were bursting at the seams with meaning. On the other hand, those who desired intimacy and deeper connection may have been overestimating the possibilities of sex within their social context, not just because they were in a subordinate position, but because the dominant order already held a constrained and tightly regulated view of "normal" and "fulfilling" relationship. I do not wish to denigrate either pole (or anyone in between), or to imply that they didn't know what they were talking about or lived in false consciousness. Rather, I wish to suggest that their arguments about the meaning of gay sex were more *normative* than *descriptive*. That is, they were statements of what gay sex *ought* to mean, rather than what it actually meant (bearing in mind the Deweyan notion of "meaning": how the physical sex act was situated in a symbolic order and social context and how the individual experienced that relation).

For gay men during this period, choosing to have sex and to be open about the fact that they were sexually active, to form relationships with other gay men, and to participate in broader forms of gay male social interaction involved a transformation at every level, indeed, a restructuring of gay men's very feelings. Participating in a community of gay men (or not) involved an emotional investment of some kind, be it adamant opposition or gung-ho support or anywhere in between. But more than that, gay men invested in community building in the hope of forming real, intimate bonds with other gay men. The relationship of individual gay men to each other in their emerging community necessarily transformed them as they experienced their same-sex desire, sex, and relationship in a different kind of social environment, one in which the tensions did not revolve around avoiding police interference or passing to keep one's job. Instead, gay men's focus had begun to shift to thinking about what other gay men thought of them and whether or not they were accepted by other gay men. Ironically, the gradual removal of outside threats actually complicated the process of forming gay community and relationships with other gay men by allowing the social space for gay men to seriously consider *each other* instead of "the Man" as a threat to their well-being. Whereas with the official public and with symbolic domination, the struggle was to assert one's existence against a concerted and well-orchestrated effort to keep homosexuals in their abject position, the gay male community and counter-publicity already assumed that an individual was gay, that there was nothing wrong with being gay, and that truly supportive social environments were possible for gay men. This meant that the interpersonal conflicts in and of themselves did not necessary automatically exclude an individual, but it also meant that when gay men felt rejected by the community, they felt it all the more personally, as the social environment that should welcome and nurture them seemed to say "No" to them with a greater force than the rejection of the dominant culture.

The longing for intimacy and for closer connection with other gay men reflects the opening up of experience as gay men struggled out from under the domination. In other words, as their environment opened up and gave them more space to experience themselves and to explore the possibilities of gay life, gay men expressed and acted out the needs and desires that the dominant culture had denied them. Again, the longing for a sense of community pushes us to look at the realm of feeling, the affective side of experience, where in the unending interaction with the complex environment, experience involved feelings at every point on the circuit. So although we find a distinct lack of affect-laden bonds in the arguments gay men had with each other over community, we find that they expressed deep needs for such bonds and such affective relationships. Gay men, through their communicative interaction, were indeed searching for the affect-laden bonds.

The experience of these processes of trying to establish sexual connection, relationship, intimacy, and tight social bonds, from the communal to the interpersonal, ultimately became a system wherein gay men could produce the various and contradictory meanings that they ascribed to their life-long friendships and relationships, sexual or otherwise. When viewed from the standpoint of Dewey's organic theory of knowledge, the process of gay community building in 1960s San Francisco was part and parcel to the process of meaning production. When knowledge and cognition are seen as arising in a circuit of experience within an obdurate and social environment—indeed, inextricably linked to that environment—the meanings gay men ascribed to their relationships can be seen as the complicated relationship between experience, social interaction, feeling, affect-laden bonds, communicative interaction, and behavior and practice within the social environment. Indeed, all of these things taken together *is meaning itself.* The production of meaning has the personal quality of making experience intelligible and therefore meaning*ful.* So the meaning of sex is as much an experience itself—and all that that entails as an activity-undergoing—as it is the discursive explanation of an experience. The meanings of gay sex and relationships emerged out of the confluence of gay men's experience of institutional repression, their experiences of community building and participation therein, and their values as they were formed in a state of need and desire and problems in their experience of their social environments. Some gay men wanted to reduce the meaning of sex to its bare minimum, because they wanted acceptance or recognition in the dominant culture, or because they accepted dominant moralities about sex acts, or because they didn't want to be *different.* Other men desired an expansive meaning of gay sex, because they wanted it to consummate their desires for relationship and intimacy. In all the meanings they ascribed and worked out, *gay* could never be the same after this period, because it now included an *open, public* connection among gay men to each other, as lovers, friends, life-partners, and communities, whatever that might ultimately look like. Nonetheless, from the evidence these men left behind, the quest to make gay sex, and by extension gayness itself, into something *more,* seems to have been the most elusive of desires to fulfill.

Notes

1. See Peter M. Nardi, *Gay Men's Friendships: Invincible Communities* (Chicago: University of Chicago Press, 1999).

2. Wrote one author, "The first [major problem after coming out] was finding a lover." *VR* Nov. 1970, 39, 43–44. Not all agreed that a significant romantic relationship was of utmost importance. *Vanguard* argued a few years earlier that many gay men were

only "half alive" because they were waiting for Prince Charming to carry them away. "Give up, Mary. The secret, the power to overthrow your loneliness is within. Put [your]self aside and learn to love others." *VG* March 1967. But perhaps simply learning to love others wasn't enough. That *Vanguard*'s would make such an argument in the first place reveals the primacy of the question in gay men's mind.

3. He argued that sex was a collection of "potent forces that govern physical relationships between complex personalities. I believe these laws do apply to the variant. I'm not sure how exactly or to what extent. But I know what I observe." *TN* Oct. 28, 1963.

4. "As James Baldwin says in *Nobody Knows My Name*, 'It does not take long, after all, to discover that sex is only sex, that there are few things on earth more futile or more deadening than a meaningless round of conquests.'" *TN* Oct. 28, 1963.

5. *Town Talk* asked when people would realize "that prejudice does not equal tolerance, and that satisfaction in love relationships does not equal degeneracy. These absurd and invalid equations will disappear as human beings learn not to fear the sexual instinct, but to use it as well." *TT* Jan. 1965, 1–2, 4.

6. Writing under the name Army, one man wrote, "Sex has nothing to do with morality. There is nothing sacred about sex. No act is moral or immoral per se merely because it is a sexual act. . . . Sex is good for everybody; sex is not sinful. It is morally neutral." *VR* Sept. 1967, 16–17.

7. See also *VR* June 1972, 34–35. *Vanguard* also published several articles insisting on the spiritual goodness of sex. *VG* 1.7, 29: "I choose to feel that the sexual revolution is emotionally honest and basically good. . . . Contrary to common belief, the homosexual act in itself is not necessarily a sin." See especially Dr. Fredrick C. Wood Jr. "Sex within the Created Order," *VG* 1.8, 5–6.

8. "Science will tell us that any normal healthy man has sexual drives." *VR* Dec. 1969, 20–21.

9. "[I find gay men] who can accept sex or leave it alone with equal feeling," wrote one man. *VR* Oct. 1970, 48.

10. See Phyllis Lyon, "Sex Can Be Fun: Life in a Sex and Drug Forum" *VR* Nov. 1970. "We are all . . . victims of myth and misinformation about human sexuality." The forum came up with three starting assumptions for teachers of sexuality. 1) sex can be talked about casually and helpfully; 2) ok to show and view images of sex acts; 3) teachers should have low guilt. "The Forum also takes an aesthetic view of human sexuality. . . . When sex is shown and talked about 'not clinically, but casually and nonjudgmentally,' humans can be assisted with their sexual problems. . . . The revolutions sweeping America—homosexual, black, women, sexual, youth—all seek freedom for the individual."

11. "Cole analyzes the philosophy of male promiscuity with a fellow he meets in the shower. . . . Cole: 'That's a heresy. Isn't sex meaningless this way?' Blond Boy: 'So who wants meaningfulness all the time? I want the meaning of all sorts of experiences with a lot of different individuals. If that's so meaningless, that's also tough. I enjoy it.'" *VR* Aug. 1971, 46–47.

12. See *VR* April 1972, 13.

13. The homosexual "places his emphasis in object relationships on physical sameness, rather than contrast." *VR* June 1972.

14. "And perhaps what we have called sexual 'orientation' probably just means that we have learned to play certain kinds of music well, and have not yet turned onto other music." *SFFP* Dec. 22–Jan. 7, 1970, 3–5.

15. "The 'missionary position' . . . purpose of the creation of offspring, is the first presupposition of everything Western culture represents . . . patriarchy, capitalism, nationalism, imperialism, fascism. From it come the thought patterns of active/passive, dominant/submissive, I/you, we/they, top/bottom, greater/lesser, win/lose." *GS* Oct. 1970, 4.

16. "[S]ex for us is more a matter of communication. And, through our experience with different people, we develop a wide range of skills and a broad perspective on sexual means of relating to people. . . . [G]ay men welcome the opportunity for intimate relationship with many people and experience is more highly valued." *GS* April 1972, 10.

17. "[Gay sex] might on one occasion be a quick release of tension and on another occasion be a leisurely expression of the deep love two men have for each other. . . . We tend not to condemn the quick sex release any more than the quick grabbing of a hamburger. . . . Sex is the potential means for the deepest sharing between human beings, but that potential is not destroyed or robbed by more casual experiences in bed."

18. For example, "Furthermore, you do not 'make' a homosexual by having a sexual experience with him or her. Too many people think that homosexuality is all physical . . . they leave out the important mental and emotional parts of his nature." *VR* Sept. 1969, 20–21, 30.

19. "We give preference to the genitality because of its orgiastic gratification, whereas it is the emotional satisfaction from extended close physical association that more appropriately meets our relational needs." *VR* Aug. 1970, 6.

20. "What separates me from the straight boy is not just the things we do in bed, but what our lives have been. When I meet an up-front Gay brother, I make a connection. I already know a lot about him." *GS* Aug.–Sept. 1970, 12.

21. Guy Strait consistently objected to hustlers and their refusal to acknowledge their sexuality and connections to the community, but he also argued consistently that prostitution should be legalized. "They [normal-appearing hustlers] are as much a variant as anyone can imagine, but they hide their natural proclivities with the surcharge for their company. They are commonly called hustlers. But they are nothing more than prostitutes and whores." *TN* Sept. 16, 1963, 1–2.

22. See for example letter from Jeff Hrock, *BAR* July 1, 1971.

23. "[H]e desires freedom, he urgently needs to be loved, and he needs money to survive." *VR* April–May 1968, 29.

24. See *VR* Oct. 1970, 4, 12. See also *VR* Feb. 1971, 11. Ron David wrote of his experiences with hustlers that he knew personally in 1971. "Hustlers—like whores—are damned by society in a love/hate relationship that despises their existence all the while it is fascinated by their life style. . . . Granted there are hustlers with all types of hang ups, just as there are all types of [etc]. . . . [Hustlers I have known] have included, among others, a straight, rugged 'man's man' ex-Marine whose eloquent quotations from Russian novelists can bring about a mental climax as well as physical; an Army deserter deep into the drug culture; a fashion model whose work has graced the S.F. Sunday Chronicle (who taught me that every part of the body can be erotically stimulated); and a Canadian ex-convict. . . . All of these people lead independent, well-directed lives. . . . They may be existentialists, but pragmatic ones. None of the defeatism, self-pity, guilt or sexual frustration evident in your Vector article are apparent. . . . I'm not necessarily advocating that everyone should rush right out to visit his corner hustler. but I would like an end to the stereotyping and antagonistic putdown that homosexuals in general and gay publications in particular seem all too ready to address toward hustlers. Vive le midnight cowboys!"

25. See Letter dated June 24, 2002, in Ormsbee's personal collection.

26. "The poor devil who is living in suburbia and who does not know the score (and often does not know the name of the game) is the one who frequents the Tea Rooms and the balcony of the theater that is showing nudie-cuties." *TN* Sept. 2, 1963, 1–2.

27. See *TN* Sept. 16, 1963, 1–2.

28. See *TN* Dec. 23, 1963, 1. See also *CN* Aug. 3, 1964, 6–8.

29. For Strait, these men were "the T-Room Queen and the Park Queen . . . '"the married man' down the peninsula who is straight except occasionally, . . . the person who cannot face his proclivities and reacts to them with violence and brutality towards his fellow man." *CN* Aug. 3, 1964, 6–8.

30. Richard M. Morton, of Petaluma, wrote, "We were not put here to suck and fuck our lives away! You know and I know that there has to be more to life than impartial and nameless intercourses." *GS* Oct.–Nov. 1971, 13. One *Vector* writer suggested an evaluative question: "Does it reflect in the slightest degree the humanized homosexual—or 'homophile'—which so many have worked so damned hard to achieve." *VR* July 1970, 10–11.

31. One man explained that two men sharing orgasms was "an absolute antithesis" to straight, reproductive sex. "[T]he act of 69-ing involving two persons of the same sex" was the perfect antithesis because "the totality of its mutuality creates the condition for the expansion of the act to include more than two persons without subtracting from anyone's degree of complete involvement: expansion into a community of persons sharing in the same orgasmic act of mutual affection." *GS* Oct. 1970, 4.

32. *Vector* included line drawings in its 1967 calendars, such as a water-skier or a young man in Halloween costume; these were not associated with advertising.

33. See *VR* Sept. 1970; ad copy read, "We proudly serve the Gay Community with the latest, the most exciting and the best in male films available"; March 1971 ad for a gay movie house included explicit sex.

34. See *VR* April–May 1968

35. See *VR* March 1969, 28; ad for Turk Street News Stand included edited images of young men having sex, March 1970, 26; ad for Le Salon had bare erect cocks, March 1970; another Turk Street ad included *Big D. . . Magazine* with an image of an young Asian man, and *Target* depicts a man bent over spreading his cheeks but the genitals covered, Aug. 1970, 4. By 1972, the Le Salon ads had explicit images of gay sex including oral and anal sex acts. See *VR* Feb. 1972, 55.

36. *VR* April 1971, 18–19.

37. Interestingly, Hal Call, often considered among the most conservative gay activists of the 1950s and 1960s had a photolab in the back of his store where he made copies of homemade photographs (according to a conversation with Willie Walker of the GLBTHS). There are also two books written on the history of gay pornography through this period. See F. Valentine Hooven, *Beefcake: The Muscle Magazines of America, 1950–1970* (Köln, Germany: Taschen, 1995); and Thomas Waugh, *Out/Lines: Underground Gay Graphics before Stonewall* (Vancouver, Canada: Arsenal Pulp Press, 2002).

38. I am uncomfortable with this word because it seems to carry with it anti-sex, anti-imagery value judgments. However, without employing cumbersome phrases or descriptors, I'm at a loss of another term to use. But I do so with the insistence that my intended use should not be taken in any way to imply a value stance for or against pornography per se.

39. From Roberta K., *VR* Jan.–Feb. 1968, 16–18: "For a person with some imagination, the use of printed matter, text or photography, can be far more fulfilling than an actual encounter with another individual. . . .With pornography, however, there is no such

disappointment. The scene is there, raw and naked, and the activities are just as you want them." From Larry Brinkin, "Pornography is not detrimental. The 'average' adult, if he were going to do something antisocial, would do it without being influenced by written words. Many gay people, far more than care to admit it, are sexually aroused by erotica, particularly, as an inducement to masturbation. this is not restricted to homosexuals however." And from Xerxes, "A certain amount of pornography can be titillating, but beyond that it is boring because of its repetitiousness. . . . That makes pornography enticing to most persons is the child's thrill of doing something 'naughty' and forbidden."

40. This despite his confession a year later that when he lived in Chicago, he had "four file drawers of nudes, sex action shots, and writings stayed in the apartment at all times." *CN* 4.4, 8–9.

41. Hal Call, owner of Adonis Bookstore, "explains that pornography is mainly produced for the lonely and unloved who can fantasize in to romantic or sexual infatuation as a substitute for real experience." *VR* April 1971, 18–19.

42. See *CN* 4.4, 8–9. In 1971, the Presidents Commission on Obscenity and Pornography recommended that pornography be decriminalized and argued that it was not harmful to the public. The Nixon Administration rejected the report. See *VR* April 1971, 18–19. The particular concerns of gay men to obscenity laws was explained thusly: "Homosexuals do not vary from heterosexuals in their attitude toward obscenity and pornography; homosexuals do register greater concern when it appears that an attitude is based more upon emotionality than rationality. It is the non-intellectual, emotional view of homosexuality that has created so much unhappiness and hostility between the homosexual and the heterosexual in our society." *VR* June 1971, 13.

43. A *Vector* writer argued, "So-called 'pornography' obviously fills a deep public need or else the demand would not be so great or sales so high. . . . [Censors] should concentrate their attention not on the suppliers, but on the public to ascertain what need is being fulfilled and determining a way more acceptable to them in which the need can be satisfied without pornography." *VR* May 1966, 11. Gay men also had access to pornographic literature, especially gay pulp fiction. Disappointed Reader, for example, was offended by a book review of a pulp novel that he found to be "disgusting, obscene, and in extremely bad taste" in its campy litany of the sexual exploits of a straight man who enjoyed sex with other men. See *VR* July 1966, 4. Indeed, gay pulp provoked a particular kind of ire from gay men who found it offensive not in its sexuality but in its representation of gayness. For one reviewer, gay pulp literature only represented gay men as "Closet Queens" or the "Gay Grotesque" where straight authors "save" gay characters in the end. See *VR* June 1970, 26, 29, 32–33. "Perhaps part of the hang-up about erotica is its quality or lack of it. The story lines with few exceptions are weak. The descriptions tiresome. . . . The heroes seldom have less than 9-inch phalluses and generally can ejaculate at least twenty-five times daily." *VR* April 1971, 18–19.

44. In 1968, S.B. argued that "if pornography is your bag, I could care less one way or the other because you have to carry your bag, but it is not a homosexual bag. Any connection that is established between the homophile movement and pornography is a disservice to the movement and an affront to the majority of homosexuals who are not interested in pornography." *VR* Jan.–Feb. 1968, 16–18.

45. "To the extent that pornography is visual, it represents more a male than female interest." *VR* May 1971, 54–56.

46. A SIR board member defended the editorial choice. "*Vector* is the number one homosexual publication in America today. It is proper, in the context of this particular Open Forum, that such a photo be shown." *VR* Jan.–Feb. 1968, 16–18. This board mem-

ber found an explicit connection between homosexuality and pornography, albeit a highly qualified one.

47. *VR* Feb.–March 1968, 24–25. Leo Laurence and T.M.E. agreed. See *VR* April–May 1968, 29.

48. W.W. Sherman wished that the courts would divorce the ideas of sex and nudity from pornography and "assume the positive attitude that the beauty and eloquence of all in this realm are absolutely pure and wonderful." *VR* Feb.–March 1968, 24–25.

49. George Caldwell of Chicago congratulated SIR for its bravery and then asked that even more explicit images and descriptions appear. "Such discussions in your Open Forum section would be just as proper as Auto Racing or horse enthusiasts having their own publications."

50. "As the pseudo-civil rights liberal is exposed when he gasps at the sight of the racially mixed couple on the street, your presentation shocks and boggles the *Vector* reader who will pay ten times the value of a Market Street paperback or a hazy photo depicting what he could be enjoying with his lover at no financial cost—you have unmasked us all." *VR* April–May 1968, 29.

51. See *VR* May 1970, 21.

52. One Canadian reader worried because in Toronto, gay men "play it cool" and the covers were too obvious. *VR* June 1970, 37.

53. Satisfied Reader argued, "The primary reading public for *Vector* is gay, not straight. The reaction of the straight public should be of secondary, if any, importance to the *Vector* staff. Straight society controls our behavior more than enough already. Should straight considerations censure OUR magazine?" *VR* July 1970, 9. Satisfied Reader argued that the nude covers were the most universal aspect of the magazine, elevating pornography to the level of that which unified all gay men.

54. "It is my cursory estimation that you are trying to force on the 'square' the same thing they have tried to force on us for many years. [If you don't appreciate the male form] there must be something wrong with you." The editor was replaced after only four issues. In 1972, *Vector* actually took credit for starting a trend when *Cosmopolitan* printed its nude centerfold of Burt Reynolds. See *VR* May 1972, 50.

55. "Hate is pornographic but easily tolerated in our society." *VR* Jan.–Feb. 1968, 16–18.

56. See letter from SIR Board Member.

57. "'Pornography' is only a word. . . . A limp penis is okay, and a half-hard penis is okay, but a fully erect penis becomes 'pornography.' Such nonsense!"

58. See *VR* May 1971, 54–46.

59. "Americans will go on having sex—with or without erotica. Kids will continue to learn about sex, whether it's at home, in a classroom, in a basement or from watching dogs in the school yard." *VR* April 1971, 18–19.

60. See *TT* Sept. 1965, 1, 4.

61. "If Americans were not interested in sex—there would be no pornography." *VR* April 1971, 18–19.

62. Even the religious gays got into the argument as Dr. Paul Roberts argued that anti-nudity was an evil idea introduced by Satan. See *VR* Oct. 1971, 21.

63. An anonymous reader argued that outside a real-life sexual context, the "male body loses its sex appeal." *VR* March 1972, 16.

64. "A hard dick is something very beautiful." *GS* April 1972, 10.

65. One man wrote, "I think that a 19-year-old kid is good for more than a quick roll in the bushes of Huntington Park. . . . But then again, I'm one of those idiot radicals that

sees nothing disgusting about a frontal nude (no matter how large or small the cock) and I am inclined to question why I should design my life to please those that do." *VR* April 1970, 26.

66. See letter from Louise Kauffman, *VR* Dec. 1970, 6.

67. See *VR* Oct. 1970, 9.

68. See *GS* Jan. 1972, 2.

69. One *Gay Sunshine* writer, Rink, tried to submit photos of himself to a modeling agency commonly used by *Vector* and reported that rather than being judged on his looks, it was all about the money. He was asked to be a model and encouraged to bring in other young men. If he did, he would receive a cut of their first year's earnings. He then reported that models are "procured" to "perform" at social gatherings. See *GS* Jan. 1972, 2.

70. "No one I talked to was able to completely insulate himself no matter how much he tried. Buying or selling degraded them all." *GS* Feb.–March 1972, 3.

71. Nonetheless, *Gay Sunshine* contained its fair share of explicit depictions of men and gay sex. To be fair, however, these were almost always line drawings and done by Gay Sunshine members. They were never, as far as I could tell from the publications, professionally done by modeling agencies. These images themselves are often tied to the counterculture of the day, as in the calendar depicting a gay zodiac.

72. For example, a regular column, Café Society, reported in the Aug. 5, 1963 about a rumor mill at bars such as the Tool Box, Black Cat, and the Jumping Frog; that José (first name only) planned to put on *Anthony and Cleopatra* for the 6th of July. Such columns often used campy humor to make its point: "Jose privately told me that he has spent slightly less that $40 million on this production, but he did not have the expense of Liz Taylor either." Connecting the Bay Area to other communities, Strait reported from bars in Tulsa, Dallas, and Los Angeles, referring to bars where men go to be seen as "Eyeball Palaces." Michelle, a drag queen, tried to get some "muscle men" to appear on stage with her at the opening of the Gym, a new bar, but only two of five agreed. This feature idea running down bar events was carried on by both *Vector* and the *Bay Area Reporter*.

73. Ads often reflected the sexual nature of their clientele, as in the Miracle Mile Christmas ads that featured the male symbol; the first image of a shirtless man was a line drawing of a shirtless cowboy in an ad for a bar in Phoenix in *The LCE News*; and later, ads featured photographs of naked young men as part of their ads, as in the ad for the Waterfront in *VR* Dec. 1968, 19. An ad appeared for the Miracle Mile (i.e., Folsom Street, south of Market) for Ramrod, the Stud, Covered Wagon, and Febe's; each in a male symbol as Xmas ornament in *VR* Dec. 1968, 19. Dave's Bathhouse began advertising in *Vector* with nudes in 1970; and a photo spread of "Greg and David" featured them together in a bathhouse in the city, *VR* Feb. 1972.

74. "In the homosexual pickup spot there is a variance of understanding of homosexuality itself. In the pickup spot you will find the married man from the suburb who strays from his ordinary bed only from time to time and when he does he is not at all as choosy as the full-time homosexual. The pickup spot patron merely wants to go to bed sexually—the gay bar cruiser is looking for the possibility of a lover. . . . [Bars cater to 'types'] . . . the trade of the 21-to-25 year old crowd; another the bike rider crowd; another the hair dresser crowd; another the office worker crowd, and so on. . . . The man who is accustomed to the pickups in the pickup spots does not have the knowledge of the life to distinguish this typing." *CN* 4.5, 6–7.

75. In a real gay bar, "there is a freedom of speech that does not exist in the ordinary homosexual hangout. It is rather common in the gay bar to speak in the idiom and to speak rather freely of sex habit and sex actions. In a bar known to be full of your own

kind, it is not necessary to hide anything, whereas in a homosexual pickup spot there are many who engage in homosexual acts but consider themselves not at all homosexuals." *CN* 4.5, 6–7.

76. One writer explained, "I enjoy this type of bar because its occupants seem to be in a more relaxed fraternal atmosphere that is never found in other establishments. Once accepted in the leather group one is never left out of conversation or meeting new faces. . . . There are no false pretenses, usually a tee-shirt and jeans or levis are acceptable. Western gear seems to still be 'in' as the American cowboy still retains a strong masculine image. . . . It should be noted that though leather plays an important factor in this association it does not mean that all people wearing leather are sadist or masochist. The signs of symbols of S&M are a language all their own. [hanky code]." *VR* June 1968, 5.

77. A *Vector* writer echoed the sentiment that bars provided a safe social space. "What a relief to become part of a gay crowd in a bar when we can no longer stand it and we have got to relax. . . . We are living a difference that society never lets us forget." *VR* March 1965, 2. When the Big Basket opened on Polk Street, *Vector* reported, "For the first time in our bejeweled city, persons of like temperaments can get together without fear of police harassment or civilian intimidation, and dance up a storm, wear what they like, and get involved with other people who think and feel as they do." *VR* Aug. 1968, 16–18.

78. See Chapter 6.

79. "The people who come here are MEN and want to continue being identified as such. . . . *Vector* does not share the opinion that wearing leather is necessarily 'masculine drag.'" *VR* June 1968, 16–17. Another reader complained about the "sissy-types" who flocked to the leather bars, which caused them to close because the leather guys have to try to find a place to "be by themselves." A writer calling himself "S.M." echoed, "Bitchy comments really start to fly when the doorman at one of the more popular leather bars admits people wearing leather before those dressed in more conservative garb." S.M. revealed the gendered tension in gay male sexual practices as they played out in leather bars. "[M]ost of the leather boys are going to go home with a man and not some poor excuse for one, such as is found all too often in these [other] bars."

80. Aceydecy of New York argued with Strait about why some men seek out public, anonymous sex, blaming it on the exclusive feeling at gay bars. "Maybe some hang around in public places because they have been frozen out of so-called friendlier places by the 'clique.'" *TN* Oct. 14, 1963. Nearly ten years later, *BAR* asked, "Now, how many of these same strangers [to San Francisco] leave these establishments [gay bars] with the warm glow of friendship (not alcoholic) that we as a community hope to convey?" *BAR*, July 1, 1971.

81. For example, "'Today, we have mainly a bar-oriented culture,' Gale continued. 'People have to get drunk to relate to each other. Once the counter-culture is built, it will be more meaningful, more beautiful.'" *SFFP* Jan. 1970.

82. *AG* reported that only 45 percent of its readers felt that gay bars met their personal needs. See *AG* Jan. 7, 1971.

83. "I recognize them [bars and baths] as the product of our oppression, and it seems to me tragic that if two women or men wish to dance together they have to go to a special place." *VR* April 1972, 13. And *Gay Sunshine* noted "that gays had to develop separate institutions like the baths and the bars so they would have some place to meet each other 'discreetly' . . . without offending bigoted straights with their lewd and lascivious behavior." *GS* Oct.–Nov. 1971, 6.

84. "Head" was the insider term for "hippie," the term members of the counterculture used to refer to themselves and those who "got it."

85. Indeed, for this libber, gay liberation was "the only meaningful alternative" to
bars. "The bar scene is a game. It is a great circus managed by straight and gay capitalists
out to make a buck. . . . The bar scene in San Francisco is at once a refuge and a nirvana
for Plasticgays from every crossroads hamlet in Amerika. Used to play the game of the
bars Ghetto-gays soon lose all perspective of reality."

86. Such critiques were not unique to the libbers, and in fact can be seen in the early
1960s in Guy Strait's publications. "75% of [gay bars] were opened as ordinary bars and
then business got so bad that the owners hired a bartender to 'turn it on' as a gay bar." *CN*
4.5 1964, 6–7. Libbers' critiques were merely more pointed, but not new to the San Francisco gay male community. Steve Ginsburg of Berkeley wrote, "The bars are ours; ask
Ruthie and Joe Pigs about that and why they charge the highest price of any bar for beer,
60¢." *GS* April–May 1971, 16. Smedly leveled the same kind of critique at the YMCA,
which had served as a de facto bathhouse in San Francisco at least since World War II.
The Y publicly eschewed gay men, but then encouraged their patronage and charged
them money to enter and have sex in their showers, locker rooms, and bathrooms. "We
men, queered by the inhumanity of American life, queer ourselves in the YMCA, making
ourselves into sexual objects for our own self-exploitation or the exploitation of others."
GS Aug.–Sept. 1970, 8.

87. *Gay Sunshine* also directly attacked specific bars they saw as being especially
exploitive, such as The Shed, where a young gay man was assaulted in January 1972.
"Alternatives to this exploitative scene are slowly evolving and we suggest that you support these." *GS* Feb.–March 1972, 3.

88. "Those institutions lend themselves to that kind of a life. And now we really
don't need the one night stands in our heads. I think we're liberated beyond that point.
They came about because of guilt. . . . But we're left with institutions which lend themselves only to one night stands." *GS* Dec. 1971–Jan. 1972, 1, 13.

89. Although *Gay Sunshine* spent a lot of space criticizing bar culture, some of its
members were sensitive to the complicated relationship gay men had to their bars. "I
think so many people try to get rid of their loneliness and get caught up in the bar syndrome. . . . Maybe gay lib has criticized the bars too much. We've got to provide alternatives." *GS* Dec. 1971–Jan. 1972, 1, 13.

90. "The institutions in our lives—the bars, the baths, the parks, the street cruising—
all seem to be geared toward the quick trick." *GS* Jan. 1972, 2.

91. "It's not that I'm condemning street cruising or parks or baths or even bars.
Without them we'd be left as completely sex starved as Victorian England." *GS* Jan.
1972, 11.

92. "When I go to the baths or the bars, I show concern for no more than dim shad-
ows of people. . . . Maybe this is the best I can do at the moment. . . . 'This is not living—
it's shooting up and getting stoned.'" *IA* 1.1, 2.

93. "Then I was in his arms. We were kissing. . . . A woman's voice broke through
to us, 'You can't do that here. This is a respectable place. If you are going to kiss and
hold hands, you will have to leave.'" *IA* 1.3, 10.

94. In their review of CBS's documentary about homosexuality, they reported that
gay men were incapable of "fulfilling relationship with a woman or for that matter with a
man." See *VR* April 1967, 20–21, 29.

95. See *VR* April 1967, 20–21, 29. Many gay men simply did not believe that a real
love between gay men was possible. Kevin Macre argued that gay men can't have true

love because they are too selfish. "I don't think that the emotions and physical responses of gay people are on as high a plane as straight people. . . . When we follow some of the good standards that the heterosexual world has set up on love and start dating before we 'fall in love' when we stop meeting on a Monday and tricking that night and then falling in love on Tuesday and moving in together on Wednesday then we might have healthy love." *VR* March–April 1968, 16–18. Fred the ex-gay man argued that gay male relationships were devoid of love, and based on "sharp jealousy, fear, and hatred" instead. *VR* July 1970, 18–19, 41.

96. "Tony and I were both struck by the fact of the desperation of the people. Everybody there was looking around, you know, hunting, looking very lonely. . . . The people there were acting like gay people act. They were lonely, by themselves, afraid to make any real contact. What they wanted to do was find a trick." *GS* Dec. 1971–Jan. 1972, 1, 13.

97. Another writer declared, "But damn it! I don't want to be so terribly, terribly lonely anymore either." *GS* Jan. 1972, 11. In counter-distinction to these sentiments, *Ads Gayzette*'s reader survey reported that only 31 percent of respondents felt that gay life was "cold and unfriendly."

98. *VR* Nov. 1970, 39, 43–44.

99. "We have put all our stress on problems of personal liberation. And we've been trying to liberate ourselves out of problems that have no solution." *GS* Dec. 1971–Jan. 1972, 1, 13.

100. "We must begin to relate to each other as human beings, one to another, men and men, women and men. Break down the walls the YMCA's have created in our heads, in our very bodies. We queers know what's on the other side of the partition. I am. Let's take a good look, brother, maybe some day we'll see someone else, someone we like, another human being working his way out into a world he too can create. Let's take what we inherited and make it into a more decent, a more real way of life." *GS* Aug.–Sept. 1970, 8. Likewise, Disappointed wrote that "I also feel that those of us who are seeking something more are entitled to this new extension to the gay scene to prevent our reflecting [sic] back to our youth." *AG* Feb. 25, 1971, 7.

101. One writer, F.H., argued that gay men were too immature to have "deep and meaningful bonds" and because of guilt over being gay, they were incapable of even imagining a life-long relationship with another man. For F.H., this was a form of "alienation and self doubt plants the seeds of the 'one-night-stand' and 'playing it just for kicks.'" *VR* March–April 1968, 16–18.

102. See *VR* June 1968, 12.

103. Gale Whittington argued that the bar culture, for him evidence of oppression, prevented real intimate relationship; but "'Once the counterculture is built, it will be more meaningful, more beautiful.'" *SFFP* Jan. 1970.

104. "Our relationships on the job, in school, at church could never be whole because it was not safe to express our sexual interests there. Therefore, at the end of the day or at the end of the week we went to where we knew gay people congregated: certain bars, baths, and parks. . . . Society permitted only these meeting places because they were the means by which we were kept in our place. By restricting our meeting, society forced us to act our roles in our search for each other that supported heterosexual stereotypes of us. For example they wanted to believe that we are more impersonal in our sexual relationships. . . . First they made it dangerous for us to be open about sex in our regular relationships. Then they provided meeting places, which, because we were so easily exposed, were also dangerous. Anonymity became necessary for survival. . . . Impersonal sex be-

came an imposed way of life. . . . Our oppression reached into our bedrooms." *GS* April 1972, 10.

105. Morgan Pinney felt that the poor way he was treated by men he dated amounted to self-hatred, and revealed "a great lack of respect for the gay relationship." *GS* Oct. 1970, 11. Pinney wanted gay men to adopt a personal ethic of total honesty with each other in terms of their relationships and sexual encounters. "Any other practice only serves to continue the humanly destructive myths that gay sex is only for quick tricks, for a couple of hours, that another man is but a cock to suck and then discard like a banana peel." Libbers argued that these sexual and relational differences arose not out of gayness per se, but out of gay men's relationship to the dominant culture. See *GS* April 1972, 10.

106. See for example *SFFGP* Dec. 1970, 3, a picture of Charles Thorp and his boyfriend; and *GS* Nov. 1970, 10–11, two-page spread of the famous Richard Avedon portrait of Allan Ginsberg and his boyfriend holding each other in the nude; *VR* Oct. 1971, 5, an anonymous photograph of two men, one behind the other, leaning on him, outside with their shirts off in Levis; and photos of David Clayton and Earl (Rick) Stokes, a "married" gay male couple, *VR* Dec. 1971, 4.

107. "The institutions in our lives—the bars, the baths, the parks, the street cruising—all seem to be geared toward the quick trick. . . . Our only intention is to allow you to make yourself known, to make it known that you are seeking a meaningful relationship with someone." *GS* Jan. 1972, 2.

108. For example, W.H. noted "I feel that homosexual love is real, or as real as heterosexual love. . . . [But] because gay people do not have families and both have a source of income, it is more difficult for such partnerships to last." *VR* March–April 1968, 16–18.

109. See *VR* Jan. 1969, 7, 22.

110. "Or it may be that homosexual love is bound to be, as it was in more open times, a band of men, a brotherhood, and that the commune and a 'group marriage' scene is the sane and 'normal' way for homosexuals." *AA* July 20, 1970.

111. One letter from Dan H. explained, "Love is the strong personal attachment based on ties of kinship (father/son or brother/brother) or ardent and impassioned affection (sex) or sympathetic understanding (aged couples or priest/parishioner)." *VR* March–April 1968, 16–18.

112. "Rather than a 'shot of masculinity' it is affection and emotional satiety that the homosexual craves (and don't we all?) and which, if he does not have, can result in emotional disruption and personality regression." *VR* Oct. 1970, 48. One man wrote of his nightly ritual. "I get off the Polk Street bus several blocks before my stop. To cruise. That's what it is—cruising. but in my mind, I just want to walk home slowly. In my mind, I picture meeting some nice young man standing alongside building and we'll chat very harmoniously and we'll walk on to my place and, and, etc. And Someday far in the future, when he and I are still lovers, I'll be saying to someone, 'Oh, I met him one evening walking.' It has never happened yet, of course. . . . Home now. Same solitary scene. A book. Sleep. Well, tomorrow is another day." *GS* Jan. 1972, 11.

113. But other men simply argued from their experience that love and sex were disjointed. Steve Edwards argued that "I can say that my lover and I have a more meaningful relationship than one based merely on sex and sex alone. . . . It is a love that transcends the purely physical attraction, the only binding force between so many couples, both gay and straight. Love is very rare . . . in both worlds." *VR* March–April 1968, 16–18.

114. See *VR* July 1967, 5. When *Vector* interviewed some of the local "heads," Taurameni argued that "The real human being, then, puts the emphasis on love [not sex]." *VR* July 1967, 5. Indeed, the meaning of sex and the relationship between sex and love (relationship) was a major theme of the interview with these hippie leaders. "LEON: People think that because they are communicating sexually that that's it. . . . It's so restrictive limiting to concentrate only on that one"; "NOEL: . . . Man, a screw is a screw, but let's not kid ourselves into thinking it's anything more if it isn't"; "LEON: . . . how can there be love when you don't know the person, when you haven't accepted the total person?"; "NOEL: . . . The full realization that the other person is constantly growing and if there is love, you will accept al the directions that person may grow in."

115. John Smith: "I've seen a great deal of unhappiness come as a result of attempts to become a 'free soul.' Simply accepting the truth about one's self at last does not make one a 'free soul.' . . . A little inhibition is still a good thing and a dedication of [sic] some kind of reasonable personal morality is essential to keeping self-respect." *TN* Oct. 28, 1963.

116. "A cock in the mouth becomes a virtual phallic pacifier. It may not be success or happiness but it will do until the real thing comes along. . . . How much better it would be if I could be content without having sex in such frequent and large amounts, biding my time until sex happened as part of a total intimate relationship. Ah, then it would be sweet indeed." *GS* Jan. 1972, 11.

117. "Liberation for gay people is to define for ourselves how and with whom we live, instead of measuring our relationships be straight values." *SFFP* Dec. 22–Jan. 7, 1970, 3–5. The radical Christians agreed. "And it may be that each of these ways is right for the right individual. . . . We'll never know unless we cut away the shit and prepare open and unafraid, to discover the true nature of ourselves and our brothers. . . . We can only do this together, clashing ideas and feelings together, on a battlefield of love." *AA* July 20, 1970.

118. "If they were married, they might talk it out and find out why one wants sex with someone other than his partner." *VR* Feb. 1970, 27.

119. "Gay people must stop measuring their self-respect by how well they mimic straight marriages. Gay marriage will have the same problems as straight tones, except in burlesque." *SFFP* Dec. 22–Jan. 7, 1970, 3–5.

120. Although rare, there was also discussion of gay men forming families and raising children together. "Homosexuals are capable of and do find real love, and how wonderful it would be if homosexuals could adopt children, who are homeless and unloved. It would give children love, and solve the lonely problems for many gay people." *VR* March–April 1968, 16–18. The issue was revisited in a February 1972 article in which the author argued that the urge to parent was actually not connected to reproduction; and he pointed to gay men's tendency to go into "caring" professions as evidence of their submerged parenting instinct. "Many of these occupations allow psychological compensation for the absence of offspring." *VR* Feb. 1972, 24. The difficulty, of course, was how to have children. "The problem for the male homosexual is much greater as the difficulty of finding a woman willing to have a child and give it up." The article addresses some primary concerns, namely that a child's sexuality is not determined by the sexuality of the parents; and that two homosexual parents were more desirable for a child than a single heterosexual parent.

121. Two Peaceful Lovers insisted that "it does and will work if you deeply want it to. It's not camp, it's serious business and lots of fun." *AG* Dec. 17, 1970.

122. "If you can begin your new friendship, however, by presenting as honest a portrayal of yourself as possible, you have cleared a hurdle." *CN* 4.1 (Oct. 1964), 4, 10. Perhaps the first in a long line of self-help advice for gay men seeking significant, long-term relationships, "The Homosexual Ethic" series gave readers a list of questions to ask themselves to find the right partner and advised against "quickie friendships." "Ask yourself first—will he aid your development and growth? Can he help you become a better person through understanding yourself? Is he the type of person you would be proud to introduce to friends? Will he probably make life happier for you?"

123. "There is the jealousy over the attentions your partner gives someone else. . . . You cannot completely possess another's body and soul. . . . Are you really angry because of his interest in that person or angry that you didn't make out?" *CN* 4.2 (Nov. 1964), 6–7. This sentiment was later echoed by "One Who Loved Not Wisely but Too Well," *VR* March–April 1968, 16–18.

124. "We are not tied down to each other, nor do we have completely free reins to indulge excessively. In other words, we feel we are truly married and very much in love, a feeling (even after 8 1/2 years together) which seems to constantly grow stronger." *VR* March–April 1968, 16–18.

125. "Sex alone fades away, but love endures forever. This 'modern marriage' arrangement certainly isn't easy to accept." *VR* March–April 1968, 16–18.

126. Whitman argued for "a new pluralistic, role-free social structure for ourselves. It must contain both the physical space and spiritual freedom for people to live alone, live together for a while, live together for a long time, either as couples or in larger numbers; and the ability to flow easily from one of these states to another as our needs change." *SFFP* Dec. 22–Jan. 7, 1970, 3–5.

127. "Frequently my 'married' gay friends criticize me for my partners are many and varied. My motives are constantly being analyzed. Many people like me do not sustain lengthy love affairs for many reasons. . . . But it seems that my married friends would prefer me to masturbate . . . until I find my 'true love.'"

128. Even Rossi wrote, "What I like is married men. They like to meet a person and develop a discreet affair and they always have to go home, thank God."

129. "Sex doesn't have to be, you know, that once you suck somebody's cock, you've got to be married to them. . . . Sure there's a place for casual sex, but I think that's all we've got." *GS* Dec. 1971–Jan. 1972, 1, 13.

130. "The only reason people ever band together is because organization gives them the power to satisfy their desires or to attain realization of their needs." *VG* 2.2. Zack Mansfield defined a true community as one where "people are getting together to satisfy real needs honestly, then it's a community." *GS* Dec. 1971–Jan. 1972, 1, 13. And for Morgan Pinney, real needs could only be met by a community that met "a real need to feel some sort of contact with other human beings."

131. Although it was never expressed in this way in the historical record, I feel strongly that the gay men approached community building as an end-in-view and not an end-in-itself by *necessity*. Their efforts to create community were constantly confronted by difficulties and frequently profound disappointment as the community failed to meet the desired ends. Thus, community formation was from the beginning of LCE a process of trial and error, of moving closer and closer to the kind of community various groups of individuals hoped to create, but never quite getting there. The most difficult (and in some ways the most emotionally violent) effects of this process was the conflict between different community formations as they were embodied in various groups, especially SIR vs. Gay Liberation. In the end, by the late 1970s, most overarching community organiza-

tions were gone, and only highly specific gay organizations remained by the time AIDS hit in the early 1980s.

132. "A basic desire of every person is to satisfy the feeling that he belongs. This task for a homosexual takes on gigantic proportions." *VR* March 1965, 2.

133. Through political activism, members would gain a sense of belonging to a common cause. By Intellectual Belonging, he meant that "Some of the best minds in the world are members of our Community. Why doesn't *The News* have a column on our heritage? We are not an isolated world, [a] little group in a specific social time element. We need to know these things to develop every-day pride." *TN* Oct. 14, 1963, 7–8. And by Social Belonging, he hoped that social spaces for variants, based on a Dutch model, could be developed to provide the grounds for real community development.

134. "I do feel for myself that my involvement in Gay Sunshine is where I belong—in this kind of creative activity." *GS* Dec. 1971–Jan. 1972, 1, 13.

135. See for example Harry Hay, *VR* May 1967, 21, 25: "[Social purpose of a gay community is] to enable homosexuals to establish and maintain for themselves in our society, pace for living in which to work and play as free citizens."

136. D.H. wrote, "I, like many of us, have no family per se. Can any active homosexual truthfully say they enjoy a close family relationship? . . . this organization [SIR] is truly my family." *VR* Nov. 1967, 12–13.

137. ". . . a new society of men and women who have enough love in their hearts to accept anybody different from themselves. There is a movement. The Movement. It is made up mostly of young people who are aware that our society is sick, and must be re-made into the new mold of the Aquarian Age." *SFFP* Oct. 1, 1969, 12.

138. "Emmaus House is an attempt to give spiritual significance to the homosexual. In a sense, it is a search for God in man. It is an attempt to seek Christ within each human being. It is an attempt at building a faith in which all may contribute and participate." *IA* 1.1, 1.

139. And a few years later, "Our Gay souls have nearly been stomped to death in that desert called America. If we are to bloom we can only do it together. I need you brother, because brother you are all I have." *GS* Aug.–Sept. 1970, 12.

140. Among the positive roles a gay community should play, Harry Hay lists, "To discover unequivocating words and phrases *for ourselves* by which to clearly articulate what we have always known about the meanings and values of homosexuality, and to teach *one another* the potential of homosexuality as a basis for a creative way of life." *VR* May 1967, 21, 25, emphasis mine.

141. Milton Fritz argued that developing a sense of pride among homosexuals would defeat the dangers of creating tight group boundaries that would exclude some and include others, or what men had earlier called "ingroupness."

142. See *VR* Oct. 1970, 38.

143. The Emmaus House saw gay community as a chosen family of gay individuals, using the metaphor of a family to underscore the kinds of bonds they hoped that gay men would be able to form with each other under the aegis of their organization. By framing community membership as a choice, Emmaus House created a space where "individuality and difference will bring people together in an involvement community." *IA* 1.2, 2. *I Am* argued that "the hardest part about being gay is the fear and the loneliness. There is no excuse for it anymore. . . . You as a gay brother or sister have an obligation to become one with your fellows." *IA* 1.2, 3. Adopting the familial "brother" and "sister" which had risen to prominence in the counter culture both underscored the perception that gay men

and women shared a deeper relationship than they might think and served to actually create those bonds among gay men and women.

6

Gay Masculinities

Has my sister been coerced by the straights—why has he accepted their upper- and middle-class dogmatic thinking that Gay is bad—to look it—act it—is shameful? . . . [Straights] are forcing my sisters and brothers to act and look straight IN ORDER TO FORM A MORE PERFECT UNION CONCEIVED IN SLAVERY OF THE MIND; AND DEDICATED TO THE PROPOSTION THAT TO LOOK QUEER IS AN AFFRONT AGAINST MANKIND, AND ALL MEN? ARE CREATED EQUAL. BULLSHIT!

—from *San Francisco Gay Free Press*, Dec. 1970

To recognize diversity in masculinities is not enough. We must also recognize the *relations* between the different kinds of masculinity: relations of alliance, dominance, and subordination. These relationships are constructed through practices that exclude and include, that intimidate, exploit, and so on. There is a gender politics within masculinity.

—R.W. Connell, *Masculinities* 1995 (2005)

The meanings of sex and intimacy arose from gay men's deepest hopes, fears, and desires for what *gay* should mean in their lives, and for the kinds of social possibilities that the community should provide and that the counter-public should fight for. But the stakes were far higher in the struggle over the meaning of gay masculinity. Whereas gender regulation in the dominant culture sought to enforce appropriate gendered practices and behavior, in short, to keep men in line with dominant expectations; and whereas adherence to dominant expectations carried with it certain social rewards in esteem and social power; gay men found themselves by definition outside the boundaries of acceptable masculinity, from Cold War America to the counterculture. Gay men's sexual desires and sex

acts precluded them from masculinity and from the rewards of masculinity before they even started.

In considering gay men's sexual practices and their gender, we discover the
core difference between the domination of gay men and the domination of other
subordinate groups. Pierre Bourdieu explains that what makes the domination of
gay men different is that it's their sex acts are marked for symbolic difference,
but that they are not a visible, readily intelligible sign of difference. He connects
the domination of gay people to how their sex acts subvert the most basic, sacred dominance of masculinity as the dominant, penetrating principle. Gay sex,
especially between two men, becomes the symbolic equivalent of a religious
violation, the feminization of the masculine through penetration. Bourdieu goes
on to observe that the dominant masculine principle is reproduced in gay culture
through the way they express gender (i.e., their gendered behavior and practices)
and the way they organize their sexual relationships. Homophobia, for Bourdieu,
functions like a religious taboo, one where the male-male sex act stands for the
unthinkable inversion of the gender order.[1]

As discussed in Chapter 1, Bourdieu's symbolic domination goes a long
way to help us understand the experiences of gay men grappling with the dominant gender order. In the introduction to *Masculine Domination*, Bourdieu points
to the phenomenon of submission, that the gentle domination of symbols results
in social situations of intolerable injustice, perpetuated over time, because those
who internalize the symbols acquiesce to their dominance.[2] What happens
among San Francisco's gay men after 1961 is a gradual public refusal on the
part of many gay men to accept the dominant gendered order that happens
alongside and simultaneously with a continued adherence to the dominant masculinity of the larger society. This creates a split among gay men, as the masculinities they create are constantly in an unsettled and vexed relationship with
masculine domination. Having already begun in a place outside of dominant
gender, these gay men began a decade's long argument about what masculinity
(and gender writ large) should mean for gay men, which both reproduced dominant masculinity and created new gay masculinities.

R.W. Connell, probably the preeminent theorist of masculinity, has argued
that gender is more than a set of accepted norms, but is rather continually re-
made in social action and supported by institutions. It is contested and therefore
continually, actively enforced in the smallest of interactional modes, and different contexts can produce different kinds of masculinity. But it is not merely that
there are different kinds of masculinity, but rather that these different kinds of
masculinities are in relationship with each other and that they are not equal.
Some forms of masculine practice and expression have dominance over others
and become hegemonic. For Connell, homophobia is more than an affect. It is
embodied in social practice that excludes and rewards based on gendered behavior, especially of men.[3] Masculinity is not a passive result of socialization, but
an active—for Connell dialectic—process where men (and boys) respond to
their social environments by constructive a masculinity to meet their social
needs in those contexts. During the 1960s, San Francisco's gay men underwent a

layered experience of domination, one in which they were implicated in and accused by masculinity. Into the gay counter-public, they brought with them the hegemonic masculinity from the dominant American culture as well as the masculinity gleaned from their class, race, ethnic, and religious contexts and put them all into play with gayness. These would be for any American man of the period already conflicted and contradictory. But for gay men, they experienced masculinity from the position of outsider, someone who had, by their very being, violated the most basic tenets of the dominant masculinity. They were, in short, a feminized and therefore dominated gender. From within this dynamic, gay men struggled to reclaim their place in the dominant masculine order, to undercut and deny the dominant masculine order by rejecting its masculinity and power. In following both of these goals, gay men were also necessarily producing a range of gay masculinities, and inevitably, some of those gay masculinities vied for hegemony over the gendering of the gay male community.

Women and the Gay Counter-Public

For gay men, gender seemed to carry the weight of their domination, as it was the primary marker whereby the police and the lay-public identified them; that is to say, their violation of accepted gender norms of masculinity made them visible in public as gay men. Some men felt that, as men, their sexuality was a bigger threat to the dominant culture and put greater oppressive force on them, compared to lesbians, notion found across the political spectrum.[4] The counter-public and its communities provided a social context for gay men to struggle with each other about masculinity and it also forced a kind of interaction with gay women that problematized their relationship to masculinity in a different way that many gay men found uncomfortable. As gender played such a huge role in gay men's experience of themselves, they were also blind to it in many ways. As with racism, gay men through the period seem to have been largely unaware of their own sexism, and commonly excluded women from their definitions of gay and homosexual.[5] Overt social exclusion of women did occur, but the most pervasive form of sexism consisted of women's exclusion *conceptually* from the contents of the organizational communities, which tended to focus almost exclusively on those issues most important to gay men, such as police entrapment and male pornography.

SIR was ostensibly a gender-neutral organization, and had enjoyed relatively good relationships with lesbians in the city. For example, a bowling club started between the men of SIR and the women of DOB in the spring of 1965.[6] But SIR's committees were geared toward male members, with the exception of one committee called Women in SIR, formed in August 1968.[7] Women were routinely excluded from other kinds of activities, such as the regular discussion group.[8] *Vector* was filled with images of naked men, gay male camp, and arguments among gay men about the formation of the community, but rarely addressed the issues faced by lesbians directly (or even indirectly). "[I]f *Vector* is 'a voice for the homosexual community' why has it 99% male copy and photos?" asked one female reader (*VR* Oct. 1970, 6).[9] By the late 1960s, many women found their inclusion in the magazines to be patronizing and half-hearted attempts at inclusion.[10] Gay liberation papers did better, with the occasional articles by and about lesbians; *Gay Sunshine*'s first few issues especially had much of interest to lesbians.[11] However, as time wore on, *SFFP* and *GS* both became predominantly male in their content. Thus, lesbians were most often invisible, a kind of present-absence, in the dominant discourses of the community, which had become a de facto male community.[12] What ended up happening was the simultaneous growth of two parallel but unequal gay communities, one gay male and the other lesbian, which often overlapped in interest and organization, but which retained distinctive needs and sub-cultures that continued to differentiate them even as they tried to act together in a counter-public. Some men felt this split more keenly than others, and hoped for a tighter integration of the sexes.[13] There persisted through the period a weak but ever-present desire to bring the gay men and women of the city together "so that the Gay society in San Francisco can really be strengthened to the point of better relations with our fellow Gays" (*BAR* Dec. 1, 1971). More than the social divide, it was felt by some that a male-only movement would be weaker in the face of the dominant culture.[14] The result, however, was a group of men deciding what the role of women should be, thereby reproducing masculine domination within the gay community that they experienced in the larger society.

The relationship of lesbians to gay men had grown more and more tense over the decade. In the early 1960s, the Daughters of Bilitis were sometimes mentioned in Guy Strait's papers,[15] and even more rarely, something of interest specifically to a lesbian audience was published. By the mid-1960s, some lesbians were beginning to demand their place in the movement; 1966 was a pivotal year, with both Del Martin's essay "I Am a Lesbian"[16] and an article from S. Willer, President of the Daughters of Bilitis, explaining why gay women's alliances were stronger with the women's movement.[17] For Willer, gay men and women had different political needs; whereas gay men were concerned with police harassment, lesbians were more affected by job discrimination and social inequality. She feared ultimately that gay men would not be allies in the struggle for gender equality and that they may even resist it; in other words, she feared gay men's sexism.[18]

As gay women in San Francisco became more aware of their *womanness* vis-à-vis the dominant culture, joined the burgeoning feminist movements, and participated in a series of demonstrations for women's rights—in short, as they had their own feminist awakenings—they became more and more biting in their critique of the gay men running the gay organizations and building the gay community. In October 1970, Del Martin—a longtime lesbian activist, one of the original founders of the Daughters of Bilitis, CRH, Citizens Alert, and CHF—resigned from her post at *Vector*. In her article explaining her resignation, Martin exclaimed that she had "been forced to the realization that I have no brothers in the homophile movement," when SIR's gay men refused to support women's rights or even discuss the oppression of women in their meetings (*VR* Oct. 1970, 35–37).[19] She blasted the bars and organizations that excluded women or relegated them to second-class citizenship. "Goodbye to the gay bars that discriminate against women. Goodbye to those that 'allow' them in only if they dress up in skirts," she wrote.[20] Martin had seen this kind of sexism in all of the organizations she had worked in, including those she helped form, such as the CRH. And she was equally critically of gay liberation. "They applauded the Lesbians who wished to establish common cause with them. . . . But somehow we are left with the feeling their applause was for the disruption of the meeting, not its purpose." She concluded that until gay men come to grips with women's issues "*their* revolution cannot be ours. *Their* liberation would only further en- slave us." So she bid farewell to the gay movement and to gay community. "'Gay is good,' but not good enough—so long as it is limited to white males only."

Late in the period, some gay male activists drew explicit connections be- tween the women's rights movement and the gay rights movement. But connect- ing the two in practice proved a difficult task.[21] In 1971, Gene Damon wrote to *Vector* to explain the role of *Ladder*, the lesbian publication of the Daughters of Bilitis, and to clarify why women no longer participated in the gay rights movement. "Much of the time, material of interest to or a concern with male homosexuals was carried [in the old *Ladder*]. In fact, from 1964–1966, there was more male than female homosexual coverage and nothing on women in general" (*VR* May 1971). Now, gay women were reclaiming their publication and asserting their common bond with other women, rather than with gay men. Lesbians had begun to feel that their deepest bond was with other women, gay and straight, and the gay men were part of the problem, not the solution.[22] By the summer of 1972, radical feminism and lesbian feminism had transformed the lesbian community and were carrying gay women on a parallel but unique course.[23] During this period, at least some gay men wanted lesbians to stay in the community, fighting sexism with their presence.[24] In an article entitled "Sex- ism and Lesbians,"[25] Martin did attempt to enlighten gay men, explaining to them the ways that they were sexist in their community building. She suggested that if gay men wanted to understand women, they would have to get together in consciousness-raising groups and face their own sexism; and in so doing, gay men would have to overcome their sexism before lesbians would come back to the community.[26]

As the 1960s progressed, another group of women became more visible: the male-to-female transsexual. It was during this period that the transsexual com- munity began to really take root; San Francisco had a vital and growing com- munity of transgendered individuals that ranged from drag to transsexual, with every permutation in between.[27] Gay men didn't have a language yet for talking about transsexuality, sliding uneasily between transvestite, drag, sex change, and she-male. But as early as 1967, *Vector* was trying to educate its readers. "It should be noted that transvestism doesn't necessarily relate to sex identification whereas drag usually does. A 'transsexual' is one who has attempted to legally (and biologically?) change his sex and has no relation to drag" (*VR* April 1967, 16–17). A transsexual woman calling herself "A. Tenderloin" wrote to *Vector* in 1968 and explained what it was like to want to change sexes and why she had made that decision and how liberating it had been. "I live constantly in the clothes of a woman although I am biological male. . . . The majority of my life was spent trying to play a role that I didn't fit. Though I was born with a male appendage, I couldn't consider myself a male. I don't consider myself a male. . . . All I can think about is that I'm really me now, and I like me" (*VR* April–May 1968, 29).[28] In general, *Vector* remained relatively positive toward transsexuality, most likely because its readers distanced themselves from any relationship to it.[29] For the most part, gay publications treated transsexuals as oddities or curiosities.[30]

As their lesbian sisters asserted themselves and began voicing their domination as women, rather than as homosexuals, some gay men began to take notice. Carl Whitman in particular argued that, because of their different relationship to male-dominated society, gay women would obviously see things differently than gay men. But for gay men, thinking about sexism brought them to a new understanding of their own domination, not necessarily of women. Acknowledging the chauvinism that gay men have, Whitman argued that chauvinists are also the biggest homophobes.[31] With straight masculinity as a common enemy, some gay men began rethinking the meaning of masculine gender and maleness in relationship to their gayness. Freedom became seeing oneself without the lens of sexism; and for the authenticity demanded by gay liberation, a "human way of looking at [oneself]" (*GS* Aug.–Sept. 1970, 14).[32] Because he is not sexually interested in a woman, wrote one gay libber, a gay man might never actually attempt to understand a woman or her point of view. Among gay men, liberation from sexism became a point of evaluation, that is, a way that gay men came to judge each other within the counter-public. *The Effeminist* attacked Berkeley Men's Liberation for being merely a more subtle version of sexist oppression.[33] More than any other, *The Effeminist* took the feminist theory ball and ran with it, attempting to rethink gender altogether for gay men. The radical gay Christians often argued for androgyny for gay men as a revolutionary force, but it was a reluctant recommendation insofar as dominant forms of masculinity repudiated feminine qualities such as "affection, tenderness, stability, responsibility, freedom from aggression" (*TE* May 1971, 1). Of course, some men reacted strongly against this focus on sexism, even seeing it as denying the humanity of straight men.[34] These uneasy formulations of a gay-male feminism expose the always unsettled relationship gay men had with masculinity writ large. The presence of gay women seems to have revealed to gay men both their internalization of masculine domination and their subordination to it.[35]

Drag, Leather, and Masculinity

The concentration of gay male life in particular geographical neighborhoods[36] enabled both the survival of older gay male cultural practices *and* the criticism and rethinking of those practices. Within the emerging gay counter-public and community, the gendered meanings of older gay male cultural practices were the center of the struggles over the meaning of gay-maleness in general, and the bedrock upon which new practices and meanings were built. By and large, gay male cultural practices during this period had persisted from the World War II era and before, stretching back into the nineteenth century, most notably for this discussion of gay masculinities, the practices of drag, "trade" sex, and biker, leather, and S/M practices. Gay men fought heatedly over the meanings of these practices in their new social contexts, struggling to eliminate or preserve or to accommodate the accretion of past practices and meanings.[37] Although the containment of homosexuality by the official public greatly affected their experiences,[38] gay men constantly resisted the means of control on the ground in their daily lives, by wrestling to make something more meaningful to their experiences, including a rethinking of the meaning of drag and leather.

From the evidence left in their publications, the process of accrual of new forms with old ones seems to be more complex than a simple layering of practices; older practices endured, but with meanings that shifted to match changing environments, needs, experiences, and desires of gay men in this period. By 1972, gay male practices included forms that emerged of their own during the 1960s, seemingly without knowledge of older gay male practices, but bearing striking resemblance to them (especially among gay libbers). Gay men *consciously* created the meanings for the practices that would satisfy the desires they felt; and these changed continually, both at the group and individual levels, as the needs and circumstances changed. As cultural practices that made gay men stand out in the minds of the dominant culture, and were seen as evidence of their "sickness," drag and leather had come to stand in for gay men's domination. In as much as both practices are deeply rooted in gender performances, they also served as the focal point for battles over gay masculinities, revealing a deep and abiding angst among gay men over their gender identities. Their responses to drag and leather ranged from deep shame to self-conscious, in-your-face revelry. But always they revealed an underlying unease about gender. My purpose here is not to critique or examine drag and leather cultures per se, but rather to explore the struggles gay men were having over the *meaning* of those practices during the 1960s.

For both leather and drag, the arguments revolved around the individual's adjustment to society or to himself, that he felt inadequate in some way. Does participation in drag or leather mean that you are maladjusted and don't fully accept yourself as a gay man,[39] or does it mean that you are liberated, free to express a gay male gender in ways that challenge and undermine the symbolic order of the larger society? This question was never (and has never been) settled among gay men. Gay men assigned several competing but interrelated meanings to drag and leather. For some they were a perfectly appropriate expression of gay-maleness; for others they belied anxiety, inadequacy, and maladjustment. For some drag and leather were creative expressions; for others they were oppressive and restricted gay male expression. For many men, both were merely a flaunting of difference or an escape from the reality of biological sex, leading directly to the common insistence by many that "IT IS ALL DRAG" (from Jeff Hrock *BAR* July 1, 1971). Far and away, drag- and leather-style gender nonconformity, be it the adoption of hyper-masculine expression or of a "femininized" gay masculinity, received constant and biting critique across the political spectrum. Libbers were just as likely to find drag regressive and to protest a drag show as they were to celebrate genderfuck; liberal or "assimilationist" gay men were as likely to throw a drag Imperial Ball as they were to fear that men in drag would incur the wrath of the police department. Be that as it were, drag and leather cultures remained a central and salient feature of gay male practice through the period[40]—what changed, then, were the meanings gay men ascribed to the practices, sometimes adding to and sometimes rejecting outright the older meanings and sometimes producing altogether new meanings.

Drag was often seen as anathema to gay masculinity, or at best, trivial fun; and leather was seen as an expression of dominant expectations of masculinity. They were also seen as attempts by the practitioners as attempts to achieve some kind of gender that may have been lacking.[41] Drag was also construed as a creative art, a source of pleasure, a form of self-expression; or conversely, an escape from reality, a denial of masculinity,[42] a threat to gay men's social position. Even by the end of the period, many drag balls and Imperial Courts through the period sometimes were received as "unifying" events. "The Coitilion, as we all know, demonstrated the unity and togetherness of San Francisco's homosexuals in dramatic terms" (*BAR* July 15, 1971). To be clear, gay men argued vehemently about the meaning of drag, which points to something deeper going on here.[43]

A new kind of drag practice grew out of the counterculture and the culture of "revolution" prominent in the Bay Area in the late 1960s, "genderfuck." Genderfuck was in many ways like drag, in that it took the outward signs of feminine gender performance (e.g., hair, makeup, clothing, mannerisms, etc.) and put them on unexpected or inappropriately sexed bodies and in unexpected and challenging ways. But whereas drag was often a campy imitation of femininity (in some men's estimation), genderfuck, according to its practitioners, was a self-conscious play and mixing of gendered cultural signs. The most famous genderfuck institution of the city was the Cockettes.[44] Genderfuck ignited the imaginations of many libbers, who saw it as something new and different from drag.[45] For A.D., writing in *Gay Sunshine*, genderfuck was a creative act where an individual's masculinity and femininity were mutually emphasized; A.D.'s comments reveal a central gendered value of the revolutionaries of genderlessness, or at least of gender neutrality in expression.[46] By the time this article was written, the Cockettes had already gone to New York to take their show to the national stage. But Hibiscus argued that something more important was happening with genderfuck in San Francisco—it was creativity, expression, resistance, and community.[47] The similarities to more traditional forms of drag notwithstanding, these men felt that their genderfuck was different, and they saw themselves as truly free, truly creative, and expressing something more genuine than drag did.

But gay libbers were of two minds about drag practices, seeing genderfuck as somehow fundamentally different from older drag styles, they say drag as evidence of a "gay establishment" that perpetuated negative stereotypes and unwittingly oppressed gay men. The feeling that drag was anathema to liberation was so strong that in October 1969 a group of libbers zapped the Tavern Guild's Beaux Arts Ball, a yearly fundraising event featuring drag queens and a show. They carried signs reading "Do it in the streets!" "Out of the closets, into the streets," "Wear your gown all year around," "How would you like to be Queen for a day?" "Come together right now," "Identification not exploitation," "Some of my best friends are," "Do it now," "Liberate and Drag ¡Si!, Tavern Guild No!" (see *SFFP* Nov. 1, 1969, 1). The "guerillas," as they called themselves, thought they were protesting the dominant culture, that dressing in drag was evidence of oppression. As part of their protest of the drag ball, they distributed a pamphlet entitled "Anti-Establishmentarianism"[48] that criticized the "gay establishment" for perpetuating ghettoization for the financial gain of a few, rather than working for social change that would grant "freedom for homosexuals to live and develop their life styles" (11). For these gay men and women, drag balls promoted the false value of "discretion" and kept the gay and straight worlds separate. Part of their critique was to insist that drag should be on the streets and not in a private gathering; drag balls were seen as a denial of the reality of homosexuality. Gay men in drag were, in short, "AUNTIE TOMS."

To be more explicit, gay men across the political divide saw drag as effeminate, that is, as un-masculine. This pitted drag against leather, in many gay men's minds, as they privileged one over the other in an effort to maintain their grip on masculinity.[49] Although San Francisco's drag culture had grown out of the gender-entertainment of the Barbary Coast in the late nineteenth century,[50] publicity had put new kinds of political pressures on gender-transgressive practices, namely by linking them to gay men's domination and putting them in competing with a full recognition of gay men by the official public. The conflict was evident everywhere, as "effeminate" gay men were castigated even as drag and genderfuck shows were sponsored by gay organizations. In the same pages of any given publication, you could find an argument about "swishes" (effeminate gay men) counterbalanced by campy jokes and pictures of drag queens. Many readers complained about the coverage of the drag community.[51] Guy Strait defended drag as an old and normal part of American life, but also worried that effeminacy would prevent the normalization of the homosexual.[52] Drag was seen as a negative stereotype of gender and femininity that *Vector* reproduced through its coverage of drag events, even as SIR claimed that "not all" gay men are "like that."[53] Gay men often objected to the coverage of drag because they felt it reflected poorly on all of them, effeminizing them all. J.B.

wrote, "You claim to represent the Gay Community, but it seems you are more interested in these fags and drags. . . . You seem to be trying to impress the public that the Gay Community are a bunch of Drag Queens and Fairies as a whole" (*BAR* June 15, 1971).

Drag became for some the gender line in the sand, a boundary intended to keep some men out of the counter-public.[54] Many men believed firmly that drag was an obstacle to liberation because of the image of effeminacy and weakness it portrayed to the dominant culture.[55] One gay "radical" argued that drag was a fantasy that could never provide fulfillment, giving the now-classic argument that if gay men desired women, they'd be straight. For him, there was no room for drag in the revolution.[56] Some libbers even resented the presence of "transvestites" at GLF meetings and refused to speak to them or acknowledge them.[57] One GLF drag queen, Lilly Rose, they were "always yelling at me as just a Gay male—not counting drag. 'You are born a man, why can't you be a man.' . . . I was informed that my whole purpose was to castrate gay men. I am also 'straight-male oriented' and I am a-s-e-x-u-a-l (a sexual what?). What do you girls who know me as Madame Arianne think about that?" (*GS* March 1971, 6). For some gay revolutionaries, drag was a sign of an inferior, feminine gay identity, one whose object was seen to be straight men and lacking an authentic sexuality.[58] The response to drag across the political spectrum reveals both the power of masculine domination, the internalization of symbolic forms of masculinity carried into the gay community, and the formations of hegemonic masculinities within the gay community itself. Conversely, drag was not merely a counter-hegemony to the dominant order, but also a counter-masculinity within the gay community.

Whereas drag was experienced by detractors as a feminization of gay masculinity, leather was experienced as a full-throated celebration of the most fundamental images of dominant masculinity. In short, leather came to stand for a gay *hyper*-masculinity. For example, a columnist for *Ads Gayzette* wanted to see more about Western and leather men[59] covered, what he called the "masculine happenings" of the community.[60] But leather culture, just because it was marked as "masculine," wasn't exempt from heavy critique. Some men read it as "Another hang-up" or "the 'I want a REAL man' syndrome. (I hate 'nellies,' dig 'butches,' etc.)" (*VR* May 1967, 13). Men outside the leather sub-culture derided it as another form of self-hatred, one that accepted the dominant notions of "acceptable" male dress; in its most severe, leather culture was seen as evidence of stunted development and unthinking boorishness.[61] One biker, Stan Hunter, responded simply that if he was going to ride a motorcycle, he needed to dress appropriately and it had nothing to do with masculinity.[62]

More commonly, men simply thought that leather was about identification with masculinity, part of their sexual and gender persona. They defended the S/M practices often associated with leather culture as merely the expression of certain kinds of sexual desires.[63] Many participants in the culture often denied this connection with masculinity, arguing that they are actually just average gay guys.[64] Letter writer Pierre argued that gay men chose leather because it met their hidden needs. "[The] super-butch gay set plays at their secret rites; display-ing insignia, chains on the right or left (which, like the flower worn over the ear, no one seems to remember which side means what), the jargon understandable only to the insider, the initiation ceremonies. To the new cultists, these offer instant identity" (*VR* June 1968, 16–17). For Pierre, leather played the role of providing identity and image to homosexuals, who as a group have to create their own. "[S]o let's not put leatherella down 'per se.'"[65] Like drag, however, gay libbers often saw leather culture as another hangover from the previous gen-eration, oppressive and anti-liberation as a practice. In terms of gender, like drag, leather entered the gay counter-publicity as another facet in the emerging array of gay masculinities and took its place as part of a hegemonic gay mascu-linity, as the drag and leather communities saw themselves at odds, and as the leather community more often than not fell on the side of the dominant form of gay masculinity, that is, one which, at least on its surface, conformed to the ex-pectations of masculine domination.

"Normal" or "Obvious?": Toward a Hegemonic Gay Masculinity

The San Francisco Police Department and the California Alcoholic Beverages Commission actually had training programs to teach agents the "signs of homo-sexuality" so that they could effectively entrap gay men. Both in bars and in public spaces, undercover agents assessed and chose potential marks according to their behaviors, to the degree to which they could be effectively judged as homosexual. Conversely, many gay men relied on their abilities to pass as straight not only to avoid arrest but just to keep their jobs and housing. Other gay men expressed their sexuality (and gender, as we shall see) in such a way that passing was simply not an option. But most gay men traversed the spectrum of gender and sexual expression, adjusting and adapting their behaviors with times and places, both to avoid direct intervention of the state and to establish their place in a hierarchy of gay men. This was a hierarchy of gay expression, or colloquially, a hierarchy of *how gay* a man was. Laid bare, however, it was the vying for hegemony of various kinds of gay masculinity and the efforts to ex-press that power over nonconforming gay men.

Although this hierarchy had its roots in the 1950s, during the 1960s, the de-bate about how gay one should act in public reached a fevered pitch and did not fall easily into political boundaries. Men across the political spectrum had all sorts of reactions to gender and sexual expression and odd alliances were formed across political fences in regards to gender expression and "obviousness." Recall also that many gay men valued integration into the dominant culture, that the public sphere should expand to make room for them and that the best means to this end was to carefully monitor their own and each other's behavior so that they appeared to be respectable to the dominant culture. By the late 1960s, as openness or "coming out" came to be seen as the surest means to securing gay publicity, an inverse position had emerged, that acting gay was its own good, and that expression of one's gayness was a right citizenship and of personhood. Interestingly, both positions denounced closetedness, but for different reasons. For those who valued respectability, remaining secret was ultimately unnecessary inasmuch as homosexuals were virtually normal; whereas for those who valued "gay" expression, to remain closeted was to internalize the hatred of the dominant culture. Regardless of this difference in rationale, both sides acknowledged that keeping one's homosexuality secret was a survival technique, and many advocated non-judgment and tolerance of the closeted. Despite cries for understanding, an individual's relative "gayness"—i.e., their intelligibility as gay—became the primary means whereby an individual's fitness for the community and counter-public could be judged.

What resulted was an intricate cultural field of gay expression, where a particular practice would have a degree of privilege assigned to it and a positive or negative value assigned in relationship to masculine domination of the larger society and to the emerging hegemonic gay masculinity, depending on who and where and why. Although these masculinities changed over time and across space and differed contextually and among individuals, they were always closely allied to the masculine formations of the dominant culture. And so an intense cultural debate about gender and sexual expression erupted, one which still infuses the gay male community to this day and which often divided an individual gay man from himself. One letter to the editor in 1963 from a self-proclaimed "obvious social variant" declared that he was not ashamed of his "variance," but also was embarrassed by other kinds of gender expression that made gay men more obvious, such as wearing tight pants to make his genitals visible.[66]

As victims of domination, gay men were quick to blame each other for the repressive actions of the state, mostly by pointing to gay men who were "obviously" gay. Recalling that the sex act is not readily discernible in day-to-day social interaction, gender expression becomes the primary means whereby a gay man's sexuality is intelligible in social interaction. Given the context of domination, it is no wonder that gay male social interaction focused on the gendered behavior of their fellows. The emergence of the counter-publicity and the institutions of the gay organizations provided the social spaces necessary for new forms of gay masculinity to emerge and for particular gay masculinities to rise to hegemonic positions among gay men, enforced both symbolically (e.g., through articles in the gay publications) and through social interaction (e.g., ostracism or zapping non-conforming gay men). From the beginning of the LCE, gay men who were obviously gay, effeminate in some way, were seen as the *reason* the official public and its agents actively repressed gay men.[67] Guy Strait went so far as to argue that gay men who were "normal" (that is, their gender expression conformed and didn't make them visible) paid a far higher price than the obvious.

Still in 1969, the CHF had some problems getting people to man the picket of States Steamship because many gay men in the city thought that someone who was "obviously" gay brought domination upon themselves and deserved what they got.[68] In an effort to explain the behavior of the "obvious" deviates, many blamed obviousness on a kind of psychological disorder, where the obvious homosexual simply wanted to be noticed.[69] *Town Talk* even suggested that the best way to get rid of swishes was to ignore them.[70] For many, coming out at all was itself a psychological defect. In this construction of gayness, anyone who was "obviously" gay was sick, morally degraded because this way of being gay was, supposedly, all about getting attention. Not just swishes were obvious, however. Strait argued that those who personified hyper-masculine traits were just as obviously gay.[71] The comparison of the "normal" to the "obvious" was inevitable here, where the normal homosexual has self-control and a stable life, but the swish is unreliable and unstable.[72] And so "normal" (i.e., those who could blend in to the dominant culture and pass) came to receive the moral valence of "good," and the "obvious" was "bad."

Thus, the hegemonic gay masculinity, across the political spectrum, seems to have been a masculinity that would be perceived as "normal."[73] When one man visited a GLF meeting, he reported to *Vector* that he was impressed by "the total *lack of obviously homosexual mannerisms*; it was in many ways a meeting of the youth movement, not the 'homophile'" (*VR* Oct. 1970, 38, emphasis mine). Earlier, one man calling himself Responsible argued against not just swishes, but any gay man who differentiated the community from the norm.[74] What acting "normal" really boiled down to was the power of masculine domination to reach into gay male interactions and to regulate their behavior and to push them into policing each others' gender.[75] By 1972, the value of "normal" had morphed into the valuing of "butch" or a self-consciously masculine gender expression for gay men.[76]

Derogatory slang terms for the "obvious" circulated freely in the gay publications—swishes, drags, sweater set, fems, hair-burners, limp-wristed, etc. The *LCE News* would make it clear that there were "elements" within the community that were undesirable and perhaps even detrimental to the project of liberation. Letter after letter to the numerous publications begged the "swishes" to be discreet.[77] And when a publication had some sort of obviously gay content (e.g., it was about drag or was campy), inevitably readers would respond that it was in "extremely bad taste" or obscene or simply that it destroyed the image of the homosexual.[78] Appropriate gender expression was coequal with respectability early in the decade,[79] and liberation later in the decade. Yet as gender always is, this was a contested position. Many men also insisted on the "normality" of effeminate men, and resisted the hegemonic gay masculinity.[80] Guy Strait's position on effeminate, obvious men, was somewhat tortured, arguing that they were at once harmless, that they had the "right to swish", but also that they were freaks and detrimental to the movement.[81] He even argued that the swish reproduced the stereotype that allowed "normal" homosexual men to hide[82]; and that, because Americans could laugh at a swish, they didn't feel threatened by him.[83]

But many gay men disagreed, feeling that the swish was dangerous and the source of anti-gay violence.[84]

Inasmuch as "obviousness" was based in gender expression, gay men found that, like their forebears in previous decades, they could "pass" among straight people by carefully monitoring their mannerism and speech to conform to dominant expectations of masculine behavior. Gay men's views on passing were decidedly mixed. Some gay men saw the ability to pass as a virtue, evidence of the fitness and masculinity of the individual gay man; on the other side of this spectrum, other gay men felt that passing was evidence of self-hatred and internalized oppression, that is, as the antithesis of liberation. "Hypocrites?" wrote one man. "Of course. But of a type far more disgusting. These people malign and deny their own kind in a type of behavior that we all find unforgivable" (*TN* Aug. 5, 1963, 2–3). Passing as straight remained a highly volatile issue, whether from the standpoint of one who valued respectability or one who valued gay expression. Passing might involve simply wearing a baseball cap[85] or it might be an outright refusal of identity.[86] When gay liberation came onto the scene, the concept of being obvious or normal had shifted to a question of consciousness and freedom. Libbers' arguments against passing were accepting a dominated image of themselves, imposed from the outside[87]; this was worse than being straight, it was choosing to imitate the oppressor.[88] Passing as straight became a key boundary of exclusion. Curiously, depending on the context and the masculinity at play, passing could either be the expected norm, that is to say, a gender expression that could "pass" as straight was valued and enforced; or it could be seen as a sign of false consciousness and the rationale for exclusion itself. Although they had different reasons for rejecting passing, gay men across the political spectrum curiously rejected passing even as they simultaneously produced a hegemonic masculinity.

We usually speak of the closet as the result of exterior oppression, the reaction of gay men whose difference is marked by an invisible sign (the sex act and sexual desire) even as the dominant social order enforces the invisibility by withholding status, esteem, and recognition or by outright violence. But among the gay men of San Francisco, the "closet"—that is, the choice to hide one's homosexuality and choose to maintain the invisibility and the secrecy—was also a social tool of the gay counter-public. As we have just seen with the notion of passing, gay men who had embraced the counter-public and the community adopted the closet as a way of drawing social boundaries. The closet became the primary mechanism whereby "good gays" were distinguished against "bad gays."

This was not limited to the later gay libbers. As suggested with their attitudes about passing, the League of Civil Education early in the 1960s was already constructing a different kind of closet door among the city's gay men, rooted in their distrust of gay men who refused to engage in the struggle for freedom. Here, the ire was moved from the "swishes" to the "closet queens."[89] The Closet Queen, then, was universally derided all along the political spectrum, as being incapable of relationship and of having low self-esteem, and more importantly, of being regressive and detrimental to the movement.[90] The "radical" gay men of the early 1970s argued, following Whitman's "Gay Manifesto," that closeted gay men were the worst kind of gays and a result of being ghettoized from straight society.[91] Their argument about the closet dovetailed with their desire for *authenticity*, the belief that if you were only true to yourself, honest about your desires, your core being, you would find true happiness. The closet, then, was the barrier that prevented an authentic gayness.[92] The hypocrisy, for example, of a gay employer who refused to hire a known homosexual was unacceptable.[93] The closeted man was one who from the safety of his closet had become nothing more than a voyeur.[94] Closet queens were seen those who benefited from the movement but refused to participate.[95] And in worst case scenarios, they refused to get involved when a gay man was getting bashed right in front of them.[96]

Closeted men were thus in the position of having to defend themselves, which the frequently did. Through the responses of men who chose to remain in the closet, we gain an insight into not only the oppression that obviates the need to be in the closet, but also the *pleasure* that some men experienced by maintaining their secret. Many men argued that they preferred[97] the closet for any number of reasons, ranging from it allowed them to be bisexual[98] to the feeling that the closet held open the possibilities for greater choices.[99] Of course, it was never clear exactly who was a "covert homosexual,"[100] simply because every gay man knew that, of necessity, he must at times "act straight," and because the enforcing power of the public sphere was often connected to justifications for remaining closeted.[101] In other words, the closet could provide the means for survival, social, economic,[102] and even physical. Other gay men simply led domestic, partnered lives and didn't want to join the movement or the community.[103] And finally, some gay men intimated the pleasure of living a life where they appeared "normal" and had a sex life that revolved around public cruising and anonymous sex. They saw no contradiction in what they were doing and claimed to enjoy it. Although it was rare, the realities of their shared domination did often temper the critiques leveled at closeted men.[104]

Whereas early in the period, men whose gayness was intelligible to the outside world had defended themselves in terms of their right to act that way and by comparing themselves to the harm brought about by closeted individuals and hustlers; in the late 1960s, some gay men took a different tack and began arguing that being blatantly gay was itself a value, something to be prized, another possible *means* of effecting gay liberation. By the early 1970s, the "Blatant is Beautiful" motif appeared often across the political spectrum, but mostly in gay lib publications. This view of blatancy was far from universally accepted among any community activists, regardless of their political values; but it became a powerful part of some men's notion of gayness.[105] Thus, not only being open about one's sexuality, but *acting gay* would become, for some, the key to liberation and, indeed, the very core of gayness itself. For therein lay the only route to freedom from socially dictated roles and norms, the freedom to choose how one wanted to be gay. In this mode, acting gay became an act of defiance against the dominant culture.[106] "Sister" Brian Chavez, Charles Thorp's boyfriend, wrote a piece for *Gay Sunshine* in which he argued that "Blatant Is Beautiful!" Chavez wanted more than just to angrily flaunt gayness in straight peoples' faces. He wanted gay men to accept their gayness, embrace it in themselves and others.[107]

For many gay men, blatant meant more than dress style or mannerisms, it meant being affectionate with other gay men and it meant nourishing the "Gay soul." Here we find another set of meanings for gay, ones that revolve around the meaning of the closet and an individual man's gendered behavior. We find here a deep contradiction between the devaluing of effeminacy, which we find across the political spectrum, and an understanding that effeminacy is one of the key markers of a visible "queerness."[108] The degree to which one was "obvious" was both a means of exclusion, especially where that involved effeminate behavior; but being "blatant" was prized in the later period as an act of radical self-acceptance. Undergirding this entire conversation are assumptions about masculinity and outright efforts to enforce certain forms of gay masculinity within the counter-public. While clearly, effeminacy was subordinated, the coming out of the closet and blatancy destabilized the emerging hegemonic gay masculinity, as it insisted onthe goodness of acting gay, which is to behave publicly as one would in private. And so *gay* is torn between the two sides of the closet and among competing and unsettled gay masculinities.

Gayness and Masculinity

A general anxiety over masculinity bled over into discussions about the meaning of gayness and its connection to gender identity. By the 1970s, some gay men were arguing that there was simply something different about the way gay men *did* gender.[109] The gay publications had all started thinking seriously about gender and were trying to distance themselves from simplistic appeals to masculine or feminine gender and gender's connection to homosexuality.[110] What gay men ended up with was a delicate dance with each other around the acceptable boundaries of gender expression as they tried to think through what it was exactly they found attractive and repulsive in their own and each other's gender.[111] *Vanguard*, not surprisingly, lamented that there was even a gender "choice" to be made, wondering why you had to choose between admiriable qualities of either masculine or feminie. Why not both?[112] Gay Sunshine began to speak of gender identity and expression as being extremely plastic and fluid.[113] That notion was perhaps overly hopeful, given how many activists from all sides of the political spectrum heaped embarrassment and chastisement upon drag queens and the "leather set" for their defiance of gender norms.[114] As a result of all this gender anxiety, gay men seemed always to attempt to come out with pride about being gay, while at the same time apologizing for or being defensive about their gender expression.[115] On the other hand, a few others, like Jeff Hrock, simply wanted it all. "I love saying this: I am a leather guy. I am a cowboy, 'bona fide.'

I am a drag queen. But more importantly, I am a human being, who believes that everyone should be able to pick his own life style and enjoy it. Regardless. And it might surprise you to know, JB [an anti-drag letter writer], that I'm also a pretty good man" (*BAR* July 1, 1971).

Many of the men in the early 1970s had become intensely critical of masculinity and wanted gay men to disavow traditional masculinity, connecting it to larger social systems of oppression and violence, including war.[116] Many "radical" activists intensely distrusted their straight counterparts, accusing them of using them in the same way they used straight women. This further fueled their critique of dominant forms of masculinity.[117] But even Guy Strait saw the strictures of masculine gender, seeing masculinity as a system of restriction that puts unreasonable demands on individuals.[118] Given the environment that on one hand relegated women to second-class citizen status and on the other hand equated gay men with femininity, it would have been unimaginable that images, practices, and cultural signs of masculinity not be tied up in the definitions of gay. For gay men, these signs became even more prominent and pervasive than the old drag queen used to be.[119] With their masculinity so unsure, many gay men strove to surround themselves with the signs of masculinity. *Vector* described the SOMA neighborhood as the location of a number of bars with "a different type of atmosphere" that "centered around a more pronounced accent on masculinity identification" (*VR* June 1968, 16–17).[120] Motorcycling, leather, and cowboy bars came to be seen as the loci of a kind of gay masculinity and served as the practices that marked a gay man's masculinity within the community.

At the same time, many were annoyed with these outer trappings of gay masculinity, and bucked against its growing hegemony. They thought there must be something more authentic and real that gay men were lacking in their gender practices, sometimes going so far as to argue that gay masculinity was a mere façade of manhood and not a real masculinity at all.[121] As gay men argued about the connection between gayness and masculinity, they also had to figure out what masculinity was in the first place. They knew from their own undergoing of masculine domination and self-imposed hyper-vigilance what the rules of masculinity were.[122] They knew, for example, that truly masculine boys didn't get good grades and were well behaved. But they also couldn't deny the sexual appeal of the "butch looking guys" who worked on cars and played sports. While the resisted the notion that gayness necessarily meant effeminacy, they also struggled with the sense that there was some intuitive, yet impossible-to-define connection between gay identity and masculinity. They attached community connection, activism, and group belonging to a gay masculinity, or rather something they desired of gay masculinity.[123] One writer wanted *Vector* to transform itself into a men's magazine with a "whole male concept" to appeal to all aspects of "an agreeable male existence whether heterosexual or homosexual" (*VR* May 1970, 21).

Gay men also saw masculinity as a kind of cult, a worship of an unattainable and perhaps undesirable ideal, as expressed for example in leather sub-culture. Richard M. Morton experienced the masculinity of the leather sub-culture to be an impossible ideal, an unreachable goal.[124] But for him, the line between real men and what I have been calling hegemonic images of real men was blurry. Where should gay men even begin to find themselves in that mess? For *The Effeminist* gay and masculine went hand in hand, but in completely un-expected ways. "But I am a faggot (not a woman, a faggot) who is discovering that he is male—and it's a wonderful discovery, my maleness. I feel my freedom moving inside me: '. . . It's good enough just to be male. . .' Right" (*TE* 1.2).[125] And so the conversation naturally evolved beyond the meaning of masculinity to what exactly a *gay masculinity* was or should or could be.

Effeminacy, Masculinity, and the Power of Gender

What these later men were thinking of as "sexism" was in fact a pattern among gay men of the devaluation of femininity writ large, not just of women. As we have seen, one of the primary means whereby gay men were able to negotiate the dangers of the public sphere was by passing as straight, which for all intents and purposes, translated into behaving "masculinely" or at least within the stan-dard expectations of masculinity. The gay libbers were perhaps simply more self-aware, but by no means immune from this form of gender oppression. In-deed, the fear, rejection, or outright oppression of femininity as a behavioral practice or as any sign of gayness at all transcended all political and community boundaries; it seems to have been the one unifying characteristic among all the communities. One gay libber admitted that he was a male chauvinist and then acknowledged the way his fear of femininity affected his social interactions with other gay men and how such fear influenced his own behaviors, making him less authentic.[126]

As we have seen, the swish, the effeminate gay man, bore the brunt of much anger during the 1960s; this is the consequence of the gender values that infused gay male community formation. For the older generation, an effeminate gay man couldn't possibly be genuine or "authentic" in their presentation, but was the attention seeker, the flaunter, or the flamboyant.[127] In the LCE publications, effeminate behavior was flogged constantly as silly, a parody, weak.[128] For Strait, there was no real possibility of a feminine man, only an act.[129] Thus, ef-feminacy for some gay men could not possibly be an acceptable form of gay masculinity, because it was by definition a lie. We find throughout the period a deeply felt contradiction between the idea that masculinity should naturally flow from being a man (i.e., from having a penis) and the reality that gay men's sex-ual desires and sex acts defied the very notion of masculinity by definition. Could a man who had sex with other men ever be masculine? By insisting that effeminate gay men were merely play-acting at femininity, gay men of the pe-riod were revealing their own dis-ease with the naturalness of gender by re-inscribing it in the face of contradictory experience. Many men's feelings toward the effeminate rose to the level of violence.[130] Meanwhile, gay men with "revolutionary" values were often more self-reflexive in their fear and hatred of effeminacy, which is to say that they feared and hated it, but were willing to ask themselves why.[131]

As we saw earlier, a few men who valued "blatancy" actually praised effeminacy. "The whole society is against us—we have survived. This my Brothers and Sisters is the strength of our bodies and our souls—this is the strength of a people called 'effeminate'" (*GS* Nov. 1970, 8-9). One article read as a kind of manifesto for effeminate gay masculinity.[132] As evidenced by self-identified effeminate men's anger at other gay men, most gay men must have eschewed effeminate behavior. Many found it necessary to defend or prove their masculinity. And even gay libbers saw effeminacy as a sign of the inability to stand up to the dominant culture. These gay libbers argued that for a gay man to be effeminate was to give in to stereotypes and oppression. For them, gay liberation meant liberation from the effeminate. For example, one gay libber argued that "The gay liberation movement has been an escape from the old fairyland and Judy Garland and from the traditional gay subculture. . . . 'Princess syndrome' is a good name because it sizes up the fem-identification, the fantasy imager, the egocentricity, and the cultural conservatism of the tired old gay trip" (*GS* Jan. 1972, 3).

What emerged in the gay male community, then, was an uneasy relationship to masculinity itself, wherein gay men drew in/out boundaries based on the relative (and arbitrary) assignation of masculinity. Gay publications of the time worked constantly to assert the masculinity of their constituents and, consciously or not, to claim a hegemonic gay masculinity. This grew out of the contradictions between experiencing masculine domination of the American society writ large, knowing that they were never going to *be* masculine, at least not wholly so, and yet still desiring masculinity. The fretted about whether or not homosexuality would hinder a gay athlete on the field of competition, whether or not a gay man could actually *be* masculine given that masculinity required attraction to and sex with women. And yet they asserted their masculine privilege vis-a-vis lesbians within the community, drawing clear lines to exclude biological women, drag queens, and effeminate gay men, even as they were critical of how masculinity effected their domination. Drag queens asserted a different kind of masculinity, one which pointed to the artifice of femininity and, by extension masculinity; the leather and S/M subcultures asserted a hypermasculinity, even as many gay men understood leather to be another form of drag. They could not help but simultaneously reproduce masculine domination in the gay community and reformulate and recreate masculinity as they lived lives in defiance of their domination.

Notes

1. Pierre Bourdieu, *Masculine Domination* (Palo Alto: Stanford University Press, 2002 [1998]): 119.

2. Bourdieu, 4.

3. R.W. Connell, *Masculinities*, 2nd Edition (Cambridge, UK: Polity Press, 2005 [1995]), 40.

4. One gay libber observed, "I feel the need [for liberation] is greater with men. Women have no leaded concept of femininity which they must live up to. Gay girls are not as universally hated and feared as gay guys because they are not a threat to anybody's femininity. And straight men are utterly fascinated with them." *SFFP* Oct. 1, 1969, 12.

5. An unsigned letter to *Vector* opined, "When I first heard the term, 'homophile' I was attracted to it. It seemed to indicate an interest in male relationship, male bonding, masculinity and male problems in general. Cooperation and understanding between men is exceedingly rare and anything or anyone who seems to counteract this trend has my support." *VR* May 1970, 21. For him, homosexuals were men, full stop.

6. The first match resulted in a 2–1 victory for the lesbians of DoB. See *VR* March 1965.

7. *Vector* had begun a short-lived column for women, Fluff, Buff & Butch, written by Michelle Duloc and René Autil in June 1969. Sandy Johnson was the first Chairwoman of Women in SIR. See *VR* Aug. 1968, 11: "I feel strongly that we girls need an organization like SIR as bad as the boys do. . . . The major goal of the new group is to encourage women to participate in all SIR committees and to attend its calendar events. (Women are now on five committees and one is on the SIR board.)"

8. See *VR* March 1967, 13: "There should be no prejudice against one sex by the other, through SIR. . . . So I feel that meetings such as the Conversation Group, which excludes certain persons, should have no place on SIR's calendar. . . . Otherwise we destroy the whole purpose of the supposed SOCIETY FOR INDIVIDUAL RIGHTS."

9. In 1970, *Vector*'s editor attempted to regularly publish lesbian poetry, but that lasted a scant three issues. Such efforts met with harsh criticism.

10. When a "woman's page" was proposed in 1969, Del Martin shot back, "In actuality, it was just another put down, relegating women to a particular section and not involving them in the mainstream of SIR's activities." *VR* Sept. 1969, 10.

11. See for example "About Lesbians," reprinted from RAT [a New York gay liberation paper] in *GS* March 1971, 4.

12. "Lesbians are homosexuals, something which is often forgotten when people talk about homosexuals." *VR* March 1969, 13. "We have failed to attract and involve women in the organization." *VR* Feb. 1970, 9, 19.

13. One writer who had just moved to San Francisco from Los Angeles noticed immediately the gender division in the community. He was disappointed "to see the great barrier between the guys and girls in the Gay society. [In Southern California] the girls went to the guys' bars and the boys went to the girls' bars and they mixed very well. It was like one big happy family. . . . The girls stay in their little corners and the guys stay in theirs. . . . Why can't the Gay capital of the United States (San Francisco) do it too?" *BAR* Dec. 1, 1971.

14. Nelson S. Chuang wrote, "Indeed, we need both sexes to present to the society an overall picture of our all-together oneness—a oneness in soul as well as in purpose." *VR* July 1968, 16–17.

15. See for example *TN* Dec. 23, 1963, 2.

16. See *VR* Oct. 1966, 9: "I am a lesbian. These words tell very little about me actually. But they conjure up a picture to most people of a caricature of a perverted masculine, aggressive woman vampire who preys upon members of her own sex. . . . They do not see me as a woman, very much like any other woman, who is seeking an identity as a person, as a creative member of society. . . . I am a Lesbian. These words do not come easily. They are the result of months, sometimes years of soul searching. . . . They separate me from much that I hold dear in life. for the measure of who I am immediately drops in the sight of my fellow human beings, despite the fact that I am still the same loving person, the same dear friend they knew before I put the label to what I feel deep inside of me. . . . I am a Lesbian. . . . I repeat the words loudly and defiantly. And I feel for the first time I am on the threshold of profound meaning. I see a glimmering of who I am. . . . I am a Lesbian. In the excitation that follows any moment of self-knowledge so dearly bought, I am eager to share this experience of wonder and expectations. . . . I play the buffoon, I act out the behavior they expect of me. . . . I move into the mysterious Lesbian underground for sanctuary in the hope of finding acceptance and security. . . . I am a Lesbian. . . . I am not satisfied with the boundaries of the Lesbian world. I am a citizen, a part of society, and I have need to express myself in the much larger sense of community. . . . I am a Lesbian. . . . I know the richness, the fulfillment of a love relationship that has been bound in the love of God if not by man in his church sanctuary or his courtroom. I know the spirit of adventure and the growth of personality in a love relationship that transcends society and church condemnations. . . . I am a Lesbian. . . . You fear me because you have misgivings that knowing, understanding and accepting me might somehow change you. And it will. It will not change a heterosexual into a homosexual any more than the homosexual has been changed in your prisons and on your psychiatrists' couches. But it will end truth to what is now the lie of the 'Christian' brotherhood of man."

17. Willer asserted that "the problems of the male homosexual and the female homosexual differ considerably," and that "lesbian interest is more closely linked with the women's civil rights movement than with the homosexual civil liberties movement." *VR* Oct. 1966, 8. She argued that gay women had agreed reluctantly to join with gay men in a common cause, but "although the lesbian occupies a 'privileged' place among homosexuals, she occupies an under-privileged place in the world."

18. "Lesbians have agreed (with reservations) to join in common cause with the male homosexual—her role in society has been one of mediator between the male homosexual and society. . . . In these ways we show our willingness to assist the male homosexual in seeking to alleviate the problems our society has inflicted on him. There has been little evidence, however, that the male homosexual has any intention of making common cause with us. . . . We suspect that should the male homosexual achieve his particular objectives in regard to his homosexuality he may possibly become a more adamant foe of women's rights than the heterosexual male has been."

Interestingly, Willer was actually conservative in her values where sexuality was concerned. She felt that militant activity would ultimately be counter-productive to the struggle for gay rights and urged gay men to find other means to their ends. She wrote, "Demonstration which define the homosexual as a unique minority defeat the very cause for which the homosexual strives—to be considered an integral part of society. . . . Demonstrations that emphasize the uniqueness of the homosexual may provide an outlet for some homosexuals' hostilities, but, having acted out his revolt, he loses a part of the drive that might have been available for more constructive approaches to problem solving." She then made four demands of gay men: 1) commit to women's rights; 2) commit to respect women as full people; 3) change the movement so that its focus is on sexual issues that concern both sexes; and 4) acknowledge that though women are fewer in the movement, their concerns are of equal import.

19. "[SIR] would not address themselves to the underlying reason for the existence of separate women's organization—that the female homosexual faces sex discrimination not only in the heterosexual world, but within the homophile community. . . . Goodbye to the wasteful, meaningless verbiage of empty resolutions made by hollow men of self-proclaimed privilege. They neither speak for us nor to us. . . . Goodbye, my alienated brothers. Goodbye to the lame chauvinists of the homophile movement who are so wrapped up in the 'cause' they espouse that they have lost sight of the people for whom the cause came into being. . . . As they cling to their old ideas and their old values in a time that calls for radical change I must bid them farewell. . . . Women are invisible. There is only one credential for acceptance in the homophile 'brotherhood'—the handle Mayor Alioto couldn't find on Woman's day. . . . Goodbye, too, (temporarily, I trust) to my sisters who demean themselves by accepting 'women's status' in these groups. . . . Goodbye to *Vector*. Goodbye to the 'Police Beat'—the defense of washroom sex and pornographic movies. that was never my bag anyway. Goodbye to the Women's Page. . . . Goodbye to the biased male point of view. . . . Goodbye to Halloween Balls, the drag shows and parties. . . . While we were laughing at ourselves we became the laughing stock—and lost the personhood we were seeking. It is time to stop mimicking the heterosexual society we've been trying to escape. It is time to get our heads together to find out *who we really are*."

20. "Gay Liberationists are right when they observe that gay bars ghettoize the homophile community. But there is no time or place for forming friendships for exchanging ideas for camaraderie—only for dispensing of drinks and sex partners."

21. Del Martin insisted that it was "time that the male homosexual recognized and supported his 'sister' in the additional discrimination she faces, just because she is a woman!" *VR* Sept. 1969, 10. Martin continued to write on feminist issues for *Vector*, educating her brothers on the issues that women faced in society. In "Lesbian Dilemma— Homophile or Women's Liberation?" *VR* Sept. 1970, 39, Martin laid out, in a report of a national Daughters of Bilitis conference, some of the basic arguments of feminist thought at the time. "'Once women are liberated from child bearing, there will be a need for a change in cultural values and a need for a choice of alternate life styles,' Miss [Caroline] Bird stated [author of *Born Female*]. . . . [Phyllis Lyon said] 'Indeed, the Lesbian does find herself betwixt and between . . . the homophile and the women's movements. And the Lesbian' dilemma is that, while she may offer her services and her loyalties to both, she is rarely *truly* accepted in either. . . . [The feminist movement] increasingly sensitive to Lesbianism as a political statement. . . . [Del Martin said] 'For all of the popular stereotypes of male homosexuals as having feminine characteristics, they are men, live almost exclusively in a man's world and display the same male chauvinism as heterosexual men.'"

22. "[M]ost Lesbians are in women's liberation rather than gay liberation; where they are in gay liberation they are in very separate caucuses. . . . This is in no way rejecting homosexual males, nor indeed heterosexual males. It is our view that only through the complete attaining of human rights for all women can humanity exist in the future." *VR* May 1971.

23. For an introduction to the history of lesbians during this time, see Lillian Faderman, *Odd Girls and Twilight Lovers: A History of Lesbian Life in Twentieth Century*

America (New York: Penguin, 1991), especially Chapter 9 "Lesbian Nation: Creating a Women-Identified-Women Community in the 1970s."

24. See *GS* Oct. 1970, 9.

25. See *VR* Jan. 1971, 28–29: "[Martin fought] to get them [gay men] to realize that the reason there are so few women up front is that homosexual men have been just as oppressive to lesbians as heterosexual men have been to women in general. [The Daughters of Bilitis was formed to meet needs not] met by homophile organizations that claim to be 'open' to both men and women. . . . [A SIR program] was poorly supported by male homosexuals. Why? Because it was conceived, planned and pulled off by women. Male homosexuals had been upstaged by—Lesbians. . . . First of all, to those of you who have asked for advice on what to do, I would suggest that you get together in 'men only' sessions and find out where your heads are really at. . . . At least have the decency to point out that there is a female viewpoint, that seminars on homosexuality should have a separate session on Lesbianism put on by women and refer research—something else to offer to the general subject of homosexuality. It is interesting to note that spokeswomen for the homophile movement can speak just as knowledgeably about male homosexuality as about Lesbianism. . . . But male homosexuals seem to have tunnel (penis) vision. . . . groups must include both men and women. At a recent meeting of the Homosexual Action Forum it adopted a policy that wherever possible two separate sessions should be set up—one on male homosexuality and one on Lesbianism. . . . Secondly, . . . it will be up to you to renew contact and sustain communication once it is re-established. For the Lesbian's first priority now is to the women's movements. . . . Thirdly, and hardest of all, you will have to change your reading speech and thought patterns. . . . Do you still speak of lesbians as dykes, 'the girls,' as butches and femmes? . . . Women are fed up with role play. they are rejecting pseudo caricatures and becoming the real persons they always were."

26. As already stated, most of the sexism of this period took the shape of the assumptions made about women and of women's invisibility to the gay men running the movement. Rarely, overtly sexist material would also appear. For example, Guy Strait complained that Chicago censorship boards were run by "housewives with spotty educational backgrounds." See *TN* May 27, 1963, 1.

A 1970 article by tried to explain the effeminization of men in terms of women's power. "[Something] was wrong sexually with the young American male. . . . The destruction of the Hero had begun with the advance of equal rights for women and the gradual shift of the country towards the permissiveness of the matriarchy. . . . And again, the idea of the Hero as Breadwinner was slowly being challenged. . . . Finally, the concept of the Hero as Warrior has been destroyed. . . . The hero, then, helped to underline one's masculine status." See *VR* Aug. 1970, 10–11.

27. For a history of transsexuality in the United States through the 1970s, including much good treatment of San Francisco, see Jane Meyerowitz, *How Sex Changed: A History of Transsexuality in the United States* (Cambridge, Mass.: Harvard University Press, 2002).

28. In addition, at least one man wrote to *Vector* in hopes of finding a transsexual community. Several popular films about transsexuals came out during this period, including *The Story of Christine Jorgensen* and *I Want What I Want*. Reviewers for *Vector* found them to be informative and interesting films.

29. "Dr. Inderhaus," a medical column, stated quite simply that "Transsexuals are not homosexually oriented," and therefore not homosexual. Dr. Inderhaus informed readers that transsexualism was characterized quite simply by the "very deeply held belief on

the part of the transsexual that he (she) is, despite physical appearances to the contrary, a member of the opposite sex." He assured readers that transsexuals have little interest in sex and that cross-dressing was completely different and could not lead to the desire to change one's sex. *VR* May 1972, 17.

For the most part, then, gay publications treated transsexuals as oddities or curiosities. The only outright anti-transsexual writing I found was, ironically, in *Vanguard*. The Glide-sponsored organization actually included many transsexuals in the Tenderloin district, so it makes sense that Sam Furgeson would rub elbows with them, but his negative reaction is somewhat curious in comparison with *Vector*'s treatment. Argued Furgeson, "I believe a person who is born a physical male should actively live as a male. Although I, for instance, am a homosexual (who occasionally enjoys the 'fem' part of sexual acts), I see no reason to live in drag or do anything that would make me thought of as a woman. I can't find in myself to see how anyone can live in the dress of the opposite sex." *VG* 1.9 (July 1967). Oblivious to the irony, Furgeson concluded that the transsexual should conclude from the rejection of both gay and straight society that her theory of her gender was wrong.

Interestingly, I could find no mention of transsexuality in the gay liberation press through June 1972.

30. The only outright anti-transsexual writing I found was, ironically, in *Vanguard*. The Glide-sponsored organization actually included many transsexuals in the Tenderloin district, so it makes sense that Sam Furgeson would rub elbows with them, but his negative reaction is somewhat curious in comparison with *Vector*'s treatment. Argued Furgeson, "I believe a person who is born a physical male should actively live as a male. Although I, for instance, am a homosexual (who occasionally enjoys the 'fem' part of sexual acts), I see no reason to live in drag or do anything that would make me thought of as a woman. I can't find in myself to see how anyone can live in the dress of the opposite sex." *VG* 1.9 (July 1967). Oblivious to the irony, Furgeson concluded that the transsexual should conclude from the rejection of both gay and straight society that her theory of her gender was wrong.

31. "We can junk it much more easily than straight men can. For we understand oppression. We have largely opted out of a system which oppresses women daily. . . . We have a common enemy: The big male chauvinists are also the big anti-gays." *SFFP* Dec. 22–Jan. 7, 1970, 3–5.

32. The cover of the August–September issue of *Gay Sunshine* had an etching of a naked man and a naked woman with broken shackles. The caption read, "Gay Brothers and Sisters Unite! Free ourselves! Smash Sexism!"

33. See *GS* June–July 1971, 2, 5.

34. "I cannot accept the way that gay liberation people totally deny the humanity of straight men. . . . Of course, straight men wield power and have privileges. . . . [I]s it not possible that a straight man may be unable to express himself homosexually? For this, is he to be condemned as a person? I cannot find the emotional basis to cut myself off from straight men who, over the years, have been my friends." *GS* June–July 1971, 2, 5.

35. As the 1960s dragged on, another gender grew more visible: the transsexual. It was during this period that the transsexual community was really just in fetal form; San Francisco had a vital and growing community of transgendered individuals that ranged from drag to transsexual, with every permutation in between. For a history of transsexuality in the United States through the 1970s, including much good treatment of San Francisco, see Jane Meyerowitz, *How Sex Changed* (Cambridge: Harvard UP, 2002). Gay men didn't have a language yet for talking about transsexuality, sliding uneasily between

transvestite, drag, sex change, and she-male. But as early as 1967, *Vector* was trying to educate its readers. "It should be noted that transvestism doesn't necessarily relate to sex identification whereas drag usually does. A 'transsexual' is one who has attempted to legally (and biologically?) change his sex and has no relation to drag." *VR* April 1967, 16–17. A transsexual woman calling herself A. Tenderloin wrote to *Vector* in 1968 and explained her experience as a MTF.

See letter from A. Tenderloin, *VR* April–May 1968, 29: "I live constantly in the clothes of a woman although I am biological male. . . . The majority of my life was spent trying to play a role that I didn't fit. though I was born with a male appendage, I couldn't consider myself a male. I don't consider myself a male. . . . Biologically a male and psychologically a female. . . . I am now a woman with a few abnormalities which can be corrected surgically. . . . [I]t's really enjoyable having found an identity and firmly following it. . . . All I can think about is that I'm really me now, and I like me." At least one man wrote to *Vector* in hopes of finding a transsexual community.

36. Namely, in North Beach and along Polk Gulch in the early 1960s, the increasing gay presence South of Market in the industrial areas, and in the early 1970s, the occupation of Eureka Valley (renamed The Castro).

37. Nan Boyd has dramatically shown how certain practices, especially cross-gender performance and bar association, persisted through the first sixty years of the twentieth century; and Eve Sedgwick has argued persuasively that older forms of culture do not simply pass away, but persist through a process of accretion. In his effort to answer Sedgwick's critique of his theory of gay history, David Halperin presents a rubric of four forms of structuring same-sex relationships. But this approach of sort of laying out a handful of options society has for organizing same-sexuality appears more and more ham-handed when put into play with the experiences of gay men, especially in a time period when they were leaving such prolific historical evidence. See Boyd, *Wide Open Town*; David Halperin, *How to Do the History of Homosexuality* (Chicago: Chicago University Press, 2001), 104–110; and Eve Sedgwick, *The Epistemology of the Closet* (Berkeley: California University Press, 1990).

38. See Chapter 1 and Chapter 7.

39. John N. argued that "any invert who adopts leather or drag as the way he will present himself to the gay community is either not completely reconciled to his sexual orientation or is trying, through various forms of garb and mannerisms, to bolster his own fears of an inadequate presentation of himself to the rest of the homophile community." *VR* June 1968, 16–17.

40. Drag performances at specialized bars and clubs had morphed during the 1960s into drag balls and the Imperial Court system in San Francisco, often as fundraisers for various causes or organizations. And popular queens often served as emcees for gay events and fundraising activities throughout the city (see for example *TT* Oct. 1964, 1), a practice that continues to this day. Coverage of these events was constant throughout the period, beginning with Guy Strait and through the *BAR* and the early 1970s. The liberation papers, however, rarely covered drag events other than their zapping of them, and criticized drag extensively. Even genderfuck wasn't free from their critical gaze, as we've seen. For the consistency of drag and its survival through the period, see *VR* Jan. 1970 the announcement of a Coit Club Mardi Gras party with "costumes" (10); and Jan. 1971 report on SIR's "Revolution" musical review, which included drag and nudity (35).

41. See *VR* April 1967, 16–17

42. When Tim Hillary argued that men in drag were denying the reality of their sex, The Polish Prince(ss) responded, "If drag be a mentality to escape from reality, then what of alcohol, television, a rough night of sex, or plain camping?" *VR* July 1970, 36.

43. The unease of the community and its split over the issue of drag grew clear in an informal poll taken by *Vector* as part of its special forum on drag. " (1) Have you ever worn drag? 62 yes, 108 no; (2) Is drag detrimental to the homophile community? 94 yes, 76 no; (3) should drags be confined only to theatrical productions? 77 yes, 93 no; (4) Should drags be tolerated in the Tenderloin and other public places? 66 yes, 104 no; (5) Would heterosexuals accept the homophile more readily if there was less drag? 109 yes, 61 no." See *VR* April 1967, 16–17.

44. See *GS* Nov. 1970, 17 and *VR* June 1971.

45. A.D. wrote, "Whatever you call it, it is not just drag. As valid as drag is, the 'Cockettes' and the 'Angels of Light' . . . are into something quite different." *GS* Jan. 1972, 10.

46. Hibiscus, a Cockettes performer, argued, "No, I really like being a man. I never really had the desire to be a woman. But I like beautiful things. Costumes and things." *GS* Jan. 1972, 10.

47. "[In San Francisco] the audience continues to create. The STUD is a hip gay bar in San Francisco. . . . Today, the STUD is gay street theatre at its best most nights of the week. Smoke a joint, go to the bar, buy a beer (or don't) and just stand there. You feel the excitement of live theater as you watch the arrival, one after the other, of fabulously costumed and outrageously liberated long-haired men (and now, happily, women)."

48. Reprinted in full in *SFFP* Nov. 1 1969, 11.

49. One writer complained, "SIR members, presumably a liberal-minded group, seem to find 'leather' a more acceptable than 'drag.'" *VR* May 1967, 13.

50. See Boyd, *Wide Open Town.*

51. See for example *TN* July 22, 1963, 3.

52. See *CN* Aug. 17, 1964, 7. He also argues here that drag has nothing to do with sexual desire and that most drag queens aren't sexual at all anyway. See also *CN* 4.6, 6–7.

53. In a review of an upcoming book by Dennis Altman, one man agreed with Altman's premise that drag was a capitulation to oppression. "The parade of drag queens and other mad types, in *Vector* and elsewhere, become tiresome when SIR proclaims, 'Of course the typical homosexual isn't really like that.' Does SIR really enforce stereotypes or does it attempt to tear them down?" *VR* Jan. 1972, 32.

54. See for example, "[T]he homosexual who dresses as a woman for the purpose of solicitation or to declare his femininity should be rejected by SIR. . . . He should not be allowed to damage our image as responsible men." From Jim Ramp, *VR* April 1967, 16–17.

55. See for example *VR* May 1970, 12–13; May 1971, 4;

56. *VR* May 1970, 12–13.

57. Steve Ginsburg argued that "If I or someone else don't want to talk to a TV or drag [at a GLF meeting], that's our right. Try men's clothes." *GS* April–May 1971, 16. Lilly Rose, a drag queen and GLF activist, complained that the day after a meeting, "in the street I would pass the same person and they would smile and keep on truckin', or they would just totally ignore me and keep on truckin'." *GS* March 1971, 6.

58. Some drag queens responded with humor. Mavis agreed that drag should be kept in check. "There are enough ugly women roaming the streets now." *VR* April 1967, 16–17. Ginger Snap wrote with a wink, "For as much as we lady's [drag queens] (one way or another) enjoy our own thing, we still are, and as long as it's there swinging, we are

men." *BAR* Oct. 1, 1971. Other men shared Strait's more lax attitude, and argued simply that it was a possible form of expression for gay men. R.W. Clark wrote, "Anyone should be able to dress anyway he wishes. . . . 'The clothes make the man.' If those clothes happen to be women's clothes, then that's the image the man wants to project. Let him." *VR* April 1967, 16–17. Many made simple appeals to tolerance, to creating a Community that would be open to gender diversity. An anonymous letter writer argued more forcefully, "The time has come for us—WHATEVER DRAG WE MAY WEAR—to as least have the courtesy to let people enjoy their own scene—in their own way. . . . WHETHER WE LIKE IT OR NOT, WE ARE ALL BROTHERS AND SISTERS. TRY ACTING LIKE IT." *BAR* July 1, 1971.

59. Typically, these would include a broad range of men dressed in clothing culturally marked as masculine, ranging from biker uniforms, to cowboy outfits, to blue-collar laborer and military uniforms. Such sub-communities often had specific localities in the bars that catered to their tastes.

60. See *AG* June 10, 1970, 1.

61. See for example letter from Mike S., *VR* June 1968, 16–17.

62. "Thank God that we can still dress as we please for our hours of recreation and pleasure. . . . Come off it, May. What's your real hang-up?" *VR* Dec. 1967, 31. See also letter from "An Organized Group of Motorcycle Enthusiasts," *VR* June 1968, 16–17.

63. One such writer goes on to defend the S/M practices of some forms of leather culture in terms of the desires of the participants. "Others require a masculine physical domination and yet for others it seems to be just an evening of good time with the aid of 'poppers.'" *VR* June 1968, 5. Related but not coextensive with the leather community was S/M as a gay sexual practice. By the early 1970s, S/M was treated relatively positively by the gay press, although with some distancing from the practice. The regular column Dr. Inderhaus sought to dispel misunderstandings about S/M, in *VR* May 1971, 44–45: "To be sure, the vast majority of 'sado-masochist' activities are confined to the display of fantasy-oriented garb and accessories. The mere touch of cold leather to warm naked skin has sent thousands of wads through their happy trajectories. [List of those symbols] . . . found in homes and 'dungeons' of the proponent. . . . However, the confusion of fantasy and reality, especially when intensified by the injudicious use of drugs . . . can result in inexpert infliction of injury. . . ."

64. "Most motorcyclists do not attempt to project a 'super-masculine' image . . . but if you take the time to get to know the bike-riding, 'leather boys,' we think you will probably find them more 'normal' than the couple who live next door." *VR* June 1968, 16–17.

65. Another writer wrote in the same Forum, "The homosexual community must make an effort to understand these persons [leather community] and their individuality as much as any other 'type' of homosexual and thus, erase the intimidations which are frequently felt by the men in leather." And *GS* May 1972, 7: "Gay people who have struggled with their awareness of the masculine-feminine role dichotomy in society sometimes scorn the leather cultists as 'un-liberated' or 'immature' almost as if they were a breed apart. More often than not, however, they have killed it by silence on the subject altogether. Peter [Fisher] is quick to let us know that people who wear leather (drag?) and engage in S&M sex are different only in their sexual tastes. We have too often looked askance, and from the outside, at this phenomenon."

66. "When I walk down the street, I am not attempting to fool anyone. People look at me and know what I am. I am not going under false colors. Are you?" *TN* June 10, 1963. "I am not ashamed of being an obvious social variant." But he also argued that the

gender/sexual expression of other gay men, who strained to appear masculine, was as attention grabbing as his own. "I am talking about the ones who make their privates the most obvious thing about them [those who wear tight pants, apparently as a sign of masculinity]. I am talking about the ones who pose against doorways and lamp posts, taking advantage of lighting and posing and Clorox [bleaching hair] to show off their supposed prowess. These will not admit, even to themselves that they are in the same class as myself."

In a review of a doctoral dissertation, The Overt Male Homosexual: A Primary Description of a Self-Selected Population, *Vector* reported "no striking characteristics of the sample that would make them obviously identifiable from other male members of society." See *VR* April 1971, 5.

67. Strait argued, "They [the obvious] seem to believe that since they may live differently from the rest of society that none of the laws are intended for them. . . . It is such actions by a few uncouth, unmindful people that causes a whole group of individuals to be ostracized from the rest of society." *LCEN* May 14, 1962. See especially See "The Undesirables," *LCEN* Nov. 26, 1962. Also, "The more reserved variant is almost 100% in favor of deporting or jailing or crucifying [the obvious]. They make a convenient target for their wrath." *TN* Sept. 16, 1963, 1–2. A guest editorial made the argument that effeminate and publicly recognizable variants "are an abomination and a source of trouble for all mankind" that tarnished the public image of the "normal" homosexual. *LCEN* March 4, 1962.

68. See *CHFN* May 13, 1969.

69. A.F.K. wrote, "Believe it or not, we have our share of disturbed members in this breed, and it is this group of insatiable attention seekers that consistently keeps us in hot water." *TN* Sept. 2, 1963, 1–2.

70. "Our suggestion: While urging ourselves and others to avoid behavior and manners which bring ridicule or scorn upon us, let's otherwise pay less attention, and voice less fear of that which is different. Nothing deflates a swish's sails so much as to be unnoticed." *TT* Nov. 1964, 1–2.

71. "Who are they kidding? Then there are the tight-pants types who feel that if they show all to everyone, that they will be looked upon as a real 'he-man.' Possibly to a hick from the back-country they do personify the masculine traits, but they are not kidding the general public" *TN* Dec. 23, 1963, 1.

72. "Where the ordinary homosexual can be depended upon to moderate certain phases of his life, the wanton swish can also be depended upon to let the world know in high register tones." *CN* Aug. 3, 1964, 6–8.

73. Asking for no more nude covers on *Vector* and explaining why gay men in Toronto aren't persecuted, Ron H. Smith made what was, to him, an obvious claim that "the homosexual segment here plays it cool." *VR* June 1970, 37.

74. "When will [*Vector*] take a positive stand against the terrible over-masculine 'super-men' that parade around in leather and other ugly dirty clothes? These immature, underdeveloped neurotics are creating a very detrimental image for the homosexual community. Let's all dress neatly in shirts and tie." *VR* Oct. 1967, 32–33.

75. "Straights, and many, many gays are offended by your paper. . . . 'If these faggots speak for the gays—get rid of them.'" From Thomas M. Edwards, *BAR* Jan. 15, 1972.

76. Addressing the arrests of gay men in the city, J.B. illustrates this gendered articulation of "normal": "You say 'united we stand—etc.' but who gets picked up by the police? Mostly undesirable shits who carry on in public, making asses of themselves, and

who are of no asset to any community. Most *butch gays despise these* characters." *BAR* June 15, 1971, emphasis mine.

77. See for example *CN* 4.4, 5;

78. See for example *CN* Aug. 3, 1964, 6–8.

79. Mike Newton asked, "Is it necessary for mature adult homosexuals to turn every social occasion to a 'fairyland costume event with prizes for the best-Tressed and Dressed Drag Queen? . . . When will the homophile organization trying to improve our image begin to do so and stop acting like sophomoric children?" *VR* Oct. 1967, 32–33. See also *VR* March 1970, 12–13: "I implore the *Vector* staff, the militant, the drag queen and other blatant homosexuals who make themselves unpalatable in the eyes of the heterosexual majority to 'cool it.' . . . I think *Vector* should work to show how like the heterosexual the homosexual really is. It should de-emphasize the obsession with the large penis, and make more of the serious side of the homophile movement."

80. An article in *Town Talk* in 1965 pinned the Community's distrust of "swishes" on their effeminacy. Answering an editorial in the *News Call Bulletin*, *Town Talk* editors ask, "Why are we so disturbed when we see the age-old manifestation of effeminacy in some males? It has existed as long as man has." *TT* Nov. 1964, 1–2.

81. "No one deplores the freaks of their set more than those involved in attempting to fade in the background. But this is America. Fortunately or unfortunately, depending on whether you are a 210-pounder [woman] who enjoys waddling down Market Street or a Hair Fairy who feels that he must be a freak in order to gain attention." *CN* 4.4, 5.

82. See *TN* Sept. 16, 1963, 1–2.

83. See *CN* Aug. 23, 1964, 6–8.

84. If they were victims, it was their own fault. "To the Hair Fairies of the country: Go ahead and make a freak of yourself if you must. But when the time comes that you must pay for your display of disregard for the feelings of others, don't expect any sympathy from your fellow homosexuals." *CN* 4.4, 5. Responding to an article about a gay man's experience in the Air Force, Fred James of San Francisco wrote, "Private Korinsky deserved to get in trouble. He was [a] flamboyant and disgusting person, a discredit to self-respecting homosexuals. . . . Why can't silly queens learn that they should keep their mouths shut and act like men." *VR* Oct. 1971, 9.

85. See *TN* Aug. 5, 1963, 3.

86. "They are not <u>one</u>, they merely have a number of friends who are. They would not want to be considered anything other than ordinary, red-blooded, All-American Men." *TN* Sept. 16, 1963, 1–2.

87. "You are strangely content with your role because it is a heterosexual role— everyone assumes that you are like the 'norm.' It is easy for most homosexuals to 'pass.' However, you should remember that you are not being accepted for yourself—you are being accepted as someone other than you true self." *VR* Dec. 1969, 10.

88. "Nothing is so pathetic as a Black who denies his culture, . . . unless it's one of our Gay brothers who denies his Gayness to get along in this straight plastic culture. Both have become less than men and have sunk to the level of imitations. . . . All too many of our brothers SUCCEED in passing. They become straighter than the straight." *SFFP* Nov. 1, 1969. Passing as straight and remaining in the closet became a moral litmus test for gay men. "[I]t is inexcusable to dress 'butch' in male-case and 'fem' in the female case just to pass. It is also inexcusable to dress in these ways to play straight or that you are made more desirable by appearing Straight." *GS* Oct. 1970, 9. It is important to note that this conflict cut across political boundaries. Gay libbers themselves were not above this critique. For example, describing the crowd at a national GLF meeting, one partici-

pant observed, "I looked around me and noticed that many of the 'heavy Gay Lib' people could easily pass for straight. Only a few Gay people were Blatant-on-Sight. Straight society has oppressed our people that some Gay people still try to blend in with Straights." *GS* Oct. 1970, 9. Passing, then, became a gloss for internalized oppression, where the values of the straight society had become self-regulating within gay men. See *SFFP* Jan. 1970, 2. "Until they stop abiding by the straight norm: 'we will accept you if you look like us, act like us, speak like us, and don't touch us' there can be no Gay liberated." *SFGFP* Dec. 1970, 5.

89. "The married man from the suburbs is far more often in trouble and is the cause of trouble. The screaming ones are the source of embarrassment to us but the general public is not disturbed by them." *TN* Sept. 2, 1963, 1–2. Guy Strait argued that instead of the swishes or the normal, passing variants, the problem laid with "those who do not know what they are or will not admit it even to themselves that they are sex deviates." *TN* June 10, 1963. When Rev. Williams spoke to SIR, he argued that those who were secret, who refused to become part of the Community because they refused to be seen for what they are, were of no help to the movement. See *VR* Jan. 1965, 10.

90. Ibid.

91. "To pretend to be straight sexually, or to pretend to be straight socially, is probably the most damaging pattern of behavior in the [gay] ghetto. It has many forms—the married guy who makes it on the side secretly; the guy who will go to bed once but who won't develop any gay relationships; the pretender at work or school or home who changes the gender of the friend he's talking about; the guy who'll suck cock in the bushes but who won't come home with you. Closet Queenery must end." *SFFP* Dec. 22–Jan. 7, 1970, 3–5.

92. For the gay libbers, passing was merely playing a role dictated by society. "When as gays we realize that our role-playing and possessiveness are obsolete, and we begin living and relating to each other as free unique original beings . . . we will be much happier. We have always been revolutionaries by the very fact of our existence. By our very existence, we set an example for straight men and women. You don't set a good example (or find inner satisfaction) by aping the worst traits of the oppressor; that only multiplies the negativity. To set a good example to realize our inner selves, we know that we must act out our private dreams and personal hopes." *GS* Oct.–Nov. 1971, 3.

93. See *VR* Feb. 1971, 6.

94. Ibid.

95. "[They] deplore those awfully honest demonstrations and rightful demands, who refuse to register to vote in a 'gay' bar, who don't go to SIR meetings because they once had a run-in with one bitchy member." *VR* Aug. 1971, 9.

96. When Charles Thorp was attacked on Polk St., scores of gay men just watched and did nothing to help. "The important part of these incidents was, though, that about 20 street-sissies were standing near enough to help and what did they do? Look toward the fight—then look shocked and then go back to their cruising. My dreams, my fantasies, were CRUSHED—there is no Gay Community in San Francisco. My Community is only Fairyland." *SFGFP* Dec. 1970, 5.

97. Closet Case wrote, "Can't we say with a sense of certainty that most homosexual people are *invisibly* gay and that they prefer it that way?" *VR* July 1970, 9.

98. Aceydecy argued that he was bisexual, not closeted, and "If variants are supposed to be so liberal, why do some insist that bi's are committing a crime unless they leave their wives or girlfriends and come all the way over to the other side?" *TN* Oct. 14, 1963.

99. "Many of our community prefer to remain anonymous and this right of privacy is as basic as the right to choice of selection. . . . But whether this desire is based on family, job, or simply on preference, it does not mean one must stick his head in the sand." *TT* Sept. 1965, 5.

100. See *VR* Jan. 1971, 4.

101. "Since what they are doing with their partners is forbidden, wrong, illegal, and perverse, in the eyes of the straight world, they reject the accepted moral, ethical, and legal codes in this particular area." *VR* Jan. 1966, 8.

"We lie so that we may live. Whether it is to our boss, or the draft board, or the civil service, we rarely can afford to divulge the simple truth of our homosexuality. . . . [W]e find ourselves wallowing in a mire of untruths. (A simple question 'What did you do last Saturday night?' may produce a whole string of lies.)" *VR* Jan. 1966, 1.

102. "I am a professional man and I have responsibilities that clearly require that I keep my homosexuality concealed insofar as possible. Yet I suffer from no low self-esteem, I do not attack my brother homosexuals in word or deed, and I make every effort to support legitimate homosexual causes." *VR* March 1971, 31.

103. "We are annoyed at the often used clichés and references to two gentlemen as 'closet queen' just because they happen to be content living with each other and are not interested in your co-called 'gay bar set.' . . . My friend and I met during the closing days of World War II, when he was a pilot. I was his navigator ad we fell in love with each other during a brief leave in Honolulu . . .though he was married to a Navy Nurse, who divorced him because she too had fallen in love with a Lieut. commander WAVE. We have lived together ever since the end of WWII and resent the fairy tales that homosexual marriages are one-night or short term affairs." From Myrt and Marge, *VR* Dec. 1968, 16–18.

104. "For whether it be old ones, young ones, the tight pants or the makeup, the leather or other costumes, we are going to have to come to the realization that we are in the same boat, and if we do not start getting it under way we are all going to become victims of people such as your Chief Parker [Chief of Police in Los Angeles who was notorious for violence against gay men and African Americans] or Dave Heyler [Publisher of *The Los Angeles Citizen-News*, not affiliated with the LCE's publication. Heyler was a Christian whose paper was aimed at warning the general public about the menace of the homosexual in West Hollywood]." *TN* June 10, 1963, 55. Dan Hallard urged, "All of us are afraid of being arrested; but before we tremble and cower we should think, logically, whether there is any basis for possible arrest. . . . [I]t doesn't matter who the arrested people are, nor who the conservative, clean-cut gay by-standers think they are, if they applaud the arrests of any gays, long hair or short, queen or butch, then their heads are not on right." *VR* Sept. 1971, 36. And some gay libbers advocated not "giving up on our brothers and sisters who have accepted their oppression, but by continuing to hammer at the chains that bind all of us." *SFFP* Nov. 1, 1969. The "Gay Manifesto" urged temperance in leveling criticism at closeted brothers and sisters. "Our fear of coming out is not totally paranoid: the stakes are high. . . . Closet queen is a blanket term covering a multitude of patterns of defense. . . . We are all closet queens in one way or another, and all of us had to come out. . . . They alone can decide WHEN and HOW [to come out]" *SFFP* Dec. 22–Jan. 7, 1970, 3–5.

105. Carl Whitman argued that those who were blatant were the community's first martyrs and that gays should blame straight society, not the openly gay person, for their suffering. See *SFFP* Dec. 22–Jan. 7, 1970, 3–5. One self-identified drag queen wrote in the *BAR* to convince the "masculine types in leather" that they owed a debt to the drag

queens. From Jeff Hrock (Boy) / Roxanne (Girl), *BAR* July 1, 1971: "[quoting Jose Sarria] 'All of you leather boys please remember this. Years ago, when SF was up-tight about the gay scene, it was those "tired old drag queens" who led the fight, much as the civil rightist are doing today. They were the ones, out of their closets, who said to the SFPD, Bust me, and then they fought.' So every time you pass a drag queen who is trying to do something, instead of passing judgment, say thanks. WITHOUT WHAT THEY DID THEN, AND ARE TRYING TO DO NOW, THERE WOULD BE NO 'MIRACLE MILE,' THERE WOULD NOT BE THE GENERAL ACCEPTANCE OF OUR COMMUNITY THAT THERE IS NOW, and as a matter of fact, there wouldn't be much of anything of the world that had been created and nurtured for ALL OF US, and BY ALL OF US."

106. "I am proud of the way I look. . . . I dig flouting it in straights' faces—if it makes him sick—all the better—at least he has reacted to me. . . . I'm pissed at every Gay who refuses to accept himself. I'm pissed at anyone who refuses to stand behind me and fight with me for my rights. I am queer. I want to be queer. I'm pissed at my own repressed fright at not martyring myself to my employer . . . who says, 'It's OK if you're a little Gay—but don't act Gay here.' I've got to act Gay because I am. I act as a person—I react as a faggot. And every time I give in to the oppression of a straight or a Gay—I am sickened at my own setback and failure and lack of confidence in my own truth. . . . I WANT ARMIES OF EYELASH QUEENS MARCHING ON BROOKS BROTHERS." See also *GS* Oct. 1970, 9.

107. "The Age of Blatantness is up on/in us Brothers and Sisters. Take a stand and show you Fairy Wings or Construction Helmets!" *GS* Oct. 1970, 9. Again, this was the key to liberation. "Gays won't be treated as beautiful human beings until even the most 'Flaming Faggots' and 'Diesel Dykes' are respected in Our community, as well as in Straight society." Blatancy often carried even more significance for its advocates. One man noted of his friend, he "seemed so much 'freer' when he was Blatant. It's really sad that our people cop-out on us in their dress style even."

108. Gay men often used the word queer during this period, but not in the way that current queer theorists might use it. For them, it was rather an ironic term, understood that gay men were literally *queer*, or different from the dominant forms of masculinity; to embrace one's queerness was to embrace and celebrate one's difference. Although it had a political inflection, the idea was more about the individual's relationship to his difference and to his relationship with the closet and masculine domination.

109. See *VR* Aug. 1970, 6. In his experience, Ron Baylor insisted that there was just something different about gay men's gender, something *gay*. "I admit that there are homosexual men as masculine as former President Lyndon Johnson, but in most cases there is something about homosexuals that is different. I have made a study of them and I find that most of them have a different walk and small hands." *VR* Jan. 1971, 30–31. Baylor's "small hands" theory aside, the importance here is that he felt or experienced homosexual gender as being fundamentally different.

110. One 1971 article ran down a few expert opinions. Psychiatrist Warren J. Gadpaille argued that there was an "'indelible sense of maleness or femaleness . . . by about 30 months of age. Research has also shown that core gender identity depends overwhelmingly upon the child's rearing, not upon its biological sex'" *VR* March 1971, 38–39. And Dr. Martin Hoffman argued that "an effeminate boy may or may not be pre-homosexual . . . I want to emphasize however, that most pre-homosexual students are not identifiable as such. They seem quite normal, and some pre-homosexual boys are (contrary to stereotype) very good at sports." *VR* March 1971, 38–9.

111. "It is unfortunate that we have trapped ourselves in a bag of masculine aggressive versus feminine passivity when we are actually concerned with degrees of our defensiveness toward others—regardless of sex or sexual orientation." *VR* June 1972.

112. "Even as children we are taught that we must choose. We must select the 'good' sexual pattern or the 'bad.' Inevitably we will lack either the softness of women or the virility of men in our sexual affairs." *VG* 1.9, 25. Others agreed. "What is perverted is that nifty dualistic concept masculine/feminine, into which all behavior is neatly divided." *GS* Oct.–Nov. 1971, 7.

113. "[H]undreds of other similar matters determine whether you're 'masculine' or 'feminine.' It takes an unusually secure person to undo all this conditioning, even when he really wants to. It is easier for the gay person, who surrounds himself with other gay people, to shake this cultural baggage. His friends do not make the traditional expectations of him." *GS* April 1972, 10.

114. By the 1970s, one of the most common responses to anxiety concerning the connection of gender expression and gay identity was to change the meaning of drag itself. Jeff Hrock, drag-named Roxanne, explained, "1. What 'drag' really is, is a costume. 2. What leather, as we know, it is also a costume. 3. What the western trip is (me, too) is also a costume. THEREFORE: IT IS ALL DRAG." *BAR* July 1, 1971.

115. One illustration of this common practice: "Don't get me wrong. I was not exactly a flaming faggot. I drove a tractor, plowed the fields, tossed bales of hay into the gay loft and joined the Future Farmers of America," wrote one man. *GS* Oct.–Nov. 1971, 7.

116. "Fags? We fags, why do we join the 'men' of the military? Duty to country? Patriotism? Pride? To prove we're men? We ain't men, we're faggots, and the sooner every male on this earth realizes that and admits it the sooner there will be no more wars, militaries, nor wasted trillions for defenses and armaments for the senseless murder of innocent human lives. The heterosexual man. . . . That's the myth, that's what Nixonism is." *GS* Feb.–March 1972, 10.

117. "[A]ny discussion of sexuality where straight males are involved must be taken with a grain of salt, and even regarded with great suspicion. Especially when the discussion centers around other sexualities than their own." *TE* May 1971, 1, 4.

118. Others weren't so critical of masculinity as they were of its decline. "[Something] was wrong sexually with the young American male. . . . The destruction of the Hero had begun with the advance of equal rights for women and the gradual shift of the country towards the permissiveness of the matriarchy. . . . And again, the idea of the Hero as Breadwinner was slowly being challenged. . . . Finally, the concept of the Hero as Warrior has been destroyed. . . . The hero, then, helped to underline one's masculine status." *VR* Aug. 1970, 10–11.

119. For example, "More than one man has joined the United States Marine Corps to assure himself of his masculinity." *CN* Aug. 17, 1964, 7.

120. "To a stranger, it would seem that these were not places where homosexuals congregate. . . . The theme seems to be centered around a more pronounced accent on masculinity identification using motorcycle or cowboy attire. . . . The people who come here are MEN and want to continue being identified as such. . . . Others wear leather because they just like its feeling and associated masculine implications. Probably others wear leather merely as a means of social entrance into this group in hopes of finding other men. *Vector* does not share the opinion that wearing leather is necessarily 'masculine drag.'"

121. Laura Livingwell bemoaned the loss of the "All-American male" who conducted himself with "Simple honesty, dignity, and self-respect . . . During college years, it was grand just to walk around campus and gaze at the beautiful American male, free from any adornments other than his masculine beauty. I fail to find these persons in San Francisco and find instead boys dressed up as girls, or men following the Marlon Brando stereotype of the motorcyclist completely attired in leather. Give me the good old American male and bring back the sincere, wholesomeness to which I had grown accustomed." *VR* June 1968, 16–17.

122. "Behold, the lad who is less than the all-American lad is BAD." *VR* Dec. 1969, 33.

123. An anonymous letter writer noted, "When I first heard the term 'homophile' I was attracted to it. It seemed to indicate an interest in male relationship, male bonding, masculinity and male problems in general. Cooperation and understanding between men is exceedingly rare and anything or anyone who seems to counteract this trend has my support." *VR* May 1970, 21.

124. "There is no Man alive (yesterday, today, or tomorrow) that can successfully live up to (or down) the image, that Hollywood and 5th Avenue have decreed to be 'the' Man," he wrote. *GS* Oct.–Nov. 1971, 13. He felt he was compensating for a masculinity he didn't have by adopting the leather biker image.

125. For Elijah, discovering his maleness was not the acceptance of exterior notions of masculinity, but the discovery of his own reality. "That I am a person. That I am a male human being, a biologically (?) male member of a species. That I am not defined by my relationship to another male or by my relationship to a female. I am not defined with or by or over against any other. . . . That is, I am not the other half of a couple. I am not a unit of a group, or of a society; or even of a world. I am an individual member of us."

126. "I hope my barriers against femininity and especially queens can be broken down so I can relate to them and be more natural in my own mannerisms, speech, and mode of dress. maybe one way to break down these barriers is to go to drag occasionally—something I've never done and which would freak me." *GS* Aug.–Sept. 1970, 14.

127. See for example *TN* Aug. 19, 1963, 3–4; *CN* Aug. 3, 1964, 6–8.

128. See for example letter from "Manly," *VR* April–May 1968, 29.

129. Strait, like many of these public figures of the period, spoke out of both sides of his mouth. While pointing out their universal scorn, he also defends their rights to be effeminate. And in one case, he even lauds an effeminate man as a hero for the community for his honesty and integrity. See *CN* Aug. 3, 1964, 8: "TO JIM [a tribute to a swish]: Through all your difficulties brought about by your determination to live as you see fit you have remained exactly as you are and want to be; you have the respect everyone with whom you have come in contact for your honesty, forthrightness and integrity; you have stood against everyone for what you feel is the right of a person to be what he is and express it as such; you have attempted to moderate your appearance without sacrificing your principles of what you feel is your inherent right as an American citizen; you have made no attempt to deceive anyone as to what you feel is right and honest. Therefore, the Editor and the Associate Editor salute Jim Flynagan as a friend and as a person of integrity and honesty."

130. An anonymous letter read, "You should be arrested for defending those awful freaks on Market Street. They should be treated exactly the same manner as Hitler treated the Jews." *CN* 4.5, 3.

131. "What do I most fear? . . . When I really dig out my fears, I think I most fear becoming a woman. . . . I tell myself I have to be butch; my body has to look and feel

strong; my clothes have to be masculine; my mannerisms cannot be feminine; . . .I can't associate with feminine guys—especially queens—because there is something 'wrong' with them." *GS* Aug.–Sept. 1970, 14.

132. "I hear being said to me, 'Gay sister, I am so ashamed of you and embare-assed [sic] by you and I don't accept you or your god-fucked-up-right to dress and make up as you PLEASE!' And when I hear a sister or brother tell me that he is ashamed of me because I am Gay and look and act like a fairy (and I am—I like it—I want to look like it)—I get sick—I want to SCREAM!" *SFGFP* Dec. 1970, 5.

7

The Meaning of Gay

We Gay males discover our histories, our lives. The Man suppressed our existence and isolated us from one another. We discovered we were human and
they called it homosexuality. We discovered what it means to be a man in
America and they called it self-hate. We discovered ourselves, and they said we
were afraid of women. We discovered their secret, their empty and vicious
lives, and they called us outlaws.

—from *The Effeminist* 1.2 (1971)

I know of no way in which intelligence or mind could arise or could have
arisen, other than through the internalization by the individual of social processes of experience and behavior, that is, through the internalization of the conversation of significant gestures, as made possible by the individual's taking the
attitudes of other individuals toward himself and toward what is being thought
about.

—George Herbert Mead, *Mind, Self, and Society,* 1934

When Rev. Williams instructed SIR members in 1965 to ask themselves, "Who
are we?" he hit upon the most important point of articulation between the individual struggling to make sense of his desires in a hostile environment and the
emerging communities he might have circulated in. Williams clarified, "Homosexuals must face what they are and who they are. . . . I mean by this what I call
'gut' understanding, in a sense the deepest part of existence which gives the
individual his orientation [direction, not sexuality] and his community a center
of mutual concern and interest. What does it mean to be a homosexual?" (*VR*
Jan. 1965, 4). What, indeed? Surely, this question was not new or unique to the
gay men of the 1960s, as other men with same-sex desires in other times and
places have had to ask themselves similar questions. Different societies have

253

responded to these questions of a meaning-full "identity" with varying degrees of repression and accommodation, which allowed for different kinds of satisfying (or at least good-enough) answers. Indeed, it is a historical gaff of grand proportions to argue that same-sex attracted men only had identities after World War II.[1]

As the 1970s dawned, gay men of every political ilk insisted more and more loudly that only they could speak for themselves, that only they were qualified to give definitions, only they were qualified to assign meaning, and only they were capable of understanding what it meant to be gay—for it was *their* feelings and desires, *their* interior lives, *their* experience of domination, and *their* sexuality. The question of why an individual would be homosexual has vexed Western science since at least the mid-nineteenth century, and by the end of the 1960s, gay men were using their own experiences in combination with what they had gleaned from scientific studies to assert their own theories of the etiology of homosexuality. These theories of the origins of same-sex desire were inevitably connected to different ideas about what gayness would mean in their own time and place. A handful of general categories emerged as coherent and meaningful for them between 1961 and 1972: a democratic *choice* (lifestyle, taste, proclivity); *genetic* (inborn); *natural* (connected to the larger, natural historical world, but sometimes with more spiritual understanding of "natural"); and *acquired* (learned, cultural). From their active-undergoing of domination, gay men constantly had to reevaluate the meaning of their same-sex desire for sex and relationships with other men. Domination played together with how they positioned themselves vis-à-vis community building and the gay counter-public to form their basic stances on the origins and therefore meaning of homosexuality. These four general categories of meaning often overlapped and individuals and groups seem to have held contradictory meanings simultaneously, or to have adopted and shed meanings as they were situationally expedient.

In contexts where traditional citizenship and recognition were the predominant values, the idea that homosexuality was merely a sexual *democratic choice*, a taste like any other, held sway.[2] Guy Strait compared homosexuality to liking escargot when one's parents do not like eating snails.[3] Adopted tacitly by the LCE, the democratic choice model of sexuality argued, in effect, that the origin of homosexuality should be irrelevant in the official public sphere, as it should be an individual right to choose to be gay. Thus, homosexuality was seen as "among the valid choices people can choose is homosexual experience" (*TT* Sept. 1965, 1, 4). The experience of oppression by the state combined with the desire for integration and full citizenship in the public sphere made sexuality *intelligible as a choice*, one best determined by individuals without interference from an outside group or institution.[4] One writer even argued that as homosexuality became a valid choice in American culture, there would be a noted increase in homosexuality, because many men refused the homosexual choice simply because society forbade it.[5] If same-sex sex were a matter of taste and choice, this also made situational homosexuality intellible to gay men.[6] Later in the period, gay men continued to use the choice argument as an inroad to the public sphere, insisting that homosexuality was merely one lifestyle choice among many, and therefore should not fall under the purview of governmental control.[7] But for many gay men, the argument of choice failed to answer fundamental questions about their sexuality; while individuals may indeed chose their sexual partners, it doesn't explain why they make the choices they do.[8]

References to the inherency of homosexuality, to its inbornness, first began to circulate in the gay press in the mid-1960s.[9] This *genetic* categorization enabled gay men to claim power over their sexuality and to confront the dominant psychopathological definition of homosexuality as "sickness." Here, homosexuality was seen as instinctual and hereditary, as an instinct.[10] For some, this turn to instinct pointed up a beauty or a kind of spiritual experience of sexuality.[11] When same-sex desire was construed as hereditary, it was also often seen as a *capacity*, a theme that will emerge throughout the latter part of the decade as many gay men saw themselves as being *gifted* to be able to love other men. In 1971, *Vector* ran a story about the causes of homosexuality and quoted Evelyn Hooker's famous article in which she argues that gay men turn to genetics as a means to justify their homosexuality to the larger society (see *VR* April 1971, 5).[12] Although its prominence among gay men declined during the 1960s, the feeling that their gayness was inborn remained a strong recurring idea, where homosexuality was experienced as a kind of truth of the self.[13] Numerous men expressed the feeling that they had known they were different for most of their lives.[14] The genetic view of homosexuality led to explanations of gay men's anxiety[15] and in one case proposals for how society can deal with the "genetic carriers of homosexuality."[16]

Gay men also refused dominant explanations of homosexuality in the particular way they appealed to *Nature* to explain it. Nature functioned as a kind of catchall category for gay men's struggle to make their sexualities intelligible to themselves and to situate themselves with self-respect vis-à-vis the dominant culture.[17] They argued that their existence was natural, despite not being able to reproduce together.[18] Many gay men took the naturalness of their sexuality a step further, finding in nature the meaning of gayness as something that just *is* that needs no explanation.[19] In an overlap with the *genetic* category, gay men argued that they simply *were* gay, that to desire and have sex with another man was simply the most normal, *natural* thing they could do. Importantly, the naturalness of their sexuality conflicted with their experiences of growing up in a straight world.[20] Despite these intense pressures, "we found it impossible to deny the profound emotion of love for our own kind." So for many gay men, the experience of growing up in America is at odds with who they were naturally born to be.[21] The argument came down to what exactly "natural" might mean, and what part of homosexuality was natural. Many argued in the 1970s that the naturalness of gayness lay in its the capacity to love someone of the same sex— the aptitude for same-sex love was natural.[22] And for those who valued authenticity as an end of gay counter-publicity, this nature was deeply personal and deeply connected to the self.[23]

Still others rejected both the genetic and the natural arguments, which they saw as a "degrading, demeaning, dehumanizing . . . 'anatomy is destiny' theory. Our genital organs are our appendages; we are not appendages of our genital organs" (VR June 1972). For them, gayness was a matter of choice, but with the added weight of cultural conditioning behind it.[24] Here, some men felt that it was their domination that made homosexuality so salient for them; otherwise, it would be a minor part of existence.[25] Critics of the genetic model argued that biological explanations failed to elicit the depth of their experience, to account for what they had lived.[26] As early as 1965, Town Talk anchored sexuality in social mores. "Heterosexuality is not a scientific norm, but a value norm, and value norms are subject to change" (TT Sept. 1965, 1, 4). Many of these arguments of values were rooted in Freudian conceptions of the self, and his notion of polymorphous perversity and fundamental bisexuality shaped in the relationships of the family. Here we find an oft-repeated notion that bisexuality is actually the default position of human beings.[27] This kind of sexual blank slate was most fully embraced by gay libbers who felt that human beings were naturally bisexual, that Freud's polymorphous perversity suggested an ideal state without sexual categories based on sexual object choice at all.[28]

It is not my purpose to answer the ponderous etiological question here but to highlight the problems gay men had as they created new categories that would make intelligible their sexual desire, their experience of sex acts, their undergoing of domination, and their lives in the emerging counter-public and community, trying to make sense of it all *with each other*. The questions they asked each other were many and varied: If homosexuality is a choice, why is heterosexuality not a real choice for homosexuals? If it's genetic or instinctual, then why not seek to cure it as one does other genetic diseases? If it's natural, why are homosexuals so different from each other—why is behavior and desire so diverse among homosexuals? If it's socially determined, where does the desire come from and why isn't it simple to switch one's desired object? The conflict over the nature and meaning of homosexuality went round and round (and continues to do so) among gay men as no explanation seemed to fully give voice to their experience of homosexuality and all of them left the individual and community open to further oppression. "[A]ll homosexuals have been forced to question the validity of the rationalizations that have made the homosexual community pliable and weak in the past" (CHFN May 13, 1969). Thus, gay men did not settle on any stable explanation or definition of their homosexuality for neither the complex environment nor their own desires could allow it, inasmuch as each of these explanations makes sense in a given context. Rather, they created in the 1960s in San Francisco a matrix of possibilities, an array of meanings of *gay* that made sense to them in their context and made their lives manageable and meaningful.

A Gay History and Folk Anthropology

The project of creating an expansive and meaningful gayness led many men to connect their lives and experiences with the past and with men in other times and places, that is, they worked to create a *gay history* and a *folk anthropology of homosexuality*. Whereas academics often work to distinguish among different kinds of homosexuality, the different social roles and meanings of homosexuality across time and among different cultures, gay men were seeking connection to and a kind of psychic communion with homosexuality in other times and places. This was, in effect, an expansion of the meaning of gay, that created bonds, real or imagined, and made of "gay" a blanket term uniting men who love and have sex with men across time and space. This contraction of time and space produced, in scholarly terms, inappropriate and unempirical matrix of homosexuality; yet it was a newly expanded category that created for these gay men the affect, or feeling, of being part of something that transcended their own grounding in San Francisco, U.S.A., in the middle of the Cold War enduring yet another bar raid, legal battle, excommunication, firing, or shunning. And so they began to speak of a gay "culture." While culture can be a vexed category of analysis, here I'm more concerned with what these men meant by the term. For them, a gay culture was a set of practices, feelings, art, and especially a history that united, in their estimation, gay men across cultures and through time.

Many gay men apparently understood that membership in the emerging gay community was different from other communities they'd grown up in, because every gay man had to *choose* to attach himself to the community, inasmuch as no gay man is born into a gay culture.[29] *Agape in Action* worried that when homosexuals eventually found a community of other homosexuals, they would have been so distorted by the dominant culture that the culture they would find would be without depth or real meaning. They wanted gays to embark on a journey of discovery of sorts, to find out what a homosexual "really" was, an authentic gayness. For many libbers, the new gay culture needed to be an authentic gay culture, one that would reject the distinction between homosexual and heterosexual and develop instead a new self-identity and lifestyle.[30] That it had to be something new seemed obvious to gay libbers who had embraced "revolution" as an end.[31] They felt that gayness should mean existing outside of definitions, thereby granting the possibility to be or make themselves into whatever they desired. This often had a sense of separatism to it, that for true cultural and psychic liberation to occur, it had to be outside of existing boundaries.[32]

So the gay-culture-to-be, the promise of the coming culture, became a source of pride and of revolutionary possibility, and with it came alternate views of European and American history that emphasized the existence and persistence of gay men. Indeed, the idea that there was a historical foundation upon which a healthy gay culture could be built permeated the publications, across the political spectrum, beginning in 1969. *SFFP* referred to an "antique cultural heritage with its distinctive and dignified literary and visual and performing arts forms"

(Dec. 7, 1969, 7). And *The Effeminist* argued that the invisibility of gay history was evidence not that it didn't exist, but that the dominant culture wanted to keep gay men from knowing their own history.[33] So the act of creating or "discovering" gay culture was to battle the dominant culture.[34]

Instead of relying on outmoded ways of being homosexual, these men hoped to establish a full-fledged gay culture,[35] often distinguishing between "homosexuals" and a new "gay man," where the former accepted his life as defined by the dominant society and the latter chose his own self-definitions.[36] As I have already amply shown, the gay libbers saw themselves as advanced beyond and superior to older gay men and the "gay establishment" they represented; gay libbers saw themselves as doing the real work of re-imagining gay male life. They often felt that the modes of being gay from the early 1960s and earlier were destructive to the gay soul and the source of alienation. "Gay Liberation, on the other hand, wants to destroy the system of gay bars altogether. To be free to continue patterns of alienation [of the gay bars]. . . is to be free to destroy human lives." (*AA* Feb. 1971). Liberation became for these men a way to end alienation as they saw it.

But creating a new "liberated" gay male culture presented problems of its own. At least one man saw that such hard definitions of authentic culture could end up creating an alienation perpetrated by gay liberation itself.[37] Remembering that the primary complaint among gay men at the time was that the "gay lifestyle" as it was constituted in the early 1970s failed to meet their basic needs, many gay men felt that gay liberation wasn't really any different, but was merely putting old wine into new bottles. Whereas the old gay life was a ghettoized life of tightly structured scripts that categorized the individual gay men and shunted him into a box (or bar, as it were), for many, gay liberation was simply another kind of ghettoization with new and different tight scripts and a different box to fit into.[38] Despite these difficulties, men across the political spectrum looked to literature, art, and especially history as the source of a cultural grounding for gay men.

Publishing gay literature and thought appeared as one priority. Speaking of a proposed gay literary and scholarly journal, "The Gay Community will attempt 'to bring homosexuals together over thought and creativity—publishing work in progress or planned in mathematics, social and natural sciences, history, religion, philosophy, trades and crafts'" (*SFFP* Nov. 1, 1969, 15). But as cultural sources for gay men, literature and art presented as many problems as they solved. Were artistic representations, for example, accurate? Were the broad and open enough to stand in for an archetypal gay man?[39] Another problem was that, more often than not, the means of producing art were in the hands of straight people, who had final say over the value and marketing of the product.[40] Dirk Vanden argued that until gay men control the production of their art, straight publishers would "blue-pencil those [gay] heroes' humanity right out of existence" (*VR* July 1970, 10–11).[41] Along with this insistence for control of publication came an effort to reclaim gay authors of the past, including Homer, Sappho, Marcel Proust,[42] Allen Ginsberg, James Baldwin, Tennessee Williams, etc.[43] They spoke of a gay literary style that united the writings of gay men through time, and hoped that they could elevate the esteem and value of such a gay style.[44]

For some gay men, these authors of the past set the way for their own sense of self and a uniquely gay world view; they saw in them a heritage that was all there own, a touchstone for creating a gayness that had a past, a depth, and a potential future.[45] As part of this movement was also an interest in gay theater, which saw among other things, the formation of Berkeley's Gay Liberation Theater. Stevens Crandall, GLT's founder, hoped that gay theater would be a kind of cultural guerilla practice, both undercutting the power of domination and raising the consciousness of gay men and women.[46] Crandall felt that in its raw form, theater was the most direct, most human way to effect cultural change, both within and without the gay community. So poets, playwrights, and novelists offered what seemed to be a very real alternative to the dominant culture that they had been raised with and the possibility of re-conceiving of the world in their own terms.

A few gay men also began to speak of music as a possible locus of gay culture, some arguing that gay men had a special relationship to music. Don Burton was a gay folk singer in the city who described how listening to Joan Baez inspired him to write from his own experiences instead of simply repeating the tropes of folk music. "I was singing about peace, when I was sick to my stomach with fear, the fear every homosexual learns. . . . [So] I wrote about the love I felt for a man, but I was too afraid of laughter to ever sing my songs to anyone, even my mother" (*SFFP* Oct. 16, 1969, 11). Another man, J.B. Harding, an academic, argued that gay men had a special relationship to pop music,[47] that music was a powerful force in gay men's lives for their creation of a group identity through aesthetic consumption. "This gratification which occurs at unconscious levels does not operate logically, as stated earlier, and it therefore does not know that there is no such thing as Gay music, and thus produces esteem for the listener who participates. . . . The more detectable a song is as Gay, the greater its gratification to Gays" (*BAR* Jan. 15, 1972).

Most common and perhaps most powerful way gay men sought a cultural heritage was their look to the past for a feeling of connectedness through a *gay history*, which would be both a history of gay men themselves and history with a gay sensibility. "It is time they learn of the rich and ancient culture of the Gay people" (*SFFP* Dec. 7, 1969, 7). Gay men often felt that the dominant culture had stolen from their history the chance to know of gay historical figures' noble acts, either by excluding gay men or by desexualizing them when they are included in the dominant history, thereby depriving gay men of positive historical role models.[48] Much of this historical attention focused on the influence of gay men in the arts and letters, as noted earlier.[49] As gay men tried to think about what their culture would mean, in the standard sense of culture as their arts and intellectual achievements, they broadened their debates about what gay could mean and the value of being gay in American culture.

Harry d'Turk wrote several pieces in *Citizens News* about historical figures including Oscar Wilde, Walt Whitman, and Marcel Proust.[50] "Walt Whitman specifically disavowed any 'morbid inference' was to be made from his poems. How, then, shall we understand his lines?" (*CN* June 22, 1964, 5), he asked. This is the question often begged in the treatment of homosexuality in history: What do you do with historical figures who had no conception of gayness or homosexuality or who, like Whitman, publicly denied they had sex or desired other men? Gay men confronted this question head on outside of academia in the pages of these publications, claiming as their own historical figures who, within academia, provoked intense debate among professional historians and social scientists. One book published in 1964 claimed historical figures as gay all "those alleged to have been actively homosexual, occasionally homosexual, bisexual or completely sublimated" (*CN* Aug. 3, 1964).[51]

History became, for many, the key to understanding gay life, and by the 1970s nearly every issue of every publication had some sort of historical article in its pages.[52] Magnus Hirschfield, the German sexologist, was lauded as a closeted homosexual who fought for homosexual rights before anyone knew what that was.[53] *Gay Sunshine* sought to resurrect an Egyptian pharaoh, Akhenaten, as the first "de-closeted homosexual" in history who was persecuted and killed for taking a boy-queen when Nefertiti died (Oct.–Nov. 1971). Another little-known homosexual historical figure, Roger Casement, became a proto-type for a homosexual ethic, as he seemed to have lived out both a homosexual life and an anti-imperialist politic as he fought against the oppression and dehumanization of the African and Brazilian men he loved. When he returned to Ireland and became a nationalist, the British government used his diaries to discredit him as a homosexual. After reading his diaries, Silverstein suggested that Casement was an example of the centrality of homosexuality in gay men's lives and in the structure of their ethics.[54]

The idea of "gay history" wasn't new with the libbers, and stretches all the way back to 1961 in this period, and at least through the early formations of the Mattachine Society in the late 1940s. In point of fact, this effort for same-sex attracted men to seek and claim their own history traces well back at least into the nineteenth century, e.g., the German Karl Ulrichs. So while the libbers undertook to reclaim a gay history, they were actually participating in an old and ongoing effort. It seems, however, that the publicity and community of the early 1970s created a different urgency for the project and also produced a ground where the notion of a gay history could take hold to such an extent that it would eventually become an array of academic sub-disciplines. As the gay libbers sought to re-imagine gay life and create something new, especially what it should mean to be a gay man, they went down the same roads that gay men had gone down before, looking to the arts, literature, and history for substantive ideas about gayness. And in the process created a kind of folk anthropology of homosexuality, which is to say, they sought to explain in universal terms the experience and effect of same-sex desire and same-sex sex among human men across different cultures. They appropriated and integrated men of the past and men from different cultures into their own understanding of gay, and used it as a basis for a much broader and a more psychically deep (that is affectively laden), connected gayness.

In contrast, as we have seen throughout this book, there was always resistance to the new and expanding meanings of gay that were emerging through the period. Whether motivated by fear or by the fact that many men felt satisfaction in the lives they already had, the resistance was a constant presence in the gay publications. In fact, some gay men wanted nothing to do with any kind of gay culture or community at all. It is possible that these men overlap with those who sought as an end to gay publicity a total integration into American society and who saw community building as superfluous to gaining the rights of personhood. But it is also possible that they held other motives altogether. Regardless, what remains for us to analyze is their refusal and their stated reasons for refusing. As have seen, this stretches all the way back to the LCE days, when men objected to the idea of a "gay community", that there could possibly be anything that united homosexuals in a cohesive group beyond their shared legal needs. The same kind of sentiment persisted through the period, and we see it surfacing even in the early 1970s.[55] Another form of refusal came in the disavowal of discernible gay behaviors. One man who went to a gay liberation meeting for the first time noted that he was impressed by "the total lack of obviously homosexual mannerisms" (*VR* Oct. 1970, 38).

From wanting more association with straight people to disavowing gay behaviors, many gay men struggled against being part of a movement that they felt pigeon-holed them or subjected them to scrutiny or divided them from the society they longed to be part of.[56] A man calling himself Disillusioned was disturbed that the gay publication's images of homosexuality were seen as representative, because he felt strongly that it did not represent him or his experiences. Indeed, "outness" itself was a difficult social stance to take for many gay men. Keir Storey, a Seattle man, objected to the frequent use of the term "closet queen" in *Vector* because he felt it didn't accurately describe his experience of gayness. For him, personal choice and difficult circumstances were both legitimate reasons not to publicly be part of a gay community.[57] Another writer felt that the gay publicity of SIR was one of spectacle and voyeurism that served to bait the strait press but did little else of value.[58] And Michael Cooke, a CHF organizer, complained that when the Steamship Company fired a gay employee, the gay community was unresponsive. If the community could do nothing but party, as Cooke saw it, what was the use of a community?[59] The gay culture as it was constituted, for Cooke and men like him, was empty of what he needed from it. For men like Cooke, gay culture was quite simply "fucked up" (see *SFFP* Oct. 1, 1969, 12).

The Evolution of Gay

In the 1950s, the Mattachine Society and *ONE Magazine* had used the term "homophile" to refer to men and women who were attracted to and had sex and relationships with people of the same sex. This was an effort to spin homosexuality away from the pathologizing discourses of psychiatry and the criminal discourses of the law. In sum, to put a positive valence on same-sexuality by associating it with *philia*, or love. During the 1960s, the issue of how members of the movement should label themselves took on far more than mere semantic arguments, as the meanings associated with various labels and categories structured the experiences of gay men in their environments. Beginning with homophile, the periodicals of the period used such labels as social variant, homosexual, deviant, and ultimately gay to make sense of their evolving experiences as they took on the task of defining their own lives in the face of their domination in the official public sphere. These categories served as a way to make sense of their political differences, as we have already seen; but more importantly, they came to serve as the means whereby individuals could make sense of their own experiences, their active-undergoing of being homosexual in a homophobic environment.

The early members of the LCE and readers of their publications tried to come up with ways to think about their homosexuality and to think of themselves *as* homosexuals that would both embody their particular views of democracy and leave their individual differences in tact, in order to bring them into the fold of American democracy. They frequently employed the 1950s term "homophile"; but just as often they sought to divorce themselves from this term, which they saw as inflammatory and inaccurate as it was employed by the Mattachine Society, against which they saw themselves acting. Valuing integration and full citizenship, they tended to think in quasi-sociological terms, seeing themselves as "social variants" or sometimes "social deviants."[60] But the term "homosexual" itself was almost never used until mid-1964; and even more rare were the many slang terms that were already commonly circulating in the bar communities of the period, most notably, "gay." In this early period where publicity seemed to demand a certain respectability, Strait's papers downplayed the explicit difference of homosexuality that he perceived to provoke the oppression he was fighting.[61] In his publications, he used any term or word *except* those that were most descriptive and which gay men themselves used to define themselves. This imprecision of terms often led to a perceived lack of substantive coverage about what gay men's lives were really like.[62]

Although the LCE's reluctance to call a spade a spade waned as the decade reached mid-point, the values and fears that drove such vagueness did not. Gay men who insisted that they really *were* normal after all continued to make themselves heard and had a powerful sway in some parts of the gay community. Many of these men were veterans of the Mattachine Society in San Francisco from the late 1950s, but had become disillusioned with the Society's unwillingness to confront directly the police force and the justice department in the city. But they also carried with them the core values and views of the Mattachine Society: citizenship and respectability, that gay men were only minimally different, choosing a different lifestyle and publicly active. Echoing Mattachine's arguments from the 1950s, these early publications argued publicly that there was no difference between gay and straight folks except one little "proclivity." From there, the LCE publications built his arguments about homosexuality around the idea of "personal choice." We have seen, however, that parallel meanings of homosexuality survived not only in the LCE, but also in many men (even some among the gay libbers) through the period. So the idea of the "social variant" passed into the night with the demise of the LCE and the gradual marginalization of Guy Strait within the gay publication mini-industry in San Francisco; but the category's *meaning*, that is, the values that drove that category and structured gay men's practices and interactions remained very much a part of gay men's struggle for identification. By the time SIR formed, they had reverted back to the Mattachine's category, "homophile," but SIR employed the term in ways that expanded it past its usage in the older organization. SIR used homophile to describe communities, organizations, and activities; it used it when speaking of public actions; it used it when speaking of love and sex; it used it when speaking of gay cultures such as drag and leather and camp and even pornography. So SIR took up the word "homophile" and made it into a fully formed cultural identity associated with its own organizational structures, values, and practices, but extended its meaning and import into the lives and cultural practices of individual gay men.

Coined in the late 1860s in by a Hungarian sexologist, the word "homosexual" as a category of human beings has had quite a career.[63] By the mid-twentieth century, many gay men, especially those who had either been in therapy or who in an effort to understand themselves had researched the topic, knew of the category "homosexual." Especially in the context of the post–World War II purge from the military and civil service, "homosexual" as a category of mental disease was used commonly among gay men in San Francisco. It was the word bandied about by the ABC in the 1950s as they sought ways to bring down gay bars and it had been written into the rules the ABC used, which forbade homosexual conduct in establishments that served alcohol. Gay men's relationship to the idea of "homosexual" as a category was thus a troubled one in the 1960s. Was it a disease, a crime, or a sexual identity?

By 1964, *Citizens News* used the term homosexual regularly. Following its clinical history from the military and psychiatric professional usage, "homosexual" maintained among gay men a more clinical usage through much of the period. It was seen most often in purely analytical terms merely to distinguish gay men by the fact they had sex with other men.[64] Thus, arguments using the category "homosexuality" often circulated around defining a "true" homosexual.[65] This enabled gay men to distinguish between "homosexual conduct or behavior" and "true homosexuality" as they struggled to understand what made them different, as it seemed experientially to be constitutionally different from a mere sexual episode or event.[66]

Employing "homosexual" in this way, as an analytical category for distinguishing among men who had sex with other men, allowed gay men to distance themselves from the clinical, psychiatric baggage of the word.[67] By the 1970s, gay men were actively rejecting the pathology associated with "homosexual" as a category, refusing that content and actively re-injecting it with a content that matched their experiences of *being, living,* and *acting* homosexual.[68] Despite this shift, it continued to be difficult to separate the term from the power it carried among those in the medical field or in the law. "The See-er has seen Gay Liberation most simply as liberation from being 'homosexual.' Homosexuality is a category thrust upon people who sexually enjoy other people of the same sex. It is a repressive category" (*IA* 1.2, 2).

"Homosexual," then, was a label used in various ways, most often wrested from its pathology and used to address homosexuality's basic form: sex between people of the same sex. Because gay men used the term in so many ways, but also in such generic ways, it was often denied what I call *meaning-power,* that is, of the ability of meanings to continually structure relationships and interactions.[69] In this way, homosexuality often became the term used when they wanted to emphasize the *naturalness* or even banality of same-sex attraction or of sex between men.[70] The word was, however, always sexual by definition, never separated from the aspect of desired object.[71] Ultimately, it was at the end of the period in the pages of *San Francisco Free Press* and other liberation publications that the categories "homosexual" and "gay" were conflated and the meaning of homosexual began to shift.

That "homosexual" had changed was made clear when the CHF attempted to get a non-discrimination clause put into a ballot measure in the fall of 1969 and they purposefully used the words "homosexual orientation" in the language of their petition "because obscuring the word homosexual would defeat this purpose and only propagate the ashamedness uptight people, gay and straight, contain within themselves" (*SFFP* Oct. 16, 1969, 1, 5). Indeed, SIR's board eventually rescinded its support of the CHF drive because of the use of the word "homosexual" in the ballot initiative, which they felt was "too inflammatory" for the general public at that time. But "homosexual" was here to stay as an out-and-proud word. Over the following few years, however, many preferred the term "Gay as opposed to homosexual" (*SFGFP* Nov. 1970, 4–5, 12) in order to refuse once and for all the "scientific" baggage of the term and to make gay men into something more than "sex machines." For gay libbers, the idea of "gay" afforded them the power to define themselves, to take control of the symbolic world that infused their life and to create the meanings (that is, the complex relationship between the symbolic and the interactional worlds) that made sense and were fulfilling to them.[72]

The most powerful category label by the 1970s was "gay," which had come to stand for a public, self-aware, and communal form of male-male sexuality, embodied in the oft-repeated slogan, "Gay Is Good." But like "homophile" and "homosexual" before it, "gay" was a hotly contested term as gay men struggled over what exactly it would mean to call themselves gay, or to actually *be* gay. By 1972, the usage of homosexual had bled over into the usage of "gay," and the two had come to be used almost interchangeably across the political spectrum, and despite the preference for "gay" in the liberation press. Also by 1972, gay men across the political spectrum were using these two words almost exclusively to describe themselves, and the battles had shifted to be over the meanings of "gay" and "homosexual" as "homophile" fell into complete disuse. Like SIR's previous usage of "homophile," "gay" had come to be imbued with much more than mere sexual desire and practice. It was a people, the members of a community, a counter-publicity, and a culture. Indeed, usage of "gay" (and increasingly of "homosexual") was a *constituting effect* of the emergence of a gay male community and its concomitant culture. By constituting effect, I mean that it was neither a "cause" of gay culture, in any sort of discursively determined way; nor was it only an effect, chronologically following the emergence of the culture. Rather, as gay men struggled for recognition and to create a community, they needed words that described their experience of social difference, of membership in that community, and of self-understanding or identity. The word "gay" had been in usage for at least sixty years by the time gay men in 1960s San Francisco started using the word publicly.[73] What is key here is how the very publicity and communal experience of gay men changed the meaning of the word "gay" (and by association, the word "homosexual") and how that word and arguments over its meaning in turn came to structure communal relations and interactions.

"Gay" (and 1970s-style "homosexual") came to connote something far larger than a sexual proclivity, but also a particular relationship with the dominant culture, relationships within a gay community, gay practices which had evolved and accrued new meanings, and a sexual self, all emerging out of the process of gay men working out with each other what their lives would mean, always in relationship to the dominant culture, in their counter-publicity and its related community.[74] Homosexuality and gayness came to be *more* than they had been and this new meaning-power guided subsequent generations through the morass of making sense of themselves and their environments, to good or ill. But for homosexual and gay to become "something more," it had to be continually reworked, constantly massaged to do and be more and especially to separate it from the dominant culture's vastly negative misrepresentations of homosexuality.[75] This notion of homosexuality as a "capacity" or an "ability to love"—rather than either a choice or an inborn trait—became dominant for a brief period in the Bay Area's publications in the early 1970s. This was obviously a direct contradiction of the medical, pathologizing definitions of homosexuality that saw it as deficient, perverted, diseased.[76] Importantly, "gay" and "homosexual" in their expanded form obviously had to be more than just sexual desire or behavior.

For gay/homosexual to become the linguistic signs for this "more," a gay culture had to be built or at least defined. We have already seen how gay men struggled over their various sexual and social practices and how they drew in and out boundaries within the community, often based on these cultural differences among them. Many gay men from across the political spectrum had rejected as best they could most previous gay cultures. So gay/homosexual had come to mean a culture that was continually reformed as individuals made their way from their birth communities and into something new that would be, hopefully, nurturing to their true selves as gay individuals. This process of adopting what came to be thought of as a gay identity meant, beyond doubt, coming out of the negative or incomplete images of their "selves" that gay men had received in their birth communities. But the contents of that gayness were anything but clear and were, in fact, the very focus of most of the battles over meaning I have examined here in this book.

Further, the move to "gay," inflected with the *authenticity* ascribed to it within the liberation movement, brought with it an increasing emphasis on the process of self-knowledge, the path one must tread to be "truly" gay, usually a process of "discovery" of one's true identity.[77] This discovery was often linked to a particular cultural value system vis-à-vis sexual desire and community affiliation, often emphasized by capitalizing the word. Nick Benton even described discovering a gay identity as being "born again," entering the baptismal waters a homosexual and emerging Gay,[78] where gay came to stand for the birth of a new culture, a new lifestyle, a new mode of being. This version of the positive meaning-power of "gay" endured after him, as the "free ground for the development of a gay identity." As gay men had begun thinking about "gay pride" and as they formulated it in relationship to "authentic" gayness, so they began to associate gay identity with an inner beauty of gay personhood in opposition to the "respectable" homosexual and in defiance of the "straight world."[79] Gay liberation had to be more than its politics and social activities, it had to, at the psychic level, liberate "the Gay Soul from the fear of the Straight Pig." For, "A Gay Soul is a beautiful thing. It's a gift of personhood, a gift of the Spirit" (*AA* Jan. 5, 1971).

Finally, many men came to believe that the very experience of same-sex attraction gave gay men different values, a different perspective on life in opposition to and outside of the dominant world view, which, they believed, led to misunderstandings between gay and straight people, and to the oppression of gay men.[80] When Michael Silverstein, professor of sociology, was fired from CSU Hayward in 1971, he described his relationships with his students as being from a different value system based in his gay experience, and that for him to act authentically, he had to interact with his students as a gay man would.[81] From the early 1960s idea of "social variant"—basically indistinguishable from the general public in all but their "proclivities"—gay man had produced a "Gay Soul," a culturally distinct kind of human being. From within that broad range of possible meanings, homosexual men worked ceaselessly to understand their experiences as they had them and to create new kinds of meanings that could infuse their entire lives with gayness and where gayness would be inseparable from other aspects of being human. Both the narrowest and the broadest meanings of homosexuality and gay-maleness produced experiences both of freedom and of domination. It was never answered (rightly so) where along this continuum one *should* fall, although many had their opinions. What remained, however, was an open question, where gayness was a flexible field of possibilities that could be expanded or contracted depending on political necessity, in-the-moment needs, conflicting identity demands, community participation, social context, or personal desire.

Gayness as Identity

Since I'm writing this forty years after *gay* became an identity, or more accurately, a process of self-identification, it can be difficult to clearly ascertain the shift that occurred during this period. One possibility is that the shift was a matter of salience, that is, the degree to which one's homosexuality was central to self-conception and to which it interpenetrated other aspects of the individual's life. By examining the development of the notion of gayness during this period and combining it with the emotional and social expectations gay men had of gayness, it becomes useful to see the emergence of gay identity as a degree of salience that emerged out of the interactions of gay men during a particular time period and, from my research, the transformation of homosexual subcultures into a gay counter-public. To assert a gay identity, as I described previously, felt like a kind of liberation for gay men in and of itself, a sense that they had control over who they were and the lives they wanted; that is, gayness became a mode of being in the world.[82] But claiming such an identity often meant automatic disenfranchisement in the official public and association with men and women you may not particularly like or have much in common with. At its worst, "gay" might simply be a nebulous identity with no valuable or meaningful content.

In his recent argument about the end of the closet, Steven Seidman divided identities into two kinds: core and thread. The men writing about gayness in the late 1960s were expressing a core identity, one that affects or defines all aspects of life, which one carries from context to context. A thread identity, by contrast, "is important for self-defining in only *some* situations."[83] This, he argues, is what has changed for gay men since Stonewall. As the closet has been less and less enforced by the state, gay men and women have less and less a need for gay identity to be a core identity where "it will shape an individual's decisions about friends, residence, social activities, and employment." Although this conception of a gay core identity bears out to some degree in the 1960s, the arguments gay men were actually having with each other over their identities belie a complicated and fluid identity that could range from barely existent to core and anywhere in between, depending on the individual, his values, and the context. Seidman's argument that participating in an urban gay community meant "fashioning a life around a core gay identity" doesn't actually hold up to the experiences gay men were having as they tried to figure out what exactly a "gay" identity should even mean and how important it should be in a gay man's life.

In other words, gay men were arguing with each other about whether "gay" should be, to use Seidman's terms, a core or a thread identity or indeed, an identity at all throughout the entire period between 1961 and 1972. It seems that gay men moved in and out of various kinds of identities, and they did so consciously to meet changing needs in a changing environment. For my purposes here, the interpretive problem arises when you begin to try to categorize men's experiences empirically what into a core or thread identity. For example, does an oppressive society produce a de facto core identity in its abject members? Or what do you do with the gay men who argued against a core identity, but were actively engaged in a gay male community that seemed to have made it a de facto core identity? And what of men who desired integration and acceptance into the dominant society, who had to constantly monitor behavior to fit in, thereby again making it a de facto core identity despite their eschewal?

What the traces these men left in their publications seem to indicate, however, is that the identification process, as a process, is fragmented and differentiated over time and among contexts. From their arguments, it's a reasonable extrapolation that individuals moved in and out of situations or times when their gayness was core and others where it would fade into the background as a thread identity, and anywhere in between. Although this seems to just be what Seidman meant by a thread identity, I would argue that the distinction between core and thread may actually not be useful as a category of analysis as a social fact, at least not in the 1960s, because gay men seemed to move in and out of gayness as an identification, both as groups and as individuals. This is difficult to support empirically, because it is difficult to follow an individual through time to see how he would have identified. But given the breadth of arguments put forth throughout the period, I find it reasonable to infer that identification was a process that was context- and affect dependent, depending on the individual and his circumstances. So the relative "core-ness" or "thread-ness" was not a historical function of the period, but rather a function of the particular experience and the meanings individuals and groups were trying to create in "gayness."

Interestingly, it seems to have been in "gay" settings where "gayness" faded into the background, and other demarcating factors rose to the surface as core identity markers (e.g., drag queen, butch, bottom,[84] conservative, or black).[85] In other words, core-ness or thread-ness seem to themselves be context-specific effects of interaction rather than empirically sustainable social facts. For the gay men of this period, "gayness" had evolved by the early 1970s into a symbolic effort to imbue their experiences as gay men with meaning; gayness also stood in for political ends, ranging between total equality with heterosexuality to something altogether different from heterosexuality. So "coming out of the closet" was not merely a choice of core identities, or a choice between a core or a thread identity; rather, coming out was a *meaning-making move*, one of the more significant social interactions that lent meaning and significance to the word "gay" and to its related practices and communities. To be clear, I mean not a rational choice here, but an experience-driven choice, an activity-undergoing in a particular environment that enabled a range of identification possibilities.[86]

On the other hand, for many men, the adoption of a gay identity or identifying with other gay men was anathema to their desires, so they refused the identification. Throughout the period, many gay men hoped that straight folks would simply take the time to understand that they simply desired other men.[87] So as we have seen, a common reaction to gay-as-identity was to say it was no identity at all—gays are just like straights and many forms of gay life needed to be done away with, stripping homosexuality down to its bare sexual desire. For those refusing identity, a common strategy downplayed the core-ness of a sexual identity as "only one facet of the whole person" (*VR* Dec. 1968, 34–35).[88] Those who refused a gay identity felt it as a proscription on their selves, a limit to who they could be or become. It is reasonable to assume there were still others, whose voices we do not directly here in the gay publications, reduced their sexual desires to the bare sex act and actively refused any and all identification, community interaction, and social contact with gay men at all outside of meeting their sexual needs. Traces of these men remain in the many men wrote of the frustrating experience of having sex with a man who afterwards denied any same-sex desire at all, let alone a gay identity[89]; and many gay men wrote of their resentment toward straight-identifying men who had sex with men, such as hustlers and their johns, or married men who had sex with men in public places. Another refusal of gay identity came from those who felt a true liberation would be a liberation from all sexual identity categories altogether.[90] This was a point of conflict in the community, as those who chose a gay identification saw this refusal of identity as leading to emotional problems for the individual, because they were denying their true selves, a kind of disingenuousness or even a lie.[91]

If identification as "gay" were to mean any thing and if the community were to support the full personhood of gay men, then those things that had defined a man's gayness had to be thought through and assigned significance. Meaning-making never happens in a vacuum, but rather in the soup of knowledge and social relationships and personal feelings and significantly in a complex environment. The experiences of oppression—from family to the state, from the psychiatrist's couch to the pulpit—propelled gay men toward something that could heal the pain and ruptures in their lives. The search for publicity and community served to reshape gay men's relationships to their social environments at multiple levels, which in turn allowed them to *rethink themselves*: literally, to produce new knowledge about gayness to bring their experiences of sexuality and their environment inline with each other.

Meanings of a Gay "Self"

A letter to the editor from a police vice officer whose assignment was to entrap homosexuals in bars appeared in Guy Strait's paper in 1963. The anonymous writer seemed to be having an identity crisis of his own. "But I cannot bring myself to arrest another man for wanting to be with his own kind," he wrote (*TN* June 24, 1963, 3). In a sort of coming out tale, the officer wrote of accepting an advance when off duty, and of the strong desire for a close (if not sexual) relationship with a man. "I am not and probably never will be what you would call a 'confirmed social variant,'" he insists. "What constitutes a variant anyhow?" For those who insisted that gayness meant more than gay sex, this really became the central question: what does it really mean to be gay? This question reaches back to the beginning of the period and for decades before that, and ties in to all the cultural arguments gay men had with each other about their counter-public, their community, gay male sexual practices, intimacy, and their identity. Is the gay man simply a citizen like every other American? Should he be "responsible" like any other good citizen, that is, should he conform to social and cultural expectations? Or is he fundamentally different from most citizens? Is he revolutionary? Liberal? White? Is he a member of a meaningful community outside the usual affiliations enjoyed by American males? All of these questions and more circulated around the men engaged in the complicated task of meaning-making.

As the process of gay self-identification evolved, the meaning of gayness came increasingly to be located in the "self." This gay self began in an embryonic phase in the early 1960s. First, in the early counter-public's publications we find the oft-repeated call for the sexual variants to recognize themselves as being *different* from the general population (the very definition of deviant, which was often employed at the time). Writers often connected the recognition of difference with a normative position in the value of knowing one's self and especially being conscious of one's desires, as they created a juxtaposition between those whose behavior was motivated consciously and those whose behavior was accompanied by denial. And second, that "variant" self had to be anchored in some kind of ethical framework based in respect for the self; in the early 1960s, this was often paired with urges to live ethically and follow social rules, tying back to respectability as a *means* to achieve the ends of the counter-public.[92] Gay men also seem to have understood that the process of self-respect would be part of an individual's personal journey.[93]

By mid-1960s, the moral guidelines of recognizing one's difference and then following ethical guidelines of respectability became increasingly dissatisfying for those who felt that "homosexuality has a positive functional purpose in the life of man" (*VR* Sept. 1971, 30–31). Out of this desire grew a more fully recognizable notion of a gay self, one that was fundamentally different from other kinds of selves. This was not the first time such an idea had existed; Edward Carpenter had entertained such notions in his theories of democracy at the turn of the twentieth century, and in California, Harry Hay, one of the originators of the Mattachine Society and later of the Radical Faeries, made much the same argument. But in this time and place, there were a series of small but significant differences, anchored in the fact that they were circulating in a full-blown gay publicity. First, they argued that the gay self must come from gay men and from no one else.[94] The gay self was, for these men, always, pro-

foundly, and strongly humanized; this was often done subtly through representations of gay men,[95] but could also be accomplished explicitly in the rhetoric they
employed to describe it. One young man described his experiences discovering
his gay self during college. "[B]ut I couldn't censor myself enough [at college].
My Gay self was showing through. And my Gay self was me," he wrote. "The
bodying forth of your being is the birth of your power, and your power is your
body emerging from the eclipse of its shadow, like a flower" (*GS* Aug.–Sept.
1970, 13). To be clear, there was always the counter-point circulating, too, that
homosexuality was only *one* part of a whole person,[96] but this seemed to be the
minority position by the 1970s, at least as it was represented in the gay press.

Concomitant with the gay self arose the idea of self-hatred, that men who
refused gay-as-identity were suffering from a form of self-denial or internalized
hatred. But self-hatred was deployed across the political spectrum and by various men for widely different reasons. Gay men who enjoyed older practices
such as leather and drag saw gay liberationists as being self-hating for refusing
the pleasures of gay sub-cultures. They saw gay liberation as a bunch of "homosexuals who themselves hold a low opinion of homosexuality. Some of us see
this as the problem underlying gay militancy: if you can't love yourself then
you'll get everyone else to dislike you through hostile behavior" (*VR* Jan. 1971,
4). A few gay libbers actually admitted to experiencing self-hatred, in moments
of clarity and almost in a confessional tone.[97] For their part, the gay "radicals"
also leveled their icy stares at older gay men and blasted them for their inability
to accept new and, for them, more authentic gay identities. Gay traditionalists, as
they called adherents of older gay cultural forms, "are unable to imagine that
gay is good. . . . They desperately want to be heterosexual, but they believe the
hand of cruel fate is set against them" (*GS* Jan. 1972, 3). Indeed, all around the
circles of gay men in the public sphere this became one of the most common
slams leveled at political opponents: *they* refuse a gay identity, which is their
true or authentic self, and are therefore inferior or bad gays.

As we saw in Chapters 2 and 3, gay "pride" was seen as a possible *means* to
achieving freedom of personhood. Whereas ideas of pride first appear in the
LCE publications, as the meaning of gay expanded and moved toward the process of self-identification, so did gay *pride* take on new meanings. If there was a
gay self, that gay self had to be rescued from the clutches of the dominant culture and raised to its rightful state of conceptual integration and psychic wholeness. Whatever their political means and ends or their relationship to gay liberation, with very few exceptions it seems that these activists and their publications
saw identity-building to be as important as community building, and by extension, the building of Gay Pride.[98]

The emergence of this self-acknowledging process and its central role in
gay publicity really started before 1961, as the self-acknowledgement became a
part of the strategies of earlier forms counter-publicity and indeed of the homosexual communities that came before. Nonetheless, it took on deep personal
significance for the gay men willing to "come out" in the 1960s.[99] In discussions
of their pride or esteem of themselves as homosexuals, they connected the per-

sonal, the experiential, and the political aspects of their gayness. In the early 1960s, they focused on the act of self-disclosure, of admitting to oneself and coming to an understanding of oneself as a homosexual, an act seen as difficult but liberating.[100] By the late 1960s, discussions had turned to efforts to make the act of revelation meaningful in itself by making same-sex desire itself intelligible in larger and more public ways.[101] Here, the gay self was *felt* and *experienced* and undeniable, an ever present difference and for some the source of their happiness.[102] At the same time, most writers were aware of how complicated self-awareness could be, given the realities of the social world gay men inhabited.[103] Choosing to live life true to your feelings, to *be* gay, meant "fac[ing] almost unbearable feelings of guilt as a result of his own sexual predestination" (*VR* April 1969, 13–14, 25). Many knew that the self-recognition process came at different times for different men in different circumstances.[104] For other gay men, this awareness of the gay self and self-recognition must expand and extend outward to be useful and good.[105]

Out of these early notions of self-acceptance arose full-fledged gay pride, a pride in the gay self that held a significance often lost in today's parades and rainbow flags. Recalling the feelings of guilt, shame, loneliness, sadness, and even suicidality—the detrimental affects of symbolic domination—one man wrote when he became aware of his desires, "initially, my reaction was a violent one of guilt, taught to me by an oppressive moral-social background. I was hurt and bleeding. I was being driven towards insanity toward a hatred of my society and my race" (*VR* Nov. 1970, 39, 43–44). But these gay men believed such negative feelings could be overcome by putting a *positive affect* in their place. "I am happy to have a letter from you when you say that you are not ashamed of what you are. Shame must be connected with something that is evil. Your situation is not evil so long as there is no intent to do harm or unkindness to others" (*TN* Aug. 19, 1963, 3–4). Throwing off shame was the first step to gaining self-respect[106] and self-love.[107] So pride was not an event, but an affective normative, an call to deny the power of the dominant symbolic order and of the official public and to replace the very structure of feeling with that of a gay self.

But pride was something that had to be achieved, the result of work, both through self-conscious meaning-making and through activities and experiences that contradicted the effects of being dominated.[108] Gay men had numerous strategies for achieving pride, that ranged from reading books, to participating in zaps.[109] Gay men found the negative affect resulting from symbolic domination, however, to be persistent and pervasive, and they never ceased to talk about it through the period. They fought against inferiority complexes,[110] guilt, worthlessness, fearing that gay men and women without pride, i.e., still dominated, would be dangerous to their movement.[111] It was not always easy to speak about the nature of guilt, however, as some men were ashamed of each other, not themselves. Thus, pride, whatever shape that might take, would require not just work, but vigilance to establish and maintain. Some gay men saw this is a concerted effort to reclaim and create a gay male history and cultural heritage, as we saw earlier.

This emphasis on self-acceptance coupled with a positive affect of pride increased as the decade progressed, and the means whereby the various organizations sought to instill pride became yet another source of conflict among gay men. Before long, self-acceptance was nearly always coupled with the idea of pride. Cecil Williams told gay men in a sermon in 1968, "It's time that Homosexuals begin to understand themselves more, begin to accept themselves more, and say to the world (including their parents): 'I'm a homosexual, and I'm proud of it'" (*VR* Nov. 1968, 5). Demonstrators began using the idea of pride in San Francisco at the 1969 protest at the *Examiner*'s office.[112] By 1969, pride was no longer simply the positive affect to counter guilt and shame and self-hatred, nor was pride merely a goal for the community. Pride was the key to gay freedom. When the Committee for Homosexual Freedom began, the group proposed a gay academic journal, in which "[W]e must develop the tools of pride to plant well the seeds of freedom—one day we will harvest our seeds and feed ourselves meal of plenty. On that day we will be truly free" (*CHFN*, Oct. 16, 1969). For their part, some gay liberation activists saw their movements as the true source of gay pride, of a lasting and meaningful self-acceptance.[113] And this, as we have seen, led to the projects of personhood freedom: living openly. "'How can I be myself and love myself unless I'm willing to be open? I want everyone to know who I am. I'm learning to love myself'" (*SFFP* Oct. 16, 1969, 8).

Not surprisingly, just as they had compared themselves to the African American civil rights movement in creating their counter-publicity, so too did they see in the notion of Black Power and Black Pride a model for how Gay Pride should be structured socially and how it should feel.[114] In identifying with blackness, as we have already seen, they constantly and unintentional reaffirmed of the *whiteness* of this form of gay identity, inasmuch as they identified with blackness but their own racially diverse fellows remained virtually invisible. By the late 1960s, the comparisons with African American experience were expanding. Charles Thorp described on several different occasions in both *Vector* and *San Francisco Gay Free Press* his experience of growing up gay and how early on he identified with black culture, even calling himself a "white Negro."[115] Thorp's message for gay men was to see that black folks had come to a true sense of pride in themselves and their heritage and people; and so could gay men.

Out of this greatly expanded and black-inflected notion of gay pride came the now cliché slogan, "Gay Is Good." As trite and somewhat meaningless as it may appear to contemporary, jaded eyes, these words carried powerful impact in their context, for they were a direct refusal of their opposite, the dominant cultural meaning assigned to homosexuality, that gay is bad. Rev. Williams, again, gave the slogan a leg up in a speech. "If black is beautiful, then gay is good," he said.[116] The idea had stunning power in the lives of many men, allowing them to make the public declaration of their sexuality and to claim their gay selves in social interaction. "Really believing that GAY IS GOOD!, I faced my family and closest straight friends honestly, as a homosexual" (*VR* Jan. 1969, 13). It's power as language, it was hoped, would extend to an "affirmation that one's life can be worthwhile in spite of the struggle he must face in this restricted culture at this time in history" (*VR* Sept. 1969, 20–21, 30). When a SIR official proposed what should be the primary goals of homosexuals in society in 1970, one of these was to "remove the mask" off of gay life, for there is nothing bad about it. We are, he argued, "normal healthy, worthy, beautiful people who have our ups and downs our gay moments and our sad moments. I am convinced that it is only as enough of us do that, that we will change our sick gay image into our real image as beautiful people" (*VR* July 1970, 39).[117] The image of a Good, Beautiful, Proud gayness arose out of the hopes and desires of a generation of men who wanted a gaynnes that would infuse their lives and give them meaning, even "the total personality of the individual and the total fabric of the social order" (*GS* Nov. 1970, 16).

Open Gayness vs. Closeted Gayness

We have already seen how gender was used as a primary means to maintain the closet door for various and contradictory reasons both within and without the community. But activists were examining the whole notion of the closet critically, asking themselves, if there is a gay self and if a big part of liberation comes from throwing off the negative affect of oppression and claiming pride in oneself and one's gay brothers and sisters, then what do we do with the closet? A metaphor circulating among gay men at least since the 1920s,[118] the closet took on special significance in the 1960s as their political and social imperatives switched from a keeping a secret code of identification of others "in the life" to staking a claim in the public sphere and openly expressing one's sexuality and, by extension, one's identity, what I have called in this book *gay publicity*. We have already seen that the closet had been from the beginning of the period a sore spot for gay men participating in the counter-public, such that closeted men were shunned or shamed in community building and definitely excluded from the definition of a "good gay." It is clear that "open" and "out" was the privileged form of gayness by the late 1960s and that closeted men were viewed as "self-hating." Yet many men rejected the notion that you had to come out or declare openly in any way your sexuality to have a healthy gay identity.[119] And so gay men had to work out whether or not *gay* could or should ever also mean *closeted* (or, as I discussed earlier, passing).

The dominant view among gay men, at least among those participating in the community and the counter-public, was that coming out was the key to freedom and fighting back against domination.[120] Coming out became, at least for the men writing in the gay periodicals, participating in some minimal way in the counter-publicity, the door to love, to feeling freely and authentically, to the ability to live in beauty, to what I have summarized as *freedom of personhood*. The problem, of course, was that gay men lived in a real world and in a complex social environment that required discretion and sometimes outright secrecy for safety and often for the protection of their very lives. They had to constantly combat the symbolic domination of the official public, mass culture, religion, etc., such that many men were at least selectively closeted.[121] For some of the gay libbers, closeted men did not, maybe even could not, understand their own oppression, living under a sort of false consciousness.[122] And as we've seen several times already, the feared that the closeted among them were dangerous to the success of the movement and the authenticity of their gay brothers.[123] They also believed that violent homophobes were often latent (that is, un-self-aware) homosexuals.[124]

There flowed nonetheless an undercurrent of tolerance for the closeted, as all gay men had to be selectively closeted to negotiate the world they lived in. And this often gave way to understanding and compassion for their closeted brothers. One *SFGFP* article compared closet queens to babies, arguing that they cannot come out until "those who are strongest make the way safer for those who are too sensitive" (*SFGFP* Nov. 1970, 4–5, 12). Gay men seemed especially sensitive to the closet-effects on youth and young men.[125] Some men, however, simply had an aversion to adopting a gay identity; indeed, as we have seen, not only did some gay men actively eschew a gay identity, but they consciously chose to remain in the closet, much to the chagrin of activists across the political spectrum. Again, the realities of men's lives were that many had to consciously choose not to be known. For some, such as military personnel, passing was a necessity for their own safety.[126] In many ways, the arguments about coming out were abstract, because given the social environment in which they lived, all gay men knew that coming out would carry with it consequences, sometimes severe. On the mild side, the discomfort of neighbors "is one of the penalties that the nonconformist must be prepared to bear" (*TN* Aug. 19, 1963, 3–4). For men with wives and girlfriends, coming out as gay would mean ending those relationships. Others knew that it meant a loss of family.[127] Some feared institutionalization in psychiatric or penal facilities (rightly so).[128] So coming out was vitally important, but knowing the complexity of coming out, many gay men were willing to leave the decision to personal discretion and comfort. Until the early 1970s, outing someone else was strictly taboo in the community.

The closet and passing as straight, then, were means to many different kinds of ends during the period, from keeping one's job to staying alive to managing the discomfort of being "out." Perhaps a closeted man simply wanted anonymous sex and nothing more; but more common were the risks, what was at stake if he were found out.[129] If being gay meant being out, the difficulty across the board was the practical side: when and where do you come out without ostracizing yourself or exposing yourself to danger? And so across the spectrum, gay men strategized on when, where, and how to come out, cautioning each other to pay attention to circumstances when it would be ill advised, such as to co-workers.[130] Yet the question remained, when do you come out? Answers ranged from when straight people are causing problems for you with their ignorance, to maintaining your own sanity.[131]

Many "out" gay men, as they had come to be called by the early 1970s, took aim at the closet and fired with everything they had. To them, closeted men were as much an enemy as the straight world. When a SIR member was beaten to death at Land's End in 1967, "Of the many gay persons in the area that day who saw the beating and murder of Stoltz, not one came forward to testify" (*VR* June 1967, 17). This was seen as an acquiescence to violence, and activist SIR members accused the closeted men who refused to help Stoltz while he was being beaten and later refused to testify as considering violence "part of the game of being gay and it is the victim's fault if it happens" (*VR* June 1967, 17). Being closeted also meant that there was always a social distance, a disconnect that could never be bridged.[132] Being closeted could mean being relegated to certain areas of the city and only certain kinds of social interaction with other gay men. Closeted men were seen as guilt-ridden and having low self-esteem.[133] There were portrayed as having higher drug and alcohol addictions, higher suicide rates, and less of an ability to reconcile their personal lives with the rest of life. If liberation meant adopting a gay identity, embracing the gay self, and having gay pride, then the whole process hung on the ability of the individual to come out, confront his domination, and join the counter-public. For gay libbers, if you refused to come out, you consciously bypassed your own liberation.[134] And as we saw in Chapter 5, the worst of all the closet queens was the hustler, who uses gay men for his own financial gain and personal gratification.[135]

By the 1970s, coming out was itself the fundamental act of liberation. But coming out was complicated for the libbers, as the negative affect of growing up gay in American is not so easily overcome. "The trouble is, however, the guilt, fear, self-hatred too often remain even though the gay may have 'come out' from repressing his feelings to expressing them" (*GS* Nov. 1970, 16). Not only did coming out not necessarily cure the negative affect of oppression, but it also didn't keep gay men from falling into what many gay libbers saw as "bad" practices of going to bars, cruising for sex, or worst participating in drag or leather sub-cultures. Thus, for gay libbers, to be truly free meant to come out *and* reject the sexual practices discussed earlier, which were "oppressive" in another world where "Gay is Good."

Openness overlapped with notions of being "blatant" in one's gender and sexual expression in public.[136] Many men were defiant in their rhetoric about living openly, refusing the morality and mores of the dominant society.[137] And they spoke in glowing terms of the personal benefits of coming out, which ranged from curing physical ills such as insomnia, to the emotional benefits of peace of mind and psychological wholeness. They described it as stepping into the Light for the first time in their lives and as the feeling of having a burden lifted. And often as the feeling of being fully human for the first time.[138] By the time of the first Gay Pride Parade in San Francisco, *outness* had become a measure of the quality of one's *gayness* among most activist gay men across the political spectrum, even taking into account the often necessary practice of passing. The purpose wasn't merely to expose one's own sexuality publicly—"I am not advocating that you must reveal your homosexuality to everyone just for the sake of letting people know that YOU are homosexual" (*VR* Dec. 1969, 10)—but for the good of the cause. Through the combination of gay men's efforts to form a counter-publicity, to build a community, and to imbue their experiences and practices with meaning, gayness expanded to an identification process, complete with a *gay self, gay pride*, and a social practice of *coming out*. Inversely, a gay man's outness came to stand for the degree to which his gayness was fully developed and to his general trustworthiness within the counter-public and community. It must be noted, however, that it was never clear what exactly constituted "coming out" and whether or not anyone was ever actually done "coming out." Coming out before 1972 seemed to have little if any effect on the social environment that oppressed gay men, so the worth or meaning of coming out was never clear.

In the context of their multi-level struggle against the official public sphere and symbolic domination and in their work with each other for counter-publicity, community, and meaning, gay men created a kind of gay male identity, but one which could be picked up and put down situationally and strategically. The various categories they adopted, from "social variant" to homophile, from homosexual to gay, reflected the situated needs of the men who filled those categories with meaning in various times and places, and to various ends. The words or categories themselves are less important than the ongoing efforts to make them meaningful and how those categories and labels made experiences intelligible and provided for gay men the ability at an individual and communal level to create meaningful responses to the problems they faced because of their sexual desires, sex acts, relationships, practices, and social interactions. To meet the ends of integration and respectability, early formulations of homophile and Strait's notion of "variant" worked well as strategic self-conceptions; but for community building, the category had to be expanded beyond "sexual proclivity"; and for outright transformation of self and society, "gay" had to take on the most profound psychological significance. That all of these meanings (if not their category labels) survived the period and that all of those ends still circulate as possibilities among gay men in the twenty-first century demonstrate their usefulness (or at least their good-enough-ness) in dealing with same-sex attraction in a heteronormative culture. But regardless of what their individual positions were on a given issue, gay men were deeply concerned with the mode of conceiving of their "selves," demonstrating the "coreness" of their gayness to their lived *active-undergoing*, their experience of American, Californian, and San Franciscan society in the 1960s.

Gay identity itself became a multi-layered means, directly confronting pathologizing, regulating discourses of religion, medicine, and the media by giving gay men the tools to conceive of themselves as something more than mentally ill or criminal. Gay activists hoped that gay identity, as it came to be constituted by 1972, would instill in men a sense of pride, enabling a self-acceptance, a peace of mind, and happiness. It is key, however, that none of these identity categories was stable at any time. All of them in their contexts were hotly contested from within and without organizations, from across the spectrum of gay men in San Francisco and beyond. The diversity of meanings ascribed to such things as gay sex, coming out, and gender reveal not a disunity or a failure of consensus building, but rather the inherent diversity of gay men at the level of experience. These were all value judgments arising from gay men's gut-level assessments of their environments and their experienced problems within those environments. In other words, the positions men took on such issues as coming out or gender expression arose directly from the way they underwent the relationship to their own feelings, their various communities, and the American public sphere. Gay was as gay did; or more aptly put, gay was as gay experienced.

Notes

1. See David Halperin, "Forgetting Foucault," in *How to do the History of Homosexuality* (Chicago: University of Chicago Press, 2002).

2. See *TN* May 17, 1963, 1.

3. See *TN* Aug. 19, 1963, 3–4. Strait argued for job non-discrimination on the basis that "Homosexuality, in the main, is a way of life, either by choice or by inclination, and it has no bearing whatsoever on ability." *CN* May 25, 1964, 8–9; here, he changed culinary analogies: it is much more like eating turnips than escargot.

4. Thomas M. Edwards even argued that some men choose homosexuality in order to avoid their civic and social responsibilities. See Oct. 1967, 18–19.

5. See *VR* April 1968, 20–21.

6. Most notably in Alfred Kinsey's highly influential *Sexual Behavior in the Human Male* (Philadelphia: W.B. Saunders, 1948). "I have met considerable number of persons who were formerly homosexual. . . . [H]omosexuality is not a permanent state with every person who happens at any particular time to be homosexual." *VR* Jan. 1969, 16–17.

7. They often found help from "experts." See for example *VR* Feb. 1972, 11: "'Homosexuality is not a disease. . . It is a way of life,' says Gina Allen and Clement Martin in their recent book, *Intimacy*. . . . And it is evident to me that homosexual relationships are as valid, beautiful, joyful and natural as heterosexual ones, and at times just as painful and frustrating as well. What do [experts who are pro homosexual] have in common? The answer is our Humanist religion."

8. "The current 'up front' attitude among some homosexuals is that homosexuality is their preference. This is a social attitude adopted to express the right of every man to freedom of choice, but it still doesn't explain the choice." *VR* June 1972.

9. Not surprisingly, many gay men rested their arguments for heredity on Havelock Ellis. "To begin with, it must be realized that a determining hereditary factor operates in the development of homosexuality. Havelock Ellis preferred to say that there is a 'predisposition,' and used the parallel between homosexuality and color-blindness." *VR* March–April 1968, 20–21.

10. See for example *TT* Jan. 1965, 1–2, 4. Another man quoted Ralph Waldo Emerson to connect instinct to happiness in life: "If the single man plant himself indomitably

on his instincts, and there abide, the huge world will come round to him.'" See *TN* Aug. 19, 1963, 3–4.

11. "True homosexuals today, enduring the ceaseless ignorant drivel of psychiatry and knowing that none of such exorcisms in any way even begin to touch the core of that singing glory they carry within themselves, must now at last recognize that overpowering call within—as just such an instinct." *VG* 2.1.

12. In the late 1950s, Hooker found that the majority of the Los Angeles gay men she interviewed believed they were "born that way"; more important, her study revealed that gay men had the same emotional stability as their straight counterparts, revealing no difference whatsoever in their rates of emotional disturbance or mental illness. Her published works on the topic are numerous.

13. Tom Mauer wrote in response to a young man that had written to Ann Landers, "Whatever you do, Woody, let your sexual orientation come out of you! It's there; you can't change it nor can any therapist. What you can do is discover what it is. But if you choose a sexual life style that violates your sexual orientation, you'll make a tragedy of your life and undoubtedly one or two other lives as well." *VR* April 1971, 20–21.

14. Wrote one man, "For as long as I can remember, I knew I was somehow different" *VR* Aug. 1971, 36–37. Boris Korinsky, writing about his discharge from the military, quipped, "I can't remember ever not being a homosexual." *VR* Sept. 1971, 10–11. And "Jackie" described his childhood in Texas where his parents accepted early on that he was different. "Perhaps my childhood wasn't an exciting one, certainly there were no great emotional problems, but from the moment my body first became aware of sex, I have been solely oriented towards men. I don't blame this on anyone, for to me there is no blame, because homosexuality is natural to me. And I am glad." *VR* Nov. 1967, 12–13.

15. "Men who are genetically homosexual but who have been socially conditioned to view homosexuality negatively will have a high degree of anxiety," *VR* Jan. 1972, 14.

16. See review of Norman C. Murphy, Anxiety, Homosexual Attitude, Duration of Time since Initial Explicitly Sexual Response, and Number of Explicitly Sexual Responses in VR Jan. 1972, 14: "What does Murphy believe to be the significance of his studies and findings. He stops just short of genetic manipulation and makes his recommendations toward compensation: if you are a homosexual 'carrier,' adoption of a heterosexual child; social education toward a more positive attitude concerning homosexuality; special tranquilizers for homosexuals; finding the best social environment for homosexuals; new forms of behavioral conditions (he calls this 'manipulation of nervous tissue')." See VR Jan. 1972, 14. An earlier Vector had warned readers against genetic explanations of homosexuality: "What must be of great concern is that the secrets of the bio-chemical nature of conditioning of man is on the verge of being discovered. In the hands of our present misguided societal leadership, me could find such potent knowledge misused, wherein the very worth of natural man is destroyed." VR Jan. 1969, 16–17.

17. For some, the argument for naturalness made obvious sense in terms of the anti-sodomy laws throughout the United States. See for example, VR June 1972, 34–35: ". . . unequal justice from state to state. . . . For example, in Idaho you may receive ten years in jail for a single act of anal copulation while in Illinois there is no penalty for the same act. Words such as 'unnatural acts' and 'crimes against nature' are frequently used in legislation which permits a judge or jury o determine what is sexually 'unnatural' or 'against nature.'"

18. Lou Harrison argued that gay men will always exist because their existence is natural; nature reproduces gay men even though they can't reproduce themselves. "Our

ranks are continually and regularly replenished from nature." *VR* Oct. 1967, 18–19. Another man noted simply that homosexuality was common throughout the animal kingdom, making the very idea of "abnormality" absurd. See *VR* Feb.–March 1967, 11.

19. You, Homosexual, are you perverse? Is it unnatural for you to view the brawny
lad with a delightful eye? Are you going against YOUR NATURE when you express
yourself sexually? . . . My hunger for food, my thirst for water, my desire for homo sex is
MY NATURE. Laws do not quiet my appetite. Prison will not quench my thirst, reinte-
gration will not appease my sexual nature. I be that which I be. Please burn all the
witches, dismember all the heretics, destroy all non-Aryans, build barbed wire fences
around all the cities, then, my country confiscate my innards. But only then. *VR* Oct.
1967, 23.

20. "We knew, without being knowledgeable, that it was not 'ordinary' to feel such
deep desire and passion for 'one of our own kind.' . . . those with a deep rooted homosexual predilection eventually recognize that the practices in the barn-bush-basement
[with friends] meant more to them than they did to their playmates." *VR* Oct. 1968, 6.

21. "The American fantasy of growing up straight with no question of an alternative
way of life is not realistically concerned with the way persons are naturally born or
made." *VR* Nov. 1968, 5. Thus, "We declare that love between those of the same sex,
however incomprehensible, absurd, or even abhorrent it is to the feelings of 'normal'
people, is neither a vice nor a disease, it is not a mockery of nature, but a manifestation of
nature; it is an erotic variation that has been observed among all peoples on earth since
the dawn of human thought." *VG* 1.7, 2, 5, original in all caps.

22. See letter from Martha Shelley, *GS* Aug.–Sept. 1970, 12.

23. "...a plausible assumption was that with no cultural pressure in either direction,
fifty percent of children would grow up to be mainly heterosexual and fifty percent homosexual. Or there is the possibility that adult sexual preferences might conform to the
normal curve distribution." *VR* March 1969, 16–17. "And what is natural, the
straight/queer world had better begin to realize is not some immutable, cosmic law laid
down by God or some such. What is natural is what springs from the inner source of each
person's being." *GS* Oct.–Nov. 1971, 7.

24. "[P]sychological social and cultural factors outweigh constitutional and glandu-
lar factors in producing sexual orientations." *VR* March 1969, 16–17.

25. "Our homosexuality is a crucial part of our identity, not because of anything intrinsic, but because social oppression has made it so." *VR* Jan. 1972, 32.

26. "But this [genetic explanation of homosexuality] is at best superficial because
the reality of being goes to the core of a personality and this has ultimately nothing to do
with genetics." *VR* Jan. 1969, 7, 22.

27. See also *VR* Nov. 1965, 6: "Benson contends that man can be either homosexual,
heterosexual or bisexual; the choice is his. To assert that exclusive homosexuality is a
perversion, while exclusive heterosexuality is 'normal' is to recognize the norm of sexuality a being a created, value-laden concept. Created by heterosexuals to force others to
recognize their false values."

28. Carl Whitman would eventually argue that "Nature leaves undefined the object
of sexual desire. The gender of that object has been imposed socially." *SFFP* Dec. 22–
Jan. 7, 1970, 3–5. For some, this meant that sexual object choice was indeed mutable,
whereas for others, the social explanation did not necessarily mean that homosexuality
was mutable. "The individual whose identity is psycho-dynamically involved in homosexuality will remain so oriented." *VR* Sept. 1971, 30–31.

29. "We are born blind and unimagined. We are only just beginning to create a culture and an identity. . . . But homosexuals have always been born separate and isolated from their brothers, each feeling like the only Martian on earth, a stranger in his own family." *AA* July 20, 1970.

30. See *AA* Feb. 1971.

31. "How can we exist but by coming from our exile in space, rather than trying to make whole new truth out of old lies, figs out of thistles?" *GS* Aug.–Sept. 1970, 13.

32. "The time has come, however, to start creating new life-styles—a gay community, in which the repressive strains of the straight society are absent." *GS* Nov. 1970, 17.

33. See *TE* 1.2, 11.

34. "We must get outside the system of mechanized insanity and we must manifest our own world!" *IA* 1.1, 1.

35. "'If people enjoy the sterile, closety life, they should stay there, but I don't think they really enjoy it,' [said Gale Whittington]. By building counter-culture we can show the closet queens something better than the [gay] establishment." *SFFP* Jan. 1970.

36. See *AA* Feb. 1971.

37. "I want to be part of a movement that will not alienate the average gay person. One gay brother who has had passing contact with gay liberation said to me recently, 'They want to take away everything we have, but they offer nothing in return.'" *GS* June–July 1971, 2, 5.

38. See *IA* 1.1, 4–5.

39. For example, James H. Ramp, in his review of Christopher Isherwood's *A Single Man*, worried that readers would think his characters were "representative of us all" *VR* March 1966, 6.

40. One gay author argued that straight publishers simply don't get what being gay in America means and they certainly don't understand gay sex; they fake it and end up facilely perpetuating old stereotypes in their editorial choices. What was needed was a strictly gay literary tradition, "a genre written by gay authors for a strictly gay audience, no holds barred, telling it like it is or should be, and *put out by a gay publisher.*" *VR* June 1970, 26, 29, 32–33. See also *VR* July 1970, 10–11.

41. See also *SFFP* Dec. 7, 1969, 7.

42. See *CN*, April 6, 1964, 7.

43. See *SFFP* Dec. 7, 1969, 7.

44. "The professor stated that the Gay literary style, with its distinguishing characteristic of the free intermixture of ideas, emotion, and facts, can be traced from Homer and Sappho throughout history to the contemporary works of Allen Ginsburg, James Baldwin, and Tennessee Williams. With this proud heritage it is nothing less than shocking to read in the autobiography of a famous contemporary black Gay novelist, 'I was corrupted by a white man in a subway toilet when I was eleven years old. That's why I am the way I am.' The decadent heterosexual society did a good job of keeping him in the closet of shame. With his 3000 year literary heritage he is proud to be Black but ashamed to be Gay, even though is writing style is 99% Gay. This writer needs to be liberated and turn his shame to pride." *SFFP* Dec. 7, 1969, 7.

45. "We have in our . . . homosexual American heritage beautiful concepts of God and creation such as Walt Whitman's 'Out of the Cradle endlessly Rocking' and 'Crossing Brooklyn Ferry.' Why must we be saddled and subjected with the Judaic-Christian bigotries?" *VR* July 1967, 13.

46. See *SFFP* Oct. 16, 1969, 4. "Gay Liberation Theatre . . . is still confronted not only with turning on the straights but with creating an awareness of our oppression in the

minds of our own gay community and with effecting a solution to our position in the rest of the hip community." *SFFP* Oct. 16, 1969, 8.

47. "We see, however, that the preference of Gays in the main for the 'top ten' so to speak is clearly different from the 'top ten' most often heard in certain heterosexual discotheques." *BAR* Jan. 15, 1972.

48. Mike Silverstein argued, "This society denies us our gay heroes. . . . If these homosexuals are too important to be excluded, their homosexuality is either ignored or heatedly denied. . . . This is the case with such people as Edmund Carpenter, Friedrich Caspar Ulrichs, and the subject of this article, Roger Casement." *GS* Aug.–Sept. 1970, 16.

49. "Isn't it true we've had most of our known history in the arts and also most of our acceptance is the arts. In fact, isn't it more honest to say Gay is Creativity rather than Gay is Good. Gay is a life-style. It is how we live. It is our oppression. It is our Tiffany Lamps and our guns. Gay is our history and the history we are just beginning to become" *SFGFP* Nov. 1970, 4–5, 12.

50. See *CN* March 9, 1964, 1; June 22, 1964, 5.

51. Review of Noel I. Garde's *Jonathon to Gide: The Homosexual in History.*

52. See *TE* 1.2, 11.

53. See *CN* 4.8, 4.

54. "Roger Casement made love to the men of the Congo and Peru [sic] and because he was a good man; his affection for individual Africans and Indians led to a sympathy for their enslavement. It was his sexuality that led him to encounter 'natives' as sex partners and people, and his compassion required that he then attempt to end their oppression. His homosexuality was not irrelevant to his accomplishments, it occasioned [them]." *GS* Aug.–Sept. 1970, 16.

55. "The morbid days of 'The Boys in the Band' are gone, said the president [of SIR]. It is time we get away from the over-emphasis on everything being 'gay,' and calling one another 'queens'; that we begin to associate more with non-homosexuals." *VR* July 1970, 31.

56. While this desire to belong could be dismissed as false-consciousness (and often was by contemporaries), it was a rather wide-spread feeling gay men expressed throughout this period, pointing perhaps to more complex dynamics of the relationship between selfhood, identity, and the dominant culture.

57. "Yet I suffer from no low self-esteem, I do not attack my brother homosexuals in word or deed, and I make every effort to support legitimate homosexual causes. . . . I admire those who do meet the homosexual-identity problem head-on; I am sure they are rewarded by an inner peace and social freedom unknown to those of us who do not or cannot make the ultimate admission." *VR* March 1971, 31.

58. In his response to an article by a Mr. Bowers in *The Saturday Review*, he wrote of SIR and *Vector*, "The gay world described by Mr. Bowers with its affected customs and manners, its ghetto institutions, its stuntmen such as the student body president in high heels or the gay evangelist in collar and clerical 'drag,' its Merle Miller . . . types who flutter 'out of their closets' now that it is safe, like debutants making their formal entrances into the 'Gay' society, its die-hard gay awareness classes, its revival-like observances of Gay Pride Week and Christopher Street Parade, the public spectacle of its gay wedding ceremonies—this colorful gay world is delightful. . . . No wonder . . . the popular press have baited. But why should *Vector*?" *VR* April 1972, 6.

59. "People [of CHF], you're beautiful. . . . But from the gay community—nothing. It was almost as hard to relate to their musical comedy atmosphere as to the straight world." *CHFN* Apr. 22, 1969.

60. In this vein, also sometimes "nonconformist." See for example, *TN* Aug. 19, 1963, 3–4.

61. "A frank appraisal of the social variant is in order. . . . [T]he variant is uninformed and is ready to blame almost everyone but himself for his plight" *TN* Sept. 16, 1963, 1–2.

62. See for example letter from W.E.B., *TN* Oct. 14, 1963, 7.

63. And too much power has been granted it by interpreters of Michel Foucault's, *History of Sexuality*.

64. See for example *VR* Sept. 1970, 26;

65. "True homosexuality is a complex condition that must be differentiated from episodic behavior entered into for a variety of conscious motivations." *VR* Sept. 1970, 26. Interestingly, this kind of distinction was emerging simultaneously in academic circles among sociologists studying deviance. Edwin Lemert specifically distinguished between "rule breaking" and deviance proper, which includes a stable identity formed around deviant behavior. See also *VR* Jan. 1972, 14.

66. See for example *TT* Jan. 1966, 1, 5: "But more disastrous is it to be accused of homosexual conduct or orientation once sworn in and on active duty."

67. *VR* Jan. 1971, 30–31.

68. For example, one book review noted, "'Homosexuality is not a disease. . . . It is a way of life,' says Gina Allen and Clement Martin in their recent book, *Intimacy*. . . . And it is evident to me that homosexual relationships are as valid, beautiful, joyful and natural as heterosexual ones, and at times just as painful and frustrating as well." *VR* Feb. 1972, 11.

69. For example, argued one man, "We do not feel that homosexuality is a noble way of life. Nor do we find it an ignoble way of life. We do not find homosexuality a desirable way of life, nor do we find it an undesirable way of life. It is merely another way of life. . . . For those who have chosen or who find themselves in that way of life, we find it as rewarding as any other way of life" *CN* May 25, 1964, 8–9.

70. "I believe homosexuality needs no defense per se," wrote one man. *VR* Nov. 1965, 6. "Homosexuality is not a condition—it is a sex act like any other socially nonconforming sex act—and it is performed by an infinite variety of persons under an infinite variety of circumstances; homosexual persons are not a class; their minority status stems solely form society's label, and the willingness of homosexual lifestyle cultists to continue to act the part."

71. "You don't have to be homosexual to love another man. . . . It's an expression of brotherly love, not necessarily sexual, unless and although it can be that too, depending on how you express your love or come across. . . . Homosexuality is the capability of two members of the same sex loving each other in a way which is determined consensual and mutual in feeling by both persons; and therefore expressed by love in sex that assures a metaphysical well-being for both in their principles and practice." *SFGFP* Dec. 1970, 5.

72. "We don't even need you any more. We'll define ourselves, thank you. And we won't do it just in terms of sexuality, either. We are not homosexual, we are gay. No, I mean Gay. And it isn't homosexuality that we're talking about, it's gayness. . . . We know who you are now, and we won't trust you or submit to your subtleties again." *AA* Oct. 28, 1970, 7–8. And *The Effeminist* echoed, "We Gay people reserve the right to create our own lives. We are learning to struggle and to build. . . . They know they can regu-

late homosexuality; they thought it up, they can polish it any way they want to. But they can't get a hold on the Gay people anymore, no. We're fighting back." *TE* 1.2, 11. One gay man described his personal journey as the journey from homosexual to gay. "I think I have changed from being homosexual to being gay. When I was homosexual, I felt my need to relate to men could be fulfilled only in the secrecy of a gay bar or cruising in the dark of the night. . . . So when in straight circles—which was most of the time—I felt inadequate." *GS* Aug.–Sept. 1970, 14.

73. See George Chauncey, *Gay New York: Gender, Urban Culture, and the Making of the Gay Male World, 1890–1940* (New York: Basic Books, 1994), 14–21.

74. By 1972, *Vector* could claim that "The homosexual movement has been the center of the change in our attitudes toward sex for the last twenty years. . . . From shrinking, closeted creatures who shunned the light and open air they have emerged to play the role of proud militants." *VR* April 1972, 6.

75. For example, Carl Whitman had something to say about this. For him, "We have to realize that our loving each other is a good thing. . . . It is not a makeshift in the absence of the opposite sex; it is not hatred for the opposite sex; it is not genetic; it is not the result of broken homes. . . . HOMOSEXUALITY IS THE CAPACITY TO LOVE SOMEONE OF THE SAME SEX." *SFFP* Dec. 22–Jan. 7, 1970, 3–5.

76. See also *GS* Oct. 1970, 4.

77. For example, "They [gay liberation] also assisted many young homosexuals in discovering their identity." *SFFP* Nov.1, 1969, 7.

78. See *AA* Feb. 1971.

79. "[Gay] Beauty isn't respectable; the straight world doesn't dig it, because it doesn't fit into a world of concrete playgrounds and computerized cafeterias. . . . And I push homosexual beauty. That's where my head is at. I'd like to talk to the people at the Symposium, all those beautiful, concerned mixed-up people, and tell them they don't have to apologize any more. Gay is good, baby!" *SFFP* Nov. 1, 1969, 11.

80. "Gays have different values than straights. . . . He [Gale Whittington, founder of CHF] meant the sociological definition of value, which Random House defines as 'the ideas, customs, institutions, etc., of a people.' At a taped interview for KTLA, Gale made it clear that the family is a straight institution not part of the value system of Gay people. He noted that the unwarranted and outmoded idolization of the family and romantic love by the mass media and government and churches has been used as an instrument of cultural suppression of the Gay people." *SFFP* Dec. 7, 1969, 7.

81. "I was aware that I was doing it because I was Gay. I liked my students too much to give up the possibility of relating to them as people. The only alternative were to relate to them as full humans—potential lovers, by giving up authority or by engaging in the sublimated sado-masochistic teacher-student relationship that is so common in the college." *GS* March 1971, 3.

82. "I started having sex with guys and enjoying it instead of feeling what I had just done was wrong. I discovered anger within myself and started to express it. . . . I discovered the joy of doing things with gay guys other than going to bed . . . feeling in my life that wasn't completely associated with an intellectual trip or with my expectations, but which came from the sensuality of my body and from the new way of relating. And so I became gay." *GS* Aug.–Sept. 1970, 14. "Why not a Gay Way," asked an *I Am* writer. "A fulfilling, 'whole' life for homosexuals. . . . I speak about Gay Self-determination: Coming out of the closet, not just physically (or sexually); but physically, psychologically, and emotionally: Coming all the way out of the closet." *IA* 1.1, 4–5.

83. Steven Seidman, *Beyond the Closet: The Transofrmation of Gay and Lesbian Life* (New York: Routledge, 2002), 10, emphasis added.

84. Receptive partner in anal sex.

85. This seems to align with the sociological notion of the *hidden ethnicity*, where one's identities are only salient in contexts where they are challenged or minoritized.

86. "We must all begin to see what Gay means and what Straight means. And this can be begun if we Gays begin to admit to ourselves, to another person, and finally to the World that we are what we are. There is something really god-like in that admission. The world may well be waiting for the Word." *SFFP* Jan. 1970, 2.

87. "They would find that we share the same frustrations, the same empty lives, the same sense of guilt, sinfulness and meaninglessness foisted on us all by our hypocritical society." *VR* Jan. 1965, 5.

88. See also letter from Robert H., *VR* June 1969, 24.

89. See *VR* June 1969, 10.

90. James L. Stoll declared, "[W]e are *sexual*, not homosexual or heterosexual . . . and no form of sexual expression is better or worse than any other (as long as it is consensual, honest, and humane)." *VR* Oct. 1971, 9, emphasis mine.

91. "Homosexuals who do not accept themselves as being gay, men who like other men but keep these feelings secret, these persons may find themselves in trouble with their own guilt feelings." *VR* Jan. 1969, 16–17. "For the homosexuals [in older movements] themselves did not really believe they were the same as Middle America. . . . One senses a tension between the desire to conform and a strong camp 'Boys-in-the-Band' mannerism that is beneath those protestations of respectability." *VR* Oct. 1970, 38.

92. Jack Parrish again, "However, the more we assert ourselves and stand up for our rights with quiet dignity and self-respect, the more likely we will begin to respect ourselves. And, as our image of ourselves [improves], so will the heterosexual community's [image of us]." *VR* July 1966, 4.

93. "[T]he complexity of it [coming out/self-awareness] varies a great deal and each of our readers could tell his/her own story about their adjustment to homosexuality." *VR* Aug. 1971, 36–37.

94. "I am convinced that a homosexual alone is capable of relating what it IS to be a homosexual. No psychoanalyst can relate it, nor any priest, nor any sociologist, nor any heterosexual." *VR* March–April 1968, 15.

95. One *Vector* cover portrayed a naked youth curled in fetal position against a cracked cement wall. Wrote the editor, "*Vector* views this photograph by Walter Render as an artistic interpretation of the homosexual's loneness. The figure has been forced into 'a corner' but is bent in thoughtfulness, rather than submission." *VR* Sept. 1969, cover and masthead.

96. "In truth, homosexuality is but an aspect of a person's being. Surely, too, it is an irresistible and integral part of a person's being. Were it otherwise, the enormous pressure of culture against its expression would prevent that expression." *VR* Aug. 1968, 7. See also letter from Walther Sherman, *VR* Dec. 1970, 6: "What Charles McCabe misses (November *Vector*) is that life (gay or straight) is what you make of it. Just being homosexual doesn't spell out your doom. . . . Sexuality is only a fragment of our total existence."

97. "I still have barriers toward feeling gay guys are my brother in the struggle. In gay liberation meetings I sometimes feel 'better' than the other guys. . . . My mind's eye still views me as straight much of the time." *GS* Aug.–Sept. 1970, 14.

98. "[T]o find the answers in our search for identity, recognition, and appreciation, we must be willing to guide each other as a brotherhood of friends through any and all personal and administrative road-blocks. Together we can do this, and together we will." *VG* Feb. 1967.

99. Raymond A. Loom, from Chicago, wrote, "You see, I am a social variant and I have been ever since I was 14. I am not ashamed of being what I am, and I have no intention of changing, but I would like to know how to live in a society that condemns me and my kind, how to combat those who militate against us." *TN* Aug. 19, 1963, 3.

100. Men writing letters to Guy Strait's papers enacted a sort of ritualized self-acknowledgement, as when A.F.K. wrote, "For some thirty years, I have been aware of what I am and settled down with 'the thing'; and for twenty-five years I have been a qualified Psychiatric Social Worker in good standing." *TN* Sept. 2, 1963, 1–2.

101. "But one way or another, we found it impossible to deny the profound emotion of love for our own kind. . . . But such prayers [that God would change us] went unanswered for our bodies were wiser than the mores of society and they told us that what we felt was good and what we experienced was satisfying." *VR* Oct. 1968, 6.

102. "We knew, without being knowledgeable, that it was not 'ordinary' to feel such deep desire and passion for 'one of our own kind.' . . . Those with a deep rooted homosexual predilection eventually recognize that the practices in the barn-bush-basement [with friends] meant more to them than they did to their playmates." *VR* Oct. 1968, 6. See also *VR* Aug. 1971, 36–37 and *VR* Dec. 1971, 5.

103. "Fortunately, I faced reality and gained self-respect at an early age. However, I understand and sympathize with those who've been brainwashed by 'straight' society and feel unsure of themselves." From B.A., *VR* Jan. 1969, 27.

104. One young man wrote, "I began to realize my homosexuality at 15. I also realized that others might not discover it in their teens at all. At my age, people are usually not aware of their homosexuality, or they are fighting the first signs of it." *VR* Nov. 1970, 39, 43–44. For this young gay libber, knowing he was gay was easy. "[T]he most difficult part of being a teenage homosexual—finding an identity."

105. "[W]e do not mean a power over other people, but that power over our own lives which we receive, personally and in our community, as we grow in the consciousness of our heritage and our own human dignity." *SFFP* Dec. 7, 1969.

106. See letter from John Smith, *TN* Oct. 28 1963.

107. See letter from Dan H., *VR* March–April 1968, 16–18: "The first perhaps is that you cannot love another without having love for yourself . . . a true love and respect for yourself. Too many of us have not risen above society's contempt and resulting guilt to find genuine love of one's self. Without this you cannot love another."

108. Given that gay men were so diverse, coming from every imaginable background, the "degree of misery or happiness in their lives depends on their level of consciousness. Self-acceptance in a hostile society is not easily won." *VR* July 1970, 12.

109. *Town Talk* praised one such book for giving gay men the tools they needed to take a "a first step toward his unashamed self-recognition and to his emergence as a whole person." *TT* Sept. 1965, 1, 4. R.O.D. Benson's book, *In Defense of Homosexuality* received equally glowing reviews in *Vector*; Benson hoped his book would be a weapon of self-defense in the hands of every homosexual. See *VR* Nov. 1965, 6. Frank J. Howell reviewed *Homosexual Behavior Among Males: A Cross-Cultural and Cross-Species Investigation* and claimed that upon reading the book, a "psychic relief will be his [the reader's], i.e., 'Man, it is all right to be you.'" *VR* Feb.–March 1968, 11. And one of the founders of the *SFFP* had plans to write a book "dedicated to the young, confused, re-

jected, alienated, unloved homosexual. . . . But all too often he does not accept himself or his sexuality. . . . He can find happiness only if he accepts and loves himself and through that love can learn to truly love other persons." *SFFP* Oct. 1, 1969, 12.

110. "To some degree, almost every 'gay person' has an inferiority complex." *VR* Jan. 1969, 27.

111. "He must value his worth as an individual first of all . . . one who is trying to cope with being a 'unique' male or female in a society which is not always friendly to his natural motivations. . . . Some of our worst enemies are insecure homosexuals." *VR* Sept. 1969, 20–21, 30.

112. See *VR* Dec. 1969, 9.

113. "Gay Lib provides him with a way of accepting himself that semi-private and adult-oriented liberal groups can not." *VR* Oct. 1970, 38.

114. For example, "Just as negroes become Negro, queers become Queer." *VR* Aug. 1968, 7.

115. "I became in substance a Negro. I had to live like a Negro (in oppression) so I became aware of his problems and I began to understand the Negro's plight. . . . For in a sense, my skin was not like everyone else's. . . . [F]or me as a teenager, I want to question the homosexual community by saying that—the Negroes are saying, 'I'm Black and I'm proud' and saying it loud. Also they say 'Black is Beautiful.' And it IS beauty! Well, what are our people saying? Inside I know I'm saying, 'I'm a homosexual and I'm proud.' And for me 'Male is Beautiful.' What is the rest of the community saying?" *VR* Dec. 1968, 34–35. This was only the first time of at least three these words would appear in print in the gay press of San Francisco.

116. For Williams, "the Church has a responsibility to create a new concept (other than pervert) for homosexuals, a concept that will allow gay people to become fully human individuals free of fear and guilt about their homosexuality." *VR* Nov. 1968, 5.

117. Leo Laurence described a vital side-effect of activism in his article "Total Commitment to Be Gay." "Our picket line is beginning to show the public the beauty in homosexuality as they see our marchers singing freedom songs, laughing, holding hands, and even kissing in public." *CHFN* Apr. 29, 1969.

118. See Chauncey, *Gay New York.*

119. Robert H. of San Francisco wrote, "[A] person who must announce to the world that he is Gay is no more mature and secure than the guy posing as straight to impress the heterosexual world." *VR* June 1969, 24.

120. "When a person comes out, the dam is burst. He can get in touch with all his emotions. He feels his loves more deeply, his pleasures more keenly, and his anger in a clean and honest form—he is no longer fighting himself." *VR* March 1972, 31. Jerry Weiss continued this theme. "When you finally become aware of the natural world around you, how beautiful life can be if lived openly, how much fun it is to give, to think of others before yourself, the double life becomes intolerable." *CHFN* Apr. 29, 1969. Leo Laurence agreed. "I was leading the typical 'double-life.' . . . I honestly feel now that GAY IS GOOD." *VR* Jan. 1969, 16–17.

121. Guy Strait had wondered early on, "The whole point must lie in whether or not the person involved can *realize* his variance." *TN* Sept. 16, 1963, 1–2, emphasis mine. M.D. complained about a book by a Dr. Reuben that claimed a cure for homosexuality in 1970. "The most tragic aspect of this outright lie is the many latent homosexuals who will continue to live with their suppressed pain and the terrible blow this strikes against all of our efforts to enlighten an already prejudiced public." *VR* Aug. 1970, 9.

122. "They all are [oppressed], but, then, many refuse to believe it. By living double lives, . . . obligingly hiding their activities from free and public exercise . . .so they believe that the unhappiness they experience in the homosexual dimension of their lives (loneliness, fear of aging, superficiality) is due to the inevitability of their lamentable condition, rather than due to a social political mentality of across-the-board oppression of all things not white, straight, middle class, pro-establishment." *GS* Aug.–Sept. 1970, 2.

123. A closeted man "often acts in a destructive way toward himself and other homosexuals. He accommodates his homosexuality on the personal level by rejecting homosexuality on the public or professional level." *VR* Jan. 1971, 4. See for example *VR* April 1972, 13.

124. "Many, many brutal cops and sadistic Marine sergeants are persons who are fighting their own despised natures." *SFFP* Nov. 1, 1969, 15. "It seems especially unfortunate that 'out of our closets' may have become just another cliché mouthed by closeted homosexuals." *GS* Oct. 1970, 13.

125. "At no period of the homosexual's life is this [oppression] more apparent or serious than when, as a youth, he must face himself and his sex desires. Because of the very nature of his sex drives, the homosexual is forced to hide from his parents." *VR* Nov. 1968, 16–18. Charles Thorp echoed the devastating feelings of many gay youth of the time when he explained, "[N]ot only do you *feel* alone, but you *are* alone." *VR* Nov. 1970, 39, 43–44.

126. One man, Korinsky, led a very interesting career in the military which he described as making the transition from passing to blatant in a couple of years. "[A sergeant warned me:] 'Don't be too campy. Be careful or you'll get in trouble. . . . In my own way, I became a gay militant. . . . I was gay by my actions and the gay things that I said. . . . By June '70, I was very anti-Army, anti-Vietnam, and very gay. . . . I even joined with some straight friends to put out a base 'underground' newspaper [at Fort Riley in KS]. We put out nine issues, one a week. It was anti-war, anti-Army and for some strange reason, pro-Gay. . . . By day I was wild enough but now at night I ran the Army's mimeo machine to get out a contraband newspaper." *VR* Sept. 1971, 10–11.

Ramon Contreras, described how he felt it necessary to pass to a certain degree during the State Line's protest in May of 1969. "Yet at all times, I maintained a façade of straightness when confronting straight society because American concepts of how to behave and believe had been inculcated into me: to be proper always, to have possessions more than most, to have a job that provides a class status higher than most, and faith that the conventional channels of the established American political system provides an access to justice for all." *CHFN* May 13, 1969.

127. Staying away from home "is one of the prices I must pay for being honest with myself," wrote another closeted man. *CN* June 22, 1964, 6.

128. Lee Roberts related how when he came out to his family, "no one suspected a thing about me until the day I wanted to finally break away from the cloying atmosphere of my family and making a clean break of it, [I] told all. . . . My father tried to have me committed to a mental hospital." *VR* Nov. 1968, 16–18.

129. "I'm safe where I am; I have a good job in the financial district. My lover of 15 years is with a bank; we have a nice home and flower garden in Marin County in a safe area with respectable neighbors." *VR* March 1970, 12–13.

130. One man reported, "For years, I have been intentionally excluded from regular social activities of the sizeable 'in group' at work. One host once said: 'I don't want that faggot in my house.'" *VR* Jan. 1969, 13. When he and his boyfriend did attend a holiday party, they "played it cool" and mixed with other people at the party. Discussions about

coming out at work often provoked controversy. "Persons with a high homosexual profile are particularly incensed that professional men do not publicly declare their sexual orientation and confront public opinion. . . . Revelation is an individual responsibility and decision" *VR* Jan. 1971, 4. Following their perceived association with other movements, *Gay Sunshine* saw coming out at work as their connection to the working class. David Charles wrote, "Our silence is submissive and destructive to ourselves and others who may be gay. . . . This is where gay power lies, in the working class. This is where gays are most hidden and also where the majority of gays are" *GS* June–July 1971, 14. The article concluded, "Working class gays UNITE!"

Interestingly, *Vector* reported that a survey of employers revealed that "However, many responses included comments which indicated the concern about sexuality was often whether one 'appeared' to be homosexual rather than the orientation itself." *VR* June 1971, 17.

131. Dan argued that "if their [straight person's] ignorance is causing problems then I feel they must be told." *VR* March 1971, 37. Jerome Verriel, of Seattle, wrote an alternative response in *Vector* to an Ann Lander's column that had appeared in national newspapers in which she sent a gay young man who asked if he should come out to reparative therapy. "Dear Woody: Don't' fight it. They only help that you require is self-understanding and the ability to be honest with yourself. . . . In my experience, a homosexual cannot be totally 'cured' of his desires. . . . Don't just trick, find real love." *VR* April 1971, 20–21. John Broadhurst advised Woody, "Allow yourself time to grow up and decide how strong you are able to overtly identify with the homophile minority group."

132. "So he [a young, closeted gay] is conscious of a tension in every conversation with them [straights]." *VR* Dec. 1967, 10.

133. *VR* April–May 1968, 29; Jan. 1971, 4.

134. "I would say to [the closeted] that it [coming out] is much less difficult than they might imagine; that they will feel immensely better and happier for it; and that this is the greatest single contribution any of us can make to the gay cause. We can only overcome oppression by others once we are able to overcome the oppression within ourselves that makes us afraid to be open about who we are." *VR* April 1972, 13.

135. "The hustler who does not realize his condition and who preys on his own kind, even though he will not admit they are his own kind, constitutes the greatest threat to the variant." *TN* Sept. 16, 1963, 1–2. For many, the hustler was simply a criminal who refused to take care of himself. "The prostitute from experiences with fellow citizens and jail mates is well aware of this [danger]. Yet he persists. Obviously, there is some other factor, in the case of prostitution, which makes this criminal behavior worthwhile in spite of its comparable monetary inequalities." *VR* Feb. 1971, 11. They argued often that a hustler was a broken person, one incapable of feeling affection, and so frustrated and hostile. "[T]he young male prostitute knows that he is desired for his body and so he attempts love at that level." Thus, many gay men (regardless of whether or not they paid for hustlers) could see themselves not only as morally superior, but as healthier and even *more gay* than hustlers. "[H]e allows himself to be used sexually and then discarded, the damage is so great to his ego or self-esteem that he is not able eventually to function as a hustler." Only slightly more tolerated were closeted married men who had sex with men on the side. Gay men dealt with this by explaining to themselves how a gay man could be married in the first place. "Hence the theory that one may be behaviorally conditioned from a same to a contrasting sexual object without damage to the individual. What actually occurs in such a conditioning is that the object becomes desexualized. . . . The het-

erosexually conditioned homosexual finds himself engaging in heterosexual masturbation using an object of the opposite sex." *VR* June 1972.

136. See Chapter 6.

137. "I will not faun before the graven image of public morality. I will not distort my nature in the name of self-denial. I will not give up living in the name of security, acceptance or instant suicide. . . . Never, for one particle of time, ignore the sense of affirmation which accepts both joy and sadness, and peace and terror as the two sides of the coin called living." *VR* Jan. 1965, 6.

138. Some examples: Leo E. Laurence wrote, "As a result I no longer have chronic insomnia. I no longer feel depressed most of the time. I am sick neither physically or mentally." *VR* Jan. 1969, 16–17. In thinking about a popular writer who had admitted publicly his homosexuality, a reviewer mused, "Will he destroy his closet or merely step out of it? . . . It's like emerging from a pitch dark cave onto a brightly lighted seashore." *VR* March 1971, 45. George Mendenhall was outed by the *San Francisco Chronicle* in 1971, and he found to his surprise, "It has given us more confidence in working side-by-side with people who might still reject homosexuality but who accept your editor as a human being. And that is the way that we look at ourselves . . . first, human beings; secondarily, homosexual." *VR* Aug. 1971, 4.

Conclusion

Meaning, Desire, and the Future of Gay

To learn to be human is to develop through the give and take of communication an effective sense of being an individually distinctive member of a community; one who understand and appreciates its beliefs, desires, and methods, and who contributes to a further conversion of organic powers into human resources and values.

—John Dewey, *The Public and Its Problems*, 1927

To examine the lives of gay men between 1961 and 1972 is to see a historical moment when men and women were actively engaged in shaping the meaning of their experiences as homosexual individuals. Gay-maleness was the emergence of something new and different in quality and social function than what had gone on before; it was built upon meanings gay men had created during the 1950s and yet it was substantively different. Homosexuality as a social phenomenon—complete with cultural signs and geographical locations—rather than a disease or crime was only just emerging into the dominant culture's awareness, especially after the June 23, 1964 issue of *LIFE Magazine*. But activist gay men and women were working consciously to make such a social, public homosexuality a reality, to transform their complex environment into one which would nurture and sustain the consummation of their desires, in other words, one free from domination and abjection. Such a transformed environment would allow them to freely explore their homosexuality and make of it what they would without interference, violence, and emotional battering. Study of such a historical moment of emergence, during which various groups of activist gay men actively sought a counter-publicity, enables the interpretation of the blending of the sub-cultural formations of gayness prior to 1961 with the emerging and contested public forms; it uncovers the process whereby a particular, domi-

291

nant meanings of gay maleness, gay male publicity, came to be a relatively stable feature of the American cultural landscape by 1972.

I began this project seeking to map out the central features of gay-maleness that had emerged by the time of the 1972 gay pride parade in San Francisco and which has had the surprising strength, the longevity, to sustain itself through the past forty years, through ongoing battles with a homophobic official public and even the devastation of AIDS. What comes from the evidence is an unsettled, fluid gayness wherein different formations of gayness seek to establish a dominance or hegemony among gay men, but which succeeded only in some contexts. What I found instead was that the 1960s were a period of the *expansion* of the meaning of gay, as more and more aspects of social and personal life and individual psychology were implicated and imbricated into gayness as the decade wore on; and concomitantly, that many men from various contexts resisted that expansion and struggled to minimize or contain their homosexuality, to keep it as detached as possible from other aspects of their lives. Clearly, any individual men could fall at any place along the spectrum between expansion and minimization, and it is possible that his position could change over time or even from situation to situation. Gayness in this view becomes not an identity or political movement, but an ever expanding and contracting set of interconnections in the social world and psychologies of gay men.

It was the emerging counter-publicity and the desire to build community that enabled this ballooning-shrinking gayness, as they increased the number, quality, and kind of social contacts and interactions available to San Francisco's gay men. As counter-publicity and community worked, or rather, as gay men created them, they enabled a new degree of social interaction, as gay men gained the chance to encounter and interact with men of various backgrounds and in new and more complex ways, in interaction with various gay organizations, overlapping and conflicting gay politics, and of course, always under the domination of the symbolic order and the official public. This emergent and growing interaction necessarily increased the possible meanings of gay, by changing the nature and number of gay men's interactions. In short, they gave gave men a growing range of choices for how they could make their same-sex desires and behaviors intelligible, based on the extent to which an individual gay men (or a group) wanted his gayness to interpenetrate with other areas of his life.

As the decade progressed, this changed the nature of the "homosexual role"[1] in San Francisco, and in conjunction with other gay communities and movements around the country, in American society at large. Whereas the official public continued to dominate and control the homosexual role, gay men alongside gay women were constantly challenging the official public's authority to and legitimacy in controlling it, claiming that right for themselves. Out of their efforts to wrest control of the homosexual role from the dominant society, gay activists ended by creating a new kind of homosexuality, marked by the fact that it was contested by those assigned to it.

By focusing on the meaning-making process that arose out of counter-publicity and community building in relationship with a dominating symbolic order and official public, I found that the 1960s was not a story of a bifurcated gay politics (i.e., "assimilationist" vs. "radical," which I have discussed at length in this book), but rather was the story of a shift in the socially necessary concerns of gay men. Early in this period, gay men and women were focused on creating a gay publicity per se. Their efforts were aimed at getting people involved, convincing their like-others that they had a stake in the public and should engage with it, and in creating organizations that fostered the emerging counter-publicity. This was clearly in response to the realities of their environment, and the evident need to devise and flesh out a public-facing gayness. In the mid-decade, some gay men had enough of a gay publicity formed that they were speaking of a new kind of gay community, one in which a gay public could form affect-laden bonds through shared interests. And late in the decade, the gay counter-publicity and community were formed well enough (albeit unevenly and unfinished) that other gay men, often but not exclusively younger, were free to consider issues of gay authenticity, brotherhood, identity, and Pride. The shift, then, was a matter of changing emphasis in relationship to a changing context as the decade wore on. So the gayness that arose between 1961 and 1972 in San Francisco was an incredibly flexible and open gayness, always fraught with power struggles among gay men and in relationship to the dominant society, that enabled the full range of meaning, in G.H. Mead's sense, for individual gay men to situate themselves in.

In examining the meanings gay men ascribed to their gayness in the 1960s and early 1970s, only traces of their thoughts and feelings, captured in the historical record, stand as witness to their experience. But these linguistic, cognitive aspects of meaning formation are in many ways only the visible evidence of the complex process that produced meaningfulness for their experience. For Dewey, thought—and by extension culture and the cognitive-linguistic communications about thought—is only one part of a process of experience. "Thought was not a thing but a division of labor within experience, a mediating, 'instrumental' function depending 'upon unreflective antecedents for its existence, and upon a consequent experience for its final test' (*SLT* 367)."[2] Gay men's undergoing of events, the *experience* of gayness, was the entire circuit of the interaction and transaction between the individual and his environment.

The "thought" which arose from that experience, of which the historical record has left traces, indeed all the evidence available for a critical inquiry, is the *mediation* between the experience of agents, acting purposefully in their environment to transform it to remediate the domination of the public sphere, the state, in their lives. "Knowing [for Dewey] was a *mediating* function capable of rendering judgments to guide actions that would transform problematic non-cognitive situations into ongoing, unproblematic, non-cognitive experience."[3] For gay men, it was the non-cognitive experience of being gay from within their abjection—the feelings, the activity-undergoings—which gave rise to their knowledge of being gay, that is to say, of being *different* in a way that was salient to both them and the dominant culture. That salience of difference enabled simultaneously the repression of the expression of sexual difference and the imposition of symbolic domination where gay men were denied access to the most basic kinds of personhood accorded to full members of the public sphere. The experience of abjection brought with it the process of "reflective inquiry," where gay men were able to think about their situation and to act purposefully to transform their environment to accommodate them and to enable the consummation of their desires, sexual and otherwise.

As organizations grew and proliferated in San Francisco and as more and more gay men became members of them, the consciousness that gay men indeed constituted a public grew. Indeed, as the period between 1961–1972 progressed, the argument quickly shifted from whether or not gay men had enough in common to form a political bloc to an implicit assumption that they did indeed exist. As it happened, it was the formation of the public that engendered its existence in the minds of gay men. For Dewey, any society necessarily consists of many publics that wax and wane depending on circumstances. A public, for Dewey, was the group of individuals who experienced the consequences of others' social actions, when they were diffuse, enduring, and broad in their effect. For gay men, effects of particular kids of actions between, say, the police and a gay man or between a hustler and the gay john he beat up, necessarily made them a possible public. What changed in 1961 was the conscious effort of gay men to move beyond the methods employed by the Mattachine Society to seek to form a counter-public that could challenge the social transactions that had such damaging effects on them as individuals and as a group.

Circumstances created by the regulatory discourses of law, medicine, and religion had combined with the repressive actions of the state to produce an environment in which a new public, a gay counter-public, had to form to answer the effects of those modes of behavior in the larger American public. Thus, the environment had evolved to a point where gay men's associations could grow beyond their bar sub-cultures into something new and more powerful. Because the state and other cultural organization were so tightly organized against the formation of the public, it was constantly threatened with fading into an inchoate collection of individuals, such as had existed prior to 1961. Dewey notes that in a well-organized state, "To form itself, the [new] public has to break existing political forms. This is hard to do because these forms are themselves the regular means of instituting change. The public which generated political forms is passing away, but the power and lust of possession remains in the hands of the officers and agencies which the dying public instituted."[4] The American public was just beginning to face, in 1972, the implications of the formation of the gay counter-public, and the transformation of the institutions have been slow indeed.

Concurrent with (and perhaps as a consequence of) their effort to form a counter-public, gay men and women also began to think of forming a new kind of community. At first, this community consisted merely of a political bloc, the group necessary to evoke change; but by 1965, some men were already greatly expanding their understanding of gay community, imagining it into being as an association of individuals with much in common, where other needs besides their "sexual proclivities" could be met, such as facilitating the formation of friendship, providing creative and social outlets, and fostering gay men's developing identities. And by the time revolutionary values were added to the mix, gay community had become the location of something unique and special to the American social scene, that fostered meaning-making for same-sex attracted peoples per say. However individual gay men conceived of the community, or the meanings they ascribed to it, it undoubtedly existed by the mid-1960s and had a great power in the lives of gay men, inside and outside of the activist organizations. Dewey felt that the existence of such communities was vital to the development of individuals and the achievement of an individual good.

Many gay men wrote of their feelings of community within organization, and the liberating effect it had on them emotionally and intellectually to understand themselves as part of a larger community. At the same time, many men rejected membership in a community and distanced themselves from its formation. Interestingly, both groups of men participated in the communication within the community, arguing about the meanings of community itself in addition to the meanings of any number of other practices and situations salient and important to gay men. Thus, even those who understood themselves as being outside the community benefited by engaging with the community in working out for themselves oppositional identities and values. As Dewey noted, the primary function of a community is to provide the context wherein such beneficial conversations can occur.

Gay community formation had at its core social interactions in the form of the institutions, the cooperative action gay men took, the ways the differentiated themselves from each other, and in their intense conflicts over ends and means in the public sphere and over the meaning of gayness. Those meanings constituted a cognitive aspect of gay community, as there emerged from their debates the expanding notions of identity of the members of the community and the ideologies that should structure it. But at the heart of a community in an abject social position, the affective aspect rose to the most prominence. Gay men *felt* themselves to be members of a community, or if they did not, they felt the presence of a community of some sort. The feeling of that membership was a consummatory experience for many, as they sought the recognition of like others and the validation of their desires for sex and relationships with men, and for their practices as gay men. Such a consummatory experience offered a kind of security in their selves that they had not been able to find outside the community, with the exceptions of the same kinds of safety offered by the small, subcultural associations that existed prior to the 1960s. Dewey noted, "Whenever there is a conjoint activity whose consequences are appreciated as good by all singular persons who take part in it, and where the realization of the good is such as to effect an energetic desire and effort to sustain it in being just because it is a good shared by all, there is in so far a community."[5] Even from the experiences of gay men who did not actively participate in activist organizations, they were nonetheless affected by the existence of a community, whose presence was felt as the mode of discussing homosexuality in the public sphere changed and as the nature of interaction between gay men shifted because of the emerging community.

As gay men continued to engaged the same kinds of negative misrepresentations of homosexuality they had been enduring at least since World War II, they began to create for themselves a public context within their communities to deal with the harmful effects in new and creative ways. The community and counter-publicity, emerging in a social space where important arguments could be had, allowed gay men to talk about their experience of same-sex desire, their experience of oppression, and their reactions to medical, legal, and religious discourses of homosexuality. The social spaces afforded by community and counter-publicity brought together individuals engaged in the same kinds of struggles with their experiences of symbolic domination, and eventually produced for gay men an environment where they could simply reject those meanings prescribed from outside and to produce new meanings of gayness.[6] For Dewey, meaning arose directly out of communal interaction; indeed, it could not exist without it. The meaning of gay desires and practices accrued as gay men debated the potential conflicts of those desires and practices, and indeed came to associate gay desires and practices with their potential consequences. Having sex with another man, dressing in drag, going to a gay bar, or participating in a "zap" action were marked necessarily by the meaning they acquired in their communal setting.

Growing ever more intense through the period, gay men argued amongst themselves about the very meaning of their gayness itself. When they argued that gayness was inherited and biological, or when they insisted that it was a choice to be made legitimately, or when they insisted on its naturalness or on its chosenness, they were engaging not in a literal search for the cause or source of their homosexuality, but for its meaning. Among other things, to argue that it was a choice was to say that within the public sphere it should be a legitimized choice of a free individual in the society; to argue that it was natural was to alleviate the potential guilt inherited from other environments in which homosexuality was laden with sickness and disease; to argue it was enculturated was to hope that all sexuality was a cultural phenomenon and that it could become malleable, thereby liberating all people in a revolutionary vision of radical sexual freedom; and to argue that it was genetic was to remove psychic responsibility for having being a degenerate, less-than-human man. Each of these possible iterations of the meaning of same-sex desire has meaning in a social context, carries weight because of the environment within which it was formed, and provided status and consummatory experience within a community of gay men. This is to say nothing of the literal etiology of homosexuality, but of the meaningful role that etiological arguments play in their context. Ultimately, gay men assigned meanings to their desires and practices as made their experiences of their desires intelligible and as facilitated their continued satisfying consummation.

Hegemonic Gayness

Many gay men felt various kinds of power and domination within the gay community as the circulated in arenas where they were not welcome or where they did not fit in the dominant values of that particular milieu (as when the drag queen was chastised by GLF members at a meeting in Berkeley, or when a man described how the men in a leather bar rejected him because he didn't look the part). There were also certain articulations of values that seem to have had power among gay men because they matched the values of the dominant symbolic order and/or the official public, such that gay men who valued their positions as professional, middle-class white men, or those who valued respectability, or those with "normal" sexual habits or gender presentations seem to have occupied a privileged position in some parts of the gay community, but by no means all. The relationship of such men to the official public belies the near impossibility of establishing a dominant or hegemonic position within an abject counter-public. Gay community was, by definition, subordinate and dominated both institutionally and symbolically, which made any claim for dominance within the gay counter-public or within the gay community always tenuous, always uncertain. Further, the kinds of powers gay men could exert against each other were always circumscribed by their relationship to the dominant society. There was no clear hegemonic gay-maleness by 1972.

On the other hand, what becomes clear is that gay men of that period established the terms of an ongoing debate among themselves and future generations of gay men, and that the terms of that debate became the historic center-poles of gay-maleness. Although the answers to the questions seem to have remained open, the questions continue to be asked to greater and lesser degrees depending on the positions of the men engaged in the debate. Gay men argued about what the status of a gay man *should* be in the American official public sphere; they argued about what their ends and means should be vis-à-vis the official public; what freedom should mean, and what rights they were entitled to; they argued about the meaning of community, the pros and cons of membership, and the strategies to establish and maintain it; they argued about who counted and was worthy of being gay in terms of race, gender, social class and age; they argued about appropriate gender presentation, appropriate sexual outlets, and appropriate sub-cultural practices (e.g., leather and S/M); and they argued about their identities, the salience and significance of having a core gay identity. In the formation of their new public and in the gathering together of a community, gay men created the social context that could foster the consummation of their same-sex desires and facilitate the production of meaning that made their desires intelligible in positive and individuating, as well as limiting and constraining, ways.

Matrices of Desire and Multitudes of Values

Of primary importance throughout this process were the *desires* of gay men at play in their actions. Often in studying homosexuality, the question of desire rests at the level of sexual attraction and the consummation of sexual desire, especially where the very category "homosexual" is seen as being unstable or in question. What, indeed, is a homosexual? Is it a man who desires other men sexually? Or is it a man who has sex with other men? Or is it both? Or is it neither; must a man *identify* as homosexual in order to be one, regardless of his desires or sexual behaviors? However, such a view of desire is strictly limited to questions of sexual affect and behavior and is epistemologically linked to the process of categorization (not to mention verification and authentication).[7] This limited notion of desire, in attempting to analyze the social interactions of homosexuals and the meanings they produce, limits interpretive scope. Surely this was the definition of homosexuality as it came down in the official discourses of sexology through medicine and psychiatry, in their will to know, to discipline life into intelligible sexual categories. Guy Hocquenghem rejected this psychiatric definition of desire, homosexual desire, as he argued instead that there is no qualitative difference between heterosexual desire and homosexual desire: desire simply *is*.[8] Even as Eve Sedgwick insists that we're all sexually different in our innumerably multiple reactions to sex and sexual situations, and even as Hocquenghem insists that desire is polyvocal at its source and that homosexual is an exterior categorization of the effects of many kinds of sexual desires, they both remain firmly in the realm of the *sexual*.

Of course, the sexual desires of gay men and their relationship to sexual desire, their feelings about it, and their understandings of particular sex acts and practices are all central to a group actively persecuted for their sexuality. However, desire must be rethought in much larger terms to understand why and how *this* homosexuality, *this* gay-maleness came to be between 1961 and 1972; such a narrow understanding of desire could never explain the struggles for meaning or for identity or for community, nor could it explain why and how gay men fought for recognition in the public sphere. To answer that problem, we must greatly expand our understanding of desire and both its individual and social functions. To do this, I return to John Dewey and the pragmatic theory of knowledge, his organism-environment model of knowledge production.

All impulses seek expression and consummation. Dewey argues that there are three possible expressions of impulse: 1) it can simply be explosively discharged, unconsciously and undirected; 2) it can be incorporated and directed through habit into the stream of human activity; or 3) it can be suppressed, having no place in the habit of the individual or society in question.[9] Recall that Dewey argued that impulses are of no interest to social scientists because they are unintelligible of themselves. What *is* intelligible is *desire*. Desire, then, becomes what "arises only when 'there is something the matter,' when there is some 'trouble' in an existing situation. . . . There is something lacking, wanting, in the existing situation as it stands, an absence which produces conflict in the elements that do exist."[10] In other words, desire arises when impulses cannot be habitually expressed or consummated, when habit is foiled, when our predispositions don't function to answer our impulses, when for environmental (material or social) reasons we cannot consummate our impulses. Thus, impulses exist as the *sina qua non* of desire; but they are not, themselves, desire. Desire "includes foreseen consequences along with ideas in the form of signs of the measures . . . required to bring the ends into existence."[11]

At that point, impulses become desires: they are rendered conscious and they are given conscious content; they become the objects of valuation and are therefore subject to moral evaluation. Thus, all discreet desires are linked into larger systems of desire; they are founded in the material relations of the complex environment, both obdurate and social, and are inseparable from it. Desire so conceived also explains valuation, the process whereby an object (material, relational, or ideational) becomes a value either as an end-in-view or as a means to a particular end-in-view. Thus, desires can be verified, for they are inextricably linked to objects (contents) in a specific context and tied to the behaviors that directly precede it. Effort to consummate the desire is the "essence of the tension involved in desire."[12] Dewey calls this "effort-behavior" and notes that its consequences are observable. Therefore the "adequacy of the desire" that inspired the effort-behavior is subject to evaluation through its effects.

For my exploration into the emergence of the meaning of gay, this is the desire that must be brought to the fore. What is key to understanding the production of the meaning of gay between 1961 and 1972 and literally *the* means to understand gay male experience is that when we speak of impulses, sex is merely the most obvious impulse at play but not the only impulse and not necessarily the most important one. For this reason, in each of the preceding chapters, I have sought to tease out the multiple aspects of gay male life, paying particular attention to the *affective* quality of their experience (in addition to the discursive contents of their arguments), as well as to the conflicts or the points of rupture they experienced as they sought to lend meaning to their experiences. I have also focused in on their strategies or proposed strategies as well as brief descriptions of their actual actions both in the public sphere and in their own communities. I have also striven to bring out the details of where gay men's lives intersected with the dominant culture and the effect that such interaction had; for indeed, the dominant culture *was* the complex environment within which gay men lived.

So the various forms of social interaction as they emerged during this period—from the transformation of the older communities, to the harassment of the police, to the election of officials and attempts to reform the law, to organizational formation and activities, to in-fighting and competition over means and ends, and the hard-fought battles for the substance of gay community—all of these are the *effort-behaviors* of individuals attempting to work out the consummation of their desires in an environment set up specifically to prevent that consummation. Obviously, we are talking about much more than the simple desire to suck a cock or fuck; such sexual desires had had means of consummation already. What changed was the emergence of new and more powerful desires than the bare, same-sex sexual practice. These gay men desired a different environment in which to have sex; they desired a different social context within which to meet each other; they desired social and relational bonds with each other that were proscribed by the environment as it was; they desired full participation in the official public sphere, i.e., citizenship, *as* gay men; they desired community and companionship, understanding and communal recognition; they desired self-esteem and self-love; they desired identity.

All of gay men's desires (and by extension their values) were both ends-in-view and means to other ends, or as Dewey called them, ends-as-means (values). And all of them mixed with other desires: the desire to be masculine, the desire to be a drag queen, the desire to be normal, the desire to express oneself a-normally (e.g., campy), the desire to be a minority, the desire not to be a minority, the desire to identify with Black folks, the desire to be respectable, the desire to transform society, the desire to be left alone, the desire to integrate. All of what I have discussed here in this book are reflections of the *desires* of gay men in the 1960s in terms of their effort-behaviors to consummate them. What we get, then, is not "homosexual desire" at the center of an "identity movement." We get a complicated matrix of overlapping and therefore competing desires, as each issue that gay men debated was articulated through their desires. So as a gay man articulates his gayness and his own publicity, it becomes a process of him situating his desires (values) in relationship to his social context in a particular time. To make it more complicated, because desires are fluid and the circumstances that evoke them are constantly changing, and because the communication that gives them meaning is ongoing, gay men's particular valuation of any given practice or their values driving publicity, or their desires for possible outcomes change from time to time and place to place.

Desire, then, is the constitutive feature of gay male meaning-making, not in its sexual form, but in the relationship of multiple social, communal, cultural, emotional, psychological, and sexual desires, which bubble to the surface in a communicative interaction wherein desires can be expressed and enacted in the counter-public, the community, and the public sphere. Desires and symbolic interaction, then, gave rise to various meanings of gay in a particular historical moment when gay men could no longer suppress their impulses. They insisted on expressing and integrating their desires into their habitual behavior; and this was a *habitualness* that they insisted must be public in its nature. For Dewey, "To desire an object was, in effect, to argue that that object as an end-in-view would when actively pursued and achieved, resolve the troubled situation in which the agent currently found himself. Because all such judgments were subject to empirical test by measuring the consequences of the end-achieved against the consequences predicted by the end-in-view they were subject to verification or refutation and could be then said to be warranted or unwarranted."[13] And so gay men's desires, their struggles with each other over meanings, became the end in view of a counter-publicity and community that supported an ongoing debate about desire that continues to this day.

Toward an Effective Freedom for Gay Men

What remains unclear from the period is what exactly a gay liberation might look or feel like. The gay libbers of the day argued that it was to be free from the domination of a straight society.[14] The members of LCE and early SIR members thought it meant getting rights, changing the law, and ending police harassment. Was gay liberation achieved by 1972? Is it achieved now? How would we know we had it when it happened? Gay men had articulated by early in the 1960s an idea of a kind of freedom that would allow them to pursue the most personal aspects of their individuation in peace and that would allow them to generate positive meanings for their same sex desires and relationships. Although it was never articulated in any clear form, from 1961 through 1972, there was a pervasive sense among gay men that they lacked something important to their very *Selves* in the society as it was constituted. I have called this value a "freedom of personhood" for purposes of clarity and consistency.

The difficulty, then, lies in determining what a gay liberation, a freedom of personhood for gay men, might look like. For Dewey, the ethic of self-realization, the ideal for a democratic community, served as the ideal or principle whereby things could be morally evaluated. "IN THE REALIZATION OF INDIVIDUALITY THERE IS FOUND ALSO THE NEEDED REALIZATION OF SOME COMMUNITY OF PERSONS OF WHICH THE INDIVIDUAL IS A MEMBER; AND, CONVERSELY, THE AGENT WHO DULY SATISFIES THE COMMUNITY IN WHICH HE SHARES, BY THAT SAME CONDUCT SATISFIES HIMSELF."[15] The ethic of self-realization, for Dewey, requires the realization of a community within which the individual can be realized. When gay men and women began to push outward from their conceptions of a gay public, they also expanded what they wanted from their gay community. Whereas they began with a community limited as a political bloc, they soon found that such a community failed to answer all of their needs and desires, all that was lacking them as abject members of the larger American society. Ethically, for Dewey, the individual will find self-realization at he strives for the realization of his community. So gay liberation must consist of access to such a community or to the resources necessary to create and sustain such a community.

Key in gay men's experiences was that they experienced the lack of freedom in social terms, that the meanings generated from outside their experiences by individuals who weren't gay and that outsiders acted to physically repress their self-expression and the consummation of their desires. If bondage, constriction, domination were experienced as social, then perhaps "liberation" must be conceived as its social inverse. To think through these problems, I turn again to John Dewey and attempt to adapt his notions of democracy, community, and freedom for the questions I have posed here. For Dewey, freedom must be always an adjective, not a metaphysical quality; it must be an apt description of an actual circumstance and experience, never an abstracted ideal. Freedom for gay men would then becomes *effective*, or in other words, capable of creation and cause, within a social environment. "Since actual, that is, *effective rights* and demands are products of interactions, and are not found in the original and isolated constitutions of human nature, whether moral or psychological, mere elimination of obstructions is not enough."[16] Thus, an effective freedom necessarily means a transformation of the social arrangements that would allow for gay men to act upon their individual matrix of desire for self-realization, or what Dewey called individuality.

The social context within which individuation or self-realization might be possible for gay men, would require access to the social goods necessary for such realization, and if Dewey is correct, access on some level to a community that would foster the gay man's individuation. Thus, for Dewey, equality must be qualitative, not quantitative: the value of a gay man's individuality to the public sphere should be considered immeasurable and cannot be reduced to a structural equality. A democratic community for Dewey would be a community of individuals striving to express their individuality to the best of their ability. So equality must be an equality of access to the social and cultural tools and milieus necessary for the realization of the individual.[17] In *Ethics*, Dewey argued that "Effective freedom also required as the condition of its exercise 'positive control of the resources necessary to carry purposes into effect, possession of the means to satisfy desires; and mental equipment with the trained powers of initiative and reflection required for free preference and for circumspect and far-seeing desires.'"[18] Gay liberation, then, must mean more than simply being free from the obstacles that prevented gay men from meeting, having sex, or forming organizations. Structural freedom maintains the possibility of a vast inequality of power. For Dewey, a true freedom would require access to the tools of "deliberation and invention" necessarily to consciously consider and choose appropriate means and ends to the satisfaction of personal desires within a communal context.

Gayness is inherently social, not just in its discursive content (although that may also be the case), but in its acting out, in its performance. The meanings of gayness only arise socially in the actions of gay individuals with others, gay or otherwise. Gay liberation must mean, then, access to a social environment in which associations with other individuals nurture sexual difference, where the social function of the individual as individual members of a community. Effective freedom exists only in a social environment, a community affiliation, where individual difference can grow. Paradoxically, individuality can only exist in a community context; and a community depends on the individuality of its members to flourish. For Dewey, this was "associated living," and it was a social good, in the moral sense. "Habits, customs, and social institutions were to be judged according to the degree to which they contributed to the 'development of a qualitative enhancement of associated living'"[19] For Dewey, then, a social practice was to be judged a moral good when it "contributes positively to free intercourse, to unhampered exchange of ideas, to mutual respect and friendship and love—in short to those modes of behaving which make life richer and more worth living for everybody concerned; and conversely any custom or institution which impedes progress toward these goals is to be judged bad." As we have seen, the gay community as it was constituted in 1972 was deeply fractured by the moralizing bent of gay men in their contexts of symbolic domination. Whether purposefully or as a reaction to their experiences, they maintained a constant state of agitated evaluation in contexts were appraisal may not have been necessary, and drew swift and rigid lines of demarcations between their evaluative communities.

It is unclear if a gay community will survive a banalization of sexual difference, as the American drive for conformity is still a powerful thread in American culture; perhaps emerging social forms will negate the need for a gay community and counter-publicity, once and for all eliminating the "troubles" which brought gay men to a consciousness of their gayness and oppression in the first place, evoking their desires for something more for themselves. But it is worth considering that the maintenance of a democratic gay community might be a worthwhile end-in-view in its function of providing the context wherein same-sex attracted men can debate and create meanings of their experiences in their difference. It is unclear whether an environment without a gay community would be capable of providing the social milieu necessary for gay men to achieve a self-realization or individuation, in the Deweyan sense. If history is an clue, the answer is probably not; scholars are watching the social interaction with gayness in highly tolerant societies such as the Netherlands for answers.

For Dewey, a community cannot meet its deepest potential unless it remains a face-to-face community with a physical location for interaction to occur.[20] The depth and breadth of debate fostered by the gay community between 1961 and 1972 and the multitude of possible desires that arose out of gay men's interactions with each other are testament to the power of a community to proliferate the possible iterations of gay-maleness and enable the expression and consummation of desires. That they were highly conflicted should not disturb us, as conflict is not only inevitable in human interaction, but, when conducted ethically, an invaluable tool for appropriate valuations (appraisals) to occur. Indeed, although sometimes the evaluative actions of the gay men of the early 1970s bordered on the unethical in their dealings with fellow community members, in my opinion, a democratic community must also enable the evaluation of modes of being a gay man. Perhaps work of future community activists should lie in reformulating a community to answer the needs of gay men in a significantly less hostile environment; or perhaps it should center around reformulation of the gay community such that it more closely resembles the ideal "democratic community," where evaluations would be more carefully and appropriately directed and where diversity of gay male expression could be accepted within a context of qualitative equality and effective freedom.

Notes

1. See Mary McIntosh, "The Homosexual Role" in *Social Problems* (1968): 182–92.

2. John Dewey, *Studies in Logical Theory,* quoted in Robert B. Westbrook, *John Dewey and American Democracy* (Ithaca: Cornell University Press, 1991), 76.

3. Westbrook, 128.

4. John Dewey, *The Public and Its Problems* [1927], in *John Dewey: The Later Works, 1925–1953,* Vol. 2, edited by Jo Ann Boydston (Carbondale: Southern Illinois UP, 1988), 255.

5. Ibid., 365–6.

6. The Mattachine Society and the Daughters of Bilitis had also directly engaged the dominating effect of these discourses in the 1950s. What had begun to change in 1961 was the nature of the social space wherein that engagement took place and the scope of who was involved in the debate. Whereas the conversation in the 1950s had been greatly limited to a small group of organization member and under the aegis of straight advocates, the 1960s and '70s dialogue occurred in a much broader public created by different kinds of organizations and the publications and public actions that broadened the possible participants exponentially.

7. Eve Sedgwick addresses the weaknesses of this conceptualization as it relates to our "knowledge" of homosexuality as a category in "Introduction: Axiomatic" in *Epistemology of the Closet* (Berkeley: California University Press, 1990): see 22–27.

8. See Guy Hocquenghem, *Homosexual Desire* [1972] (Durham: Duke University Press, 1993).

9. See Westbrook's explanation, 291.

10. John Dewey, *Theory of Valuation* [1939] in *The Later Works: Vol. 13* ed. by Jo Ann Boydstong (Southern Illinois UP: Carbondale, 1991): 220.

11. See Ibid., 207.

12. Ibid., 205.

13. Quoted in Westbrook, 408.

14. See *SFFP* Dec. 22–Jan. 7, 1970, 3–5: "GAY LIBERATION: 1. Free ourselves: come out, everywhere; initiate self-defense and political activity; initiate community institutions to think. 2. Turn other gay people on: talk all the time; understand, accept, forgive. 3. Free the homosexual in everyone: we'll be getting a lot of shit from threatened latents; be gentle and keep talking and acting free. 4. We've been playing an act for a long time: we're consummate actors. Now we can begin TO BE, and it'll be a good show!"

15. John Dewey, *Outlines of a Critical Theory of Ethics,* quoted in Westbrook, 62 (emphasis in original).

16. From John Dewey, "Philosophies of Freedom," quoted in Westbrook, 363.

17. See Westbrook, 365, for a discussion of Dewey's notion of equality.

18. Dewey, *Outlines of a Critical Theory,* quoted in Westbrook, 165.

19. Westbrook, 247.

20. See Westbrook, 314, for a description of Dewey's notion of the role of community in the formation of new publics.

Appendix

San Francisco and the United States as Environment, 1961–1972

The Bay Area—including Oakland, Berkeley, and San Jose—hosted a loosely connected gay sub-culture well before the end of World War II[1]; and the city of San Francisco had taken a strong role in defining homosexuality for the entire nation by 1964.[2] Many of the gay men flocking to San Francisco during the 1960s and early 1970s found what they were looking for here. "Shall I come home or shall I make my home in San Francisco where homosexuals are not caged and exhibited as freaks," asked one man of *Citizens News* readers (June 22, 1964, 6). By 1970, *San Francisco Free Press* argued that "San Francisco is a refugee camp for homosexuals. We have fled here from every part of the nation, and like refugees elsewhere, we came not because it is so great here, but because it was so bad there" (Dec. 22–Jan. 7, 1970, 3–5). The city and the region had become a haven of sorts for gay men from across the country, where they could meet men and women like themselves and form communities and escape oppression in less open environments around the country.[3] Wrote Tony Tanner, "Coming from an area of great bigotry, I was looking for a place of love and freedom. I have not been disappointed in my search. I thank everyone I have come in contact within your community. . . . Everything I ever dreamed of finding in San Francisco is here. It is truly a city of love" (*BAR* July 15, 1971).

The feeling was not, however, universal. Many men complained about their relative safety in San Francisco, believing that it caused complacency among activists and confined them to a "respectable" ghetto in the city.[4] One activist lamented, "San Francisco probably is not the place where true gay liberation is going to make great stands, because we have the history of being a very liberal city. It's been a very good city for homosexuals: that is, our ghetto has been defined. It's been a better ghetto than any place else, but it's still a ghetto" (*GS* Dec. 1971–Jan. 1972, 1, 13). On the other hand, some found that the city's relative safety nourished gay men and women, allowing a dialogue to take place that would foster community building.[5] Still others found the city a harsh and unwelcoming place. Vogue Lansing, a drag queen, wrote, "[P]eople had told me so much about how FREE and HAPPY it is [in San Francisco]. After I arrived, I found out different! . . . NEVER before now have I had such a fear of Police. Never before have I wished harm for any people, until now" (*BAR* Nov. 1, 1971). But most echoed the sentiments of another drag queen, Laura Livingwell. "Nonetheless, I would not live anywhere else in the entire world as San Francisco is the center of the earth! Fairies are wonderful! Isn't it grand?" (*VR* June 1968, 16–17).

The relative safety of San Francisco enabled a somewhat more open gay male culture to develop, so the city's gay male experience was related to but distinct from those in other cities, such as the federal harassment in Washington, D.C., or the mafia control of New York City. Gay and lesbian cultures had been nurtured by the permissiveness of the city dating back to the nineteenth Century. San Francisco's diverse and transient populations gave rise to a live-and-let live sensibility, an anti-Prohibition public sentiment, and a resistance to the social purity movement of the early twentieth century. San Francisco's popular culture during the early twentieth century centered on gender and sexual entertainments and sex work; parallel and related was the growth of race tourism, where Chinese and other "oriental" spectacles drew audiences who were titillated by the sexualized and racial transgressions of the stage. These racial-sexual entertainments were a fertile social network wherein the city's earliest gay and lesbian bars could grow and flourish, providing the milieu for what Nan Boyd calls "a politics of everyday life" for gay men and lesbians.[6]

In the 1950s, San Francisco had become the headquarters for a new activist group, the Mattachine Society. The Society had formed several years earlier in Los Angeles, when anti-homosexual sentiment had been on the rise around the country, as the Federal government sought to expel all homosexuals from its payroll between 1948 until 1969.[7] A small group of radical men felt increasing social pressure and sought a way to counteract the anti-homosexual hysteria of the early Cold War years. Led by the labor activist Harry Hay, this small group of men sought to create an organization modeled on the Communist Party, with small independent "cells" as its organizing structure and with consciousness raising as a central part of its purpose. The founders felt that homosexuality was a unique way of being human, and that homosexuals had something special to offer society; they coined the word "homophile" to separate themselves from the pathology associated with the term "homosexual." A few short years after its formal inception, a far more conservative group of men who eschewed the founders' connections to radicalism, took over the Society and designed a different strategy. Rather than seeing homosexuals as profoundly different, these activists saw them as relatively similar to other Americans; their strategy was to seek out heterosexual experts to represent the homosexual cause to the public. The new president, Hal Call, moved the headquarters to San Francisco. In the mid-1950s, the few lesbians who had been able to participate in the Mattachine Society had grown weary of fighting for a voice within the male-dominated group; and other lesbians desired a social space to rub elbows with gay women besides in a bar. With a handful of their friends, Phyllis Lyon and Del Martin, a San Francisco couple, founded the Daughters of Bilitis in 1955 as a women's group focusing on the specific needs of homophile women. These two homophile groups would ultimately lay the cultural and organizational groundwork for the creation of a new kind of homosexual, visible, public, and communal.

Following the McCarthy trials and the release of the Kinsey reports on human sexuality in the late 1940s and early 1950s, popular interest in the nature of homosexuality mounted. Popular sociology and psychology books began to appear as did novels and pulp fiction with homosexual themes. By the end of the 1950s, newspapers around the country had begun running stories about homosexuals suspected of treason, victims of blackmail, drawn to molest children and snare the unwary. Meanwhile, the homophile organizations worked behind the scenes to try to influence the public representations of homosexuals and to change the way homosexuality was treated in official legal and medical texts. The American press located "the homosexual" in San Francisco, and the press had begun to shift its language to use the word "gay" along side "homosexual." In June 1964, *LIFE Magazine* published its now infamous cover story, "Gay San Francisco" which permanently changed the use of the word "gay" in the American popular consciousness and declared San Francisco the "gay capital of America." Thus was born a nationalized cultural connection of "gay" with a location—even a capital—and a kind of diffuse identity that reached across the United States, that could be imagined and formed anywhere in the nation while being geographically located in a specific city and region. As evidenced by the explosion of gay bars in the city during the 1960s, there was a substantial migration into the city of men from across the United States who came equipped to see themselves as "gay" and with the expectation of finding a community wherein they could find recognition and acceptance.[8]

By the late 1950s, owners of gay bars were actively fighting the regulation of the state authorities on homosexual gatherings and alcohol consumption, winning several key legal victories. This brought gay life in the city to public attention during the 1959 mayoral campaign. Democratic candidate Russ Wolden accused the Republican mayor of making the city safe haven for homosexuals. The tactic backfired, as the press pooh-poohed Wolden for sensationalizing his campaign. But it had the consequence of making the gay and lesbian population of the city vulnerable, as the incumbent mayor, George Christopher, responded by stepping up his efforts to root out vice in the city and restore the city's national reputation. In December of that year, the California Supreme Court affirmed that homosexuals had a right to congregate and consume alcohol, so the state's Alcoholic Beverage Control Department had to prove "illicit sexual activity" on the premises to revoke a liquor license. Thus began a decade-long police crackdown on gay bars in San Francisco, as new methods were employed to accuse gay men and women of lewd public sexual acts in order to arrest them and close down the city's gay bars. It was in this social environment that the significant shifts took place, wherein the city's gay men turned to publicity and community building, and began to generate new meanings of gay-maleness.

The events, social movements, and cultural trends of the San Francisco Bay Area and of the United States at large shaped gay men's environment, creating more than a mere backdrop to their discrimination or struggle for meaning. In many key ways, these larger cultural trends constituted the very experiences that proved problematic for gay men, pushing them to act to resolve the discomfort they felt being gay in America, or more specifically, gay in San Francisco. Both in with the men I spoke with and in the words men left in the publications, several key 1960s issues came up over and over again, as they described their experiences. The contradictions of Cold War culture, especially the pressure to conform to "mainstream" values; the war in Vietnam; the African American Civil Rights Movement; and the counterculture and hippie movement all arise continuously. These events and trends, then, shaped the context within which homosexual men would work out what it would mean to be gay. Howard Brick has called American culture of the 1960s "the age of contradiction," a push-pull between optimism and pessimism, between individualism and conformism.[9] Brick's notion of contradiction provides an invaluable insight into the dynamic and polarized arguments that gay men would have with each other throughout the decade.

Importantly, at the center of gay men's struggle for meaning was the dialectic between Cold War conformism and the ever-increasing resistance to it. Not surprisingly, this tension shaped gay male interaction, where as individuals and as a group they often swung between the poles of conformism and repudiation of what they saw as American culture, square, straight, "the man," suburban, mainstream. Those gay men who subscribed to Cold War ideals of patriotism and anti-communism often found themselves caught between a conformism they valued and a repulsion they felt by virtue of being rejected by the mainstream. Gay men as a group were assigned a subordinate or dominated status within Cold War American society and culture. In his discussion of the impact of the Cold War on the development of gay and lesbian activism, Robert J. Corber has argued that the anti-homosexual edge of McCarthyism of the previous decade had consolidated American homophobia. Corber breaks down Cold War culture into three main areas: national security and anti-communism, "organization man" and conformism, and the emphasis on the "American Way."[10] Although dying out by the mid-1960s, anti-communism continued to feed gay men's fear of their government and their mistrust of the official public sphere. For example, Harry Hay, one of the founders of the Mattachine Society, explained that 1950s anti-communist paranoia exorcised its demons on gay men, like a modern-day inquisition[11]. By the early 1960s, gay men in San Francisco had begun to turn anti-communist rhetoric on its head, using it in creative ways against their op- pressors in the official public. They compared American anti-sex and anti- obscenity campaigns to a communist regime, and argued that a truly free and democratic nation necessarily included sexual freedom. As Guy Strait noted, "To disagree with the Establishment now is just slightly short of sacrilegious" (*TN* Dec. 6, 1963, 1–2). Gay men were by definition outside Cold War norms and so were perceived as de facto non-conformists, regardless of their own po- litical orientation.

With the Cold War as a permeating theme in American life during the 1960s, major social struggles on the ground entered San Francisco gay men's consciousness and in some cases provided a framework for their debates about issues more directly related to their experiences as gay men. For example, ever aware of the dangers of censorship, Guy Strait criticized the Kennedy admini- stration for its control of the media during the Bay of Pigs crisis.[12] And follow- ing Kennedy's assassination, many gay men feared that they would be blamed for the president's murder by implication, because Jack Ruby's personal life- style had the outward appearance of being gay.[13] The Watts uprising in Los An- geles resonated with gay men who sympathized with those African Americans who rose up against their oppression.[14] And in 1968, the suppression of civil rights and free speech at the 1968 Democratic National Convention in Chicago seemed to some gay men to spell the end of civil democracy.[15] By the end of the 1960s, the repressive events of 1968 on one hand and the push to conform on the other stirred feelings of anger and promoted a willingness to fight outright against the controlling culture of the official public sphere, to move toward a more direct and confrontational stance with "the mainstream."[16] The proximity and visibility of groups and movements with which many gay men identified had a great impact on the way gay men interpreted their experiences and enacted their publicity.

During this period, the military, of course, vigorously defended itself against the intrusion of homosexuality or any association with it. The trend of discharging homosexual service men and women as unfit had begun during World War II[17] and continues to this day. *The News* reported that 20,000 men a year were rejected from the armed services because "they have been accused of being homosexuals or of associating with them" (Dec. 6, 1963, 2). Whether or not the number is accurate, it points to the widespread feeling of being singled out and rejected. The military was known to trick service members into confes- sions, promising honorable discharges. One discharged young man calling him- self Edward,[18] wrote a letter to his mother, published in the *Citizens News*, de- scribing his discharge. "I was taken before the interrogators who gave me a grilling the likes of which I did not know could exist in the United States. . . . I was also told that they would notify you and that I would be court-martialed and might have to serve from 5 to 10 years [if I didn't confess]. . . . This merely for being a homosexual." On Treasure Island in the San Francisco Bay, the Lavender Barracks, as they were called by San Francisco gay men, were used to house soldiers and sailors discharged for homosexuality. The military closed the facility in 1967.[19]

As the war in Vietnam escalated, the contradictions between the desire to conform and the desire to rebel intensified among gay men. "I would think twice before trotting myself over to (you know where) to get shot at by both sides," wrote An Ex-Sailor (*VR* may 1966, 7). It became a quandary for gay men who desired to serve: Should they check the "homosexual" box and get out of service or should they leave it blank and take their chances on the inside? *Town Talk* writers, in general more conformist, nonetheless found themselves likewise conflicted, arguing that the draft revealed that the government at once hated and loved single gay men.[20] At the height of the Vietnam War, gay libbers held conferences of gay vets who gathered to tell their stories of being gay in the military. They told of gang rapes, beatings, and murders—pushing suspected gays from helicopters, throwing them overboard of ships, and "accidental shootings" on the front lines. At these conferences, *Gay Sunshine* argued that gay vets found comfort with each other and were more likely to see to the heart of the military culture and understand its hypocrisy. But ultimately, the contradictions were too much for men like Ralph Hall. "Fags? We fags, why do we join the 'men' of the military? Duty to country? Patriotism? Pride? To prove we're men? We ain't men, we're faggots" (Feb.–March 1972, 10).

Perhaps the only national movement more as influential as Cold War and the anti-war movement was the African American Civil Rights movement, which shaped how gay men would conceive of their emerging opposition to the official public sphere and might shape a social movement centered around sexuality. A major shift in American cultural consciousness had begun in the 1950s, when African Americans stepped up their demands for public recognition through their campaigns of non-violent resistance in the South. By 1961, the Civil Rights movement had firmly entered the minds of gay men in San Francisco, and they had begun to identify with the Black struggle for freedom and full citizenship. This conscious identification with the racial "other" often expanded to identification with Jews in Nazi Germany and, in the early 1970s, with women, but most consistently through the decade, gay men saw themselves as a kind of "black" person, regardless of their racial identity, and African American struggles served as inspirational touchstones both imaginatively and literally as their movement grew.

Identification with African Americans as fellow oppressed groups lent to San Francisco's gay men new ways to conceive of their position within American society. Cecil Williams, a veteran civil rights activist and African American minister from Kansas City, Missouri, had moved to San Francisco and taken a position at Glide Memorial Methodist church in the Tenderloin. He provided meeting spaces for the Society for Individual Rights and for Vanguard, he actively sought gay, lesbian, and transgender worshippers, he and his staff spearheaded campaigns to help gay street kids, and he spoke at gay rights meetings and wrote articles for gay publications throughout the 1960s and beyond. His influence on the gay rights movement in the city cannot be underestimated. Early in SIR's history, Williams wrote an article for *Vector* in which he said, "Our society rejects many more people than it affirms. The Negro, the homosexual, the Mexican, the farm worker, the poor and deprived in general, the drunks: you name it—the list of people society doesn't like is almost endless" (Jan. 1965, 9). Williams' participation in a gay forum such as *Vector* expanded for gay men the possibilities of whom them could identify with in their experience of oppression.[21]

The LCE News often rhetorically placed police brutality of gays alongside police brutality of African Americans.[22] Watching the treatment of blacks by the police and the government often provoked awareness in gay men of their own situation. In June of 1963, there was a protest march up Market Street "against the withholding of civil rights from American Citizens all over the nation, with particular interest on Birmingham and San Francisco" ("Parade," *TN* June 10, 1963). Guy Strait used the Civil Rights movement to note the hypocrisy of of Police Chief Tom Cahill's speech at the rally, when the SFPD regularly trampled the rights of homosexuals in the city. "Frankly, we fail to see the difference between Birmingham Police Dogs and California Police Dogs." Awareness of race issues in San Francisco was mixed and sometimes inaccurate and often unknowingly racist. "In San Francisco, we do not have 'nigger towns' [sic]. Of course out in the Fillmore District and at Hunters Point we have huge areas that are devoted to low-income Negroid groupings" (*CN* March 9, 1964, 1–2). But just as often, race was used with a sense of irony: "We have all sorts of racial tolerance. Even Willie Mays was allowed to buy a house in a totally white neighborhood. Of course he had to threaten legal action." Gay men often ignored that many of their own number were black, and the gay press drew comparisons with African Americans from the perspective that blackness was different from gayness.

Using the Civil Rights movement, gay men were able to conceive of themselves as having collective problems and therefore possible collective means to address those problems. "It is an understanding that, as humans, as tax-payers, as voters, as just plain Americans, the homosexual is almost as respectable as the Negro." (*CN*, 4.4 (Jan. 1964), 5). In *Vanguard*, the similarities between blacks and gays were laid out in terms of the battles waged. "The Negro does not want supremacy nor privacy. He wishes equality. . . . Queer Citizens Alert! The Negro and the gay are fighting for the same exact thing: FREEDOM! . . . We are on the same side. . . . We must help each other as we fight" (*VG* 1.6). In comparing the two movements, writers often saw inspiration in the black movement that fought for the place of African Americans in society, whereas the homosexual was seen as a helpless victim who slinks away rather than fights, because "when he should be alive with love and friendship, he is filled with hate and fear" (*VR* Jan. 1965, 5).

But the differences between black oppression and gay oppression were also apparent. Gay men seem to have known that whereas blackness was immedi-

ately apparent, gayness could be hidden.[23] Identification with African Americans
was uneasy, as heterosexual black folks often resisted the association of homosexuals with their struggle for racial justice, often seeing homosexuality as a
"white thing." And homophobia within the black community also threw up barriers that prevented more material coalitions that might have been. After a run-in
at a black church in Oakland, white gay men naively "were shocked that Negroes have no empathy with homosexuals or their problems. . . . They dispar-
aged us as less than human, as a detriment to society" (*VR* Oct. 1968, 8-9). One
writer commented glibly on graffiti he saw on a Berkeley bathroom wall. "'Kill
all white homos! I hate whites! Kill! Kill! Whitey! P.S., I see why white girls are
preferring blacks. At least they're real men.'" (*VR* April 1970, 6).[24] Despite
these problems, several African American men like Cecil Williams and Willie
Brown, and ultimately Huey Newton, compared the black struggle to gay men's
struggle.[25] Leo Laurence, during his short tenure as editor of *Vector*, argued, "As
a member of the Black community, too often we have been advised that now is
not the time. . . . I think the homosexual community and other persons interested
in sexual freedom will have to adopt the techniques, tactics, and commitment
that has been generated in some quarters under the heading of Black Power" (*VR*
April 1969, 5, 14). So the identification with African Americans was uneasy at
best and racist at worst; but its impact on gay men's efforts to make meaning out
of their experience is undeniable.

The radical political movements in Berkeley and the counterculture in San
Francisco served as hotbeds for conflict, debate, and creativity among gay men.
The movements of the Bay Area grew from the Students for a Democratic Society and the Berkeley Free Speech Movement, to the anti-war movement, and
finally the women's movement of the early 1970s. Gay men looked to them with
a mixture of hope and fear: hope for new ways of engaging the public for recognition, and fear of backlash and dissolution of the society many gay men simply
wanted to be a part of. For example, responses to the Free Speech actions at
University of California across the bay provoked responses ranging from outright condemnation to worshipful praise of the bravery of the youth.[26] Many
men argued against aligning with the counter culture or the radicals.[27] Others
argued that such identifications with radicalism could never be successful for
gay men, because, ultimately, the goals were different.[28] But for younger gay
men and for gay men who saw in these movements the key to their liberation,
the confrontation and willful refusal to conform, as it was expounded in radicalism and the counter culture, were the best hope for a better future. Even some
members of SIR, which had up until the late 1960s taken a more reformist tack
against the status quo, were swayed by some of radicalism's arguments.

The culture created by the Berkeley Free Speech movement would rever-
berate through the end of the 1960s and into the early 1970s, with the emergence
of local independent radical papers (such as the *Berkeley Barb*[29]) and later campus protests at San Francisco State University,[30] leading to the anti-war movement. Actions against the Vietnam war played a central role in the development
of some gay men's political activity,[31] they often appeared in the pages of gay

publications, including in paid advertisements[32] and as thought pieces arguing about what gay liberation might and should ultimately mean. The *San Francisco Free Press* ran an article with pictures following a peace rally in Golden Gate Park from November 15, 1969, in which Rev. Michael Francis Irkin mused about what the fight for peace should bring to gay men's consciousness of themselves as revolutionaries.[33] And the Third World movement was just getting underway as gay liberation took hold in the Bay Area. "The struggles of the peoples of the world is our fight as well" (*SFGFP* Dec. 1970, 14). And finally by the early 1970s, some gay men would finally identify with the women's movement.[34] They argued that gay men had a common oppressor with women, "the male heterosexual, who is the major oppressor of us all" (*VR* March 1972, 4). Thus, identification with other abject groups allowed gay men to conceive of themselves not merely as a minority group (their status alone did that), but as a group capable of action and transformation in the official public sphere. Interestingly, the socialist underpinnings of all these movements emerged from time to time in the publications of the early 1970s, revealing the association of much of gay thinking with leftist academic thought.[35]

Closely related to the political movements of the 1960s was the burgeoning counterculture movement in mid-1960s San Francisco; the counterculture, or hippie movement, had in some ways an even greater impact on gay men living in San Francisco than the radical political movements, as it offered an example of not only how to be different, but also how to be comfortable in one's differences. Here, generational differences among gay men were among the most apparent, not in whether or not they liked the hippie movement, but rather in their relationship to it. Young gay men in the early 1970s were simply products of their youth culture. On June 28, 1970, young gays in the city held a "Gay-in" in Golden Gate Park, and *Gay Sunshine* ran a photo of some of the participants in their inaugural issue (Aug.–Sept. 1970, cover). Evident in their clothing, hair, and beards, these gay men and women were deeply connected to the counterculture of the period. Older gay men, on the other hand, had to confront the meaning of the counterculture and assimilate it into their understandings of themselves. In their writings about the hippies, gay men of all ages seemed to both embrace the hippie aesthetic and ideal and simultaneously to be wary of it. "Freedom in dress codes, drugs, long hair, and colorful clothing for males, rock music, and a generally liberated outlook toward life are elements of the hip movement that have had a deep effect on the development of Gay liberation" (*SFFP*, 1.9 (Summer 1970), 12). Many of the core values of the so-called hip movement would find their way to the center of the debates about gay identity in the early 1970s. Among the countercultural values most important to gay men, as evidenced in their writings from the period, were first, that a "way of life" could be consciously and expressly created in counter-distinction to the dominant culture; second, that human beings should organize their social relationships with love; and third, that human beings had a right to be, or in other words, that a counterculture could provide a social space necessary for people to be their "authentic" selves. As these countercultural values made their way into the gay public, they often served as standards whereby many gay men judged each other's authenticity in their gayness and sexual politics.[36]

In the mid-60s, when the hip movement was new and still a relatively local phenomenon, the hippies faced police raids and violence in the Haight-Ashbury district; gay men began to identify with them as fellow-oppressed, because of their lifestyle, and argued that gay men should support the rights of hippies to live as they wanted.[37] Most of this early discussion about the hippie movement idealized its countercultural values and sought to figure out what gay men should take from it. *Vector* ran a special issue on hippies in July 1967, the "Summer of Love," complete with a readers comment section and an interview with some of the city's male leaders in the hippie movement—"The Poet," Leon Christopher, Tauremeni (described as a poet and mystic), and David Noel— wherein they explained the philosophies of the movement as they saw it. The ideals of universal love and acceptance especially appealed to gay men who found in them an argument for *authenticity*, as a way to think about gayness as a kind of self-expression. Many saw hippies as examples of how to shake off the strictures of society to be who you wanted to be, and the hippie ethical system also resonated with some gay men. "It's easy to be a hippie, man. Just love," wrote one gay youth (*VG* 1.6).

But to gay men's consternation, these ideals of the "whole human" and of "letting love be" were also laced with a distrust of homosexuals. SIR's 1967 interview revealed the hippies' uneasy view of gay men, where the hippies were as likely as not to be anti-gay in their rhetoric, even as the gay men of SIR tried to ally with them. One hippie interviewed in *Vector,* Noel, complained that "homos seem to want to wear their sexuality like a badge," and Tauremeni argued that hippies were trying to fight for a new culture, but that "homos are bound and determined to imitate society," and therefore not aligned with hippies at all (*VR* July 1967, 5). The next month, a gay man worried, "As a group, hippies place homosexuals in the same bag that the overall established community does" (*VR* Aug. 1967, 13). Despite this implied rejection by the hippies, San Francisco's gay men experienced the presence and interaction with hippies, and out of that experience grew a continued identification with hippies' tension with the police and with their humanist and expansive.

Many older gay men positioned themselves in a more antagonistic relationship to the goings-on in Golden Gate Park during the so-called "summer of love." When asked if the gay community should identify with the hippies, some argued that the hippies had merely dropped out and were lazy freeloaders. The follow-up *Vector* issue contained a scathing critique of the counterculture by Bill Beardemphl, who panned the hippies' "ostrich-like escapism from reality through use of various stimulants, drugs and narcotics; their inability to understand the social organization and its needs; and their intellectual irrelevance to today's and tomorrow's human potentials by reverting to an immature, primitive religious mysticism" (Aug. 1967, 13). He saw the ideals of the counterculture as "hip but hackneyed ramblings about love and lust." And many other gay men were worried about the image of the gay community if it publicly identified with the hippies.[38] One man I interviewed, Niles, simply waved his hand dismissively and rolled his eyes when I asked him if the hippie movement had affected his life as a gay man in the 1960s.[39]

Interestingly, it was the young gay men who admired the counterculture movement who leveled one of the most biting critiques. They felt that despite the ideals of the hippies, that Haight-Ashbury would simply become another system of conformity where "authenticity" would be judged by superficial appearance. "Haight-Ashbury must not be a rebellion from conformity to conformity. . . . If [people moving to the Haight] look square, are they going to get the same treatment as the local squares?" (*VG* 1.6). Indeed, Leon had commented in the *Vector* interview, that "a lot of hippie-looking people are really so pathetically square," and therefore not *authentic* or *real* hippies (*VR* July 1967, 5). In the end, although there was much that could be admired in the hippie movement, some gay men concluded that "the gay community must maintain a distance socially and organizationally in order that both movements may survive independently" (*VR* July 1967, 14–15). One of my informants, Amos, reported that by 1969, the hippie movement had changed dramatically, and the culture of love and openness had been replaced by a drug culture; and what had been a relatively open-minded attitude toward gay men was replaced by distrust, anger, and homophobia.[40] Amos described what he called the "hippie uniform" that was a sign, for him, of exclusion and conformity that marked the end of the ideals that had been so important to him in the mid-1960s.

Other gay men had a completely different kind of experience with hippies. As the counterculture grew, gay men who already lived in the Haight-Ashbury neighborhood had an unexpected connection to young hippies: the flophouses. Gay men had been living in the Haight for many years, and by the early 1960s, many popular gay bars and restaurants were there. Amos lived in the Haight during the early hippie movement, but had remained aloof from the gay community. An art professor at a local university in his late thirties, at the end of the 1960s he began to have his first sexual experiences when he let young hippie men live in his home with him. He maintained a very open relationship with the young men, some of whom were also gay but most of whom were not.[41] When the hippie culture diverted toward drugs and conformism, Amos continued to open his house to young men, but he moved to the other side of Buena Vista hill, in an exodus of gay men that at the time was quickly transforming Eureka Valley into the Castro neighborhood. "Though never admitted, one of the reasons why the hippies' Haight worked as well as it did was not so much due to the politically oriented 'diggers' as it was to the gay shopkeepers, clerks, and just plain residents who contributed food, clothing, and money to the strays on their doorstep. . . . Most of the time it was out of the goodness of some queen's heart" (*GS* March 1971, 6). In the early years of the hip movement, such flophouses, where older gay men opened their home to young hippie men, were quite common, connecting generations of gay men with the values and ideas of the movement.

In the end, the importance of the hippie movement for many gay men was that its ideals of authenticity (which became oppressive in their own right for many) actually opened up many gay men to embrace what they felt was their authentic selves as gay. This move to embrace authenticity as a value helped many man step out of the closet with confidence. Mickey, in his late twenties at the time, recalled calling himself a "gay-hippie" because it seemed more complete than simply "gay"; he would ultimately spend ten years in various hippie communes in the Bay Area.[42] Jake remembers the younger hippie men as being so much freer than he was that he envied them. "It was a pleasure to be around them, eager as I was to achieve such a relaxed, open state of being."[43] In his early thirties when he moved to San Francisco in 1967, Jake found the hippie movement in "full bloom." "I forced myself to relax and become more open, consciously aiming at a casual presentation of self as gay, neither hiding nor flaunting this part of me." Jake had felt that he was a "defective" human being; the hippie movement allowed him to shed that weight and feel that "I was as much human being as everyone around me."

Throughout this book, the themes and influences of these larger cultural goings-on have been apparent and recurring. The struggle to place oneself along a continuum between conformity and rebellion in the larger context of the 1960s informed gay men's efforts to understand what "gay" should mean on the individual level and to society as a whole. The power of Cold War visions of America and democracy infused their understanding of their experiences of oppression and their place in the institutions of 1960s America and California. The Vietnam War exerted itself into gay men's consciousness as World War II and Korean War veterans and as possible draftees into the Vietnam War; it shaped their styles of political activism in the early years of the 1970s; and it raised questions about justice and equality that bled into their discussions about gay rights. The African American Civil Rights movement and gay men's identification with blacks provided a framework for conceiving of themselves as a community and as an oppressed minority. The radical movements, especially in Berkeley, furnished the fertile ground for intellectual critique and for political organizing. And finally, the counterculture and hippie movement provided a model for how to live outside the norm and inspired many gay men with the idea that gayness might be part of an "authentic" self that they had to seek out and express. Obviously, the cultural and social milieu of San Francisco between 1961 and 1972 served as a rich ground out of which gay men could create a meaningful gayness.

Notes

1. For this overview of San Francisco's gay history, I rely on Elizabeth A. Armstrong, *Forging Gay Identities: Organizing in San Francisco, 1950–1994* (Chicago: Chicago University Press, 2002); Nan Boyd, *Wide Open Town: A History of Queer San Francisco to 1965* (Berkeley: California University Press, 2003); John D'Emilio, *Sexual Politics, Sexual Communities: The Making of a Homosexual Minority in the United States, 1940–1970* (Chicago: Chicago University Press, 1983); Martin D. Meeker, *Contacts Desired: Gay and Lesbian Communications and Community, 1940s–1970s* (Chicago: Chicago University Press, 2005); Gayle S. Rubin, "The Valley of the Kings: Leathermen in San Francisco, 1960–1990" Ph.D. Dissertation, University of Michigan, 1994; Gayle S. Rubin, "The Miracle Mile: South of Market and Gay Male Leather, 1962–1997," in *Reclaiming San Francisco: History, Politics, Culture*, edited by James Brook, Chris Carlsson, and Nancy J. Peters, 242–72 (San Francisco: City Lights Press, 1998); and Susan Stryker and Jim Van Buskirk, *Gay by the Bay: A History of Queer Culture in San Francisco Bay Area* (San Francisco: Chronicle Books, 1996).

2. See Meeker, 151–196.

3. *VR* June 1971, 34–35; *GS* Dec. 1971–Jan. 1972, 1, 13.

4. *VR* March 1970, 12–13.

5. *GS* Feb.–March 1972, 2, 7.

6. See Boyd, *Wide Open Town.*

7. See David K. Johnson, *The Lavender Scare: The Cold War Persecution of Gays and Lesbians in the Federal Government* (Chicago: University of Chicago Press, 2004).

8. See Meeker, *Contacts Desired.*

9. See Howard Brick, *Age of Contradiction: American Thought and Culture in the 1960s* (Ithaca: Cornell University Press, 1998).

10. Rober J. Corber, *Homosexuality in Cold War America: Resistance and the Crisis of Masculinity* (Durham: Duke University Press, 1997), 2.

11. *VR* May 1967, 21, 25. See *TN* May 27, 1962, 3 and 4. By the late 1960s, only the John Birch Society still regularly conflated homosexuality with Communism in the public sphere. See *VR* March 1969 for a reprint of "The Fall from Decency to Degradation," an article written by George S. Shuyler, an African-American John Bircher. In it, Shuyler claims that homosexuals are pawns of the Soviet Union seeking to pervert the moral soul of the United States.

12. See *TN* May 27, 1962, 3 and 4.

13. See *TN* Dec. 6, 1963, 1–2; and *CN* 4.1 (Oct. 1964), 6.

14. See *VR* Oct. 1965, 2 and Nov. 1965, 4.

15. See *VR* Sept. 1969, 23–24.

16. *SFFP* Nov. 1, 1969, 10.

17. For a detailed account of World War II and gay men and women in the military, see Allan Bérubé, *Coming Out under Fire: The History of Gay Men and Women in World War Two* (New York: Plume, 1990).

18. It is unclear in the text if this was a real person or a fictional account created by Strait to make his point.

19. See *VR* Dec. 1967, 6.

20. Jan. 1966, 1, 5.

21. In the early 1970s, some gay men would finally identify with the women's movement; however, the identification with feminism and women in general was frought with major tensions around gender identity. They argued that gay men had a common oppressor with women, "the male heterosexual, who is the major oppressor of us all." *VR* March 1972, 4. Thus, identification with other abject groups allowed gay men to conceive of themselves not merely as a minority group (their status alone did that), but as a group capable of action and transformation in the official public sphere. The issue of gender will be a recurring theme throughout the book.

22. See for example *TN* May 13, 1963, 1.

23. See for example Bill Plath, *VR* April 1970, 6.

24. Another report quoted an article from *The Humanist* magazine in which Dick Gregory accused lesbians of raping black children arrested in Birmingham. See *VR* Oct. 1968, 8–9.

25. For a treatment of Huey Newton's famous speech concerning gay rights (and his uneasy insistence that he was not gay himself), see *GS* Oct. 1970, 4.

26. *CN* 3.23, 7.

27. *VR* Oct. 1967, 18–19

28. See *VR* Sept. 1969, 20–21, 30.

29. See "Truth Comes Up Like Thunder: Out of Berkeley Across the Bay" *VR* July 1967, 11. "The *Berkeley Barb* thrives on exposés about sex, race relations, civil wrongs, misbehavior of the fuzz, napalm vigils, the Diggers, the Grape Strike, hanky panky in the University of California, sit-ins, be-ins, folk rock, bells, flowers, feathers and beads."

30. For coverage of the student walkouts at SFSU demanding coverage of black studies by the university, see *VR* Jan. 1969, 5–6.

31. See Suran, "Coming Out Against the War." While his argument that anti-war activism was a source for gay activism is well taken, his conclusions may be overstated: many other factors influenced the emergence of a radical gay political movement and many other movements had preceded that radical movement.

32. See for example *VR* Sept. 1969, 23.

33. See *SFFP* Dec. 7, 1969.

34. *AA* July 20, 1970, 1

35. See for example, *GS* June–July 1971, 2, 5.

36. See for example *VR* Oct. 1970

37. See for example *VG* 1.7, 30 and *VR* July 1967, 14–15.

38. See letter from anonymous, *VR* Aug. 1970, 23.

39. Recorded interview, August 2003.

40. Letter dated May 27, 2002.

41. Letter dated May 27, 2002; and recorded interview, July 2002.

42. Letter dated May 28, 2002.

43. Letter dated December 12, 2002.

Bibliography

Abelove, Henry. "The Queering of Lesbian/Gay History." *Radical History Review* (1995): 46–55

———, Michele Aina Barale, and David M. Halperin. *The Lesbian and Gay Studies Reader*. New York: Routledge, 1993.

Adam, Barry D. *The Rise of a Gay and Lesbian Movement*. Boston: Twayne, 1987.

———. "Love and Sex in Constructing Identity Among Men Who Have Sex With Men." *International Journal of Sexuality and Gender Studies* 5 (2000): 325–39.

Adler, Sy, and Johanna Brenner. "Gender and Space: Lesbians and Gay Men in the City." *International Journal of Urban and Regional Research* 16 (1992): 24–34.

Alexander, Jonathan. "Beyond Identity: Queer Values and Community." *Journal of Gay, Lesbian, and Bisexual Identity* 4 (1999): 293–314.

Almaguer, Thomás. "Chicano Men: A Cartography of Homosexual Identity and Behavior." In *The Lesbian and Gay Studies Reader*, edited by Henry Abelove, Michele Aina Barale, and David M. Halperin, 255–73. New York: Routledge, 1993.

Altman, Dennis. *Homosexual Oppression and Liberation*. New York: Avon Books, 1971.

Appiah, K. Anthony. "Race, Culture, Identity: Misunderstood Connections." In *Color Conscious: The Political Morality of Race*, 30–105. Princeton: Princeton UP, 1996.

Armstrong, Elizabeth Ann. "Multiplying Identities: Identity Elaboration in San Francisco's Lesbian/Gay Organizations, 1964–1994." Ph.D. Dissertation, University of California, Berkeley, 1999.

———. *Forging Gay Identities: Organizing Sexuality in San Francisco, 1950–1994*. Chicago: University of Chicago Press, 2002.

Aronowitz, Stanley. "Against the Liberal State: ACT-UP and the Emergence of Postmodern Politics." In *Social Postmodernism: Beyond Identity Politics*, edited by Linda Nicholson and Steven S. Seidman, 357–83. Cambridge: Cambridge UP, 1995.

Badgett, M. V. Lee. "Thinking Homo/Economically." In *A Queer World: The Center for Gay and Lesbian Studies Reader*, edited by Martin Duberman, 467–76. New York: New York University Press, 1997.

Bailey, Robert W. *Gay Politics, Urban Politics*. New York: Columbia UP, 1999.

———. "Sexual Identity and Urban Space: Economic Structure and Political Action." In *Sexual Identities/Queer Politics*, edited by Mark Blasius. Princeton: Princeton UP,

2001.

Beam, Joseph. "Making Ourselves from Scratch." In *The Columbia Reader on Lesbians and Gay Men in Media, Society, and Politics*, edited by Larry Gross and Lillian Faderman, 79–80. New York: Columbia UP, 1999.

Beemyn, Brent, ed. *Creating a Place for Ourselves: Lesbian, Gay, and Bisexual Community Histories*. New York: Routledge, 1997.

Berlant, Lauren, and Elizabeth Freeman. "Queer Nationality." In *Fear of a Queer Planet: Queer Politics and Social Theory*, edited by Michael Warner, 193–229. Minneapolis: Minnesota UP, 1993.

Bérubé, Allan. "The History of the Bathhouses." In *Policing Public Sex: Queer Politics and the Future of AIDS Activism*, edited by Dangerous Bedfellows. Boston: South End Press, 1996.

Birch, Keith. "The Politics of Autonomy." In *Homosexuality: Power and Politics*, edited by The Gay Left Collective, 85–92. New York: Allison and Busby, 1980.

Blasius, Mark. "Introduction." *GLQ: A Journal of Lesbian and Gay Studies* 3 (1996–1997): 337–56.

———, ed. *Sexual Identities/Queer Politics*. Princeton: Princeton UP, 2001.

———. "An Ethos of Gay and Lesbian Living." In *Sexual Identities/Queer Politics*, edited by Mark Blasius. Princeton: Princeton UP, 2001.

Blumenfeld, Warren J. "Beyond Identity Politics." *Journal of Gay, Lesbian, and Bisexual Identity* 4 (1999): 369–72.

Bourdieu, Pierre. *Masculine Domination* [1998]. Palo Alto: Stanford UP, 2001.

Boyd, Nan Alamillo. *Wide Open Town: A History of Queer San Francisco to 1965*. Berkeley: University of California Press, 2004.

Boykin, Keith. *One More River to Cross: Black and Gay in America*. New York: Anchor Books, 1996.

Bravmann, Scott. "Telling (Hi)Stories: Rethinking the Lesbian and Gay Historical Imagination." *OUT/LOOK: A National Lesbian & Gay Quarterly* Spring 1990.

———. "Postmodernism and Queer Identities." In *Queer Theory/ Sociology*, edited by Steven S. Seidman. Cambridge: Blackwell, 1996.

Browning, Frank. *A Queer Geography: Journeys Toward a Sexual Self*. New York: Noonday Press, 1996.

Bullough, Vern L. "Alfred Kinsey and the Kinsey Report; Historical Overview and Lasting Contributions." *Journal of Sex Research* 35 (1998): 127–31.

Butler, Judith. "Imitation and Gender Insubordination." *In The Lesbian and Gay Studies Reader*, edited by Henry Abelove, Michele Aina Barale, and David M. Halperin, 307–20. New York: Routledge, 1993.

———. "Merely Cultural." *Social Text* (1997): 265–77.

Canaday, Margot. *The Straight State: Sexuality and Citizenship in Twentieth-Century America*. Princeton: Princeton University Press, 2009.

Cant, Bob, and Nigel Young. "New Politics, Old Struggles." In *Homosexuality: Power and Politics*, edited by The Gay Left Collective, 116–27. New York: Allison and Busby, 1980.

Cerullo, Margaret. "Hope and Terror: The Paradox of Gay and Lesbian Politics in the 90s." *Radical America* 24 (1990): 10–16.

Champagne, John. "Seven Speculations On Queers and Class." *Journal of Homosexuality* 26 (1993): 159–74.

Chauncy, George Jr. *Gay New York: Gender, Urban Culture, and the Making of the Gay World, 1890–1940*. New York: Basic Books, 1995.

Clark, Danae. "Commodity Lesbianism." In *The Lesbian and Gay Studies Reader*, edited by Henry Abelove, Michele Aina Barale, and David M. Halperin, 186–201. New York: Routledge, 1993.

Clarke, Cheryl. "The Failure to Transform: Homophobia in the Black Community." In *Home Girls: A Black Feminist Anthology*, edited by B. Smith. New York: Kitchen Table Press, 1983.

———, Martin Duberman, Jim Kepner, Karl Bruce Knapper, Joan Nestle, and Carmen Vazquez. "Twenty-Five Years After Stonewall: Looking Backward, Moving Forward." In *A Queer World: The Center for Gay and Lesbian Studies Reader*, edited by Martin Duberman, 262–82. New York: New York University Press, 1997.

Cohen, Cathy J. "Punks, Bulldaggers, and Welfare Queens: The Radical Potential of Queer Politics?" In *Sexual Identities/Queer Politics*, edited by Mark Blasius. Princeton: Princeton UP, 2001.

Cohen, Ed. "Who Are 'We'? Gay 'Identity' As Political (E)Motion (A Theoretical Rumination)." In *Inside/Out: Lesbian Theories, Gay Theories*, edited by Diana Fuss, 71–92. New York: Routledge, 1991.

Conerly, Gregory. "Policing the Boundaries: Defining Black Lesbian/Gay Identity and Community Relationships." Ph.D. Dissertation, University of Iowa, 1997.

Connell, R.W. *Masculinities*, 2nd Edition [1995]. Cambridge, UK: Polity Press, 2005.

Corber, Robert J. *Homosexuality in Cold War America: Resistance and the Crisis of Masculinity*. Durham: Duke University Press, 1997.

Cornwall, Richard R. "Incorporating Social Identities into Economic Theory: How Economics Can Come Out of Its Closet." In *A Queer World: The Center for Gay and Lesbian Studies Reader*, edited by Martin Duberman, 477–501. New York: New York University Press, 1997.

Cruikshank, Margaret. *The Gay and Lesbian Liberation Movement*. New York: Routledge, 1992.

Davis, Madeline D., and Elizabeth Labovsky Kennedy. "Oral History and the Study of Sexuality in the Lesbian Community: Buffalo, New York, 1940–1960." *Feminist Studies* 12 (1986): 7–26.

Deitcher, David. *The Question of Equality: Lesbian and Gay Politics in America since Stonewall*. New York: Scribner, 1995.

Delaney, Samuel R. *Times Square Red, Times Square Blue*. New York: New York University Press, 1999.

D'Emilio, John. *Sexual Politics, Sexual Communities*. Chicago: Chicago UP, 1983.

———. "Gay Politics and Community in San Francisco Since World War II." In *Hidden from History: Reclaiming the Gay and Lesbian Past*, edited by Martin Duberman, Martha Vicinus, and George Jr. Chauncy. New York: New American Library, 1989.

———. "After Stonewall." In *Making Trouble: Essays on Gay History, Politics, and the University*, edited by John D'Emilio. New York: Routledge, 1992.

———. *Making Trouble: Essays on Gay History, Politics, and the University*. New York: Routledge, 1992.

———. "Capitalism and Gay Identity" [1980]. In *Making Trouble: Essays on Gay History, Politics, and the University*, edited by John D'Emilio. New York: Routledge, 1992.

———. "Dreams Deferred: The Birth and Betrayal of America's First Gay Liberation Movement." In *Making Trouble: Essays on Gay History, Politics, and the University*, edited by John D'Emilio. New York: Routledge, 1992.

———. "The Homosexual Menace: The Politics of Sexuality in Cold War America." In *Making Trouble: Essays on Gay History, Politics, and the University*, edited by John D'Emilio. New York: Routledge, 1992.

————. "Gay Politics, Gay Community: San Francisco's Experience." In *Making Trouble: Essays on Gay History, Politics, and the University*, edited by John D'Emilio. New York: Routledge, 1992.

————. "Gay History: A New Field of Study." In *Making Trouble: Essays on Gay History, Politics, and the University*, edited by John D'Emilio. New York: Routledge, 1992.

————. "Making and Unmaking Minorities: The Tension Between Gay History and Politics." In *Making Trouble: Essays on Gay History, Politics, and the University*, edited by John D'Emilio. New York: Routledge, 1992.

————. "Homophobia and the Trajectory of Postwar American Radicalism: The Career of Bayard Rustin." *Radical History Review* 62 (1995): 81–103.

D'Eugelli, A. R., and C. J. Patterson, eds. *Lesbian, Gay and Bisexual Identities over the Lifespan: Psychological Perspectives*. New York: Oxford UP, 1995.

Dewey, John. *Human Nature and Conduct* [1922]. Toronto: Dover Books, 2002.

————. *The Public and Its Problems* [1927]. In *John Dewey: The Later Works, 1925–1953, Vol. 2*, edited by Jo Ann Boydston. Carbondale: Southern Illinois UP, 1988.

————. *Experience and Nature* [1929 (1925)]. In *The Later Works, 1925–1953: Volume 1: 1925*, edited by Jo Ann Boydston. Carbondale: Southern Illinois University Press, 1988.

————. *The Quest for Certainty* [1929]. In *The Later Works, 1925–1953: Volume 4: 1929*, edited by Jo Ann Boydston. Carbondale: Southern Illinois University Press, 1984.

————. *Individualism Old and New* [1930]. In *John Dewey: The Later Works, 1925–1953*, Vol. 5, edited by Jo Ann Boydston. Carbondale: Southern Illinois UP: 1988.

————. *Freedom and Culture* [1938]. Amherst: Prometheus Books, 1989.

————. *Theory of Valuation* [1939]. In *The Later Works, 1925–1953: Volume 13: 1938–1939*, edited by Jo Ann Boydston. Carbondale: Southern Illinois University Press, 1988.

Dobinson, Cheryl. "Confessions of an Identity Junkie." *Journal of Gay, Lesbian, and Bisexual Identity* 4 (1999): 265–69.

Duberman, Martin. *Stonewall*. New York: Plume, 1993.

————, ed. *A Queer World: The Center for Gay and Lesbian Studies Reader*. New York: New York University Press, 1997.

Du Bois, W.E.B. *The Souls of Black Folk* [1903]. New York: Dover, 1994.

Dugan, Kimberly Beth. "Culture and Movement-Countermovement Dynamics: The Struggle over Gay, Lesbian and Bisexual Rights." Ph.D. Dissertation, Ohio State University, 1999.

Duggan, Lisa. "Making It Perfectly Queer." *Socialist Review* 22 (1992): 11–31.

————. "The Discipline Problem: Queer Theory Meets Lesbian and Gay History." *GLQ: A Journal of Lesbian and Gay Studies* 2:3 (1995).

Duttmann, Alexander Garcia. "The Culture of Polemic: Misrecognizing Recognition." *Radical Philosophy* 81 (1997): 27–30.

Duyvendak, Jan Willem. "The Depoliticization of the Dutch Gay Identity, or Why Dutch Gays Aren't Queer." In *Queer Theory/ Sociology*, edited by Steven S. Seidman. Cambridge: Blackwell, 1996.

Eaklor, Vicki L. "Learning from History: A Queer Problem." *Journal of Gay, Lesbian, and Bisexual Identity* 3 (1998): 195–211.

Edelman, Lee. "Seeing Things: Representation, the Scene of Surveillance, and the Spectacle of Gay Male Sex"." In *Homographesis: Essays in Gay Literary and Cultural Theory*, edited by Lee Edelman. New York: Routledge, 1994.

————. "Tearooms and Sympathy, or, the Epistemology of the Water Closet." In *The Lesbian and Gay Studies Reader*, edited by Henry Abelove, Michele Aina Barale, and David M. Halperin, 553–76. New York: Routledge, 1994.

Eliason, Michele J., and Kris Morgan. "Lesbians Define Themselves: Diversity in Lesbian Identification." *Journal of Gay, Lesbian, and Bisexual Identity* 3 (1998): 47–63.

Epstein, Barbara. "Why Poststructuralism Is a Dead End For Progressive Thought." *Socialist Review* 25 (1995): 83–119.

Epstein, Steven. "Gay Politics, Ethnic Identity: The Limits of Social Constructionism." *Socialist Review* 17 (1987): 9–54.

Escoffier, Jeffery, Regina Kunzel, and Molly McGarry, eds. "The Queer Issue." *Radical History Review* (1995).

————. "Homosexuality and the Sociological Imagination: The 1950s and 1960s." In *A Queer World: The Center for Gay and Lesbian Studies Reader*, edited by Martin Duberman, 248–61. New York: New York University Press, 1997.

————. *American Homo: Community and Perversity*. Berkeley: California UP, 1997.

Esterberg, Kristin G. "From Accommodation to Liberation: A Social Movement Analysis of Lesbians in the Homophile Movement." *Gender & Society* 8 (1994): 424–43.

Etzioni, Amitai. "Is Bowling Together Sociologically Lite?" *Contemporary Sociology* 30:3 (May 2001): 223–224.

Evans, Len. "Alfred Kinsey and Homosexuality in the 1950s: The Recollections of Samuel Morris Steward as Told to Len Evans." *Journal of the History of Sexuality* 9 (2000): 474–91.

Eylath, Gwenn C. "Marching and Watching: The Sociological Meaning of the Gay, Lesbian, Bisexual and Transgender Pride March." Ph.D. Dissertation, Brandeis University, 1997.

Faderman, Lillian. *Odd Girls and Twilight Lovers: A History of Lesbian Life in Twentieth-Century America*. New York: Penguin, 1991.

Fenster, Mark. "Queer Punk Fanzines: Identity, Community, and the Articulation of Homosexuality and Hardcore." *Journal of Communication Inquiry* 17 (1993): 73–94.

Foucault, Michele. *Discipline and Punish: The Birth of the Prison* [1975], translated by Alan Sheridan [1977]. New York: Vintage Books, 1995.

————. *The History of Sexuality, An Introduction, Vol. 1* [1976]. New York: Vintage, 1990.

Fraser, Nancy. "Rethinking the Public Sphere: A Contribution to the Critique of the Actually Existing Democracy." In *Habermas and the Public Sphere*, edited by Craig Calhoun. Cambridge, Mass.: MIT Press, 1992.

———— "Politics, Culture, and the Public Sphere: Toward a Postmodern Conception." In *Social Postmodernism: Beyond Identity Politics*, edited by Linda Nicholson and Steven S. Seidman, 287–314. Cambridge: Cambridge UP, 1995.

————, ed. "Heterosexism, Misrecognition, and Capitalism: A Response to Judith Butler." *Social Text* (1997): 279–89.

Freedman, Estelle. "'The Burning of Letters Continues': Elusive Identities and the Historical Construction of Sexuality." *Journal of Women's History* 9.

Freitas, Anthony J. "Belongings: Citizenship, Sexuality, and the Market." In *Everyday Inequalities: Critical Inquiries*, edited by Jody O'Brien and Judith A. Howard, 361–84. Cambridge, MA: Blackwell, 1998.

————, Susan Kaiser, and Tania Hammidi. "Communities, Commodities, Cultural Space, and Style." *Journal of Homosexuality* 31 (1996): 83–107.

Fuss, Diana. "Pink Freud." *GLQ: A Journal of Lesbian and Gay Studies* 2 (1995): 1–9.

Gamson, Joshua. "Must Identity Movements Self-Destruct? A Queer Dilemma." In

Queer Theory/ Sociology, edited by Steven S. Seidman. Vol. 42. Cambridge: Blackwell, 1995.

———. "Messages of Exclusion: Gender, Movements, and Symbolic Boundaries." *Gender & Society* 11 (1997): 178–99.

Gates, Henry Louis. "The Black Man's Burden." In *Fear of a Queer Planet: Queer Politics and Social Theory*, edited by Michael Warner, 230–38. Minneapolis: Minnesota UP, 1993.

The Gay Left Collective, ed. *Homosexuality: Power and Politics*. New York: Allison and Busby, 1980.

Geertz, Clifford. *The Interpretation of Cultures* [1973]. New York: Basic Books, 2000.

Gilmartin, Katie. "'We Weren't Bar People': Middle-Class Lesbian Identities and Cultural Spaces." *GLQ: A Journal of Lesbian and Gay Studies* 3 (1996): 1–51.

Gluckman, Amy, and Betsy Reed. "The Gay Marketing Moment." In *A Queer World: The Center for Gay and Lesbian Studies Reader*, edited by Martin Duberman, 519–25. New York: New York University Press, 1997.

Goffman, Erving. *Stigma: Notes on the Management of Spoiled Identity* [1963]. New York: Touchstone, 1986.

Goldstein, Anne B. "Homosexual Identity and Gay Rights." *In A Queer World: The Center for Gay and Lesbian Studies Reader*, edited by Martin Duberman, 399–405. New York: New York University Press, 1997.

Greene, B., comp. *Ethnic and Cultural Diversity among Lesbians and Gay Men*. Thousand Oaks, CA: SAGE Publications, 1997.

Gross, Larry, and Lillian Faderman, eds. *The Columbia Reader on Lesbians and Gay Men in Media, Society, and Politics*. New York: Columbia UP, 1999.

Grossman, Arnold H. "The Virtual and Actual Identities of Older Lesbians." In *A Queer World: The Center for Gay and Lesbian Studies Reader*, edited by Martin Duberman, 615–26. New York: New York University Press, 1997.

Haider-Markel, Donald P., and Kenneth J. Meier. "The Politics of Gay and Lesbian Rights: Expanding the Scope of the Conflict." *Journal of Politics* 58 (1996): 332–49.

Hall, Stuart. "In Defense of Theory." In *People's History and Socialist Theory*, edited by Raphael Samuel, 380. New York: Routledge, 1981.

———. "Deviance, Politics, and the Media." *In The Lesbian and Gay Studies Reader*, edited by Henry Abelove, Michele Aina Barale, and David M. Halperin, 62–90. New York: Routledge, 1993.

Halperin, David M. "Is There a History of Sexuality." *In The Lesbian and Gay Studies Reader*, edited by Henry Abelove, Michele Aina Barale, and David M. Halperin, 416–32. New York: Routledge, 1993.

———. "Historicizing the Subject of Desire: Sexual Preferences and Erotic Identities in the Pseudo-Lucianic Erotes." In *Foucault and the Writing of History*, edited by Jan Goldstein. Cambridge: Blackwell, 1994.

———. *Saint=Foucault: Towards a Gay Hagiography*. New York: Oxford UP, 1995.

———. "Forgetting Foucault" [1998]. In *How to do the History of Homosexuality*. Chicago: University of Chicago Press, 2002.

Hanawa, Yukiko. "Inciting Sites of Political Interventions: Queer 'n Asian." In *A Queer World: The Center for Gay and Lesbian Studies Reader*, edited by Martin Duberman, 39–62. New York: New York University Press, 1997.

Harper, Philip Brian. "Gay Male Identities, Personal Privacy, and Relations of Public Exchange: Notes On Directions for Queer Critique." *Social Text* (1997).

———, Anne McClintock, Jose Esteban Munoz, and Trash Rosen, eds. "Queer Transitions of Race, Nation, and Gender." *Social Text* (1997).

Harris, Daniel. *The Rise and Fall of Gay Culture*. New York: Bantam Books, 1997.

Hennessy, Rosemary. "Queer Visibility in Commodity Culture." In *Social Postmodernism: Beyond Identity Politics*, edited by Linda Nicholson and Steven S. Seidman, 142–86. Cambridge: Cambridge UP, 1995.

———. *Profit and Pleasure: Sexual Identities in Late Capitalism*. New York: Routledge, 2000.

Herdt, Gilbert. "Third Genders, Third Sexes." *In A Queer World: The Center for Gay and Lesbian Studies Reader*, edited by Martin Duberman, 100–107. New York: New York University Press, 1997.

Hocquenghem, Guy. *Homosexual Desire*. Duke UP, 1993 [1972].

Hollibaugh, Amber. "Right to Rebel." In *Homosexuality: Power and Politics*, edited by Jeffrey Weeks, 205–15. London: Allison & Busby, 1980.

Hooven, F. Valentine. *Beefcake: The Muscle Magazines of America, 1950–1970*. Köln, Germany: Taschen, 1995.

Humm, Andrew. "The Personal Politics of Lesbian and Gay Liberation." *Social Policy* 11 (1980): 40–45.

Humphreys, Laud. *Tearoom Trade: Impersonal Sex in Public Places*, Revised Edition. New York: Aldine de Gruyter, 1975.

Ingebretsen, Edward. "Gone Shopping: The Commercialization of Same-Sex Desire." *Journal of Gay, Lesbian, and Bisexual Identity* 4 (1999): 125–48.

Ingram, Gordon Bren, Anne-Marie Bouthillette, and Yolanda Retter, eds. *Queers in Space: Communities/Public Places/Sites of Resistance*. Seattle: Bay Press, 1997.

Irvine, Janice M. "A Place in the Rainbow: Theorizing Lesbian and Gay Culture." In *Queer Theory/ Sociology*, edited by Steven S. Seidman. Cambridge: Blackwell, 1996.

Jackson, Earl. "The Responsibility of and to Differences: Theorizing Race and Ethnicity in Lesbian and Gay Studies." In *Beyond a Dream Deferred; Multicultural Education and the Politics of Excellence*, edited by Becky W. Thompson and Sangeeta Tyagi, 131–61. Minneapolis: Minnesota UP, 1993.

Jackson, Katrice, and Lester B. Brown. "Lesbian of African Heritage: Coming Out in the Straight Community." *Journal of Gay and Lesbian Social Services* 5 (1996): 53–67.

Jagose, Annamarie. *Queer Theory: An Introduction*. New York: New York University Press, 1996.

James, William. *The Varieties of Religious Experience: A Study in Human Nature* [1902]. Mineola: Dover Publications, 2002.

Jenness, Valerie. "Social Movement Growth, Domain Expansion, and Framing Processes: The Gay/Lesbian Movement and Violence Against Gays and Lesbians As a Social Problem." *Social Problems* 42 (1995): 145–70.

Johnson, David K. *The Lavender Scare: The Cold War Persecution of Gays and Lesbians in the Federal Government*. Chicago: University of Chicago Press, 2004.

Kaplan, Morris B. *Sexual Justice: Democratic Citizenship and the Politics of Desire*. New York: Routledge, 1997.

Katz, Jonathan Ned. "'Homosexual' and 'Heterosexual': Questioning the Terms." In *A Queer World: The Center for Gay and Lesbian Studies Reader*, edited by Martin Duberman, 177–80. New York: New York University Press, 1997.

Kayal, Philip M. "Communalization and Homophile Organization Membership: Gay Volunteerism Before and During AIDS." *Journal of Gay and Lesbian Social Services* 1 (1994): 33–57.

Kennedy, Elizabeth Labovsky, and Madeline D. Davis. *Boots of Leather, Slippers of*

Gold. New York: Routledge, 1993.

———. "Telling Tales: Oral History and the Construction of Pre-Stonewall Lesbian History." In *A Queer World: The Center for Gay and Lesbian Studies Reader*, edited by Martin Duberman, 181–98. New York: New York University Press, 1997.

Kinsey, Alfred. *Sexual Behavior in the Human Male*. Philadelphia: W.B. Saunders, 1948.

Kirsch, Max H. *Queer Theory and Social Change*. New York: Rutledge, 2000.

Kissack, Terence. "Freaking Fag Revolutionaries." *Radical History Review* 62 (1995): 104–34.

Krupat, Kitty. "Out of Labor's Dark Age: Sexual Politics Comes to the Workplace." *Social Text* 61 (1999): 9–29.

Leap, William L. "Staking a Claim On History and Culture: Recent Studies in the Anthropology of Homosexuality." *Anthropological Quarterly* 71 (1998): 150–54.

———, ed. *Public Sex/Gay Spaces*. New York: Columbia UP, 1999.

LeVay, Simon, and Elisabeth Nonas. *City of Friends: A Portrait of the Gay and Lesbian Community in America*. Boston: Massachusetts Institute of Technology, 1995.

Macnair, Ray H. "The Diversity Functions of Organizations That Confront Oppression: The Evolution of Three Social Movements." *Journal of Community Practice* 7 (2000): 2.

Marcus, Eric. *Making History: The Struggle for Gay and Lesbian Equal Rights, 1945–1990, An Oral History*. New York: Harper Collins, 1993.

Marsiglia, Flavio Francisco. "Homosexuality and Latinos/as: Towards an Integration of Identities." *Journal of Gay and Lesbian Social Services* 8 (1998): 113–25.

Maynard, Steven. "Respect Your Elders, Know Your Past: History and the Queer Theorists." *Radical History Review* Fall (1999): 56–78.

McIntosh, Mary. "The Homosexual Role." *Social Problems* (1968): 182–92.

Mead, George Herbert. *Mind Self and Society: From the Standpoint of a Social Behaviorist* [1934], edited by Charles W. Morris. Chicago: University of Chicago Press, 1962.

Meeker, Martin D., Jr. "Come Out West: Communication and the Gay and Lesbian Migration to San Francisco, 1940s–1960s." Ph.D. Dissertation, University of Southern California, 2000.

———. "Behind the Mask of Respectability: Reconsidering the Mattachine Society and Male Homophile Practice, 1950s and 1960s." *The Journal of the History of Sexuality* 10, No. 1 (2001): 78–116.

———. *Contacts Desired: Gay and Lesbian Communications and Community, 1940s–1970s*. Chicago: Chicago University Press, 2005.

Meyerowitz, Jane. *How Sex Changed*. Cambridge: Harvard UP, 2002.

Mill, John Stuart. *On Liberty* [1859]. New York: Penguin, 1974.

Moorhead, Cari. "Queering Identities: The Roles of Integrity and Belonging in Becoming Ourselves." *Journal of Gay, Lesbian, and Bisexual Identity* 4 (1999): 327–43.

Morgan, Tracy D. "Pages of Whiteness: Race, Physique Magazines, and the Emergence of Public Gay Culture." In *Homographesis: Essays in Gay Literary and Cultural Theory*, edited by Lee Edelman, 280–97. New York: Routledge, 1994.

Mort, Frank. "Sexuality: Regulation and Contestation." In *Homosexuality: Power and Politics*, edited by The Gay Left Collective, 38–51. New York: Allison and Busby, 1980.

Morton, Donald, ed. *The Material Queer: A LesBiGay Cultural Studies Reader*. Boulder: Westview Press, 1996.

Murphy, Bianca Cody. "Difference and Diversity: Gay and Lesbian Couples." In *A Queer World: The Center for Gay and Lesbian Studies Reader*, edited by Martin Duberman, 345–57. New York: New York University Press, 1997.

Namaste, Ki. "'Tragic Misreadings': Queer Theory's Erasure of Transgender Subjectivity." In *Homographesis: Essays in Gay Literary and Cultural Theory*, edited by Lee Edelman, 183–203. New York: Routledge, 1994.

———. "The Politics of Inside/Out: Queer Theory, Poststructuralism, and a Sociological Approach to Sexuality." In *Queer Theory/ Sociology*, edited by Steven S. Seidman. Vol. 12. Cambridge: Blackwell, 1994.

Nardi, Peter M. *Gay Men's Friendships: Invincible Communities.* Chicago: University of Chicago Press, 1999.

Nelkin, Dorothy, and Susan M. Lindee. "Creating Natural Distinctions." In *A Queer World: The Center for Gay and Lesbian Studies Reader*, edited by Martin Duberman, 309–17. New York: New York University Press, 1997.

Nicholson, Linda, and Steven S. Seidman. *Social Postmodernism: Beyond Identity Politics.* Cambridge: Cambridge UP, 1995.

Ordona, Trinity A. "Coming Out Together: An Ethnohistory of the Asian and Pacific Islander Queer Women's and Transgendered People's Movement of San Francisco." Ph.D. Dissertation, Santa Cruz: University of California, 2000.

Parker, Andrew, ed. *Nationalisms and Sexualities.* New York: Routledge, 1992.

Penaloza, Lisa. "We're Here, We're Queer, and We're Going Shopping! A Critical Perspective On the Accommodation of Gays and Lesbians in the U.S. Marketplace." *Journal of Homosexuality* 31 (1996): 9–41.

Penn, Donna, ed. "Queer: Theorizing Politics and History." *Radical History Review* (1995): 24–42.

———. "The Present and Future of Recuperating the Past." *GLQ: A Journal of Lesbian and Gay Studies* 2 (1995): 279–305.

Phelan, Shane. "The Space of Justice; Lesbians and Democratic Politics." In *Social Postmodernism: Beyond Identity Politics*, edited by Linda Nicholson and Steven S. Seidman, 332–56. Cambridge: Cambridge UP, 1995.

Piore, Michael. "Economic Identity/Sexual Identity." In *A Queer World: The Center for Gay and Lesbian Studies Reader*, edited by Martin Duberman, 502–13. New York: New York University Press, 1997.

Pitts, Victoria. "Visibly Queer: Body Technologies and Sexual Politics." *Sociological Quarterly* 41 (2000): 443–63.

Raffo, Susan. *Queerly Classed.* Boston: South End Press, 1997.

Rich, Adrienne. "Compulsory Heterosexuality and Lesbian Existence." *In The Lesbian and Gay Studies Reader*, edited by Henry Abelove, Michele Aina Barale, and David M. Halperin, 227–54. New York: Routledge, 1993.

Richards, David A. J. "Sexual Preference As a Suspect Classification." *In A Queer World: The Center for Gay and Lesbian Studies Reader*, edited by Martin Duberman, 406–17. New York: New York University Press, 1997.

———. *Identity and the Case for Gay Rights: Race, Gender, Religion as Analogies.* Chicago: Chicago UP, 1999.

Rimmerman, Craig A. *From Identity to Politics: The Lesbian and Gay Movements in the United States.* Philadelphia : Temple UP, 2002.

Romo-Carmona, Mariana. "Latina Lesbians." *In A Queer World: The Center for Gay and Lesbian Studies Reader*, edited by Martin Duberman, 35–38. New York: New York University Press, 1997.

Roscoe, Will. "Gender Diversity in Native North America: Notes Toward a Unified Analysis." In *A Queer World: The Center for Gay and Lesbian Studies Reader*, edited by Martin Duberman, 65–81. New York: New York University Press, 1997.

Rubin, Gayle S. "Thinking Sex: Notes for a Radical Theory of the Politics of Sexuality" [1984]. In *The Lesbian and Gay Studies Reader*, edited by Henry Abelove, Michele Aina Barale, and David M. Halperin, 3–44. New York: Routledge, 1993.

———. "The Valley of the Kings: Leathermen in San Francisco, 1960–1990." Ph.D. Dissertation, University of Michigan, 1994.

———. "The Miracle Mile: South of Market and Gay Male Leather, 1962–1997." In *Reclaiming San Francisco: History, Politics, Culture*, edited by James Brook, Chris Carlsson, and Nancy J. Peters, 247–72. San Francisco: City Lights, 1998.

Scott, Joan W. "The Evidence of Experience." In *The Lesbian and Gay Studies Reader*, edited by Henry Abelove, Michele Aina Barale, and David M. Halperin. New York: Routledge, 1993.

Sedgwick, Eve Kosofsky. *Epistemology of the Closet*. Berkeley: California UP, 1990.

Seidman, Steven S. "The Case of Antigay Politics: The Failure of the Left." *Dissent* 35 (1988): 487–89.

———. "Identity and Politics in a 'Postmodern' Gay Culture: Some Historical and Conceptual Notes." In *Fear of a Queer Planet: Queer Politics and Social Theory*, edited by Michael Warner, 105–42. Minneapolis: Minnesota UP, 1993.

———. "Queer Pedagogy/Queer-Ing Sociology." *Critical Sociology* 20 (1994): 169–76.

———. "Deconstructing Queer Theory or the Undertheorization of the Social and the Ethical." In *Social Postmodernism: Beyond Identity Politics*, edited by Linda Nicholson and Steven S. Seidman, 116–41. Cambridge: Cambridge UP, 1995.

———, ed. *Queer Theory/Sociology*. Cambridge: Blackwell, 1996.

———, Chet Meeks, and Francie Traschen. "Beyond the Closet? The Changing Social Meaning of Homosexuality in the Unisted States." *Sexualities* 2 (1999): 9–34.

Sender, Katherine. "Selling Sexual Subjectivities: Audiences Respond to Gay Window Advertising." *Critical Studies in Mass Communication* 16 (1999): 172–96.

Simpson, M., ed. *Anti-Gay*. London: Freedom Editions, 1996.

Sinfield, Alan. "Sexuality and Subcultures in the Wake of Welfare Capitalism." *Radical Philosophy* 66 (1994): 40–43.

Smith, Ralph R., and Russel Windes. "Identity in Political Context: Lesbian/Gay Representation in the Public Sphere." *Journal of Homosexuality* 37 (1999): 25–45.

Stein, Arlene. "Becoming Lesbian: Identity Work and the Performance of Sexuality." In *The Columbia Reader on Lesbians and Gay Men in Media, Society, and Politics*, edited by Larry Gross and Lillian Faderman, 81–91. New York: Columbia UP, 1999.

Streitmatter, Rodger. "The Advocate: Setting the Standard for the Gay Liberation Press." *Journalism History* 19 (1993): 93–102.

———. *Unspeakable: The Rise of the Gay and Lesbian Press in America*. New York: Faber & Faber, 1993.

———. "Lesbian and Gay Press: Raising a Militant Voice in the 1960s." *American Journalism* 12 (1995): 142–61.

———. "Creating a Venue for the 'Love That Dare Not Speak Its Name': Origins of the Gay and Lesbian Press." *Journalism and Mass Communication Quarterly* 72 (1995): 436–47.

Strub, Sean. "The Growth of the Gay and Lesbian Market." In *A Queer World: The Center for Gay and Lesbian Studies Reader*, edited by Martin Duberman, 514–18. New York: New York University Press, 1997.

Stryker, Susan, and Jim Van Buskirk. *Gay by the Bay: A History of Queer Culture in the San Francisco Bay Area*. San Francisco: Chronicle Books, 1996.

Suran, Justin David. "Coming Out against the War: Antimilitarism and the Politicization of Homosexuality in the Era of Vietnam." *American Quarterly* 53, No. 2 (Sept.

2001): 452–488.

Sweeney, John J. "The Growing Alliance Between Gay and Union Activists." *Social Text* 61 (1999): 31–38.

Teal, Donn. *The Gay Militants*. New York: St. Martins Press, 1995 [1971].

Thompson, Mark. *Leatherfolk: Radical Sex, People, Politics, and Practice*. Boston: Alyson, 1991.

Thorp, John. "The Social Construction of Homosexuality." *Phoenix* 46 (1992): 54–61.

Trend, David, ed. "Queer Subjects." *Socialist Review* 25 (1995).

Trumbach, Randolph. "Are Modern Western Lesbian Women and Gay Men a Third Gender?" *In A Queer World: The Center for Gay and Lesbian Studies Reader*, edited by Martin Duberman, 87–99. New York: New York University Press, 1997.

Tucker, Scott. *The Queer Question: Essays on Desire and Democracy*. Boston: South End Press, 1997.

Umphrey, Martha M. "The Trouble With Harry Thaw." *Radical History Review* (1995).

Valadez, Gilbert. "A Discourse Within: Multicultural Inclusion in the Lesbian and Gay Community." Ph.D. Dissertation, University of San Francisco, 1996.

Waring, Henry Ross. "Media System Dependency and Identity: The Development of America's Gay and Lesbian Alternative Media and the Transformation of Homosexuality." Ph.D. Dissertation, University of Southern California, 1996.

Warner, Michael, "The Mass Public and the Mass Subject." In *Habermas and the Public Sphere*, edited by Craig Calhoun. Boston: MIT Press, 1992.

———, ed. *Fear of a Queer Planet: Queer Politics and Social Theory*. Minneapolis: Minnesota UP, 1993.

———. "Introduction." In *Fear of a Queer Planet: Queer Politics and Social Theory*, edited by Michael Warner, vii–xxxi. Minneapolis: Minnesota UP, 1993.

———. *The Trouble with Normal: Sex, Politics, and the Ethics of Queer Life*. New York: Free Press, 1999.

Waugh, Thomas. *Out/Lines: Underground Gay Graphics before Stonewall*. Vancouver, Canada: Arsenal Pulp Press, 2002.

Weeks, Jeffrey, ed. *Homosexuality: Power and Politics*. Allison & Busby, 1980.

———. "Capitalism and the Organization of Sex." *In Homosexuality: Power and Politics*, edited by The Gay Left Collective, 11–20. New York: Allison and Busby, 1980.

———. "Sexual Identification Is a Strange Thing." In *Social Theory: The Multicultural and Classic Readings*, ed., edited by C. Lemert. Boulder: Westview Press, 1991/1993.

West, Cornell. "Cornel West On Heterosexism and Transformation: An Interview." *Harvard Education Review* 66 (1996): 356–67.

Westbrook, Robert B. *John Dewey and American Democracy*. Ithaca: Cornell University Press, 1991.

Weston, Kathy. *Families We Choose: Lesbians, Gays, and Kinship*. New York: Columbia UP, 1991.

———. "Get Thee to a Big City: Sexual Imaginary and the Great Gay Migration." *GLQ: A Journal of Lesbian and Gay Studies* 2 (1995): 253–77.

Whitehead, Harriet. "The Bow and the Burden Strap: A New Look At Institutionalized Homosexuality in Native North America." In *The Lesbian and Gay Studies Reader*, edited by Henry Abelove, Michele Aina Barale, and David M. Halperin, 498–527. New York: Routledge, 1993.

Wishik, Heather R. "Life Maps: Tracking Individual Gender and Sexual Identity Construction in the Contexts of Cultures, Relationships, and Desires." *Journal of Gay, Lesbian, and Bisexual Identity* 1 (1996): 129–52.

Bibliography

Woods, Gregory. "We're Here, We're Queer, and We're Not Going Catalogue Shopping." In *A Queer Romance: Lesbians, Gay Men and Popular Culture*, edited by Paul Burston and Colin Richardson, 147–63. New York: Routledge, 1995.

Woods, James. "The Different Dilemmas of Lesbian and Gay Professionals." In *A Queer World: The Center for Gay and Lesbian Studies Reader*, edited by Martin Duberman, 508–13. New York: New York University Press, 1997.

Zicklin, Gilbert. "Media, Science, and Sexual Ideology: The Promotion of Sexual Stability." In *A Queer World: The Center for Gay and Lesbian Studies Reader*, edited by Martin Duberman, 381–96. New York: New York University Press, 1997.

Index

About the Author

J. Todd Ormsbee received his Ph.D. in American Studies from the University of Kansas in 2004. He has been an assistant professor of American Studies at San Jose State University since 2005, where he teaches a broad range of courses in American society and culture.

Breinigsville, PA USA
24 February 2010
233065BV00007B/1/P